Writing in a Visual Age

LEE ODELL
Rensselaer Polytechnic Institute

SUSAN M. KATZ
North Carolina State University

BEDFORD/ST. MARTIN'S
Boston ▪ New York

For Bedford/St. Martin's

Senior Developmental Editors: Kristin Bowen/Carolyn Lengel
Senior Production Editor: Shuli Traub
Senior Production Supervisor: Nancy Myers
Senior Marketing Manager: Richard Cadman
Art Director: Lucy Krikorian
Text and Cover Design: Delgado and Company, Inc.
Copy Editors: Alice Vigliani/Wendy Polhemus-Annibell
Picture Research: Alice Lundoff
Cover Photos: directional buttons/keypad: © Steven Puetzer/Photonica; woman taking photograph: © Brandan Harman/Photonica; minidiscs in cases: © Neo Vision/Photonica
Composition: TechBooks/GTS
Printing and Binding: R.R. Donnelley & Sons Company

President: Joan E. Feinberg
Editorial Director: Denise B. Wydra
Editor in Chief: Nancy Perry
Director of Marketing: Karen Melton Soeltz
Director of Editing, Design, and Production: Marcia Cohen
Managing Editor: Erica T. Appel

Library of Congress Control Number: 2004101197

Manufactured in the United States of America.

1 0 9 8 7 6
f e d c b a

For information, write: Bedford/St. Martin's, 75 Arlington Street, Boston, MA 02116   (617-399-4000)

ISBN: 0-312-39497-7

EAN: 978-0-312-39497-4

Acknowledgments
Acknowledgments and copyrights appear at the back of the book on pp. 741–743, which constitute an extension of the copyright page.

Preface

New technologies have transformed our understanding of what it means to compose. The design, formatting, graphing, and illustration tools available in the average word processor were unthinkable just a few years ago, and the options available for Web documents or Power-Point presentations are even more impressive. Not surprisingly, this ability to use visuals and design to create effective documents is rapidly turning into a requirement: both in college courses and in the real world, most writers today are expected to work with more than just words. And so the writing course is heroically expanding to develop writers who are not just literate but visually literate.

Our backgrounds in composition and rhetoric prepared us to teach students how to understand and write verbal texts. Visual communication, by contrast, required us to answer unfamiliar questions—about how to choose an appropriate illustration, for example, or how to design a page or screen so as to make information as accessible as possible. Soon, however, we came to two realizations. The first was that while students' technological skills surpassed our own, many of these less-experienced writers didn't know how to use visual information effectively. The second was that principles from our work with verbal texts (the concept of "voice," for example) could guide students' efforts to work with visual elements and to integrate those elements seamlessly into written documents. As a result of these realizations, we began work on this book to help our students communicate effectively in a culture where visual rhetoric is as important as verbal rhetoric.

Like many writing instructors, we had long recognized the importance of asking students in writing courses to reflect on nonverbal messages in a wide variety of materials such as ads, brochures, and Web sites. But students today are already working with visually sophisticated texts—print documents incorporating tables and figures, materials on the Web, PowerPoint presentations, and so on. Consequently, we decided not only to help students become critical readers of visual texts but also to show them how to integrate visual information (pictures, charts and graphs, page layout) into all of the major assignments we ask them to do.

We have found that students who benefit from this new advice on integrating visuals still need a textbook that takes a practical, step-by-step approach to the various kinds of writing that first-year students are often asked to do. Thus, using the work of both students and professionals to illustrate strategies, *Writing in a Visual Age* guides students through the entire writing process for each assignment, from the earliest stages of composing to producing a finished draft and reflecting on their progress as writers. In order to communicate effectively, writers must have a clear sense of their audience, and this book gives extra attention to helping students develop an understanding of rhetorical context. The book also leads student writers through specific discovery strategies that can help them formulate and articulate their ideas for each type of writing, not in an isolated chapter but as an integral part of the work students do for a given assignment. And as students work through these important early stages and toward the completion of each assignment, this book shows them how visual rhetoric can be an integral part of each stage.

Special Features

> **Specific guidance in integrating visual information into the writing process.** *Writing in a Visual Age* uses sample texts, by both student and professional writers, to show ways students can use visual information to accomplish basic rhetorical goals such as engaging an audience's attention, creating an appropriate voice, or elaborating on a point. In addition to the ongoing advice throughout the assignment chapters, a full chapter on designing pages and screens explains principles of layout and design and gives guidelines for using visuals (tables, photos, headings, charts, and so on). The illustrated Introduction asks students to consider the broad range of visual texts they'll be called on to read and compose, while giving an overview of how to use this book.

> **Real-world readings.** Visually interesting readings are presented much as they were in the original magazine, newspaper, or other print or electronic source—illustrating writers' strategies not just with their words but also with layout and other visual elements. Questions and discussion that surround the readings focus on strategies that students may use later to write their own effective texts.

> **Strategies for composing in specific genres.** Each of the assignment chapters in Part 1 present specific, targeted strategies for meeting the demands of writing in six familiar genres: profiles, reports, position papers, evaluations, proposals, and instructions. Strategies for accomplishing a practical goal—gathering information for a report, for example—appear in easy-to-follow and easy-to-find charts that are illustrated with examples from the chapter's readings. The inside back cover offers a quick reference to genre-specific model texts and strategies.

> **Unique guides to writing focused on practical rhetorical concerns.** Each chapter in Part 1 offers step-by-step guidance on all aspects of

creating a draft—exploring a topic, analyzing context, developing the topic, engaging an audience, creating an appropriate voice, providing structure, designing the document, integrating visual information, and concluding. Students are also encouraged to work through the conclusion of the composing process by getting feedback, revising their work, and reflecting on their progress as writers.

> **Detailed instruction for considering contexts for writing.** *Writing in a Visual Age* gives special attention to understanding audience, circumstances, and purposes. Each chapter in Part 1 provides an explanation of the contexts in which texts in a particular genre are likely to appear, a visual analysis of a published text in that genre that successfully integrates visual and verbal information, and an overview on analyzing context illustrated by an example from a student's work. Students learn to pay attention not only to the situations in which their audience will likely be reading but also to the knowledge, needs, and values with which their audience is likely to approach the students' work. Questions for Analyzing Context appear in each assignment chapter, and samples completed by students show how other writers thought through a context analysis.

> **Innovative, practical design.** A clear, visual presentation, featuring boxes, bulleted lists, and consistent use of color, gives students an easy way to find the information they need in every chapter. In addition, the inside front cover presents a graphic overview of the featured information in the assignment chapters.

> **Extensive coverage of research.** Four chapters in Part 2 provide detailed information about research, from beginning to conduct research to completing a documented text. One chapter introduces library and Internet research, while another offers advice on conducting interviews and other field research. A third chapter gives students valuable instruction in evaluating information, whether from print, electronic, or other sources. Finally, a chapter on MLA and APA documentation features a complete annotated student MLA paper and extensive coverage of documenting sources, along with worksheets (downloadable on the book companion Web site) that simplify the job of compiling a working bibliography.

> **Detailed guidance for special writing situations.** In addition to composing texts such as reports or proposals, students need to be able to communicate effectively in e-mail and on examinations. They may also need to create portfolios of their work, write for community organizations, and make oral presentations. Each of these topics is discussed in a separate chapter in Part 3 that not only provides useful advice but also illustrates that advice with specific examples from student or professional work.

> **Student voices showcased throughout.** *Writing in a Visual Age* features the voices and work of student writers. Samples of student essays and worksheets provide practical models for each kind of assignment, and dialogues with students highlight the choices they made during different stages of the writing process.

Supplements

Book Companion Site at bedfordstmartins.com/visualage

Links throughout the book direct students to extensive new media resources for *Writing in a Visual Age*. Students have access to a range of tools to help them at different stages of assignments.

> ❯ Interactive visual activities for each chapter in Part 1 give students practice analyzing how visual information interacts with written text. Extending

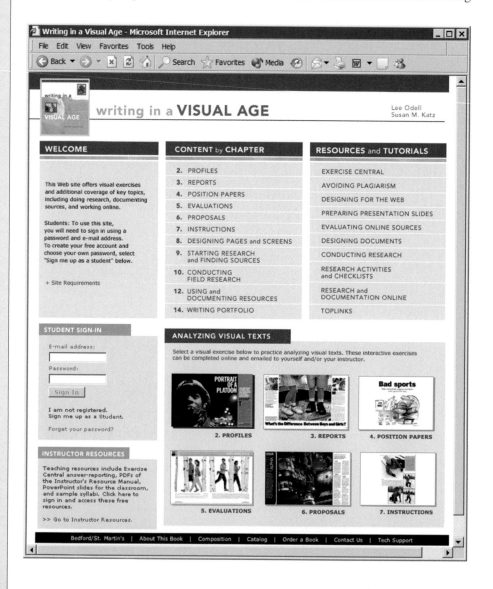

the visual analysis presented in each genre chapter, these activities provide guidance for working with visual information and a brief writing prompt that asks students to draw conclusions based on their analyses.

> Downloadable worksheets offer space for students to work with concepts from each assignment chapter. Key questions are available as PDFs for students to download, or as editable files for instructors to customize.

> Additional resources for students on the site include Exercise Central (interactive grammar exercises), additional model essays, research help and links, and more.

> Online support for instructors includes a downloadable *Instructor's Resource Manual*, PowerPoint slides, and more.

Instructor's Resource Manual

We recognize that *Writing in a Visual Age* is somewhat different from most composition texts, so the *Instructor's Resource Manual*, written by Susan Katz, accompanies this textbook and includes a great deal of support information. Although instructors who are new to teaching composition are the most likely readers, even experienced instructors may enjoy the variety of classroom activities and complementary assignments that are included in these pages. The manual is divided into three parts.

> **Part 1: teaching strategies.** The first chapter in this part includes suggestions, based on our combined years of teaching writing, for creating a syllabus, planning lessons, managing the classroom, and so forth. The second chapter provides general information about assessing and evaluating student work, creating rubrics, and writing comments, as well as specific information about assessing the role of visuals in student work. The third chapter provides sample syllabi for one- and two-term courses, including several thematic options.

> **Part 2: suggestions for teaching *Writing in a Visual Age*.** The first chapter in this part provides an overview of all the features common to the six assignment chapters in the textbook. Next, individual chapters cover each of the genre-based chapters in the book, offering activities to supplement those in each assignment chapter and ideas for varying the assignments.

> **Part 3: teaching resources.** The third part of the manual consists of two chapters. The first provides cross-references to activities for each of the major concepts presented. The second chapter lists additional resources for teaching this course available to you through Bedford/St. Martin's.

ix Visual Exercises CD-ROM

Available free when packaged with *Writing in a Visual Age* (ISBN 0-312-43322-0), this innovative CD-ROM introduces the fundamentals of visual composition. Students can analyze and manipulate the elements of visuals, gaining a more thorough understanding of how visual rhetoric works.

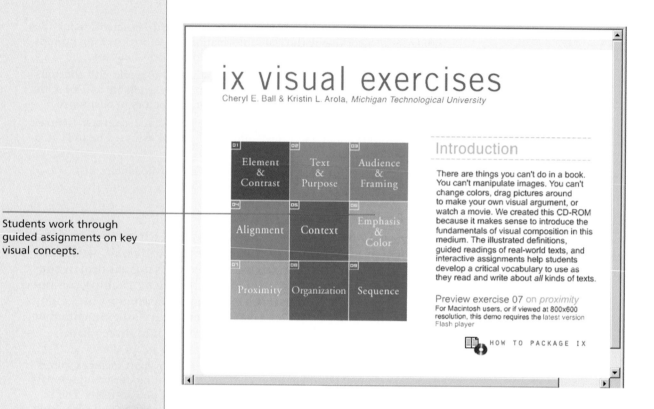

Students work through guided assignments on key visual concepts.

Acknowledgments

Many people have helped us make this book a reality. We are especially indebted to students who have allowed us to use their work as sample papers in this book: Ryan Flori, Stephanie Guzik, MaryBeth Rajczewski, Nathan Swinton, Margaret Tomeo, Amanda L. Zimpfer, and Max Zujewski. We are also grateful to the other students who have contributed other materials to the book and the Web site: Holly Adams, Ryan Balzer, Laura Beyer, Simone Billings, Matthew Blake, Joshua Patrick Brien, Nathan Burstein, Michelle Williams Chipley, Jonathan Dance, Justin Ferrazzano, Crystal L. Gilson, Ivan Hall, Diane Kalendra, Joshua Khouvy, Aaron Kline, JoyceLynn Lagula, Michael Laurino, Carolyn Leverett, Adam Lowry, Kristy Megill, Jenny Ming, David Nicolai, Tiffany Beth Peters, Donna Phillips, John David Roberts, Shirl Rogers, Raghav Sachdev, Kevin Sichler, Natasha Sim, David Stepp, and Patrick Vitarius.

We are grateful to colleagues whose ideas and discussion have helped us with this book: Simone Billings, Donna Phillips, Barbara Lewis, Andreas Karatsolis, Ken Denberg, Shaun Slattery, Jason Waite, Sandrine Dincki, Jennifer King, and Gabriele Bechtel. We also want to thank the following reviewers for their valuable insights and suggestions over the course of the book's development: Kenneth M. Autrey, Francis Marion University; Cheryl E. Ball, Michigan Technological University; Marilyn Bauer, Leeward Community College; Tammie Borland, Wynantskill High School; Richard Bullock, Wright State University; Warren Keith Duffy, University of Massachusetts, Dartmouth; Sarah Farris, University of Houston, Downtown; Elizabeth Gardner, Millersville University; Mary Gormley, Johnson and Wales University; Kathie Gossett, University of Illinois, Urbana-Champaign; Dene Grigar, Texas Women's University; Sybille Gruber, Northern Arizona University; Dan Hefko, University of Illinois, Urbana-Champaign; Maurice Hunt, Baylor University; Gesa Kirsch, Bentley College; Karla S. Kitalong, University of Central Florida; Catherine Latterell, Pennsylvania State University, Altoona; Barbara J. Lewis, Siena College; David Mair, University of Oklahoma; Miles McCrimmon, John Sargent Reynolds Community College; Libby Miles, University of Rhode Island; Gardner Rogers, University of Illinois, Urbana-Champaign; Bridget F. Ruetenik, Purdue University; Michael J. Salvo, Northeastern University; Peter Sands, University of Wisconsin, Milwaukee; Beckey Stamm, Columbus State Community College; and Anne Wysocki, Michigan Technological University. We think that their comments have done much to make our work more useful to students and instructors alike.

We are deeply grateful to a number of people at Bedford/St. Martin's: Chuck Christensen and Joan Feinberg, who supported this project from the very outset, and Nancy Perry and Denise Wydra, who kept the big picture in focus; Marilyn Moller, who encouraged us to begin this project; Diana Puglisi, who guided us through initial drafts of the manuscript; Kristin Bowen, who helped us make major improvements; Carolyn Lengel, who helped us with finishing touches; Shuli Traub, who patiently saw us through the production process; Erica Appel, who guided the book toward publication; and Nancy Myers, who gave painstaking attention to every detail. We also want to thank Paul Stenis, Nick Carbone, Rae Guimond, and Jennifer Smith for their work on the book's Web site; Lisa Delgado for her innovative book design; and Sandy Schechter, Elisabeth Gehrlein, Alice Lundoff, and Joan Scafarello for securing permissions for all of the text and art. We are also grateful to all of the other editors and in-house people who made contributions large and small: Judy Voss, Barbara Flanagan, Richard Cadman, Keith Paine, Pam Ozaroff, Alice Vigliani, Wendy Polhemus-Annibell, and Stephanie Butler.

Susan wishes to thank Paul for his love and his support when she was working on yet another revision. Lee wishes to thank Geraldine Anderson, Arthur Bushing, and Richard Young—whose influence continues to this day—and, of course, Linda, whose love and patience have made so much possible. Finally, both of us acknowledge our indebtedness to students we have worked with over the years. We think we have helped our students become better writers; we know they have helped us become better teachers.

Contents in Brief

Contents

Writing
in a Visual Age

1
Introduction to *Writing in a Visual Age*

EWSPAPERS. MAGAZINES. BOOKS. E-MAIL. POSTERS. SIGNS. TESTS. T-SHIRTS. LABELS. BILLBOARDS.

Brochures. Web sites. Everywhere you go, everywhere you look, messages are calling for your attention. Just think how many different texts you see in any given day. Some of them grab your attention, and some you ignore. Some of them you *have* to read, and some you *choose* to read. Why are some texts so appealing or important? Why are some texts so much more effective than others? This chapter will help you answer these and other questions about texts that you read. More important, understanding these concepts will help you achieve the goal of this course: to become a better writer yourself.

Although you often hear that we live in a visual age, messages have always been conveyed visually. How a text looks—its color, arrangement, size, and the images it contains—has always contributed to its meaning. Even a quick glance at the texts on these pages tells you a great deal. Without reading any of the words, you can tell the difference between a magazine and a Web site, between something serious and something entertaining, between something you would find interesting and something you would choose to ignore. Texts such as these are created by teams that include people such as writers, editors, designers, typographers, and art directors.

Habitat for Humanity
New York City
2003 Annual Report

What's changed over the past few decades, especially with texts such as the ones on these pages that have a somewhat limited or specialized audience, is that more and more often the roles of the author, editor, designer, and producer are all being played by one person. In addition, the integration of visuals into text is becoming the standard for many print and online documents. That's because there are more opportunities for individuals to control the appearance of the texts they create through the use of a wide variety of electronic tools.

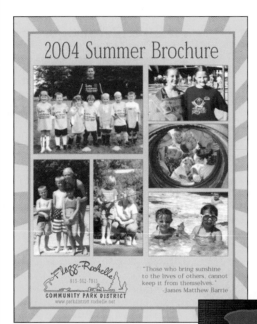

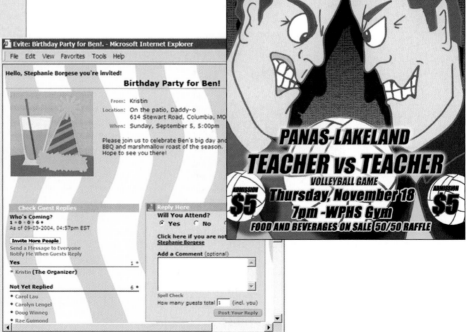

In the course of your college career and in your professional life, you will be asked to produce documents that take advantage of all available resources—whether they are words or images—to convey your message as powerfully as possible. To be successful you will need to understand what influences readers, and you will need to make effective use of available tools, much as the student-produced texts on these pages do. This book is designed to help you learn how to create effective, influential texts that integrate words and images.

Kristy Megill
English 111, Dr. Katz
Due 2/11/04

Could You Be the Next Victim?

PICTURE THIS—you just stepped out of the library after a late night session of cramming. You are walking through the brickyard towards your dorm at 12:30 at night when all of a sudden two men run up behind you, shove you to the ground, and rip your book bag off your shoulders. By the time you realize what just happened, the two men are long on their way and with your stuff!

Well you may think I just made that up, but actually, this did happen to an N.C. State student less than a month ago and if you are not careful, you may be next. Throughout the month of January there were two robberies and one assault reported on the N.C. State Campus. Since we can assume that N.C. State's campus is not considered one of the safest areas, especially at night, students and faculty need to take more precautions and be aware.

On January 16 at 1:30 a.m., there was another mugging, except in this case, an N.C. State student was shot in the leg. Once again the two black male suspects got away. This incident took place on Hillsborough St. at the Wachovia Bank.

Crime obviously is the major problem, but what are the causes? One of the causes to this problem includes the lack of protection from campus security. Since public safety insists on not patrolling the campus at night, there is going to be more crime. Also since there are not enough lights or emergency phones around, a higher chance of muggings is likely to occur. Criminals usually like to gather in dark places where they can't be seen too well. If

someone is suspicious of another individual then he or she is going to have to run a hundred yards just to get to an emergency phone. Another cause is the fact that people are not aware of their surroundings and do not take precautions. Most other students or teachers walk from one place to another without being alert. The problem is that ...

Margaret Tomeo
Professor Odell
English 102
March 22, 2004

ACL: The Curse of Women Athletes

"I knew right away exactly what I did." (McCallum and Gelin 44).

After hearing a rip in her right knee, Tiffany Woosley, a shooting guard for the University of Tennessee Lady Vols, knew she had torn her ACL, or anterior cruciate ligament. She was performing a simple jump shot and landed incorrectly—and her injury caused her to miss the rest of the season. This has become the story for too many women athletes, including Woosley's teammate Nikki McCray, an All-American forward who tore her ACL in a pickup game (McCallum and Gelin). Duke University's Monique Currie tore her ACL in a

pre-season game, possibly ruining their hopes for a big season (See Fig.1). And Brandi Chastain missed her 1987 and 1988 college soccer seasons after having surgery for the ACL in both knees (Patrick). ACL tears are turning into an epidemic among women athletes at all levels of sports, especially among high school and college players. As the number of women competing in sports continues to increase, understanding the causes of this common injury will enable us to help these athletes reduce their risk.

Fig. 1. Photograph of Monique Currie. From Nick Wass, "No. 1 Blue Devils Counting on Currie," by Jim Reedy, Washington Post 16 Mar. 2004: D1. Monique Currie and her knee brace illustrate that women athletes at all levels are susceptible to injury.

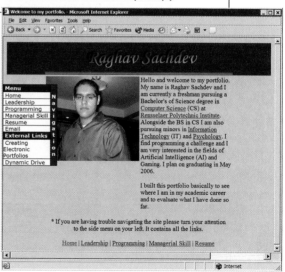

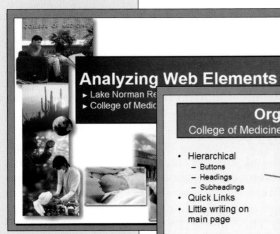

Analyzing Web Elements
- Lake Norman Re...
- College of Medic...

Organization
College of Medicine at the University of Arizona

- Hierarchical
  - Buttons
  - Headings
  - Subheadings
- Quick Links
- Little writing on main page

Organization
Lake Norman Regional Medical Center

- Hierarchical
  - Pull-down Menus
  - Headings
  - Subheadings
- Site map
- Select writing

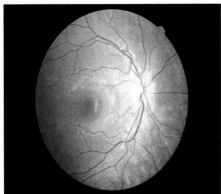

COVER STORY

NATION OF DEGENERATION

Macular degeneration is the leading cause of blindness in Americans over the age of 55. Many are asking – "What is macular degeneration?"
By Holly Adams

Margaret James was diagnosed with macular degeneration at the age of 62. Now, only three years after her diagnosis, the grandmother of five and retired English teacher can no longer enjoy the everyday tasks so many take for granted. Her collection of literary classics remains untouched, collecting dust on the bookshelves. Her 1999 Honda Accord has been parked in her garage for over a year. She can no longer enjoy "babysitting" her grandchildren or watching movies at the local theater with her circle of friends.

"You never realize how much you take something for granted until it's gone," said James of her lost sight. "I'll never be the same. My life will never be the same. It's devastating."

HEALTH OF THE NATION A picture of a normal, healthy retina taken with a special camera. Eye doctors use this type of picture to evaluate the health of a patient's eye.

COVER STORY

many are unaware of the effects of macular degeneration and that it is an incurable eye disease.

"The first time I had ever heard of the disease was when my optometrist diagnosed me with macular degeneration," says James. "It is such a common disease; why hasn't everyone heard about it?" There are ways to lower your chances of getting macular degeneration. People need to be educated before it is too late, like in my case."

The number of macular degeneration cases will increase in the coming years due to aging baby boomers and the increase in life expectancy. Macular

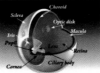

ANATOMY OF THE EYE The macula is the center of the retina and is very close to the optic disc (the area where the optic nerve enters the eye).

degeneration is expected to take on epidemic proportions in the next 20 years.

What is age-related macular degeneration?

Age-related macular degeneration (AMD) is a disease that affects the central portion of the retina known as the macula. The macula is a thin layer in the back of the eye, which records images and sends them to the brain by way of the optic nerve. The deterioration of this part of the eye results in distorted vision and blind spots, which makes everyday functions difficult.

Since the macula controls central vision, other wise known as "straight ahead" vision, such tasks as driving a car, reading, recognizing faces and seeing fine details are impossible.

People with AMD may experience blurred vision, loss of central vision and the appearance of straight lines as wavy. In some cases, the disease progresses slowly

TIME, April 20, 2004   47

A DIFFERENT VIEW Normal vision (left) versus the vision of a person with AMD (right)

and causes slight changes in a patient's vision. However, the loss of vision in both eyes could be caused if the disease progresses at a faster rate.

The seriousness of the disease is dependent on the type of AMD a person has - dry AMD or wet AMD.

Dry vs. Wet AMD

A majority of those affected by AMD experience the dry form of the disease, which is the gradual decay of cells in the macula. Early signs of dry AMD are drusen, windows in the retina caused by growth in the retinal membrane.

may lose vision due to dry AMD while the other eye may not. Changes in a person's overall vision might not be impaired if dry AMD has only infected one eye.

Wet AMD is the more serious form of the disease and only affects a small proportion of AMD patients. However, it accounts for almost all of the cases that end in blindness.

The wet form of AMD is caused by the formation of abnormal blood vessels behind the macula. These blood vessels can leak fluid

Writing Visually

Whether you realize it or not, you already know quite a bit about how words and images work together to convey meaning. You laugh at cartoons, add emoticons to your instant messages, follow maps, and respond to flyers posted on campus bulletin boards. While these examples come from everyday life, you also have experience with the role of visuals in school-based documents. Textbooks and other course materials are filled with photographs, drawings, charts, tables, and graphs, all designed to help you understand some event, concept, or relationship. What you may not have experienced, however, is creating texts of your own that use visuals effectively.

Until very recently, most writing textbooks have had little to say about the look of written text. They advised students about such matters as the appearance of the bibliography or cover page, but for the most part these textbooks have concentrated on helping students develop and express ideas effectively through written language. That advice remains vitally important because *writers still write*. But now that's not all they have to do. Today's writers also must find ways to use visual information as part of the messages they want to convey.

This emphasis on visuals is an outcome of the age in which we live: computers allow us to do things with type and graphics that once were possible only for skilled graphic artists. Internet service providers make it possible for people around the world to access the World Wide Web, with all its opportunities for visiting—and designing—visually interesting Web sites. As you try to formulate and express your own ideas, you can draw on a wide array of visual resources: pictures, colors, type styles, page or screen layouts, and so on. The challenge is in learning how to use these resources effectively, in finding ways to integrate visual and written information so that they work together to create a unified text. This book is designed to help you see how you can use visual information as part of your "writing."

Writing in Context

Throughout this book, and especially in the chapters in Part 1, you will find a focus on the contexts for writing. All good writing responds to a context: a particular audience, the circumstances under which that audience will encounter the text, and the purposes that a text was designed to achieve. You may not have thought much about context before because most of the texts you've produced have existed within an academic context. That is, most of the writing you have done to this point has been for one type of audience (teachers), under one set of circumstances (the requirements of an assignment written for an instructor who has to read your work), for some type of academic purpose (to demonstrate what you have learned or what you need to learn). However, all that is about to change. In this and other courses, and in your life after college, you will need to adapt your writing for a wide variety of contexts.

You'll learn more about understanding context as you read chapters and work on the assignments in Part 1 of this book. In these chapters, you'll find analyses of the contexts for sample documents, activities that will help you analyze context on your own, and suggestions for analyzing the context of documents that you are producing. For now, a few examples using the texts from the beginning of this chapter will demonstrate the three elements of context: audience, circumstances, and purposes.

Audience

Every text is created for a specific audience—designed to make some specific person or group of people stop and read. This concept of audience will become more clear if you think about the intended readers for some of the texts at the beginning of this chapter. Take a close look at the *Newsweek* cover (p. 4) and try to decide who you think would be likely to read the cover story, "Lawsuit Hell: How Fear of Litigation Is Paralyzing Our Professions."

Obviously professionals similar to the ones depicted on the cover—ministers, physicians, law-enforcement officers—are likely to read this article. Going one step further, we can say that other professionals who are not shown—such as dentists, engineers, and teachers—may want to read the article to see how their professions are being affected by a fear of lawsuits. Other readers would include students thinking of entering a profession, the parents or spouses of professionals, or possibly even individuals considering suing a professional. Another category of readers would include the lawyers who are involved in representing litigants on both sides of these cases. What's important, however, is not simply knowing that there are these diverse groups of potential readers but identifying the characteristics the members of these groups share that would make them interested in reading the information that this report presents. In this specific example, the readers are likely to share the following characteristics.

> ❯ A recognition that the number of lawsuits against professionals is on the rise.
> ❯ A familiarity with the costs—both financial and emotional—that come from being involved in litigation.
> ❯ A personal or professional concern with lawsuits.
> ❯ A desire to know if there is anything they can do to prevent or minimize litigation problems.

Before you begin to write your own texts, you need to analyze your audience, determining characteristics that will allow you to write a more appropriate, relevant text. Understanding your audience tells you what your readers already know about your topic and what they want (or need) to know about the topic. The key point is: there is no such thing as a "general audience." The more clearly and thoroughly you are able to identify and describe your audience, the more effectively you will be able to create a text that members of that audience will find engaging and worthwhile.

Circumstances

As a writer, when you think about circumstances you should try to think about the way that your reader's purpose may differ from your purpose. First of all, you have to think about how your reader's encounter with a text is an event within a series of events. That is, a text always exists in chronological relationship to other events, and those other events will affect the reader's decision about reading. For example, if you were to see a magazine article on breast cancer and you had recently learned that your mother has breast cancer, you would be more likely to read the article than if you had never known anyone with the disease.

Further, a writer needs to think about why a reader might want or need to read a particular document. Is the reader trying to make a decision about what movie to see or who to vote for? Is the reader concerned about some current event, such as a new highway or a corporate scandal? Is the reader trying to learn how to accomplish some task, such as creating a PowerPoint presentation or assembling a bicycle?

Looking once more at the texts that opened this chapter, think about the possible circumstances under which readers might encounter the "2004 Summer Brochure" (p. 6). This brochure describes a variety of summer activities sponsored by the Rochelle, Illinois, Community Park District. Readers are likely parents and children who want to participate in these activities. The readers are people who are looking for things to do outdoors in a park setting—swimming lessons, bike tours, golf outings, and so forth. Parents who work might also be looking for activities that will keep children occupied during the summer break, such as day camps or other youth activities.

These brochures are likely distributed via mail to the homes of the town's residents or given out to elementary and middle-school children. They might be in display racks at the supermarket or in public buildings, such as the library or town hall. Wherever they are found, the bright colors and cheerful photographs grab the attention of the reader and provide an obvious message about the contents—a message that will be recognized immediately by readers who are thinking about what to do in the summer. Also, since the brochure is sponsored by a community organization, the name and logo are likely to be familiar to residents, which will add credibility to the document and provide parents with a sense of security about entrusting their children to this organization.

What you need to think about as you plan any document is the type of situation your readers are likely to be in at the time they encounter a text. Where are they physically, emotionally, intellectually? How much time do they have to spend on reading? How do they feel about this topic? What else are they likely to have read or heard about this topic? What is important to them with regard to this topic?

Purposes

It seems fairly obvious that writers have a purpose in mind when they sit down to write—they may be writing for pleasure, to fulfill an assignment (in school or at work), to demonstrate how to do something, to share newfound information or ideas, or to stay in touch with friends and family. Before you begin to write, you need to clearly define your purpose so that you can make reasoned decisions about how to achieve that purpose. For example, if you're trying to convince your boss to let you take on a particular new project, you need to present evidence that will support your request. If you're trying to teach your readers how to use a PDA, you need to create a logical sequence of steps. To consider purpose, take a look at Raghav Sachdev's personal Web site included in the montage on p. 8. What do you think the writer's purpose was for this Web text? What do you think Sachdev did to achieve his purpose?

There are at least three purposes for the Web site, two of which are obvious and one of which isn't. The first obvious purpose, as Sachdev explains, is "to see where I am in my academic career and to evaluate what I have done so far." The second is to present himself in the most favorable light possible. This Web site is an electronic portfolio—a Web site that Sachdev will probably maintain throughout his college years and use when he applies for jobs or possibly to graduate school. The site will introduce him to employers (or admissions officers), presenting his credentials and experiences. The third and less obvious purpose is that Sachdev designed this site for a course on electronic portfolios, so he needed to meet the criteria set forth by the instructor.

Sachdev tries to achieve his purposes through a variety of visual and verbal means. He includes a photograph of himself, which personalizes the page. He incorporates links to relevant organizations—his school and three academic departments—for readers who are interested in learning more about his academic life. A navigation bar across the bottom links to information about career-related skills, including programming, leadership experiences, and managerial abilities, as well as his résumé. He also provides internal and external links along the left-hand side so readers can learn more about him and his interests.

Throughout this book you'll learn more about how to identify and understand audience, circumstances, and purposes, and you'll also learn how to take that information and use it to meet a series of objectives that all writers need to address.

Focusing on a Writer's Objectives

Regardless of the type of text being written—a report for school, a letter to your grandmother, a proposal for your employer, a newsletter for your sorority—there are certain objectives all writers have to achieve if they want to produce an effective document. These objectives form the framework for all of the chapters in Part 1 of this book, and you'll see them emphasized throughout the book because they are important to any type of writing. The objectives work as a set of goals in drafting any document, and when you achieve your objectives as a writer—using both words and images—you will produce appropriate, relevant, functional texts in any setting.

Keep in mind that you will not try to meet these objectives one at a time or even in the same way for every writing project or assignment. There are many different strategies that you can use to achieve the objectives, and throughout this book you'll find descriptions of these strategies and suggestions for choosing the most appropriate ones. Your decisions about the best way to meet the objectives will be based on the context for your document. The chapters in Part 1 will guide you in understanding your context and using that knowledge to meet the objectives described below.

Developing a Topic

In any writing situation, you have some kind of subject that you're writing about, and you need to find some way to develop that topic for your text. In other words, you have to think of things to say about the topic. Most writers—students and professionals alike—begin a writing project with the fear that they won't have enough to say to meet the needs of the assignment or task. Part 1 offers many strategies for developing a topic that vary depending on the kind of text you are creating.

Engaging an Audience

What does it mean to engage an audience? To get your readers' attention, to get them involved or interested enough to start reading, you need an effective introduction to your text. People don't *have* to read what you've written, so you need to persuade them to do so. In newspapers, magazines, and Web sites, for example, writers may place striking photographs or other visuals at the beginning, but there are other effective techniques.

Creating an Appropriate Voice

Whether you realize it or not, every text has a *voice*. The voice of a text reflects a personality, a set of attitudes, or even the literal sound of a person speaking. Read the following sentence aloud several times, trying to reflect each voice described.

"John spent $10,000 on a new boat," she said
{
angrily.
laughingly.
hysterically.
enviously.
mysteriously.

As you read these sentences, notice how you change the emphasis on different words, use different inflections, and adjust your pace. These sentences contain explicit cues about the kind of voice to give to the words. Yet writers create voice even when they're not writing dialogue. Just read aloud any of the texts shown on the beginning pages of this chapter. Do you hear the different voices? In your own writing you'll want to create an appropriate voice, depending on your audience, circumstances, and purposes.

Providing Structure

The structure of a document tells readers what to expect and helps them find information easily. A table of contents provides structure for navigating a book or electronic text, as do headings and layouts. You may not have thought a lot about providing structure in your own documents, but you will need to meet this objective as you create more complex and sophisticated texts.

Concluding the Text

All good things come to an end. But you don't want to just end your text; you want your conclusion to reinforce your purpose for writing. Reading the conclusions of many different texts will help you figure out which strategy for concluding works (or doesn't work) for your text.

Designing and Integrating Visual Information

Today's writers don't just string words together. They create posters, flyers, brochures, and Web sites. They produce reports that contain charts and graphs. They scan photographs and integrate them with words. They use various features of type (different fonts, bold, italics, and so on) to create headings and links that help draw readers' attention to important points. As you work through the assignments in Part 1, you'll find advice on paying attention to the design of your work and on choosing appropriate design elements from a host of possibilities.

A Sample Student Text

To give you an idea of how the six objectives lead to effective communication, let's examine a highly effective student report, written for a course much like the one you are taking now. Look closely at the opening section of this report on the following page.

Margaret Tomeo chose her topic—anterior cruciate ligament (ACL) injuries—because she was concerned about one type of injury that is common among women athletes. But what exactly makes her text effective? First, she quickly captures the interest of her readers, engaging them in a variety of ways. For example, she begins with a brief quotation from a woman athlete who suffered an ACL injury. This quotation and the description that follows in the next paragraph give the report credibility: readers learn of one athlete's firsthand experience with the injury. Tomeo's opening also creates in readers an emotional, sympathetic response to the athlete's experience.

Another way that Tomeo engages her audience is through a catchy title. The acronym *ACL*, which will be recognized by readers familiar with this type of injury, is followed by a strong statement about the injury (she calls it a "curse"). The title will be seen as valid by readers who know something about ACL injuries and will likely intrigue readers who are not familiar with them.

The second paragraph provides information about the athlete quoted in paragraph 1 and another injured athlete and cites anecdotal evidence of other such injuries. All of this evidence heightens readers' awareness of the widespread nature of the problem and leads directly to the thesis statement that ends the paragraph: "As the number of women competing in sports continues to increase, understanding the causes of this common injury will enable us to help these athletes reduce their risk." The thesis statement explicitly creates the expectation that readers will learn more about the causes of ACL injuries and may even learn how to avoid these problems. Readers who are concerned about ACL injuries—either for themselves or for friends or relatives—now have a good reason to continue reading Tomeo's report.

Yet another obvious way that Margaret engages her audience is by incorporating a photograph of a female athlete wearing a knee brace. The photo serves to attract the attention of women who play basketball

Margaret Tomeo
Professor Odell
English 102
March 22, 2004

ACL: The Curse of Women Athletes

"I knew right away exactly what I did." (McCallum and Gelin 44).

After hearing a rip in her right knee, Tiffany Woosley, a shooting guard for the University of Tennessee Lady Vols, knew she had torn her ACL, or anterior cruciate ligament. She was performing a simple jump shot and landed incorrectly—and her injury caused her to miss the rest of the season. This has become the story for too many women athletes, including Woosley's teammate Nikki McCray, an All-American forward who tore her ACL in a pickup game (McCallum and Gelin). Duke University's Monique Currie tore her ACL in a

pre-season game, possibly ruining their hopes for a big season (See Fig.1). And Brandi Chastain missed her 1987 and 1988 college soccer seasons after having surgery for the ACL in both knees (Patrick). ACL tears are turning into an epidemic among women athletes at all levels of sports, especially among high school and college players. As the number of women competing in sports continues to increase, understanding the causes of this common injury will enable us to help these athletes reduce their risk.

Fig. 1. Photograph of Monique Currie. From Nick Wass, "No. 1 Blue Devils Counting on Currie," by Jim Reedy, Washington Post 16 Mar. 2004: D1. Monique Currie and her knee brace illustrate that women athletes at all levels are susceptible to injury.

Title features an acronym and dramatic word choice.

Introduction begins with a cryptic quotation.

Anecdote provides evidence of injury.

Photograph of woman athlete wearing knee brace attracts readers' attention.

Caption provides source and reinforces concern.

Thesis statement creates expectations of report contents.

and similar sports, fans of women's basketball, women who have suffered knee injuries, and the families and friends of women athletes.

A Sample Student Context Analysis

Later on as you read the entire report (found in Chapter 3), you will note how Tomeo met all of the objectives outlined above. At this point, understand that while Tomeo was an excellent student, she wasn't born knowing how to engage an audience. She learned what to do to produce an effective report from working with the materials provided in this textbook. Specifically, she learned how to think about the context for her report by completing a context analysis. Then she learned some specific strategies that helped her figure out how to meet the objectives.

EXCERPTS FROM MARGARET TOMEO'S CONTEXT ANALYSIS

Audience Knowledge, Values, and Needs

What sort of experiences (personal or secondhand) have my readers had with my topic?

Most likely they know someone who has experienced an ACL tear.

Margaret assumes her readers already know a bit about this injury.

Circumstances

Are there any recent events that might motivate my audience to read my report? If so, what are they?

A teammate or a friend who plays a sport may have just suffered an ACL tear; my readers will be curious about this injury if they know someone who has torn their ACL recently or is wearing a brace. They may have read about it in the paper or seen it on TV. It has happened to many professional female athletes, especially basketball players (Rebecca Lobo) and soccer players (Brandi Chastain), and even Michelle Yeoh, a movie actress.

Her readers are likely to feel a personal connection to and interest in this topic.

Readers will want to know the effect ACL will have on their friends or relatives who have suffered the injury.

In addition to the personal connection, readers may have heard something about this injury in news reports about famous people with ACL tears.

Purposes

What purposes am I trying to accomplish in writing my report? What overall impression do I want to leave my reader with?

I'm trying to make my readers aware of this common problem so that they can help themselves and others reduce the risk of the injury. I hope my readers will incorporate my advice into their sports and/or workouts.

Margaret's readers will want to avoid the injury themselves or help others avoid it.

A portion of the context analysis that Tomeo completed before she began writing her report appears on p. 18. (To see Tomeo's full context analysis, turn to p. 151 in Chapter 3.) As you scan the excerpt reproduced here, notice that the questions ask you to think about the three aspects of context that are relevant to all documents: audience, circumstances, and purposes. In each Part 1 chapter, after you've chosen a topic for your assignment, you'll be guided to answer a set of these questions for analyzing context.

Using Strategies to Meet Your Objectives

In every chapter in Part 1, you'll find a variety of strategies that you can use to meet your objectives as a writer, and the work you do answering the questions for analyzing context will help you choose the most appropriate strategies. Green "how-to" boxes throughout these chapters present strategies specifically designed to help with the particular kind of writing discussed in the chapter. Each box includes not only several strategies to help you meet a given objective but also examples from the chapter's readings.

Samples from Strategy Boxes

Below, you'll find two samples taken from strategy boxes in Chapter 3, Reports. These boxes discuss two strategies—relating to readers and establishing conflict—that will help writers of reports engage an audience.

The first sample appears in the How to Relate to Readers strategy box. The left-hand column discusses a way of relating to readers of a report. The right-hand column then explains how Margaret Tomeo used the strategy in her paper on ACL injuries.

How to Relate to Readers

Strategies

Include an easily recognizable visual. If this visual also creates a conflict, so much the better. But the conflict and other important elements of the picture or graphic must remind readers of something they know, care about, or need.

Examples

Sometimes writers create visual images with words, but Tomeo does it with a photograph of a well-known woman athlete wearing a type of brace that most athletes will recognize as symptomatic of knee injury.

The second sample is taken from the How to Establish Conflict strategy box. On the left-hand side is one method that the writer of a report might use to show readers what they don't know about a subject. On the right, an example taken from Tomeo's paper shows how she used this strategy.

How to Establish Conflict

Strategies

Tell a story about actions that conflict with what readers expect or that dramatizes a problem about which readers are concerned. This sort of beginning must be filled with specific, credible details; otherwise, readers may dismiss it as too sensationalist.

Examples

Although Tomeo expects her readers to be familiar with ACL, they may not realize how pervasive such injuries have become. Her introduction lists facts about the incidence of this injury and ends with a comment about causation that readers may not have thought about.

You'll find boxes such as these—often with several strategies in each box and always accompanied by examples from the readings—throughout the chapters in Part 1. As you work on your assignments in Part 1, these boxes will give you ideas about how to meet your objectives. Try out different strategies to see which ones seem the most promising for your audience, circumstances, and purposes. Since the examples in these boxes always come from a reading, you may want to refer back to the reading itself to get more ideas. Keep in mind that you will not use all of the strategies for any one assignment. Also remember that strategies from one chapter may help you achieve the objectives for an assignment in another chapter. For example, you may learn in Chapter 3 how to include an easily recognizable visual that might engage the audience for a proposal (an assignment in Chapter 6).

Using *Writing in a Visual Age*

It's unlikely that your instructor will ask you to read every chapter in *Writing in a Visual Age*, but you will benefit from knowing all the types of information the book contains. You may find that you can use some of the chapters in Parts 2 and 3 as resources to help you with assignments in Part 1, or you may use ideas from any of the chapters for assignments in other courses. The rest of this chapter provides an overview of the material you will find in this book.

Part 1: Writing Assignments

The chapters in Part 1 introduce you to six different types of projects.

> profiles
> reports

> position papers
> evaluations
> proposals
> instructions

Each chapter follows a similar format, first discussing what it is that makes this type of text different from others. Chapter 3, for example, points to the unique characteristics that make a report different from other types of writing, reviewing the elements that make a report particularly effective. In the Reading to Write section, you'll read sample texts, or readings, written by professionals and students, that exemplify those characteristics. Each reading is followed by questions designed to get you thinking about its features and suggestions for thinking about topics for your assignment. Throughout each chapter, the readings are used to demonstrate the strategies writers employ to meet their objectives.

Next, you'll be given an assignment (which your instructor may modify) and guidelines for creating a text of your own. The Guide to Writing portion of each chapter includes explanations, analyses, and activities— all aimed toward helping you learn the strategies that the writers of the sample readings used to achieve their objectives. Throughout the Guide you'll also encounter purple boxes titled Working on the Assignment that provide specific suggestions for composing your own text.

Each chapter's Guide to Writing is divided into three sections—Getting Started, Drafting, and Finishing Up—that represent the logical and chronological nature of the writing process. (That is, you cannot begin writing until you select a topic, and you cannot revise your draft until you write one.) However, note also that writing is *not* a linear process. You will move back and forth through the process, returning to review and assess aspects of each assignment. The three parts of the process point to the things you need to do to create your text, and you will recognize them as obvious once they're pointed out to you in the following paragraphs.

First, getting started involves two tasks: selecting a topic and analyzing the context for your work. Many students have a hard time figuring out what they should write about. The chapters in Part 1 feature activities designed to help you brainstorm lists of topics—whether on your own or with other students. Getting started also involves narrowing the field and focusing on a topic that will satisfy the requirements of the assignment as well as analyzing the context for the assignment. In other words, you need to consider the audience you're trying to address, the circumstances in which your readers will encounter your text, and your purposes for writing this text for that audience. Completing the context analysis, and revising it as you become more familiar with your topic, will allow you to analyze your context, plan your text, and make decisions appropriate for your audience, circumstances, and purposes.

Once you select a topic and analyze the context for your work, you can move on to drafting your assignment. As you draft, the advice in each chapter in Part 1 will help you focus on and meet the six objectives introduced earlier in this chapter. The green-shaded boxes present practical strategies alongside analysis of professional and student texts that use the strategies to meet the objectives. Studying these strategies and examples will give you ideas that you can incorporate in your own work. In addition, you'll encounter purple-shaded Working on the Assignment boxes throughout each Part 1 chapter that will guide you through drafting your assignment. These boxes offer brief directions, explaining what you can do to complete the assignment while ensuring that you meet all of the objectives.

After you have written your draft and met the objectives to the best of your ability, it's time to finish up. What that means is you need to get some help to see how well you have met those objectives. One of the best ways to accomplish this is to ask a classmate to review your paper. A peer review will help ensure that you have met the criteria established by your instructor for the assignment. You may find it makes the most sense to swap papers with a classmate, because as you read your classmate's paper, you'll be reminded of the criteria yourself. Once you have feedback from a classmate or other reviewer, it's time to revise your paper and submit the final version to your instructor. You may also have feedback from your instructor to take into consideration, such as notes the instructor wrote on your draft or that you made during a conference. Pay close attention to the feedback you've received from all sources, incorporating the best suggestions into your final paper. Keep in mind your audience, circumstances, and purposes as you revise.

As you work through the chapters in Part 1, complete any of the individual or group activities that your instructor assigns as well as the tasks suggested in the Working on the Assignment boxes as you encounter them in the chapter. Doing each assignment in small increments will enable you to work with a variety of strategies, choose the ones that work best for your particular topic and context, and make the most of your time and effort in this course.

While your instructor may not require you to read and complete the assignments in all six chapters of Part 1, you may find it helpful to refer back to the chapters when you have assignments for these types of documents in other courses. For example, you might use Chapter 4 to write a position paper for a history course, or you might consult Chapter 7 to write the instructions for software you designed for a computer science course.

Part 2: Strategies for Design and Research

Part 2 includes five resource chapters. Although your instructor may not assign all of these chapters, you can take advantage of the material as you need it for this or other courses.

Chapter 8, Designing Pages and Screens, opens Part 2 with an overview of some of the most important elements of visual presentation. Here you'll find a wealth of information about layout: explanations and descriptions of the major elements of layout (such as columns and white space), the principles of page design (such as tension and alignment), and other important details (such as page numbering and indenting). In addition, you'll learn how to choose or create graphics and figure out how and where to insert them. The chapter covers both pictorial graphics, such as photographs and drawings, and representational graphics, such as pie charts and bar graphs. Suggestions for working with color and choosing fonts for the most effective presentation are also provided.

The other four chapters in Part 2 all pertain to conducting research. Chapter 9, Doing Research, guides you through library and Internet research: how to find the information you need, sort through your results, and organize your data. When your assignments call for primary research, you'll want to read Chapter 10, Conducting Field Research, which explains how to conduct interviews, surveys, and observational research.

Chapter 11, Evaluating Sources and Taking Notes, will help you evaluate the credibility of your sources. In an era when anyone with a computer and Internet access can create a Web site, it has become increasingly important to determine the validity and trustworthiness of sources. Chapter 11 analyzes the credibility of a variety of sources and provides guidelines for analyzing your own sources. This chapter also makes suggestions for taking notes as you do your research, including tips for creating and organizing quotations, paraphrases, and summaries and avoiding plagiarism.

Chapter 12, Using and Documenting Sources, has two major components. The first section of the chapter provides a sample student paper that models how one student met the writer's objectives for a research report. The second section focuses on documenting sources and formatting in-text citations and reference lists in the MLA (Modern Language Association) and the APA (American Psychological Association) styles.

Part 3: Strategies for Special Writing Situations

The chapters in Part 3 introduce you to communicating in specific situations. Chapter 13, Writing for the Classroom, focuses on the types of writing you will most likely be asked to do in other courses. Specifically, the chapter gives you suggestions for responding to three types of academic writing assignments: assigned essays, in-class writing (including essay exams), and electronic writing. Although you may be familiar with these types of writing, you may find that the expectations are different in college courses than in your prior academic experience.

For some courses, you may be asked to produce a portfolio of your writing, or you may need to create a portfolio later when you begin to look for a job. Chapter 14, Writing Portfolios, helps you think about how to choose materials to include, write required texts, and organize a print or electronic writing portfolio.

Chapter 15, Writing for the Community, describes how writing outside the academic environment differs from typical academic writing. This chapter responds to a growing interest in service-learning courses that ask students to do "real" work in "real" environments, such as in nonprofit and community-based organizations. Here you will learn how to adapt your writing to meet the needs of an audience that wants and needs your work.

Finally, Chapter 16, Making Oral Presentations, focuses on the differences between presenting information orally and in writing. Using model texts, the chapter shows what will and will not work in oral presentations. Your instructor may not assign this chapter, but you will find it helpful for the presentations you'll be asked to make in other courses and in your career.

The Glossary of Visual and Rhetorical Terms at the back of the book provides definitions for key terms that appear throughout this text. In addition to writing-related terms, the glossary includes definitions, examples, and cross-references for many terms related to visuals and design.

Writing Assignments

2
Profiles

N EXPLANATION OF HOW A POLITICIAN WENT FROM A CHILD- HOOD ON WELFARE TO A CAREER

in the U.S. Senate, a photo-essay about one night in a hospital emergency room, an account of a reporter's experiences on a road in a distant country, a story about a children's television personality, an account of what makes a friend truly exceptional. Different subjects, different page layouts, different messages. What they have in common, however, is that they are all profiles—efforts to capture in words and images the unique character or spirit of a person, a place, or the activities that go on in a place.

Typically, the term *profile* is applied to stories about people, in which writers convey the unique experiences and qualities of an individual. Sometimes the person being profiled is an individual whose name and position many readers will recognize, and sometimes the subject is known only to a few people until the writer profiles him or her for a larger public. But people, whether famous or obscure, are not the only possible subjects for profiles. A place may also have a personality or a distinctive atmosphere that readers will be curious about. Indeed, some of the profiles in the

"Once upon a time, a long time ago, a man took off his jacket and put on a sweater. Then he took off his shoes and put on a pair of sneakers. His name was Fred Rogers. He was starting a television program."

– Tom Junod,
"Can You Say . . . 'Hero'?"

27

Reading to Write section of this chapter will take you into unfamiliar situations, increasing your understanding not only of these situations but also of the people and activities associated with them.

No matter what the topic is—a person, place, or activity—profiles have one basic goal: to provide readers with an insider's view of the topic. That is, profiles try to give readers a sense of experiencing the topic for themselves: hearing someone speak candidly, observing activities that happen spontaneously, or reaching understandings that are not readily apparent to people who are not insiders. In part, creating such an experience entails providing readers with information—verifiable facts about a person, place, or activity. But it also entails choosing facts that evoke emotions, attitudes, and/or values, conveying the full richness of an experience.

Providing an Insider's View

Think back to the last time you saw a television reporter interview someone who had just been through a profoundly moving experience— winning (or losing) an Olympic gold medal, for example, or surviving a natural disaster. Almost invariably the first question asked was something like, "How does it feel to . . . ?" or "What was it like to . . . ?" or "What did you think when . . . ?" Blunt as such questions might be, they reflect a fundamental desire to become insiders, to go behind the scenes and experience as directly and powerfully as possible something that for most people may be completely beyond their daily experience. To do this, you will need to apply some of the following questions to your topic.

> What is special or distinctive about the person, place, or activity about which you are writing?

> How does your topic relate to things your readers know about, care about, or have experienced? Why should readers care about your topic?

> What emotions, attitudes, or values does your topic evoke?

> How do other people—especially insiders who know your topic well—view the topic? What do they say about it? How do they react to it? What do their words and actions tell you about the topic?

> What surprises you (and, potentially, your readers) the most about the topic?

> How did the person, place, or activity become the way he or she or it is? What forces shaped your topic? What factors contributed to its unique or surprising character?

In order to answer these questions effectively, you have to develop a thorough understanding of the context in which your profile will be read.

Profiles in Context

To answer questions like "What is special about this subject?" or "Why should readers care?" you need to think about the context in which your profile will be read. Who do you hope will read the profile? What would they want to gain by reading it? Under what circumstances will they encounter the profile? In terms of your experience with other school assignments, your answer to these questions may seem obvious: your reader is usually your instructor, someone who has given an assignment in part to help you become a better writer. Your reader will encounter your writing when it comes in along with all the other writing submitted by your classmates. Your purpose is to show that you are learning something about writing—or perhaps simply to earn a good grade.

There's just enough truth in this answer to make it misleading. Of course your work will be assigned and graded by your instructor. But in the writing you do for this course and beyond, it will ultimately be most useful to take a broader view of context. Begin with the assumption that you are writing for someone who is not obliged to read what you have written. You have to earn this person's interest and attention, in part by making your work appeal to what he or she knows and cares about and in part by relating your work to the reader's current circumstances—events he or she may have experienced personally, read about, or seen in movies or on television. Further, you have to develop a clear sense of your purpose in writing, an understanding of what you hope to do for the reader. As you learn to think carefully about the context for your writing, you will grow as a writer. And you should improve your grades, as well.

Audience

The two previous paragraphs use the term *reader* as though you will be writing for a single individual. Throughout this book, you will find advice to begin thinking of your audience by identifying a specific individual (or a small group of individuals). This approach will make it easier to determine what your audience knows about your subject and the values or needs that might prompt someone like that individual to read what you have written.

Your understanding of your audience will vary widely, depending on the characteristics of the individual you envision reading your profile.

But remember that readers of profiles are likely to share at least one characteristic: they want to become insiders, go behind the scenes, get past the superficial or the obvious. They want answers to such questions as "What is this person really like? What is special about a particular place or the activities that go on there?" Your readers will want factual answers that are part of a public record or that can be corroborated by other observers. But the readers of your profile may also welcome your personal observations or reactions, just so long as all this information adds up to a valid, insightful overall impression.

Circumstances

Sometimes circumstances make it easy to interest a reader in the subject of your profile. Is the person you want to profile engaged in a political campaign or a personal scandal (or both)? Is he or she receiving widespread attention because of a scientific discovery, a trial, or a performance in movies or on television? Is the place the site of a war or a newly discovered vacation spot? Is the activity something your reader has recently heard about or experienced, either personally or through reading or other media? If so, and if your reader is aware of these circumstances, he or she may be eager to read what you have written.

But what of topics your reader has never heard of or been interested in? In these cases, you will have to work harder to interest your reader. Part of the way to do this is to show how that person, place, or activity relates to your reader's circumstances—the events and experiences he or she is aware of, either personally or vicariously. Would your audience be willing to read a profile of a hospital emergency room? Perhaps—if members of your audience have ever had to go to an emergency room, have read accounts of random violence in some large cities, or are familiar with the television program *ER*. Part of your job as a writer is to discover your readers' experiences—personal or vicarious—and show how your profile's topic relates to those experiences.

Purposes

A profile writer's basic purpose is to give readers an insider's view of the person, place, or activity that is the focus of the profile. Beyond this, the writer's purpose may vary widely. For instance, consider the profiles found in this chapter. In one, the writer tries to convince a sophisticated, potentially skeptical group of readers that the children's television personality Mr. Rogers was, in fact, a hero, someone who could command the respect of adults as well as children. In another, a television news anchor conveys his sense of the sadness and devastation of war-ravaged Afghanistan. In yet another, a student explains why and how one of her classmates provided a profound personal influence. When you write a profile, you will have a specific purpose in mind. Different as the purposes of profile-writers can be, in all cases their readers should come away with a dominant impression, a strong sense of what a person, place, or activity is really like, and why that topic matters.

 ## For Collaboration

Think about situations in which you are an insider. Perhaps you play a sport your classmates don't know much about, or you have an unusual hobby or job. Perhaps you've spent time in a place your classmates haven't been to. Make a list of some of the details that you know as an insider but that would not be apparent to someone who is an outsider to the sport, job, hobby, or place. Using your insider knowledge, get together with several classmates and explain what is distinctive or special about your topic. Try to give them an insider's view of that topic.

Visual Information in Context

In subsequent chapters of this book, you will learn how writers—including you—can make use of a wide range of visual elements: page or screen layout, for example, and charts, graphs, and tables. This chapter will concentrate on photographs, the kind of visual that appears most frequently in profiles. Typically, people regard photographs as sources of factual information, assuming that the camera doesn't lie. Sometimes this assumption is valid; the picture taken in a "photo finish," for example, is often the most reliable way to determine the winner of a horse race. But current technology makes it possible to alter not only the impression a photograph makes but also its content. Even without the use of special technology, the way a picture is taken conveys not only what the photographer sees but also certain emotions, attitudes, and values.

This is not to discredit the use of photographs. Indeed, they can contribute greatly to the overall effectiveness of many types of writing. However, photographic images, like every other aspect of a text, should be read carefully. In reading the photographs that accompany a profile, the key question is this: How does the impression created by the photograph (or series of photographs) contribute to an understanding of the unique qualities of the person, place, or activity being profiled? This is a very broad question, and it is helpful to look for three kinds of answers: those relating to the photograph's composition (the arrangement of visual elements within the picture), selection of details, and accompanying description, if any.

> For more information on the effective uses of these visual elements, see **Chapter 8.**

Questions to Ask When Reading Visual Information in Profiles

How is the picture composed? That is, what people or objects are shown, and how are they located in relation to each other? What attitudes are suggested by the way the picture is composed? Will those attitudes make sense to the audience? More specifically:

> What is the focal point of the picture? To whom or what is the reader's eye drawn first? What people or objects are particularly noticeable because they are near the center of the photograph, in the foreground (relatively close to the camera), or distinct in size, color, or some other physical characteristic?

> What viewing angle is represented? When the person or object in the picture is shown as if someone is looking up at it from below, the viewing angle usually makes the subject seem important or powerful. If the perspective is that of looking downward, the angle tends to make viewers seem relatively strong or important and the subject seem weak or unimportant.

> Who or what occupies the upper half of the picture? Who or what occupies the lower half? As a rule, people or objects in the upper half of a picture seem more important or powerful than people or objects in the lower half.

> What kinds of lines and shapes appear in the photograph? Especially notice diagonal lines or sharp, jagged ones. Diagonal lines can suggest movement or threat; jagged lines often create tension or anxiety. Shapes that appear ready to collide, collapse, or crush other shapes can have similar effects.

> If the picture is in color, what associations do those colors have? Warm colors such as red and orange typically evoke strong emotional reactions; cool colors such as blue have a calming effect; dark colors suggest something sinister or gloomy. If the picture is in black and white, which parts of it are relatively light, and which are relatively dark?

What kinds of details appear in the photograph? What associations might they have for the reader? Are any significant details missing? How are the details similar to or different from what the audience knows or expects?

> If people are depicted, what is most noticeable about their facial expressions, gestures, posture, clothing, or size relative to other people or objects in the picture?

❭ If an object is depicted, what aspects of its size, color, or other physical characteristics make it stand out?

❭ What relationships are suggested? For example, does the picture juxtapose very different objects or people? Does it include details suggesting that one person or object is going to affect some other person or object?

❭ What is the physical setting or scene?

❭ What attitudes, emotions, or values is the reader likely to associate with the people or objects and the physical setting?

● **If the photograph is captioned, does the caption add to the reader's understanding of the people or objects depicted?**

❭ Does the caption explain what is going on in the photograph?

❭ Does the caption express or imply emotions, attitudes, or values?

❭ Is the name of the photographer, date of the picture, or the source of the image emphasized? Prominent display of such information can suggest newsworthiness, academic or historical significance, or commercial importance.

 ## Exercise

Bring to class a profile that contains several striking pictures. Identify the effect these pictures create and, by answering some of the questions discussed above, try to determine how the effect is achieved. Be prepared to show the pictures to your classmates and explain how they create a particular effect and what they add to the impressions conveyed through the written text.

FIGURE 2.1
**Visual Elements in
"The Road to Kabul,"
a Profile in a
Magazine**

● **Image** The girl's face and the tank behind her are the *focal point* drawing viewers' attention. In this composition, it is impossible to focus on the girl without seeing the tank, and vice versa.

● **Image** Details in the photo show a desolate landscape, military equipment, and a seemingly vulnerable child—all details that have a strong emotional impact.

● **Caption** The article title functions as a caption for the photo, although a more detailed caption appears on a facing page.

● **Caption** The boldfaced introductory sentences also helps readers locate the scene shown in the photo.

THE ROAD TO KABUL

More than 20 years after his first journey to Afghanistan, **DAN RATHER** returned to the war zone. Here, the CBS anchor writes about how the devastated country has changed—and how it hasn't

38   TV GUIDE FEBRUARY 2, 2002

Sample Analysis | The Road to Kabul

Later in this chapter, the profile "The Road to Kabul" begins with a photograph of a young girl in the foreground (relatively close to the camera) and two tanks in the background (see Figure 2.1). Readers may have a lot of questions about this photograph. For instance, the girl appears to be standing in a road. Is this actually the road—or a road—that leads to Kabul? Was the photograph posed? Or did the photographer just happen to be in the right place at the right time? Readers have no way to answer such questions. Nevertheless, the photograph is striking; it evokes strong feelings and seems to provide some insight into the plight of Afghan citizens. To see how and why the photograph has this effect, consider the annotations that analyze its composition, details, and captions.

The composition of this image is likely to create a strong emotional reaction that is consistent with the view developed in the written text: war-torn Afghanistan is a place of great human suffering, even among those who are not combatants in the war. As you can see, the focal point of the picture includes two objects located just above the center of the photograph: the face of the young girl in the foreground, and the nearer tank in the background. Because the child is in the foreground, she appears relatively large. But the power and menace of the tank are suggested not simply by its presence but by the fact that it occupies the upper half of the picture, a location that emphasizes its dominant,

threatening relationship to the child. This relationship is also emphasized by the slightly diagonal line formed by the front of the tank. Whether or not the tank is actually moving, diagonal lines suggest movement—which, in this case, appears to bring the tank dangerously close to the child.

The details in the picture make the child seem especially vulnerable. She is completely defenseless, and there is no indication that she is aware of the tank (she appears to be gazing off into the distance) or that the tank commander is aware of her. The setting is particularly disturbing. The girl is not in any of the usual places one might expect to find a child (in the yard of her home, for example) but rather in the middle of a road that appears to be heavily trafficked with military vehicles. Thus the picture echoes the mood of human dislocation, devastation, and despair that will be suggested in much of the written text.

As the title of the profile, "The Road to Kabul," appears prominently below the picture, readers will associate the road in the title with the road in the photograph. Although magazine captions are often positioned below photographs, the caption for this picture, "A girl near old Soviet Army tanks," appears inconspicuously on the facing page (see p. 46). Although the tank is old, it is still large and threatening. If readers notice this caption, it will reinforce their first impressions.

Exercise › **bedfordstmartins.com/visualage**
*Click on **CHAPTER 2** › **VISUALS***

For practice analyzing the visual information in another sample profile, see the visual exercises on the companion Web site for this book.

Reading to Write

In your principal assignment for this chapter, you will write a profile that provides an insider's view on either a topic of your choice or one selected by your instructor. You will draw on various sources such as readings, personal experiences, and interviews in order to satisfy your readers' curiosity about what a particular person, place, or activity is like.

The following profiles, which come from a wide range of sources, will help you see some of the strategies you might use in your own profile. In addition, the variety of subjects covered here may suggest some of the different kinds of topics about which you might write.

Each reading is followed by questions (Reflecting on What You Have Read) that will start you thinking about what is involved in creating an effective profile. Also, at the end of each profile you will find a Thinking Ahead prompt, suggesting ways a given reading might help you decide on a topic for your own profile. The subsequent sections of the chapter will help you get started on your assignment, compose a draft, and assess and revise that draft.

› **bedfordstmartins.com/
visualage**

*For additional examples
of profiles, click on*
CHAPTER 2 › **EXAMPLES**

This profile of Senator Patty Murray appeared in *People* magazine, in a series of profiles of women who serve in the U.S. Senate. Throughout the profile, authors Thomas Fields-Meyer, Elizabeth Velez, and Mary Boone emphasize Senator Murray's reputation as "a one-time soccer mom who represents the interests of ordinary folks." Why do you suppose the authors gave this emphasis to their profile?

From Welfare to Washington

THOMAS FIELDS-MEYER, ELIZABETH VELEZ, MARY BOONE

Once told that a mom with kids had no place in politics, Patty Murray carves out a powerful niche in the U.S. Senate

In the 10th of PEOPLE'S occasional series on the 13 women currently in the U.S. Senate, we profile Washington Democrat Patty Murray. Raised in a tiny town by parents of modest means, she could not afford even such basics as health care. On the Hill since 1993, she has made it her duty to put the needs of average families first.

Patty Murray was a young mother of two when she first visited the Washington State Senate in the early '80s. Then a homemaker, she had come to fight against budget cuts for an educational program that had helped her improve her parenting skills. "I was trying to figure out why these people couldn't understand what was happening with kids and families," she says. "And I realized that I was looking down on all these old bald heads."

She lost the battle, at least temporarily. But the encounter helped spur Murray, 51, to enter local politics a few years later, starting down a path that would lead her to the U.S. Senate. There she has made a name for herself as a one-time soccer mom who represents the interests of ordinary folks. "She didn't create this image to win a political race," says

Murray "never tries to be something she's not," says Sen. Tom Daschle, a fan.

"She's gutsy," a colleague says of Murray
(at a Yakima, Wash., apple farm).

Sid Snyder, majority leader of the state senate. "That's who she is."

Those feelings shaped her political priorities—such as the Family & Medical Leave Act she helped pass in her first year in D.C. and the education bill she successfully sponsored in 1998, aimed at hiring 100,000 new teachers nationally. Her achievements have brought her increasing clout. Appointed last December as the first woman to chair the Democratic Senatorial Campaign Committee, she was charged with raising funds for the party's upcoming Senate races. Since the Sept. 11 attacks, she has a new challenge, chairing the Senate Appropriations Subcommittee on Transportation, which oversees legislation regarding the nation's airports—such as the airline-security bill the Senate unanimously passed in October. Terry McAuliffe, chair of the Democratic National Committee, says Murray's sensitivity and determination will make her a major player. "Because she's so unassuming, she's often underestimated," he says. "But she is up and coming—one of the Senate's shining stars."

Murray was born in 1950, one of twin sisters, to David Johns, a dime-store manager, and his homemaker wife, Beverly (both deceased), in the rural community of Bothell, Wash. The family—Murray has five other siblings besides her twin—got by but couldn't afford to buy health insurance or even visit a clinic. "We suffered through measles, chicken pox and everything else that kids get," says Murray, "and we never went to see a doctor." Still, the children gained a civic sense. Beverly cleaned the local church every Sunday morning, and the family regularly took food to poor families. "My parents taught me that we have an obligation to something bigger than ourselves," says Murray.

They also instilled a strong work ethic in their children, who labored in a variety of jobs from picking strawberries to helping in the store. "We all worked," says Murray's twin sister, Peggy Zehnder, a seventh-grade teacher in Bellingham, Wash., "because that's what we needed to do." It became even more important when Patty was 16 and her family learned that her father had multiple sclerosis. "It was heart stopping," says Murray. "It made us understand that you have to be able to rely on yourself and your family."

With David incapacitated, the Johnses went on welfare briefly, and then Beverly took an accounting course with government aid and got a job as a bookkeeper for a ferry company. That experience gave Murray an appreciation for how government can help in times of need. "Without the social services that allowed her to get the training she needed and get a job," says Murray, "my family wouldn't have made it."

"Women have to work harder in the Senate than men," says Murray (winning in '98).

As a teenager Patty escaped into   7
books and played flute and piccolo in the
school band but had no interest in politics beyond becoming secretary of a girls'
service club. Then, as a Washington State
University freshman, she successfully led
a 1968 protest against a dress code
requiring skirts each night at dinner.

It was also at WSU that she met Rob   8
Murray, whom she married in 1972. She
worked as a secretary to help put him
through his last years of school. Rob,
now 51, was in the Coast Guard and
went on to work loading ship cargo, and
they settled in Shoreline, a bedroom
suburb north of Seattle, where she
became a full-time mom to their son
Randy, born in 1976, and daughter Sara,
born three years later.

Murray was volunteering at a state-   9
funded cooperative preschool when
she learned that the legislature was
going to cancel the program's funding.
Murray drove with the kids 72 miles to
Olympia to complain. But when she
met with a legislator, she says, "I was
told that I could not make a difference,
that I was just a mom in tennis shoes."
She took that as a challenge. "A mom
in tennis shoes has as much right to

make policy as these guys in tasseled
shoes," says Murray, who enlisted
friends and made enough calls to
restore funding.

Inspired by that success, she ran for   10
the school board in Shoreline, losing
by 300 votes. But when the candidate
she had opposed died three months
later, she was appointed to fill his term
and stayed for seven years, eventually
becoming president. Despite an economic slump and a public eager to see
lower taxes, she spoke out for public-
school funding. "It wasn't a popular
view, and I admired her bravery for
that," says Jack Rogers, a retired
Shoreline school administrator. In 1988
she was elected to the state senate,
where she helped pass one of the
nation's first state family-leave laws.
Buoyed by her success, she ran for the
U.S. Senate in 1992, challenging five-
term Republican Congressman Rod
Chandler for the seat vacated by
Democrat Brock Adams. She was dramatically outspent, but her populist
message appealed to voters, and she
took 54 percent of the vote.

In the capital she learned that   11
women still had to prove themselves.
"A woman, when she gets elected, they

A top advocate for education, Murray visited a Seattle school in September.

Husband Rob (with Patty and grandson Aidan) admires his wife's "quiet, inner strength."

with their kids," says chief aide Ben McMakin. "When she calls me at home about work stuff, she actually apologizes." Her own balancing act has become more complicated. After son Randy graduated in 1995 from a Virginia high school, husband Rob and daughter Sara returned to Shoreline, where Rob, who resumed a job as a computer-systems director, "can be seen as his own person," says Murray.

She returns there most weekends, hiking, salmon fishing with her family and visiting constituents. During the week, she e-mails her family daily. She takes satisfaction in the work but never forgets that it was family that got her into this in the first place. "The people I meet in Washington, D.C., aren't going to care about me when I leave here," she says. "My family will."

12

wonder if she really knows anything," says Murray. What she did know was the difficulty of balancing work and family. "She wants her staff to be home

Reflecting on What You Have Read

1 It would come as no surprise to most readers to learn that a politician (or, for that matter, anyone else) cultivates a public image that does not reflect his or her private life. In what ways do the authors of this profile try to convince you that Senator Murray's public image and private life are one and the same? Do they succeed in convincing you? Why or why not?

2 To what extent do the photographs of Senator Murray convey an image of someone who represents the interests of "ordinary" citizens? What aspects of the photographs help create this image?

3 Look closely at the captions that accompany the photographs. What do those captions add to your understanding of or attitudes toward Senator Murray?

4 How does this profile explain Senator Murray's reasons for becoming interested in politics? Why might this explanation seem especially appealing to readers of *People* magazine?

5 The authors of this profile go into detail about the challenges Senator Murray has faced as a child and as a parent. What reasons do you see for including information about these challenges?

**Thinking
Ahead**

The authors of "From Welfare to Washington" try to give readers a sense not only of what a public figure is like but also of why this particular person has certain characteristics. Think about people in public life such as politicians, athletes, and historical figures. Are there any about whom you wonder, in effect, "What makes this person tick?" What background influences and motivations cause this person to act a certain way or attain certain achievements? Is there anyone you'd like to research for the writing assignment in this chapter?

Many people know about hospital emergency rooms through the television program *ER*, but relatively few people have actually spent much time in one. In the May 5, 2002, *New York Times Magazine* piece "E.R. Unscripted," author Robert Mackey and photographer Naomi Harris introduce readers to an actual emergency room in an inner-city hospital. As you read and view this profile, think about why the profile has the term *unscripted* in its title.

E.R. Unscripted

ROBERT MACKEY AND NAOMI HARRIS

In this episode, Dr. Sandra Scott works through the night at one of New York City's busiest trauma centers.

Sandra Scott's night begins with a resuscitation and ends, after dawn, with a pile of paperwork. In between is a 12-hour shift at Kings County Hospital Center in Brooklyn. Scott, a 34-year-old specialist in emergency medicine, has worked at Kings County since 1998. Because Kings County is a publicly financed hospital in a low-income neighborhood, many who come in are uninsured, but the hospital is obliged to treat them. Which means that Scott sees a wider range of cases than doctors in most E.R.'s. In addition to dealing with cuts and bullet wounds, on any given night Scott will treat everything from miscarriages and S.T.D.'s to dental problems and what one patient believed was sleep disturbance caused by a spell.

The work is exhausting, but Scott has turned down cushier offers outside the city. "I like taking care of uninsured patients," she says. "My experience in more private settings is that the patients are maybe overeducated. They pick up a *Cosmo* magazine and it tells them that Xanax is good for them, and then you have to explain to them why you don't want to give them Xanax. Patients here, they're pretty grateful." Scott, who grew up in Louisiana, also recently started a rape crisis center at the hospital and spends part of her vacation each year in Haiti, teaching medicine in Port-au-Prince and treating patients in the countryside. She came to Kings County, she says, "because New York City emergency medicine sounded glamorous at the time." When I ask her if it still seems glamorous after four years, she looks at the popping flashbulbs and smiles. "Well," she says, "you're here."

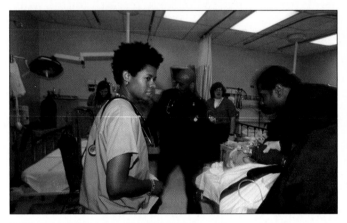

7:42 p.m. Early in the shift, Eli D'Attilo, an 84-year-old man with advanced Alzheimer's, is brought in by paramedics and E.M.T.s, who began resuscitating him at his nursing home. D'Attilo had signed a living will asking that "heroic measures" not be taken to keep him alive, but until they get clearance from the hospital to honor this, Scott and her colleagues must do everything they can to keep D'Attilo from dying.

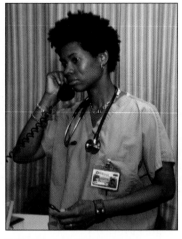

8:20 p.m. While resuscitation continues on D'Attilo, Scott calls the hospital administration. "What can we do to stop this?" she asks. She is told to keep D'Attilo on a respirator, but they can stop treating aggressively. "We developed a relationship with the family," Scott says. "We told them we were hoping he would die while in our care."

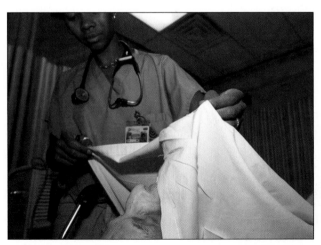

12:40 a.m. As expected, Eli D'Attilo dies on Scott's shift. She pronounces the death, then goes to call his son. "My father didn't just fall asleep," Joseph says. "It took him three and a half years to die." Thankfully, the care in his father's final hours was "very, very excellent," he says. "You'd think Kings County would be the pits, but it was the Cadillac."

12:43 a.m. Diobenton Delmas, 25, comes in after being slashed during an attempted carjacking. Delmas, whose wound stretches from his collarbone to his armpit, seems unshaken by it all. "That's what happens when you're driving those Navigators," he says. "They want those Navigators."

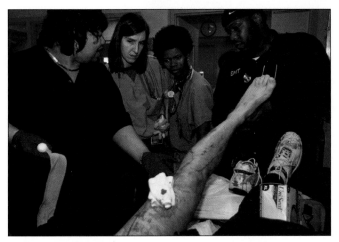

1:02 a.m. Scott examines Roman Mantachev, a Russian tennis instructor who has arrived with a deep wound in his leg. Mantachev claims that he was attacked in the street by people he didn't know. "He was saying they took a stick and poked it through his skin," Scott says, "but it turned out it was from a nice big, fat kitchen knife."

7:25 a.m. By the end of Scott's 12-hour shift, Delmas and Mantachev have been discharged. Scott leaves with a bag packed for a few days in Miami. "It's always nice to finish a shift," she says. "The best thing is just stepping outside."

Reflecting on What You Have Read

❯ For more on analyzing the composition of a photograph, see the questions on p. 32.

1   After reading and viewing this profile, what impressions do you have of Dr. Sandra Scott? What aspects of the written text and the photographs lead you to form this impression?

2   Notice the quotations in the captions that accompany the photographs. What reason(s) do you see for including these quotations?

3   Consider the composition of the photograph that accompanies the caption beginning "1:02 a.m." What does the composition tell you about the patient?

4   Most of the activities that take place in the emergency room are shocking or sad. But the author expresses no reactions to any of them; he just records what people do and say. Would this profile be more effective if it included his personal reactions? Why or why not?

5   What is your reaction to the final image of Dr. Scott? How do the composition and details of the picture help create this reaction? What does the caption contribute to your reaction?

Thinking Ahead

In "E.R. Unscripted," Robert Mackey and Naomi Harris profile an unfamiliar but important workplace, conveying a sense not only of the activities that go on there but also of the people who work there. Think about places where you have worked, places that have a distinct atmosphere or that employ people with interesting personalities or life stories. Looking ahead to your own writing, consider using both photographs and written text to help readers appreciate the unique qualities of an activity that goes on in one of those special places.

On September 11, 2001, religious extremists carried out a surprise attack on the United States by hijacking four commercial airplanes with the intention of crashing them into buildings that were symbols of American power. The attack caused the deaths of everyone on board the airplanes—hundreds of people—and thousands more in and around the World Trade Center in New York and the Pentagon in Washington, D.C. In an effort to root out the terrorists responsible for the attack, American troops soon were engaged in combat in Afghanistan, an already war-torn country that most Americans knew little about at the time.

In his February 2, 2002, profile "The Road to Kabul," television journalist Dan Rather tries to give readers of *TV Guide* a sense of what that ravaged country is like. As you read this profile, notice passages that succeed in giving a strong impression of Afghanistan and the Afghan people. How does Rather's writing accomplish this objective?

THE ROAD TO KABUL

More than 20 years after his first journey to Afghanistan, DAN RATHER returned to the war zone. Here, the CBS anchor writes about how the devastated country has changed—and how it hasn't

TV GUIDE FEBRUARY 2, 2002

AFGHANISTAN'S CAPITAL CITY LIES IN A valley surrounded by mountains. To the north rises the storied Hindu Kush range. To the southwest lie more mountains. Kabul sits below, where the Panjshir Valley opens to the plain.

In early December, as our Scandinavian pilots spiraled our Beech 1900 turboprop down to Bagram Airbase, 35 miles outside Kabul, sun glinted off newly snow-capped peaks. The pilots had insisted on making this "corkscrew" approach in order to maximize distance from—and minimize exposure to—any Taliban holdouts lurking in the mountains with shoulder-fired antiaircraft weapons.

A dusty haze hung over the city. The plane sliced through it, revealing a ghostly airfield. We could make out the smashed remains of MiGs, burned-out buildings, a cratered runway here, another rocky one there. As we taxied, we got a close-up look at the devastation: the ruined planes, the debris of trucks, armored vehicles and what were once antiaircraft batteries. One had a sense of passing through a graveyard. Dozens of Afghans swept the tarmac by hand in search of mines.

We hadn't gotten more than three feet from the plane when we were encircled by Northern Alliance soldiers, all wearing the trademark black-and-white scarves, the hats and mismatched camouflage outfits we'd seen on TV for weeks. I noticed how battle-hardened they looked: lean and leathery, with very white teeth. They scowled as they approached but seemed uncertain as to what they should do next. First, they warned us against straying. "Mines," they said. Then they demanded to see our entrance visas. If such things existed for Afghanistan, we did not have them.

We had been told in Pakistan that advance elements of the U.S. Army's 10th Mountain Division would be at this air base to do what British Marines had not been able to do: gain control of it from the newly victorious Northern Alliance. [*Britain's offer to deploy peacekeeping troops had been rebuffed by the Northern Alliance prior to the arrival of U.S. soldiers to help secure the air base for humanitarian aid in December.*] I asked what appeared to be the only Alliance man on the tarmac who spoke English if there were

Afghanistan, now (clockwise from left): A girl near old Soviet Army tanks; United Front's **Abdullah Abdullah** and **Rather**; Kabul residents living amid the ruins

any American soldiers around and, if so, if we could talk to them. He just stared at me. As the baggage search went on, we asked again several times. Finally, the English speaker said, "You might see some at the gate on your way out." With another long stare, he added, "But you can't stop and talk to them. It's not allowed."

Correspondent Liz Palmer and our other CBS News colleagues already in Kabul had hired two Toyota four-wheel-drive vehicles to come meet us. We got them loaded up and, with our Northern Alliance escort–keeper, headed out.

No pavement: An Afghan man outside Kabul

At the first gate, there they were: two American soldiers in full camouflage gear with M-16 rifles. Both were privates, both about 19 years old. We told our driver to stop. Over the protests of our "escort," he did. We got out with the camera rolling. Two more American soldiers seemed to come out of nowhere, then a third: a major, a captain and a sergeant-major. They were surprised to see us, friendly but wary. A confusing and in some ways comic scene ensued, with us trying to talk to the soldiers and several Northern Alliance men trying to prevent it, joined by a man who seemed to be something akin to the local neighborhood mayor, along with his entourage.

The "mayor," through his interpreter,

insisted that we cease and desist, get back in our vehicles and move out immediately. We ducked, dodged and did the old side shuffle as our efforts to interview the U.S. troops proceeded in fits and starts, but an edgy situation quickly got edgier. It was a volatile mix: the Americans, the fighters from the North and the locals. The Northern Alliance didn't like having Americans on their turf and were letting that be known in ways big and small. Their general attitude was: "Thank you very much for your air strikes and other help that have made us the liberators of Kabul and the North. Now please get lost."

No one, to our knowledge, had done any television interviews with American troops on the ground in Afghanistan before this. As we rode out toward the main gate and the road to Kabul, we slapped fives and laughed. Sometimes even tiny victories can be sweet.

There weren't any Americans at the end of the road leading from the airport, only Northern Alliance fighters and some local gunmen manning the gate. As we eased past, a couple of teenagers put their hands on the windows of our vehicle, staring in at us. It was our first encounter with the Afghan people's raw curiosity about Americans.

The way to Kabul stretched ahead— long, dirty and tailbone-bustingly bumpy. No pavement. Plenty of bomb craters. Whole portions of the road seeming as if they were about to slide away. We drove through miles of choking, throat-scratching dust as thick as fog. Around us, a brown moonscape, with towering brown mountains in the distance. In between, only rocks and rubble. The sweep of the plains, punctuated by the occasional ruins of dried-mud

AP/WIDE WORLD

watchtowers, gave the whole scene a medieval feel. But it was overlaid with the remains of modern warfare: overturned tanks, the twisted carcasses of demolished armored vehicles. Up ahead, men dressed in rags hoisted Russian-made weapons to their shoulders as they watched our vehicle pass.

Ninety minutes went by before we covered the 35 miles to Kabul, and even that was only because our wheelman drove like a contestant in a demolition derby. About a third of the way there, we saw the Tank Man looming before us. He squatted on a rock, next to a stream and an old tank he had captured from the Taliban. He sat between two bombed-out bridges, wearing a thousand-yard stare. He wouldn't give the tank up, he said, because he expected that he would need it again. He had been living there for four weeks, alone, in his broken-down, armored Winnebago. He had come from Kabul, headed for the air base. With the bridges out, he was forced to try to rumble across the wide stream. When the overheated tank engine hit the cold stream water, it blew a rod or something.

The Tank Man helped us ford the stream with our four-wheel-drives. When we tipped him, he did not smile: He just put his hand briefly over his heart in the traditional Afghan gesture of appreciation and returned to his rock and his thousand-yard stare.

As we approached Kabul, small roadside stands appeared, selling everything from meat on hooks to balloons floating in bunches. We also saw what at first looked like dirty piles of rags beside the road: women, begging with hands outstretched. I worried about the children I saw walking along the street—they were so little, so close to traffic and so

Left begging: Afghan children in Kabul

often unaccompanied by adults.

Our driver started to give us a kind of tragic tour of Kabul's highlights—where this person had been hanged or that man had been beaten. We passed the soccer stadium, where thousands had watched the Taliban shoot women for their "transgressions."

Kabul, like the surrounding countryside, was brown. Three years of drought and disrepair had exposed the city to strong winds full of windblown topsoil and smoke from wood fires. Clean water was not always available, and when it was, it often came only in buckets. We tried to establish what routine we could: a shower or a bath or even a sponge bath, then a change into clean clothes for sleeping. We averaged two to three hours of sleep a night. And we were quickly reminded how much we took for granted at home. My first hot shower in days, at a rented house, was heavenly. Peanut butter and jelly spread over the inside of a big piece of Afghan bread became a great feast.

I had been in Afghanistan 20 years before. Despite all that the country had endured in the years in between, I was struck by many of the same qualities in the Afghan people that I had witnessed on my (Continued on page 51)

THE ROAD TO KABUL

(Continued from page 42)

first trip. After so much war, a grimmer culture could be expected. Instead, the Afghans had retained their openness and their wonderful sense of the absurd. They still loved to laugh. Humor and warmth were the weapons everyday people used to endure what had been for them a very long war.

That isn't to say that the Afghans aren't ferocious warriors. They are. And they are equally ferocious survivors, ingenious when it comes to getting by in difficult times. The colorful satellite dishes pieced together from hair-spray and air-freshener cans, now springing up for sale everywhere, are a testament to this improvisational spirit and to how much the people crave contact with the rest of the world.

Many of Afghanistan's men are gone. In war, a country's best men often go first. They die or return home without limbs or eyesight. So it has been in Afghanistan for more than 20 years. So it is today. You see them along the roads, on the streets and in the alleys of villages and cities: the broken men, many begging, some too proud to stick out their hands but begging just the same. You can see it in the eyes.

The many war widows are mostly at home, or at a mosque, weeping, wailing and praying. Sometimes you see orphans running in packs, the smaller ones begging or scavenging for food, the older ones fighting and stealing. Etched in my mind forever are the faces of the children we met as they played among the tombstones at the cemetery outside of Kabul. They all knew which of the graves held warriors and which held victims. They knew how the people had died and when and where. One little girl about 2½ years old sat on a tomb, swinging her legs idly. Two graves over, her brother leaned against a tombstone, gazing at the sky.

And then there was 19-year-old Raffi Khetab and his dog-eared English dictionary, tossing out ancient slang like "shake a leg," "don't let the cat out of the bag" and, his favorite, "all that jazz." He wanted to fit in when he made it to the USA. Slim as his chances are, he is absolutely convinced that some way, somehow, he will beat the odds. I hope he does. And I hope that, if he does, he finds America to be all that he wants it to be.

Looking for reporting help, we went to the local television station. There was little help to be had. The station, built by the Russians in the 1970s and 1980s, was a bombed-out, shot-up hulk.

In war, a country's best men often go first. They die or return home without limbs or eyesight. So it has been in Afghanistan.

The station's oversize, typically Russian satellite dish had been disabled by Taliban explosives. What was left of it stood against the sky like a monument from another age. The onetime local TV news anchor—a compact, handsome young man who spoke good English— agreed to help us while he waited to get back on the air with his own work. There was sadness in his tight smiles. I think he thought his anchoring days were finished, but he could not or would not give up hope.

To be in Afghanistan again was to feel anew just how awful, how truly awful, is war. From the Tank Man to the orphans of war to the Northern Alliance foreign minister we interviewed when we first arrived in Kabul, the eyes were vacant but for the hurt and fear of the hunted. Everywhere we went in Afghanistan, day and night, we could feel those haunted eyes upon us. ■

Dan Rather anchors the CBS Evening News.

Reflecting on What You Have Read

1 There are many journalists who could have written a piece on Afghanistan. Why might *TV Guide* be especially interested in a profile written by Dan Rather?

2 Unlike Robert Mackey in "E.R. Unscripted," Rather frequently tells readers how he reacted to aspects of the place he is profiling. Why do you think he includes his own feelings and reactions?

3 There likely were many photographs that could have been used at the beginning of this profile. What effect is achieved by beginning the profile with a photograph of a young child standing almost directly in the path of a tank?

4 Notice the physical settings in most of the photographs. What impressions do they create? At the beginning of the profile, Rather uses words to give an overview of the region (Kabul "lies in a valley surrounded by mountains"; "sun glinted off newly snow-capped peaks"). Do you think Rather is justified in using words to give this overview rather than including an aerial photograph of the region? Why or why not?

5 In some cases, Rather talks about groups of people: for example, the maimed veterans of Afghan's wars; the "war widows"; and the orphans who beg or scavenge for food. But occasionally he focuses on individuals: the Tank Man; a nineteen-year-old with a "dog-eared English dictionary"; a former TV news anchor near his bombed-out station. What reasons do you see for focusing on these individuals? What do they add to your general understanding of Afghanistan and its citizens?

6 In a couple of instances, Rather talks not about Afghanistan but about his own actions: "slapping fives" with his colleagues; taking a hot shower; eating a piece of bread spread with peanut butter and jelly. Do you think that Rather's accounts of his own actions contribute to readers' understanding of what life is like on "the road to Kabul"? Why or why not?

Thinking Ahead

In "The Road to Kabul," Dan Rather profiles a place that most readers of *TV Guide* would find remote and exotic. If you have been to such a place, it might serve as a good topic for a profile. But as you think of a possible topic, be careful not to overlook places that are less exotic—a favorite vacation spot, for example, or a place where you and your friends like to hang out. What is important is that the place has a distinct character—a personality—that invites strong reactions from those who visit it.

For over three decades, the television program *Mister Rogers' Neighborhood* made Fred Rogers a hero and role model for many children in the United States. Unfortunately, childhood heroes and role models do not always hold up under the scrutiny of adults, who are quick to spot flaws or imperfections that children may overlook. In the following profile, which appeared in *Esquire* magazine before Fred Rogers's death in February 2003, author Tom Junod views Rogers from the perspective of a slightly skeptical adult. As you read Junod's profile, notice how his admiration for Rogers competes with his perception of qualities that, to an adult, might seem less than heroic.

Can You Say . . . "Hero"?

TOM JUNOD

Fred Rogers has been doing the same small good thing for a very long time

Once upon a time, a little boy loved a stuffed animal whose name was Old Rabbit. It was so old, in fact, that it was really an unstuffed animal, so old that even back then with the little boy's brain still nice and fresh he had no memory of it as "Young Rabbit" or even "Rabbit"; so old that Old Rabbit was barely a rabbit at all, but rather a greasy hunk of skin without eyes and ears, with a single red stitch where its tongue used to be. The little boy didn't know why he loved Old Rabbit; he just did, and the night he threw it out the car window was the night he learned how to pray. He would grow up to become a great prayer, this little boy, but only intermittently, only fitfully, praying only when fear and desperation drove him to it, and the night he threw Old Rabbit into the darkness was the night that set the pattern, the night that taught him how. He prayed for Old Rabbit's safe return, and when, hours later, his mother and father came home with the filthy, precious strip of rabbity roadkill, he learned not only that prayers are sometimes answered but also the kind of severe effort they entail, the kind of endless

1

frantic summoning. And so when he threw Old Rabbit out the car window the *next time,* it was gone for good. . . .

   Once upon a time, a long time ago, a man took off his jacket and put on a sweater. Then he took off his shoes and put on a pair of sneakers. His name was Fred Rogers. He was starting a television program, aimed at children, called *Mister Rogers' Neighborhood.* He had been on television before, but only as the voices and movements of puppets, on a program called *The Children's Corner.*

2

Now he was stepping in front of the camera as Mister Rogers, and he wanted to do things right, and whatever he did right, he wanted to repeat. And so, once upon a time, Fred Rogers took off his jacket and put on a sweater his mother had made him, a cardigan with a zipper. Then he took off his shoes and put on a pair of navy-blue canvas boating sneakers. He did the same thing the next day, and then the next . . . until he had done the same things, *those* things, 865 times, at the beginning of 865 television programs, over a span of thirty-one years. The first time I met Mister Rogers, he told me a story of how deeply his simple gestures had been felt, and received. He had just come back from visiting Koko, the gorilla who has learned—or who has been taught—American Sign Language. Koko watches television. Koko watches *Mister Rogers' Neighborhood*, and when Mister Rogers, in his sweater and sneakers, entered the place where she lives, Koko immediately folded him in her long, black arms, as though he were a child, and then . . . "She took my *shoes* off, Tom," Mister Rogers said.

   Koko was much bigger than Mister Rogers. She weighed 280 pounds, and Mister Rogers weighed 143. Koko weighed 280 pounds because she is a gorilla, and Mister Rogers weighed 143 pounds because he has weighed 143 pounds as long as he has been Mister Rogers, because once upon a time, around thirty-one years ago, Mister Rogers stepped on a scale, and the scale told him that Mister Rogers weighs 143 pounds. No, not that he *weighed* 143 pounds, but that he *weighs* 143 pounds. . . . And so, every day, Mister Rogers refuses to do anything that would make his weight change—he neither drinks, nor smokes, nor eats flesh of any kind, nor goes to bed late at night, nor sleeps late in the morning, nor even watches television—and every

3

morning, when he swims, he steps on a scale in his bathing suit and his bathing cap and his goggles, and the scale tells him he weighs 143 pounds. This has happened so many times that Mister Rogers has come to see that number as a gift, as a destiny fulfilled, because, as he says, "the number 143 means 'I love you.' It takes one letter to say 'I' and four letters to say 'love' and three letters to say 'you.' One hundred and forty-three. 'I love you.' Isn't that wonderful?"

The first time I called Mister Rogers on the telephone, I woke him up from his nap. He takes a nap every day in the late afternoon—just as he wakes up every morning at five-thirty to read and study and write and pray for the legions who have requested his prayers; just as he goes to bed at nine-thirty at night and sleeps eight hours without interrup-

4

tion. On this afternoon, the end of a hot, yellow day in New York City, he was very tired, and when I asked if I could go to his apartment and see him, he paused for a moment and said shyly, "Well, Tom, I'm in my bathrobe, if you don't mind." I told him I didn't mind, and when, five minutes later, I took the elevator to his floor, well, sure enough, there was Mister Rogers, silver-haired, standing in the golden door at the end of the hallway and wearing eyeglasses and suede moccasins with rawhide laces and a flimsy old blue-and-yellow bathrobe that revealed whatever part of his skinny white calves his dark-blue dress socks didn't hide. "Welcome, Tom," he said with a slight bow, and bade me follow him inside, where he lay down—no, *stretched out,* as though he had known me all his life—on a couch upholstered with gold velveteen. He rested his head on a small pillow and kept his eyes closed while he explained that he had bought the apartment thirty years before for $11,000 and kept it for whenever he came to New York on business for the Neighborhood. I sat in an old armchair and looked around. The place was drab and dim, with the smell of stalled air and a stain of daguerreo-type sunlight on its closed, slatted blinds, and Mister Rogers looked so at home in its gloomy familiarity that I thought he was going to fall back asleep when suddenly the phone rang, startling him. "Oh, hello, my dear," he said when he picked it up, and then he said that he had a visitor, someone who wanted to learn more about the Neighborhood. "Would you like to speak to him?" he asked, and then handed me the phone. "It's Joanne," he said. I took the phone and spoke to a woman—his wife, the mother of his two sons—whose voice was hearty and almost whooping in its forthrightness and who spoke to me as though she had known me for a long time and was making the effort to keep up the acquaintance. When I handed him back the phone, he said, "Bye, my dear," and hung up and curled on the couch like a cat, with his bare calves swirled underneath him and one of his hands gripping his ankle, so that he looked as languorous as an odalisque. There was an energy to him, however, a fearlessness, an unashamed insistence on intimacy, and though I tried to ask him questions about himself, he always turned the questions back on me, and

> **[T]he train was crowded with children who were going home from school. Though of all races, the schoolchildren were mostly black and Latino, and they didn't even approach Mister Rogers and ask him for his autograph. They just sang. They sang, all at once, all together, the song he sings at the start of his program, "Won't You Be My Neighbor?" and turned the clattering train into a single soft, runaway choir.**

when I finally got him to talk about the puppets that were the comfort of his lonely boyhood, he looked at me, his gray-blue eyes at once mild and steady, and asked, "What about you, Tom? Did you have any special friends growing up?"

"Special friends?" 5

"Yes," he said. "Maybe a puppet, or a 6 special toy, or maybe just a stuffed animal you loved very much. Did you have a special friend like that, Tom?"

"Yes, Mister Rogers." 7

"Did your special friend have a name, 8 Tom?"

"Yes, Mister Rogers. His name was 9 Old Rabbit."

"Old Rabbit. Oh, and I'll bet the two 10 of you were together since he was a very young rabbit. Would you like to tell me about Old Rabbit, Tom?"

And it was just about then, when I was 11 spilling the beans about my special friend, that Mister Rogers rose from his corner of the couch and stood suddenly in front of me with a small black camera in hand. "Can I take your picture, Tom?" he asked. "I'd like to take your picture. I like to take pictures of all my new friends, so that I can show them to Joanne. . . ." And then, in the dark room, there was a wallop of white light, and Mister Rogers disappeared behind it. . . .

Once upon a time, Mister Rogers 12 went to New York City and got caught in the rain. He didn't have an umbrella, and he couldn't find a taxi, either, so he ducked with a friend into the subway and got on one of the trains. It was late in the day, and the train was crowded with children who were going home from school. Though of all races, the schoolchildren were mostly black and Latino, and they didn't even approach Mister Rogers and ask him for his autograph. They just sang. They sang, all at once, all together, the song he sings at the start of his program, "Won't You Be My Neighbor?" and turned the clattering train into a single soft, runaway choir.

He finds me, of course, at Penn Sta- 13 tion. He finds me, because that's what Mister Rogers *does*—he looks, and then he finds. I'm standing against a wall, listening to a bunch of mooks from Long

Island discuss the strange word—χαρις—he has written down on each of the autographs he gave them. First mook: "He says it's the Greek word for grace." Second mook: "Huh. That's cool. I'm glad I know that. Now, what the fuck is grace?" First mook: "Looks like you're gonna have to break down and buy a dictionary." Second mook: "Fuck that. What I'm buying is a ticket to the fucking *Lotto*. I just met Mister Rogers—this is *definitely* my lucky day." I'm listening to these guys when, from thirty feet away, I notice Mister Rogers looking around for someone and know, immediately, that he is looking for me. He is on one knee in front of a little girl who is hoarding, in her arms, a small stuffed animal, sky-blue, a bunny.

"Remind you of anyone, Tom?" he   14
says when I approach the two of them. He is not speaking of the little girl.

"Yes, Mister Rogers."   15

"Looks a little bit like . . . *Old Rabbit,*   16
doesn't it, Tom?"

"Yes, Mister Rogers."   17

"I thought so." Then he turns back to   18
the little girl. "This man's name is Tom. When he was your age, he had a rabbit, too, and he loved it very much. Its name was Old Rabbit. What is yours named?"

The little girl eyes me suspiciously,   19
and then Mister Rogers. She goes a little knock-kneed, directs a thumb toward her mouth. "Bunny Wunny," she says.

"Oh, that's a *nice* name," Mister   20
Rogers says, and then goes to the Thirty-fourth Street escalator to climb it one last time for the cameras. When he reaches the street, he looks right at the lens, as he always does, and says, speaking of the Neighborhood, "Let's go back to my place," and then makes a right turn toward Seventh Avenue, except that this time he just *keeps going,* and suddenly Margy Whitmer [his producer] is saying, "Where is Fred? Where is Fred?" and Fred, he's a hundred yards away, in his sneakers and his purple sweater, and the only thing anyone sees of him is his gray head bobbing up and down amid all the other heads, the hundreds of them, the thousands, the millions, disappearing into the city and its swelter.

Once upon a time, a little boy with a   21
big sword went into battle against Mister Rogers. Or maybe, if the truth be told, Mister Rogers went into battle against a little boy with a big sword, for Mister Rogers didn't *like* the big sword. It was one of those swords that really isn't a sword at all; it was a big plastic contraption with lights and sound effects, and it was the kind of sword used in defense of the universe by the heroes of the television shows that the little boy liked to watch. The little boy with the big sword did not watch Mister Rogers. In fact, the little boy with the

big sword didn't know who Mister Rogers *was,* and so when Mister Rogers knelt down in front of him, the little boy with the big sword looked past him and through him, and when Mister Rogers said, "Oh, my, that's a big sword you have," the boy didn't answer, and finally his mother got embarrassed and said, "Oh, honey, c'mon, that's *Mister Rogers,*" and felt his head for fever. Of course, she knew who Mister Rogers was, because she had grown up with him, and she knew that he was good for her son, and so now, with her little boy zombie-eyed under his blond bangs, she apologized, saying to Mister Rogers that she knew he was in a rush and that she knew he was here in Penn Station taping his program and that her son usually wasn't *like* this, he was probably just tired. . . . Except that Mister Rogers wasn't going anywhere. Yes, sure, he was taping, and right there, in Penn Station in New York City, were rings of other children wiggling in wait for him, but right now his patient gray eyes were fixed on the little boy with the big sword, and so he stayed there, on one knee, until the little boy's eyes finally focused on Mister Rogers, and he said, "It's not a sword; it's a death ray." A death ray! Oh, honey, Mommy *knew* you could do it. . . . And so now, encouraged, Mommy said, "Do you want to give Mister Rogers a hug, honey?" But the boy was shaking his head no, and Mister Rogers was sneaking his face past the big sword and the armor of the little boy's eyes and whispering something in his ear—something that, while not changing his mind about the hug, made the little boy look at Mister Rogers in a new way, with the eyes of a child at last, and nod his head yes.

22 We were heading back to his apartment in a taxi when I asked him what he had said.

23 "Oh, I just knew that whenever you see a little boy carrying something like that, it means that he wants to show people that he's strong on the outside.

24 "I just wanted to let him know that he was strong on the inside, too.

25 "And so that's what I told him.

26 "I said, 'Do you know that you're strong on the inside, too?'

27 "Maybe it was something he needed to hear." . . .

28 **Once upon a time,** there was a little boy born blind, and so, defenseless in the world, he suffered the abuses of the defenseless, and when he grew up and became a man, he looked back and realized that he'd had no childhood at all, and that if he were ever to have a childhood, he would have to start having it now, in his forties. So the first thing he did was rechristen himself "Joybubbles"; the second thing he did was declare himself five years old forever; and the third thing he did was make a pilgrimage to Pittsburgh, where the University of Pittsburgh's Information Sciences Library keeps a Mister Rogers archive. It has all 865 programs, in both color and black and white, and for two months this past spring, Joybubbles went to the library every day for ten hours and watched the Neighborhood's every episode, plus specials—or, since he is blind, *listened* to every episode, *imagined* every episode. Until one night, Mister Rogers came to him, in what he calls a visitation—"I was dreaming, but I was awake"—and offered to teach him how to pray.

29 "But Mister Rogers, I *can't* pray," Joybubbles said, "because every time I try to pray, I forget the words."

30 "I know that," Mister Rogers said, "and that's why the prayer I'm going to teach you has only three words."

31 "What prayer is that, Mister Rogers? What kind of prayer has only three words?"

32 "Thank you, God," Mister Rogers said.

The walls of Mister Rogers' Neighbor- 33
hood are light blue and fleeced with
clouds. They are tall—as tall as the
cinder-block walls they are designed to
hide—and they encompass the Neighborhood's entire stage set, from the
flimsy yellow house where Mister
Rogers comes to visit, to the closet
where he finds his sweaters, to the
Neighborhood of Make-Believe, where
he goes to dream. The blue walls are the
ends of the daylit universe he has made,
and yet Mister Rogers can't *see* them—
or at least can't know them—because he
was born blind to color. He doesn't
know the color of his walls, and one day,
when I caught him looking toward his
painted skies. I asked him to tell me
what color they *are,* and he said, "I
imagine they're *blue,* Tom." Then he
looked at me and smiled. "I imagine
they're blue."

He has spent thirty-one years imagin- 34
ing and reimagining those walls—the
walls that have both penned him in and
set him free. You would think it would
be easy by now, being Mister Rogers;
you would think that one morning he
would wake up and think, Okay, all I
have to do is be *nice* for my allotted half
hour today, and then I'll just take the
rest of the day off. . . . But no, Mister
Rogers is a stubborn man, and so on the
day I ask about the color of his sky, he
has already gotten up at five-thirty,
already prayed for those who have
asked for his prayers, already read,
already written, already swum, already
weighed himself, already sent out cards
for the birthdays he never forgets,
already called any number of people
who depend on him for comfort, already
cried when he read the letter of a
mother whose child was buried with a
picture of Mister Rogers in his casket,
already played for twenty minutes with
an autistic boy who has come, with his
father, all the way from Boise, Idaho, to
meet him. The boy had never spoken,

until one day he said, "X the Owl,"
which is the name of one of Mister
Rogers's puppets, and he had never
looked his father in the eye until one
day his father had said, "Let's go to the
Neighborhood of Make-Believe," and
now the boy is speaking and reading,
and the father has come to thank Mister
Rogers for saving his son's life. . . . And
by this time, well, it's nine-thirty in the
morning, time for Mister Rogers to take
off his jacket and his shoes and put on
his sweater and his sneakers and start
taping another visit to the Neighborhood. He writes all his own scripts, but
on this day, when he receives a visit
from Mrs. McFeely and a springer
spaniel, she says that she has to bring
the dog "back to his owner," and Mister
Rogers makes a face. The cameras stop,
and he says, "I don't like the word *owner*
there. It's not a good word. Let's change
it to 'bring the dog *home*.'" And so the
change is made, and the taping resumes,
and this is how it goes all day, a life
unfolding within a clasp of unfath-
omable governance, and once, when I
lose sight of him, I ask Margy Whitmer
where he is, and she says, "Right over
your shoulder, where he always is," and
when I turn around, Mister Rogers is facing me, child-stealthy, with a small black
camera in his hand, to take another picture for the album that he will give me
when I take my leave of him.

Yes, it should be easy being Mister 35
Rogers, but when four o'clock rolls
around, well, Mister Rogers is *tired*, and
so he sneaks over to the piano and
starts playing, with dexterous, pale fingers, the music that used to end a 1940s
newsreel and that has now become the
music he plays to signal to the cast and
crew that a day's taping has wrapped.
On this day, however, he is premature
by a considerable extent, and so Margy,
who has been with Mister Rogers
since 1983—because nobody who
works for Mister Rogers ever *leaves* the

Neighborhood—comes running over, papers in hand, and says, "Not so fast there, buster."

"Oh, please, sister," Mister Rogers says. "I'm done." [36]

And now Margy comes up behind him and massages his shoulders. "No, you're not," she says. "*Roy* Rogers is done. *Mister* Rogers still has a ways to go." . . . [37]

Once upon a time, a man named Fred Rogers decided that he wanted to live in heaven. Heaven is the place where good people go when they die, but this man, Fred Rogers, didn't want to *go* to heaven; he wanted to *live* in heaven, here, now, in this world, and so one day, when he was talking about all the people he had loved in this life, he looked at me and said, "The connections we make in the course of a life—maybe that's what *heaven* is, Tom. We make so *many* connections here on earth. Look at us—I've just met you, but I'm invested in who you are and who you will be, and I can't help it." [38]

The next afternoon, I went to his office in Pittsburgh. He was sitting on a couch, under a framed rendering of the Greek word for grace and a biblical phrase written in Hebrew that means "I am my beloved's, and my beloved is mine." A woman was with him, sitting in a big chair. Her name was Deb. She was very pretty. She had a long face and a dark blush to her skin. She had curls in her hair and stars at the centers of her eyes. She was a minister at Fred Rogers's church. She spent much of her time tending to the sick and the dying. Fred Rogers loved her very much, and so, out of nowhere, he smiled and put his hand over hers. "Will you be with me when I die?" he asked her, and when she said yes, he said, "Oh, thank you, my dear." Then, with his hand still over hers and his eyes looking straight into hers, he said, "Deb, do you know what a great prayer you are? Do you know that about [39]

yourself? Your prayers are just wonderful." Then he looked at me. I was sitting in a small chair by the door, and he said, "Tom, would you close the door, please?" I closed the door and sat back down. "Thanks, my dear," he said to me, then turned back to Deb. "Now, Deb, I'd like to ask you a favor," he said. "Would you lead us? Would you lead us in prayer?"

Deb stiffened for a second, and she let out a breath, and her color got deeper. "Oh, I don't know, Fred," she said. "I don't know if I want to put on a *performance*." . . . [40]

Fred never stopped looking at her or let go of her hand. "It's not a performance. It's just a meeting of friends," he said. He moved his hand from her wrist to her palm and extended his other hand to me. I took it, and then put my hand around her free hand. His hand was warm, hers was cool, and we bowed our heads, and closed our eyes, and I heard Deb's voice calling out for the grace of God. What is grace? I'm not certain; all I know is that my heart felt like a spike, and then, in that room, it opened and felt like an umbrella. I had never prayed like that before, ever. I had always been a great prayer, a powerful one, but only fitfully, only out of guilt, only when fear and desperation drove me to it . . . and it hit me, right then, with my eyes closed, that this was the moment Fred Rogers—Mister Rogers— had been leading me to from the moment he answered the door of his apartment in his bathrobe and asked me about Old Rabbit. Once upon a time, you see, I lost something, and prayed to get it back, but when I lost it the second time, I didn't, and now this was it, the missing word, the unuttered promise, the prayer I'd been waiting to say a very long time. [41]

"Thank you, God," Mister Rogers said. [42]

Reflecting on What You Have Read

1 If you read the title of this piece aloud, the three dots (ellipses) that precede the word *hero* might indicate a hesitation about using that word to describe a children's television personality. The title also seems to mimic the slow, deliberate way new concepts or words were defined for viewers of *Mister Rogers' Neighborhood.* Why might Junod express this hesitation when writing for readers of *Esquire* magazine?

2 In recounting his first meeting with Mr. Rogers, Junod notes some unflattering details about Mr. Rogers's physical appearance (for example, "a flimsy old blue-and-yellow bathrobe that revealed whatever part of his skinny white calves his dark-blue dress socks didn't hide"). Is Junod justified in including such details? Why or why not? Presumably, he could have captured some of these details in a photograph. Do you think Junod should have included such a photograph? Why or why not?

3 Apparently, Mr. Rogers likes to take pictures. But the pictures included in Junod's profile are of Mr. Rogers's face, a cardigan sweater on a hanger, and Mr. Rogers in the Neighborhood. What reasons do you see for including these pictures and not some of the ones Mr. Rogers took during the interview? Why not include pictures of him talking with the children in Penn Station?

4 Junod begins his profile with a story that turns out to refer to his own childhood experience. What does Junod accomplish by beginning in this manner?

5 Throughout his profile, Junod almost always refers to his subject as "Mister Rogers" rather than "Fred" or "Rogers." What is the effect of using this name? Does this practice seem justified? Why or why not?

6 After spending a good bit of time with his subject, Junod comes away profoundly impressed. Do you share Junod's reactions? What is there in the text (and in your own experience) that leads you to share (or reject) Junod's reactions?

Thinking Ahead

Think of people you admired greatly when you were a child, and consider reviewing your impressions of one of them now that you have a more mature perspective. Spend some time talking with, observing, and—if possible—reading about this person. In what ways do your childhood impressions still seem valid? In what ways have they changed?

It may seem that the most interesting subjects for a profile would be people who are extremely well known. That is not necessarily the case, as Stephanie Guzik shows in the following profile of Diane Turcotte, a fellow college student whose life is not limited to the time she spends "Behind a Plain White Lab Coat." As you read this profile, notice the different ways Guzik helps readers see how remarkable Diane Turcotte is.

Stephanie Guzik

Behind a Plain White Lab Coat

After an exhausting day of classes one Monday afternoon early 1
in the semester, I decided to walk across campus to the cell culture lab to feed my fibroblast cells. As I lazily walked up the three flights of stairs to the biology floor and wandered slowly into room 309, I saw Diane Turcotte's smiling face peer up from her computer screen. According to our instructor, George, Diane was the pride of our Cancer Cell Group. He often told me, "You could learn a lot from that girl. She's a wonderful, dedicated member of this group," and I always had to hold back from asking, "What could this senior possibly teach me about this program that you couldn't?" I always seemed to run into Diane whenever I went to the lab; in fact, it often made me wonder if she ever left.

On this particular Monday afternoon, Diane was waiting for the 2
components of a reagent solution to dissolve in a beaker of distilled water and writing a paper for one of her classes in the meantime. "Hey Steph!" she called out cheerfully. "How was your day?" I looked at her, feeling somewhat dazed, and replied, "How in the world can you be so extremely perky after classes on a Monday?" She just smiled and went back to her paper. I put down my bag, grabbed my lab notebook, and went across the hall into the sterile culture lab, closing the door behind me.

I prepared myself in the lab, setting up all my equipment, wash- 3
ing my hands, and putting on my plain white lab coat. I logged into

the lab in the notebook that we keep on top of the refrigerator and went to open up the incubator. I took my two large culture flasks off the second shelf and looked at them under the microscope. One appeared very clear, with a good growth of cells, while the other had black blotches floating in the bright orange growth medium. I wasn't sure what to do, but I fed my cells anyway, cleaned up the lab, and left, saying goodbye to a still-perky Diane as I walked out.

Thursday rolled around and it was once again time to feed my cells. After class, I wandered over to the lab, trudged up the stairs, and walked slowly down the hall. Once again, Diane was in room 309, this time waiting for proteins to run through her polyacrilamide gel. "Is today any better?" she asked. "Well, it's not a Monday; we'll put it that way," I replied as I put my things down and went back into the sterile lab across the hall. I prepared everything again and went to 4

Fig. 1. Diane at work in the lab.

open up the incubator in the lab. As I swung the door open, I immediately noticed a flask on the second shelf with bright yellow growth medium: a clear sign of contamination. My stomach dropped as I saw the letters SG on the bottom of the flask. I took out both of my cultures and saw that the one was bright yellow and the other was cloudy orange, which meant I had killed all the cells I had been growing for almost three weeks. I closed the incubator, took off my plain white lab coat, and went back into room 309 with both of my flasks.

Diane was hunched over her gel, waiting patiently for the proteins to be pulled to the bottom by the current running through the apparatus. She saw me as I walked in, somewhat frustrated. I quietly asked, "Does this happen to you?" Diane took one look at the flasks I held outstretched and understood. She smiled and replied, "Actually, this is perfect timing. I've been growing roller bottles of cells for about a month now and had finally gotten a culture to grow, but today I came in and they had all 'jumped off.' So I get to start all over too. Come on, let's go." She turned off the current running through her gel, took the apparatus apart, and walked past me into the sterile lab. I put down my contaminated flasks long enough to put on my lab coat again. Still frustrated, I squirted bleach into my two flasks to kill off all the bacteria and remaining cells, while Diane washed her hands and put on her plain white lab coat. We sat there together in that lab, passaging new cells from one flask into another, for a little under an hour. In that hour, I began to understand what our instructor had been talking about. 5

As we sat down at the sterile hoods to begin working, Diane said, "Stephanie, you can't give up. That's what I've learned in this place. I've spent three years in this room, and no matter how many flasks and roller bottles I've gone through, no matter how many cells I've stained incorrectly, no matter how many gels I've run, I finally realized that getting frustrated over this stuff is completely pointless. Cell culture is not your whole life. There's so much beyond this one little room that is much more important than passaging these cells into a new flask." 6

It struck me as funny that this woman who I had seen so many 7
times in the lab was talking about everything outside of the lab. But
one hour in the lab talking with Diane convinced me that she is not
only the amazing and dedicated cell culturist George told me about,
but also such an active participant in so many campus activities that
she far outshines every other student I have met in my time here. I
came to realize that behind Diane's plain white lab coat is a woman
who has had a full life at college, who has experienced everything,
and who has made her time on campus one to remember and
cherish. Behind it was someone I wanted to be like.

Whereas I simply go to class, go to the lab, go back to my dorm, 8
and occasionally go out with my friends (and to this point thought
that I was doing pretty well!), I discovered that Diane has an entire
spectrum of things to do once she walks down that staircase out of
the lab. Our college is known to have students who struggle to do
well in their classes and struggle even more to have a good time
while at school because classes outweigh the rest of their activities.
Diane has certainly overcome that challenge.

Diane told me she's taking a Senior Advanced Lab course based 9
in Molecular Biology, a Statistical Analysis course, and Immunology
and Human Physiology. In all, she said, it adds up to seventeen hours
of class time each week, not including the several hours of homework required by each class. It was clear to me that even though she
is a senior, Diane had chosen courses that are quite difficult and
time-consuming—unlike other seniors, who coast through their last
two semesters with less intellectually challenging courses like Introduction to Sculpture. The only response I could manage was, "That's
amazing." "It's not too bad," Diane replied. "I just go to class, do all of
my work after class either here or in the library, and then I have time
to do everything else I want to do." *Everything else? What else could
there be,* I wondered. *I'm having enough of a hard time balancing
school, the lab, and my sorority.*

Diane belongs to the same sorority I do on campus, so I know 10
how much time she spends at the house. She has been a member

Fig. 2. Sorority sisters after a formal. Diane is the third from the left in the middle row.

since her freshman year and is so kind and enthusiastic that all the sisters adore her. I have yet to find a sister who has anything bad to say about Diane, and I believe Melissa put it best when she told me, "Diane is just your average, run-of-the-mill amazing person."

Until I started working in the Cancer Cell Group, I never would   11 have guessed that Diane was so involved in academics, simply because the majority of people on our campus who are extremely involved in their courses don't seem very happy or relaxed. However, Diane is an exception. During recruitment periods for our sorority, she is constantly at the house, socializing with the sisters and the potential members. She is so relaxed that no one could guess that she'd be heading back to the lab afterwards. When recruitment is over, Diane can still be found hanging out at the house a few times during the week or getting ice cream at the local Friendly's with some of the other senior sisters.

Although I knew about Diane's sorority involvement, before this 12 afternoon in the lab I had no idea that she cared about any activities beyond that and her coursework. But she told me about several other groups on campus that are important to her. First, there's CASA—the Chinese American Student Association. When Diane came to college, she initially wanted to be a member of the Vietnamese Student Association, but since our campus didn't have one, she decided to join CASA instead to "embrace her Asian ethnicity." "It's really nice to be able to associate with people that have a similar background to me," Diane said. "I grew up in a house that embraced Vietnamese culture, and I wanted to continue that feeling once I got to campus."

Second, she told me about TriBeta, which is a national Biology 13 Honor Society. Our campus has not established a definite chapter of TriBeta, but Diane, along with some other biology students, is working very hard to get the campus TriBeta group recognized nationally. For the past year she has acted as the secretary of the campus TriBeta group, and she is currently in the process of contacting the representative who will come examine our facilities to make sure that we have met the national society's requirements. She is also actively recruiting students to become a part of the group she helped establish. "Right now, TriBeta is a lot of work just because we don't have our chapter established yet, but once the menial labor is done, it should be a lot of fun," she said enthusiastically.

After she told me about her involvement in CASA and TriBeta, I 14 was expecting Diane to say something along the lines of "Between those groups and my coursework, I'm fairly busy." Instead, she continued, "I'm also part of the Order of Omega for being a sorority sister and for meeting the requirements." Although Diane said this modestly, I personally know that being a member of this, the national Greek Honor Society, is much more than "meeting requirements"; it has to do with being a leader, being active—basically being amazing in one way or another.

Finally, Diane added that she lives at home, which is close to 15 campus, and spends as much time as she can with her family and her two nephews. She usually goes home for dinner and spends a little time with her parents, then goes back to the lab to work for most of the night. *I have trouble seeing my friends on a weekly basis,* I thought, *but she makes sure she spends time with her family every night. How does she do it? How can she be so active on campus, so wonderful in her coursework, and yet so involved at home?* I just didn't get it. While I sat there absorbing what Diane had told me, she decided to add that she also does work-study for our instructor, spending some time testing new products that George is considering for purchase, purifying reagents that the group uses on a regular basis, and organizing and cleaning the lab. Was I sitting next to some sort of machine? "Oh, and I also had to study for my GRE's all semester because I wasn't sure if I wanted to go to graduate school or go directly into a lab to work." After Diane took the exam and thought about it a lot, she decided to look for a research position and work for a few years. *Yes, indeed, there is a machine behind that plain white lab coat,* I decided. *There has to be. No one could possibly be so active and yet seem so relaxed at the same time.*

There was an awkward silence after Diane told me about every- 16 thing she did. I didn't know what to say. All I could think of was "wow," but somehow I didn't feel that would do any justice to what I had just heard.

As we were doing our final steps for the passaging, I decided to 17 ask, "So what about sleep? Do you ever sleep?" Diane just smiled, like she always does, and said, "Of course I sleep. It's not always as much as I'd like, and it's not as much as some of the other students on campus, but I get my rest. Sometimes I'm in the lab for anywhere from 5 to 24 hours in a day doing protocols, so when it's a busy night with work and with the lab, I get anywhere from no sleep to 3 hours. On nights when I'm not quite so busy, I get around 6 hours. It's not so bad once you get used to it." *No sleep? Who does that?* That's all I could think as we capped up our flasks and labeled them with the date and our initials.

By that time, it was around 7 o'clock. I was completely exhausted and still trying to absorb everything Diane had just told me. We put our flasks in the incubator—mine on the second shelf and hers on the top shelf. We cleaned up the hoods and all our materials. We washed our hands. We took off our plain white lab coats. 18

Then I followed Diane out of the sterile lab and into room 309. She went back over to her gel as I put away my lab notebook. As she sat there preparing her gel for a Western blot protocol, which would take about another five hours or so, I thought to myself, *The poor thing is going to be stuck in the lab all night again.* But then I realized that whereas I would be "stuck" in the lab, she would simply "be" in the lab, enjoying just one of the many tasks in the busy life that she leads. 19

As I put my bag on my back, Diane said with a smile, "Are you going out tomorrow night?" This time, I smiled back. "I know a couple of the sisters are going out, and Vanessa and I definitely are. Would you like to come with us?" As always, Diane smiled, looked at her gel, and said, "If all goes well with this thing, I'm with you. Just let me know what time." 20

"Of course," I said, and turned to walk out the door. "Have a good night," I added. As I walked to the door I heard Diane say, "You too. Don't forget, there's a whole different place outside of that door. Take advantage of it while you can." I smiled and slowly walked out of room 309, down the hallway, and down the stairs in a better mood than I had been at any other time during the past few weeks. I felt inspired, still touched by my conversation with the amazing woman I had discovered hidden behind a plain white lab coat. 21

Reflecting on What You Have Read

1 When Stephanie's instructor tells her that "you could learn a lot from that girl," Stephanie is at first doubtful, as she reveals in the first paragraph of her profile. Why do you think Stephanie decided to express her doubts so early in the profile?

2 What are some of the ways in which Stephanie contrasts her actions and reactions with Diane's? What do those contrasts tell you about Diane?

3 Notice the questions Stephanie asks—of herself and of Diane. How do they add to your understanding of Diane?

4 Look closely at the pictures Stephanie includes in her profile, considering both composition and details. In what ways do these pictures succeed (or fail) in reinforcing the attitudes Stephanie conveys in her written text?

Thinking Ahead

Think about someone you know well—a classmate, coworker, or family member, for example. What qualities set this person apart? For example, how does he or she confront problems that seem overwhelming to most other people? What is distinctive about this person's daily routines? How do other people react to this person? Can you get pictures that show what this person is like? It may be that someone you see every day would be a good subject for a profile.

Assignment

Profile

Write a profile of a person, place, or activity that will reveal to readers the characteristics that you think make him or her or it remarkable. The person, place, or activity you choose should invite strong reactions—admiration, respect, or appreciation. You may write about topics that inspire mixed feelings, but you will probably do best if you avoid topics about which you have only negative emotions.

Throughout the Guide to Writing a Profile are Working on the Assignment boxes.

These boxes provide guided advice for developing your profile. However, your instructor may have specific requirements about how long the profile should be, what sort of topic to write about, whether you should prepare the profile as a print or online document (or as an oral presentation), and whether you should include or exclude any particular visual elements. Be sure you understand those requirements before you start working on the assignment.

Guide to Writing a Profile

First, the bad news: there is no set of steps that will inevitably lead you to write a successful profile—or any other type of writing, for that matter. The composing process is just too complicated and unpredictable for that. The good news, however, is that you can apply some very useful guidelines and strategies that will greatly increase your chances of finding something interesting to say and saying it effectively.

The remainder of this chapter will help you through the process of creating a profile that reveals an insider's view of an interesting subject. The first step is covered in Getting Started—selecting a topic and analyzing the context in which your profile will be read. Then you will experiment with many of the verbal and visual strategies illustrated in profiles you were introduced to in Reading to Write, and you will use them in the Drafting section. These strategies can help you work toward the writer's objectives of developing your topic (that is, finding something to say), writing an introduction that will engage readers' interest, creating an appropriate voice, providing a clear structure, concluding your profile effectively, and designing your profile and integrating visual elements. Finally, in Finishing Up you will receive guidance in creating a review draft, assessing your work carefully, and using that assessment to revise your profile.

Guide to Writing a Profile

Getting Started

Sometimes when people receive a writing assignment, the first thing they do is procrastinate, hoping that they will eventually feel inspired to start writing. Inspiration is a good thing, but it usually occurs only after you have invested a certain amount of work in an assignment. To get started on this work, you will first select a topic and then begin to analyze the context in which your profile will be read.

Selecting a Topic

Perhaps you already have a profile topic in mind, and it will turn out to be the topic you actually write about. But don't count on it. The process of finding a good topic—whether for the assignment in this chapter or for any other writing assignment—is usually a little more complicated and time-consuming than that. In general, it's best to start with lots of possible topics and then winnow the list down to something you really want to write about. You may make a couple of false starts, working on topics that prove too limited or too uninteresting. It's all right if that happens—unless it happens the night before the assignment is due.

Working on the Assignment

Selecting a Topic

One way to find a subject for your profile is to read profiles others have written. For example, skim over all the profiles in Reading to Write. Do the topics remind you of comparable people, places, or activities? Also, read the Thinking Ahead prompts that follow each profile; perhaps one of these contains a suggestion that will help you generate ideas. After this preliminary work, try the following activities.

> **Brainstorm on paper,** writing quickly in response to the following questions: Who are some people you really admire? Think of people who are currently in the news. Also think of historical figures as well as people you know personally. Are there some places or activities that have special meaning for you or whose distinctive characteristics (their atmosphere, the people associated with them, the events that typically occur there) make a lasting impression? For the moment, do not worry about how good your answers sound. In brainstorming, the primary goal is quantity, so just list as many ideas as you can. You can go back later and sift through the list, looking for ideas that seem especially workable and interesting.

> **Review what you have written,** selecting a few topics that made a strong impression on you.

> **Discuss** these topics with a small group or the entire class. Try to explain what is remarkable or distinctive about the topics you identified.

> **Brainstorm again,** focusing on one specific topic. Write answers to questions such as the following: What makes it special? What are the impressions it has left on you? Why did it leave those impressions?

> **Explain** to a small group of classmates what your impressions are and why you have them. Do your classmates see why this person, place, or activity is so remarkable? Would they be interested in reading about it? Can they help you think of people who would be interested in reading about it?

Once you have identified a topic that you might like to write a profile about, you need to do some preliminary data gathering. Try the following activities, making notes about what you learn.

> **Examine your own experience.** Have you had any personal contact with this person or place? Have you taken part in this activity or observed it personally? If so, do you have any anecdotes that help define its special character?

> **Talk with others** who may know something about your topic. What are their experiences? Can they tell you any good stories about your topic? Can they provide any factual information that surprises you or adds to your understanding of the topic?

> **Do a quick survey of your library's databases, and look on the Internet.** Does it seem likely that you'll be able to find good stories that illustrate the distinctive qualities of your topic? Without too much digging, can you find background information on those qualities?

> **Look for good photographs.** Can you find or take any photographs that will help readers appreciate how significant your topic is?

If you have trouble finding plenty of information that supports the unique, remarkable qualities of your profile topic,

continued

continued

consider looking for another topic. And even if you are finding plenty of interesting information, the preliminary work is still not finished. You need to start thinking about the context in which your profile will be read.

STUDENT DIALOGUE: SELECTING A TOPIC

Writing in a Visual Age: You give the impression that you decided almost immediately that you wanted to write your profile about Diane. Is that true? If so, how did you decide to write about her?

Stephanie Guzik: I had toyed with other ideas for the profile, about famous people or a vacation spot I know of, but I also thought of Diane initially for the profile. She is such a great role model and I admire her so much that I figured it would be easy to give a firsthand view of what a great person she really is. Also, when I first started thinking about the paper, I looked into the other topic ideas and didn't come up with much information that would be useful. I decided it would be better to write about someone I know directly so I could give my perspective as well as input from other people she's close with (our instructor, other sorority sisters, and so on). After I thought about it, Diane just seemed like the obvious choice for my topic.

Analyzing Context

In selecting a topic, you have been focusing on one basic question: *Can I find information that interests me and gives me a sense of the distinctive character of a certain person, place, or activity?* The other part of getting started is thinking about the context in which your profile will be read—the audience you hope to reach, the circumstances in which the audience members will encounter your profile, and the purposes you hope to accomplish by writing the profile. It will be easiest to analyze the context for your profile by first thinking in terms of one or two individual readers who are typical of the larger group you hope to reach.

After identifying a typical individual, you need to answer questions about the audience members' knowledge, values, and needs; expectations for content, layout, and format; and the circumstances in which they will encounter your profile. You should also answer questions about your purpose for doing this type of writing. By considering these questions, you analyze the context for your profile and establish a basis for making wise decisions about what to say and how to say it.

<table>
<tr><td style="vertical-align:top">

Questions for Analyzing Context

</td><td>

Audience knowledge, values, and needs

> What sorts of experiences (personal or secondhand) have my readers had with my topic?

> How does my topic relate to things my readers know, value, or care about?

> Do my readers have any biases or preconceptions concerning my topic? If so, what are they, and do I have any information that will correct (or reinforce) those attitudes?

Audience expectations for content

> What questions are my readers likely to want to have answered?

> What kinds of information are my readers likely to value?

Audience expectations for layout or format

> Which reading in this chapter comes closest to looking the way my readers will expect my profile to look?

> Are there any visual features (for example, photographs) my readers are likely to expect or appreciate?

> Are there ways in which my profile will look different from the readings in this chapter?

Circumstances

> Are there any recent events that might motivate my audience to read my profile? If so, what are they?

> If not, what sort of background information should I provide at the beginning of my profile?

Purposes

> What purposes am I trying to accomplish in writing my profile? (See discussion of purposes, p. 30.) What overall impression do I want to leave my readers with?

> What sort of voice do I want readers to hear when they read my profile? (For a discussion of voice, see p. 88 of this chapter.)

</td></tr>
</table>

> bedfordstmartins.com/ visualage

To download these questions as a worksheet, click on **CHAPTER 2** › **WORKSHEETS**

As you learn more about your profile topic, your understanding of context may change. In fact, you may decide to target an altogether different audience if you discover important aspects of the topic that might not mean much to the audience you originally envisioned. However, you need to begin thinking about context now. Try to answer this question: *Can I think of a specific individual or small group of people who would actually have a desire to read about the subject of my profile?* If the answer is no, consider changing your topic. It will be hard to write a good profile if you can't think of anyone who would be interested in reading it.

Analyzing Context

After identifying a specific reader, you can begin thinking about the context for your profile by taking the following steps.

Draw on your knowledge of yourself in order to begin understanding your reader. What makes this topic appeal to you? How does it appeal to your values, interests, and attitudes? Is it likely that your reader shares any of these values, interests, and attitudes?

Talk with your reader or with someone who is as similar to that reader as possible. What

does this reader already know about your topic? Does he or she have any preconceptions or misconceptions? Has your reader had any personal experiences that would make him or her receptive (or hostile) to your profile topic?

Identify the circumstances in which your reader will encounter your profile. Has anything happened recently to prompt his or her interest? For example, has your subject recently been in the news? Is your subject associated with someone or something that has been in the news?

As you work on the profile, your understanding of your audience may change. For example, you may get a clearer idea of what the audience knows or expects, or you may revise your ideas about the sort of format that is appropriate. Consequently, you may want to revise your responses to the Questions for Analyzing Context as you work on the profile. But for now, be as specific as possible.

STUDENT CONTEXT ANALYSIS

Here's how Stephanie Guzik answered these questions for the profile she wrote, "Behind a Plain White Lab Coat" (p. 60).

Audience Knowledge, Values, and Needs

What sorts of experiences (personal or secondhand) have my readers had with my topic?

The students who would potentially be reading this article would have an idea of how much work is involved in college. They would know the amount of homework associated with classes and the time commitment required for participating in college-level extracurricular activities.

How does my topic relate to things my readers know, value, or care about?

My readers know that college comes with many responsibilities that are very hard to balance. This profile tells of one college student beating the odds. Diane is simply what every college student would strive to be: very successful in class, but still able to enjoy her time at college by being involved in everything she has an interest in.

STUDENT CONTEXT ANALYSIS

Do my readers have any biases or preconceptions concerning my topic? If so, what are they, and do I have any information that will correct (or reinforce) those attitudes?	*The college students that I know (including myself) would all love to be able to do well in class but still have a life outside of class. A common misconception is that there's no way to accomplish that goal. Either you're tied up with work and never have a social life, or your life is simply social and not much else. This profile exemplifies how a college student has gotten the best of both worlds. She works when she needs to and does extremely well in class because of it, but she's also involved in several groups on campus as well as a sorority.*

Audience Expectations for Content

What questions are my readers likely to want to have answered?	*What is so special about this student?* *How much does she actually do in class and on campus?* *How is she able to balance so many things during college?* *Why is she looked so highly upon by the writer?*
What kinds of information are my readers likely to value?	*Students are intrigued by other students and what they do. They like to compare themselves to others. By including personal anecdotes in this paper, I make sure that the audience is more likely to relate to the paper as if they knew Diane.*

Audience Expectations for Layout or Format

Which reading in this chapter comes closest to looking the way my readers will expect my profile to look?	*"From Welfare to Washington" probably comes closest to looking like I want my profile to look. It has the human interest pictures that seem appropriate for my readers.*
Are there any visual features (for example, photographs) my readers are likely to expect or appreciate?	*I chose photographs to highlight what I wrote about Diane. Readers will appreciate them because they put a face with the story. The pictures of Diane in the lab show where she spends most of her time and show her in action while working with her cells. The picture of Diane at the formal shows her having fun with her sisters and provides an image of her as more than just a student—she's also involved in many activities and enjoys having fun with her friends.*
Are there ways in which my profile will look different from the readings in this chapter?	*I'm not going to have multiple columns.*

continued

STUDENT CONTEXT ANALYSIS

continued

Circumstances

Are there any recent events that might motivate my audience to read my profile? If so, what are they? If not, what sort of background information should I provide at the beginning of my profile?

Since the students that would be reading this profile would most likely be in school or just about to go back to school, there isn't a recent event that would make them be more apt to read the article. However, if they read it before starting a new semester, they may be inclined to become more involved on campus.

Purposes

What purposes am I trying to accomplish in writing my profile? What overall impression do I want to leave my readers with?

Overall, I want my readers to admire Diane as much as I do. She is what most college students consider successful, but unlikely. Most college students focus on either work or fun, but most don't balance the two. Diane has established a strong academic life with a balanced social life and several on-campus activities. I think my profile will inspire some readers to become more active on campus and to strive to have a fuller life while in college.

What sort of voice do I want readers to hear when they read my profile?

I want readers to know how much I admire her, but I don't want to sound like she's too good to be true.

Drafting

With ideas about what you might say about your topic and a sense of the specific audience you want to target, you can create a good draft of your profile. The next section of this chapter presents strategies you can use for developing your topic, engaging your audience, creating an appropriate voice, providing structure, and concluding effectively. There are also suggestions that will help you design your profile, making appropriate use of visual features such as photographs and page layout. As will always be the case in this book, you will have opportunities to learn about these strategies by taking a close look at some texts that provide good examples. You may be able to refine or add to these lists of strategies by analyzing other profiles that you think are engaging and effective.

Developing Your Topic

You will find that narrative, or story-telling, strategies are important in developing the content of almost any profile. You can use these strategies most effectively if you begin by gathering information, drawing on secondary sources, your personal experience, or both.

Gathering Information

If you have chosen to write about a well-known person, place, or activity, you should have little trouble finding information from other writers. You might check the library for biographies or databases, using an electronic database service such as Wilson Select or LexisNexis. You might also do an Internet search using search engines such as Google, Yahoo!, and AltaVista. Make a list of the possible sources you find. To determine which books, articles, and Web sites you might want to investigate, look at the tables of contents of books, scan the first few paragraphs of articles, or notice the topics listed on the homepage of Web sites. Ask yourself which ones seem likely to provide facts, details, or stories that will help present a unique insider's view of your topic. Also, ask yourself how credible a given source appears to be.

You need not read through to the end of a source that initially seems irrelevant or unconvincing, but in general you should keep complete bibliographic information so that you can locate a piece again if you need to come back to it for more information. Record the author's name, the title of the piece (article, book, Web site), and all the other relevant information (URL of a Web site and the date you accessed it, for example, or date and page number of a magazine article). You should also write down key facts and phrases you want to quote directly, and you should summarize other important information.

If you are writing about a person or place known only to you and a few other people, you will have to draw heavily on your own experiences. Even if you are writing about a well-known topic, you should look for opportunities to draw on your personal experiences. What have you observed about your subject? What have you heard other people say about it? What experiences made it so memorable for you or others? As is the case with materials you have read, be careful not to rely entirely on your memory. Keep notes, quoting and summarizing what people say and recording what you observe.

As you gather information, be on the lookout for photographs or other visuals that will help you explain what makes your profile topic unique and interesting. Or consider taking your own photographs to reveal something of its character. If you plan to reproduce visuals from secondary sources, be sure to record the photographer's name and the date the picture was taken, as well as any other information about it (along with source information for the print source or Web site that included the image). Credit the sources in a caption, in your text, or in a note at the end of your profile.

❯ For more details about using library material, see **Chapter 9.**

❯ For more on evaluating the credibility of a source, see **Chapter 11.**

❯ For more advice on taking notes, see **Chapter 11.**

❯ For more advice on working with photographs, see **Chapter 8.**

STUDENT DIALOGUE: GATHERING VISUALS

Writing in a Visual Age: One of the photographs you included was a group picture of Diane and some of her sorority sisters at a formal dance. Where did you find this photograph, and why did you include it?

Stephanie Guzik: I got the picture of the sisters off of one of the senior members' Web sites. It was taken at a formal last fall that I had attended, where I got my first glimpse into the sorority. I had found a few other photographs of Diane with some sorority sisters, but this one seemed like the perfect fit. It shows Diane right in the middle of a group of girls having a great time together. In the profile, I wanted to make sure that Diane was seen in many lights: academic, extracurricular, family, and friends. This picture showed exactly what I wanted to portray by her being a sister in the sorority, having fun with friends, and being able to hold a balanced life socially and academically.

Working on the Assignment

Developing Your Topic

After spending a couple of hours doing some preliminary information-gathering, you should ask yourself some crucial questions: *Is this topic as interesting as I originally thought? Did I find myself getting enthused as I read or thought about it? Can I think of anyone else who might find this as interesting as I do?* If the answer to one or more of these questions is no, you may need to do a bit more reading. If this additional reading doesn't change your answer, you should probably consider cutting your losses; give up on this topic and look for another one. That's difficult to do, especially when you have invested a certain amount of effort in gathering information. But it's not nearly as difficult as trying to force yourself to write a good profile on a topic that simply doesn't interest you.

Once you are reasonably confident that you have a good topic for your profile, you should become a little more systematic in your information-gathering, using the following strategies to guide your reading and thinking.

How to Gather Information

Strategies	Examples
Look for written and visual information that your readers know, can recognize, or care about. People understand new information by relating it to what they already know. Consequently, the more remote your topic is from your readers' personal experience, the more important it is to show how your subject is similar to or different from things they already know or care about.	*Readers of "The Road to Kabul" (p. 45) may know little about Afghanistan, but they have seen tanks, and they can certainly sympathize with a child standing alone, apparently in the path of an oncoming tank. Similarly, college students who read "Behind a Plain White Lab Coat" (p. 60) may not know Diane, the subject of that profile, but they certainly know what it is like to have yet one more job to do after a long day of classes.*
Find out about some of your subject's more impressive accomplishments or characteristics. If you do a thorough job of gathering information, you will probably have more information than you can include. This is a good problem to have; it will allow you to select only those accomplishments or characteristics that will be especially meaningful to your readers.	*Dr. Sandra Scott ("E.R. Unscripted," p. 41) has an exhausting job at "one of New York City's busiest trauma centers." The fact that she rejected "cushier offers" at other hospitals gives some insight into her dedication to helping people who have little access to other medical care.*
Look for background information that makes your subject unique. Readers like to know how people achieved what they did or how something evolved into its current state. Profiles of people often include a narrative explaining the obstacles the subject overcame in reaching a position of prominence. But this background information may also explain the personal or cultural forces that led a person to act in a certain way.	*"From Welfare to Washington" (p. 37) explains some of the early experiences that shaped Senator Murray's character.*

Creating an Exploratory Draft

At this point you should be about ready to write an exploratory draft, one that will help you determine how well you understand your profile topic and what you need to do to convey your view of that person, place, or activity to the appropriate audience.

Creating an Exploratory Draft

Before you begin the exploratory draft, review the information you gathered to get a good sense of what you found. Go back to any sources you are doubtful about to clarify your ideas and make sure the information is correct. Also confirm the source and accuracy of any quotations you may want to use. This extra check of your sources will help you gain confidence, prevent errors, and save time later on.

Then take a look at the context analysis you completed, answering the questions on p. 74. Are there some questions that aren't completed very well? For example, are you lacking information about your readers' knowledge, needs, and values? Do you have a good sense of what your readers will expect in terms of content, both verbal and visual? Finish completing your responses to the best of your ability.

Once again, review the notes you took and the materials you gathered. Read closely and underline or mark key facts (quotes, stories, statistics) that convey an insider's perspective on the topic. After doing this, set aside twenty to thirty minutes and write as rapidly as you can (without interruption), completing the following sentences.

> "One thing that makes my topic so remarkable/impressive is _____." Without stopping to look back at the information

you gathered, elaborate on that statement as much as you can.

> "Something else that makes my topic so remarkable/impressive is _____." Then continue to elaborate as much as possible from memory. Keep doing this for at least twenty minutes.

After you have done this exploratory work, read or show what you have written to other students (either a small group or the entire class). Ask your classmates to answer the following questions.

> What details give a particularly clear impression of the person, place, or activity that is the topic of my profile?

> Are any passages unclear or confusing? If so, which ones are they, and what makes them unclear or confusing?

> Are there passages in which my intended readers would appreciate more detail? If so, where are these passages, and what details might be helpful? Would a photograph be useful at any of these points?

After considering your classmates' responses, determine whether there are places where you might use some of the strategies explained earlier to give readers more insight into your profile topic. Use your classmates' responses to guide you in deciding whether or how to add to, delete, or modify information in your exploratory draft.

Using Narrative

Almost all profiles use some narrative. After all, it's hard to talk about a person or place without mentioning what people do and say. Usually stories or anecdotes about people reveal something significant—not only what happens but when, where, and why something happens. As a rule, narratives entail some sort of conflict—within a character, between characters, or between a character and his or her environment. As you look for stories to use in your profile, remember that not all stories are equally useful. You should choose stories that provide some original insight into the unique qualities of the subject you are profiling.

The following charts introduce some of the strategies writers can use in telling stories that profile a person or a place. However, because a good story is always richer and more engaging than any summary or analysis, you might want to reread the profiles "The Road to Kabul" and "Can You Say . . . 'Hero'?" In the first profile, Dan Rather gives readers a sense of what it is like to travel in a distant country, Afghanistan, that has been ravaged by many years of war. In the second profile, Tom Junod has the difficult task of getting sophisticated adult readers to share his profound admiration for a personality from a children's television program.

❯ For additional narrative strategies and examples, see **Chapter 3,** pp. 160–162.

As you read the following charts, think of ways the strategies they explain might help you tell stories about your profile subject.

How to Use Narratives about People

Strategies

Anticipate reactions—especially negative reactions—readers are likely to have to the person about whom you are telling your story. If you are writing about a well-known or controversial person, readers may have formed impressions that are quite different from the ones you want to convey. Or readers may be skeptical, particularly if they feel they are reading about someone who is too good to be true. You may need to acknowledge these negative reactions and show how they do not represent the entire truth about your subject.

Describe the conflicts the people in your story face, and explain how they respond to those conflicts. One of the best ways to learn about a person is to see how he or she deals with adversity. Tell your readers what your profile subject says and does in solving problems, overcoming difficulties, or dealing with unpleasant people.

Examples

"Can You Say . . . 'Hero'?" (p. 51), a profile of television personality Mr. Rogers, carefully acknowledges the apparent frailty and ordinary physical qualities of the subject. This demonstrates that author Tom Junod is not someone who gushes over a celebrity or is taken in by a carefully contrived TV image. Thus the sophisticated, somewhat skeptical readers of Esquire *are more likely to trust Junod when he explains the powerful ways he is affected by what Mr. Rogers says and does.*

One episode in "Can You Say . . . 'Hero'?" begins with this sentence: "Once upon a time, a little boy with a big sword went into battle against Mister Rogers." At first this child refuses to acknowledge Mr. Rogers's presence, but Junod narrates how Mr. Rogers waits patiently and ultimately wins the "battle" by saying something that "made the little boy look at Mister Rogers . . . with the eyes of a child at last, and nod his head yes." Junod concludes this anecdote by letting Mr. Rogers explain: "I said, 'Do you know that you're strong on the inside, too?' Maybe it was something he needed to hear."

continued

How to Use Narratives about People

continued

Strategies	Examples
Locate the person in a scene that suggests something of his or her personality or distinctive qualities. The scene may be one in which your subject typically appears or one that differs from his or her usual setting. The important thing is to choose a scene that reveals aspects of the person's character or personality.	*Junod's first interview with Mr. Rogers took place in a New York apartment that was "drab and dim, with the smell of stalled air and a stain of daguerreotype sunlight on its closed, slatted blinds"—a very humble setting that contrasts effectively with the remarkable powers of perception Mr. Rogers displays during this interview.*
Observe the person closely, noticing details that not only set him or her apart from others but that differ from the details readers may have observed for themselves.	*Junod observes Mr. Rogers as he appeared just after awakening from a nap, "wearing eyeglasses and suede moccasins with rawhide laces and a flimsy old blue-and-yellow bathrobe that revealed whatever part of his skinny white calves his dark-blue dress socks didn't hide." He then tells how Mr. Rogers turns the table on his interviewer, making Junod the one who reveals personal, even embarrassing, details about himself.*
Show how people react to the person. What do people say to and about him or her? What sort of actions does this person seem to inspire in others?	*Junod lets readers see how a wide range of people react to Mr. Rogers. These include children on a subway who spontaneously sing the theme song of Mr. Rogers's television program and a "mook" who says that he's going to buy a lottery ticket because "I just met Mister Rogers—this is definitely my lucky day."*
Tell about the person's prior experiences, especially incorporating stories that illustrate or explain his or her personality, attitudes, status, or actions.	*Junod recounts several stories from Mr. Rogers's past. Perhaps none is more indicative of the extent of Mr. Rogers's influence than a story in which he visited a gorilla named Koko who had learned American Sign Language and regularly watched Mister Rogers' Neighborhood. When Mr. Rogers met Koko, she took him in her arms "as though he were a child" and then, following the ritual with which the program begins each day, removed Mr. Rogers's shoes.*

STUDENT DIALOGUE: USING NARRATIVE

Writing in a Visual Age: In the fourth paragraph of your profile, you narrate a brief incident in which you discover that something went wrong with your experiment. Why did you include both your reaction and Diane's?

Stephanie Guzik: I included both of our reactions to the dying culture as a means of contrast. Whereas I was upset about the dead culture, Diane took it in stride and convinced me that it wasn't the end of the world. I carried that thought throughout the paper, focusing on the difference between Diane and myself (representing most college students who are just trying to make it through). That situation in the lab also brought up the idea of how caring Diane is and how much of a mentor she is.

Working on the Assignment

Using Narratives about a Person

If you are writing a profile about a person, find or write a narrative that reveals something significant about the person. Bring this narrative to class, and be prepared to answer the following questions.

❯ What does this narrative reveal about the subject of my profile?

❯ Would the narrative offer my readers an insider's view of the subject of my profile?

❯ What strategies were used in developing this narrative?

❯ Are there additional strategies that might make the narrative more effective?

❯ How might this narrative add to (or change) the impressions I expressed in my exploratory draft?

How to Use Narratives about Places and Activities

Strategies

Describe the place from different distances and perspectives. With your mind's eye, zoom in to focus on a specific detail or move back to take a panoramic look. Also, notice details that would be important to different kinds of people. For example, in looking at a beach, what details would a sunbather notice? a windsurfing instructor? a lifeguard?

Look for ways to complement your written observations with photographs.

Examples

"The Road to Kabul" (p. 45) begins with Rather describing what he sees from his plane, noting first the surrounding "snow-capped peaks" and then the "dusty haze" that hangs over the city of Kabul. Only as he lands does he get a "close-up look at the devastation: the ruined planes, the debris of trucks, armored vehicles and what were once antiaircraft batteries."

continued

How to Use Narratives about Places and Activities

continued

Strategies	Examples
Tell about (or show photographs of) the inhabitants of the place or people who take part in the activity. Make sure readers can see what's remarkable about their appearance, actions, words, and attitudes.	*"E.R. Unscripted" (p. 41) shows the full range of patients who come through Dr. Scott's emergency room in a twelve-hour period. Captions with each photograph help convey each patient's personality.*
Talk about the conflicts or difficulties you encountered, but only insofar as your experiences convey some impression of the place or activity you are describing. Perhaps, for example, inhabitants of the place went to some trouble to help you find a lost billfold or gave you a place to stay until you could make other arrangements. That sort of experience may say a lot about the subject of your profile.	*Rather tells of the difficulty he and his colleagues have in trying to interview U.S. troops. Faced with hostile Northern Alliance soldiers who want to prevent the interview, Rather and his colleagues persist as long as they dare. Rather concludes this narrative with the comment: "As we rode out toward the main gate . . . we slapped fives and laughed. Sometimes even tiny victories can be sweet."*
Notice incongruities. Pay attention to things that surprise you, that seem out of place or inconsistent with what people might expect.	*In "E.R. Unscripted," Mackey records that a patient "whose wound stretches from his collarbone to his armpit, seems unshaken by it all" and even flirts with Dr. Scott, who is treating him.*
Record your impressions and reactions, either directly or indirectly through figurative language or visual images. You may or may not want to state your impressions directly. In either case, use the sort of written and visual information that will enable readers to share the experience as fully as possible.	*When he entered Kabul, Rather tells us: "I worried about the children I saw walking along the street—they were so little, so close to traffic and so often unaccompanied by adults." Reflecting on the devastation in Afghanistan, Rather comments: "One had a sense of passing through a graveyard." Later, as he travels toward Kabul, Rather says: "We drove through miles of choking, throat-scratching dust as thick as fog. Around us, a brown moonscape, with towering brown mountains in the distance."*

Using Narratives about a Place or Activity

If you are writing a profile about a place or activity, find a narrative someone else has written or write your own narrative that reveals something significant about the place or activity. Bring this narrative to class, and be prepared to answer the following questions.

> What does this narrative reveal about the topic of my profile?

> Would the narrative help my readers feel that they were developing an insider's view of my profile topic?

> What strategies were used in developing this narrative?

> Are there additional strategies that might make the narrative more effective?

> How might this narrative add to (or change) the impressions I expressed in my exploratory draft?

Engaging Your Audience: Writing an Introduction

Why would you read a profile? Because you are interested in the person or place that is its subject? Well, maybe. If you are a fan of, say, a particular movie star or you are looking for information about a place you might want to visit, you might be drawn to anything that mentions the movie star or the vacation spot. But notice that none of the profiles in this chapter count on this sort of automatic attraction. Most likely, neither would any profile you might choose to read on your own. Instead, profile writers themselves have to motivate their readers, giving them strong incentives to stop and read rather than skip on to the next article.

The key to motivating readers lies in observing two basic principles.

> Readers must be able to relate the topic to something they know, value, or need.
> Readers must feel some conflict—tension, question, uncertainty—that prompts them to read further.

Relating to Readers

The profiles in the Reading to Write section of this chapter display a variety of strategies for relating to readers. Here are three strategies that will help your own writing relate to—or develop common ground with—your readers.

How to Relate to Readers

Strategies	Examples
Begin by referring to something the reader knows about, appreciates, or can recognize. Such references can take the form of both written text and visual images.	*"Can You Say . . . 'Hero'?" (p. 51) begins with two visual images. First, a cardigan sweater that children for the last thirty years have seen Mr. Rogers put on each day. Lest there be any doubt about whose cardigan sweater it is, the familiar image of Mr. Rogers appears on the facing page.*
Create a scene the reader can visualize.	*Most readers of "The Road to Kabul" (p. 45) have never been to Afghanistan, but most are likely to have seen snow-capped mountain peaks and cities enveloped in haze.*
Create a voice the reader can recognize. (For more on voice, see p. 88.)	*The very title "Can You Say . . . 'Hero'?" suggests the scenario of an adult talking to a small child, as does the first line of the profile: "Once upon a time . . . "*

Establishing Conflict

In addition to establishing a relationship with your readers—in effect, getting them "on your side"—you should present or suggest a conflict that will motivate them to keep reading. The following list illustrates strategies for doing this.

How to Establish Conflict

Strategies	Examples
Juxtapose two dissimilar things. Most experiences are complex; things are rarely all good or all bad, all significant or all trivial. Readers sometimes appreciate a subject more fully when they see the extremes that it involves.	*"E.R. Unscripted" (p. 41) refers to two extremes of Dr. Scott's nightly work, which "begins with a resuscitation and ends, after dawn, with a pile of paperwork."* *The initial photograph in "The Road to Kabul" (p. 45) juxtaposes an unaccompanied, vulnerable child against the military might associated with a tank.*

How to Establish Conflict

Strategies	Examples
Tell a story that shows a conflict or problem. The story should not be long or complicated, but it should introduce one or more key people and show them disagreeing with each other, facing some serious obstacle, or grappling with a problem.	*"Can You Say . . . 'Hero'?" (p. 51) begins with a story in which a child becomes separated from a much-loved toy animal. "From Welfare to Washington" (p. 37) begins with a confrontation between a young homemaker and a group of "old bald heads," state legislators who had cut the funding for an educational program the homemaker valued.*
Suggest a contrast between what the reader knows and what the writer is going to say. One of the principal reasons people read profiles is to gain insight that they may not otherwise have. If you can make readers aware that your information will take them beyond what they currently know, without belittling them, you will appeal strongly to their desire to be insiders.	*The word* unscripted *in the title "E.R. Unscripted" implies that the writer will take the reader beyond the impressions created by a television program—where problems are under the control of writers and are usually resolved within one or two hour-long episodes.*

Working on the Assignment

Engaging Your Audience

> Look on the Web, in magazines, and in books to find a profile in which the first few paragraphs do a good job of engaging a reader's interest. Be prepared to show this profile to your classmates and explain your answers to the following questions: What assumptions does the writer appear to be making about the reader's knowledge, needs, and/or values? What aspects of the beginning of the profile would appeal to a person with the knowledge, needs, and/or values you have identified?

> Review—and, if necessary, revise—your context analysis, being careful to describe your reader's knowledge, needs, and/or values.

> Using one or more of the strategies explained above, write one or more introductory paragraphs that seem likely to engage the attention of the audience you have described. Consider using a photograph along with these paragraphs.

> Bring this introductory material to class, along with your context analysis.

> Ask your classmates to tell you whether the introduction you have written (and perhaps the photograph you have included) seems likely to engage the intended audience.

> Also ask your classmates whether they can think of other strategies to engage your audience.

Creating an Appropriate Voice

In telling stories about Fred Rogers, author Tom Junod creates a very personal voice, frequently using the pronoun *I* and conveying his own reactions. A personal voice also appears in "The Road to Kabul" and "Behind a Plain White Lab Coat." By contrast, the profiles "From Welfare to Washington" and "E. R. Unscripted" make no reference to *I* or *we*; nor do they indicate explicitly how the writer (or photographer) felt about the subject of the profile. What accounts for this difference? Why would some authors decide to create a personal voice while others do not? More to the point, how do you decide whether or not to create a personal voice when you write a profile?

Your answer will depend on your answer to one further question. Will your readers need to understand your personal experiences and reactions in order for you to achieve your purpose in writing your profile? For the author of "Behind a Plain White Lab Coat," the answer was clearly yes. Stephanie Guzik was aware that most members of her audience would need to know about her personal experiences with the subject of her profile—a fellow student at her college—in order to understand her purpose in writing the piece. But for the authors of the profile of Senator Patty Murray ("From Welfare to Washington"), on the other hand, the answer was no. Their goal was to show how someone rose from relative obscurity to a position of national importance. To do this they could draw on secondary sources (news articles and biographies of the senator) and on the comments of those who can talk authoritatively about Murray's political accomplishments (Senator Tom Daschle, for instance). Indeed, using secondary sources can be a good way to add depth and perspective to your profile.

When authors have personal experiences with their subjects, those experiences can sometimes give readers unique insights. Both Dan Rather in "The Road to Kabul" and Tom Junod in "Can You Say . . . 'Hero'?" write about subjects for which they could probably find a lot of secondary sources. But both writers draw principally on their personal experiences. Rather does so because he is writing for readers of *TV Guide*, people who will appreciate the expertise he brings to his topic. His personal experience and reactions enable readers to go beyond the brief glimpses of Afghanistan they see in accounts on the evening news. Similarly, Junod sees aspects of Mr. Rogers that are inaccessible to people who know the man only as a television personality.

Whether or not they create a personal voice, all the profiles in this chapter display distinctive attitudes toward their subjects.

❯ For strategies involving secondary sources, see p. 77 of this chapter or p. 155 in **Chapter 3**.

How to Create an Appropriate Voice

Strategies	Examples
Choose details that exemplify the attitudes you want to convey. There may be times when you need to come right out and state your attitude toward your subject. But more important, choose details that will let readers see for themselves the kinds of emotions or attitudes your subject inspires.	*Mackey, the author of "E.R. Unscripted" (p. 41), clearly admires the emergency room doctor Sandra Scott and presents her as dedicated to practicing medicine in a chaotic environment. But he never explicitly says either of these things. Instead, he chooses details that illustrate the chaos and stress. He notes, for example, that "In addition to dealing with cuts and bullet wounds, on any given night Scott will treat everything from miscarriages and S.T.D.'s to dental problems and what one patient believed was sleep disturbance caused by a spell."*
Allow your subject to speak for himself or herself, displaying the attributes you admire. Be selective; listen for comments that in just a few words convey some important attitude or character trait.	*In "Can You Say . . . 'Hero'?" (p. 51), Junod recounts how Mr. Rogers overcame the hostility of the young child with a plastic sword. In response to Junod's questioning, Mr. Rogers says: "Oh, I just knew that whenever you see a little boy carrying something like that, it means that he wants to show people that he's strong on the outside. I just wanted him to know that he was strong on the inside, too. . . . [so] I said, 'Do you know that you're strong on the inside, too?' Maybe it was something he needed to hear."*
Let others comment on your subject, expressing the attitudes you wish to convey. Especially look for comments from people who can speak authoritatively about your subject. Again, be selective. Choose only those comments that express your point more succinctly or effectively than you can.	*The authors of "From Welfare to Washington" (p. 37) want readers to see Senator Murray as someone who genuinely "represents the interests of ordinary folks." To convey this impression, they cite comments from other political leaders: "'She didn't create this image to win a political race,' says Sid Snyder, majority leader of the state senate. 'That's who she is.'"*
Choose photographs that imply your impressions of or attitudes toward the subject of your profile. Pay special attention to the composition of these photographs and to the details they include (and exclude).	*"Behind a Plain White Lab Coat" (p. 60) includes a photograph that shows Diane in a different setting, reinforcing the point that her life is not limited to a science lab.*

Creating an Appropriate Voice

If you have not already begun to do so, think about the voice you want to convey in your profile. What are your attitudes toward your subject? How personal do you want your voice to be? To find answers to these questions, follow these steps.

> Review your context analysis (revise it if you need to).

> List some of the words and phrases you hope readers would use to describe the voice in your profile.

> Show both the context analysis and the list of words and phrases to someone else (a classmate or your instructor); ask this person to tell you whether the voice you hope to create makes sense, given what your analysis says about your intended audience and purpose.

> Using what you learn from your classmate or instructor, revise the list of words that describe the voice you want to create.

> Ask someone (a classmate, your instructor, or a friend) to read a section of your draft aloud, and listen to the sound of his or her voice. Can you hear the attitude you want to create in the sound of this reader's voice? If you can, good. If you can't, look closely at your draft to see what words and phrases you need to change in order to create the voice you want.

> Ask someone to read your introductory paragraph(s) (aloud or silently) and then list the words he or she would use to describe the voice you're trying to create. Does this reader's list match yours? On the basis of what this reader tells you, decide whether you need to revise either your conception of the voice you want to create or your introduction. Or do you need to revise both?

STUDENT DIALOGUE: CREATING AN APPROPRIATE VOICE

Writing in a Visual Age: In several places, you interject questions in italics that run through your mind as you talk with Diane. What was your purpose in including these questions? What do they say about you and your attitudes toward Diane?

Stephanie Guzik: The highlighted thoughts italicized in the text continue to add contrast between myself and Diane. Whereas I often struggle to balance my work, sorority, and friends, Diane somehow finds time to do that and much more without much stress. In writing the paper, I could imagine several questions that readers might raise about how Diane actually manages to do everything. Therefore, I interjected these italicized thoughts, which the reader could most likely relate to while reading the paper.

Name: Jessica Miller   Time: 10:40

Delivery: obesity, environmental factors
          ideas come through clearly, avoid "uh"- work to
          have transitions btw. ideas

Content: fast food, physical activity, good info.

Structure: forecast main ideas? solutions clear - more about what
           the average person can do, then talk about solutions twice?

Visual(s): ppt. slides clear, proofread - "heart" = "heat"
           - watch time! practice to find a time that works.
           - why have the statistics at the end?   C-   28/40
           - included too much information...

Providing Structure

One of your main objectives as a writer is to let readers "see" the structure of your work. Specifically, you need to make the work accessible, giving readers cues that make it easy to understand what you're getting at and to find the information they want or need. You also need to create clear expectations, giving readers a sense of where you're headed in a given passage. Finally, you often need to create links that show how one paragraph (or a larger section of text) relates to the passages that precede or follow it.

You may already be familiar with some of the best ways of providing structure—using thesis statements, placing topic sentences near the beginning of paragraphs, and using words that forecast the content of an upcoming paragraph or series of paragraphs. In addition, the profiles in Reading to Write use a variety of other strategies to make the work accessible, create clear expectations, and indicate links between paragraphs or longer sections.

Making Information Accessible

In some situations, readers will not read every word of the texts you create. Instead, they may scan for information about specific points. Consequently, part of your responsibility as a writer is to make it easy for readers to find what they are looking for. The following list describes several strategies you can use to make information accessible.

How to Make Information Accessible

Strategies	Examples
Use thesis statements and topic sentences. Not all profiles have thesis statements, nor do all paragraphs have topic sentences. But when authors do use a thesis statement, they tend to put it near the end of the introductory paragraph(s) of their profile. When authors use a topic sentence, they tend to put it at or near the beginning of a paragraph.	*The authors of "From Welfare to Washington" (p. 37) assert their thesis near the end of the second paragraph: "There [in the Senate] she has made a name for herself as a one-time soccer mom who represents the interests of ordinary people." And they begin the third paragraph with an explicit topic sentence: "Those feelings [as a representative of "ordinary folks"] shaped her political priorities." Junod does not provide an explicit thesis statement, although his attitude toward Mr. Rogers is clearly suggested by the title "Can You Say . . . 'Hero'?" (p. 51).*

continued

How to Make Information Accessible

continued

Strategies	Examples
Group related details together to form a dominant impression. Think of your profile as consisting of related "chunks" of information, groups of closely related facts that add up to a point you want to make or an impression you want to convey.	*In "The Road to Kabul" (p. 45), Rather begins one paragraph by noting: "The way to Kabul stretched ahead—long, dirty and tailbone-bustingly bumpy. No pavement. Plenty of bomb craters." The remainder of the paragraph mentions details of sights along the road ("overturned tanks, the twisted carcasses of demolished armored vehicles") that convey the impression of a region devastated by war.*
Break up a narrative into discrete episodes. Think of your narrative as consisting of a series of mini-dramas, much like the scenes of a television program, movie, or play.	*Junod presents a series of vignettes, each revealing some new aspect of Mr. Rogers's personality. Each vignette is preceded by an extra line of white space and begins with words (such as "Once upon a time") set in a typeface and style that stand out from the rest of the text.*
Use pictures with clear, informative captions. Some pictures are indeed worth a thousand words, but a picture is not much good if readers don't understand why it's there. Be sure to include a caption indicating what the picture shows (who, what, when, where, and so on).	*Each photograph in "From Welfare to Washington" includes a caption that clearly suggests some facet of Senator Murray's personality.*

Working on the Assignment

Creating Thesis Statements and Topic Sentences

Although it's true that not all profiles have thesis statements and not all paragraphs have topic sentences, readers of any type of writing usually want to know what you're getting at—either the point you are making or the impression you are trying to create. One way to help readers is to use explicit thesis statements and/or topic sentences.

How do you come up with thesis statements? Read back over your notes and your exploratory draft. Then complete this sentence: *The main point/main impression I'm trying to get across is _____.* Show this sentence to your instructor and/or your classmates, and ask whether it accurately reflects the content in your draft. If it does, that's fine. You probably have the thesis you want to support in your profile. If not, you can change the sentence, change the content of what you have written, or change both.

Working on the
Assignment

The same procedure works for creating topic sentences for paragraphs. Read over each paragraph, and then complete this sentence: *The main point I'm making in this paragraph is _____*. Then check to see whether the content of the paragraph actually supports or illustrates this point. If it doesn't, you may need to change the sentence, change the content that follows it, or both.

How will you know whether you need to use a thesis statement and topic sentences in your profile? The answer will depend in part on the instructor's goals for your writing class. If you're in doubt about this, ask the instructor. Also ask the instructor or your classmates to read your profile and tell you what they see as the main point of the profile or of any given paragraph. If they can tell you, even without seeing a thesis statement or topic sentence, then you might not need to use them.

Creating Expectations

Several of the strategies for providing structure (using thesis statements, topic sentences, and forecasting words) also help create expectations. In addition, the following list includes other strategies that will help readers anticipate what you are going to say in a given section of text.

How to Create Expectations

Strategies

Establish a pattern, and repeat it throughout your profile. The most common patterns are (1) to make assertions and then elaborate and (2) to ask questions and then provide answers. But—as the examples in the right-hand column suggest—these patterns can take many different forms.

Examples

In "E.R. Unscripted" (p. 41), after the two introductory paragraphs, there is a series of photographs, each accompanied by an informative caption.

"The Road to Kabul" (p. 45) frequently identifies challenges and then explains how they were overcome.

Another pattern appears in "Can You Say . . . 'Hero'?" (p. 51). Junod consistently tells stories about his encounters with Mr. Rogers, ending each story with an insight into Mr. Rogers's personality—in effect, a punch line. (Note that Junod's strategy of asserting his point at the end of an episode rather than at the beginning is not easy to put into practice. If you want readers to be willing to wait for the punch line of your stories, you have to be a really good storyteller. For more strategies that can help with storytelling, see p. 160 of Chapter 3.)

continued

How to Create Expectations

continued

Strategies	Examples
Use photographs that imply attitudes or impressions that will be developed in the written text. It is not enough to have a clear picture of the person, place, or activity you are profiling. The picture must somehow—through facial expressions, posture, dress, actions, or surroundings—suggest a point of view you will make explicit in the written text.	*At the beginning of "The Road to Kabul," the sadness and harshness of life in Afghanistan are established in a photograph of a solitary child, apparently standing in or near the path of an oncoming tank.*
Use forecasting words or phrases. These terms appear near the beginning of a section of text and indicate the topic to be covered. They often appear in thesis statements or topic sentences. They may also introduce longer passages within the main part of the profile.	*After acknowledging that the Afghans ("The Road to Kabul") are "ferocious warriors," Rather observes that they are "equally ferocious survivors." The next several paragraphs describe some of the ways in which Afghans are surviving.*

Creating Links

Even though readers may not read every word of your profile, they still will want to have a sense of flow, of how a given paragraph or set of paragraphs relates to the passages that precede and follow it. Here are several strategies to create links that will give readers a sense of flow.

How to Create Links

Strategies	Examples
Use transition words or phrases. Use words that indicate when, where, or why something happened.	*"E.R. Unscripted" (p. 41) includes the precise time at which each photograph was taken. "The Road to Kabul" (p. 45) marks each stage of Rather's journey with some sort of signpost: "At the first gate [to the airport] . . ."; "About a third of the way there [to Kabul] . . ."; "As we approached Kabul. . . ."*

How to Create Links

Strategies

Begin a new paragraph by referring to information contained in the preceding paragraph, especially if the new paragraph corrects or amplifies an impression created by the preceding paragraph.

Examples

In "From Welfare to Washington" (p. 37), the authors recount Senator Murray's success in defeating legislators' efforts to cut funding for a preschool program. They begin the next paragraph with these words: "Inspired by that success, she ran for the school board."

Midway through "The Road to Kabul," Rather comments on the openness, warmth, and good humor of people in Afghanistan. In the next paragraph, he corrects an impression that readers might have formed: "That isn't to say that the Afghans aren't ferocious warriors. They are."

In a profile of a person, place, or activity, return to the same person in several instances, each time adding some new information or insight.

To give "E.R. Unscripted" a feeling of coherence, Mackey and photographer Naomi Harris not only focus on Dr. Scott but also on several patients—such as Eli D'Attilo, who dies during the night, and his family.

Working on the Assignment

Providing Structure

Bring to class a copy of a profile that does a good job of making its structure very clear. Be prepared to show your instructor and/or classmates how the author(s) enabled you to see the structure of the profile. After identifying strategies other writers have used, review your exploratory draft, looking for ways you might use some of these strategies to make the structure of your own profile clear.

Concluding Your Profile

Because the goal of a profile is to give readers an insider's view of the topic, you need to create an impression of and convey an attitude toward your topic. The conclusion should reinforce that impression and solidify that attitude. The profiles in Reading to Write suggest a variety of strategies that can help you end with something memorable that reinforces or extends the message(s) you have sought to convey.

How to Conclude

Strategies	Examples
Create an evocative image. Using words and/or visual images, try to leave the reader with the overall impression you have sought to create throughout the profile.	*"E.R. Unscripted" (p. 41) concludes with a photograph of Dr. Scott leaving the hospital alone, in a seemingly endless hospital corridor.*
Refer to a detail you mentioned earlier, adding new information about it.	*The end of "Can You Say . . . 'Hero'?" (p. 51) returns to the story of Old Rabbit, suggesting that Mr. Rogers led Junod to a new understanding of that story. In light of this understanding, Junod finds himself saying the prayer he had previously heard Mr. Rogers advise a child to pray: "Thank you, God."*
End with a quote from the person you are profiling (or a revealing quote from someone involved in the place or activity you are writing about). Don't use just any quote. Use a comment that reveals something important about the subject's personality or character.	*The final paragraph of "From Welfare to Washington" (p. 37) acknowledges that although Patty Murray finds satisfaction in her work as a senator, she places primary importance on her family: "'The people I meet in Washington, D.C., aren't going to care about me when I leave here,' she says. 'My family will.'"*
Frame your profile. Come back to an image or idea you mention at the beginning of the profile, but expand upon that image, giving it additional meaning.	*The conclusion of "Behind a Plain White Lab Coat" (p. 60) returns to Diane in the setting where readers first saw her—in the lab. But at this point Guzik has provided the details that let readers take Diane seriously when she says: "Don't forget, there's a whole different place outside of that door [to the lab]. Take advantage of it while you can."*

 Exercise

Bring to class a profile you find interesting and informative. Does its conclusion reflect any of the strategies identified above? If not, how does it conclude? What strategies are apparent in the conclusion? Be prepared to explain your answer to your classmates.

Working on the Assignment

Concluding Your Profile

Using a strategy identified earlier (or a different strategy from a profile you have analyzed), write a conclusion for your profile. Share your draft with some classmates or your instructor, and ask for their response. Can they identify the strategy, and do they think it is appropriate? If not, what strategy would they recommend? Would that conclusion reinforce or extend the dominant impression created throughout your profile?

Designing Your Profile and Integrating Visual Information

Most of the profiles in this chapter are relatively conventional in design. Some of them make effective use of photographs (especially captioned photographs), but they do not display the range of visual features found in other types of writing: bulleted lists, headings, inset boxes, or charts. (One exception is "Can You Say . . . 'Hero'?"—which uses pull quotes, or lines of text "pulled out" and set in boxes for emphasis.)

Check with your instructor about the visual features that are appropriate for the profile you are writing; bear in mind the goals of the course and your intended audience. If you decide to include photographs, be sure to observe the following guidelines.

> Photographs should not only depict the subject of your profile; they should also convey the same attitude or tone you create in the written text. For example, a profile of a place that you find romantic or exotic should include photographs that convey these impressions.

> Unless the photograph is self-explanatory (as in "The Road to Kabul"), you should use a caption that either indicates what is going on (as in "E.R. Unscripted") or expresses an attitude or some other characteristic you want to associate with your profile subject (as in "From Welfare to Washington").

> If you use photographs that you have not taken yourself, be sure to give appropriate credit, following the guidelines on p. 77.

Working on the Assignment

Integrating Photographs

Find some photographs that you think convey the attitudes or impressions you hope to communicate through the written text of your profile. Create captions for these photographs. Bring the photographs and captions to class. Show the photographs to your classmates, and ask what messages the photographs convey to them. Then show both the photographs and the captions to your classmates. Ask them to tell you

continued

Working on the Assignment

continued

whether the captions either (1) explain clearly and succinctly what is going on in the photographs, or (2) indicate an attitude that seems consistent with the photographs. If your classmates' reactions differ greatly from your own, you might need to look for other photographs—or get additional reactions from people who are as similar as possible to your intended readers.

Finishing Up

By now, you should have some strong impressions and views of the topic of your profile. Next, create a review draft to convey those impressions as effectively as possible. After writing this draft, assess it carefully—not only by critiquing it yourself but also by getting others' perspectives in a final review. Then, use what you learn from this assessment to make revisions in content, organization, style, and/or format.

Creating a Review Draft

Your review draft is not final, but neither is it a rough draft. It should represent the best work you are capable of doing at this point. Before you start writing, look back at your context analysis. If your understanding of that context has changed revise the context analysis and keep your analysis in mind as you decide what to say and how to say it.

Also, look back at your exploratory draft. Ask yourself whether it conveys the basic impression you want the reader to have. Notice points at which you want to improve upon this exploratory draft, perhaps adding some details—written or visual—and perhaps deleting others. Look for places at which narratives would clarify or emphasize an important quality of the person, place, or activity you are profiling. Especially if your concept of your audience or purpose has changed substantially since you began, you may need to go back to your notes or sources for pertinent stories or details. And remember that for any secondary source (a magazine, a Web site, and so on), you have to document these sources appropriately.

⟩ For advice on documenting sources, see **Chapter 12.**

Also look at your introductory and concluding paragraphs. Does the introductory material establish the voice you want to create? Does it seem likely to engage the intended audience? Does the conclusion reinforce the basic impression you want to convey?

As you work on the review draft, take pains to make the structure clear. It may help to make an informal outline indicating your main points and the impressions you want to convey. Use the strategies described on pp. 91–95 to make your work accessible, create clear expectations for your readers, and link paragraphs or larger sections of text.

Getting a Final Review

Once you have made your review draft as complete and polished as possible, have it reviewed by one or more people who understand the principles (analyzing context, engaging readers, and so on) that you have been working with in this chapter. These reviewers might include your instructor, your classmates, and/or a tutor in your school's writing center.

> Give the reviewer a copy of your draft, one he or she can make notes on.
> Give the reviewer a copy of your context analysis. If necessary, revise that analysis before giving it to the reviewer.
> Ask the reviewer to begin his or her response by answering the following questions. (1) What is the overall impression you get of the topic of my profile? (2) What words would you use to describe the person, place, or activity I am writing about? (3) Given what I say in my context analysis, how likely does it seem that this impression will come through clearly and be interesting to my intended audience?
> Ask the reviewer to adopt the perspective of the audience described in your context analysis and then use the following checklist in commenting on your work.

Checklist for Final Review

> bedfordstmartins.com/
> visualage
>
> *To download the check-list as a worksheet, click on* **CHAPTER 2** > **WORKSHEETS**

1 In my context analysis, please highlight any statements that give you a good sense of the knowledge, values, and needs of my intended audience. (For an example, see p. 74.) Please indicate any statements that need to be clarified.

2 In my context analysis, please highlight any statements that give you a good sense of the circumstances, purposes, and expected format for my profile. (For an example of a good context analysis, see p. 74.) Please indicate any statements that need to be clarified.

3 In what specific passages have I developed my topic thoroughly, creating a clear, dominant impression of my subject? What are some passages in which I could make that impression clearer or more effective? What are some strategies (explained on pp. 81–84) I might use to do this? Do the photographs I have used contribute to the impression I am trying to create?

4 What portions of my introduction seem likely to engage the interest of my intended audience? What are some strategies (explained on pp. 86–87) that might make the introduction more engaging?

5 How would you describe the voice I have created? At what points does that voice seem appropriate, given my intended audience and profile topic? What strategies (explained on p. 89) might help me make the voice clearer or more appropriate?

6 What are some words or phrases that provide a clear structure for my profile, making information accessible, creating clear expectations for readers, and indicating links between paragraphs or larger sections of text? What strategies (explained on pp. 91–95) might I use to make the structure of my profile clearer?

7 How does the conclusion of my profile reinforce or extend the dominant impression I am trying to create? What strategies (explained on p. 96) might I use to make my conclusion more effective?

8 If the profile includes photographs or other visual elements, what do they contribute to the overall impression conveyed in the profile? Do the images have appropriate captions?

If possible, ask the reviewer to talk with you about your review draft as well as make notes on it. During this conversation, make careful notes about what the reviewer finds to be clear or unclear, interesting or uninteresting; also note any suggestions he or she makes. You may be tempted to argue with the reviewer or explain something you feel he or she has misunderstood. Try not to do so. Instead, ask why the reviewer makes a particular suggestion or what causes him or her to misunderstand or disagree with something you have said.

Revising Your Profile

Once you have a good idea of how the reviewer responds to your profile (after you have listened without explaining, arguing, or making judgments), go back through your notes on your reviewer's comments. Bearing in mind your intended audience and purpose, decide which comments are most valid. Then use the strategies referred to in the Checklist for Final Review.

After resolving all the issues that need attention, proofread carefully and correct any typographical or formatting errors. Then submit this final draft to your instructor.

Taking Stock of Where You Are

Although you will find differences among the writing assignments in this book, there are also some important similarities. For example, you always have to analyze the intended audience, write an introduction that will engage that particular audience, and so forth. Each assignment in *Writing in a Visual Age* will teach you strategies that can help you grow as a writer and improve your work on subsequent assignments. This will be especially true if you make a conscious effort to assess your development as a writer as you go along.

To help with this assessment and growth, continually review what you're learning and try to determine what you need to work harder on in the future. Once your instructor has returned the final draft of your work, think back over all the comments you received—from classmates as well as your instructor—and write out answers to the following questions. (You might want to keep these in a journal or a special section of a notebook.)

> bedfordstmartins.com/
> **visualage**
>
> *To download these quesions as a worksheet, click on* **CHAPTER 2** › **WORKSHEETS**

Questions for Assessing Your Growth as a Writer

- What appears to be my greatest area of strength?
- Where am I having the greatest difficulty?
- What am I learning about the process of writing?
- What am I learning about giving and receiving feedback on writing?
- What have I learned from writing a profile that I can use in my next assignment for this course, for another course, or for work?

SAMPLE STUDENT ASSESSMENT

Here's how Stephanie Guzik answered these questions for the profile she wrote on Diane Turcotte (p. 60).

What appears to be my greatest area of strength?

I feel that my strength is (other than meeting a deadline) providing a personal look into the subject by using personal experiences, thoughts, and feelings.

Where am I having the greatest difficulty?

My greatest difficulty (other than evaluating my writing like this) is wanting to add too much information in too short a time. After I initially wrote the paper, there were several sections that I had to take out; they had information that originally seemed pertinent but when I reviewed it, didn't seem as important as I had thought.

What am I learning about the process of writing?

In writing this paper, I learned how to add personal touches to my writing. Whereas other papers I've written are devoid of emotion or personal thoughts, I was able to incorporate what I thought of Diane into this paper.

What am I learning about giving and receiving feedback on writing?

While I was writing this paper, I talked several times with people about what I should change and what I should do with what I had written. It was a little harder with this paper to accept criticism without thinking about it, simply because my own personal thoughts and feelings were involved in writing the paper. However, I learned to take the criticism and rather than completely change what I had written, I simply altered what I had already written to compensate for whatever comments had been made.

What have I learned from writing a profile that I can use in my next assignment for this course, for another course, or for work?

Writing the profile was definitely a breath of fresh air compared to other pieces of writing. However, I feel that from writing this paper, I will be able to incorporate more feeling into my other papers, although indirectly. I can use my thoughts to guide my writing rather than just providing facts about the topic.

3
Reports

THE FOCUS IN THIS CHAPTER IS ON REPORTING: CONVEYING INFOR-MATION THAT READERS WILL find accurate, credible, and reasonably comprehensive. As you will see later in the chapter, this information may take different forms—visuals (charts, graphs, pictures), for example, as well as written texts. This information may also come from different sources—perhaps from your own personal experiences and observations as well as secondary sources such as statements from recognized authorities, results of surveys or experiments, or firsthand accounts of observers who are in a good position to report accurately and fairly. In all cases, however, reports must provide factual information.

Moreover, reports must provide factual information that matters to a specific person or a particular group of people. When writing a report, it will not be helpful to think of addressing a general reader. Instead, you will need to identify a specific audience and provide members of this audience with information that addresses their unique concerns or questions and that contributes substantially to their understanding of the topic. In other words, you must provide your audience with factual information they will see as meaningful.

" 'Here we live like pigs and eat like dogs,' says Son Li, 66, who arrived four years ago and works 12-hour shifts seven days a week as a clothes hanger in a sweatshop on Lafayette Street...."

– Edward Barnes,
"Slaves of New York"

103

Providing Meaningful Information

To a very large measure, your ability to provide readers with meaningful information depends on your ability to answer questions they are likely to have. For example, your audience may ask such questions as the following.

> Why should I read this report? How does it relate to things I know or care about?

> How does this report add to (or challenge) what I already know, believe, or value?

> Can I trust what the writer of this report is saying? Is the information derived from credible sources?

> Does the writer appear to know what he or she is talking about? That is, does the writer have the experience or knowledge to speak authoritatively on this topic?

> Is there likely to be more than one perspective on this topic? If so, has the writer represented these other perspectives fairly?

> Does the report answer questions that matter to me or tell me how people are trying to solve problems I am concerned with?

Are these the right questions to ask? Are there other questions about the topic that are even more compelling and important? One of the best ways to find out is to read widely and talk with people who know something about the topic. As you do this, pay attention to facts or details that surprise or perplex or intrigue you. Ask yourself (and answer) such questions as these: Why does this fact surprise me? How is it different from or similar to what I expected? Typically, the effort to answer one question leads to still other questions and answers.

In addition to gathering information about your topic, you will need to learn about the specific audience you hope to reach. What do the members of this audience currently know? More important, what kinds of questions are they likely to have? What aspects of your topic are likely to confuse or bother them? What additional questions are likely to occur to them as they read your report?

All these questions invite one more: How, as a writer, do you go about answering so many different questions? You will find that answers can come from a wide variety of sources: your own experience and observations, your reading of print and online materials, and interviews with people who are well informed about your topic. To create a good report, you will probably need to explore all these sources, and later in this chapter you will experiment with different strategies for doing so. Ultimately, you may decide that some sources are more appropriate and more useful than others. This decision, like other writing decisions you'll make, will rest on your understanding of the context for your report.

Reports in Context

Sometimes writers do not have to think consciously about the context for their work, especially when they are trying to accomplish a clearly defined purpose for a single audience whose characteristics they know well. Often, however, writers have to be able to function effectively in a variety of contexts, addressing the concerns of a range of audiences in various circumstances. You may have noticed, for example, that different instructors sometimes look for different things in your writing. This does not indicate that the instructors are being arbitrary; rather, it indicates that different academic disciplines have different notions of what constitutes good writing and evidence. Some disciplines, for example, value only data that can be determined experimentally, analyzed statistically, and presented in tables and graphs. Other disciplines value personal observation, whether it is recorded verbally or visually; still others insist on careful analysis of what scholars have previously determined and sometimes discourage the use of visual elements. Consequently, you must adapt your report writing for different academic contexts.

The obligation to adapt your work according to the context becomes even more pronounced when writing reports at work or in other communities. In these settings, people may approach your reports with widely differing attitudes, knowledge, and purposes for reading. Some readers may value essay-like reports; others may expect to get information from an easy-to-read brochure or from a Web site with lots of links. To communicate effectively, you need to understand your audience's expectations and act accordingly. When you work on the writing assignment for this chapter, you will gain practice in understanding your audience's expectations, and more, in the Analyzing Context section.

Audience

In other courses, you may have been asked to write for a general reader or for someone who happens to be interested in a particular topic. But these scenarios are not very realistic. Is there such a thing as a general reader? Try to think of something you have read that is intended for a general reader. A newspaper? Probably not. After all, a person who reads the lifestyle section may not read the sports section, and a person who reads about basketball might not read about figure skating. Moreover, the readers of one newspaper may differ widely from readers of another.

What about the audiences for whom you write in college? Can you identify a general reader among your college instructors? Again, probably not. Admittedly, all your instructors will appreciate writing that is free from grammatical errors and written in an appropriate style, and they will also expect you to provide evidence for your claims. But what constitutes credible evidence, and what constitutes an appropriate style? For a biology instructor, evidence will probably include the results of an experiment, presented in charts or tables; the instructor may also expect you to use specialized terminology and avoid personal pronouns such as *I*, *we*, or *you*. By contrast, a literature instructor is likely to value accurate references to a literary text and may encourage the use of personal pronouns.

It is likely that you will write for people who will differ in the amount of knowledge they have about the topic; their values or attitudes; the circumstances in which they will read, listen to, or watch your report; and the purposes they hope to accomplish by doing so. As a rule, readers of reports are not simply reading to acquire information. They often hope to use that information in some way—they may be seeking reassurance, for example, or looking for a sound basis for making a decision. If you want your report to be effective, you will need to analyze the audience and anticipate the multiple purposes its members might have for reading the report.

Circumstances

As you think about your audience, also think about the circumstances in which your audience will encounter your report. When, where, and in what form will the report appear? Are there any recent events that are prompting you to write your report or that might make your audience want to read your report? Sometimes reports will be assigned by a teacher, a supervisor, or a client; they may be expecting the report to look like a conventional essay and to appear (or arrive via e-mail) by a certain time and date. In other cases, however, the audience may not even know the report is being written and may encounter it unexpectedly—as part of a Web site, for example, or as a brochure in a doctor's office, an article in a magazine, a pamphlet distributed by a business or social organization, or a brief fact sheet.

In all cases, circumstances will affect the content, appearance, and tone or voice of the report. In most cases, timing will be especially important. But timeliness is also an important concern for reports that are not written for academic or workplace assignments. For example, to interest nonscientists in an explanation of how DNA coding works, a writer might mention the role of DNA evidence in solving a murder case. Similarly, reports on anorexia or bulimia may be especially valuable to readers who have friends or family members affected by these disorders. The reports that are most likely to be read and valued either convey new information about topics that have long mattered to readers or touch on topics, issues, or problems that are currently on readers' minds.

Purposes

Up to this point in your schooling, your main purposes in writing a report may have been simple and straightforward. Perhaps you wrote a report to find out as much as possible about a topic that interested you. Or you may have tried to show your instructor that you understood a particular concept or procedure, such as the conventions people must follow in writing an academic essay. These are perfectly reasonable purposes. But as you begin to write reports for communities beyond school, including work, you will discover that these purposes are only part of the larger picture of report writing.

Along with the basic goal of informing readers, reports usually have specific purposes, such as the following.

> ❯ To make readers aware that a serious problem exists
> ❯ To inform readers of a solution to a problem about which they are concerned
> ❯ To provide readers with facts they can use in making a decision
> ❯ To challenge readers' preconceptions
> ❯ To make readers aware of a situation or trend that is likely to affect them personally
> ❯ To reassure readers who are concerned about a particular topic
> ❯ To make a favorable impression on readers

In accomplishing these purposes, you also have to remember that your primary obligation in a report is to provide a credible and reliable account of a topic that matters to both you and your readers.

Visual Information in Context

As you will see from the examples in the Reading to Write section of this chapter, a good report may make extensive use of visual information—not just images (photographs or drawings), graphs, and tables, but also columns, quotations pulled out of the main body of the text (pull quotes), different sizes and colors of type, special text set off in boxes, and so on. Visuals can be an important part of a report, but they are not an end in themselves. Consequently, you should never use a visual element just so you can say you used one. Instead, choose visuals that make sense in relation to your topic and the context in which your report will be read.

 For Collaboration

The bulleted list of specific purposes for reports above is by no means complete. Try adding to it. Read (or listen to or watch on TV) several different reports. Ask yourself whether the authors of these reports are trying to accomplish one or more of the purposes mentioned in this list. What other purposes might they be trying to accomplish? Then, working with one or two classmates, list the purposes for the reports you found.

When writers of reports use visual information well, it will help readers find answers to their questions, contribute to the credibility of the report, and convey a coherent attitude toward the topic. Of course, visuals may also be unclear, inappropriate, or irrelevant, so you should take care to evaluate the visual information found in a report.

To anticipate your readers' needs in terms of the visual information you include in a report, consider four basic, context-related questions.

> What should the overall look of the page or screen be? (For example, how many columns should it have? Should it include pictures?)

> Is this overall look consistent with what the intended readers expect?

> Do all the visual elements on the page or screen help the intended readers find answers to the questions that matter to them?

> What does the visual information reveal about my understanding of readers and the topic?

You can answer these questions for your own projects by reading a variety of reports and thinking about their page layout; images; and charts, graphs, maps, and tables.

> For more information on the effective uses of these visual elements, see **Chapter 8.**

Questions to Ask When Reading Visual Information in Reports

● **Does the layout (arrangement) of the page or screen make it easy for the intended readers to find the information they want or need?**

> What kind of information dominates—visual or verbal?

> Are there headings? If so, do they give a clear idea of the information that will appear in the text that follows each heading?

> Are there charts, sidebars (inset boxes of text), or pull quotes (highlighted quotations from the text)? If so, do they serve a real purpose, such as emphasizing key information or answering questions that readers may have?

> Are there variations in the size and style of type? If there are variations, what functions do they serve? Does type appear in color?

> How many columns are there? What sorts of publications are likely to use this number of columns? Does the width of each column make the text easy to read?

● **If there are images (photographs, diagrams, or other drawings), what questions do they answer? What attitudes do they convey? How likely is it that readers will recognize and appreciate these attitudes?**

> What kinds of details are included in the image? Are any significant details missing? Does the picture contain extraneous information?

> What viewing angle is represented? When the person or object is shown as if the viewer is looking up at it from below, this viewing angle usually makes the subject seem important, powerful, or threatening. If the perspective is that of looking downward, the angle tends to make the subject seem weak or unimportant. If the image lets viewers look head-on, the position is usually one of equality.

> What colors are used? Is there anything surprising or distinctive about them? Warm colors such as red and orange tend to evoke strong emotional reactions and a sense of danger or urgency, whereas cool colors such as blue have a more calming effect. Also, dark colors suggest something sinister or gloomy, and pastels suggest innocence, childhood, or safety.

> What kinds of lines and shapes are apparent? Diagonal lines can suggest movement or threat; jagged lines often create tension or anxiety. Tilting, top-heavy, or pinched shapes can also evoke negative emotional reactions. Other lines and forms can suggest balance and stability.

> Is the image clearly explained through the use of a title, caption, or accompanying description?

> Can the reader find a clear relationship between the image and the text?

If there are charts, graphs, maps, or tables, how informative and relevant are they?

> Can the reader easily see the point of a given chart, graph, map, or table?

> Can the reader easily find the most important information?

> Does the chart, graph, map, or table contain any distracting colors or unnecessary special effects?

> Is the chart, graph, map, or table clearly labeled and, if necessary, explained with a title, legend, or key?

> Are the units of measurement clear and consistent? If symbols are used, is their meaning clear?

> Is the chart, graph, map, or table clearly related to the text?

> Does the chart, graph, map, or table help readers compare and contrast different data?

 Exercise

Bring to class a report that presents information in a visual and interesting way. It might contain images—photographs and drawings—or graphs, diagrams, maps, or tables. Or it might make special use of text, by setting it off with columns, or color, as pull quotes, or boxed in sidebars, for example. Consider the effects these visual elements create by answering the questions listed above. Then try to determine how these effects are created. Be prepared to explain how the visual elements create a particular effect and how they add to the impressions conveyed through the report's written text.

FIGURE 3.1
Visual Elements in "Weapons of Mass Disruption," a Report in a Magazine

● **Map** Shaded areas on map answer reader's question: How large an area would be affected?

● **Map** Connotations of reddish elliptical circles contrast with connotations of green in rectangle.

● **Map** Uses colors that create emotional associations: different shades of red suggest differing amounts of danger.

● **Caption** Caption explains meaning of visual elements; forms part of a visual unit.

● **Layout** Heading forecasts content.

● **Layout** Size, color, and style of type make heading stand out.

● **Layout** Column width makes type easy to read; minimal white space suggests serious, in-depth coverage of the topic.

● **Image** Reddish-orange clothing signals danger; black masks make workers seem less human, more intimidating.

● **Image** Viewing angle makes workers look large, imposing.

● **Image** Diagonal lines in posture and leg movement suggest urgency.

● **Layout** Source credits are small and isolated, making content of visuals more important than who created them.

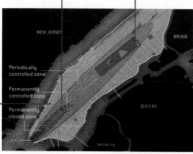

NOXIOUS PLUME of hot fallout spreads over New York City's Manhattan Island after the simulated detonation of a radioactive cesium-based dirty bomb (assuming a wind from the southwest). The highlighted zones would be expected to have radiation levels comparable to those that caused the closing of contaminated regions around the damaged Chernobyl nuclear power plant.

ticles. From past incidents, we know that if the material is an alpha emitter, such as plutonium or americium, it could become lodged in victims' lungs for years and lead to long-term radiation exposure. But if evacuees are decontaminated quickly, thoroughly washing their skin and disposing of contaminated clothing, the total exposure will be minimal.

Dust from a radiological weapon would remain trapped for extended periods in cracks and crevices on the surfaces of buildings, sidewalks and streets, and some would have been swept into the interiors of buildings. Certain materials that could be used in a radiological attack, such as cesium 137, chemically bind to glass, concrete and asphalt. More than 15 years after the 1986 Chernobyl disaster, in which a Soviet nuclear power plant underwent a meltdown, cesium is still affixed to the sidewalks of many Scandinavian cities that were downwind of the disaster. Fortunately, the radiation exposure from underfoot is fairly low, increasing the cancer death risk by less than one in 10,000.

If the material contains alpha emitters, the long-term health risk comes from breathing radioactive dust suspended in the air by wind, the action of tires or pedestrian traffic. In Kiev, more than 100 kilometers from Chernobyl, dust in the streets still contains low levels of plutonium. Should the material remaining in the area contain cesium 137 or other gamma emitters, anyone entering a contaminated area would be exposed to low-level radiation because, unlike alpha rays, gamma rays penetrate clothing and skin.

Consider the dispersal of 3,500 curies of cesium 137 by an explosion at the lower tip of Manhattan Island. Sources capable of delivering this much radiation have been "orphaned" in the former Soviet Union; the U.S. recently committed $25 million, in partnership with Russia, to track these materials down. Such a source, if acquired by terrorists, would be difficult to handle, requiring some shielding to prevent a builder from receiving an incapacitating radiation dose. But the cesium would already be in powder form, making dispersion relatively easy.

80 SCIENTIFIC AMERICAN

If this source were prepared and then exploded, about 800 square kilometers would be contaminated above the strict EPA decontamination guidelines. The disaster would not be of Chernobyl's magnitude; it would release less radiation overall, and none in the form of potent short-lived isotopes such as iodine 131. But its strategic placement would wreak havoc. Over an area of about 20 city blocks, there would be a one-in-10 increased risk of death from cancer for residents living in the area (without decontamination) for 30 years, a 50 percent increase over the background rate. A broader area of 15 square kilometers—varying from four to 20 square kilometers, depending on the weather—would be contaminated above the relocation threshold recommended by the International Commission on Radiological Protection and accepted by the NRC. If these standards were relaxed and the relocation threshold were the same as that used around Chernobyl, the area affected would still be roughly 100 city blocks. The property value of this area is estimated in the hundreds of billions of dollars.

Decontamination Procedures

REMOVAL OF URBAN RADIOACTIVE contamination has never been performed on a large scale because no one has ever had to deal with the consequences of a radiological attack. Our current knowledge of how to cleanse an urban area is based on experience from smaller-scale industrial operations and from cold war–era studies on the aftermath of nuclear war.

The cleanup effort would initially involve removing loose contamination—radioactive dust particles settled on surfaces or lodged in interstices. Relatively low cost mechanical techniques such as vacuuming or pressure washing should be effective. More invasive, higher-cost surface-removal techniques, such as sandblasting, would be necessary where hot dust has penetrated deep into more porous materials. In some cases, sidewalks and asphalt may have to be removed. The top layer

COSTLY CLEANUP EFFORTS will follow any use of a dirty bomb. Hazmat-suited workers will have to scrub fallout from surfaces with water jets, vacuums and sandblasters, as well as remove contaminated plants and soil.

NOVEMBER 2002

SARA CHEN [top]; YUN JAI-HYOUNG AP Photo [bottom]

Sample Analysis   Weapons of Mass Disruption

Later in this chapter, the report "Weapons of Mass Disruption" goes into some detail about dirty bombs. The following brief analysis of one page of this article, shown as it originally appeared in *Scientific American*, will help you see several ways the questions for reading visual information can be applied to a specific report.

Visual information is used effectively throughout "Weapons of Mass Disruption," but one page is especially rich in such information (see Figure 3.1). The page begins in the middle of an explanation of how a radioactive dust cloud might spread over a metropolitan area—in this case, New York City.

The layout here is especially effective. The one heading on the page (Decontamination Procedures) clearly indicates what the following paragraphs will discuss, and it is reinforced by the opening words immediately below: "Removal of urban radioactive contamination. . . ." Further, the heading is easy to notice because the type in which it is printed differs in size and style from the type that precedes and follows it. The text is printed in two columns of moderate width, each occupying half the page. Readers will have encountered this basic layout many times before and will find it relatively easy to read. *Scientific American*'s two-column layout allows for a significant amount of text on a page, giving a serious impression, while using images and a format that readers would find in a typical newsmagazine.

In at least two respects, the visuals are very informative. First, they answer questions raised by the text they accompany. The text in the left-hand column explains the different kinds of fallout produced by a dirty bomb. How big an area might the bomb affect? This question is answered in the unusual map with the caption beginning "noxious plume." The map shows how fallout might be dispersed over the heart of New York City, a likely target for terrorist attack. The text in the right-hand column describes a cleanup procedure that would be different from anything most people have ever seen. What would that cleanup look like? The image with the caption beginning "costly cleanup efforts" shows a group of workers wearing hazmat (hazardous material) suits.

This informative quality is enhanced by the use of captions and—in the case of the map—labels. For example, the text accompanying the map explains the different colored areas on the map and suggests the severity of the damage by comparing it with damage experienced in the aftermath of the 1986 Chernobyl nuclear plant disaster. Further, the map has self-explanatory labels identifying the surrounding areas (Brooklyn, New Jersey) and differences in the ways various areas of the city would be affected (the "permanently closed zone," for example).

In addition to conveying information, each visual implies an attitude toward its related subject matter. If you have always thought of maps as objective representations, this one may be somewhat of a surprise. Consider that for many people New York City is an intimidating, threatening place. But in the map, the viewing angle, or perspective, allows readers to look down on the city rather than up at its intimidating skyscrapers. This perspective excludes overwhelming details—crowds, traffic, and skyscrapers literally disappear from view.

What readers see instead is a profound threat to the city, a threat heightened by the use of color. The area of greatest danger (the "blast site") is appropriately labeled in red, a color often used to suggest danger. As the radioactive cloud moves away from the blast site, the colors are still tinged with red, but they become lighter, indicating that the danger diminishes as distance from the blast increases. Yet even the lightest of these colors contrasts effectively with Central Park, the rectangular area depicted in green. Often associated with springtime, renewal, and life, this color contrasts with the danger and death represented by the reddish cloud of radioactive dust. The city is thus made to seem threatened rather than threatening, vulnerable rather than intimidating.

In contrast, the image of cleanup workers makes ordinary human beings seem more intimidating. The viewing angle here has the reader looking slightly upward, making the workers seem imposing. This quality is enhanced by the details that are excluded from the picture. None of the workers' human qualities are apparent. Their faces, for example, are covered by flat, dark masks.

The urgency of the workers' situation is suggested through the slight diagonal lines apparent in their posture and stride and in the color of their hazmat suits. The workers are not standing still; they are depicted in mid-stride, their bodies bent slightly forward as is often the case when people are in a hurry. The workers' suits are a bright orangey red, a color that highway construction workers and hunters often wear to protect themselves from danger. In this context, the color is especially appropriate since the workers themselves may be in great danger. The effect of this color is enhanced because it stands out vividly against the white background that occupies almost two-thirds of the image.

Exercise › **bedfordstmartins.com/visualage**
Click on **CHAPTER 3** › **VISUALS**

For practice analyzing the visual information in another sample report, see the visual exercises on the companion Web site for this book.

Reading to Write

› **bedfordstmartins.com/ visualage**

For additional examples of reports, click on
CHAPTER 3 › **EXAMPLES**

In your principal assignment for this chapter, you will write a report on a topic of your choice or one selected by your instructor that identifies issues that matter to your intended audience. You will draw on various sources (readings, personal experiences, interviews) to answer those questions in ways your audience will find credible and informative.

The following reports will help you see not only some of the strategies you might use, but also the different kinds of topics about which you might write. Each reading is followed by questions (Reflecting on What You Have Read) that will help you think about what is involved in making a credible, informative report; also, a Thinking Ahead prompt will suggest ways to decide on a topic for your own report. The subsequent sections of the chapter focus on starting your assignment, composing a draft, and assessing and revising that draft.

One reason people read reports is to gain new insight into a topic about which they already have some information. Writing in *Newsweek*, the authors of the following report assume that most of their readers know that college students drink, sometimes to excess. But the authors also assume that their readers may be unaware of developments in this area: (1) a Harvard study showing that binge drinking is on the increase among college students, and (2) a variety of efforts colleges are taking to reduce alcohol consumption on campus.

Before you start reading, glance briefly at the report—a reproduction of the original page in *Newsweek*—and consider these questions: What initial impressions does the general layout of the page create? How credible do you expect the report to be? Consider as you read how your initial expectations are challenged or justified.

EDUCATION

Bellying Up to the Bar

A new Harvard study finds that binge drinking is still a big problem on many college campuses

ANDREW LICHTENSTEIN

Wild ones: *Keg parties still rule on many campuses*

BY CLAUDIA KALB AND
JOHN McCORMICK

FOUR YEARS AGO A HARVARD RE-
search team issued a shocking report
about alcohol abuse among college
students. Last week Harvard was
back with a new assessment—and the news
wasn't good. Despite years of national publicity about the problem, the percentage of
students who binge-drink—consuming five
or more drinks in a sitting for men, and four
or more for women—has declined only
from 44 to 43 percent. Other details were
even more damning: half of all bingers do
so regularly—at least three times within a
two-week period. And one-third *more* students now admit they drink just to get
drunk. "Maybe I'm expecting change too
fast," says Henry Wechsler, the study's
lead author and an expert on alcohol abuse
at the Harvard School of Public Health,
"but I am disappointed."

Are colleges doing enough to crack down
on risky drinking? The stakes are high:
cases like the notorious alcohol poisonings
at LSU and MIT last year kill an estimated
50 students annually. Although some
schools present comprehensive programs
to educate students about the dangers of
drinking, many campuses offer only perfunctory efforts. College presidents are
caught between the desire to act boldly and
the fear that heavy-handed actions will

scare off prospective students. David Anderson, a George Mason University researcher who tracks college alcohol policies, says that in 1997, the average school
spent just $13,300 to discourage substance
abuse. Typical efforts: freshman-orienta-
tion workshops and alcohol-awareness
pamphlets. Many college presidents dele-
gate their alcohol programs to administrators already overburdened with other
tasks. Says Anderson: "It's no wonder
we're not making much progress."

The picture's not entirely bleak. William
DeJong, head of the Higher Education Center for Alcohol and Other Drug Prevention
in Newton, Mass., says that after years of
relying on educational efforts, administrators are now turning to more innovative
strategies. Many schools, such as the Uni-

versity of North Carolina at Chapel Hill, offer substance-free dorm rooms. Colleges
are also teaming with neighborhood bars to
ban happy-hour advertising on campus and
to enforce drinking laws. Some schools are
offering nonalcoholic "mocktail" parties.
Others, like Clark University in Worcester,
Mass., have turned campus pubs into coffeehouses. The trend shows some promise:
the number of students who don't drink has
grown from 16 to 19 percent. "I'm not ready
to proclaim victory," says DeJong, but efforts are "definitely improving."

Dangerous drinking is at its worst in fraternities and sororities, where four out of
five members acknowledge that they binge.
But it's possible the situation will improve
there, too. Wechsler collected his most recent data early in 1997. But that was before
the highly publicized deaths last fall of
pledges Benjamin Wynne at LSU and Scott
Krueger at MIT. Several national fraternities have announced plans to ban alcohol in
chapter houses.

Some experts argue that demonizing millions of binge drinkers makes it appear as if
high-risk drinking is the norm. Michael
Haines, a campus-health official at Northern Illinois University, says a more effective
approach is to use advertising to hammer
home the positive side of Wechsler's numbers: the fact that many students do drink
responsibly. That message lets NIU's
22,000 students view heavy
drinking not as the norm, but as
aberrant. In 1989, 45 percent of
the school's students said they
binged—but on average they
guessed that 70 percent of
their peers did. Nine years later
Haines can point to some successes. Students now estimate more reasonably that
33 percent of them binge—and
the share who actually do has
plummeted to 25 percent. Inspired by Haines's campaign,
dozens of schools are now exploring this so-called social-norms approach. "We want to tell students what
they're doing right," he says, "and grow
more of that behavior."

Public pressure can change students'
drinking habits. Lloyd Johnston, a University of Michigan researcher who has surveyed college drinkers nationwide since
1980, says the percentage who binged
dropped through the '80s and into the mid-
'90s, largely because of widespread publicity about the dangers of drunken driving
and other alcohol-abuse problems. About
two years ago, however, the numbers started climbing back up slightly. The only good
news, Johnston says, is that dangerous
drinking begins to subside after the age of
22. Provided, of course, that young people
make it that far.   ■

When the Party's Over...

The more college students drink, the more they're at
risk. Some alcohol-related problems that were reported after bingeing:

	NON-BINGERS	OCCASIONAL BINGERS	FREQUENT BINGERS
Drove after drinking	20%	43%	59%
Memory lapses	10	29	56
Got behind in schoolwork	9	25	48
Unplanned sexual activity	10	24	45

SOURCE: THE HARVARD SCHOOL OF PUBLIC HEALTH COLLEGE ALCOHOL STUDY

Reflecting on What You Have Read

1 What questions does this report answer? Does it neglect to answer any questions that you think are important? If so, what would those questions be, and why do you think they are important?

2 What is your reaction to the two people in the photograph at the beginning of the article? How is your reaction influenced by the details included in (and excluded from) this photograph? How is your reaction influenced by the viewing angle, colors, and caption? What reasons might *Newsweek* have had for including this picture?

3 Notice the table (When the Party's Over . . .). What questions does it answer? What difference would it make if the author omitted the table and summarized its information in a paragraph or two?

4 What overall impression does this article create for readers? Are they likely to come away reassured ("the picture's not entirely bleak") or even more concerned ("binge drinking is still a big problem") than they were before reading the article? Identify specific passages in the text that justify your answers.

5 Compare this report with another binge drinking report that appears on the companion Web site for this book. Consider the visual and written content of both reports. What do the visuals and written text tell you about the audience and purpose for which each report was written?

Thinking Ahead

The report on binge drinking discusses a social trend that is likely to matter to a great many readers. As you think of topics for your own report, consider reporting on such a trend. You might follow up on the topic of binge drinking: Have college students' drinking patterns changed since the *Newsweek* article appeared several years ago? Have schools developed new ways of responding to this trend? Or you might consider investigating other trends—voting patterns of young people, for example, or incidents of road rage on highways in the United States—that are likely to be of particular interest to a specific group of readers.

From the standpoint of health, one of the major legal events of the late twentieth century was the legal settlement known as the Master Settlement Agreement that forced cigarette makers to restrict their advertising in general and to stop using ads aimed at the youth market (young people between the ages of twelve and seventeen). Two years after this decision became final, two researchers asked a logical question: Have the tobacco companies changed their advertising practices, or are they still trying to appeal to the youth market? To answer this question, researchers working for the Massachusetts Department of Public Health, Diane Turner-Bowker and William L. Hamilton, examined advertising in what they referred to as "youth magazines." The following report of their research appeared on the Web site *Campaign for Tobacco Free Kids*. As you read, consider this question: Do you think that the magazines studied can be appropriately called youth magazines?

Address | | ▼ | → Go

CIGARETTE ADVERTISING EXPENDITURES BEFORE AND AFTER THE MASTER SETTLEMENT AGREEMENT: PRELIMINARY FINDINGS

Diane Turner-Bowker and William L. Hamilton

The Master Settlement Agreement (MSA) between the States' Attorneys General and the tobacco industry requires the elimination of certain types of outdoor tobacco advertisements, including those found on billboards, in arenas, stadiums, shopping malls, video arcades and advertisements on private or public transit vehicles and transportation waiting areas. The MSA also forbids tobacco manufacturers from "directly or indirectly targeting youth in their promotional activities, or engaging in activities with the primary purpose of initiating, maintaining, or increasing youth smoking."[1]   1

In advertisements taken out by Philip Morris in March of 2000, the company stated: "Perhaps the most visible change is the removal of tobacco advertising from billboards in the United States. The goal of this provision is to limit the exposure of kids to tobacco advertising, a step defined by the public health community as a way to help reduce the incidence of youth smoking."[2]   2

This analysis examines cigarette advertising expenditures in January to September 1998—the three calendar quarters preceding the MSA—and January to September 1999. The purpose is to see how cigarette advertising to youth changed after the MSA was implemented.   3

Increased Magazine Advertising to Youth

Cigarette marketing to teens through magazine advertising increased after the Master Settlement Agreement took effect in November 1998. This conclusion is based on analysis of advertising   4

 Internet

Address [   ] ▼ | ➡ Go

expenditures in 29 magazines for which youth readers (aged 12–17) make up at least 5 percent of the magazine's total readership.[3] The analysis focuses on magazines with more than 15 percent youth readership, the level used by the Food and Drug Administration in establishing advertising restrictions.[4]

Cigarette Advertising in Magazines with More Than 15% of Readers Aged 12–17

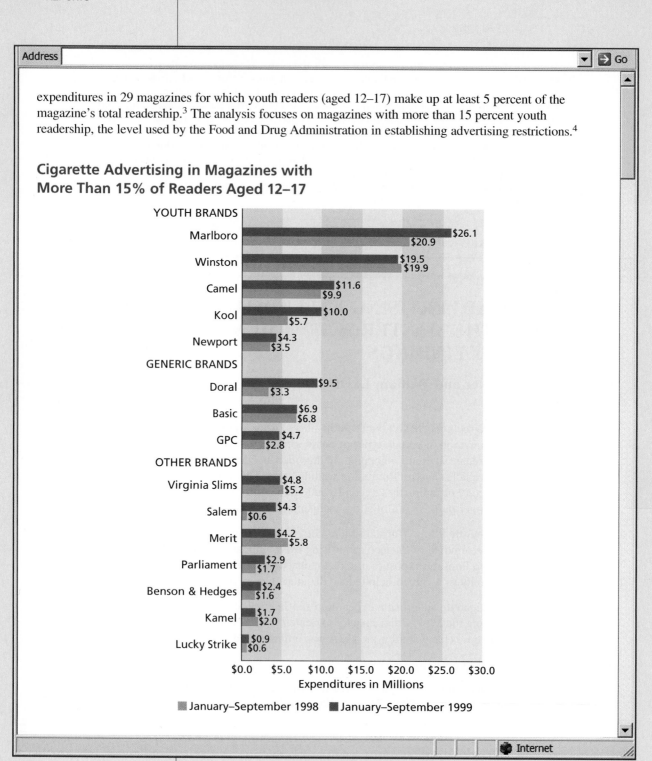

YOUTH BRANDS

Marlboro	$26.1 / $20.9
Winston	$19.5 / $19.9
Camel	$11.6 / $9.9
Kool	$10.0 / $5.7
Newport	$4.3 / $3.5

GENERIC BRANDS

Doral	$9.5 / $3.3
Basic	$6.9 / $6.8
GPC	$4.7 / $2.8

OTHER BRANDS

Virginia Slims	$4.8 / $5.2
Salem	$4.3 / $0.6
Merit	$4.2 / $5.8
Parliament	$2.9 / $1.7
Benson & Hedges	$2.4 / $1.6
Kamel	$1.7 / $2.0
Lucky Strike	$0.9 / $0.6

Expenditures in Millions
$0.0 $5.0 $10.0 $15.0 $20.0 $25.0 $30.0

■ January–September 1998 ■ January–September 1999

Internet

Address [   ] ⬇ ➡ Go

Cigarette advertising expenditures in magazines with more than 15 percent youth reader-ship increased $30 million after the MSA.

Nineteen of the 29 magazines had more than 15 percent youth readers.[5] Cigarette companies spent $119.9 million on advertising in these magazines in the first nine months of 1999. This amounts to more than a third of their total magazine advertising expenditures for the period ($314.0 million). Cigarette advertising in these 19 magazines after the settlement was almost $30 million higher than it was in the corresponding period in 1998 ($90.2 million).   5

Advertising expenditures in magazines with 5–15 percent youth readership increased $24.4 million from the pre-MSA to the post-MSA period.

In the first nine months of 1999, the ten magazines with 5–15 percent youth readership had $72.9 million in cigarette advertising. This is an increase of $24.4 million over the level for the corresponding period in 1998.   6

Magazine Advertising Increases by Brand

Much of the increased advertising in youth magazines came from the brands that have been recognized as the brands most preferred by youth. But several other brands also stepped up advertising strongly in magazines with more than 15 percent youth readership.   7

Marlboro spent $26.1 million in the first nine months of 1999 on advertising in magazines with more than 15 percent youth readers. That is the most of any single brand, and a $5.2 million increase over 1998.

During the first nine months of 1999, the five cigarette brands recognized in previous research as the leading youth brands[6] spent a combined $71.1 million on advertising in magazines with youth readership of more than 15 percent. Marlboro, Winston, and Kool are the three top spenders. Kool increased advertising by $4.3 million, or 75.8 percent, relative to the pre-MSA period.   8

Generic brands Doral and GPC dramatically increased their advertising in the 19 youth magazines. Doral nearly tripled its expenditures, from $3.3 to $9.5 million.

Basic, the third major generic brand, spent much more than Doral and GPC in 1998 in magazines with more than 15 percent youth readership. Doral far surpassed Basic in the first nine months of 1999, however, and GPC substantially narrowed the gap with Basic. The three brands combined increased their spending in these magazines by 64.5 percent from 1998 to 1999.   9

Salem, Parliament, and Benson & Hedges all had major increases in advertising in youth magazines after the MSA. Salem jumped from $0.6 million in the first nine months of 1998 to $4.3 million in the corresponding period of 1999.

Among the brands examined, only four spent less on advertising in magazines with heavy youth readership after the MSA. Only one of the four, Winston, has traditionally had a major share of the youth market, and Winston advertising declined by less than 2 percent.   10

Internet

Address [   ] ▼ Go

Grouping these brands by manufacturer shows that all four companies increased their advertising in youth magazines, but to different extents. [11]

Brown and Williamson increased its advertising in magazines with more than 15 percent youth readership by 72.1 percent, from $9.0 to $15.5 million.

RJR had the biggest increase in absolute dollars, at $11.0 million (30.9 percent). Philip Morris expenditures increased by $5.5 million. Lorillard, with just one brand in the group examined (Newport), increased its spending by $0.8 million, or 23.0 percent. [12]

---

1. Kline R, Davidson P. Advertising restrictions. In Kelder G, Davidson, editors. *The Multistate Master Settlement Agreement and the future of state and local tobacco control: An analysis of selected topics and provisions of the Multistate Master Settlement Agreement of November 23, 1998.* Boston, MA: Tobacco Control Resource Center, Inc. at Northeastern University School of Law, 1999. Available from: http://www.tobacco.neu.edu/msa/index.

2. *Boston Globe.* March 1, 2000, p. A6.

3. Data on magazine readership come from: 1998 Simmons Teen-Age Research (STARS) Weighted by Population. New York: SMRB, Inc., 1998; and 1998 Simmons Spring SMM Weighted by Population. New York: SMRB, Inc., 1998. Data on quarterly media expenditures by cigarette brand come from Competitive Media Reporting (CMR). New York: Competitive Media Reporting, 1999.

4. 21 CFR Part 801, et al. Regulations Restricting the Sale and Distribution of Cigarettes and Smokeless Tobacco Products to Protect Children and Adolescents; Proposed Rule. *Federal Register.* August 11, 1995. The regulation limited advertising to black text on a white background for any magazine or other publication except those "(1) whose readers aged 18 years or older constitute 85 percent or more of the total readership, and (2) that is read by fewer than 2 million persons under age 18" (Section 897.32).

5. This analysis includes only magazines for which the percent of youth readership is available from STARS 1998. Other magazines not examined in STARS 1998 may have more than 5 percent youth readership. Thus the total cigarette advertising in magazines with more than 5 percent or more than 15 percent youth readership is probably greater than the totals shown here. The magazines included and the percent of readers that are age 12–17 are as follows:

Magazine	Percent	Magazine	Percent
Vibe	42.23	Sports Illustrated	22.55
Sport	32.95	Outdoor Life	20.33
Spin	32.03	Glamour	19.81
Hot Rod	31.14	Vogue	18.88
Popular Science	30.10	Popular Mechanics	17.52
Sporting News	30.01	Essence	17.49
Rolling Stone	28.17	Soap Opera Digest	16.65
Motor Trend	25.21	TV Guide	16.05
Mademoiselle	23.66	Self	15.98
Elle	23.40	Field & Stream	14.60

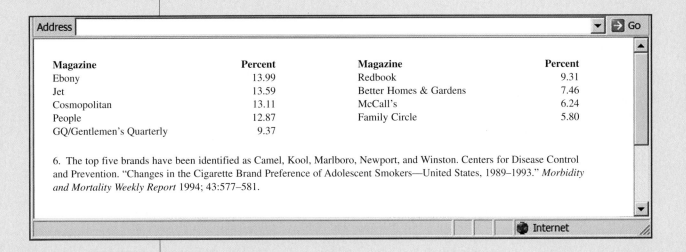

Address | ▼ | ➡ Go

Magazine	Percent	Magazine	Percent
Ebony	13.99	Redbook	9.31
Jet	13.59	Better Homes & Gardens	7.46
Cosmopolitan	13.11	McCall's	6.24
People	12.87	Family Circle	5.80
GQ/Gentlemen's Quarterly	9.37		

6. The top five brands have been identified as Camel, Kool, Marlboro, Newport, and Winston. Centers for Disease Control and Prevention. "Changes in the Cigarette Brand Preference of Adolescent Smokers—United States, 1989–1993." *Morbidity and Mortality Weekly Report* 1994; 43:577–581.

🐾 Internet

Reflecting on What You Have Read

1 The report begins with a summary of the legal agreement the tobacco companies accepted, followed by a quote from a Philip Morris advertisement. What effect is achieved by starting the report with the summary and the quote?

2 This report contains a number of statements in boldface type. What purposes might the authors have been trying to accomplish through the use of this type?

3 On what basis did the researchers select the magazines they studied? Does this basis seem fair? Why or why not?

4 The chart on p. 116 labels some brands of cigarettes as Youth Brands. What basis do the authors have for using this label? What impression do the bars under Youth Brands create? Does this impression seem justified? Why or why not?

Thinking Ahead

It is common practice for institutions to pass laws or make rules and policies that are intended to help people or make their lives better. This is true for government (national, state, and local levels) as well as for organizations (businesses, schools, religious groups, sports, and social clubs). Can you think of any such rules that have been passed by an institution you know well? For example, has your school made any changes in requirements for graduation? Have you worked at a job where you saw major policy changes implemented? If so, can you think of an audience that might benefit from a report on how (or whether) such changes are being implemented? Is there an audience that might need to know how different groups are being affected by the new rule, policy, or law?

Many people have become increasingly concerned about sweatshops: factories where employees work long hours for little pay, often in conditions that are unsafe or unsanitary. Americans often assume that sweat-shops are located solely in foreign countries, where wages are low and living conditions for most people are mis-erable. Edward Barnes's report, pub-lished in *Time*, chal-lenges this assump-tion, showing that sweatshops—many employing illegal immigrants—exist here in the United States. As you read this piece, underline passages where the information he pro-vides confirms, adds to, or challenges what you already know about sweat-shops. Also, pay care-ful attention to the photographs and the way people and their surroundings are depicted.

Slaves of New York

EDWARD BARNES

How crime and mismanaged laws have made the city the biggest magnet for Chinese illegals

Autumn in New York may be inviting to most visitors to the city, but the approach of winter is ominous for the tran-sients inhabiting a fourth-floor walk-up on the Bowery. In the heat of summer, a few at least are able to sleep on the fire escapes and the roof of the building—avoiding for a moment the circle of hell they have been assigned. The cramped and airless space

1 within is subdivided into 32 cubi-cles doled out to at least 100 men. The stink of sweat, unwashed clothing, old shoes and garbage suffuses the narrow makeshift corridors. Cooking noises mingle with the gurgle of kitchen-side urinals. On tiny TV sets, a few men watch home videos of kin and country long left behind, for some as much as a decade ago. Others stare at the

Living in airless, unhygienic cubicles in Manhattan, the Fujianese are isolated by language and fear, their nights lonely and their days occupied by ill-paid labor.

distant passion of porn tapes smuggled in from the old homeland. Each night the sounds of aching and loneliness drift down to the streets of Chinatown.

The Bowery warren is just one of scores set up to house illegal immigrants from China, men and women smuggled in to work in the teeming sweatshops and restaurants of New York City's many Chinatowns. "Here we live like pigs and eat like dogs," says Son Li, 66, who arrived four years ago and works 12-hour shifts seven days a week as a clothes hanger in a sweatshop on Lafayette Street, a few blocks away from the Bowery barracks. He says he makes about $1 an hour, when his employer pays. He has paid dearly for the privilege of working in America.

Most of the illegals have forked over as much as $48,000 each to gangsters in order to get to America. They are part

of a wave from China's coastal Fujian province; no one knows what their real numbers are. Every now and then a boat stuffed with human cargo will wash up on a beachfront community. But many other landings go undetected. Police estimate there are 300 gang-run safe houses where illegals live as they prepare to enter the workplace. New York City's Fujian association estimates there are 500,000 illegals from the province in the U.S.; the CIA puts the undocumented influx at 100,000 a year. (In comparison, the 1990 U.S. Census estimates there are 2.3 million American residents of Chinese origin.) What is certain is that for reasons both global and local, the illegals, their transporters and their employers are forgoing the boomtowns of the West Coast and homing in on New York City.

There are two reasons that New York has turned into a magnet for Chinese illegals: first, the collapse of labor-law enforcement in the city; and second, a frantic attempt by the area's garment industry to remain competitive with Third World rivals. The garment industry has always been the heart of Chinatown's economy. More than 400 garment sweatshops, often situated in hidden lofts and garrets, turn out clothes for most of the nation's major retailers. Wing Lam, head of the Chinese Staff and Workers Association, admits that Chinatown has always been a haven for illegals and sweatshops, but he says things have taken a very bad turn. "The West Coast has better wages, and the living conditions are better," he says. "But the labor laws there are enforced more strictly. The immigrants come to New York because it is lawless. The 1986 immigration act made employers responsible for hiring undocumented aliens, ceding the New York garment industry to the criminals who take advantage of illegals too afraid or unable to complain." Today, he says, it

Injured at his restaurant job and unable to work, this immigrant watches over his granddaughter at the overcrowded Bowery garret while her parents work in Chinatown.

It is not enough to survive on, but we have no choice. All New York has left is turnaround time." As a result, says Lam, "Garment shops will no longer hire documented workers because employers find they can pay undocumented workers less and not fear complaints. Besides, they know these people have to work."

New York's sweatshops 6 are often small, nonunion operations with fewer than 20 sewing machines and manned almost exclusively with illegal aliens in Chinese enclaves like Sunset Park in Brooklyn or Flushing, Queens. According to Lam, a recent Department of Labor study found that 90% of the garment shops in Chinatown were in reality sweatshops. Most of the shops in New York, about 70%, according to Lee, are owned by ethnic Chinese; and 40% of their products go to two major buyers: Wal-Mart and K Mart. Virtually all pay by piece rate, and only a handful of workers are able to produce enough to approach the minimum wage of $5.15 an hour. For most, "the pay has dropped to $2 an hour or less. Work laws are no longer enforced, and crippling injuries have soared," says Peter Kwong, a professor who studies Chinatown.

In fact, these workers are lucky to get 7 wages at all. Says Kwong: "Employers know that the workers can't complain, so they withhold wages, claiming manufacturers were slow to pay. It has become standard practice to withhold six weeks' pay or more." The vast numbers of new arrivals have depressed wages throughout Chinatown 30% in the past five years. Dishwashing jobs, for

is common for sweatshops to withhold eight weeks' pay from workers who have no government agency to turn to for help. Says Lam: "Those few who do complain find that an agreement of understanding between the Labor Department and the Immigration and Naturalization Service means that anyone who complains about wages or working conditions will be deported. It has created a plantation system where bosses can do virtually anything to workers without fear of penalty."

Manufacturers contend they must 5 find ways of going around the law in order to meet the demands of retailers who place the orders. Says Kenny Lee, head of an apparel association: "Five years ago, manufacturers would pay $4 to have a shirt that sold for $24 manufactured. Today they offer half, and if you don't take it, someone else will. There are no more big orders of thousands of garments. Those now go overseas. Instead, we get 'rescue orders,' clothes that must be in the stores in a few days, often no more than 200 pieces.

instance, which once paid $800 a month, now pay $500.

Most of the illegals are from rural districts where jobs are limited, and the temptations of China's already crowded cities—and America's streets of gold—are impossible to resist. They aren't prepared for the harshness of the life they find in New York City, according to Yung Fong Chan, a clergyman whose church serves the Fujianese immigrants. "Mental illness and suicide have both become serious problems," he says. "People, isolated from their families and forced to endure hardship they never imagined, just snap." Then there is the constant pressure from the gangs who brought them over and continue to see the immigrants as better guarantees of meal tickets than their old heroin trade. 8

Twice in the past year, gang members surrounded the Bowery quarters, blocked the fire escapes, then calmly robbed the residents of their savings. The victims didn't complain, they said, because they feared retaliation against their families in China if they caused trouble for the gangs. Says one: "We have no one to protect us. There is nothing we can do. We may as well be slaves."

Government action has been minimal. In the past five years only a handful of sweatshop owners has been prosecuted for failing to pay workers. The government failure has created an even more lawless enclave. Local cops say that as the immigrants become more desperate for money, they often turn to crime. According to Tommy Ong of the New 9

Unregulated employment agencies offer cheap jobs in restaurants, construction and garment-industry sweatshops, such as the one shown here.

York police intelligence division, the sleazy employment agencies under the Manhattan Bridge that specialize in placing illegal immigrants in jobs around the country often misrepresent and oversell the type of work available. When workers return and can't pay off their immigration debt, the gangsters (or "snakeheads") offer them a deal. The illegals describe their ex-employers' operation and return with shotguns and masks to rob the place with members of the gang. The debt is then canceled. "Local police are usually stumped, but we know exactly what happens," says Ong. "It has become a nationwide problem."

"I didn't know life here could be so hard. It is worse than what I left behind in China. Now I can't even go back."

–Yu Li, who came to the U.S. in 1995

Each tale is one of heartbreak. Yu Li [10] says she cried for nearly a year after she was brought over to find a better life. She paid gangsters to get out of China three years ago to join her husband, who had illegally entered the U.S. in 1991. She paid the snakeheads money her husband had borrowed and sent over. Almost immediately after reaching New York, she began working 17-hour days, seven days a week, at a local garment factory. But because she was new and the factory paid piece rate, she made only $1 an hour. "Sometimes we had nothing for ourselves. I made less than $100 a week." She and her husband made so little money they couldn't afford to live together. He continued to sleep on the floor of the restaurant that employed him. She slept in a basement owned by relatives. Her husband would ask angrily, "Why don't you work harder?" "But," says Yu, "I couldn't work any harder."

Yet the couple again dealt with the [11] snakeheads in order to be reunited with the three children they left behind. The price: $132,000. It was a harrowing journey. Their 14-year-old son was separated from his sisters shortly after the journey began, abandoned in Cambodia when war broke out and stuck in a Vietnam jail until he bribed his way out with $500 he had stashed away. Relatives helped pay off the snakeheads, but each month Yu has to pay $3,000 on the debt. "It is hard. We have nothing." Now they have fettered their children to their fate. "The hardest thing," she says, "is that I have had to make the children work. They should be in school, but we need the money they bring home." She sighs. "It was never this hard in China."

Reflecting on What You Have Read

1 Although Barnes is careful to document his claims about these sweat-shops, his own feelings and values are very clear. What are some passages that make his feelings and values clear? What is your reaction to these passages? To what extent do they add to or detract from the credibility of the report?

2 How would you characterize Barnes's purposes in writing this report?

3 Look closely at the people in the photographs, especially their facial expressions, clothing, and postures. How are these details similar to or different from what you expected to see? What is your reaction to these details?

4 In the essay's photographs, look at the settings in which the people are located. What details do you notice? How do they affect your reaction to the people?

5 From what angles are the people photographed? How does the viewing angle in each photograph affect your reaction?

6 Notice the picture captions—for example, the ones that accompany the photos of the grandfather and the people operating steam presses. In what ways do the captions add to or detract from the effect of the photographs?

Thinking Ahead

❯ bedfordstmartins.com/
visualage

For a very different account of sweatshops, see Bill Buford's "Sweat Is Good": click on ***CHAPTER 3*** ❯ ***EXAMPLES***

One of the main reasons people write reports is to make readers aware of a problem, especially one that readers assume pertains only to other people or exists only in other places. Edward Barnes, for example, wants readers to realize that sweatshops are a problem right here in the United States, not just in third-world countries. The nature of the problem a writer addresses may vary widely, ranging from social and economic problems such as sweatshops to personal or health problems such as anorexia and other eating disorders. As you think about topics for your report, consider these questions: Are you aware of a problem that other people tend to ignore or overlook? Can you think of readers who might need to understand how such a problem might affect them or someone they care about? Are there ways you might use visual information such as photographs and tables to inform people about this problem?

DREAD WIND: The greatest danger of a dirty bomb is not the explosive blast but the radioactive particles it projects into the air.

Ever since September 11, 2001, Americans have been acutely aware of the potential for terrorist attacks. Such attacks might take several forms, one of which could be the detonation of a dirty bomb—a conventional explosive packed with radioactive contaminants that would be released into the atmosphere. The authors of this article for *Scientific American,* Michael A. Levi and Henry C. Kelly, are physicists at the Federation of American Scientists, a Washington, D.C.– based research and advocacy organization concerned with science and public policy. As you read this November 2002 article, consider whether the visuals overstate the threat of a dirty bomb, causing more alarm than is warranted.

Weapons of Mass Disruption

MICHAEL A. LEVI AND HENRY C. KELLY

1 Although the explosion and subsequent high-rise blaze are nasty, most building residents are away at work, so nobody is seriously hurt. A parade of police cars, ambulances and fire trucks pulls up to the curb, lights flaring and sirens blaring. Emergency crews dodge bits of smoking debris and prepare to enter the stricken structure.

2 Suddenly a sensor panel on a fire truck flashes a warning. *"The radiation detectors have gone off!" a stunned fire chief roars. "It looks like a dirty bomb!"* Activity stops abruptly as alarm sweeps through the assembled crews. What appeared to be a standard fire emergency is actually a terrorist attack with a radiological weapon.

3 Alerted by radio, disaster-control agencies dispatch specially trained radiation-mitigation teams to the site. Rescue workers slip into brightly colored hazmat suits. Police officers in gas masks start to evacuate bystanders, but most of the frightened onlookers are already running away in panic, handkerchiefs over their mouths.

4 The explosive device, spiked with radioactive cesium, has released a cloud of toxic dust. When it drifts downwind, fallout settles over nearly 60 city blocks.

Buildings, sidewalks, streets and cars are quickly coated with radioactive debris. As the ventilation systems of buildings in the neighborhood suck in the dust, people inhale small amounts of carcinogenic particles.

5 After sitting abandoned and quarantined for a short period, the environs are swept by teams of workers who decontaminate surfaces with vacuums, water jets and other apparatus as part of a prolonged cleanup effort. In retrospect, the incident has caused relatively few injuries, most of which were the result of traffic accidents during the frenzied exodus. Still, fearful residents refuse to return. Business revenues and real-estate values plummet, and several buildings near ground zero have to be demolished. The final costs reach the tens of billions of dollars.

Radiological terror weapons could blow radioactive dust through cities, causing panic, boosting cancer rates and forcing costly cleanups

DIRTY VERSUS NUCLEAR BOMBS

People sometimes confuse radiological with nuclear weapons

A DIRTY BOMB is likely to be a primitive device in which TNT or fuel oil and fertilizer explosives are 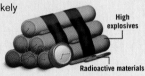 combined with highly radioactive materials. The detonated bomb vaporizes or aerosolizes the toxic isotopes, propelling them into the air.

A FISSION BOMB is a more sophisticated mechanism that relies on creating a runaway nuclear chain reaction in uranium  235 or plutonium 239. One type features tall, inward-pointing pyramids of plutonium surrounded by a shell of high explosives. When the bomb goes off, the explosives produce an imploding shock wave that drives the plutonium pieces together into a sphere containing a pellet of beryllium/polonium at the center, creating a critical mass. The resulting fission reaction causes the bomb to explode with tremendous force, sending high-energy electromagnetic waves and fallout into the air.

This kind of scenario could become a 6 reality in the not too distant future. Defending ourselves from the threat of radiological weapons has become a grim necessity. The components and know-how needed to build a dirty bomb are available, and there are fanatics out there who just might do the deed. The arrest earlier this year of Al Qaeda sympathizer José Padilla (Abdullah al Muhajir) on suspicion of plotting to construct and set off a dirty bomb gives an indication of the interest in building such a device.

A radiological weapon, or dirty 7 bomb, is typically a crude device comprising conventional explosives, such as TNT or a fuel oil/fertilizer mixture, laced with highly radioactive materials. The explosives generate a pulse of heat that vaporizes or aerosolizes radioactive material and propels it across a wide area.

Weapons experts consider radiologi- 8 cal bombs a messy but potentially effective technology that could cause tremendous psychological damage, exploiting the public's fears of invisible radiation. Not weapons of mass destruction but weapons of mass disruption, these devices could wreak economic havoc by making target areas off-limits for an extended period. Radiological bombs have never been used, mainly because they have long been considered inappropriate for military purposes: their effect is too delayed and unpredictable to sway a battle.

Although they are relatively simple in 9 principle, constructing and deploying one of these mechanisms is difficult to do. It is more complicated than wrapping stolen materials around a stick of dynamite. Such a clumsy weapon might only scatter large chunks of material, limiting the area affected and making cleanup easy. An effective dirty bomb is, however, much easier to assemble than a nuclear weapon, although it would still require considerable skill. A major problem is that the builder could be fatally exposed to hot isotopes. But a deadly dose of radiation can take weeks to have an effect and so might not deter suicidal terrorists.

Radioactive Rebar

Materials that are highly radioactive are 10 employed in hundreds of medical, industrial and academic applications. There are about two million individual sources of ionizing radiation in the U.S. alone, thousands of which are of significant size. Their uses include destroying bacteria on food, sterilizing pharmaceutical products, killing cancer cells, inspecting welds, exploring for oil, and doing research in nuclear physics and engineering. The U.S. federal government encouraged the distribution of plutonium isotopes for research during the 1960s and 1970s, and much of the material is still out there because the government has not been willing to pay for its recovery.

Ionizing radiation sources, such as cobalt 60, cesium 137 and iridium 192, emit gamma rays; others, such as americium 241 and plutonium 238, produce alpha particles. These materials are often expensive, and authorities always assumed that there would be a clear economic incentive to protect them from thieves. Policymakers also expected that heavy protection of these substances would be unnecessary because no one would risk exposure to the life-threatening levels of radiation they produce.

Despite these assurances, significant quantities of materials suitable for dirty-bomb making have been found abandoned in scrap yards, vehicles and houses around the U.S. and Europe. A recent U.S. Nuclear Regulatory Commission (NRC) study reported that American business and research facilities had lost track of nearly 1,500 pieces of equipment with radioactive parts since 1996, scores of which would be big enough for a dirty bomb. Half were never recovered. Earlier this year a steel-recycling plant found a hot source mixed in with scrap metal. Several years ago radioactive cesium passed undetected through a recovery facility and was subsequently melted down and cast in steel reinforcing bars for concrete.

The International Atomic Energy Agency stated in late June that almost every nation in the world has the radioactive materials needed to build a dirty bomb. More than 100 countries lack adequate controls to prevent the theft of these materials. Late in 2001, for instance, two woodsmen in the former Soviet republic of Georgia were dosed after they found a portable radiothermal generator—a large radioactive strontium 90 source—abandoned in the woods. They used the generator as a heating device. Chechen rebels created a scare in 1995 when they placed a shielded container holding cesium 137 (taken from cancer-treatment equipment) in a Moscow park and then tipped off Russian news reporters to its location. Eight years previously, scrap scavengers broke into an abandoned cancer clinic in Goiânia, Brazil, and stole a medical device containing radioactive cesium. About 250 people were exposed to the source; eight developed radiation sickness, and four died. The incident produced 3,500 cubic meters of radioactive waste—enough to cover a football field to hip level—and left the local economy devastated.

Radiation Effects

In addition to acute health problems such as radiation sickness, radioactive materials can cause cancer. Quantifying dangerous radioactive dose levels is difficult, however, because specific health effects are uncertain.

Radiation doses are often measured in rems. Everyone receives about a quarter of a rem every year from exposure to natural sources, including cosmic rays and the uranium in granite bedrock. In general, people subjected to 100 rems or more develop radiation sickness and require immediate medical attention. Half the people exposed to 450 rems will die within 60 days. Even small doses can increase the risk of getting cancer. On average, if 2,500 people

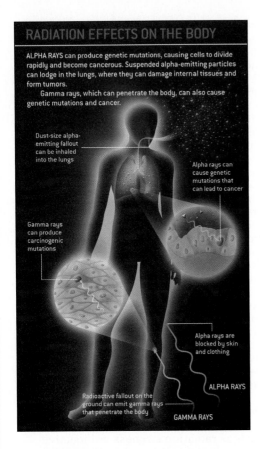

RADIATION EFFECTS ON THE BODY

ALPHA RAYS can produce genetic mutations, causing cells to divide rapidly and become cancerous. Suspended alpha-emitting particles can lodge in the lungs, where they can damage internal tissues and form tumors.

Gamma rays, which can penetrate the body, can also cause genetic mutations and cancer.

Dust-size alpha-emitting fallout can be inhaled into the lungs

Alpha rays can cause genetic mutations that can lead to cancer

Gamma rays can produce carcinogenic mutations

Alpha rays are blocked by skin and clothing

ALPHA RAYS

Radioactive fallout on the ground can emit gamma rays that penetrate the body

GAMMA RAYS

three years. The NRC typically sets a looser threshold, equivalent to a one-in-500 increased cancer death risk over 50 years. But these assessments are controversial because there are no good statistics showing how much cancer increases as a result of low levels of radiation. Currently experts estimate the hazards of exposure by assuming that the chance of developing cancer decreases in proportion to the amount of radiation received. They also presuppose that there is no minimum level of exposure that is harmless.

Hot Cloud in the City

To understand the potential impact of a dirty bomb, we examined a range of plausible attacks. We studied hypothetical dispersal scenarios and estimated the sizes of the areas that would be contaminated above various dose thresholds. To do this, we used the HOTSPOT computer code, developed at Lawrence Livermore National Laboratory, which simulates the movement of radioactive particles. The model's results were then combined with experimental and theoretical data on the effects of radiation to produce estimates of health risks and contamination.   17

A simulated dispersal depends on a range of inputs, including time of day, weather, wind speed, and scattering methods. Higher winds, for example, spread materials over a greater area, reducing the amount of contamination in any one place. To ensure that our outputs were not simply the result of specific initial conditions, we ran more than 100 dispersal scenarios. For a given radioactive source, variations in ambient conditions produced changes in our estimates by at most a factor of 10. Such an error range does not affect our basic conclusions, if only because the various factors tend to offset one another. For every factor with the potential to make a bomb's impact half as bad, there is another to make it two times worse.   18

are exposed to a single rem of radiation, one will die of an induced cancer.

Scientists and regulators have long debated what level of radiation exposure is tolerable. Federal regulations prohibit radiation workers from receiving more than five rems annually. The U.S. Environmental Protection Agency recommends that a contaminated area be abandoned if decontamination efforts cannot reduce the extra risk of cancer death to about one in 10,000. This additional risk is equivalent to having 25 chest x-rays over one's lifetime or being exposed to cosmic radiation in Denver (as opposed to sea level) for   16

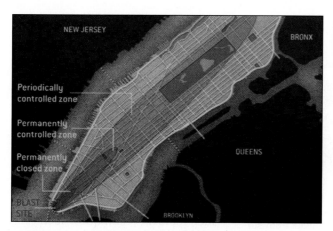

NOXIOUS PLUME of hot fallout spreads over New York City's Manhattan Island after the simulated detonation of a radioactive cesium-based dirty bomb [assuming a wind from the southwest]. The highlighted zones would be expected to have radiation levels comparable to those that caused the closing of contaminated regions around the damaged Chernobyl nuclear power plant.

If people in the vicinity of an explo- 19 sion are unable to leave the area before the dust cloud arrives, they will inhale small particles. From past incidents, we know that if the material is an alpha emitter, such as plutonium or americium, it could become lodged in victims' lungs for years and lead to long-term radiation exposure. But if evacuees are decontaminated quickly, thoroughly washing their skin and disposing of contaminated clothing, the total exposure will be minimal.

Dust from a radiological weapon 20 would remain trapped for extended periods in cracks and crevices on the surfaces of buildings, sidewalks and streets, and some would have been swept into the interiors of buildings. Certain materials that could be used in a radiological attack, such as cesium 137, chemically bind to glass, concrete and asphalt. More than 15 years after the 1986 Chernobyl disaster, in which a Soviet nuclear

power plant underwent a meltdown, cesium is still affixed to the sidewalks of many Scandinavian cities that were downwind of the disaster. Fortunately, the radiation exposure from underfoot is fairly low, increasing the cancer death risk by less than one in 10,000.

If the material contains 21 alpha emitters, the long-term health risk comes from breathing radioactive dust suspended in the air by wind, the action of tires or pedestrian traffic. In Kiev, more than 100 kilometers from Chernobyl, dust in the streets still contains low levels of plutonium. Should the material remaining in the area contain cesium 137 or other gamma emitters, anyone entering a contaminated area would be exposed to low-level radiation because, unlike alpha rays, gamma rays penetrate clothing and skin.

Consider the dispersal of 3,500 curies 22 of cesium 137 by an explosion at the lower tip of Manhattan Island. Sources capable of delivering this much radiation have been "orphaned" in the former Soviet Union; the U.S. recently committed $25 million, in partnership with Russia, to track these materials down. Such a source, if acquired by terrorists, would be difficult to handle, requiring some shielding to prevent a builder from receiving an incapacitating radiation dose. But the cesium would already be in powder form, making dispersion relatively easy.

If this source were prepared and then 23 exploded, about 800 square kilometers would be contaminated above the strict EPA decontamination guidelines. The disaster would not be of Chernobyl's magnitude; it would release less radiation

COSTLY CLEANUP EFFORTS will follow any use of a dirty bomb. Hazmat-suited workers will have to scrub fallout from surfaces with water jets, vacuums and sandblasters, as well as remove contaminated plants and soil.

overall, and none in the form of potent short-lived isotopes such as iodine 131. But its strategic placement would wreak havoc. Over an area of about 20 city blocks, there would be a one-in-10 increased risk of death from cancer for residents living in the area (without decontamination) for 30 years, a 50 percent increase over the background rate. A broader area of 15 square kilometers—varying from four to 20 square kilometers, depending on the weather—would be contaminated above the relocation threshold recommended by the International Commission on Radiological Protection and accepted by the NRC. If these standards were relaxed and the relocation threshold were the same as that used around Chernobyl, the area affected would still be roughly 100 city blocks. The property value of this area is estimated in the hundreds of billions of dollars.

Decontamination Procedures
Removal of urban radioactive contamination has never been performed on a large scale because no one has ever had to deal with the consequences of a radiological attack. Our current knowledge [24] of how to cleanse an urban area is based on experience from smaller-scale industrial operations and from cold war–era studies on the aftermath of nuclear war.

The cleanup effort would initially involve removing loose contamination—radioactive dust particles settled on surfaces or lodged in interstices. Relatively low cost mechanical techniques such as vacuuming or pressure washing should be effective. More invasive, higher-cost surface-removal techniques, such as sandblasting, would be necessary where hot dust has penetrated deep into more porous materials. In some cases, sidewalks and asphalt may have to be removed. The top layer of soil might have to be carted off-site and disposed of. Much vegetation might have to be cut down. Chemical agents such as acids might have to be used to dissolve rust and mineral deposits in which contaminants are trapped. [25]

To make the process manageable, we may need to reevaluate contamination guidelines. The strict EPA regulations are appropriate for peacetime purposes—they were developed (with public consultation) to force limits on corporate polluters. Faced with the alternative of abandoning swaths of a city, we might have to accept an increased risk. We might choose, for example, to adopt the NRC guidelines, which require cleanup of all areas where contamination would deliver a dose greater than five rems over 50 years, increasing the risk of cancer death by more than one in 500 (equivalent to a reduction of each person's life expectancy by roughly 15 days). An alternative would be to require cleanup of all areas where contamination would more than double the background radiation rate. [26]

WHAT TO DO IF ATTACKED

In the event of a radiological weapons incident, take these basic steps:

If you're inside, close your windows and turn off any external ventilation. This will stop radioactive particles from getting inside. Although filter masks are useful outside, they do not offer any added protection indoors.

If you're outside, get inside, wash up and discard your clothes. This will remove any radioactive particles. You might track in some radioactive fallout, but this danger is offset by the benefits of being indoors. You should stay inside until you're told to do otherwise by law-enforcement officials or emergency personnel. If people start fleeing the scene, it will be harder to contain contamination and to move emergency workers and equipment efficiently.

In all cases, listen for instructions from the authorities. The nature of the required response will depend on the size and type of the dirty bomb.

Iodine tablets are ineffective, because dirty bombs [unlike reactor meltdowns] would be unlikely to release radioactive iodine.

Protective Measures

Many relatively low cost, practical steps can be taken to reduce the risks from radiological weapons and minimize the effects if an attack should occur. The first step is to ensure that the materials themselves are secure. The NRC and other federal agencies are tightening the licensing process governing access to radioactive materials and the security standards for all dangerous materials. Inspections must be frequent and thorough. Programs to collect and safeguard unused materials, building on efforts such as the successful Los Alamos Offsite Source Recovery Project, need to be expanded.

Research should also be funded to identify less dangerous technologies— ion beams, for example—that can provide the food sterilization, medical and other services now supplied by radioactive materials. Increased security will raise the cost of using radioactive materials and create economic incentives for nonradioactive alternatives.

The next step would be to improve our ability to detect materials in the event that they are stolen. The U.S. ought to install an extensive array of radiation-detection systems at key points such as airports, harbors, rail stations, tunnels, highways and borders. This effort has already begun: radiation detectors from the Department of Energy's Nuclear Emergency Search Teams are being installed along the Boston–New York–Washington corridor and on the perimeter of the nation's capital. Routine checks of scrap-metal yards and landfill sites would also protect against illegal or accidental disposal of dangerous materials. In applications such as these, highly sensitive detectors are unnecessary because materials could all be checked at the entrance to a facility and would be unlikely to be shielded. Simple, inexpensive Geiger counters would suffice.

We must also ensure that the government is prepared to mitigate the impact of any radiological weapon that is actually used. An effective response to an attack requires a system capable of quickly gauging the extent of the damage, identifying appropriate responders, developing a coherent response plan, and getting the necessary personnel and equipment to the site rapidly. To help assuage fear, federal authorities should designate a single scientifically credible official who could provide consistent information about the attack.

All of this requires extensive training. Emergency and hospital personnel need to understand how to protect themselves and affected citizens during a radiological attack and be able to determine rapidly if individuals have been

exposed to radiation. Although generous funding has been made available for
instruction, the program needs a clear
management strategy.

Finally, we need to learn how to
decontaminate large urban areas and
determine the steps necessary to minimize contamination. This could mean
the difference between abandoning or
demolishing a city and getting it back in
operation after a few months of cleanup.

Although the effects of a radiological
attack are minor compared with those
of even a small nuclear weapon, a dirty
bomb could have drastic economic and
psychological consequences. Fortunately,
studying the nature of the risk gives us
the chance to take actions that could
reduce the likelihood of an event and
minimize the damage. We should begin
immediately.

32

33

MORE TO EXPLORE

**Making the Nation Safer: The Role of Science
and Technology in Countering Terrorism.** Committee on Science and Technology, National
Research Council, 2002. Available at **http://
stills.nap.edu/**

**Securing Nuclear Weapons and Materials:
Seven Steps for Immediate Action.** M. Bunn,
J. Holdren and A. Weir. Harvard University Press,
2002. Available at **www.nti.org/e_research/
securing_nuclear_weapons_and_materials_
May2002.pdf**

Senate Committee on Foreign Relations Hearing
Testimony on "Dirty Bombs and Basement Nukes."
Summary available at **www.ransac.org/
new-web-site/related/congress/hearings/
sfrc_notes.html**

Council on Foreign Relations Q&A on Dirty Bombs:
**www.terrorismanswers.com/weapons/
dirtybomb.html**

Reflecting on What You Have Read

1 This report begins with a very dramatic visual and a written scenario
that details the ways people would react upon hearing that a dirty
bomb had been detonated. How would you describe the voice, or tone,
of the visual and the scenario? Is it consistent with what you would
expect of a magazine called *Scientific American*? Does the voice seem
justified? Why or why not?

2 The heading Radioactive Rebar (p. 128) contains a word—*rebar*—that
the authors assume readers of *Scientific American* will understand.
Given that *Scientific American* has described itself as "bringing its readers unique insights about developments in science and technology for
more than 150 years," does the authors' assumption seem reasonable?
Why or why not? Further, there is relatively little mention of rebar in
the paragraphs that follow this heading. Does this seem justified to
you? Why or why not? If you are not familiar with the word *rebar*, can
you find anything in the article that explains what it is?

3 Look at the thumbnails on the next page for the first three pages of
this article as they originally appeared in *Scientific American*. Notice

the places where the color red appears on these pages. What is accomplished by using red in these places?

4 In several places the report uses inset boxes to set off certain information: Dirty Versus Nuclear Bombs; Radiation Effects on the Body; and What to Do If Attacked. What are the benefits of setting off this information from the rest of the text? Why do you think this information was even included?

5 The authors of this piece cite relatively few sources for their claims. Does this reduce the credibility of their report? Why or why not? If you were writing this report, at what points would you cite sources for your claims?

Thinking Ahead

The events of September 11, 2001, raised Americans' consciousness of one form of terrorism. However, the authors of this article draw on recent research to give insight into another form of terrorism. You might review recent issues of popular newsmagazines (*Time*, *U.S. News & World Report*, *Newsweek*, or *Slate,* for example) to identify topics for which research is producing new insights or challenging conventional assumptions.

In recent years, there has been a dramatic increase in the popularity of women's sports. Unfortunately, there has been an equally dramatic increase in the number of sports injuries to which women are especially vulnerable. In the next report, Margaret Tomeo talks about one of the most serious of these injuries: damage to a small piece of tissue in the knee, the anterior cruciate ligament, or ACL. A varsity soccer player at her university, Margaret wrote this piece with herself and her teammates in mind. On a bus trip to a soccer game, Margaret asked one of her teammates to read the report. This prompted a general discussion of ACL injuries, and several other teammates read the draft without being asked. As you read, try to determine what aspects of Margaret's report led her teammates to read the entire piece carefully.

Margaret Tomeo

ACL: The Curse of Women Athletes

"I knew right away exactly what I did" (McCallum and Gelin 44).   1

After hearing a rip in her right knee, Tiffany Woosley, a shooting   2 guard for the University of Tennessee Lady Vols, knew she had torn her ACL, or anterior cruciate ligament. She was performing a simple jump shot and landed incorrectly—and her injury caused her to miss the rest of the season. This has become the story for too many women athletes, including Woosley's teammate Nikki McCray, an All-American forward who tore her ACL in a pickup game (McCallum and Gelin). Duke University's Monique Currie tore her ACL in a pre-season game, possibly ruining their hopes for a big season. (See Fig. 1.) And Brandi Chastain missed her 1987 and 1988 college soccer seasons after having surgery for the ACL in both knees (Patrick). ACL tears are turning into an epidemic among women athletes at all levels of sports, especially among high school and college players. As the number of women competing in sports continues to increase, understanding the causes of this common injury will enable us to help these athletes reduce their risk.

What Is the ACL?

The anterior cruciate ligament, ACL for short, is a ligament in   3 the knee to which much of the stress of physical activity is transmitted.

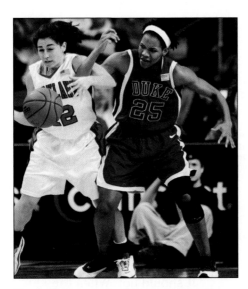

Fig. 1. Photograph of Monique Currie. From Nick Wass, "No. 1 Blue Devils Counting on Currie," by Jim Reedy, *Washington Post* 16 Mar. 2004: D1. Monique Currie and her knee brace illustrate that women athletes at all levels are susceptible to injury.

The knee depends so much on the ACL that it is one of the most vulnerable parts of the human body. When people run or walk, the knee bears the entire weight of the body, continually flexing and absorbing the shock of every step. Central to all this activity and stress is the ACL, which runs through the knee to form a cross connecting the thigh bone (femur) with the shin bone (tibia) (Wilkinson 68). (See Fig. 2.) The ACL keeps the femur aligned with the tibia when the knee is bent and prevents the tibia from sliding forward too much (Hawaleshka). It also stabilizes the knee while an athlete is running and changing directions. When an ACL tear occurs, the knee gives out and becomes unstable. This instability does not go away until the injury is treated through surgery and rehabilitation. Even after all this, athletes with torn ACLs may have problems with recurrent instability, further joint damage, and early arthritis.

When Are ACL Injuries Most Common?

ACL injuries can happen at almost any time, but the majority of ACL injuries are non-contact, resulting from "planting" on one foot or making lateral movements such as changing direction suddenly. Other movements, such as straight-knee landings and one-step stopping while the knee is hyperextended, cause tears in the anterior

4

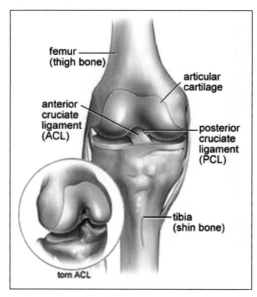

Fig. 2. Diagram of the ACL. From "What is the ACL?" *ACL Solutions,* 2002, Medical Internet Solutions, 10 Mar. 2004 <http://www.aclsolutions.com/theacl_1.php>.

cruciate ligament as well (Moeller and Lamb). The ligaments in the knee become extremely prone to injury when an athlete has exercised her quadriceps (muscles in the front of the thigh) and hamstrings (muscles in the back of the thigh) to fatigue. The muscular fatigue causes increased tibia movement at the knee and allows the knee to bend in ways in which it should not. When the ACL gives way, a player may feel and hear a pop in her knee as she collapses to the ground, unable to support her own weight.

As a player's muscles become fatigued, the player also becomes 5 mentally fatigued. When this happens, a player can lose sight of what her body can handle. As this occurs, the athlete often attempts maneuvers that her body cannot withstand. The combination of muscular and mental fatigue makes knee injuries most common in sports that involve frequent jumps, landings, rapid changes in direction, and abrupt deceleration and acceleration. Tears are most common in high-risk sports such as soccer, basketball, volleyball, field hockey, gymnastics, and skiing (Hawaleshka). Although this sort of injury can happen to both males and females, it is especially common among female athletes.

Why Are Women at a Greater Risk?

The discrepancy in the numbers of women and men suffering 6 from ACL tears is due partly to biological factors and partly to social factors. Anatomically, women are more prone to an ACL tear for several reasons. One is that women have a decreased hamstring-to-quadriceps strength ratio compared to that of men. Women's hamstring muscles are usually about half as strong as their quadriceps, whereas men's hamstrings are two-thirds as strong as their quadriceps. This muscle imbalance creates a stress on a woman's ACL because the quadriceps can overpower the hamstring, causing the tibia to be pulled too far forward (Wilkinson 69). The body depends on the hamstring to stabilize the knee, so there is greater risk of strain and injury when the hamstring is much weaker than the quadriceps.

7

Another anatomical difficulty is that women have wider hips than men, and a woman's femur, the bone connecting hip and knee, is shorter than a man's. Consequently, women's legs slope inward at the knees, placing additional stress on the anterior cruciate ligament (McCallum and Gelin 46). In women, the angle from hip to knee (the quadriceps angle, or Q-angle) is greater than the Q-angle in men. (See Fig. 3.) Men's Q-angles usually range from 11 to 13 degrees, whereas women's Q-angles can be up to 17 degrees (Moeller and Lamb). This means that in women's knees, the force of the body is not transmitted directly downward, but instead is directed at a greater angle than in men's knees. The greater the angle, the more strain on the knee and the greater risk for ACL injury.

8

Tears can also occur when a woman's femur acts as a guillotine, shearing the anterior cruciate ligament if the knee is hyperextended

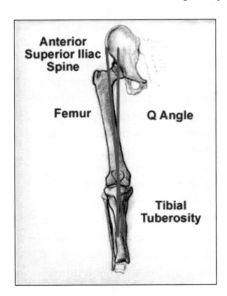

Fig. 3. Diagram of the Q-angle. From Stephen Pribut, "Runner's Knee," *Dr. Stephen M. Pribut's Sports Pages,* 22 Jan. 2004, 10 Mar. 2004 <http://www.drpribut.com/sports/spknees.html>.

(Hawaleshka). This occurs in women because of the size and shape of the femoral notch, the point through which the ACL passes in order to connect the femur to the tibia. In women, the femoral notch is narrower than the femoral notch in men. It also tends to be in the shape of an "A" whereas a man's femoral notch is shaped more like a "U." When the knee is overextended, more pressure is put on the ACL. The narrower arch, combined with its sharper angle, increases the risk that a woman's femoral arch will cut into the ACL, resulting in a tear of that ligament (McCallum and Gelin 46).

Female hormones can also have a significant effect on the anterior cruciate ligament. A 1998 University of Michigan study showed that most ACL tears occurred when estrogen levels in women were the highest (Harden and Spurgeon). Estrogen weakens the ACL cells by altering their metabolism and increasing the laxity of the muscular tissue so the ligament is easily stretched and torn (Simonian). Another study, done at UCLA, found that the anterior cruciate ligament has receptors that react to estrogen and weaken in its presence (Harden and Spurgeon). In addition, females are at a greater risk because their joints tend to be looser than those of males (Hawaleshka). 9

Not only does the female anatomy contribute to the high risk of ACL injury, but societal factors affecting body movement and muscle strength also make women more susceptible. For one thing, women generally have less exposure to physical activities and, on average, their conditioning is at a lower starting point than men's. Furthermore, many women are not taught simple motor skills early in their development and consequently maneuver the wrong way. For instance, males typically land using both legs, so that both knees absorb the impact, while females favor one-legged landings. "I'm not saying that a man would never make the same move the same way, but it's much more likely that he would've learned the right way to do it," states Iowa trainer Alex Kane. "Either because of budgetary constraints or philosophical reasons, that teaching is not going on in the physical education system. Therefore you have impaired neuromuscular coordination. The foundation is simply not there. Girls aren't taught it, and they aren't encouraged to learn it" (McCallum and Gelin 47). 10

How Can These Injuries Be Reduced?

Currently, it is still unclear how to prevent anterior cruciate lig- 11
ament injuries. But female athletes can reduce the risk of ACL tears
by learning proper motor skills, wearing the right equipment, and
undertaking a program of strength training. Mary Lloyd Ireland, MD,
director of the Kentucky Sports Medicine Clinic, suggests that
women should be encouraged to play sports as young girls and
should be taught the proper athletic techniques for actions such as
jumping and pivoting (Schnirring). Young women athletes also need
to take advantage of programs that provide special training through
local sports clinics, physical therapists, and athletic trainers.

The right equipment can also decrease the number of ACL 12
tears. Recently, manufacturers have begun trying to create a shoe
that reduces friction without eliminating grip. According to Dr. Bill
Youmans, an orthopedic consultant for the University of Tennessee,
wearing such shoes would reduce the number of ACL injuries for
men and women alike (McCallum and Gelin 48). Shoe manufacturers
are also trying to accommodate a woman's foot so that shoes fit better and provide ankle support that helps reduce excess tension on
the knee. Finally, arch supports, known as orthotics, can help keep
the foot balanced, reducing the strain on the knee.

The most important element in preventing ACL tears is appro- 13
priate strength training. Female athletes should be encouraged to
begin weight training to establish a proper relationship between
muscle groups, especially the hamstring and quadriceps. To establish this relationship, women should consider activities such as
squats and lunges, which increase muscle strength while reducing
the stress on the knee. Similarly, using the leg press machine, push-
ing the weight away from the body while lying down, is beneficial,
strengthening the lower body while not placing any strain on the
ACL. In addition, women can benefit from balancing exercises and
Plyometrics, exercises that involve training for power and explosive-
ness using rapid muscle contraction.

Paying close attention to preventative measures can reduce the 14
number of women suffering from ACL injuries and prolong their

career. If we start now, we can greatly reduce the number of anterior cruciate tears that plague so many of our female players, players such as the outstanding Tennessee shooting guard, Tiffany Woosley.

Works Cited

Harden, Blaine, and Devon Spurgeon. "Knee Injuries Abound for Female Athletes." *Washington Post* 29 Mar. 1998. 18 Mar. 2004 <http://www.wsyacy.com/knee/ACL_WP980329.html>.

Hawaleshka, Danylo. "ACL: A Real Pain in the Knee." *Maclean's* 7 Apr. 1997: 66.

McCallum, Jack and Dana Gelin. "Out of Joint." *Sports Illustrated* 13 Feb. 1995: 44-48.

Moeller, James L. and Mary M. Lamb. "Anterior Cruciate Ligament Injuries in Female Athletes: Why Are Women More Susceptible?" *The Physician and Sportsmedicine* 25.4 (1997). 3 Mar. 2004 <http://www.physsportsmed.com/issues/1997/04apr/moeller.htm>.

Patrick, Dick. "Plant, Pop, then Pain." *USA Today* 25 June 2003. 15 Mar. 2004. <http://www.usatoday.com/sports/2003-06-24-acl-cover_x.html>.

Pribut, Stephen M. "Runner's Knee." *Dr. Stephen M. Pribut's Sport Pages.* 22 Jan. 2004. 10 Mar. 2004 <http://www.drpribut.com/sports/spknees.html>.

Schnirring, Lisa. "What's New in Treating Active Women." *The Physician and Sportsmedicine.* 25.7 (1997). 19 Mar. 2004 <http://www.physsportsmed.com/issues/1997/07jul/schnirri.htm>.

Simonian, Peter. "Knee Injuries Stepped up among Women." *Health Beat* 4 May 1999. 1 Mar. 2004 <http://depts.washington.edu/hsnews/hb/hb990504.html>.

Wass, Nick. *Monique Currie.* "No. 1 Blue Devils Counting on Currie." By Jim Reedy. *Washington Post* 16 Mar. 2004: D1.

"What Is the ACL?" *ACL Solutions.com.* 2002. Medical Internet Solutions. 10 Mar. 2004 <http://www.aclsolutions.com/theacl_1.php>.

Wilkinson, Todd. "Pop, Crackle, Snap." *Women's Sports & Fitness* Apr. 1998: 68-69.

Reflecting on What You Have Read

1   Why do you think some of Margaret's teammates read her report carefully without being asked to? Can you identify certain aspects of the text that would draw them in? If so, what are they?

2   Although Margaret is an athlete, she has no training in sports medicine. Consequently, she was especially concerned about establishing her credibility in talking about this topic. What are some of the ways she attempts to do so? Do you think she succeeds? Why or why not?

3   What differences do you see between the first photograph in this report and the subsequent images? What do these differences tell you about the visuals' different functions?

4   In the third paragraph of her report, Margaret explains what the ACL does and what happens when it is damaged. But before discussing the ACL specifically, Margaret writes more generally about the knee. What does she achieve by writing about the knee before the ACL?

Thinking Ahead

As you will see on p. 148, Margaret considered several topics before deciding to write about injuries to the anterior cruciate ligament. She chose this topic because she knew it was a problem that concerned her and some of her friends. As you try to think of topics for your own report, you might try Margaret's approach: think of problems that concern you and your friends, teammates, or family. Would any of these people find it helpful to understand the cause of a particular problem and steps that could be taken to avoid or minimize it?

Assignment

Report

Write a report, either on a topic of your choice or on one selected by your instructor, that answers questions that matter to the members of your intended audience. The topic should be significant—that is, it should matter to someone else (an individual, a group, or an organization) as much as it matters to you. If you have the opportunity to choose your own topic, bear in mind the following suggestions.

> If you already know a little bit about the topic, this knowledge will give you a basis for developing some real expertise in the area you select.

> If you cannot think of an audience who wants or needs to hear what you have to

say about a particular topic, you probably should choose a different one.

Your instructor may have specific requirements about how long the report should be, what sort of topic you should write about, whether you should prepare the report as a print or online document (or as an oral presentation), and whether you should include or exclude any particular visual elements or use a particular documentation style to formally cite sources. Be sure you understand those requirements before you start working on the assignment.

Guide to Writing a Report

It's possible that all the ideas you have and all the decisions you make while writing your report will work on the first try, but you shouldn't be discouraged if things don't work out that way. Like many writers, you may find that your ideas change greatly during the course of writing a report. Your understanding of the intended audience and purposes may shift, you may find some aspects of your topic to be more interesting and worthwhile than others, or you may decide that you cannot stand the topic you initially planned to write about. That's fine. Projects do not always end up exactly the way you first envision them. Your ideas should develop—and perhaps change dramatically—especially at the beginning of a project.

The remainder of this chapter will help you through the process of creating a credible, informative report that someone will actually want or need to read. The first step is covered in Getting Started—selecting a topic and analyzing the context in which your report will be read. Then you will experiment with many of the verbal and visual strategies illustrated in reports you were introduced to in Reading to Write, and you will use them in the Drafting section. These strategies can help you work toward the writer's objectives of developing your topic (that is, finding something to say), writing an introduction that will engage readers' interest, creating an appropriate voice, providing a clear structure, concluding your report effectively, and designing your report and integrating visual elements. Finally, in Finishing Up you will receive guidance in creating a review draft, assessing your work carefully, and using that assessment to revise your report.

Getting Started

You might assume that the writing process begins when you sit down at your desk and start putting words on a piece of paper or entering them on the computer. But, in fact, the writing process begins much earlier than that, when you are trying to select a topic to write about and beginning to analyze the context in which your report will be read. If you invest some effort in selecting a topic and analyzing context, you're likely to have more success when you actually sit down to create a draft.

Selecting a Topic

You will not always have a lot of choice as to the topics you write about. Your instructor (or, eventually, an employer or a client) may say, in effect, "I want you to do a report on. . . . " In many situations, however, you will have some freedom in selecting a topic for your report. Consequently, you will have to make some choices.

> ❯ Choose a topic that is not too broad to cover in the assigned number of pages or in the number of weeks you have to work.
> ❯ Choose a topic you care about.
> ❯ Make sure your topic is one about which you can get plenty of information.

In addition, consider two more bits of advice.

> ❯ Choose a topic that matters not just to you but to someone else—an individual, a group of people, a business, or some other organization.
> ❯ Make sure your topic will let you achieve some goal in addition to gathering and presenting certain information.

These last two recommendations will have a lot to do with the ultimate success of your report. How do you carry them out? One approach is to think of topics that directly affect you and people you know. Then think about what those people might hope to gain by reading your report. For example, as you'll see below, Margaret Tomeo, the student who wrote "ACL: The Curse of Women Athletes," knew that injuries to a ligament in the knee were a potential problem not only for herself but also for other women on her soccer team. Consequently, she wanted not only to understand this problem, which could affect all of them, but also to find out what they could do to avoid it.

Another approach is to immerse yourself in a topic that interests you, gathering as much information as possible. As your understanding of the topic grows, look back at the list of purposes for reports on p. 107. Is your exploration of the topic putting you in a position to accomplish any of these purposes? Are you, for example, becoming aware of a serious problem? If so, identify a specific individual or group that is likely to be affected by it even though they are currently unaware of it. Then write a report that alerts this audience to the problem. Alternatively, if your reading and observations lead you to conclude that some people have serious and potentially harmful misconceptions about the topic, you might write a report that informs them of those misconceptions and the potential harm they may cause. Keep in mind that the list of purposes for reports is not complete. As you read (or watch) other reports, ask yourself what purposes and audiences they address. Perhaps you will decide to try to accomplish a comparable goal for a comparable audience.

If you cannot think of someone who would need or want to read a report on a given topic, find another topic. Your sense of audience and purpose will affect what you say and how you express your ideas. The more specifically you can define your audience and purpose, the greater chance you will have of creating an interesting, useful report.

Working on the Assignment

Selecting a Topic

If you're having trouble finding inspiration, you might develop good report topics by reading the Thinking Ahead prompts that follow each of the reports in Reading to Write. Even if you haven't read each report, the Thinking Ahead prompt may contain a suggestion that will help you generate ideas. Also, you can read published reports—in this chapter and in other sources—and ask yourself whether the authors of those reports failed to answer questions that you or someone else need to have answered. If so, consider writing a report that supplies the missing information.

You might also get some ideas for topics by doing these activities.

> **Brainstorm.** Writing as quickly as you can, list every topic you can think of that might have some potential as a topic for this report. For the moment, don't worry about how good these topics sound. In brainstorming, the primary goal is quantity, so just list as many potential topics as possible. You can go back later and sift through the list, looking for ideas that seem especially workable and interesting.

> **Work with a group to create a list of potential topics.** Don't worry if some of the potential topics strike you as silly; again, the goal here is quantity, not quality. As a writer, sometimes you have to clear your mind of several poor ideas in order to come up with one good idea.

> **Work with a few other students to identify two or three topics that have promise,** and then think of an audience that might be interested in each one.

> **Choose one topic you think you might focus on for this report.** Base your choice on your own ideas about a possible audience and the comments of your small group. Remember: your choice of topic may change, but you have to start somewhere.

> **Brainstorm a list of statements about the topic** you have tentatively selected. Jot down everything you already know, remember, or think about this topic.

> **Explain what you know** to your group and see what information members of the group can add, what additional questions they can think of, and what sources they suggest for you to draw on.

Once you have identified a topic that you might like to write about, you need to do some preliminary data gathering to refine it.

> **Examine your own experience.** Have you had any personal contact with the topic of your report? Have you taken part in activities associated with your topic or observed it personally? If so, do you have any anecdotes or facts that seem relevant?

> **Talk with others** who may know something about your topic. What are their experiences? Can they tell you any good stories about it? Can they provide any

continued

Working on the Assignment

continued

factual information that surprises you or adds to your understanding of the topic?

> **Do some reading.** Do a preliminary search in your library's databases (such as Lexis-Nexis, Readers' Guide Abstracts, or Wilson Select). And, of course, check out the Internet, but remember that information on the Net is not always reliable or complete. Don't try to read everything carefully at this point. Just read enough to confirm that your proposed topic is interesting and worthwhile and that there is plenty of credible material available on it.

> **Look for visual information**—images, charts, graphs, and so forth—**that provides insight into the topic for your report.**

> **Conduct a brief reality check** after doing a fair amount of reading and talking. Are you finding plenty of interesting material? Have you identified an audience that actually needs or wants to know what you have to say about the topic? Do you see a compelling reason why the audience will want to read about this topic at this particular time? If you can't answer yes to at least two of these questions, consider changing your topic or your audience. Do this now, not the night before the assignment is due.

> For more on locating and choosing appropriate visuals, see **Chapter 8.**

STUDENT DIALOGUE: SELECTING A TOPIC

Writing in a Visual Age (WVA): What topics did you consider writing about?

Margaret Tomeo (MT): Pollution, recycling, endangered species.

WVA: How did you come to choose ACL injuries as your topic?

MT: I was playing soccer at the time, and there were a couple of times ACL injuries happened to people I knew. So it was a recurring thing I kept hearing about.

WVA: At what point were you certain you had a good topic to write about?

MT: I passed my draft around on the bus on the way to a soccer game. And the girls on the team all had personal stories about ACL, but my draft had a lot of information they didn't know. They found it helpful. It appealed to them. So that showed me it was a popular topic.

Analyzing Context

Once you are reasonably sure you have a good report topic, you need to start thinking about the context in which the report will be read—the audience you hope to reach, the circumstances in which readers will encounter your report, and the purposes you hope to accomplish by writing the report. It will be easiest to analyze the context for your report by first thinking in terms of one or two individual readers who are typical of the larger group you hope to reach.

After identifying this typical individual, you need to answer questions about the audience's knowledge, values, and needs; their expectations for content, layout, and format; and the circumstances in which audience members will encounter your report. You should also answer questions about your own purpose for doing this type of writing. By asking and answering these questions, you analyze the context for your report and establish a basis for making wise decisions about what to say and how to say it.

Questions for Analyzing Context

❯ bedfordstmartins.com/ visualage

To download these questions as a worksheet, click on **CHAPTER 3** ❯ **WORKSHEETS**

Audience knowledge, values, and needs

❯ What sorts of experiences (personal or secondhand) have my readers had with my topic?

❯ How does my topic relate to things my readers know, value, or care about?

❯ Do my readers have any biases or preconceptions concerning my topic? If so, what are they, and do I have any information that will correct (or reinforce) those attitudes?

Audience expectations for content

❯ What questions are my readers likely to want to have answered?

❯ What kinds of information are my readers likely to see as credible?

Audience expectations for layout or format

❯ Which reading in this chapter comes closest to looking the way my readers will expect my report to look?

❯ Are there any visual features (for example, photographs, charts, bulleted lists) my readers are likely to expect or appreciate?

❯ Are there ways in which my report will need to look different from the readings in this chapter?

Circumstances

❯ Are there any recent events that might motivate my audience to read my report? If so, what are they?

❯ If not, what sort of background information should I provide at the beginning of my report?

❯ To see how one student responded to these questions see the student context analysis, p. 151.

- **Purposes**

  〉 What purposes am I trying to accomplish in writing my report? (See discussion of purposes, p. 106.) What overall impression do I want to leave my readers with?

  〉 What sort of voice do I want readers to hear when they read my report? (For a discussion of voice, see p. 165 of this chapter.)

  The activities in the Working on the Assignment: Analyzing Context box below will help you think through and prepare to answer the Questions for Analyzing Context above.

Analyzing Context

As with any assignment, you should think about the audience for your report as concretely as possible. Try to identify one or more individuals who are typical of the larger group you hope to reach. Then take the following steps.

Talk with one or more members of your audience. What do they already know about your topic? Do they have any preconceptions or misconceptions? Have they had any personal experiences that would make them interested in or concerned about the topic? Do they have any expectations about how the report should look? Do they, for example, expect you to cite sources? If so, what style of citations? Do they expect pictures, charts, or graphs?

Put yourself in your readers' place. Use what you are learning about your readers to answer such questions as these: *If I were in my readers' place, what questions would I want to have answered? What kinds of information would I be likely to find credible?*

Draw on your knowledge of yourself. What knowledge, experiences, and values led you to be interested in this topic? Are there any points at which you and your readers might share some knowledge, experiences, or values? What are the points at which you and your readers differ most with respect to what you know or value?

Identify the circumstances in which your readers will encounter your report. Are they aware of recent events that make the topic important? Are they likely to have read or heard other reports on your topic, especially reports that view the topic differently from yours?

As you work on the report, your understanding of your audience may change. You may, for example, get a clearer idea of what the audience knows or expects, or you may revise your ideas about the sort of format that is appropriate. Consequently, you may want to revise your responses to the Questions for Analyzing Context as you work on the report. But for now, be as specific as possible.

STUDENT CONTEXT ANALYSIS

Here's how Margaret Tomeo answered these questions for the report she wrote, "ACL: The Curse of Women Athletes" (p. 136).

Audience Knowledge, Values, and Needs

What sorts of experiences (personal or secondhand) have my readers had with my topic?

Most likely they know someone who has experienced an ACL tear.

How does my topic relate to things my readers know, value, or care about?

They are not very knowledgeable on the topic but want to learn more because they know how common the injury is. They want to learn how to be safe and prevent injuries throughout their careers.

Do my readers have any biases or preconceptions concerning my topic? If so, what are they, and do I have any information that will correct (or reinforce) those attitudes?

They may believe that the injury only occurs in younger and weaker athletes.
May feel that most people are not at risk—want to know risk factors.
Don't know that ACL tears occur more frequently in women.
May think that these injuries cannot be prevented.
Don't know that this ligament is a crucial part of the knee—don't know what it is or what it does.
Don't know how serious the injury really is.

Audience Expectations for Content

What questions are my readers likely to want to have answered?

What is the ACL? What does it do?
Why is the ACL so important?
Can these injuries be prevented? How?
Why and when do ACL tears commonly occur?
How many people are affected? How common is this injury?
Why are ACL injuries more common in women than in men?

What kinds of information are my readers likely to see as credible?

The information will have to be based on medical research.

Audience Expectations for Layout or Format

Which reading in this chapter comes closest to looking the way my readers will expect my report to look?

My report will contain headings, like the report on the tobacco settlement.

continued

STUDENT CONTEXT ANALYSIS

continued

Are there any visual features (for example, photographs, charts, bulleted lists) my readers are likely to expect or appreciate?

Are there ways in which my report will need to look different from the readings in this chapter?

Like "Bellying Up to the Bar," my report will contain visuals, but these should be more technical than human-interest.

Circumstances

Are there any recent events that might motivate my audience to read my report? If so, what are they?

If not, what sort of background information should I provide at the beginning of my report?

A teammate or a friend who plays a sport may have just suffered an ACL tear; my readers will be curious about this injury if they know someone who has torn their ACL recently or is wearing a brace. They may have read about it in the paper or seen it on TV. It has happened to many professional female athletes, especially basketball players (Rebecca Lobo) and soccer players (Brandi Chastain), and even Michelle Yeoh, a movie actress.

Purposes

What purposes am I trying to accomplish in writing my report? What overall impression do I want to leave my reader with?

What sort of voice do I want readers to hear when they read my report?

I'm trying to make my readers aware of this common problem so that they can help themselves and others reduce the risk of the injury. I hope my readers will incorporate my advice into their sports and/or workouts.

I want to sound concerned about this topic, but not too emotional. I want to sound like someone who really understands the physiology involved in this injury.

Drafting

As you did the earlier work on selecting a topic and analyzing context, you began to think about the things you might want to say in your report. Now you need to develop your initial ideas into a coherent report that someone else will want or need to read. The next few sections of this chapter outline a variety of verbal and visual strategies that will help you meet the objectives of developing your topic, engaging your audience, and so forth. As in other chapters in this book, you will be working with strategies that appear in readings found in Reading to Write. The following discussions, along with the strategies and examples lists, will help you see how specific passages reflect strategies that you can apply to your own writing. You can always add to these lists of strategies by analyzing other reports you find interesting and credible.

Developing Your Topic

In writing a report, you must develop your topic thoroughly, providing credible, reliable answers to the kinds of questions listed on p. 149 of this chapter. To do this, you will begin by gathering a great deal of information, possibly more information than you will actually use in the final version of your report. How do you gather this information and keep track of it? How do you narrow the topic and formulate a thesis? How do you formulate and articulate your ideas in a way that will seem credible and important to your audience? How can you incorporate narrative into your report? The following pages provide suggestions for ways to address these issues as you develop your topic.

Gathering Information

For certain topics and audiences you may want to draw on personal experience. But in almost all cases, you will also need to consult secondary sources such as magazine articles, government reports, surveys, and Web sites.

Draw on personal experience. You will need to be selective in drawing on personal experience because it is not appropriate for all reports. However, references to personal experience often can give readers a sense of how an abstract topic affects individuals or can establish your credentials as someone who has observed the topic firsthand. One way to gather this sort of information is to keep careful notes of what you have observed and heard, perhaps creating scenes readers can visualize or reporting stories that give the topic a human face. You can also interview people who are knowledgeable about the topic, using their words to elaborate on key points in your report.

Use secondary sources. Secondary sources include magazine articles, government reports, surveys, and Web sites. From a technological perspective, perhaps the simplest way to find these sources is to do a keyword search on the Internet. But remember: although the Net can be a useful source, it can also be problematic. For one thing, information found there has a way of disappearing because both individuals and organizations frequently modify their Web sites. Furthermore, just about anyone can say just about anything on the Net, no matter how flimsy

❯ bedfordstmartins.com/
visualage

For an excellent example of a report based entirely on personal experience, see Bill Buford's "Sweat Is Good": click on **CHAPTER 3** ❯ **EXAMPLES**

❯ For more advice on locating and evaluating good sources online, see **Chapter 11.**

> For additional information about using library and Internet resources, see **Chapter 9.** For advice on evaluating information on the Web, see **Chapter 11.**

> For suggestions about ways to locate useful visuals, see **Chapter 8.**

their credentials may be. Be careful about relying on Internet material when you cannot find any information about the organization or individual who posts the information you are considering using. Also, it is a good idea to determine whether information from a given Internet site can be corroborated by other sources.

Somewhat more reliable sources of information can be found in your school library's online or card catalogue and databases. Listings in databases are usually taken from well-known, reputable sources—government or scientific reports, newspapers, and magazines. Though none of these sources is infallible, the materials your library has chosen to subscribe to are likely to be reliable. These databases will let you search for information on specific topics, and some of them (Wilson Full Text Select, for example) may let you print out copies of articles free of charge. Many campus libraries offer access to these resources via their Web sites, so much of the information is available to browse and print from your own computer.

While consulting secondary sources, be on the lookout for pictures or other graphics that will help you develop your topic. Also, look for information to incorporate into a chart, table, or graph. You will not be able to lay out pages (or screens) until much later in the process of writing your report, but keep a careful record of this sort of information. It may prove useful when you write the final draft of your report.

STUDENT DIALOGUE: SELECTING SECONDARY SOURCES

Writing in a Visual Age (WVA): How did you decide which sources to use in your report?

Margaret Tomeo (MT): I tried to use information that I kept finding in more than one source. And if I found something in only one source, I tried to find something to back it up. I was looking for sources that matched, that had facts that were agreed on.

WVA: How did you know you were asking the right questions?

MT: I was a member of the audience, and those were the questions I would ask. I just figured that since I was a female athlete, those were the right questions.

As you look for information to develop your topic, you can use a variety of strategies such as the following.

How to Gather Information

Strategies	Examples
Draw on different sources of information. Many reports draw on the work of authorities, people who have invested a great deal of time in thinking about or investigating a particular topic. Useful as this source of information can be, it should not be your only source. Consider drawing on your own experiences and on comments from people who are involved in or concerned about your topic.	*"Cigarette Advertising Expenditures" (p. 115) presents information from several sources: the Federal Register, a company that analyzes media, a newspaper, and a legal analysis found on the Web site of a law school.*
Incorporate different types of information. Quotes are often useful, especially if they are drawn from a variety of sources; so are statistics, narratives, case histories, eyewitness accounts, and your personal observations and experiences.	*"Slaves of New York" (p. 120) includes statistics from diverse sources: the New York City Police, the CIA, and the 1990 census. It also includes one illegal immigrant's account of her personal experiences, as well as photographs of the living conditions of sweatshop workers.*
Acknowledge different perspectives on your topic. If you are writing about a complex topic, different people or groups will likely have different perspectives on it. If your report is to be credible and informative, you will have to integrate different perspectives.	*"Bellying Up to the Bar" (p. 113) cites one authority who claims that "we're not making much progress" but also cites evidence to support the claim that "the picture's not entirely bleak."*
Look for ways to represent information visually. Pictures can convey both information and attitudes; charts and tables can present a lot of information succinctly and dramatically; bulleted lists and inset boxes can provide easy access to important information. Never use visuals just for decoration. Make them an integral part of the messages you are conveying.	*This may entail photographs ("Weapons of Mass Disruption," p. 127), line drawings ("ACL: The Curse of Women Athletes," p. 136), or charts and tables ("Cigarette Advertising Expenditures").*

❯ For advice on taking notes, see **Chapter 11.**

Keep track of information. When you've done a lot of research and are getting ready to write a draft of your report, it can be very frustrating to find that you remember only part of an important quote or that you aren't sure where you found an interesting statistic. To avoid this frustration, you should do two things. First, keep detailed notes of any personal experiences you want to include in the report. Jot down responses

❯ For more on keeping a working
  bibliography, see **Chapter 9.**

to questions such as the following: What did you see or hear? What did people do or say? What was the setting?

Second, create a working bibliography. At the very least, keep complete bibliographic information for each source you read. You should record the author's name, the title of the piece (article, book, Web site), and all the information required to locate the piece if you need to come back to it for more information (the URL of the Web site and the date you accessed it, for example, or date and page number of the magazine article). You need not record all this information according to the precise guidelines of the documentation style you're using, but noting all this information will save you time later. Also note the main point of each source and how it relates to your report topic. It can be especially useful to list the main questions the source poses and summarize the answers it gives.

Creating an Exploratory Draft

After you have gathered information—doing a good bit of reading, note-taking, and reflecting—you should be ready to write an *exploratory draft*

Working on the Assignment

Creating an Exploratory Draft

Before starting the exploratory draft, take a close look at the context analysis you completed, answering the questions on p. 151. Are there some questions that aren't completed very well? For example, are you lacking information about your readers' knowledge, needs, and values? Do you have a good sense of what your readers will expect in terms of content, both verbal and visual? At this point, complete your responses to the best of your ability.

Now read back over the materials you gathered, underlining passages that seem especially informative or that answer significant questions you or your readers might have about the topic. After doing this, don't try to write a formal essay right away; don't even worry about paragraphing or organization. Just set aside twenty to thirty minutes and write as rapidly as you can in response to the following prompts.

> ❯ "One point I want to make about my topic is _____." Relying on your memory of the information you gathered, elaborate on that statement as much as you can.
> ❯ "Another point I want to make is _____." Then continue to elaborate as much as possible from memory.
> ❯ "Another point is _____."
> ❯ "Another point is _____."

Keep doing this until you have used the full twenty to thirty minutes.

After completing this exploratory work, read or show what you have written to other students (either to a small group or to the entire class). Describe the intended audience to your classmates, and then ask them to answer the following questions.

> Can you think of an audience that would want or need to read a report on this topic?

> Do any of my points seem likely to be especially interesting or informative to my audience? (If so, these points may become the thesis of the report or the topic sentences of some of the paragraphs.)

> Can you think of additional questions my audience might want to have answered?

> Can you think of other types of information I might use to elaborate on the points I am trying to make?

> Can you think of places in the report where some sort of visual (a picture, for example, or a chart) might make my report more informative or credible?

After considering your classmates' responses, determine whether there are passages where you might use one or more of the strategies explained earlier to make your report more informative or credible. Use your classmates' responses to guide you in deciding whether or how to add to, delete, or modify information you have included in your exploratory draft.

that will help determine what you currently know and what you still need to find out in order to write an effective report.

As you begin to identify questions your audience will want to have answered, you can read with an increased sense of purpose. Your awareness of these questions should help you determine what sort of information to gather from various sources. Of course, you should make note of new information that may be important for your audience's understanding of the topic.

Narrowing Your Topic and Formulating a Thesis

Your exploratory draft should help you identify some of the main points you might make in your report. Now it is time to focus your efforts, narrowing the topic so that you can produce a credible, informative report. Like the authors of the reports in Reading to Write, you should focus on one or two principal questions that (1) are likely to matter to the intended reader, and (2) can be answered credibly within the limitations (of time, energy, and overall document length) under which you are working. Your answers to these questions will eventually become the thesis you develop in the report.

Narrowing Your Topic and Formulating a Thesis

It may take a while to determine the principal question your report will answer. As you read and talk with people about your topic, occasionally stop and try to complete these two sentences.

> "The main question that really interests me is _____."

> "The reason this question is important to my audience is _____."

Your answers may change a bit each time you ask these questions. But eventually you should find yourself becoming more confident that you have a clear, focused question, which will in turn lead to a clear, focused thesis.

For example, Margaret Tomeo didn't try to write about sports injuries in general. She didn't even try to report on everything that could be said about ACL injuries. After a good bit of reading and thinking, she focused solely on two closely related questions: *What are the causes of the injury? How can it be prevented?* Her answers to these questions led to her thesis: "As the number of women competing in sports continues to increase, understanding the causes of this common injury will enable us to help these athletes reduce their risk."

Margaret narrowed her topic and found her thesis by considering her audience and zeroing in on topics that were most likely to matter to those readers. You should probably do the same: think about what your audience knows and values, and identify the questions for which they will expect or need to find answers. Then use your answers to those questions to formulate your thesis.

As you go through this process, there is a good chance that your thesis will change. If that happens, you may have to gather additional information to support your new thesis. But if you do, it is also likely that your report will be better as a result.

Formulating and Articulating Ideas

Your exploratory draft will help you begin figuring out what to say in your report. But this draft is only a beginning point for the process of formulating and articulating the ideas you will present. During this process, your ideas will probably change considerably. These changes are hard to predict, but the reports in Reading to Write (pp. 112–143) suggest some strategies that can help.

How to Formulate and Articulate Ideas

Strategies	Examples
Notice comparisons and/or contrasts. One of the ways people understand anything is to see how a person, idea, action, or place is similar to or different from something else. It can be especially helpful to compare or contrast something that is new to readers with something they already know or care about.	*"Cigarette Advertising Expenditures" (p. 115) contrasts what cigarette manufacturers claim to be doing and what they are actually doing. "Weapons of Mass Disruption" (p. 127) draws a clear distinction between dirty bombs and nuclear bombs, highlighted in a sidebar.*
Classify. Although you must avoid stereotyping, an individual entity (a person, an object, an action) is always a member of a larger class of things. It can be useful to notice the qualities the entity shares with a larger group. It can also be useful to break your topic down into subcategories or subtopics.	*"Bellying Up to the Bar" (p. 113) divides the general category of binge drinkers into subgroups: males, females, and members of fraternities and sororities. The article then notes similarities and differences among the subgroups. These subgroups are also reflected in the table When the Party's Over.*
Notice changes or trends. Technology changes, and so do individuals, social groups, institutions, societies, and people's views of the world. Explore your topic's history to discover trends or significant changes—whether in the topic, the people associated with the topic, or people's view of the topic. Determine how much your readers need to understand about these trends and changes.	*"Cigarette Advertising Expenditures" uses a bar graph to show how cigarette manufacturers increased their advertising in youth-oriented magazines. "Slaves of New York" (p. 120) reports on a large-scale trend in patterns of immigration, noting that increasing numbers of immigrants choose to live in New York.*
Look for causes and effects. Chances are the question *Why?* will occur to your readers. Therefore, notice the reasons people give for their actions, and try to identify their motives. Determine if cultural, social, or economic forces are at work. Also consider the consequences or implications associated with your topic. If something happens (an action is taken, a law is passed, a discovery is made), what is likely to happen—or what did happen—as a result?	*Having noted an immigration trend that led to "Slaves of New York," Barnes gives two reasons why this trend is occurring: the "collapse of law enforcement" in New York City and competition among garment manufacturers.*
Notice problems and solutions. One reason people read reports is to find out what is being done to solve an important problem. Identify problems associated with your topic and find out what is being done to solve them.	*"ACL: The Curse of Women Athletes" (p. 136) explains reasons female athletes are susceptible to ACL injuries and then outlines exercise programs to prevent these injuries.*

Formulating and Articulating Ideas

It may help to think of the strategies for exploring and articulating ideas as questions to answer as you read or examine your own experience with the topic.

› What kinds of contrasts do you see between people and objects, between what people say and what they do, between what you expected and what is actually the case?

› Can you begin to categorize and subcategorize the materials you are working with?

› Do you notice any trends?

› Can you find any causes for the way people act or the way things are? Do people's actions have any surprising consequences?

› What are the main problems associated with your topic? Are you identifying any solutions to those problems?

If one strategy or question doesn't turn up something interesting, try another one. Also, don't rely entirely on your memory. Use your working bibliography or copies of key materials with important points underlined.

Periodically review your notes and other materials you have collected. Bring them all to class, along with your exploratory draft. Be prepared to explain—to one or more classmates or to your instructor—how this new information is helping you elaborate on or revise points you made in the exploratory draft.

› bedfordstmartins.com/
visualage

For a report that consists almost entirely of narrative, see "Sweat Is Good." Click on **CHAPTER 3 › EXAMPLES**

Using Narrative Effectively

Elements of narrative are likely to appear in many of the reports you read, listen to, or watch. Some narratives are straightforward and dry, as in the Methods section of a laboratory report, where writers list the series of actions they took in performing an experiment. But many other reports benefit from a well-told story, one that involves specific people engaged in a series of actions that lead to conflicts, a climax, and some sort of resolution.

How to Use Narrative Effectively

Strategies

Provide some background information.
You need not provide a complete history of your subject, but do include enough background to enable readers to appreciate the predicament faced by people in the narrative.

Examples

Barnes's narrative about Yu Li ("Slaves of New York," p. 120) begins with Yu Li's account of the difficulties she and her family encountered in trying to leave China for the United States. This background makes her experiences in the United States all the more poignant and ironic.

How to Use Narrative Effectively

Strategies	Examples
Tell readers about the setting in which the story takes place. This description often happens at the beginning of a narrative, but sometimes details about the setting are revealed as the narrative progresses. Mention those aspects of the setting that help readers understand the predicament or motivations of the people in your story.	*"Slaves of New York" does not say much about the physical situations in which Yu Li and her husband live. But it reveals that her husband sleeps on the floor of a restaurant, and we can probably assume that the basement in which Yu Li lives is as unpleasant as the "Bowery warren" described. These details about setting underscore Yu Li's predicament.*
Identify the important people in your story, especially those who come into conflict with each other.	*In Barnes's narrative, the principal people are Yu Li and her husband, who appear as both heroes and victims. Other people include villains and oppressors: the gangsters and "snakeheads" who exploit would-be immigrants, the factory owners, and the officials who fail to enforce labor laws.*
Explain the important conflicts or problems the people in your report encounter, and tell what they do and say to resolve these conflicts or problems.	*There are multiple problems and conflicts in Yu Li's story: the difficulties she and her family had in reaching the United States; the harsh working conditions they encounter here; the disparities between the promise of America and the reality of some immigrants' lives in America. Perhaps the most unsettling aspect of this story is that efforts to solve these problems seem futile; there may be no good resolution for Yu Li's story.*
Tell what people say, especially when their statements reveal a lot about their personalities, motives, or current situation.	*There is little dialogue in "Slaves of New York" except for the brief exchange in which Yu Li's husband asks why she doesn't work harder. Statements that are quoted (for example, "It is hard. We have nothing.") are well chosen to represent a given person's feelings or point of view.*
Give readers some insight into why people say or do what they do.	*The motives of Yu Li and her family are clear and consistent with the classic American dream: improving one's economic and social lot in life and maintaining one's family.*

continued

How to Use Narrative Effectively

continued

Strategies

Make sure there is a point to your narrative.

Examples

Much of "Slaves of New York" deals in large numbers and in general comments about the predicament faced by immigrants who work in sweatshops. The story of Yu Li and her family allows readers to understand these workers' situation in specific, personal terms.

Working on the Assignment

Using Narrative Effectively

As you read and talk with people, look for narratives that relate to your report topic. A narrative does not need to be lengthy or complex, but it should involve at least one person who engages in actions that involve conflict. You may or may not want to use direct quotations, but you should try to give some information not only about what happened but also about why people acted and reacted as they did.

Either find or create a narrative concerning your topic. Bring the narrative to class, and be prepared to explain how it helps you answer a question your readers are likely to ask. Also be prepared to explain how it might help you elaborate on, revise, or add to something you said in your exploratory draft.

Engaging Your Audience: Writing an Introduction

Any instructor would prefer to read a report that is engaging and fulfills some purpose beyond minimally meeting the demands of an assignment. Nonetheless, you and your instructors have an implied contract: you have to complete the assignment, and they have to read what you have written.

Outside the classroom, however, the rules of the game change dramatically. No one is obliged to read your reports or even glance at them. Occasionally, readers will pick up a report because they are interested in the topic. More typically, however, you will have to motivate your readers, giving them a compelling reason to pay attention. How do you write an introduction that accomplishes this? The reports in Reading to Write suggest two basic principles.

> Let readers see how your topic relates to what they know, care about, or need.

> Establish a conflict that matters to your readers.

Relating to Readers

> For a discussion of what makes a source credible, see **Chapter 11.**

The reports in the Reading to Write section of this chapter display a variety of strategies for acting upon these two principles. Here are three strategies that will help your own writing relate to—or develop common ground with—your readers.

How to Relate to Readers

Strategies	Examples
Provide background information from a source readers will see as credible.	*"Bellying Up to the Bar" (p. 113) begins with four references to Harvard—one in the subtitle and three in the first paragraph—in an effort to get readers to take seriously the claim that binge drinking is a real problem on college campuses.*
Include an easily recognizable visual. If this visual also creates a conflict, so much the better. But the conflict and other important elements of the picture or graphic must remind readers of something they know, care about, or need.	*Sometimes writers create visual images with words, but Tomeo ("ACL: The Curse of Women Athletes," p. 136) does it with a photograph of a well-known woman athlete wearing a type of brace that most athletes will recognize as symptomatic of knee injury.*
Mention an attitude or preconception readers are likely to share. Find common ground with your readers—some shared knowledge or value that can act as a common point of departure for what you say in your report, even if you then go on to challenge that attitude or preconception.	*"Slaves of New York" (p. 120) opens by referring to an attitude shared by many visitors to New York: autumn is a particularly "inviting" time to visit the city. (Some readers may also recognize the phrase "autumn in New York" as part of an old romantic ballad about the city.)*

Establishing Conflict

In addition to letting readers see how your topic relates to what they know, care about, or need, you should create a conflict that will motivate them to read your report. The following list illustrates several strategies for doing this.

How to Establish Conflict

Strategies	Examples
Use words or visuals showing something that conflicts with what readers want, value, or expect. The best way to do this may be through the use of photographs that depict people, actions, or scenes that readers will find startling or disturbing.	*The photograph above the text in "Bellying Up to the Bar" (p. 113) presents an image of college drinking that might be disturbing even to readers who have no objections to occasional social drinking.*
Tell a story about actions that conflict with what readers expect or that dramatizes a problem about which readers are concerned. This sort of beginning must be filled with specific, credible details; otherwise, readers may dismiss it as too sensationalist.	*"Weapons of Mass Disruption" (p. 127) begins with a scenario in which a bad situation rapidly becomes far worse than police and rescue workers expected. The reference to an "explosion and subsequent high-rise blaze" is alarming, but not nearly so alarming as the revelation that the explosion released radioactive material—a potential disaster that touches on readers' worst fears about terrorism.*
Provide background information that enables you to create a conflict. You might begin by summarizing what a person, group, or institution claims to be true or claims to be doing and then noting how certain actions contradict those claims. Or you might summarize what people (especially authorities) have long believed to be the case and then suggest that recent events (or results of recent studies) contradict these beliefs.	*The first two paragraphs of "Cigarette Advertising Expenditures" (p. 115) explain what the tobacco industry is supposed to be doing, and they cite one tobacco company's claim about what it is doing. The remainder of the report documents the conflict between what the companies are doing and what they are supposed to be doing.*

If the conflict is too strong, it may offend or alienate readers. But the right amount of the right sort of conflict makes them aware of questions or problems, which will prompt them to read the rest of your report in search of answers or solutions. The right amount or type of conflict depends on your analysis of the intended audience. What works for one audience might be inappropriate for a different audience—yet another reason to take care with your context analysis.

STUDENT DIALOGUE: RELATING TO READERS

Writing in a Visual Age (WVA): Why did you use the picture of the basketball player at the beginning of your report?

Margaret Tomeo (MT): I wanted the audience to know right away that they could relate to it.

WVA: Why did you choose this particular picture?

MT: This picture was really clear. In a lot of other pictures, the brace wasn't really the center of attention. Also, you could tell exactly what she was doing. The brace was a focus of the picture.

Working on the Assignment

Engaging Your Audience

> Look on the Web, in magazines, and in newspapers to find a report in which the first few paragraphs do a good job of engaging a reader's interest. What strategy (or strategies) has the author used to gain the audience's attention? Does anything about the overall appearance of the report seem especially effective? Can you say why these strategies make sense, given the topic and the context?

> Review—and, if necessary, revise—your context analysis.

> Bearing in mind what your context analysis says about the intended audience and purpose, write two different introductions to your report, each time using a different strategy or combination of strategies for relating to readers and establishing conflict.

> Bring your draft introductions to class, along with your context analysis.

> Show your classmates the introductions and the context analysis. Ask them to tell you which introduction works better, given your topic and the context.

> Also ask your classmates whether they can think of other strategies to engage your audience.

Creating an Appropriate Voice

Another important factor in engaging and sustaining an audience's interest is the voice you create—in other words, the attitudes, personality, and even the literal sound your words create in a reader's mind. Sometimes this voice may be detached or impersonal; sometimes it may have a very personal sound, almost as though one person were speaking casually to another. In all cases, however, your voice must be credible; you must sound (and be) well informed, fair, and thoughtful. Beyond this, you may choose to sound almost any way you want (assuming that the voice you create is appropriate to the subject matter and the context for your writing).

To create an appropriate, effective voice, you have to be aware of alternatives and choose wisely among them. Some choices involve wording; as a rule, if you can think of several synonyms for a given word, you should choose the one that connotes the right personality or attitudes. For example, the people who investigate automobile accidents might be referred to as *law enforcement officers*, *police*, or *cops*, depending on the attitudes you want to express toward the investigators. Other choices involve the content of the report and related visual elements.

❯ **bedfordstmartins.com/
visualage**

*For additional reports
on binge drinking,
click on*
CHAPTER 3 ❯ **EXAMPLES**

The Web site for this book contains two reports on binge drinking, one from an academic journal (*Journal of American College Health*) and one from a weekly tabloid (*Weekly World News*). The voice of the academic report is that of scholars, people who know a great deal about the topic but refrain from inserting personal reactions and make no reference to ways the topic might affect themselves or other people they know. The first page of the report establishes the authors' credentials by indicating their academic degrees and listing the universities with which they are associated. The first page also contains some statistics and a history of the topic, with footnotes citing academic sources from which that history is drawn. There are no personal pronouns, no pictures, no emotional language. The voice seems well informed, thoughtful, and sober— exactly what one would expect in an academic report of research.

At the other extreme, the voice of the tabloid report seems sensationalist, superficial, even a little hysterical. The report shows pictures of people drinking excessively. The only statistic cited ("At least 52 percent of college students routinely drink to get high") is one that seems very alarming, and the report contains no footnotes, no history of the problem, and no reference to the authors' credentials. The language is very sensationalist: the headline uses terms such as *booze* and *getting plastered* rather than neutral phrases such as *alcohol* and *drinking excessively*.

The voice of the newsmagazine report "Bellying Up to the Bar" falls somewhere in between the voice of the other two reports, having some elements of sensationalism but sounding more rational and informative than the tabloid report. You can get a sense of the voice of each report just by reading their titles.

> From the *Journal of American College Health:* "Trends in College Binge Drinking during a Period of Increased Prevention Efforts: Findings from 4 Harvard School of Public Health College Alcohol Study Surveys: 1993–2001."
>
> From *Newsweek:* "Bellying Up to the Bar"
>
> From the *Weekly World News:* "Booze Is Destroying Our Kids"

How to Create an Appropriate Voice

Strategies	Examples
Choose words that reinforce or imply the attitudes you want to convey.	*Word choice in "Bellying Up to the Bar" (p. 113) is appropriate for the writers' audience and purpose. They use the terms* binge drinking *and* risky drinking *to refer to students' use of alcohol. A term like* getting plastered *would create a more sensationalist, negative attitude, while a phrase like* heavy episodic alcohol use *would create a more formal or academic tone.*
Decide whether personal pronouns are appropriate. The use of personal pronouns such as *I, we, us,* and *you* can help establish a personal relationship with the reader. However, personal pronouns may be inappropriate in some situations: for example, if writers address the reader as *you* only in sentences that point out what the reader has done wrong, they risk alienating the reader.	*"Bellying Up to the Bar" avoids personal pronouns for the most part but quotes authorities that use* I *and* we, *creating a more personal voice. By including quotations that use a more personal voice, the report shows that the quoted authorities share a common concern with readers.*
Decide what sort of information to include (and exclude). Your attitude and personality are reflected not only in the questions you choose to answer but also in the kinds of information you use in answering them.	*Rather than providing detailed citations of scholarly studies, "Bellying Up to the Bar" describes a Harvard study in the opening paragraph and reprints selected data in a table. Also, this report is carefully limited in scope, commenting on the drinking of a specific group: students of college age.*
Use visual elements (pictures, charts, graphs, and so on) and a page layout that are consistent with the attitudes you want to convey in the written text.	*The photograph in "Bellying Up to the Bar" presents an unflattering picture of college students drinking; inclusion of such a picture seems to indicate that this report will not display a positive or even neutral attitude toward the subject.*

Creating an Appropriate Voice

What kind of voice have you created in the exploratory writing you have done thus far? What tone do your words imply? What does that tone say about your personality, your attitudes toward the topic, and your relationship to the intended readers? To clarify and perhaps revise the voice of your report, try the following activities.

> List some of the words and phrases you hope readers would use to describe the voice in your report. The list may include attitudes and personal characteristics.

> Check with a classmate and your instructor to see whether the voice you present seems appropriate in light of the topic and what you say in your context analysis.

> Consider whether visual elements might give clues to your voice.

> Ask someone (a classmate, your instructor, or a friend) to read a section of your draft aloud, and listen to the sound of his or her voice. Can you hear the attitude you want to create in the sound of this reader's voice? If you can, good. If you can't, look closely at your draft to see what words and phrases you need to change in order to create the voice you want.

> Ask someone to read your introductory paragraph(s) (aloud or silently) and then list the words he or she would use to describe the voice you're trying to create. Does this reader's list match yours? On the basis of what this reader tells you, decide whether you need to revise either your conception of the voice you want to create or your introduction. Or do you need to revise both?

Providing Structure

People rarely read reports just for pleasure, and they are rarely willing to follow along patiently, waiting to see where you may be headed or what point you are getting at. Instead, readers sometimes just look for pieces of information that answer their questions, confirm their suspicions, or fill some gap in their understanding of the subject under discussion. And even when readers do follow the writer's line of reasoning, they do not always read every word. Instead, they make predictions about what will be said next. Given these facts, it is important for writers to make their work accessible and to create clear expectations; that is, they need to give cues that will enable readers to find certain information and anticipate what will be said next. In addition, it is important to create a sense of coherence, establishing links between one paragraph and the next.

Making Information Accessible

Remember that readers will not read every word; they may instead look for specific information. The following strategies will help you make it easy for readers to find what they are looking for.

How to Make Information Accessible

Strategies

Use thesis statements and topic sentences. Often, thesis statements occur at the end of the introductory section of a report. In some cases, the thesis may also be expressed or implied in a title or in a caption that appears near the title.

Not all paragraphs have topic sentences, and not all topic sentences appear at the beginning of a paragraph. But for much of the reporting you do, it will be a good idea to let readers know what you are getting at near the beginning of each paragraph.

Examples

"Bellying Up to the Bar" (p. 113) asserts points in either the first or second sentence of paragraphs. One exception is in the second paragraph, which asks: "Are colleges doing enough to crack down on risky drinking?" The authors' answer clearly is no; many colleges are making only "perfunctory efforts" to reduce binge drinking.

Use headings that announce the topic to be discussed or the question to be answered in a given section of text. A laboratory report, for example, should contain headings such as Methodology, Results, and Discussion. When possible, however, avoid general headings like Discussion. Instead, use headings that inform readers about the points you will make in the following discussion.

Each section of "Cigarette Advertising Expenditures" (p. 115) begins with a heading that announces the topic discussed in the following paragraphs. Each section of "ACL: The Curse of Women Athletes" (p. 136) begins with a question that is answered in the following paragraphs.

Use boldface type and white space to highlight key points.

"Cigarette Advertising Expenditures" uses special type treatments repeatedly. In one instance, boldface type highlights the amount of money spent by Marlboro, the brand for which manufacturers have spent the most advertising money.

> For more information on using type and white space effectively, see **Chapter 8.**

Creating Expectations

Studies have demonstrated that readers often try to anticipate what a writer will say next. Consequently, you should provide readers with a structure that helps them form clear, accurate expectations. To do so, use the following strategies.

How to Create Expectations

Strategies	Examples
Use forecasting words or phrases. These terms appear near the beginning of a section of text and indicate the topic to be covered. They often appear in thesis statements or topic sentences. They may also introduce longer passages within the main part of the report.	*In paragraph 17, the authors of "Weapons of Mass Disruption" (p. 127) say they combined "experimental and theoretical data . . . to produce estimates of health risks and contamination." The next paragraph explains how the authors derived their data, and subsequent paragraphs estimate the health risks from different amounts and types of contamination.*
Ask and answer questions. Once a question is established in readers' minds, it creates the expectation that an answer will be forthcoming, especially in the form of new information that expands readers' current understanding of the topic.	*Paragraph 2 of "Bellying Up to the Bar" (p. 113) asks: "Are colleges doing enough to crack down on risky drinking?" The article goes on to describe the limitations and the successes of efforts at various colleges.*

Creating Links

Even though readers may not read every word of your report, they still will want to have a sense of flow, of how a given paragraph or set of paragraphs relates to the passages that precede and follow it. Here are two strategies to create links that will give readers a sense of flow.

How to Create Links

Strategies	Examples
Use transition words or phrases.	*Examples recur throughout all the reports in Reading to Write. They include such words and phrases as* subsequently, previously, on the other hand, similarly, *and* consequently.
Use words or phrases that refer to something mentioned previously.	*In "Slaves of New York" (p. 120), this strategy links the second and third paragraphs. The second paragraph discusses illegal immigrants. The third paragraph is linked to the second by the phrase "most of the illegals."*

Providing Structure

Bring to class a copy of a report that does a good job of making its structure very clear. Be prepared to show your instructor and/or classmates how the author(s) enabled you to see the structure of the report. After identifying strategies other writers have used, review your exploratory draft, looking for ways you might use some of these strategies to make the structure of your own report clear.

Concluding Your Report

Although your instructor and some of your classmates will likely read your drafts in this course through to the end, readers of other reports may not read your conclusion, especially if they are using your work as a fact sheet or a source for specific information. But even fact sheets can have conclusions, usually titled something like For Further Reading or More to Explore. Other types of reports will require something more, if only to keep readers from assuming you have gotten tired of the topic and decided to stop. One way of concluding is suggested in a time-honored piece of advice about writing (and oral presentations, as well): *tell them what you're going to say; say it; and then tell them what you've said*. That is, conclude your report by summarizing the main ideas you presented. This is a useful strategy, but it's not the only one.

How to Conclude

Strategies

Frame the report, providing further information or comments about a topic that you mentioned at the beginning.

Examples

"Weapons of Mass Disruption" (p. 127) includes a scenario (a hypothetical narrative) in which police and rescue workers respond to the detonation of a dirty bomb. The final section returns to this topic, describing in more detail the effective response to this sort of disaster. In "ACL: The Curse of Women Athletes" (p. 136), Margaret Tomeo also frames her report by mentioning the athlete, Tiffany Woosley, whose story began the report.

continued

How to Conclude

continued

Strategies	Examples
Tell a story that dramatizes your main point. People often find it easy to remember a good story. If you can tell one that reiterates your main point, you increase the chances of readers' remembering the gist of what you said.	*Having described the predicament of sweat-shop workers, "Slaves of New York" (p. 120) concludes with the story of Yu Li and her husband, who worked seven-day weeks and still had so little money that they couldn't afford to live together.*
Reiterate your main point, perhaps using a compelling quote.	*Yu Li reiterates the author's point for him. After explaining the difficulties she and her family faced in China, Yu Li concludes her story—and the report—with these words: "It was never this hard in China."*
Mention the implications of what you have said. Readers should not come away wondering, "So what? How does all this affect me or things I care about?" It's a good idea to anticipate these questions, explaining how readers can use the information you reported to solve or avoid problems that matter to them.	*After explaining what women athletes need to do in order to avoid injury, "ACL: The Curse of Women Athletes" concludes with the hope that "if we start now, we can greatly reduce the number of anterior cruciate tears that plague so many of our female players."*
Mention "good news" and "bad news." Summarize some of the important questions your report has answered, or reiterate solutions to significant problems. Then mention questions that still need to be answered, or refer to problems that remain unsolved or may arise in the future. This can be especially useful if you want readers to continue thinking about your topic.	*The end of "Bellying Up to the Bar" (p. 113) mentions some good news (binge drinking decreased from the 1980s to the mid-1990s) and contrasts it with more recent bad news (in recent years, binge drinking has begun to increase again). The authors cite one last piece of good news (binge drinking decreases after students reach age 22) and imply one last piece of bad news (binge drinkers might not "make it that far").*

 ## Exercise

Bring to class a report you find interesting and informative. Does its conclusion reflect any of the strategies identified above? If not, how does it conclude? What strategies are apparent in the conclusion? Be prepared to explain your answer.

Working on the Assignment

Concluding Your Report

Using a strategy or strategies identified earlier (or a different strategy from a report you have analyzed), write a conclusion for your report. Share your draft with some classmates or your instructor, and ask them to tell you (1) what strategy you used in your conclusion, and (2) whether that conclusion reinforces or extends the main point conveyed in your report.

Designing Your Report and Integrating Visual Information

By now you should have decided on the major visual elements—headings, images, charts, graphs, or tables—you want to use in your report. Now it's time to think about the overall layout—where these elements will appear on the page (or screen), how many columns you will use, and whether you will include sidebars (inset boxes), pull quotes, or bulleted lists. Be sure to check with your instructor to see what guidelines he or she has for the design of your report.

Review the questions related to reading visual information in reports (p. 108). Keep these questions in mind as you consider using the following strategies to tie together all the visual elements in your report.

How to Design Your Report and Integrate Visual Information

Strategies	Examples
Decide on the number of columns you will use. Check with your instructor for specific guidelines. If none are available, see the guidelines in Chapter 8.	*Readings in this chapter illustrate a variety of page layouts, using one, two, or three columns.*
Use headings to make your work accessible. No matter what form they take, headings must give readers a clear sense of the point being made or the kind of information they will find in a given section of the report.	*Headings can take several forms: assertions, as in "Cigarette Advertising Expenditures" (p. 115); brief phrases, as in "Weapons of Mass Disruption" (p. 127); and questions, as in "ACL: The Curse of Women Athletes" (p. 136).*

continued

How to Design Your Report and Integrate Visual Information

continued

Strategies	Examples
Identify a specific function for every visual element such as charts, graphs, or pictures. Remember, visuals are not just decoration. They should convey information and attitudes that are important to your report.	*"Bellying Up to the Bar" (p. 113) uses an unflattering, bold photograph to engage readers. The table in this report is there to answer readers' likely questions. In "Weapons of Mass Disruption," the picture of workers dressed to clean up radioactive fallout from a dirty bomb conveys an attitude and sense of danger. The second diagram of the ACL in "ACL: The Curse of Women Athletes" helps readers visualize what is being described.*
Make sure pictures are located near the written text they are intended to elaborate on.	*When Tomeo ("ACL: The Curse of Women Athletes") provides a picture of the ACL, tibia, and femur, she inserts the picture right at the point where the written text discusses these components of the knee.*
Make sure photos and other visuals are appropriately captioned.	*In reports for technical or academic audiences, adding a caption means giving a visual a number—"Fig. 1," for example. (See Tomeo's report.) In most captions for reports written in the humanities, you should add a label to the figure number, giving source information, explaining what the visual represents, and why its contents are important.*

❯ For more advice on using headings and inserting captions, see **Chapter 8.**

Working on the Assignment

Designing Your Report and Integrating Visual Information

Find an example of a report (from an article in a magazine or scholarly journal, a Web site, a brochure, a book, or a pamphlet) that has visual qualities you think might serve as a model for your report. Discuss this model with your classmates and/or your instructor, pointing out specific visual features and explaining why you think they might be appropriate for your intended audience.

It can also help to sketch out how each page will look, indicating (as in the following example based on a page from "Weapons of Mass Disruption") headings, large blocks of written text, and rough sketches of the pictures, graphs, tables, and so forth that will appear on each page. Again, you should be able to explain to your classmates and/or instructor why you intend to use the visual features indicated in your sketch and why you want to arrange them in a certain way. Designers call this kind of rough sketch a mock-up.

Finishing Up

If you have not already begun to move beyond your exploratory draft, now is the time to do so. The next step is not a final draft, but neither is it a rough draft. Instead, it is a review draft; it represents the best effort you can make at this point. After completing this draft, you will need to assess it carefully not only by critiquing it yourself but also by getting others' perspectives. This means that you will subject the review draft to a final review (from one or more of your classmates or from your instructor). Then you will use this assessment to make revisions in content, organization, style, and/or format.

Creating a Review Draft

In preparation for writing the review draft, look back at the context analysis you did for your report. Has your understanding of any part of that context changed? If so, revise your context analysis and keep your analysis in mind as you decide what to say and how to say it in the review draft. Also, look back at your exploratory draft. Do you need to modify any of the points expressed there? Are there any places where you need to add information that would make your points clearer or answer questions the audience is likely to ask? Finally, review your notes and working bibliography. Make sure that quotes and other references are accurate. Also make sure that each source is appropriately cited.

As you work on your review draft, examine the introductory and concluding paragraphs. Does the introductory material establish the voice you want to create? Does it seem likely to engage the intended audience? Does the conclusion reinforce the basic point you want to convey? Do your introduction and conclusion still seem appropriate for your audience

❯ For advice on documenting
sources, see **Chapter 12.**

and topic? If not, modify them by using one or more of the strategies identified in this chapter.

In addition, take some pains to make the structure clear. It might help to make an informal outline indicating your main points. You should also use the strategies described on pp. 169–170 to make your work accessible, create clear expectations for your readers, and link paragraphs or larger sections of text.

Getting a Final Review

Once you have revised the review draft to make it as complete and polished as possible, have it reviewed by one or more people. These reviewers may include a friend or roommate, especially one who has an interest in the topic. But you should also have the draft reviewed by people (classmates or your instructor) who understand the principles (analyzing context, engaging readers, and so on) that you have been working with in this chapter.

> Give the reviewer a copy of your draft, one he or she can make notes on.
> Give the reviewer a copy of your context analysis. If necessary, revise that analysis before giving it to the reviewer.
> Ask the reviewer to begin his or her response by answering the following questions. (1) What are the main points I am making in my report? (2) Given what I say in my context analysis, how likely does it seem that this report will be informative and credible to my intended audience?
> Ask the reviewer to adopt the perspective of the audience described in your context analysis and then use the following checklist in commenting on your work.

**Checklist for
Final Review**

1 In my context analysis, please highlight any statements that give you a good sense of the knowledge, values, and needs of my intended audience. (For an example, see p. 151.) Please indicate any statements that need to be clarified.

2 In my context analysis, please highlight any statements that give you a good sense of the circumstances, purposes, and expected format for my report. (For an example of a good context analysis, see p. 151.) Please indicate any statements that need to be clarified.

3 In what specific passages have I developed my topic thoroughly, especially by answering questions my readers are likely to have? What are some passages in which you have questions about what I say, either because my writing seems unclear or because you think my audience would disagree? What are some strategies (explained on pp. 155, 159, and 160) I might use to make my report clearer, more complete, or more credible?

4 What portions of my introduction seem likely to engage the interest of my intended audience? What are some strategies (explained on pp. 163 and 164) that might make the introduction more engaging?

> **bedfordstmartins.com/
visualage**
*To download this
checklist as a
worksheet,
click on*
CHAPTER 3 › WORKSHEETS

5 How would you describe the voice I have created? At what points does that voice seem appropriate, given my intended audience and the subject matter of my report? What strategies (explained on p. 167) might help me make the voice clearer or more appropriate?

6 What are some words or phrases that provide a clear structure for my report, making information accessible, creating clear expectations for readers, and indicating links between paragraphs or larger sections of text? What strategies (explained on pp. 169 and 170) might I use to make the structure of my report clearer?

7 Is the conclusion of my report effective? What strategies (explained on p. 171) might I use to make it more effective?

8 If the report includes photographs or other visual elements, how do they help make it informative and credible? Are there any points at which I need to add more visual elements? If so, what should they be—headings, pictures, bulleted lists? At what points do I need to add or revise captions for pictures or legends for charts, graphs, and maps?

If possible, ask the reviewer to talk with you about your review draft as well as make notes on it. Be careful not to argue with the reviewer, especially if he or she raises questions or disagrees with something you have said. When this happens, try to find out why he or she is disagreeing or asking a particular question.

Revising Your Report

Up to this point, you have listened to your reviewer's comments without explaining, arguing, or making judgments about the validity of those comments. Once you have a good idea of how the reviewer responds to your report, however, you should go back through your notes on his or her comments. Bearing in mind your intended audience and purpose, decide which comments are most valid. Then use strategies referred to in the Checklist for Final Review.

After resolving all the issues that need attention, proofread carefully and correct any typographical or formatting errors. Then submit this final draft to your instructor.

Taking Stock of Where You Are

Although you will find differences among the writing assignments in this book, there are also some important similarities. For example, you always have to analyze the intended audience, write an introduction that will engage that particular audience, and so forth. Consequently, there should be a cumulative quality to the writing assignments you do from this book. Each assignment should teach you strategies that can help you grow as a writer and improve your work on subsequent assignments. But

❯ bedfordstmartins.com/
  visualage
  *To download these
  questions as a
  worksheet,
  click on*
  CHAPTER 3 › WORKSHEETS

this will only happen if you make a conscious effort to assess your development as a writer as you go along.

    To help with this assessment and growth, continually review what you're learning and try to determine what you need to work harder on in the future. Once your instructor has returned the final draft of your work, think back over all the comments you received—from classmates as well as your instructor—and write out answers to the following questions. (You might want to keep these in a journal or a special section of a notebook.)

**Questions for
Assessing Your
Growth as a Writer**

- What appears to be my greatest area of strength?
- Where am I having the greatest difficulty?
- What am I learning about the process of writing?
- What am I learning about giving and receiving feedback on writing?
- What have I learned from writing a report that I can use in my next assignment for this course, for another course, or for work?

SAMPLE STUDENT ASSESSMENT

Here's how Margaret Tomeo answered these questions for the report she wrote on ACL injuries (p. 136).

What appears to be my greatest area of strength?

I think that I'm pretty good at gaining factual information and organizing it in a clear way. I think I also kept my readers in mind when I was writing the report so that the information appealed to them and was also important to them. My audience was very specific, and I think I did a good job focusing the paper on this audience and what questions they would want answered.

Where am I having the greatest difficulty?

Sometimes I had trouble because I knew what certain things meant so I assumed that my readers also knew what they meant. I needed to clarify or describe some points better and not make assumptions. I had trouble with the voice and tone in parts of the report because I'd jump from being personal to being informative. In my first draft, my paragraphs didn't flow together that well, so I needed to improve that. After I added some introductory and concluding sentences, the report flowed a lot better.

SAMPLE STUDENT ASSESSMENT

What am I learning about the process of writing?	*The process of writing takes many steps—even choosing a topic must be developed. Start off by brainstorming to find a topic to focus on. The process of writing takes a long time and many revisions. The report that you write may seem clear to you, but what is most important is that it is clear to your audience. To make sure of this, it's important to have as much feedback as possible, so get as many people as possible to read the report and state what they feel was done well or what could be improved on.*
What am I learning about giving and receiving feedback on writing?	*Receiving feedback is important because it allows you to clarify points that may seem clear to you but are vague to others. With the feedback, I was able to learn what points I needed to improve on. For example, I knew what intrinsic and extrinsic (in my first draft) meant, but my readers did not, so I needed to replace them with terms that were clearer. Also, I learned to make my paragraphs flow together better (better conclusions and introductions—helped entire report to flow). Also, I was able to see what I was doing well throughout the report so I know what to do next time.*
What have I learned from writing a report that I can use in my next assignment for this course, for another course, or for work?	*You have to keep a specific audience in mind so that you know exactly to whom you are writing. Answering questions about the audience helps focus in on what questions the report should answer. This will also help you define the tone and voice of the report. Also, having a specific purpose in mind is important because it helps guide and focus the report. You have to choose a topic that will matter to other people, not just you. When we brainstormed and wrote down topics to write about, some topics didn't have a specific audience, so they weren't easy to write about; the papers about these topics seemed to lose focus.*

Position Papers

HOULD PEOPLE DRIVE SUVs? SHOULD U.S. LAW BE CHANGED TO ALLOW THE SALE OF HUMAN organs? Should the government provide vouchers to help families send children to private schools? These are all questions that invite opinions—texts that describe not just where an author stands on a particular issue, but also why. It is not difficult to find this type of opinion. Examples abound in most print media: newspaper editorial pages and "op-ed" pages (literally, the page opposite the editorial page), unsolicited mail (from legislators, special interest groups, community organizations), books, and columns in newspapers and magazines. You can also find people presenting opinions, and the reasoning behind their opinions, in electronic media: on television news channels, radio talk shows, e-mail and discussion forums, and Web sites. In all these cases, the authors are trying to persuade you, to influence your thoughts or actions. At the very least, they want you to come away thinking, "Hmm. I see. That makes sense." More likely, they want you to buy something, vote a certain way, or approve of a particular course of action.

Identifying the Elements of Arguments

As is the case with other kinds of writing in this book, a persuasive argument requires *evidence*—details, statistics, quotes—that your audience will see as credible. But a good argument also requires answers to the following questions.

> What *claims* do you want to make? That is, what are the main points you want readers to accept?

> What *reasons* will your audience accept in order to make a valid connection between your evidence and your claims? What principles or values will you use to help justify your claims?

> What kinds of *appeals* are most appropriate, given your audience and topic? For example, do you want to appeal to their emotions? To logic?

To understand the connections among evidence, claims, reasons, and appeals, imagine you have received a ticket for parking illegally on campus, and you want to avoid paying a fine. Imagine, further, that the evidence in your case is clear: the time on your parking meter had expired. Even so, you don't feel that you should have to pay the fine. How could you justify that opinion? Here are some reasons you might be tempted to give.

"Other cars were parked illegally, and mine is the only car that was ticketed."

"I was only there for five (or ten, or whatever) minutes."

"I did not see the sign."

These reasons might sound good, but they might not work—at least, not if parking regulations at your school assume that all people who park on campus are responsible for their own actions. In that case, what other people may or may not have done is irrelevant. If the sign was there and you didn't happen to read it, or you ignored it for only a few minutes, those are not acceptable reasons for excusing you from paying the fine.

Is there any way you would be able to avoid paying the fine? Perhaps, especially if the parking regulations also state that motorists may not be responsible for violations caused by circumstances beyond their control. You probably wouldn't have to pay a fine if you could show that your battery had gone dead and you had to call someone (other than a friend) to come jump-start your car. A persuasive argument in this case would consist of the following three parts.

Claim: "I shouldn't have to pay the fine."

Reason: The Parking Office assumes that people should not be held responsible for actions that are genuinely beyond their control.

Evidence: A receipt showing you paid a mechanic to jump-start your car at the time and location where you received the ticket.

Putting together claim, reasons, and evidence, an argument against paying the fine might go something like this: "Campus parking regulations say that we shouldn't be penalized for parking violations over which we have no control. Here's the receipt that proves my violation was caused by a dead battery. Therefore, I'm asking for the fine to be waived." This particular argument involves what the Greek philosopher Aristotle referred to as an appeal to logic, involving factual information.

 ## For Collaboration

Working with one or two classmates, find two articles or advertisements—from a newspaper, the Web, or a magazine—that present an opinion. Write down the main claim each piece is making, along with a list of the reasons given to support each claim. Then list the evidence you can find to support each opinion. Bring the articles or advertisements and your lists to class for discussion.

To appreciate what Aristotle meant by an appeal to logic, compare it to the other two types of appeal he identified: the emotional appeal and the ethical appeal. If you were to make an emotional appeal, you would try to play on your audience's emotions, perhaps by saying something like this: "You know how tough it is for college students to make ends meet, and I'm especially hard up right now. I just don't know where I'll find the money to pay this fine." If you were to make an ethical appeal, trying to show that you're a person of good character, you might say: "I always observe campus parking regulations, so I've never gotten a ticket before. In view of my excellent record, I don't think I should have to pay this fine."

Each of these three appeals represents a way to respond to questions a reader is likely to ask when assessing someone's argument.

Logical appeals

> Is the argument reasonable?
> Is the evidence credible?
> Are the reasons valid?
> Has the writer anticipated and responded to questions people are likely to ask or objections they are likely to raise?

Emotional appeals

> Why should I care about this topic?
> Does the topic affect me personally?
> Does the topic affect people or issues that I feel strongly about?

Ethical appeals

> Do I trust the person making this argument?
> Do I detect any biases that make this person's argument seem weak or suspect?
> Does this seem like someone who shares my interests and values?

Readers may not ask all of these questions all of the time. You may, for example, be taking a stand on an issue they are well aware of and feel strongly about. Members of your audience may already know why they should care about your topic. But in much of the writing you do, especially for your college career, it's likely that your readers will need to see that your argument is logical and that your claims are supported with credible evidence and reasons.

Making Persuasive Arguments

A written opinion, or position paper, has to include three very specific components if it is to succeed as an argument that persuades an audience.

> It must clearly make at least one claim about an issue so that readers know what the author's position is.

> It must be based on reasons that appeal to the audience's logic, emotions, or ethical values.

> It must provide evidence that the audience will find credible, such as factual information, examples, statistics, quotes from authorities, anecdotes, personal experience, or textual evidence (information that is quoted, paraphrased, or summarized from a written text).

In addition, there are other components that are optional—they often strengthen an argument but are not always necessary. For example, you may need to include an explicit statement of the reasons that connect the evidence to the claim (if the connection between the evidence and claim is complicated or obscure, you will probably need to spell it out). You may need to include *qualifiers* that limit your claim's scope or strength. For most claims, you should anticipate and respond to *objections*, or statements of opposing points of view. Responses to objections—a *rebuttal* or refutation—are an explanation of the evidence (and perhaps the reasons) that contradict and discredit part or all of the opposition's point of view. (In some cases, you will need to make a *concession* to a strong opposing view, and then move on to argue other points supporting your claim.)

How do you decide whether evidence will be credible? What makes a reason seem valid? Do you always have to spell out your reasons? How do you know whether you're anticipating the right questions and responding to them persuasively? How big a role should logical, ethical, and emotional appeals play in your argument? Answers to such questions depend to a large extent on your understanding of the context in which people hear or read your argument.

Opinions in Context

Throughout your life, it's likely that you'll be asked to express your opinion on a great variety of topics. Some of these opinions will be fairly inconsequential, such as where to go for dinner or which movie to see. Other opinions will shape your life: how many children you want to have; what religious activities, if any, you want to participate in; what city you want to live in; what job you'd like to find; whether graduate school does (or doesn't) make sense for you. In most of these situations, however, it's unlikely that anyone will ask you to write or present your opinion in a formalized way. Your opinion is more likely to be expressed in conversation than in a written statement.

On other occasions, however, you may want to share your opinion with a great many people, or it may become part of some type of record. In these situations, you'll likely need to make a formal presentation of your opinion—including all the necessary components of a convincing argument—either orally or in writing. For example, you may want to express your opinion on a topic of civic concern, such as the rezoning of your neighborhood to allow for a waste treatment facility or the changing of speed limits on nearby highways. Or you may want to influence a decision at work or in an organization you belong to—whether to allow employees the option of flextime, for example, or whether to undertake a new building project. Throughout this chapter, we will refer to opinions in these contexts as *position papers*.

Over the course of your academic career, many assignments will require you to take a position based on your own reading and research, information given in lectures, and your personal experience and observations. You may, for example, be asked to present and defend your interpretation of a literary text or to take a position on a given topic and present a convincing argument in support of that position. Sometimes you will be asked to make your argument in an oral presentation, and sometimes in writing. In either case, you'll always need to think about the audience you are trying to influence, the circumstances in which that audience will read or hear your opinion, and the purposes you are trying to achieve.

Audience

As with all the other kinds of writing covered in this book, your success in writing a position paper depends to a large extent on identifying your intended audience and determining what its constituents are likely to know, believe, and value. It's especially important to understand what the members of your audience value—what matters to them, what they care about—for their values will greatly influence what they consider credible evidence and valid reasons.

For an example of how different values can affect an argument, let's say you think you need to have a car, but you'll have to get financial help from your parents to buy one. Your claim is that you need a car. What kind of evidence could you gather to support that claim? Here is a statement that you might consider using as evidence.

"It takes thirty minutes to get to the mall by bus and only ten minutes by car."

Assume, for a moment, that this statement is credible to your audience. That is, your parents trust you and are willing to take your word that it takes longer to get to the mall by bus than by car. Also assume that your parents know that car ownership is an important topic; they know it matters to you, and it also matters to them. How persuasive is your statement likely to be? That depends on the kinds of reasons your parents, as your audience, are likely to accept, and that, in turn, depends on the values they hold. Let's consider this statement in more detail.

"It takes thirty minutes to get to the mall by bus and only ten minutes by car."

This piece of evidence might work if your audience recognizes the value of saving time. In that case, your argument would go something like this.

Claim: "I should have a car."

Reason: It's important not to waste time.

Evidence: Having a car will save twenty minutes in getting to the mall.

Both you and your parents might agree on the value of saving time, but there is something else going on here as well. You are only going to save time with each trip to the mall. Whether or not this evidence convinces your parents that you need a car will depend on how much value they place on frequent trips to the mall. If you have a job at the mall or expect to get one, your parents may agree that it is important enough for you to save twenty minutes per trip that they will help you buy the car. On the other hand, if you go to the mall simply to hang out with friends, your parents might think that you should spend more time studying instead. In a case like this, they may believe not only that you do not need a car but also that you should not have one.

 ## Exercise

As you read the three statements below, figure out what the claim, reason, and evidence would be for each one. Then identify someone who might be persuaded by this argument. What values would this person have to accept in order to find the argument persuasive? What values might cause someone to reject an argument based on these statements?

> I need a car because the gym is over a mile away from my dorm, and I have to go there twice a week for phys-ed class.

> I need a car because a car would make it easier to go the beach (or the mountains) with friends on weekends.

> I need a car because my friends tell me that I have a better chance of getting into a fraternity or sorority if I have a car.

It's possible that the bulleted statements listed in the preceding exercise might not work with your parents. If so, what are some arguments that might work? That would depend on your parents, but assume, for a moment, that your phys-ed class is held in the evening and that there have been several muggings recently near the gym where your class meets. Since parents are likely to value the personal safety of their children, your argument might go something like this.

Claim: "I should have a car."

Reason: It's important to take actions that will ensure my safety.

Evidence: My class schedule requires me to go to the gym twice a week for phys ed; there have been a lot of muggings near the gym; there is no bus service to the gym, and the walk to the gym takes me through the area where the muggings have occurred; there is a well-lit, safe parking area near the front door of the gym.

 ## Exercise

To make sure you're comfortable with the terminology and structure of arguments, identify a value that your parents accept. Then construct a three-step argument that contains reasons and evidence in support of the claim "I should have a car."

What we're saying about parents, of course, applies to your effort to convince any audience. No matter who that audience may be, you have to think carefully about what is important to them—what they know, believe, and value—and then support your claim with reasons and evidence that are consistent with what your audience knows, believes, and values. In other words, strive to create some kind of common ground with your readers in order to get them interested in your topic and persuade them to pay attention to your argument.

Circumstances

As you try to identify your readers' knowledge, beliefs, and values, you will also need to understand their circumstances. For position papers (and for the assignments in other chapters in this book), you will have to figure out when and where the members of your audience will encounter your position paper and how much time they will have to read or listen to it.

You will also need to give careful thought to a few key questions. For example, has anything happened recently (at school, in the community, in the business world, in the political arena) that will increase your readers' awareness of this situation (or something similar to it) or make them more interested in this topic? To continue the car example, if your parents are already aware that there have been muggings near the gym where you have a phys-ed class, you may only need to remind them of this fact. If, however, your parents aren't aware of these muggings, or if they don't realize your class meets in the evenings, you may have to provide them with more detail or at least refer to some credible sources (stories in a local newspaper, for example) to show that you are not simply repeating unsubstantiated rumors.

You should also consider whether your readers will be likely to disagree with your opinion. Will they know of arguments others have raised in opposition to your opinion? If so, you may need to anticipate and respond to points that are likely to be made by people who disagree with you. Assume, for example, that your parents don't want you to have a car because they think that having a car was one of the reasons why your cousin partied too much and flunked out of school. In this case, you might need to show significant differences between your record and your cousin's: for example, that he or she was in more extracurricular activities than you are, that he or she was never a very serious student, and that your grades have always shown you to be a much more conscientious student.

Purposes

Even if you have participated in debates or written opinions before, your purpose in doing so probably had more to do with fulfilling an academic obligation than with actually trying to persuade someone to accept your point of view. When you write position papers in the future, however, you will most likely be truly trying to persuade an audience to agree with you. In such cases, it's important to think about why you want people to agree with you. For example, are you trying to accomplish any of the following purposes?

> To make readers aware of a situation
> To challenge readers' assumptions about an issue
> To respond to a point of view you disagree with
> To gain respect for your opinions
> To encourage support for your point of view
> To change readers' opinions
> To influence readers' emotions, perhaps by alarming (or reassuring) them
> To ask readers to respond to a situation
> To convince readers to change their behavior
> To ask readers for a specific action or decision

Note that this list begins with a limited amount of involvement from your readers (you just want them to know about something) and moves to a very specific request (you want them to do what you're asking). As your purpose becomes more like the entries toward the end of the list, your argument must become more persuasive. It is harder to get someone to take a specific action than to merely read about a topic, so your evidence and reasons need to be more compelling if you are to succeed in your purpose.

Visual Information in Context

All kinds of visual elements—pictures, headings, sidebars, graphs, and so on—can be important features of position papers. Photographs, graphs, and other images in particular can serve as visual evidence, making an argument in a way that words alone could not do. As a writer you need to determine carefully the kinds of visual elements that will make sense, given your subject and the context in which you are arguing for your position.

To anticipate your readers' needs in terms of the visual information you will include in your position paper, consider four basic questions:

> What should the overall look of the page or screen be? Should it include images?

> Is this overall look consistent with what the intended readers expect?

> Do all the visual elements on the page or screen help readers understand the evidence for my position?

> What does the visual information reveal about my understanding of readers and the topic?

You can answer these questions for your own position paper by reading a variety of other arguments and thinking about their page layout; images; and charts, graphs, maps, and tables. When considering the visual elements in a position paper, it is important to ask questions about their role in the overall argument.

> For more information on the effective uses of these visual elements, see **Chapter 8.**

Questions to Ask When Reading Visual Information in Position Papers

Does the layout (arrangement) of the page or screen make it easy for the intended readers to understand the argument?

> What kind of information dominates—visual or verbal?

> Are there headings? If so, do they give a clear idea of the position or evidence that will appear in the text that follows?

> Are there charts, sidebars (inset boxes of text), or pull quotes (highlighted quotations from the text)? If so, do they serve a real purpose, such as providing evidence or answering questions that readers may have?

> Are there variations in the size and style of type? If there are variations, what functions do they serve? Does type appear in color?

● **If there are pictures, charts, or tables, what sources are they drawn from? Do those sources seem credible?**

> What kinds of information are included in the pictures, charts, or tables? Can you think of significant information that is missing?

> Do the visuals contain any extraneous information?

● **If there are images (photographs, diagrams, or other drawings), what kinds of appeals do they make? Do they reflect logical, emotional, or ethical appeals? How likely is it that readers will recognize and appreciate these appeals?**

> Are the appeals made through visuals consistent with the appeals made in the written text? Are the appeals appropriate given the writer's audience, circumstances, and purposes?

> What viewing angle is represented? What impression does the viewing angle give the reader?

> What colors are used? Is there anything surprising or distinctive about them? How do the colors contribute to the readers' impressions?

> Is the image clearly explained?

> Can the reader find a clear relationship between the image and the text?

● **If there are charts, graphs, maps, or tables, how persuasive and relevant are they?**

> Can the reader easily see the point of a given chart, graph, map, or table?

> Is the chart, graph, map, or table clearly labeled and, if necessary, explained with a title, legend, or key?

> Is the chart, graph, map, or table clearly related to the text?

> Does the chart, graph, map, or table help readers understand the argument?

 Exercise

Bring to class a position paper that presents information in an interesting visual way. It might contain images (photographs, drawings), graphs, and tables. Or it might make special use of text (by setting it off with columns, color, pull quotes, or sidebars, for example). Consider the effects these visual elements create by answering the questions listed above. Then try to determine how these effects are created. Be prepared to explain how the visual elements generate a particular effect and how they add to the impressions conveyed through the position paper's written text.

FIGURE 4.1
Visual Elements in "New Roads Are Not the Answer," a Position Paper from the Web

● **Color** Red in title and graph evokes strong emotional responses, usually a sense of danger.

● **Graphic** Cartoon cars show problem; logo spaces letters to graphically illustrate the word *sprawl*.

● **Layout** Headings forecast content.

● **Photograph** Photograph includes information reminding readers of frustrating traffic congestion, while omitting details that might appear to limit the frustration to one driver.

● **Graph** Heading supports paper's position; source of information cited; elements are clearly labeled.

● **Caption** Caption clearly and succinctly restates the point of the graph.

● **Sidebar** Heavy, dark borders suggest serious, even somber, information; colors suggest traffic warning signs that drivers are to take seriously. Typeface makes information stand out.

● **Graphic** Serene natural scene illustrates goals of organization sponsoring position paper.

● **Caption** Caption indicates the source of information.

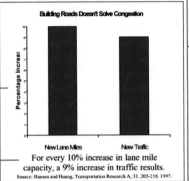

SPRAWL
HURTS US ALL

THE SIERRA CLUB'S CHALLENGE TO SPRAWL CAMPAIGN

New Roads Are Not the Answer:
Avoiding Traffic Congestion Through Transportation Choices

If You Build It, They Will Come

Traffic congestion has become an everyday reality for most Americans. Taxpayers are frustrated as more and more money is spent to expand roadways while most drivers still find themselves stuck in traffic. The average American now spends 443 hours per year behind the wheel. Why is this happening? It is called Induced Traffic. Studies show that new and expanded roads cause an increase in driving. Building new roads actually creates more congestion.

Building Roads Doesn't Solve Congestion

New Lane Miles   New Traffic

For every 10% increase in lane mile capacity, a 9% increase in traffic results.
Source: Hansen and Huang, Transportation Research A, 31. 205-218. 1997.

Wasting Time Stuck in Traffic

The rise of sprawling malls and decentralized housing explains the increased miles Americans have travelled in the last fifty years. Building more roads does not cut the amount of time we spend trapped in a car, and we must recognize that more sprawl and smog producing highways cannot fix the problem. Communities should consider the impact of induced traffic when planning their transportation future.

The Vicious Cycle of Induced Traffic

Congestion plagues a road, the road is expanded, and more people can now drive on the road. Public transit or carpool riders switch to driving, drivers switch routes and take longer trips, and congestion reappears at a greater level than before the construction. More traffic is dumped on local streets. Welcome to Induced Traffic. The short term benefits of increased road capacity result in long term suburban sprawl and reduced quality of life for residents. Roads in undeveloped areas soon attract new housing, shopping, and business centers. More people will now have to drive a longer distance in traffic to reach home, school, shopping, or work. Often, cities that spend the most on roadbuilding end up with the worst congestion.

Induced traffic immediately consumes 10-50% of new road capacity and 50-100% in four years.

Source: John Holtzclaw, "Induced Traffic Confirmed."
http://www.sierraclub.org/sprawl/transportation/seven.asp

SIERRA CLUB
FOUNDED 1892

EXPLORE, ENJOY AND PROTECT THE PLANET

● Sample Analysis | New Roads Are Not the Answer

Later in this chapter, the position paper "New Roads Are Not the Answer" makes the argument that building more roads does not alleviate traffic problems. The following brief analysis of one page of the article, shown as it originally appeared on the Sierra Club's Web site, will help you see several ways the questions for reading visual information can be applied to a specific position paper.

Many position papers use relatively few visual elements. For example, visual elements in newspaper or magazine position papers often consist solely of relatively wide columns of text and, as in the case of Ellen Goodman's piece on SUVs, a photograph of the writer. However, as "New Roads Are Not the Answer" illustrates, position papers may use a wide variety of visual elements that can make not only emotional appeals but logical and ethical appeals as well.

The layout here offers material aimed at convincing readers. Headings introduce material in each brief section succinctly, inviting readers to look further for the evidence to back up the heading's claim. In addition to the headings, three other kinds of visuals—a photograph, a bar graph, and a sidebar—break up the text and offer additional kinds of evidence for the paper's position. One of the most striking visual elements in "New Roads Are Not the Answer" is the color red, which is likely to evoke a strong emotional response, one usually associated with danger. In this position paper, the color red serves to link the warning implicit in the title with the startling statistic found in the graph labeled "Building Roads Doesn't Solve Congestion." An additional emotional appeal, found in the photograph at the top of the right-hand column, comes in part from the information the visual includes and in part from the information it excludes. The four lanes of traffic make it clear that readers are looking at a traffic jam on a major expressway. The closeness of the cars and the lit brake lights on several of the cars are likely to remind readers of the frustration most drivers feel when trapped in stop-and-go traffic. Maddening as this situation can be, however, the photograph does not show any of the facial expressions or gestures one might expect to

see when drivers are caught in this sort of situation. In this instance the omission of such details is probably a good idea. By taking a panoramic view that excludes images of individual drivers while including a large number of cars, the photographer makes it clear that the problem goes well beyond the annoyance an individual driver might feel in encountering a brief delay or small inconvenience.

Additional emotional appeals come from the sidebar at the bottom of the right-hand column. The emotional impact of problems associated with "induced traffic" is increased by the use of large, bold type surrounded by a heavy black border that is often associated with formal, often sad announcements—death notices, for example. The yellow lines that appear within the black border lighten the somber effect somewhat, but the combination of yellow and black often appears in highway warning signs—Road Slippery When Wet, for example—that are meant to be taken seriously.

Graphics at the top and bottom of the page also make emotional appeals. At the top, the cartoon cars and the sprawling typeface of the word *sprawl* graphically reinforce the idea that heavily traveled suburban roadways cause a problem. At the bottom, a contrasting graphic shows a peaceful scene from nature, with not a car in sight.

In addition to emotional appeals, visuals in this position paper also make logical and ethical appeals. Ethical appeals are evident in the relatively wide, two-column format that is usually associated with the work of columnists, writers whose opinions are likely to be highly regarded. Logical appeals come from the use of statistical data and from the inclusion of sources for that data, thereby enabling readers to verify the accuracy of claims made in the visuals. Both ethical and logical appeals are made through the clarity and simplicity of the graph in the left-hand column. Each bar is clearly labeled, and the caption restates in verbal form the information included in the columns of the graph. The information is presented in a direct, unemotional way that appeals to logic and, consequently, suggests that readers can trust the author(s) of this position paper.

Exercise › **bedfordstmartins.com/visualage**
Click on CHAPTER 4 › VISUALS

For practice in analyzing the visual information in another sample position paper, see the visual exercises on the companion Web site for this book.

Reading to Write

› **bedfordstmartins.com/ visualage**

For additional examples of position papers, click on
CHAPTER 4 › EXAMPLES

In your principal assignment for this chapter, you will write a position paper that argues persuasively in support of your opinion, either on a topic of your choice or on one selected by your instructor. Your argument will consist of not only the claim you want to make but also the evidence, reasons, and appeals that seem appropriate, given your audience and subject matter. If you have the opportunity to choose your own topic, be careful to select one about which reasonable people might reasonably disagree. You will probably need to consider objections or arguments your audience is likely to raise in opposition to what you say.

The following readings, drawn from a wide range of sources, are intended to help you see not only some of the different strategies that can be used in justifying your own opinions, but also different kinds of topics about which you might express your opinion. Each reading is followed by specific questions (Reflecting on What You Have Read) that will start you thinking about what is involved in arguing persuasively in support of your opinion. Also, at the end of each position paper you will find a Thinking Ahead prompt, suggesting ways a given reading might help you decide on a topic for your own position paper. The subsequent sections of the chapter will help you get started on your assignment, compose a draft, and assess and revise your draft.

Sport utility vehicles are among the most popular vehicles sold in the United States. Yet they are not without their detractors. As you read the following article, notice the kinds of appeals that are made in an effort to discourage the purchase of SUVs.

As a syndicated columnist, Ellen Goodman has her work published in newspapers throughout the United States. Consequently, she has to write about topics that are general enough to be of interest to a great variety of readers. Here, Goodman focuses on something that almost everyone in the United States is familiar with, but not everyone sees it in the same way. In presenting her opinion, Goodman relies on her personal experiences to argue against SUVs. Consider as you read whether you think it is appropriate to talk about an issue of national concern primarily in terms of one's own experiences.

SUVs Belong in Car Ads Only

ELLEN GOODMAN

1   For my second career, I want to write car ads. Or better yet, I want to live in a car ad.

2   In the real world, you and I creep and beep on some misnomered expressway, but in the commercial fantasy land drivers cruise along deserted, tree-lined roads.

3   We stall and crawl on city streets but the man in the Lexus races "in the fast lane"—on an elevated road that curves around skyscrapers. We circle the block looking for a place to park, but the owner of a Toyota Rav4 pulls up onto the sandy beach. We get stuck in the tunnel, but the Escalade man navigates down empty streets because "there are no roadblocks." The world of the car ads bears about as much resemblance to commuter life as the Marlboro ads bear to the cancer ward.

4   **All of this is a prelude** to a full-boil rant against the arch-enemy of commuters everywhere: Sport utility vehicles. Yes, those gas-guzzling, parking-space-hogging, bullies of the highway.

5   In this, the last gasp of the 20th century, one out of every five cars sold in America is an SUV. These sport utility vehicles are bought primarily by people whose favorite sport is shopping and whose most rugged athletic event is hauling the kids to soccer practice.

6   The sales and the size of the larger SUVs have grown at a speed that reminds me of the defense budget. In the escalating highway arms race, SUVs are sold for self-defense. Against what? Other SUVs.

7   As someone who has spent many a traffic-jammed day in the shadow of a behemoth, I am not surprised that the high and weighty are responsible for some 2,000 additional deaths a year. If a 6,000-pound Suburban hits a 1,800 pound Metro, it's going to be bad for the Metro. For that matter, if the Metro hits the Suburban it's still going to be bad for the Metro.

8   The problem with SUVs is that you can't see over them, you can't see around them, and you have to watch out for them. I am by no means the only driver of a small car who has felt intimidated by the big wheels barreling past me. Their macho reputation prompted even the Automobile Club of Southern California to issue an SUV driver tip: "Avoid a 'road warrior' mentality. Some SUV drivers operate under the false

illusion that they can ignore common rules of caution."

But the biggest and burliest of the pack aren't just safety hazards, they're environmental hazards. Until now, SUVs have been allowed to legally pollute two or three times as much as automobiles. All over suburbia there are people who conscientiously drive their empty bottles to the suburban recycling center in vehicles that get 15 miles to the gallon. There are parents putting big bucks down for a big car so the kids can be safe while the air they breathe is being polluted.

At long last some small controls are being promoted. The EPA has proposed for the first time that SUVs be treated like cars. If the agency, and the administration, has its way, a Suburban won't be allowed to emit more than a Taurus. That's an important beginning, but not the whole story.

Consider Ford, for example. The automaker produces relatively clean-burning engines. But this fall it will also introduce the humongous Excursion. It's 7 feet tall, 80 inches wide, weighs four tons and gets 10 miles to the gallon in the city. No wonder the Sierra Club calls it "the Ford Valdez." This is a nice car for taking the kids to school—if you're afraid you'll run into a tank.

Do I sound hostile? Last week a would-be SUV owner complained to *The New York Times* ethics columnist that his friends were treating him as if he were "some kind of a criminal." The ethicist wrote back: "If you're planning to drive that SUV in New York, pack a suitcase into your roomy cargo area, because you're driving straight to hell."

I wouldn't go that far, though I have wished that hot trip on at least one SUV whose bumper came to eye level with my windshield. It's one thing to have an SUV in the outback, and quite another to drive it around town. In the end, the right place for the big guy is in an ad. There, the skies are always clean, the drivers are always relaxed, and there's never, ever, another car in sight.

Reflecting on What You Have Read

1 What is Goodman's real claim in this article? How far did you have to read before you came to the claim? What do you think her purpose was in writing this column? Do you think she achieved her purpose?

2 In addition to her own driving experiences, what kind of evidence does Goodman use? Is this evidence credible? Why or why not? What kinds of reasons does this evidence reflect? Look back at the imaginary argument for buying a car (pp. 186–188). Write a sentence presenting reasons that would convince a reader to accept or reject Goodman's evidence.

3 What attitudes and personality (or voice—see pp. 242–243) does Goodman convey? Go back through the column and underline or circle the features that give you a sense of her attitudes and personality.

Thinking Ahead

Goodman identifies a fairly routine aspect of daily experience that she thinks constitutes a problem. Reflect on your own daily experience—at school, on a job, on a team, or in a club. Is there any aspect of this experience that in your opinion constitutes a significant problem? Is there an audience to whom you might express this opinion—especially an audience that might actually be able to do something to solve the problem?

Steve Sack is a nationally syndicated editorial cartoonist for the *Minneapolis Star Tribune* whose work also appears in such magazines as *Time, Newsweek,* and online in *Slate.* In this cartoon published in 2002, he asserts his position concerning SUVs. As you look closely at the cartoon, notice the ways Sack gives multiple cues regarding his opinion.

SUVs

STEVE SACK

Reflecting on What You Have Observed

1 Notice the person cleaning the windshield of the SUV. Is it safe to assume that he is the owner of the vehicle? Why or why not? Look closely at this person's face. What attitudes are suggested by the look on his face?

2 What reasons might Sack have had for drawing the license plate to read "GUZZLER"?

3 How many hoses are going into the gas tank? How does that number compare with the number of gasoline pumps? If you were Sack's editor, would you tell him to make the number of hoses equal the number of gasoline pumps? Why or why not? Would making such a change alter the type of argument Sack is presenting?

By her own admission, Ellen Goodman is writing a "full-boil rant" against sport utility vehicles. She doesn't like them, and she draws on personal experiences in letting readers know exactly how she feels. But not all topics lend themselves to this sort of approach. Sometimes writers avoid any reference to their personal opinions or experiences, presenting instead information drawn from a variety of sources other than the writer's experiences. But even so, opinion pieces can still express very strong feelings. As you read "New Roads Are Not the Answer," notice ways in which factual material conveys strong feelings.

THE SIERRA CLUB'S CHALLENGE TO SPRAWL CAMPAIGN

New Roads Are Not the Answer:
Avoiding Traffic Congestion Through Transportation Choices

If You Build It, They Will Come

Traffic congestion has become an everyday reality for most Americans. Taxpayers are frustrated as more and more money is spent to expand roadways while most drivers still find themselves stuck in traffic. The average American now spends 443 hours per year behind the wheel. Why is this happening? It is called Induced Traffic. Studies show that new and expanded roads cause an increase in driving. Building new roads actually creates more congestion.

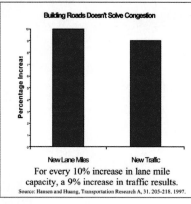

Building Roads Doesn't Solve Congestion

Percentage Increase

New Lane Miles   New Traffic

For every 10% increase in lane mile capacity, a 9% increase in traffic results.
Source: Hansen and Huang, Transportation Research A, 31. 205-218. 1997.

Wasting Time Stuck in Traffic

The rise of sprawling malls and decentralized housing explains the increased miles Americans have travelled in the last fifty years. Building more roads does not cut the amount of time we spend trapped in a car, and we must recognize that more sprawl and smog producing highways cannot fix the problem. Communities should consider the impact of induced traffic when planning their transportation future.

The Vicious Cycle of Induced Traffic

Congestion plagues a road, the road is expanded, and more people can now drive on the road. Public transit or carpool riders switch to driving, drivers switch routes and take longer trips, and congestion reappears at a greater level than before the construction. More traffic is dumped on local streets. Welcome to Induced Traffic. The short term benefits of increased road capacity result in long term suburban sprawl and reduced quality of life for residents. Roads in undeveloped areas soon attract new housing, shopping, and business centers. More people will now have to drive a longer distance in traffic to reach home, school, shopping, or work. Often, cities that spend the most on roadbuilding end up with the worst congestion.

Induced traffic immediately consumes 10-50% of new road capacity and 50-100% in four years.

Source: John Holtzclaw, "Induced Traffic Confirmed."
http://www.sierraclub.org/sprawl/transportation/seven.asp

EXPLORE, ENJOY AND PROTECT THE PLANET

Solution: Transportation Choices

Real solutions to traffic jams do not include building and widening highways. A balanced transportation program funds a variety of travel options that will provide people with more choices. The American economy added 30 million new commuters since 1980, and many have chosen to use public transit rather than drive.

Sprawl & Congestion: Long-Term Answers

- Increase funding for clean public transportation options such as fuel-efficient buses and light rail electric trains.
- Reduce funding for road and car-only projects.
- Increase funding for sidewalks and bike paths.
- Encourage Transit-Oriented Development to integrate public transit with housing and business.
- Increase public involvement in the transportation planning process so citizens' have an equal voice in their community's future.
- Encourage innovative incentive-based programs that encourage walking, biking, or car-pooling.
- Authorize zoning decisions that encourage mixed-use development.

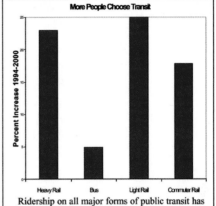

More People Choose Transit

Percent Increase 1994-2000

Heavy Rail · Bus · Light Rail · Commuter Rail

Ridership on all major forms of public transit has increased in recent years. Subways (heavy rail) and electric trains (light rail) saw the largest rise. Americans clearly want alternatives to driving.

Source: American Public Transportation Association 2000 Ridership Report

> ## 80% of commuters would prefer convenient public transit to driving.
>
> Source: Surface Transportation Policy Project, *Ten Years of Progress.*

Fight Pollution, Fight Congestion, Fight Sprawl:

More traffic, pollution, and congestion from new roads are not inevitable. Communities can plan a variety of transportation choices so residents aren't always forced to drive. Transportation policy can help enhance communities for the future and eliminate the need to build more roads.

FOR MORE INFORMATION about the Sierra Club's support for safe, clean public transportation or about the Challenge to Sprawl Campaign, please contact:
Melody Flowers,
Associate Washington Representative,
(202) 675-7915,
melody.flowers@sierraclub.org;
or Brett Hulsey, Senior Midwest Representative,
(608) 257-4994,
brett.hulsey@sierraclub.org.
www.sierraclub.org/sprawl

Experience a More Convenient Community with Travel Choices: Combining transit and development produces a mixture of land uses and easily accessible transportation options for all citizens, including bicyclists, pedestrians, children and the elderly. Visit www.sierraclub.org/sprawl/community/transformations/index.asp to see more about how transportation enhancements can transform your community.

Reflecting on What You Have Read

1 Sometimes people contend that if a text avoids references to personal feelings or experiences the text is more "objective" than a text that includes such references. How objective does "New Roads Are Not the Answer" seem to you? What basis do you have for your answer to this question?

2 Look closely at the scenes depicted in the two pictures in this position paper. How realistic do the scenes seem? How are you defining "realistic"?

3 Although this position paper never explicitly refers to personal experiences, are there passages that refer to events readers might have witnessed? Do these references add to the credibility of the piece? Why or why not?

4 Many places in the text (the phrase "vicious cycle of induced traffic," for example) seem designed to create a strong emotional reaction in readers. Do you think it is appropriate to evoke such reactions in discussing a serious problem faced by our society? Why or why not?

Thinking Ahead

This position paper questions what might appear to be a simple decision: If roads are too crowded, then the obvious decision is to build more roads. The problem, of course, is that important decisions are rarely simple. Identify some situations in which the seemingly obvious decision might not be the right one. What reasons and evidence (specifically, what appeals to logic) can you find that might persuade readers to change their minds about a decision they are confronting?

Organ transplants have become fairly common in the United States, with organs from recently deceased persons being donated to those who are seriously ill. Many people have come to accept these organ transplants as not only ethical but also essential for the health and well-being of our society. But not everyone agrees on whether the families of organ donors should receive payment for the donated organs. As a partial illustration of the ethical complexity of this issue, consider the following two contrasting opinions, one from the columnist Charles Krauthammer and one from the physician Jose Bufill.

The following *Time* magazine essay asserts that it's entirely appropriate to pay for organs. As you read "Yes, Let's Pay for Organs," notice how Charles Krauthammer, a columnist who writes frequently on ethical and social issues, recognizes his audience's potential objections by explicitly posing the questions that he thinks they might ask, and then answering those questions. See if you can identify any other strategies that Krauthammer (also a former doctor) uses to keep his audience from becoming angry or disgusted.

Yes, Let's Pay for Organs

CHARLES KRAUTHAMMER

Not from the living, which would be degrading. But the dead are a different story

Pennsylvania plans to begin paying the relatives of organ donors $300 toward funeral expenses. It would be the first jurisdiction in the country to reward organ donation. Indeed, it might even be violating a 1984 federal law that declares organs a national resource not subject to compensation. Already there are voices opposing the very idea of pricing a kidney.

It is odd that with 62,000 Americans desperately awaiting organ transplantation to

save their life, no authority had yet dared offer money for the organs of the dead in order to increase the supply for the living. If we can do anything to alleviate the catastrophic shortage of donated organs, should we not?

One objection is that Pennsylvania's idea will disproportionately affect the poor. The rich, it is argued, will not be moved by a $300 reward; it will be the poor who will succumb to the incentive and provide organs.

So what? Where is the harm? What is wrong with rewarding

people, poor or not, for a dead relative's organ? True, auctioning off organs in the market so that the poor could not afford to get them would be offensive. But this program does not restrict supply to the rich. It seeks to increase supply for all.

Moreover, everything in life that is dangerous, risky, or bad disproportionately affects the poor: slum housing, street crime, small cars, hazardous jobs. By this logic, coal mining should be outlawed because the misery and risk and diseases of coal mining disproportionately fall on people who need the money. The sons of investment bankers do not go to West Virginia to mine. (They go there to run for the Senate.) 5

No, the real objection to the Pennsylvania program is this: it crosses a fateful ethical line regarding human beings and their parts. Until now we have upheld the principle that one must not pay for human organs because doing so turns the human body—and human life—into a commodity. Violating this principle, it is said, puts us on the slippery slope to establishing a market for body parts. Auto parts, yes. Body parts, no. Start by paying people for their dead parents' kidneys, and soon we will be paying people for the spare kidneys of the living. 6

Well, what's wrong with that? the libertarians ask. Why should a destitute person not be allowed to give away a kidney that he may never need so he can live a better life? Why can't a struggling mother give her kidney so her kids can go to college? 7

The answer is that little thing called human dignity. According to the libertarians' markets-for-everything logic, a poor mother ought equally to be allowed to sell herself into slavery—or any other kind of degradation—to send her kids through college. Our society, however, draws the line and says no. We have a free society, but freedom stops at the point where you violate the very integrity of the self (which is why prostitution is illegal). 8

We cannot allow live kidneys to be sold at market. It would produce a society in which the lower orders are literally cut up to serve as spare parts for the upper. No decent society can permit that. 9

But kidneys from the dead are another matter entirely. There is a distinction between strip-mining a live person and strip-mining a dead one. To be crude about it, whereas a person is not a commodity, a dead body can be. Yes, it is treated with respect (which is why humans bury their dead). But it is not inviolable. It does not warrant the same reverence as that accorded a living soul. 10

The Pennsylvania program is not just justified, it is too timid. It seeks clean hands by paying third parties—the funeral homes—rather than giving cash directly to the relatives. Why not pay them directly? And why not $3,000 instead of $300? That might even address the rich/poor concern: after all, $3,000 is real money, even for bankers and lawyers. 11

The Pennsylvania program does cross a line. But not all slopes are slippery. There is a new line to be drawn, a very logical one: rewards for organs, yes—but not from the living. 12

The Talmud speaks of establishing a "fence" around the law, making restrictions that may not make sense in and of themselves but that serve to keep one away from more serious violations. (For example, because one is not allowed to transact with money on the Sabbath, one is not allowed even to touch money on the Sabbath.) The prohibition we have today—no selling of *any* organs, from the living or the dead—is a fence against the commoditization of human parts. Laudable, but a fence too far. We need to move the fence in and permit incentive payments for organs from the dead. 13

Why? Because there are 62,000 people desperately clinging to life, some of whom will die if we don't have the courage to move the moral line—and hold it. 14

Reflecting on What You Have Read

1 One strategy this article uses to engage the audience is an unusual visual. Is the visual better than a more realistic image of a body? Why or why not?

2 The author supports his argument by reference in paragraph 13 to the Talmud—an ancient collection of Jewish laws that is still consulted and respected today. Why do you think the author includes this reference?

3 The final paragraph of this essay appeals to readers' emotions. The author wants us to feel sympathy and change the law to save people's lives. Identify sections in which Krauthammer uses the other two types of appeals, to logic and ethics, to support his argument.

4 What circumstance prompted Krauthammer to write this essay and would prompt readers of *Time* magazine to read it?

Jose A. Bufill, author of the *Chicago Tribune* article below, is a medical oncologist—a physician who specializes in the treatment of cancer. Our society gives a great deal of authority to medical practitioners, so knowing that the writer is a physician adds instant credibility to an article dealing with the human body. However, the commentary itself does not rely on Bufill's medical knowledge. Rather, it poses an ethical question that doesn't yet have an answer. As you read the article, think about how the author's credentials affect your response.

Human Organ Donation: Gift or Graft?

JOSE A. BUFILL

1 A few days ago, while making rounds at a local hospital I chanced upon the pictures of two children tacked to a bulletin board in the intensive care unit.

One photo showed a despondent, jaundiced infant with a huge, fluid-filled belly and limp, unsettled limbs stretched out in every direction. The other showed a healthy baby beaming as he grasped his foot with his right hand and a toy with his left, as if trying to decide which to chew on first. Only after reading the note next to the photos did I realize that both were images of the same child. His mother sent the pictures with a letter thanking the hospital staff for their role in obtaining a donor liver for her son. "Thank you for giving our son back to us," she wrote. A 2 liver transplant was their only hope, and in this case, the benefit was nothing short of spectacular, clearly a gift of life.

Tissue obtained from hu- 3 mans—both living and dead—has proved to be life-saving and life-enhancing. Despite campaigns to improve public and professional awareness of the benefits of donation, the sharp upswing in demand for human organs for transplantation has not been accompanied by a corresponding increase in supply. While solutions—of both the carrot and the stick variety—have been offered to reverse the donor dearth, none has proven particularly successful, and the unmet demand for organs has fostered commercialization and, occasionally, exploitation of donors and their families. Pennsylvania, for example, recently became the first state to offer relatives of deceased people, prospective donors, financial incentives to give up the bodies of their loved ones. Documentation of paid or coerced donations from the poor of developing countries and citizens of totalitarian regimes is on the rise. In the affluent west, "market-based" organ procurement ranks among the more creative approaches that have been proposed, but is little more than a euphemism for buying and selling of body parts. Prospective "organ vendors" could "opt-in" to an organ or tissue "futures market." After their deaths, their estates would share in the substantial financial benefits currently enjoyed by a few for-profit tissue brokers. The concept of "rewarded gifting"—an oblique, contradictory term concocted to blunt the funny aftertaste that comes from knowing you've just put your innards up for sale—is unlikely to gain wide acceptance.

Before organ transplantation was possible, laws regarding disposition of a 4 dead person's body made it clear that executors of an estate could not make it an item of commerce. The reason? The body was not considered "property" in the legal sense, and therefore not a part of the person's estate. As transplantation developed into a therapeutic medical procedure, living organs from dead donors acquired value, and laws were adapted

to fit the new reality. Under the Uniform Anatomical Gift Act, which regulates procurement and distribution of human organs for medical purposes, it still is illegal to sell the dead body or its parts, but not to give them away. So some non-profit procurement groups pitch donation to surviving family members, appealing to their altruism, then charge hefty processing fees to for-profit distributors. At times, the same people run both operations. The problem is that these organizations blur the distinction between giving and selling.

Lewis Hyde, in his book 5 "The Gift: Imagination and the Erotic Life of Property," points to the existence of two "economies" operating in human relations. One is the "market economy," where commodities are valued, bought, and sold in a calculated exchange. The other is the "gift economy," where goods are given freely without calculation. Gifts cannot be purchased or traded, only bestowed on one person by another. Gifts are not capital. In a sense, the practice of organ transplantation today occupies the intersection of these two economies: one man's gift becomes another man's capital.

On the one hand, the 6 costs incurred by harvesting, processing, and transporting organs should in justice be covered, and some would argue that a reasonable profit may legitimately be made in the process. On the other hand, the organ itself, the generosity of the donor's family, and the life that is prolonged are values that resist an economic paradigm. The mother of the child in the photos came to understand that life is the ultimate gift. It is bestowed, not taken, made or earned, and it is a gift of incalculable value.

The industrial age we are 7 quickly leaving behind was characterized by the conflict of capital and labor. As the new era of biotechnology begins, the new dialectic may well be defined by the dichotomy of commodity and gift. Advances in biotechnology that allow us to manipulate human life force us to continue to put a price tag on the priceless, to confuse gift and commodity, people and property. The tension created by these contrasting values may introduce original and unexpected notions of value and wealth. We may discover in time that we have much to gain by giving away what never really belonged to us.

Reflecting on What You Have Read

1. Although this article doesn't have a striking visual like the Krauthammer article does, the opening paragraphs use a brief narrative to create a mental image that is, perhaps, even more striking than an actual visual. How does the narrative engage the audience? What are some of the characteristics of an audience that would be engaged by such a narrative? In other words, what assumptions about the audience has Bufill made that he tries to appeal to in the opening paragraphs?

2. What is Bufill's purpose in writing this article? What does he think people should do in response to the issue of organ donation? What kind of evidence does he use to try to persuade them?

3. Bufill doesn't explicitly answer the question posed in the title of this article, but the reader gets a sense of where his sympathies lie. How does Bufill demonstrate an understanding of both sides of this issue? Which side do you think he supports? Cite specific passages to justify your opinion.

Thinking Ahead

Organ transplants are just one of many relatively recent developments in medicine, and the issue of paying for organs is just one of many controversial issues associated with this field. Another is cloning. Are there any circumstances in which you think cloning of human tissue might be justified? Another controversial issue is the matter of how we pay for health care. Are health maintenance organizations (HMOs) the best way of providing health-care coverage? For other topic ideas, take a quick look through the science or health sections of popular newsmagazines. When you find a recent development that interests you, do a search of your library's databases or use a search engine such as Google or Alta Vista; you'll quickly find out whether this topic touches upon any controversial issues you might want to write about.

Vouchers are a means by which state or local governments provide money that parents can use to meet the costs of sending their children to private elementary and secondary schools. Should governments do this? Is it an appropriate use of public money? Will it help students obtain a better education? The Anti-Defamation League, a civil rights agency devoted to fighting anti-Semitism and other forms of bigotry, publishes reports and other materials defending civil rights. According to the following essay, which was posted on the Web site of the Anti-Defamation League (www.adl.org) in 2001, the answer to these questions is no. Further, this essay argues, school vouchers will also harm public schools. As you read, notice the kinds of evidence and reasons used in support of the argument. Also think of the kinds of evidence and reasons that might be used to support a contradictory point of view.

Address [   ] ▾ Go

SCHOOL VOUCHERS: THE WRONG CHOICE FOR PUBLIC EDUCATION

Anti-Defamation League

Introduction

Most Americans believe that improving our system of education should be a top priority for government at the local, state, and Federal levels. Legislators, school boards, education professionals,  parent groups, and community organizations are attempting to implement innovative ideas to rescue children from failing school systems, particularly in inner-city neighborhoods. Many such groups champion voucher programs. The standard program proposed in dozens of states across the country would distribute monetary vouchers (typically valued between $2,500–$5,000) to parents of school-age children, usually in troubled inner-city school districts. Parents could then use the vouchers towards the cost of tuition at private schools—including those dedicated to religious indoctrination.

1

Superficially, school vouchers might seem a relatively benign way to increase the options poor parents have for educating their children. In fact, vouchers pose a serious threat to values that are vital to the health of American democracy. These programs subvert the constitutional principle of separation of church and state and threaten to undermine our system of public education.

2

Vouchers Are Constitutionally Suspect

Proponents of vouchers are asking Americans to do something contrary to the very ideals upon which this country was founded. Thomas Jefferson, one of the architects of religious freedom in

3

Address [   ] ▼ ⇥ Go

America, said, "To compel a man to furnish contributions of money for the propagation of opinions which he disbelieves . . . is sinful and tyrannical." Yet voucher programs would do just that; they would force citizens—Christians, Jews, Muslims, and atheists—to pay for the religious indoctrination of schoolchildren at schools with narrow parochial agendas. In many areas, 80 percent of vouchers would be used in schools whose central mission is religious training. In most such schools, religion permeates the classroom, the lunchroom, even the football practice field. Channeling public money to these institutions flies in the face of the constitutional mandate of separation of church and state.

Supreme Court precedent supports this view. Over 50 years ago, the High Court said that the Establishment Clause requires that "[n]o tax in any amount large or small . . . be levied to support any religious activities or institutions." In 1997, the Court refused to abandon this principle, reaffirming the proposition that the government may not fund the "inculcation of religious beliefs." The Supreme Court has also held unconstitutional government programs that have the effect of advancing religion or of excessively entangling government with religion.   4

While the High Court has not yet heard a case on vouchers, it has struck down education programs that allow parents of parochial school students to recover a portion of their educational expenses from the state. And the Court has found unconstitutional any government aid that accrues to parochial schools in a way that might assist those schools in their sectarian missions. For example, it has held unconstitutional programs in which the state paid for certain secular instruction taking place in pervasively sectarian schools when such instruction was provided by the regular employees of those schools. Federal appeals courts have even prohibited the government from lending instructional materials to parochial schools. By subsidizing the tuition paid to schools dedicated to religious indoctrination, voucher programs violate the separation of church and state.   5

Still, the Constitution leaves substantial room for government programs that result in indirect benefits to religious institutions. For example, the Court has upheld programs that allow parents of children who attend sectarian schools to deduct the cost of tuition from their total income for tax purposes. Further, the Court has not struck down programs like the G.I. Bill, which pays the educational expenses of veterans of the armed forces even if they attend pervasively sectarian universities or divinity schools. These programs, though, are a far cry from the voucher initiatives that would direct public schoolchildren—and tax revenue earmarked for public education—to overwhelmingly religious institutions.   6

Vouchers Undermine Public Schools

Implementation of voucher programs sends a clear message that we are giving up on public education. Undoubtedly, vouchers would help some students. But the glory of the American system of public education is that it is for *all* children, regardless of their religion, their academic talents, or their ability to pay a fee. This policy of inclusiveness has made public schools the backbone of American democracy.   7

🌐 Internet

Address

Private schools are allowed to discriminate on a variety of grounds. These institutions regularly reject applicants because of low achievement, discipline problems, and sometimes for no reason at all. Further, some private schools promote agendas antithetical to the American ideal. Under a system of vouchers, it may be difficult to prevent schools run by extremist groups like the Nation of Islam or the Ku Klux Klan from receiving public funds to subsidize their racist and anti-Semitic agendas. Indeed, the proud legacy of *Brown v. Board of Education* may be tossed away as tax dollars are siphoned off to deliberately segregated schools. 8

Proponents of vouchers argue that these programs would allow poor students to attend good schools previously only available to the middle class. The facts tell a different story. A $2,500 voucher supplement may make the difference for some families, giving them just enough to cover the tuition at a private school (with some schools charging over $10,000 per year, they would still have to pay several thousand dollars). But voucher programs offer nothing of value to families who cannot come up with the rest of the money to cover tuition costs. 9

In many cases, voucher programs will offer students the choice between attending their current public school or attending a school run by the local church. Not all students benefit from a religious school atmosphere—even when the religion being taught is their own. For these students, voucher programs offer only one option: to remain in a public school that is likely to deteriorate even further. 10

As our country becomes increasingly diverse, the public school system stands out as an institution that unifies Americans. Under voucher programs, our educational system—and our country—would become even more Balkanized than it already is. With the help of taxpayers' dollars, private schools would be filled with well-to-do and middle-class students and a handful of the best, most motivated students from inner cities. Some public schools would be left with fewer dollars to teach the poorest of the poor and other students who, for one reason or another, were not private school material. Such a scenario can hardly benefit public education. 11

Finally, as an empirical matter, reports on the effectiveness of voucher programs have been mixed. Initial reports on Cleveland's voucher program, published by the American Federation of Teachers, suggest that it has been less effective than proponents argue. Milwaukee's program has resulted in a huge budget shortfall, leaving the public schools scrambling for funds. While some studies suggest that vouchers are good for public schools, there is, as yet, little evidence that they ultimately improve the quality of public education for those who need it most. 12

Vouchers Are Not Universally Popular

When offered the opportunity to vote on voucher-like programs, the public has consistently rejected them; voters in 19 states have rejected such proposals in referendum ballots. In the November 1998 election, for example, Colorado voters rejected a proposed constitutional amendment that would have allowed parochial schools to receive public funds through a complicated tuition tax-credit 13

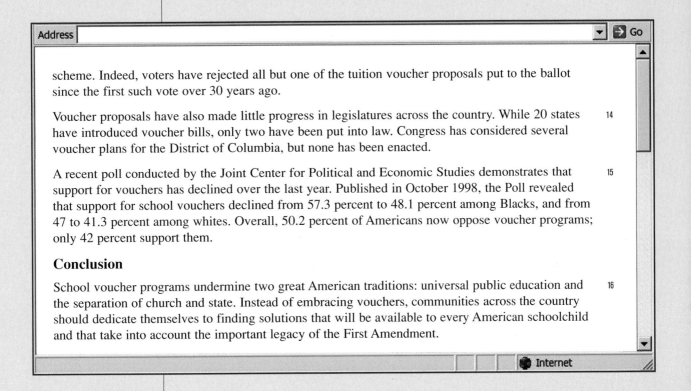

Address [   ] ▼ ➡ Go

scheme. Indeed, voters have rejected all but one of the tuition voucher proposals put to the ballot since the first such vote over 30 years ago.

Voucher proposals have also made little progress in legislatures across the country. While 20 states have introduced voucher bills, only two have been put into law. Congress has considered several voucher plans for the District of Columbia, but none has been enacted.   14

A recent poll conducted by the Joint Center for Political and Economic Studies demonstrates that support for vouchers has declined over the last year. Published in October 1998, the Poll revealed that support for school vouchers declined from 57.3 percent to 48.1 percent among Blacks, and from 47 to 41.3 percent among whites. Overall, 50.2 percent of Americans now oppose voucher programs; only 42 percent support them.   15

Conclusion

School voucher programs undermine two great American traditions: universal public education and the separation of church and state. Instead of embracing vouchers, communities across the country should dedicate themselves to finding solutions that will be available to every American schoolchild and that take into account the important legacy of the First Amendment.   16

● Internet

Reflecting on What You Have Read

1   This position paper begins by summarizing views of those who would disagree with the point that is made later in the essay. Do you think beginning in this manner is a good idea? Why or why not?

2   The claim is very easy to spot: it's in the title. What evidence does the author include to support the claim? What reasons connect the evidence to the claim? How persuasive do you find the evidence and reasons?

3   How would you characterize the voice (the attitudes and personality) reflected in this article? Identify specific passages in which you recognize this voice. What does it reveal about the writer's assumptions about the audience?

4   Under the heading "Vouchers Undermine Public Schools," the last sentence of paragraph 8 states that the use of vouchers could result in

public money being "siphoned off to deliberately segregated schools."
Do you find the reasons given in this paragraph persuasive? Why or
why not?

5   On the basis of what you have read early in this chapter about ethical,
emotional, and logical appeals, what kinds of appeals are being made
in this essay? What are the passages in which these appeals are clearest?

**Thinking
Ahead**

The implementation of school vouchers is just one example of a controversial government policy that can have immediate practical implications for
families such as yours. What are some other controversial policies that
have such implications? Can you think of an audience that does not share
your opinion on such a policy but that might be willing to listen to an
informed opinion on the topic?

The topic of gun control is so familiar and emotionally charged that it is difficult to write about thoughtfully or originally. Many people have such fixed ideas about the issue that it's virtually impossible to change their minds on it. But that's exactly what Fred LeBrun tries to do in the following position paper. LeBrun is a hunter, and he writes a column on the outdoors for the Albany, New York, *Times Union*, which is widely read by hunters and other handgun owners in the region where the newspaper is published. As you read this piece, notice how LeBrun creates common ground with his readers in the first five paragraphs and then moves to a new and perhaps unexpected position in the paragraph beginning "The verdict is so far off the wall."

Up in Arms over Decision

FRED LEBRUN

1 When it comes to the way courts and juries do things in New York, there has always been the upstate way, the downstate way, and Brooklyn.

Brooklyn's otherness was confirmed last week when a jury in federal court there returned a $560,000 liability award against 15 handgun manufacturers for the harm done to seven victims. The award was actually to just one victim, Steven Fox, 19, the only survivor among the seven.

On its face, what the jury did was about as daffy as it gets. They bought the notion, pushed by the anti-gun lobby, that the makers of legally sold guns ought to be held to some degree responsible for illegal acts done with them.

2 Immediately the vision comes to mind of ski manufacturers being held responsible for broken legs, ice skate makers liable for drownings on thin ice, and so on. The slippery slope plunges into the absurd for the lay mind in extending the product liability from this award. In reality, though, it is likely that this verdict will be tossed out because it is remarkably ridiculous, even for Brooklyn. Remarkable because in six of the seven shootings that comprise the Brooklyn case, the actual gun used was never recovered, so who knows the manufacturer[?]

3 The anti-gun crowd, of course, is rejoicing while the NRA-Second Amendment crowd is glum, as if this award is coming out of their pockets. And no doubt there is much potentially at stake here, which could eventually come out of somebody's deep pockets. There are similar lawsuits pending in four other American cities. Others will be watching the Brooklyn verdict as it goes up 4 on appeal to get in on a tobacco-like settlement, if there is one.

6 The verdict is so far off the wall that the tendency for gun owners and those defending their legitimate uses might be to dismiss everything about the suit as coming right out of a Planter's jar. But gun owners, be careful where you line up on this one, or what you cho[o]se to ignore.

7 For one, the message the jury sent might not be popular with us, or logical, or even properly directed. But it is clear. The general population is tired of the mayhem guns do to the innocent. Make it 5 stop, they say. Or else. To the extent we can bring logical oversight and accountability into play as pro-gun people, it is in our long-term best interest to do so.

Last week's verdict in Brooklyn should be a wake-up call to gun manufacturers who just might be a tad guilty of turning their backs on what happens to their products after they land in certain states.

We here in New York have 9 among the strictest handgun laws in the country. For years we've known that most of the handguns used in crimes in this state come in from other states where getting them is a snap. Those states are Georgia, Florida, the Carolinas, and Virginia. Virginia, of all places, at the back door of 8 the Capitol. Buying handguns there is as easy as buying a six-pack. We have a state police unit that spends a lot of time just tracking guns involved in New York crimes, and where they come from, so we're not guessing.

Recently, though, we've also learned that those guns were usually bought legally in the first place, then transported to New York. Not stolen. Bought legally. During the Brooklyn trial it was introduced that gun manufacturers seem to over-sell to distributors in those states, knowing that customers from more restrictive 10 states like New York will be coming a-shopping.

If it's true, I have a problem 11 with that, and so should you. Just because we understand and appreciate guns and don't demonize them, does not mean we should be taking up the cudgel for the makers.

The opposite, I think. 12 What's wrong with holding the makers to the same high standards the law in New York holds us gun owners to? Or that we hold ourselves? After all, the . . . rights they jeopardized aren't theirs. They are yours.

Reflecting on What You Have Read

1 Even if you have never heard of Fred LeBrun, there are cues in this article that identify him as a local columnist with a specific audience. Go back through the text and identify the words or phrases that connect him to a certain audience and signal that he is "one of us."

2 What is the specific event (the circumstance) that prompted LeBrun to write this article and that would prompt his audience to read it?

3 Like Ellen Goodman, LeBrun creates a distinctive voice—he starts out sarcastic and then switches to serious. What words or phrases suggest each of these voices? Do the voices seem appropriate? Why or why not?

4 In paragraph 7, LeBrun advises his readers not to ignore the message implicit in the jury's verdict. In the paragraphs that follow, what evidence and reasons does he give to support his advice?

Thinking Ahead

If you decide to write a position paper that might actually influence the thinking of someone who feels strongly (pro or con) on a topic such as gun control, try following LeBrun's example and focus on a specific court decision, one in which you can examine the evidence and reasons presented by both parties involved in the legal dispute. Then create an argument in support of your opinion in that specific case.

No one would argue that students in U.S. schools should remain ignorant of other cultures, but there is disagreement as to which cultures students should study and how much students should be taught about other values and traditions. As Nathan Swinton points out in the following essay, this topic is made especially significant by changes in the school-age population of the United States. Before you read Swinton's position paper, look at the way he described his audience and purpose for this assignment (pp. 226–227). As you read, think about how Swinton's argument reflects his sense of audience.

Nathan Swinton

Striking a Balance in Multicultural Education

With today's society becoming increasingly global and interactions between various cultures becoming more and more frequent, few can deny the benefits of possessing an awareness of other cultures. In many regions of the United States, minority groups are now accounting for significant percentages of the population, and workers today are finding the ability to speak a second language to be an advantage. Wayne Thomas and Virginia Collier report in their article "Two Languages Are Better Than One" that by the 2030s non-English-speaking students will account for approximately forty percent of the school-age population (26). This population diversity raises the question of whether to provide students with a multicultural education, commonly defined as consisting of exposure to a variety of cultures, traditions, beliefs, languages, and social groups. For most, turning a blind eye to the issue is not an option; what is in dispute, however, is the extent to which multiculturalism should be employed. Clearly, educators and parents alike want to make available to students the best schooling possible, and now more than ever, what is best seems to include developing an understanding and appreciation of cultures other than one's own.

Despite the generally acknowledged need for multicultural edu-   2
cation, advocates of its implementation take the issue to the
extreme. Often, these proponents make a case for multicultural education by imagining dire problems and express fear of what will happen in a society devoid of multicultural education. For example, in
"The Importance of Multicultural Education in a Global Society,"
Chris Garber writes, "The argument is not what would happen if multicultural education is widely implemented, but rather what will happen if it is not" (571). Without a "broader education base," he continues, "our society will not gain the cultural acceptance necessary for
the coming age of diversity" (571). Likewise, Thomas and Collier
present a similar appeal to their readers' fears, asserting in their article that "students who graduate with monocultural perspectives will
not be prepared to contribute to their societies" (23). To nip this
possible societal ill in the bud, they recommend adopting mandatory
bilingual education through immersion programs for all students,
regardless of their native language (24).

Although these points deserve consideration, the extent to   3
which they are carried renders them less than persuasive. In each of
the above instances, the authors try to frighten the reader into supporting multicultural education programs, and they paint a bleak picture of a future society that lacks cultural awareness. By creating this
slippery slope in which one societal shortcoming inevitably leads to
another, supporters of multicultural education use the fear they stim-
ulate in the reader to push forward what often are relatively extreme
changes to the current education system. Thomas and Collier, for
instance, propose at least six years of bilingual education for all students, with as much as ninety percent of instruction in the early
grades being devoted to using a second language—drastic changes
for most schools across the nation today (25). This great change to
the educational system is not the answer, though. Thomas and
Collier seem to forget that some students have difficulty learning one
language at this early age, let alone two. Additionally, the authors
make no mention of building one's cultural perspective outside the

classroom. As Angela Ferguson and Mary Howard-Hamilton point out in their discussion titled "Addressing Issues of Multiple Identities for Women of Color on College Campuses," a great deal of recognizing and understanding cultural diversity occurs without instruction from a teacher, whether it be through participation in student organizations, workshops, or social interaction in general (293). The appeal to readers' fears in arguments in favor of multicultural education overshadows such considerations and masks the extremity of the positions put forth by the authors.

If supporters of multicultural education are guilty of using scare 4 tactics in discussing the issue, then detractors are culpable of doing the same. These opponents fear multicultural education will be taken too far and worry that distinguishing cultural characteristics will be lost in a giant "melting pot" that produces one dominant and homogenous social group (Garber 569). In addition to causing the loss of one's unique cultural background, multicultural education results in traditional works being left behind, critics also believe. For example, in *Illiberal Education,* Dinesh D'Souza expresses concern that emphasizing multicultural education has led students and faculty, particularly at the university level, to show a "lack of interest, if not contempt, for the Western classics" (255). He claims that this issue is quite problematic, for "the current revolution of minority victims threatens to destroy the highest ideals of liberal education" as well as "enlightenment and understanding" (257). Similarly, Roger Kimball speaks in his book *Tenured Radicals* about a growing tendency to "decanonize" dead, white, European male authors (qtd. in Levine, 23). Thus, these opponents of multicultural education also rely on the slippery slope form of argument to create a doomsday scenario of an education system gone awry and traditional cultures and texts lost in the shuffle as a result.

Like so many pro-multicultural arguments, this opposing view 5 of multicultural education proves to be fallacious. Detractors such as D'Souza present their readers with extreme viewpoints that exaggerate the problem of cultural traditions or classical texts being left behind. Lawrence Levine tackles this issue in the chapter "Through the Looking Glass" from his book *The Opening of the American Mind,* and he directly counters D'Souza's assertions by citing recent studies showing that traditionally classic works still dominate most college courses (24). Levine concludes that neither classic texts nor minority works need be abandoned, for "curricular change and tradition can and do coexist and constitute the substance of the contemporary university" (24).

Leslie Marmon Silko makes a similar point in "Language and Literature from a Pueblo Indian Perspective." She describes the value her Pueblo culture places on words and storytelling as well as the experiences of Pueblo children going to English schools. Silko points out that though she was learning a new language and about a new culture (in the traditional "Dick and Jane" style), she did not forget about her native customs. "Whatever literature we received at school," she states, "at home the storytelling, the special regard for telling and bringing together through telling, was going on constantly" (57). In this way, both Silko and Levine illustrate the error in assuming that implementing multicultural education will result in losing certain heritages and traditional texts. 6

Without question, these supporters and opponents of multicultural education alike have the students' best interests in mind when raising these issues. Their main concern is preparing today's youth for the global society they will face in the future. Extreme solutions are not the answer to the question of whether to implement multicultural education, however. Just as it is erroneous to believe that students today will be ill-prepared for tomorrow without being immersed in intensive bilingual education, so too is it fallacious to argue that multicultural education will result in traditional practices and texts falling by the wayside. Educators need to strike a balance between the two sides, much as Mike Rose does in *Lives on the Boundary.* Teaching English to non-English-speaking youth, Rose discovered his students learned best when they were allowed to draw on their own cultural experiences and upbringings. Learning, says 7

Rose, "had to be eliciting and shaping something that was already there" (110). By allowing students to write on subjects they knew best, Rose's method of teaching neither forces the issue of learning another language nor requires students to forget their own backgrounds. His teaching method draws on the notion that each student comes to the classroom with a different set of experiences, and he encourages students to build on what they already know. Rose's example constitutes just one of the many ways in which a balance between the extremes discussed earlier can be achieved.

Although finding this balance in multicultural education may not be easy, it is necessary. Extreme positions on both sides of the issue abound, and both supporters and opponents of multicultural education present doomsday scenarios to bolster their claims; on neither side, however, are these scenarios true. While the importance of learning a second language and of understanding other cultures cannot be ignored, one must also be wary of going overboard to prep students for the global society that lies ahead. Moderation is key.

8

Works Cited

D'Souza, Dinesh. *Illiberal Education: The Politics of Race and Sex on Campus.* New York: Free, 1991. 254–57.

Ferguson, Angela D., and Mary F. Howard-Hamilton. "Addressing Issues of Multiple Identities for Women of Color on College Campuses." *Toward Acceptance: Sexual Orientation Issues on Campus.* Ed. Vernon A. Wall and Nancy J. Evans. Lanham, MD: UP of America, 2000. 283–97.

Garber, Chris. "The Importance of Multicultural Education in Global Society." *The Well-Crafted Argument.* Ed. F. D. White and S. J. Billings. New York: Houghton, 2002. 568–73.

Kimball, Roger. *Tenured Radicals: How Politics Has Corrupted Our Higher Education.* New York: Harper, 1990.

Levine, Lawrence W. "Through the Looking Glass." *The Opening of the American Mind: Canons, Culture, and History.* Boston: Beacon, 1996. 20–33.

Rose, Mike. "Literate Stirrings." *Lives on the Boundary: The Struggles and Achievements of America's Underprepared.* New York: Free, 1989. 110.

Silko, Leslie Marmon. "Language and Literature from a Pueblo Indian Perspective." *Yellow Woman and a Beauty of the Spirit.* New York: Touchstone, 1997. 57.

Thomas, Wayne P., and Virginia Collier. "Two Languages Are Better Than One." *Educational Leadership* Dec. 1997: 23–27.

Reflecting on What You Have Read

1 Nathan begins his position paper by acknowledging how important it is for students in U.S. schools to know about cultures other than their own. Given what he says about his audience on pp. 226–227, does this seem like an appropriate way for him to begin? Why or why not?

2 Do the examples Nathan cites persuade you that some advocates of multicultural education "take their issue to an extreme"? How likely does it seem that these examples would be persuasive to Nathan's intended audience? Why do you think so?

3 How successful is Nathan's ethical appeal? That is, in what ways does he succeed (or fail) in showing his intended readers that he is trustworthy and credible?

4 Do you agree with Nathan's claim in paragraph 8 that "Moderation is key" to providing effective multicultural education? What reasoning does he use to support his claim? Do you accept his reasons? Why or why not?

Thinking Ahead

Nathan's essay focuses on an issue that has the potential to change the curriculum in many colleges and universities. But it's by no means the only curriculum issue faced by schools and colleges in the United States. For example, in a time of limited budgets, many public schools are considering cutting back on their offerings in such areas as music and art. Should they be doing this? Consider your own education—in grade school, high school, or college. Have you been aware of any issues with the potential to affect the quality of education? Can you identify a specific audience for whom you might write a position paper on one of these issues?

Assignment

Position Paper

Write a position paper that argues persuasively for your opinion, either on a topic of your choice or on one selected by your instructor. Your argument should include a claim about your topic, appropriate evidence, and reasons that appeal to your audience.

If you have the opportunity to choose your own topic, it should be something that matters to you but that will also matter equally to a particular audience. You may want to think about something on your campus or in your community that bothers you and write a letter to the editor of your school or hometown newspaper.

Your instructor may have specific requirements about how long the position paper should be, what sort of topic to write about, whether you should prepare the position paper as a print or online document (or as an oral presentation), whether you should include or exclude any particular visual elements, or use a particular documentation style to formally cite sources. Be sure you understand those requirements before you start working on the assignment.

Guide to Writing a Position Paper

As you write a position paper, your ideas may change greatly, or your understanding of the intended audience and purpose may shift. In writing your opinion you may not end up exactly where you first envisioned. Your ideas and reasons should develop, especially at the beginning of a project.

The remainder of this chapter will help you through the process of creating a persuasive position paper that makes clear claims supported by good reasons and credible evidence. The first step is covered in Getting Started—selecting a topic and analyzing the context in which your position paper will be read. Then you will experiment with many of the verbal and visual strategies illustrated in the position papers you were introduced to in Reading to Write, and you will use them in the Drafting section. These strategies can help you work toward the writer's objectives of developing your topic (that is, finding something to say), writing an introduction that will engage readers' interest, creating an appropriate voice, providing a clear structure, concluding your position paper effectively, and designing your paper and integrating visual elements (giving your work a "look" that is appropriate for your topic and audience). Finally, in Finishing Up, you will receive guidance in creating a review draft, assessing your work carefully, and using that assessment to revise your position paper. You most likely will spend a different amount of time on each of these objectives, and you may focus on them in virtually any order. The process of writing is not a linear one in which you'll set down the first word of your paper and proceed in an orderly fashion directly to your conclusion. Nevertheless, you won't be descending into a trackless wilderness; all the work that you do will be contained within the simple process of getting started (selecting a topic and analyzing context), drafting your position paper, and finishing up (reviewing, assessing, and revising your work).

Guide to Writing a Position Paper

Getting Started

For this assignment, you're going to have to take a stand on some sort of issue—you're going to have to tell an audience how you believe they should think or act with regard to a particular topic. Suggestions on the following pages will help you identify a good topic for your position paper and analyze the context in which your paper will be read.

Selecting a Topic

If the instructor asks you to come up with your own topic for this assignment, you should try to think of topics that fall within the following broad categories.

> ❯ Issues you really care about
> ❯ Issues other people would or could really care about
> ❯ Issues you already know something about

If this advice sounds familiar, it's because you've seen it in other courses or read it in other chapters of this book.

When trying to think of a topic for a position paper, there's another piece of advice that might be useful.

> ❯ Try to think of issues that encompass multiple perspectives or have aspects that make it difficult for people to agree on what should be done or how they should feel.

This part of the advice suggests that you focus on something that people could argue—or debate—about. Although occasionally people take positions on topics that seem obvious, usually arguments are written on topics that *aren't* obvious. For example, you probably don't need to take a position on the value of a college education or the importance of personal hygiene. Although you could take a stand for or against either of those issues, most audiences would already agree with a "pro" argument (so there wouldn't be much point to taking a stand) and disagree with an "anti" argument (so it would be a very difficult argument to make). However, if you start paying attention to what's going on around you, you can find lots of issues that haven't been resolved.

Here is one more piece of advice.

> ❯ Try to avoid broad topics on which people's viewpoints are highly emotional and entrenched.

It's often difficult to convince readers to change their opinion about such issues as euthanasia, welfare, and capital punishment. These and many other topics are so frequently discussed that it's unlikely you would be able to bring any fresh information or insights to the debate without investing a lot more time than you'll have available for this assignment.

One good way to find a topic for your position paper is to look back at the Reading to Write section (p. 194), focusing particularly on the

Thinking Ahead prompts that follow the readings. If you are interested in some of the broad issues addressed in the readings, the Thinking Ahead questions may help you find a manageable way to write about a complex, emotionally charged subject such as gun control or health care. In any case, as you review the readings, keep these questions in mind.

> **Do I enjoy reading about this topic?** If your answer is yes, is there some aspect of the topic about which you have an opinion that you would like to share? Your opinion may differ from that of the author—in fact, having a conflicting view can lead you to identify a topic you want to write about. You might even consider responding to one of the sample readings if you disagree with the author. For example, if you value the idea of newer, faster highways or better road surfaces in your area more than you value the idea of funding additional mass transit, you might consider writing a response to "New Roads Are Not the Answer."

> **What does this topic make me think about?** Sometimes, as you read, your mind may wander a bit, leading you to discover something else that intrigues you. Normally readers try to stay focused on the text, but for the purpose of thinking about a topic, let your mind wander and see where it goes. For example, as you reread "Yes, Let's Pay for Organs" (p. 201), you might think about a friend who was in the hospital recently. That might make you think about the reason he was in the hospital. Perhaps he was injured playing football. That might take you to the topic of college sports, which might lead to recruitment and scholarships, which might be something you would like to take a stand on.

> **Where was this article published? Where might I publish my own position paper, as an essay, a letter, a brochure, or a posting on a Web site? Who would my readers be? What am I interested in that they would be interested in as well?** Position papers can appear in national media, but they may also be posted to an online discussion list, e-mailed to people who share your concerns about an issue, or tacked to a school bulletin board. If you can think of a place to publish your writing—for example, in your residence hall newsletter—it will help you define your audience and recognize the features you have in common with your readers. (For help on determining audience characteristics, see the questions on p. 224.)

> **What was the author's purpose in writing this piece? In other words, what did the author think readers should do or feel about the topic?** Each position paper presented in this chapter was written from a particular point of view on an issue; each author wanted to persuade readers to agree with that point of view. One wants "tougher" laws for SUVs; another wants states to pass laws allowing payments for organ donations. But opinions aren't just about laws. What do you see happening on your campus or in your home town that you wish were different? What could be done to make it different? How can you help bring about that change?

Working on the Assignment

Selecting a Topic

Skimming over the Reading to Write section may have given you one or more ideas about a topic for your own paper. Try to come up with at least three or four topic ideas before you make a final selection. Here are some more ways to find possible topics.

> **Brainstorm.** Writing as quickly as you can, list topics that relate to issues you care about, issues other people would care about, or issues you already know something about. Focus on issues that you know people could argue or debate about.

> **Work with a small group to create a list of potential topics.**

> **Work with a few other students to identify two or three topics that have promise,** determining whether they are topics on which reasonable people might reasonably disagree. Be careful to avoid topics about which people's opinions are so firmly set that you have no realistic chance of influencing those opinions.

> **Choose a topic from the list** based on your own position on the issue and the comments from your small group.

> **Brainstorm a list of statements about the topic** you have selected. Jot down your claim and everything you know about your topic.

> **Explain what you know** to your group and see what information or possible evidence members of the group can add.

Once you have identified a topic that you might like to write a position paper on, you need to make sure that (1) you can find plenty of factual information to support your opinion and (2) that you have a topic on which reasonable people disagree. To help with this, try the following activities, making notes about what you learn.

> **Examine your own experience.** How has your opinion been shaped by events that you have witnessed or that have happened to you? List some details about those events: Who did what? When? Why? How did you or others react to those events? What have you done, seen, or heard that influences your opinion?

> **Find out what others are saying about your topic.** Discuss your topic with friends and family. Tune in to a radio or television talk show or a community channel. What opinions do people express? What evidence and reasons do they give in support of their opinions?

> **Do some reading.** Do a preliminary search in your library's databases. Check out the Internet, but remember that information online is not always reliable or complete. Don't try to read everything carefully at this point. Just read enough to confirm that your proposed topic is interesting and worthwhile and that there is plenty of credible material available on it.

> **Look for visual information**—images, charts, graphs, and so forth—that you can use to reinforce the position you defend in your written text.

> **Conduct a brief reality check** after doing a fair amount of reading, watching, and listening. Do you have a topic that matters to you? Can you find plenty of credible reasons and evidence to present your opinion? Can you think of an audience that would at least seriously consider the position you are arguing for? If you can't answer yes to at least two of these questions, consider changing your topic or your audience. Do this now, not the night before the assignment is due.

Analyzing Context

When writing a position paper, you can assume that you're writing for people who do not share your opinion—people who either have not formed an opinion on the topic or are inclined to disagree with you. (If the audience you hope to persuade already knows, thinks, and feels exactly as you do, there's no point in writing a position paper.) But what else can you assume about the audience or the circumstances in which readers will encounter your position paper? And how should you determine the impact you want to have on the audience—should you aim simply to get readers to understand your opinion, or do you want to influence the way they will think and act on the topic?

To develop a good sense of your context in writing a position paper, you should write out answers to the following questions. As is always the case, your understanding of the audience may change as you work on the assignment. You may, for example, get a clearer idea of what they know or expect, or you may change your ideas about the sort of format that is appropriate for them. Consequently, you may want to revise your context analysis as you work on the position paper. But for now, be as specific as possible.

Questions for Analyzing Context

Audience knowledge, values, and needs

› What sorts of experiences (personal or secondhand) have my readers had with my topic?

› How does my topic relate to things my readers know, value, or care about?

› Do my readers have any biases or preconceptions concerning my topic? If so, what are they, and do I have any information that will correct (or reinforce) those attitudes?

Audience expectations for content

› What kinds of reasons are likely to appeal to the values held by my readers?

› What kinds of appeals (logical, emotional, or ethical) are they likely to respond well to?

› What questions or objections are my readers likely to want to have answered?

› What kinds of information will they see as credible?

Audience expectations for layout

› Which reading in this chapter comes closest to looking the way my readers will expect my position paper to look?

› Are there any visual features (for example, photographs, charts, bulleted lists) my readers are likely to expect or appreciate?

› Are there ways in which my position paper will look different from the readings in this chapter?

› **bedfordstmartins.com/ visualage**

To download these questions as a worksheet, click on **CHAPTER 4** › **WORKSHEETS**

- **Circumstances**
  - ❭ Are there any recent events that might motivate my audience to read my position paper? If so, what are they?
  - ❭ If not, what sort of background information should I provide at the beginning of my position paper?
- **Purposes**
  - ❭ What purposes am I trying to accomplish in writing my position paper? (See discussion of purposes on p. 189.) What overall impression do I want to leave my readers with?
  - ❭ What sort of voice do I want readers to hear when they read my position paper? (For a discussion of voice, see p. 242 of this chapter.)

The activities in the Working on the Assignment: Analyzing Context box below will help you think through and prepare to answer the Questions for Analyzing Context above.

Analyzing Context

As with any assignment, you should think about your audience as concretely as possible. Try to identify one or two individuals who are reasonably typical of the larger group of readers you hope to reach. Then take the following steps.

> **Talk with one or more members of your audience.** What do they already know about your topic? Do they have any preconceptions or misconceptions? Have they had any personal experiences that would make them receptive or hostile to your opinion?
>
> One way to begin the conversation might be to say something like, "Did you see that piece in the newspaper (or on television) on [your topic]? What was your reaction?" Try to avoid asking questions that imply the attitude or opinion you want your readers to adopt.

> **Put yourself in your reader's place.** Answer such questions as these: *If I were in my reader's place, how would I be likely to react to the arguments I want to make in this position paper? Where might I raise objections? What questions would I be likely to ask? Why might I be likely to raise these questions or objections?*

> **Draw on your knowledge of yourself.** What knowledge, experiences, and values form the basis for your own views on this topic? Are there any points at which you and your readers might share some knowledge, experiences, or values? What are the points at which you and your readers differ most?

> **Identify the circumstances in which your readers will encounter your position paper.** Are they aware of any recent events that might influence their opinions on the topic about which you are writing? Are they likely to come across your position paper as one in a series of arguments on the topic, or will your position paper be the first one they encounter on this topic?

STUDENT CONTEXT ANALYSIS

Here's how Nathan Swinton answered the Questions for Analyzing Context for the position paper he wrote, "Striking a Balance in Multicultural Education" (p. 213).

Audience Knowledge, Values, and Needs

What sorts of experiences (personal or secondhand) have my readers had with my topic?

My readers are likely to be familiar with the topic of multicultural education to some degree, although a large majority of them probably have not read the articles to which I refer very specifically and in which I situate my argument. It is also likely that, as students and educators, most have studied some aspect of multiculturalism, learned a second language, or considered the integration of multicultural works into the traditional Western canon of literature.

How does my topic relate to things my readers know, value, or care about?

My readers will likely be familiar with the debate from the 1990s about whether to instruct students in Ebonics, and they might also have heard of education reforms in the last few years that include dual-language programs for students throughout their elementary school years.

Do my readers have any biases or preconceptions? If so, what are they, and do I have any information that will correct (or reinforce) those attitudes?

I expect my audience to be partial toward implementing multicultural education in schools since that seems to be the trend today.

Audience Expectations for Content

What kinds of reasons are likely to appeal to the values held by my readers?

I think they will value reasoning that shows I'm aware of the fallacies of extreme positions (whether pro or con).

What kinds of appeals are they likely to respond well to?

They will value ethical and logical appeals; they will respond best to arguments that I am someone who has thought about the issue carefully and non-emotionally.

What questions or objections are my readers likely to want to have answered?

I think the most pressing question for my readers is, "Why is this matter important to me?"

What kinds of information will they see as credible?

I believe I can best reach my audience by using personal examples and showing how one authority's ideas are contradicted by another authority.

STUDENT CONTEXT ANALYSIS

Audience Expectations for Layout

Which reading in this chapter comes closest to looking the way my readers will expect my position paper to look?

Are there any visual features (for example, photographs, charts, bulleted lists) my readers are likely to expect or appreciate?

Are there ways in which my position paper will look different from the readings in this chapter?

My readers will expect a traditional-looking academic essay, with a list of Works Cited at the end (MLA documentation style).

My essay is not required to include headings or illustrations, as many readings in this chapter do.

Circumstances

Are there any recent events that might motivate my audience to read my position paper? If so, what are they? If not, what sort of background information should I provide at the beginning of my position paper?

I think the changing nature of America's school system is always an issue weighing on people's minds, and as today's society becomes increasingly blended with people from all sorts of backgrounds, any issue involving multiculturalism is naturally going to surface.

Purposes

What purposes am I trying to accomplish in writing my position paper? What overall impression do I want to leave my readers with?

What sort of voice do I want readers to hear when they read my position paper?

My goal in writing this piece is to demonstrate the ways in which advocates and detractors of multicultural education can and have carried their arguments to the extreme and in doing so have undermined their credibility.

I strived to achieve a calm, rational voice in my argument, one that my readers recognize as being intelligent and coming from a person who has thoughtfully and thoroughly considered the issue. I tried to avoid using any scare tactics similar to those I was pointing out in others' writing. My main strategy was to use both logical and ethical appeals, so as to make my argument logically sound and to gain my readers' trust.

Drafting

By now you've identified the subject you want to write about, you're beginning to get a good idea of who the members of your audience are and what they think about the issue, and you have a pretty good idea of the purpose you hope to accomplish in writing your position paper. You may also feel you know exactly what your position is—what is the principal claim (or thesis) you will support. But before committing yourself to a specific thesis, you'll need to work on developing your topic. This work may only reinforce your point of view, but you should be open to the possibility that your ideas may change.

The next few sections of this chapter outline a variety of strategies that will help you meet the objectives of developing your topic, engaging your audience, and so forth. As in other chapters in this book, you will be working with strategies that appear in Reading to Write. The following discussions, along with the Strategies and Examples lists, will help you see how specific passages reflect generalizable strategies that you can apply to your own writing. You can always add to these lists of strategies by analyzing other position papers you find interesting and credible.

Developing Your Topic

In writing a position paper, you must develop your topic thoroughly, providing credible, reliable answers to the kinds of questions listed on p. 223. To do this, you will begin by consulting sources and gathering information, possibly more information than you will actually use in the final version of your position paper. How do you gather the appropriate and credible information? How do you narrow the topic and formulate a thesis? How do you include all the necessary components of your argument? How can you be sure to effectively use the appropriate argumentative strategies? The following pages provide suggestions for ways to address these issues.

Gathering Information

Draw on personal experience. It's likely that you will put a lot of yourself into your position paper. The position you advocate will probably be one you personally believe in, and you may defend that position in part by reporting your own experiences and observations.

Use secondary sources. As a rule, you shouldn't try to develop your argument in a vacuum. When dealing with a significant topic (and if you aren't, why aren't you?), there's a good chance other people will have opinions and information you should consider carefully. Consequently, in developing your argument, be sure to consider not only your own experience (always a primary source of information) but also secondary sources: the evidence and reasons found in speeches, television or radio reports, magazines and books, sites on the Internet, and databases.

> For more advice on assessing the credibility of sources, see **Chapter 11.**

You may recall that in other chapters you put quite a bit of effort into finding and working with secondary sources (see pp. 77–79 of Profiles or pp. 153–156 of Reports). Now look at how Nathan Swinton's essay, "Striking a Balance in Multicultural Education," illustrates several strategies that can guide your search for secondary sources that might be useful for your position paper.

How to Gather Information

Strategies	Examples
Look for sources that help establish the importance of the issue on which you are taking a position. For some audiences, your feeling that a topic is important may not be enough. Look for information (facts, statistics, quotes, anecdotes) that provides evidence that the topic is important and that comes from sources your readers will see as credible.	*In paragraph 1 of "Striking a Balance in Multicultural Education" (p. 213), Swinton cites a 1997 report claiming that "by the 2030s non-English-speaking students will account for approximately forty percent of the school-age population." This statistic clearly suggests why it is important for U.S. schools to decide how to acknowledge the various cultures those students represent.*
Look for sources that reflect divergent points of view. As you read these sources, you may find that your own opinion changes or at least becomes more informed. You may also get a good sense of the questions or objections your readers may raise.	*Swinton cites sources that reflect three different points of view: those who go to extremes in support of multicultural education (Thomas and Collier; Garber), those who go to extremes in attacking multicultural education (D'Souza; Kimball), and those who represent what he considers a "balanced" point of view (Ferguson and Howard-Hamilton; Levine; Silko; Rose).*
Look for sources that challenge claims made in other sources. This will further refine your own understanding of the topic. It may also suggest ways to refute claims made by writers you disagree with.	*In paragraph 4, Swinton cites critic Dinesh D'Souza's claim that multicultural education will lead colleges to ignore significant works that have traditionally been featured in college curricula. But in the next paragraph, Swinton cites Levine's reference to studies that contradict D'Souza's claim.*

> **STUDENT DIALOGUE: GATHERING INFORMATION**
>
> **Writing in a Visual Age (WVA):** Why did you choose to use the secondary sources you've referred to?
>
> **Nathan Swinton (NS):** I cited those essays that best illustrated my point of how proponents and opponents of multicultural education can resort to using scare tactics or "slippery slope" forms of arguments. I wanted to refer to enough sources to make my writing sound credible and well researched, but at the same time I tried to avoid overwhelming my reader with too many sources.
>
> **WVA:** How did you decide whether a given secondary source was credible and appropriate?
>
> **NS:** I checked the authors' biographies, looking for information about what their profession is, where they live, what their background is, how they are tied to the issue, and what sort of interest they have in it. I also noted where their piece had originally appeared.

Working on the Assignment

Gathering Information

As you consult secondary sources about your topic, you should keep a working bibliography, recording the author, title, and other publication information you'll need later, either to locate a source again or to document it in your list of references or works cited. As you create this bibliography, keep the following goals in mind.

> Especially look for writers who disagree with each other or with you.
> List key claims in each source you read.
> Summarize (occasionally quoting key phrases) the evidence presented in support of these claims.

> For more on keeping a working bibliography, see **Chapter 9,** pp. 560–562.

Creating an Exploratory Draft

After you have read at least a half-dozen sources, write an *exploratory draft* of your position paper. This draft should help you recognize where you are beginning to develop some strong support for your opinion, where you can find additional evidence, where you might need to think of more compelling reasons, and perhaps even where you might need to re-think your position. Remember to draw on your own experiences and attitudes along with your secondary sources.

Working on the Assignment

Creating an Exploratory Draft

Before you begin writing an exploratory draft, take a close look at the context analysis you completed, answering the questions on p. 226. Are there some questions that aren't completed very well? For example, are you lacking information about your readers' knowledge, needs, and values? Do you have a good sense of what your readers will expect in terms of content, both verbal and visual? At this point, finish completing your responses to the best of your ability. Also review the notes you took for your working bibliography. Underline or mark key facts or reasons.

After reviewing your context analysis and your notes, set aside twenty to thirty minutes and write as rapidly as you can (without interruption), completing the following sentences.

> "The basic point I want to make is _____."
> "One reason I think this is _____."
> "The evidence that goes with this reason is _____."
> "Another reason is _____."
> "The evidence that goes with this reason is _____."

> "Another reason is _____."
> "The evidence that goes with this reason is _____."

Once you have completed this exploratory work, read or show what you have written to other students (perhaps in a small group or perhaps to the entire class). Ask your classmates to help you do the following tasks.

> Identify places where your reasons and evidence seem likely to be very persuasive to the intended audience.
> Identify places at which you need to elaborate, either by providing additional evidence or by explaining your reasons.

After considering your classmates' responses, determine whether there are passages where you might use one or more of the strategies explained earlier to justify your opinion and make your position paper more persuasive. Use your classmates' responses to guide you in deciding whether or how to add to, delete, or modify information you have included in your exploratory draft.

Formulating a Thesis

After discussing your exploratory draft with your classmates, reread the way you completed the sentence "The basic point I want to make is _____." As you listened to your classmates' comments about your draft, did you find that you wanted to modify what you had said in this sentence? If necessary, rewrite the sentence so that it expresses your position as clearly as possible. This sentence will become your *thesis*, the principal claim you want to make in your position paper. As you continue to develop your topic, you may want to revise that thesis still further. But it will serve as the starting point from which you can look for ways to argue your position as effectively as possible.

Including the Components of an Argument

As suggested earlier in this chapter, an opinion has to include two specific components if it is to succeed as an argument that persuades an audience.

> It must clearly make at least one claim about an issue so that readers know what your position is.
> It must provide evidence that supports the claim, is credible, and reflects the reasons of the audience.

In addition, there are optional components—they may strengthen your argument, but they're not always necessary. For example, your opinion may need to include one or more of the following.

> An explicit statement of the reasons connecting the evidence to the claim
> Qualifiers that limit your claim
> A statement of an opposing point of view (objection) and a rebuttal (refutation), an explanation of the evidence (and perhaps the reasons) that contradicts the opposition's point of view

Working on the Assignment

Including the Components of an Argument

Show your context analysis and your exploratory draft (along with any additional notes you have made) to your instructor or your classmates. Ask them to review your context analysis and then point to passages in the exploratory draft where you need to do one or more of the following.

> Provide evidence.
> Qualify a claim.
> Make your reasons explicit or find reasons that would be more appropriate for your intended audience.

> Respond to an objection a member of your intended audience is likely to make.

Take careful notes about what you learn from your instructor or classmates. Keep these notes in mind as you consider the traditional argumentative strategies presented on the following pages.

Using Argumentative Strategies

For examples of additional strategies for developing your topic, see the strategies for gathering information on p. 229 and for formulating and articulating ideas on p. 159 of **Chapter 3.**

The position papers in Reading to Write demonstrate many argumentative strategies—ways of formulating and justifying an opinion. Some of the more traditional strategies, most of which have been used for centuries, are well illustrated in Charles Krauthammer's "Yes, Let's Pay for Organs." But Krauthammer's strategies are by no means the only ways of developing and presenting an opinion on the topic you have chosen. Here is a list of strategies drawn not only from Krauthammer's position paper but from other readings as well.

How to Use Argumentative Strategies

Strategies	Examples
Acknowledge and respond to objections. It's very likely that your readers will test what you say, raising their own objections or objections they have heard others raise. Consequently, you should thoroughly consider potential objections while developing your topic. You can decide later the extent to which you may need to include acknowledgments of specific objections in your draft. Especially if readers' objections may be strong enough to undermine your argument, mention them and then show why they are invalid—either because they are factually incorrect or because they are based on reasons that your audience will consider dubious.	*In "Yes, Let's Pay for Organs" (p. 201), almost as soon as he introduces his opinion, Krauthammer acknowledges an objection that many people are likely to raise. In paragraph 1 he notes, "Already there are voices opposing the very idea of pricing a kidney."* *In paragraph 3 Krauthammer elaborates on this objection, stating that many people may feel that Pennsylvania's payments to families of deceased relatives who have agreed to donate their organs will have more effect on the poor than on the wealthy. Admitting that a high market price for obtaining donated organs would be "offensive," Krauthammer goes on to say, "But this program does not restrict supply to the rich. It seeks to increase supply for all" (paragraph 4).*
Cite consequences (also known as establishing causes and effects). Set up an *if . . . then . . .* situation. Show that one event is the cause or effect of the other, especially noting effects or consequences that the reader may not have intended or anticipated.	*Krauthammer concludes his argument by indicating that "if we don't have the courage to move the moral line"—that is, to allow the sale of organs from those who have died—many other people will needlessly die.* *continued*

How to Use Argumentative Strategies

continued

Strategies	Examples
Cite credible sources. Demonstrate your knowledge of the topic by drawing facts and opinions from people with sound experience and professional credentials—in other words, authorities. (For more about credibility, see Chapter 11.)	In "Up in Arms over Decision" (p. 211), LeBrun asserts that many crimes committed in New York State are committed with handguns from other states, where handgun laws are less restrictive. In support of this claim, he notes that "We have a state police unit that spends a lot of time just tracking guns involved in New York crimes, and where they come from, so we're not guessing."
Cite precedents, especially those your audience will accept as valid. It's easier to convince people if you can show that your argument has been accepted or proven in other situations.	In "Striking a Balance in Multicultural Education" (p. 213), Swinton cites the example of work done by Mike Rose with non-English-speaking young people.
Cite principle. Refer to a principle and then show how an action or situation is (or is not) consistent with that principle. Often the principle is one the audience accepts. But it is also possible to refer to a principle your audience considers faulty or unacceptable; in that case, you would show how someone else's argument is based on that faulty or unacceptable principle.	In paragraphs 8 and 9, Krauthammer mentions the principle of human dignity and suggests that paying for organs from the dead does not challenge this principle.
Consider both pro and con, good news as well as bad. You can demonstrate fairness if, no matter how strongly you feel about a topic, you consider both pro and con for any claim you make. Look for information that both supports and detracts from the claim. This will help you think through your claims, and it might give you more credibility.	In "Human Organ Donation: Gift or Graft?" (p. 203), Bufill claims: "Tissue obtained from humans—both living and dead—has proved to be life-saving and life-enhancing." But he does not ignore the sad reality that "[d]espite campaigns to improve . . . awareness . . . demand for human organs for transplantation has not been accompanied by a corresponding increase in supply" (paragraph 3).
Define key terms. Use concrete language to restrict the meaning of a key term, explaining what its limits are or what it is not. (Once in a while, you can use a dictionary to help define key terms. But dictionary definitions can be very abstract.)	In paragraph 8, Krauthammer defines the term freedom by explaining one of its limits: "We have a free society, but freedom stops at the point where you violate the very integrity of the self."

How to Use Argumentative Strategies

Strategies	Examples
Evaluate each source you cite or respond to. Use your context analysis to determine the kinds of appeals that are likely to make sense, given the knowledge, values, and needs of your audience. Then, when you want to discredit an opposing argument, consider whether the author is using emotional appeals to the exclusion of logical ones, or is relying too much on logical appeals and ignoring the emotional aspects of a situation that may concern your readers.	*In "Striking a Balance in Multicultural Education" Swinton criticizes several studies for making an unjustified emotional appeal, trying to "frighten the reader into supporting multicultural education programs" (paragraph 3).*
Make comparisons. To make your point about something (a person, an action, an idea) about which your reader may be inclined to disagree with you, show how it is similar to something else, about which your reader *does* agree with you.	*In paragraph 5, Krauthammer uses analogy to counter the argument that paying for organ donations "disproportionately affect[s] the poor"; he notes that society tolerates many things that disproportionately affect the poor: "slum housing, street crime, . . . hazardous jobs."*
Note contrasts. Tell what something is not or how it differs from other apparently similar things. This can be especially useful in defining key terms.	*Krauthammer acknowledges (paragraph 9) that it would be morally wrong to allow the sale of kidneys (and, implicitly, other organs) from living people. But in paragraph 10 he argues, "kidneys from the dead are another matter entirely."*
Point out conflicts, which may take the form of inconsistencies, paradoxes, or self-contradictions.	*As part of her criticism of SUV owners, Goodman points out in "SUVs Belong in Car Ads Only" (p. 195) that "sport utility vehicles are bought primarily by people whose favorite sport is shopping and whose most rugged athletic event is hauling the kids to soccer practice" (paragraph 5).*
Conflicts may be identified between an existing situation and the readers' values or needs.	*Goodman contends that "The problem with SUVs is that you can't see over them, you can't see around them, and you have to watch out for them" (paragraph 8).*

continued

How to Use Argumentative Strategies

continued

Strategies	Examples
Conflicts may also be identified between what the readers may believe and what the writer thinks is true or desirable.	*In "New Roads Are Not the Answer" (p. 198), the Sierra Club directly challenges many readers' assumptions that the best way to relieve traffic congestion is to build more roads.*
Provide a narrative that explains why or how something came to be.	*In "Up in Arms over Decision," LeBrun acknowledges that New York State has extremely strict gun laws. Then he explains the process by which guns become readily available to criminals in New York: lax gun laws in other states make guns available to criminals and non-criminals alike.*
Summarize your opponent's point of view and show how it is not valid. In order to argue persuasively, you need to understand thoroughly and characterize fairly the claims your opponent is likely to make. After you have summarized a counterargument fairly, you can more easily determine the kinds of information to include in order to contradict that point of view. It may also lead you to rethink your own point of view.	*In "School Vouchers: The Wrong Choice for Public Education" (p. 206), the Anti-Defamation League writes: "Proponents of vouchers argue that these programs would allow poor students to attend good schools previously only available to the middle class" (paragraph 9). The author then goes on to point out that vouchers can cover only a portion of the cost of attending an expensive private school, leaving the poorest families still unable to afford tuition at many private schools.*

 Exercise

Choose one or more of the position papers in Reading to Write (p. 194), or work with another piece your instructor assigns, and then answer this question: At what points does the author use one or more of the argumentative strategies mentioned above? Make notes on the position paper, and be prepared to explain your answer to your classmates.

STUDENT DIALOGUE: WORKING WITH OPPOSING VIEWPOINTS

Writing in a Visual Age: Although you disagree with Garber and Thomas and Collier, you summarize their positions carefully. Why did you do this?

Nathan Swinton: It bolsters my argument when I can give an opposing argument the credit it deserves and still refute it. My own argument would lose credibility were I to inadequately summarize others' points of view when discussing them, and I would likely lose some of my readers' trust had I done so.

Using Strategies for Developing an Argument

Think of all the strategies on the preceding pages as questions you can answer as you gather information and formulate your thesis. For example, you might ask yourself the following questions.

> How is my position similar to or different from something my reader knows or believes?

> What are the opposing arguments? In what ways is my opponent's view valid? In what ways is it not valid?

> What principles are pertinent to my topic? Are the things people say consistent or inconsistent with those principles?

> What objections are people likely to make when they read my position paper? How can I respond to those objections?

> If people act in a given way, what effects are those actions likely to have?

> What kinds of appeals is a given writer making? Do those appeals seem valid?

Use such questions as a guide while you read and make notes. And remember: if one strategy doesn't provide useful ideas or information, try another one. These are not rules or recipes. They are just things you can do to get yourself started with the process of gathering information and developing your argument. As you gather information, keep re-working your exploratory draft, clarifying your position and adding new evidence and reasons to strengthen your argument.

Engaging Your Audience: Writing an Introduction

In order to engage readers, writers must do two things: (1) let readers see how a topic relates to what they know, care about, and need, and (2) establish a conflict that matters to readers.

Relating to Readers

The position papers in the Reading to Write section of this chapter display a variety of strategies for engaging readers. Here are several strategies that will help your own writing relate to—or develop common ground with—your readers.

How to Relate to Readers

Strategies	Examples
Begin by making a claim that readers are likely to agree with. Whenever possible, try to find some common ground, some fact or opinion that both you and your readers accept. This will help establish you as someone with whom they have at least one thing in common. And the effort to find common ground may also lead you to re-think your own opinion.	*The beginning of "Striking a Balance in Multicultural Education" (p. 213) makes a claim that is hard to dispute, no matter how one feels about multicultural education: "With today's society becoming increasingly global and interactions between various cultures becoming more and more frequent, few can deny the benefits of possessing an awareness of other cultures."*
Acknowledge concerns or attitudes your readers are likely to have. Demonstrate that you understand your readers' worries or questions. If you show that you can, in effect, listen to your readers, you increase the likelihood that they will listen to you. Perhaps more important, as you listen to your readers, you may learn something that influences your own point of view.	*In "Up in Arms over Decision" (p. 211) LeBrun knows that his readers are likely to be dubious about any legal decision that might impinge on their right to own firearms. In his position paper, LeBrun mentions a recent jury decision that holds handgun manufacturers responsible for harm done with weapons they manufactured. Concerning this decision, LeBrun says that "On its face, what the jury did was about as daffy as it gets."*
Create a visual image readers can recognize. Some topics may seem abstract or remote from readers' personal experiences. Visual images can help make such topics less abstract, more personal. They can also help create an emotional appeal.	*"New Roads Are Not the Answer" (p. 198) begins with a photograph of a frustrating predicament (stalled traffic on an expressway) that readers are likely to recognize and respond to. "Human Organ Donation: Gift or Graft?" (p. 203) begins not with a photograph but with a description of two infants—one very sickly, the other obviously healthy. This description creates a clear visual image that is likely to stir readers' emotions.*

How to Relate to Readers

Strategies

Make sure readers can see how the conflict you have established relates to them or to things they care about. More specifically, you can refer to an action that is at odds with readers' values or sense of what is appropriate.

Alternatively, you can remind readers of a situation in which they personally have felt a conflict between the real and the ideal.

Examples

Paragraph 2 of "Up in Arms over Decision" reports on a jury verdict that penalized handgun manufacturers even though the manufacturers had done nothing illegal or, in the eyes of LeBrun's principal audience, even unethical.

Goodman uses this strategy in "SUVs Belong in Car Ads Only" (p. 195) in contrasting the ideal world of car ads with the actual, highly frustrating world in which she and her readers have to drive.

STUDENT DIALOGUE: RELATING TO READERS

Writing in a Visual Age: You begin your essay by presenting information that demonstrates the importance of understanding other cultures. What were your reasons for beginning with this information?

Nathan Swinton: My goal was to invite the readers into my essay by emphasizing the importance of the issue—I wanted to give them a reason for hearing out my argument. In addition, I hoped to establish common ground with them through this passage and let them know that I, too, understood how pressing an issue multicultural education is in today's schools.

Establishing Conflict

A conflict is at the heart of every position paper; there's no need to take a position unless there is a disagreement, a disparity between the way things are and the way they should be, or a difference among competing ideas, attitudes, or courses of action. If readers are to become engaged, if they are to read beyond the title of a position paper, they will have to be aware of that conflict. Even more important, they will have to see how that conflict affects them directly or clearly relates to what they know, care about, and need.

❯ For more examples of
establishing conflict, see
Chapter 3, p. 164.

Consider, for example, the beginning of Ellen Goodman's "SUVs Belong in Car Ads Only." Goodman makes a sharp distinction between "the real world" in which she and her readers "creep and beep on some misnomered expressway" and the idealized world of car ads in which people "cruise along deserted, tree-lined roads." If readers haven't been stuck in heavy traffic and haven't seen the sort of car ads Goodman describes, they may not understand how Goodman's position paper relates to them. And if they don't grasp this relationship, there's not much chance they will read beyond the first couple of paragraphs. They may never get to the point where Goodman begins her "full-boil rant against the archenemy of commuters everywhere: sport utility vehicles." (And those readers who drive SUVs are likely either to quit reading when they see where Goodman is heading or to continue reading only to look for places to argue with what she says.)

Goodman's way of engaging her readers shows that writers can establish conflict and relate to readers simultaneously. That is, writers can present information that conflicts with what readers know, care about, and need. In any case, you should create a conflict that will motivate people to read your position paper. The following list illustrates several strategies for doing this.

How to Establish Conflict

Strategies	Examples
Refer to widely divergent attitudes or practices. Refer to ways in which people disagree on your topic; mention conflicting actions or policies.	*"Up in Arms over Decision" (p. 211) begins by referring to different ways in which New York courts and juries do things: "the upstate way, the downstate way, and Brooklyn." LeBrun can assume that his readers in upstate New York will see the upstate way as different from and better than the other two ways.*
Create or incorporate a visual image that suggests conflict or danger. This may take the form of a picture, drawing, graph, or highly descriptive written text.	*"Human Organ Donation: Gift or Graft?" (p. 203) uses language to create two disparate images of the same child—one, a sickly, unhappy baby who desperately needed a liver transplant; the other, a healthy, happy boy who had undergone a successful transplant operation. For an example of an illustration that suggests danger, see "Yes, Let's Pay for Organs" (p. 201).*

How to Establish Conflict

Strategies	Examples
Use a "point-counterpoint" structure. Summarize the opposing point of view and then assert your own. This often takes the form of "Such-and-such appears to be true, but in reality something quite different is true." If you expect your audience to take you seriously, present the opposing point of view clearly and fairly.	*Although the author of "School Vouchers: The Wrong Choice for Public Education" (p. 206) clearly disapproves of school vouchers, he or she spends a full paragraph not only summarizing what proponents of vouchers want to do but also attributing an honorable motive to their efforts: they are "attempting to implement innovative ideas to rescue children from failing school systems, particularly in inner-city neighborhoods" (paragraph 1). In the subsequent paragraph, the writer even acknowledges that school vouchers might appear to be a good idea. Only after this acknowledgment does the writer assert his or her own position.*
Present some startling information that challenges readers' preconceptions. On many controversial topics, readers are likely to have strong opinions that are not necessarily based on factual information. One way to engage readers is to present information that challenges these opinions. This information may involve statistics, quotations, anecdotes, or eyewitness accounts, but it must be specific and come from sources your audience is likely to see as credible.	*Paragraph 1 of "Striking a Balance in Multicultural Education" (p. 213) points out that within about thirty years, "non-English-speaking students will account for approximately forty percent of the school-age population."*

Working on the Assignment

Engaging Your Audience

⟩ Look on the Web, in magazines, and in books to find a position paper in which the first few paragraphs do a good job of engaging a reader's interest. Be prepared to show this position paper to your classmates and explain your answers to the following questions: What assumptions does the writer appear to be making about the reader's knowledge, needs, and values? What aspects of the beginning of the position paper would appeal to a person with the knowledge, needs, and values you have identified?

continued

continued

❯ Review—and, if necessary, revise—your context analysis, being careful to describe your reader's knowledge, needs, and values.

❯ Using one or more of the strategies for establishing conflict or relating to readers, write one or more introductory paragraphs that seem likely to engage the attention of the audience you have

described. You may want to try more than one approach.

❯ Bring this introductory material to class, along with your context analysis. Ask your classmates to tell you whether the introduction you have written seems likely to engage the intended audience. Also ask your classmates whether they can think of other strategies to engage your audience.

Creating an Appropriate Voice

The voice of a document reflects the writer's attitude toward the topic and toward the reader. In a position paper, you're taking a stand on a particular issue, so you're either for or against something. You may feel very strongly about the issue; indeed, you may even be angry about some aspect of it. But, as a rule, it's not a good idea to be angry with your audience. In other words, make sure that you don't confuse your attitude toward the topic with your attitude toward the reader. This will become clearer if we take a look at an example.

Go back to Goodman's "SUVs Belong in Car Ads Only," and read the first three paragraphs aloud. What kind of voice do you hear? There's an informality and a friendliness to this voice, but also a sense of frustration. The informality and friendliness come from the author's use of casual language—phrases such as "Or better yet" and words such as "creep and beep" and "stall and crawl"—and from her use of first-person pronouns. She starts out talking about herself—"I want to write car ads"—in the first paragraph, shifts to "you and I" in the second paragraph, and moves on to "we" in the third paragraph. She's gradually moving from a story about herself to a story that everyone who drives in city traffic can share.

The sense of frustration comes from the parallel structure that Goodman creates throughout this section. In the opening paragraph, she presents two worlds: the real world, where someone might write car ads, and a fantasy world, where someone might live in a car ad. The next two paragraphs continue to bounce back and forth between the real world (where drivers "creep" and "stall" and "circle" and "get stuck") and the fantasy world (where drivers "cruise" and "race" and "pull up" and "navigate").

What Goodman has accomplished in this first section is to establish a voice that is friendly toward the reader. It's as if she's saying, "You and I are in this together. I know how frustrated you are—I'm frustrated, too." Once she has established her attitude toward her reader, she changes focus, now giving full voice to her attitude toward the topic. Go back and read the next two paragraphs of the article aloud.

Goodman is still informal, and she's still frustrated, but now she's angry. However, she expresses her anger not toward her audience but toward her subject, SUVs—"those gas-guzzling, parking-space-hogging, bullies of the highway." In one short sentence she has captured her feelings about this topic, using words that convey her feelings very clearly. And throughout the rest of the piece she uses words and phrases that continue to reinforce the angry, frustrated voice—such as "last gasp" and "traffic-jammed day" and "behemoth."

Such words as these make it clear that Goodman is appealing to emotions, trying to stir her audience's feelings. Her voice not only reflects the type of appeal she is making but is to a large extent determined by that appeal. If she had wanted to create a logical appeal, she would probably have created a very different type of voice. Consequently, as you think about the type of voice you want to create, also think about the type of appeal you want to make. In Goodman's position paper, you have already seen some strategies for creating the sort of voice one associates with appeals to emotion: she chooses words that have strong emotional connotations, and she mentions conflicts that capture some of the frustrations her readers are likely to feel.

Other examples in Reading to Write show a range of strategies you might use in creating a voice that is consistent with a particular type of appeal. How do you decide which type of voice (or combination of voices) to create? That depends to a great extent on the topic you are discussing and the knowledge, values, and needs of the audience you are addressing.

Emotional Appeals

When you appeal to readers' emotions, you want to create a voice that will engage your readers' feelings. Here are some strategies that will help you do so.

How to Make Emotional Appeals

Strategies	Examples
Use language and details that evoke strong emotional reactions. Different people may have very different reactions to a given word or piece of information. So before you use words and details that create strong emotional reactions, refer to the section of your context analysis in which you explain what your audience knows, values, and needs. Use that explanation to anticipate your audience's likely reaction to the specific words and details you include.	*In "Human Organ Donation: Gift or Graft?" (p. 203), Bufill begins his discussion of organ donation by describing a photograph of a child in desperate need of a liver transplant: "a despondent, jaundiced infant with a huge, fluid-filled belly and limp, unsettled limbs stretched out in every direction" (paragraph 2). Surely many people—especially parents and grandparents—will be moved by this image.*
Describe the actions of a group your readers are likely to oppose or even see as an enemy. It is especially effective if you can let readers see that you join them in opposing that enemy.	*In "Up in Arms over Decision" (p. 211), LeBrun refers to a group his readers will likely see as an opponent: the "anti-gun crowd."*
Identify consequences that are likely to inspire or alarm your readers. Help your readers see what is likely to happen if they act or speak in a certain way; help them see the potential or actual effects of an action, comment, or belief.	*"School Vouchers: The Wrong Choice for Public Education" (p. 206) contends that "vouchers undermine public schools" and cites specific ways in which vouchers would likely have this consequence for public education.*
Make comparisons that are likely to evoke strong feelings in your readers. The key phrase here is *in your readers*. A comparison that means one thing to you might mean something quite different to your readers—or it might mean nothing at all. Consider your readers' knowledge, values, and needs so that you can make comparisons that are valid from your readers' perspective.	*Describing the photograph of a healthy baby, Bufill says that the infant is "beaming as he grasped his foot with his right hand and a toy with his left, as if trying to decide which to chew on first" (paragraph 2).* *In criticizing what he sees as lax gun laws in neighboring states, LeBrun contends that "[b]uying handguns [in those states] is as easy as buying a six-pack" (paragraph 9).*

Logical Appeals

A logical appeal is diametrically opposed to an emotional appeal. Rather than trying to stir readers' emotions, an appeal to logic seeks common ground with their intellect, avoiding personal feelings and reactions as much as possible. The voice associated with this sort of appeal is likely to seem calm, unemotional, thoughtful. In making this sort of appeal, you can use some of the strategies identified earlier in this chapter: citing sources your reader will see as credible, acknowledging and responding to objections readers are likely to raise, considering more than one perspective on the issue (for example, mentioning both pros and cons), or basing your argument on principles your readers are likely to accept. The following list explains some additional ways you can make logical appeals to create an appropriate voice in your opinion.

How to Make Logical Appeals

Strategies	Examples
Summarize opposing points of view accurately and fairly. If the person with whom you are disagreeing feels you understand his or her position, that person may become more willing to consider your position. Also, your effort to summarize an opposing point of view might lead you to re-think your own point of view.	*Although Swinton feels that some critics are too extreme in their views of multicultural education, he summarizes those views carefully in "Striking a Balance in Multicultural Education" (p. 213), quoting effectively from four well-known critics of multicultural education.*
Acknowledge and refute opposing points of view. Refute counterarguments clearly, especially by mentioning a principle readers are likely to agree with, providing factual information, or citing authorities that support your point of view.	*In "Yes, Let's Pay for Organs" (p. 201), Krauthammer notes that libertarians might argue that poor people should be allowed to sell organs so that they "can live a better life." That should not be allowed, Krauthammer argues, because it undermines society's fundamental assumptions about "human dignity."*
Use impartial language to cite examples, precedents, and authorities, especially referring to institutions, organizations, or groups of people rather than to individuals. Take care when using the personal pronouns *I*, *you*, or *we*. Narratives from your own experience can be very persuasive, but be sure the story's relevance is clear and that it supports your thesis.	*"School Vouchers: The Wrong Choice for Public Education" (p. 206) frequently refers to authoritative examples and precedents ("Supreme Court precedent," for example) and talks about groups of people ("legislators, school boards, education professionals," for example) rather than naming specific individuals.*

Ethical Appeals

It is relatively easy to characterize the voices associated with emotional and logical appeals: an appeal to readers' feelings is likely to be expressed in an emotional voice; an appeal to logic is likely to be expressed in a rational, unemotional voice. But it's hard to associate any one type of voice with an ethical appeal. The goal in this type of appeal is to get the audience to trust you, to see you as one of them. If your audience feels strongly about a given subject, you may need to show them that you feel strongly about it, too. If members of your audience tend to see themselves as logical, rational, and unemotional, you may need to create a voice that displays some of these characteristics.

Even if it's not possible to identify a single voice or set of attitudes that is associated with an ethical appeal, it is possible to identify some general strategies to create a voice that will get your audience to trust you as one of them. The following list suggests a couple of strategies for doing this.

How to Make Ethical Appeals

Strategies	Examples
Use language that will establish yourself as someone readers can like and trust. If you are addressing an audience of experts, you may want to use the specialized terminology of their field; if you are using terms that are well known and agreed upon in a given field, you may not need to define them. However, if you are not addressing an expert audience, try to use language your readers hear in their daily lives; when you need to introduce specialized terms, explain them with language and examples your readers know well.	*Bufill, author of "Human Organ Donation: Gift or Graft?" (p. 203), is a physician, so presumably he could have used clinical, medical terms in describing the photograph of an unhealthy infant. In place of saying that the infant had "a huge, fluid-filled belly" (paragraph 2), for instance, he could have said the child had a* distended abdomen. *But had he done so, he would have been using medical terminology, language that is relatively unfamiliar to his audience of lay people.*
Imply that you and your readers are on the same side of a conflict. One way to do this is to identify a common enemy.	*LeBrun, in "Up in Arms over Decision" (p. 211), identifies a group (the "anti-gun crowd") to which both he and his readers are opposed.*
Another way is to use inclusive language, implying that you and your readers are on the same side in a conflict.	*In "SUVs Belong in Car Ads Only" (p. 195), Goodman uses the pronoun* we *to refer to herself and her readers and the pronoun* they *to refer to their common enemy, drivers of SUVs.*

STUDENT DIALOGUE: CREATING AN APPROPRIATE VOICE

Writing in a Visual Age: In your context analysis, you said you wanted to create a "calm, rational voice." What are some of the ways you tried to create this voice? Why was it important to create such a voice?

Nathan Swinton: My main method of creating such a voice was to give due credit to any arguments I addressed, even if I disagreed with them. I also pointed out any holes in my own argument and noted that I didn't have all the answers—for example, noting how Rose's teaching style wasn't the only possible solution. I did these things to make my readers feel I was making an educated point rather than forcing my point of view on them. Creating this voice gives me greater credibility, helps my readers to better see the merit in my argument, and increases the likelihood that they'll agree with me.

Working on the Assignment

Creating an Appropriate Voice

How do you want members of your audience to see you? Do you want them to regard you as someone who is passionately committed to a particular point of view; as someone who shares the audience's concerns and values; or as someone who takes a cool, rational approach? What are some of the words you'd like your readers to use in describing the voice you create in your position paper: *frustrated? enthusiastic? thoughtful? courteous? angry? critical?* These, of course, are not the only choices—you have the whole range of human emotion and experience to choose from. As part of making these choices, you should do the following.

〉 Review your context analysis (revise it if you need to).

〉 List some of the words and phrases you hope readers would use to describe the voice in your position paper.

〉 Show both the context analysis and the list of words and phrases to someone else (a classmate or your instructor); ask this person to tell you whether the voice you hope to create makes sense, given what your context analysis says about your intended audience and purpose.

〉 Using what you learn from your classmate or instructor, revise the list of words that describe the voice you want to create.

〉 Ask someone (a classmate, your instructor, or a friend) to read a section of your draft aloud, and listen to the sound of his or her voice. Can you hear the attitude you want to create in the sound of this reader's voice? If you can, good. If you can't, look

continued

continued

closely at your draft to see what words and phrases you need to change in order to create the voice you want.

> Ask someone to read your introductory paragraph(s) (aloud or silently) and then list the words he or she would use to describe the voice you're trying to create

and the type of appeals you're making. Does this reader's list match yours? On the basis of what this reader tells you, decide whether you need to revise either your conception of the voice you want to create or your introduction. Or do you need to revise both?

Providing Structure

Whenever you write about a complex, significant topic, there's a chance you will be uncertain about what to say or how best to say it. This is especially true when writing a position paper. As you learn more about a topic, you may start re-thinking your basic claim or thesis or even discovering that you have been mistaken about basic facts related to your topic. It is quite possible that you will go through a period of fumbling around, trying to decide exactly what your position is or groping for the words and reasons that will have the best chance of influencing the readers you hope to reach. Frustrating as it usually is, this time of fumbling and uncertainty can also be a time of testing and refining ideas, a time of growth.

For you as a writer, this process can be a good thing. But it's not necessarily an experience you want to put your readers through. As a general rule, you should make it possible for your readers to (1) identify your thesis, or your position on the topic you are writing about; (2) anticipate where your argument is headed in any given passage; and (3) see how one segment of your text relates to the segment that precedes it. In other words, you should give your work the sort of structure discussed in other chapters of this book. Make your ideas accessible, create clear expectations, and provide links between one paragraph (or section of the text) and the next.

Making Information Accessible

Remember that your readers might not read every word of the texts you create. Instead, they might look for information about specific points they are interested in. The following list suggests several ways you can make it easy for readers to find what they are looking for.

How to Make Information Accessible

Strategies	Examples
Put a thesis statement where readers will expect to find it. Often, thesis statements occur at the end of an introductory section of a position paper. In some cases, a thesis may also be expressed or implied in a title or in a caption that appears near the title. Placing a thesis statement at the end of an introduction ensures that readers do not have to look far for important information—the position you are arguing for or against in your paper.	*The title of "New Roads Are Not the Answer" (p. 198) implies the position the paper will take. The last sentence of the introductory paragraph is a direct thesis explaining the main reason why the paper will take this position: "Building new roads actually causes more congestion."*
Use headings. Let readers know the point you will make or the topic you will discuss in an upcoming section of your position paper.	*One of the clearest examples of this appears in "School Vouchers: The Wrong Choice for Public Education" (p. 206), where the headings assert the points to be made in the following paragraphs: Vouchers Are Constitutionally Suspect, Vouchers Undermine Public Schools, and Vouchers Are Not Universally Popular.*
Begin paragraphs with topic sentences. Not all paragraphs have topic sentences, and not all topic sentences appear at the beginning of a paragraph. But when you are writing a position paper, it's usually a good idea to come right out and let readers know what you are getting at, usually in the first or second sentence of a paragraph.	*In paragraph 7 of "Up in Arms over Decision" (p. 211), LeBrun begins by acknowledging that his readers might not like the "message" sent by a recent jury decision in Brooklyn. The second sentence asserts his point: "But it [the message] is clear." LeBrun then goes on to explain what he sees as that message: "The general population is tired of the mayhem guns do to the innocent. Make it stop, they say."*
Use special typefaces and white space to highlight key points.	*"New Roads Are Not the Answer" uses special type treatments repeatedly to make information easily accessible to readers. Boldface statistics stand out dramatically. Large italic typeface makes headings easy to find and read. White space divides columns and separates text from visuals.*

Creating Expectations

Studies have demonstrated that readers often try to anticipate what a writer is going to say next. Consequently, you'll want to provide your readers with a structure that helps them form clear, accurate expectations as they read. To do so, you can use the strategies in the following list.

How to Create Expectations

Strategies	Examples
Assert or strongly imply your position in the title of your position paper.	*Examples of titles that let readers immediately see what point the writers are going to make include "SUVs Belong in Car Ads Only" (p. 195), "School Vouchers: The Wrong Choice for Public Education" (p. 206), and "Striking a Balance in Multicultural Education" (p. 213).*
Assert or strongly imply your basic claim early in the text. Even if you imply your position in a title or subtitle, it's often a good idea to state your thesis at the end of the introduction. In this way, readers will not be distracted by suspense or confusion. When they know what to expect, it is easier for them to follow your argument and compare or contrast it to what they already think—and perhaps be persuaded by what you say.	*The title "School Vouchers: The Wrong Choice for Public Education" clearly indicates the basic thesis of this position paper. But that thesis is reiterated and refined at the end of the second paragraph. School vouchers are "wrong" because they "subvert the constitutional principle of separation of church and state and threaten to undermine our system of public education."*
Use forecasting words or phrases. These terms appear near the beginning of a section of text and indicate the topic to be covered. They often appear in thesis statements or in topic sentences for individual paragraphs. But they may also introduce longer passages within the main part of the position paper.	*Paragraph 2 of "Striking a Balance in Multicultural Education" notes that some proponents of multicultural education often imagine "dire problems" that will occur if schools do not promote multicultural education. The next several sentences give examples of these problems.*

Creating Links

Even though readers may not read every word of your position paper, they still will want to have a sense of flow, of how a given paragraph or set of paragraphs relates to the passages that precede and follow it. Here are two strategies to create links that will give readers a sense of flow.

How to Create Links

Strategies	Examples
Use transition words or phrases. Use words that indicate when, where, or why something happened or how ideas are connected.	*Examples occur throughout all the position papers in Reading to Write. Examples include such words as* recently, after, between, far, behind, also, but, moreover, *and* paradoxically.
Refer to a point that has been mentioned in a previous passage, and then add some new information about that point.	*In paragraphs 7 and 8 of "SUVs Belong in Car Ads Only" (p. 195), Goodman describes what she sees as the safety hazards presented by SUVs. Then she begins paragraph 9 this way: "But the biggest and burliest of the pack aren't just safety hazards, they're environmental hazards."* *In paragraph 3 of "Yes, Let's Pay for Organs" (p. 201), Krauthammer mentions one possible objection to his point of view: payment for organs may mean more to the families of poor people than to the families of rich people. Krauthammer begins the next paragraph by asking, "So what? Where is the harm?"*

Working on the Assignment

Providing Structure

Bring to class a copy of a position paper that does a good job of making its structure very clear. Be prepared to show your instructor and classmates how the author(s) enabled you to see the structure of the argument. After identifying strategies other writers have used, review your exploratory draft, looking for ways you might use some of these strategies to make the structure of your own position paper clear.

Concluding Your Position Paper

The most important thing to do in the conclusion of an argument is to say something that the audience can remember easily—perhaps something that will make them think about this topic more, or that will get them to take action. Your conclusion is a reflection of your purpose. No matter what you set out to do, now is the time to make it happen. To get some ideas for writing conclusions, look at the following strategies.

How to Conclude

Strategies	Examples
Frame your argument, returning to an idea you mentioned in the introduction.	*In the first two paragraphs of "SUVs Belong in Car Ads Only" (p. 195), Goodman talks about the "commercial fantasy land" of car ads. In the last paragraph, she refers again to this fantasy world, where "the skies are always clean, the drivers are always relaxed, and there's never, ever, another car in sight."*
Restate your main claims clearly and unequivocally.	*In "Striking a Balance in Multicultural Education" (p. 213), Swinton concludes by acknowledging that "[e]xtreme positions on both sides of the issue abound" and that "on neither side . . . are these scenarios true." He restates his main claim in response, observing that "one must also be wary of going overboard to prep students for the global society that lies ahead. Moderation is key."*
Mention the consequences of accepting or ignoring the position you have adopted.	*LeBrun's main point in "Up in Arms over Decision" (p. 211) is that gun owners should insist that gun manufacturers be held to "the same high standards" to which New York gun owners are held. LeBrun concludes by noting that if manufacturers are not held to these standards, owners may find their rights to have guns are jeopardized.*
Recommend a course of action.	*The final paragraph of "School Vouchers: The Wrong Choice for Public Education" (p. 206) urges readers not to adopt vouchers but to "dedicate themselves to finding solutions that will be available to every American schoolchild and that take into account the important legacy of the First Amendment."*

Working on the Assignment

Concluding Your Position Paper

Using a strategy identified earlier (or a different strategy from a position paper you have analyzed), write a conclusion for your position paper. Share your draft with your instructor or some classmates who have previously read your exploratory draft and your introduction. Ask your classmates to identify the strategies you have used and tell you whether the conclusion seems appropriate, given what you have said about your audience and the type of appeals you have been making in your position paper.

❯ For a sample visual argument, see "New Roads Are Not the Answer," p. 198.

Designing Your Position Paper and Integrating Visual Information

As noted earlier, many position papers make rather limited use of visual cues. However, as "New Roads Are Not the Answer" makes clear, it is possible to make extensive use of visual elements in arguing for a position. Although you should check with your instructor to determine what kinds of visuals are appropriate for your assignment, here are several strategies you might consider using.

How to Design Your Position Paper and Integrate Visual Information

Strategies

Consider using headings to introduce key points. This will make your claims more readily accessible (that is, easier to find quickly).

Examples

"New Roads Are Not the Answer" (p. 198) makes headings stand out by using large, italicized sans serif type. (For more information on styles of type, see Chapter 8.) These headings also stand out by using the same color as the header and footer, with the blue giving coherence to the important elements on the page.

continued

How to Design Your Position Paper and Integrate Visual Information

continued

Strategies	Examples
Decide on the number of columns you will use. Depending on guidelines established by your instructor, you may have several options: a single column or two columns, each of which will occupy about half the width of the page. If you are using standard 8 1/2-by-11-inch paper, avoid a three-column format; such a format can make your work difficult to read. (For more advice on using columns, see Chapter 8.)	*Sometimes position papers are designed to appear in a single column (as, for example, in the Web text "School Vouchers: The Wrong Choice for Public Education," p. 206). But often (as in the newsletter "New Roads Are Not the Answer," for example) print opinions appear in two columns, especially when published in magazines or newspapers.*
Identify the specific appeal you want each visual to make. As mentioned in the analysis of "New Roads" on p. 193, a visual may make more than one type of appeal. But you will want to make sure that each visual makes an appeal (or appeals) that reinforces those made in your written text.	*Photographs and bar graphs in "New Roads Are Not the Answer" illustrate ways visuals can make the full range of appeals—ethical and emotional as well as logical. The illustrations that appear with "Yes, Let's Pay for Organs" (p. 201) and "Human Organ Donation: Gift or Graft?" (p. 203) appeal to emotions via stark images of hearts.*
Make sure that visual elements such as pictures, charts, and graphs are located near the text they pertain to. As a rule, these visual elements elaborate on or dramatize something you've said in your written text. This effect will be lost if the visual element is too far removed from the written text to which it relates.	*In "New Roads Are Not the Answer," the picture of a traffic jam is located directly to the right of a paragraph that begins "Traffic congestion has become an everyday reality. . . ." The bar graph "Building Roads Doesn't Solve Congestion" appears immediately after the sentence "Building new roads actually creates more congestion."*
Make sure that visual elements such as pictures or graphs are appropriately labeled and captioned. These captions might take the form of a title and perhaps a sentence that encapsulates the point of the visual. If the visual is taken from another source, you should identify that source underneath the visual.	*On rare occasions, a visual—such as the picture of the traffic jam in "New Roads Are Not the Answer"—requires neither a label nor a caption. But other visuals in "New Roads" are more typical. For example, the bar graph "Building Roads Doesn't Solve Congestion" labels each element of the graph ("Percentage Increase," "New Lane Miles," and "New Traffic"). This visual also asserts the point of the graph in the caption "For every 10% increase in lane mile capacity, a 9% increase in traffic results."*

Designing Your Position Paper

Look back over the selections in Reading to Write, and identify types of visual features you might want to incorporate into your position paper. As you think about the design of your position paper, check with your instructor about the kinds of visual elements that may be appropriate for the assignment. Keeping your instructor's comments in mind, identify the visual features you want your position paper to have.

Finishing Up

After all the reading and thinking you have been doing, you should have developed a clear position on the topic you have chosen to discuss. You should now be ready to create a review draft that argues your position as clearly and persuasively as possible. Once you have created this draft, you will need to assess it carefully, not only by critiquing it yourself but also by getting others' opinions. In this process you subject your draft to a final review and then use these assessments to make any needed revisions in content, organization, style, or format.

Creating a Review Draft

In preparation for writing the review draft, look back at the context analysis you did earlier. Have you gained any new information that would lead you to revise the context analysis in any way? For example, have you learned something new about your audience's values, information that might influence the voice you create or the type of appeals you make?

Also look back at your exploratory draft, noting ways you have modified your ideas or strengthened your arguments. Ask yourself whether this draft still makes the claims you want to make and whether your arguments still seem persuasive and appropriate for the intended audience. Notice points at which you want to improve upon the exploratory draft, perhaps changing the basic points about your subject, adding or deleting details, and adding, deleting, or modifying reasons in support of your position.

As you work on your review draft, take some pains to make the structure clear. It might help to write an informal outline indicating the main points you want to make and the arguments that will support each main point. You should also use the strategies described on pp. 249–251 to make your work accessible, create clear expectations for your readers, and link paragraphs or larger sections of text.

Getting a Final Review

Once you have revised your review draft to make it complete and polished, you need to have it reviewed, preferably by one or more people who understand the principles (analyzing context, engaging readers, and so on) that you have been working with in this chapter.

> ⟩ Give the reviewer a copy of your draft, one he or she can make notes on.
> ⟩ Give the reviewer a copy of your context analysis. If necessary, revise that analysis before giving it to the reviewer.
> ⟩ Ask the reviewer to begin his or her response by answering the following question: Given what I say in my context analysis, how likely does it seem that my arguments will be persuasive to the audience I am trying to reach?
> ⟩ Ask the reviewer to adopt the perspective of the audience described in your context analysis and then use the following checklist in commenting on your work.

Checklist for Final Review

⟩ bedfordstmartins.com/
visualage

To download this checklist as a worksheet, click on
CHAPTER 4 ⟩
WORKSHEETS

1 In my context analysis, please highlight any statements that give you a good sense of the knowledge, values, and needs of my intended audience. (For an example, see p. 226). Please indicate any statements that need to be clarified.

2 In my context analysis, please highlight any statements that give you a good sense of the circumstances, purposes, and expected format for my position paper. (For an example of a good context analysis, see p. 226.) Please indicate any statements that need to be clarified.

3 In what specific passages have I developed my topic thoroughly, especially by

   (a) providing reasons and evidence that my audience will see as persuasive,

   (b) anticipating and responding to objections or questions my audience is likely to raise, and

   (c) making appropriate appeals? (For examples, see pp. 244–246.)

4 In what passages could I make my paper more persuasive? What strategies (explained on pp. 233–236) might I use to do this?

5 What portions of my introduction seem likely to engage the interest of my intended audience? What are some strategies (explained on pp. 238–241) that might make the introduction more engaging?

6 How would you describe the voice I have created? At what points does that voice seem appropriate, given my intended audience and topic? What strategies (explained on pp. 243–246) might help me make the voice clearer or more appropriate?

7 What are some words or phrases that provide a clear structure for my position paper, making information accessible, creating clear expectations for readers, and indicating links between paragraphs or larger sections of text? What strategies (explained on pp. 249–251) might I use to make the structure of my position paper clearer?

8 How does the conclusion of my position paper reinforce or extend the main claim I am trying to make? What strategies (explained on p. 252) might I use to make my conclusion more effective?

9 If the position paper includes photographs or other visual elements, what do they contribute to the persuasiveness of my argument? Do they have appropriate captions and/or explanations in the text?

If possible, ask the reviewer to talk with you about your review draft as well as make notes on it. Since position papers invite controversy, it's possible that your reviewers will disagree with one or more points you make. When this happens, your strong impulse will be to argue with your reviewers, showing them where they are wrong or have missed the point. Resist this impulse, at least at first. Instead, try to find out why they disagree with you. Once you have a good idea of what their concerns or objections are, you might respond to what they have said, asking how persuasive they find your responses.

Revising Your Position Paper

Up to this point, you have been advised to listen to reviewers' comments without explaining, arguing, or making judgments about the validity of those comments. But once you have a good idea of how your reviewers respond, it is time to go back through your notes on those comments. Bearing in mind your intended audience and purpose, decide which comments are most valid. Then use the strategies referred to in the Checklist for Final Review.

After resolving all the issues that need attention, proofread carefully and correct any typographical or formatting errors. Then submit this final draft to your instructor.

> **bedfordstmartins.com/ visualage**
>
> *To download these questions as a worksheet, click on* **CHAPTER 4 > WORKSHEETS**

Taking Stock of Where You Are

Once your instructor has returned the final draft of your work, think back over all the comments you received—from classmates as well as your instructor—and write out answers to the following questions. (You might want to keep these in a journal or in a special section of a notebook.)

Questions for Assessing Your Growth as a Writer

- What appears to be my greatest area of strength?
- Where am I having the greatest difficulty?
- What am I learning about the process of writing?
- What am I learning about giving and receiving feedback on writing?
- What have I learned from writing a position paper that I can use in my next assignment for this course, for another course, or for work?

SAMPLE STUDENT ASSESSMENT

Here's how Nathan Swinton answered these questions for the position paper he wrote on multicultural education (p. 213).

What appears to be my greatest area of strength?

What helps my writing more than anything is my preparation. I take the time to understand the articles about which I speak and then consider how best I can convey my argument to my reader. Following this strategy, I map out the course of my essay first in my head and then on scraps of paper, often forming topic or clincher sentences in my head in the process. I do all this work before composing a single word on my computer, and I set out to write my papers with confidence, keeping in mind that I know what I want to say and I just need to say it.

Where am I having the greatest difficulty?

I sometimes find myself in a writing rut when it comes to expressing thoughts or organizing my paper, using the same transition phrases or conclusions repeatedly. I also have had increasing difficulty in beginning the process of writing, and I set up a mental block that I need to be able to break through more quickly and more determinedly than I usually am able to do.

What am I learning about the process of writing?

In recent months, I've learned two important things about the nature of writing. First, writing is something that is a process and is in a state of constant change. One's writing can always be improved—an author must be able to reach that state of near-perfection and be satisfied with his or her work. Second, I've learned that one's audience is always changing. One phrase or minutia of grammar might strike the eye of one professor but completely miss that of another. Similarly, certain phrases or structural elements might appeal to a particular group of readers but not another. A writer should strive to make his or her writing as universally appealing as possible but always keep in mind the specific audience for whom the piece is being written.

SAMPLE STUDENT ASSESSMENT

What am I learning about giving and receiving feedback on writing?

I do not take criticism well, and I thrive on positive feedback. I'm somewhat stubborn when it comes to making changes to my writing, but I'm trying to make myself more open to considering others' ideas. I am much more apt to listen to an authority figure—an editor, teacher, etc.—than a peer, so I don't make as much use of peer critiques as I could or probably should, as they approach my essay from a fresh perspective and can have insightful comments to share. I recognize that this approach to writing limits me, and I'm aware that I need to be more open when it comes to feedback. Critiquing my peers' work is often beneficial since it helps me recognize both the good and the bad in their work, which I can then implement or avoid in my own work.

What have I learned from writing a position paper that I can use in my next assignment for this course, for another course, or for work?

I'm much more aware of the different approaches to making an argument and how particular argumentative methods work better in some cases than in others. I anticipate that these improvements in crafting an argument will prove beneficial for me in several ways. As the editor-in-chief of our school paper, I write editorials promoting a particular point of view and taking a stance on certain issues. I also hope to go to law school one day, and I anticipate that the ability to express an argument on paper will be of great aid in that setting.

5

Evaluations

N EVALUATION IS, QUITE SIMPLY, A JUDGMENT ABOUT A GIVEN TOPIC, AN ARGUMENT SHOWING that something is good or bad, fair or unfair, desirable or undesirable, or better or worse than something else. Writers of evaluations give clear, appropriate reasons (typically referred to as *criteria*) to justify their judgments and present specific details to show how well the topic meets (or fails to meet) certain criteria. Throughout history, people have been making value judgments in every aspect of their lives. In our society, typical value judgments might include "Professor X is a good teacher," "That movie is not worth seeing," and "The organization's plan for raising money is a smart idea." Sometimes an evaluative comment is little more than an effort to blow off steam: "That test was ridiculously unfair!" Was the test really unfair? Maybe it was. But maybe the speaker is just asking for a little sympathy or expressing frustration that was actually caused by failure to study for the test.

In other cases, however, evaluations are intended to be taken seriously, and the evaluator presents criteria that he

"A high-quality vanilla ice cream should be mild but not bland, sweet but not overpoweringly so. The dairy should be balanced with a vanilla-bean, quality vanilla-extract, or other real vanilla flavor."

– Consumer Reports, *"Cream of the Crop"*

or she believes can serve as a reliable basis for someone else's decisions and actions. In this chapter, you'll be learning how to write this more complex type of evaluation—and to understand the effects your evaluation may have. An evaluation may lead to a decision or action that is relatively trivial: "I guess I don't need to go see that new movie." But often an evaluation can have substantial consequences, affecting people's reputations, careers, or finances—think, for instance, about letters of recommendation, job-performance reviews, course evaluations, or product reviews.

If it is true that evaluations can have serious consequences for others, it is also true that they can have serious consequences for people who write them. A habit of making careless or thoughtless value judgments can cost people credibility, friendships, status, promotions, or jobs. For everyone's sake, then, an evaluation has to possess certain attributes.

> It should be balanced, acknowledging both good and bad and avoiding oversimplification.
> It should be honest, not deliberately ignoring details that challenge one's judgments and being forthright about the criteria underlying those judgments.
> It should be useful, providing readers with a sound basis for thinking and acting.

How can you make sure your evaluations are balanced, honest, and useful? First, you have to think carefully about the audience and purpose for the evaluation and carefully ground your judgments in fact. But facts rarely speak for themselves. Any effective evaluation must be based on criteria that help people answer questions of value.

Addressing Questions of Value and Criteria

People may evaluate any number of things, including products, people, policies, situations, literary works, works of art, films, and musical or dramatic performances. But all evaluations come down to one basic question of value: Is the thing—a product, for example, or an idea, a movie, or a policy—good or bad, worthy or worthless, desirable or undesirable, fair or unfair? This basic question of value may take several different forms.

> Is this thing as good as something else?
> Is it as good as someone expected or hoped?
> Is it as good as it might have been?

> Is it as good as promised?

> Is it as good as someone needs it to be?

> Is it as good as a particular set of standards requires?

Answers to questions such as these depend not only on careful observation of facts, but also on the use of clear, appropriate *criteria*—the reasons that underlie your judgment about whether something is good or bad, fair or unfair, and so forth.

General Sources of Criteria

The criteria you use as a basis for your evaluation may come from several different sources, and their persuasiveness may vary from one audience to another. As you choose from the following general sources, consider the kinds of sources your particular audience will be most likely to find convincing.

> **The evaluator's own needs and values.** A novice computer user might evaluate a piece of software on the basis of one criterion: ease of use. A more experienced computer user might rely on multiple criteria, such as excellent graphics capability and compatibility with other sophisticated technology.

> **An abstract moral or legal code.** Most legal and ethical systems frown on such acts as lying, cheating, and stealing. So in evaluating, say, a course of action, someone might ask whether that course of action violates a particular legal or ethical code. If so, that course of action is wrong or at least questionable.

> **The goals or practical needs of an organization.** If a fraternity places high value on winning at intramural sports, any plan for recruiting new members will probably be judged in terms of how likely the plan is to attract new members with exceptional athletic ability. If the fraternity is currently facing academic probation, any plan for increasing membership will almost certainly be judged in terms of how likely the plan is to attract members with strong academic records.

> **The *culture*—the shared assumptions and practices—of a group or a larger society.** Some businesses, for example, assume that they must continually change if they are to stay competitive in their fields. Consequently, when it comes time to evaluate employees, these companies may value risk-taking and innovation. Employee evaluations are likely to focus on whether employees propose new projects or more innovative ways to carry out existing projects, even if these proposals entail some degree of risk. Other companies, however, are conservative, placing more value on avoiding risk and maintaining an established routine. When these companies evaluate employees, they may ask how well a particular employee follows established procedures or whether the employee's proposals minimize risks to the company.

Exercise

Think about one type of evaluation that all students routinely encounter: grading. List some of the criteria usually used in grading. What, for example, are some reasons an instructor might have for saying that someone's work is good or bad, acceptable or unacceptable, or better or worse than another student's work? Identify some of the sources of these grading criteria.

Next, answer the following questions about grading.

〉 What do you see as some of the main purposes institutions have for assigning grades?

〉 If grades were abolished, would it be possible to accomplish those purposes in other ways?

〉 How do you think grading fits into the culture of your educational institution overall and with student culture in particular?

Evaluations in Context

Context is always important when you express a value judgment. Assume, for instance, that you and a friend are walking across campus, talking about an exam you have just taken. Both of you think the exam was extremely difficult—maybe even unfairly so. If forced to, you and your friend might admit that you probably shouldn't have waited until late last night to begin studying. Nonetheless, both of you may make some rather harsh value judgments about the exam and maybe the instructor as well. Your evaluations may or may not be fair, but you are expressing them in the relatively safe context of a private conversation with someone who shares your experience and perspective. You may speak freely, and since you are speaking rather than writing, there is no public record for others to examine or challenge.

In other situations, however, your evaluations will be written and subject to public scrutiny by people who may or may not share your feelings and experiences and who may have a direct, personal stake in what you say. In writing such evaluations as these, you are, in effect, moving into a larger and more complex context, one in which your words may have consequences—some of them unexpected—not only for your audience but for yourself as well. You will need to think carefully about key elements of this context: the audiences you intend to address, the circumstances in which they will read your evaluation, and the purposes you hope your evaluation will accomplish.

Audience

If you are evaluating a subject that matters to your intended audience, you will have to be particularly attentive to your audience's values, feelings, and personal experiences. Readers will, of course, want factual information. But judgments of what is good or bad, fair or unfair, wise or foolish, desirable or undesirable are rarely made solely on the basis of facts. Individual personalities, needs, and personal (or cultural) value systems always come into play. You may not need to worry too much about this if your evaluation exists in a very limited context (as with a close friend), where you are writing or speaking confidentially to a single individual with whom you share many experiences and attitudes. But as a general rule, you cannot automatically assume that members of your audience will be working from the same knowledge base as you are or that they are operating on the basis of the same criteria you have in mind.

The success of your evaluation will depend in large part on your ability to base your evaluation on criteria that matter to your audience. For example, if you are reviewing a restaurant for readers of a college newspaper, your criteria might include cost, size of portions, and speed of service. For subscribers to a magazine about fine dining, on the other hand, appropriate criteria might include atmosphere, the chef's training, and the extensiveness of the wine list. Remember: people may draw their criteria from different sources, ranging from their personal needs to the larger culture in which they live. Don't assume that an audience sharing some characteristics with you will necessarily share your sources of criteria. Even if you and your audience are members of the same social group, some of your readers may, for example, be operating with criteria drawn from a religious system that you may not know well.

❯ For help with analyzing your audience, see pp. 304–305.

You also need to consider whether you are likely to have a secondary audience for your evaluation—a person or group of people who are not your primary audience but who may nevertheless be interested in or affected by what you say. A hypothetical example of a secondary audience would be an instructor who happened to overhear you complaining to a friend about the unfairness of a test. A more typical example might arise when you are asked to evaluate the performance of a peer—a classmate, perhaps, or a member of an organization to which you belong. You may intend for your evaluation to be heard or read only by the person who asked you to do it, especially if your evaluation is negative. But word has a way of getting around; comments get repeated, and copies of texts get e-mailed and passed around. As you work on your evaluation for this chapter, make sure your comments will stand up to careful scrutiny by people who are not your primary audience but who might be affected by those comments.

Circumstances

People are most likely to read an evaluation when they are in circumstances that create a pressing need or motive for seeking out someone else's judgment on a question of value. Perhaps they are about to make an important decision or are uncertain of how they feel about an event that has just occurred or an era that is just ending.

The specific decisions your audience wants to make may be trivial (whether to see a particular movie, for example) or profound (whether, for instance, to hire, promote, or fire someone). Time demands may be pressing ("We must have an answer on this by five o'clock today") or virtually nonexistent ("This old car probably will run a while longer before it starts costing too much money in repairs"). Sometimes a reader's decision may have direct personal consequences ("If I say this business plan is good, am I going to lose my job if it fails?" or "Am I going to be able to look this person in the eye if I say his or her efforts aren't good enough?"). Whatever your audience's circumstances may be, you'll need to assess them carefully to ensure that your evaluation relates directly to the circumstances that matter most to readers.

Purposes

In some evaluations, writers seem to want to get something off their chest, perhaps by ranting or by "flaming" or lashing out at someone on the Internet. But for most of the writing you will do in college and your career, it's not enough simply to vent your own feelings by expressing strong judgments about good or bad, fair or unfair, sensible or foolish. In both college and career, your primary purpose in writing an evaluation is to present value judgments that readers will see as *credible*—based on criteria they accept and illustrated with factual statements they see as accurate, fair, and reliable. However, you can modify this purpose somewhat by deciding just how strongly you want to argue for the evaluation you are making.

One purpose of the reviews in the magazine *Consumer Reports*, for example, is to enable readers to form their own conclusions about consumer goods they test and rate. Although reviews usually make very clear judgments, the reviewers do not argue strongly for their conclusions. Instead, they use not only written text but also graphs and other visuals to lay out in painstaking detail the criteria and evidence underlying their evaluations. This combination of written and visual information helps readers assess for themselves the validity of the judgments in any given product review.

Other evaluative pieces (such as restaurant reviews and commentaries on social trends) are more forthrightly persuasive; the authors are likely to have a very strong opinion or reaction and may want readers to share that opinion or reaction. They may use words, details, and criteria that they know will evoke an emotional response in readers. For example, in expressing his disapproval of e-mail, one author in this chapter wants readers to share his pain and feel his annoyance. Consequently, he uses such words as *arrogance, prose at its worst,* and *overwhelm.* He also focuses on aspects of e-mail that his readers—principally adults well into their careers—are likely to find objectionable.

How strongly should your evaluation express your personal feelings or reactions? That depends in large part on your topic and what your audience expects from your review. If your audience wants experimental data on the crashworthiness of a particular SUV, you should probably omit reference to your personal reactions and be as objective as possible in presenting information about how the vehicle fared in crash tests. If, however, the audience is interested in how the vehicle looks and how pleasurable it is to drive, your personal reactions can probably play a larger role in your evaluation.

 For Collaboration

Bring to class an evaluation of a topic (a movie, a product, a restaurant, a college policy) that interests you. Think about whether the author seems to be trying to persuade readers, evoke an emotional response in them, or produce some other reaction. Share your evaluation with one or two classmates and, working together, identify the purposes of the evaluation each of you brought in.

Visual Information in Context

Typically, evaluations supplement written text with visual information, if only a set of symbols to indicate how good something is; stars, for example, are often used to indicate whether a movie or a restaurant is excellent (four stars) or terrible (one star). Other evaluations make much more extensive use of visuals, including pictures, pull quotes, sidebars (inset boxes), and tables. The kinds and amounts of visual information will vary widely, depending on the topic and the context for which the evaluation is written.

Using visual information well in an evaluation helps readers find answers to their questions, persuades them of the writer's credibility, and conveys a coherent attitude toward the topic. Of course, visuals may be unclear, inappropriate, or irrelevant, so you should take care to choose visual information wisely for your evaluation.

To anticipate what your readers will need in terms of the visual information you include in an evaluation, consider the following questions:

> Do the visual elements help the intended readers understand and accept your evaluation of the subject?

> Do the visual elements help readers see how the subject relates to their values?

> Do the visual elements meet (or fail to meet) the criteria derived from those values?

> What does the visual information reveal about your understanding of readers and the topic?

You can answer these questions for your own projects by reading a variety of evaluations and thinking about page layout; images; and charts, graphs, maps, and tables.

> For more information on the effective uses of these visual elements, see **Chapter 8.**

Questions to Ask When Reading Visual Information in Evaluations

● **Does the layout (arrangement) of the page or screen make it easy for the intended readers to find the information they want or need?**

> What kind of information dominates—visual or verbal?

> Are there headings? If so, do they give a clear idea of the information that will appear in the text that follows each heading?

> Are there visual elements, such as sidebars (inset boxes) or pull quotes? If so, do they highlight key pieces of information? Do they help readers distinguish between different kinds of information?

> Are there variations in the size and style of type? If there are variations, what functions do they serve? Does type appear in color?

> How many columns are there? What sorts of publications are likely to use this number of columns? Does the width of each column make the text easy to read?

● **If there are images (photographs, diagrams, or other illustrations), what questions do they answer? What information and attitudes do they convey? How likely is it that readers will recognize these attitudes?**

> What kinds of details are included in each image? Are any significant details missing? Does the picture contain extraneous information?

> What viewing angle is represented? When the person or object is shown as if the viewer is looking up at it from below, this viewing angle usually makes the subject seem important, powerful, or threatening. If the perspective is that of looking downward, the angle tends to make the subject seem weak or unimportant. If the image lets viewers look head-on, the position is usually one of equality.

> What colors are used? Is there anything surprising or distinctive about them? Warm colors such as red and orange tend to evoke strong emotional reactions and a sense of danger or urgency, whereas cool colors such as blue have a more calming effect. Also, dark colors suggest something sinister or gloomy, and pastels suggest innocence, childhood, or safety.

> What kinds of lines and shapes are apparent? Diagonal lines can suggest movement or threat; jagged lines often create tension or anxiety. Tilting, top-heavy, or pinched shapes can also evoke negative emotional reactions. Other lines and forms can suggest balance and stability.

> Is the subject depicted in a physical setting? If so, what does that setting imply about the subject or the people associated with it?

> Is the image clearly explained through the use of a title, a caption, or accompanying labels?

> Can the reader find a clear relationship between the image and the text?

> Are the attitudes suggested by an image consistent with the judgment expressed in the written text?

● **If there are charts, graphs, or tables, how useful and informative are they?**

> Does the chart, graph, or table help readers see how the subject of the evaluation (usually some sort of product) compares to other subjects and how well the evaluation measures up to a set of criteria?

> Does the visual contain answers to the kinds of questions the intended audience is likely to ask?

> Can the reader easily find the most important information?

> Is the chart, graph, or table clearly labeled and, if necessary, explained with a title, legend or key?

> Are the units of measurement clear and consistent? If symbols are used, is their meaning clear?

> Is the chart, graph, or table clearly related to the text?

 Exercise

Bring to class an evaluation that presents information in a visually interesting way. It might contain images (photographs or drawings), graphs, and tables. Or it might make special use of text by setting it off with columns, with color, as pull quotes, or boxed in sidebars, for example. Consider the effects these visual elements create by answering the questions listed on the preceding page. Then try to determine how these effects are created. Be prepared to explain how the visual elements create a particular effect and how they add to the impressions conveyed through the evaluation's written text.

FIGURE 5.1
Visual Elements in "Cream of the Crop," an Evaluation in *Consumer Reports*

● **Image** Photo highlights one of the favored kinds of ice cream (explained in the accompanying caption).

● **Layout** Words and images are grouped into a single unit.

● **Layout** Headings make the table and other parts of the spread (two-page layout) easy to distinguish.

● **Layout** The table dominates the spread, emphasizing the results of the evaluation.

● **Chart** Depicting "flavor and texture" scores as bars of different lengths, the chart facilitates the comparison of different products.

● **Table** Carefully chosen units of measure help readers make meaningful comparisons.

● **Layout** Subheads help readers find specific information quickly.

Sample Analysis | Cream of the Crop

Figure 5.1 shows two visual elements from "Cream of the Crop," an evaluation that uses visual information both to engage readers of *Consumer Reports* and to make the authors' value judgments clear and accessible. The dish of ice cream shown in Figure 5.1 should appeal to readers who have "come back to full-fat ice cream after trying to stem [their] cravings with reduced-fat products." The photograph includes details—the light glistening off what appear to be chocolate and butterscotch toppings, the generous helping of ice cream, the large red strawberry—suggesting that the ice cream depicted is anything but one of the "reduced-fat products" readers have grown tired of. The photograph also excludes certain kinds of details. We don't see where the dish of ice cream is located. Is the dish on a table at a restaurant? On a table in someone's home? Nor do we see a person, especially an overweight person, eating the ice cream. There are no details in the picture that might distract readers' attention from the ice cream or give readers second thoughts about eating it. Further, the ice cream appears readily accessible: the distance from which the photograph has been taken makes the ice cream relatively close to the reader; the angle of the dish (tilted toward the reader) also implies the ice cream is within easy reach. Finally, the dish of ice cream is given great prominence, in part by its size relative to the written text (the photograph takes up two-thirds of the page) and in part by its size relative to the title of the article. If readers are interested in finding a full-fat ice cream—especially one that's "worth the hit" in calories—this photograph is likely to engage their interest.

The larger portion of Figure 5.1 presents a complex but clearly labeled chart that makes it easy to compare the various brands of ice cream. Within this chart is a bar graph that indicates the judges' overall assessment of "flavor and texture." Alongside the bar graph—and also part of the larger chart—is a table that enables readers to make more specific comparisons regarding the cost, number of calories, and fat content of a serving of each ice cream product. Just above the top right-hand part of the chart, a small picture of one brand of ice cream is grouped with a caption. The image both highlights and summarizes one of the basic value judgments made in this evaluation: "Häagen-Dazs, at 73 cents a serving, was consistently excellent. Breyers Natural Vanilla was excellent, too. And at only 23 cents a serving, it's a *CR* Best Buy." Beneath the chart is a box titled "The Tests behind the Ratings," which provides background information (on how tests were conducted and on the flavor and texture of most of the ice creams tested) that may interest some readers more than others.

Exercise › **bedfordstmartins.com/visualage**
Click on **CHAPTER 5** › *VISUALS*

For practice analyzing the visual information in another sample evaluation, see the visual exercises on the companion Web site for this book.

Reading to Write

› **bedfordstmartins.com/ visualage**

For additional examples of evaluations, click on **CHAPTER 5** › *EXAMPLES*

In your principal assignment for this chapter, you will evaluate and reach a clear judgment about a subject that a specific individual or group needs or wants to have evaluated. You will select criteria that seem appropriate for your intended audience and then look closely at the subject, identifying specific details that clearly relate to your criteria.

The following readings will help you see not only some of the different strategies you might use, but also the different kinds of topics about which you might write. Each reading is followed by questions (Reflecting on What You Have Read) that will start you thinking about what is involved in making an effective evaluation; also, a Thinking Ahead prompt will suggest ways to decide on a topic for your own evaluation. The subsequent sections of the chapter focus on starting your assignment, composing a draft, and assessing and revising that draft.

De gustibus non est disputandum. That's Latin for a time-honored philosophical point: there's no arguing about matters of taste. Assume, that you think Häagen-Dazs is the best-tasting ice cream, but your friend disagrees. The Romans would say, in effect, "Okay. That's your taste. Your friend prefers Ben and Jerry's. Case closed." But *Consumer Reports (CR)* would say that both you and your friend might rethink your preferences, at least in terms of vanilla ice cream. *CR* claims that Breyers vanilla is actually the best (only by a small margin, but still the best). How can a magazine do this? After all, isn't this just a matter of personal taste? How can anybody conduct a fair evaluation of such a subjective topic?

To answer these questions, consider the following excerpt from an article in which *CR* reviews different brands of vanilla, chocolate, and coffee ice creams. Because the three flavors are reviewed similarly, this excerpt focuses on the vanilla ice creams.

Cream of the Crop

CONSUMER REPORTS

Full-fat ice cream is back in style. Which ones are worth the calories?

1   If you've come back to full-fat ice cream after trying to stem your cravings with reduced-fat products, you're not alone. The real thing is now the fastest-growing segment of all frozen dairy treats—while sales of light and lower-fat ice cream and wanna-bes like frozen yogurt have declined.

2   To help you find the products that are worth the calorie and fat hit, our trained panelists tasted 18 vanilla, 17 chocolate, and 6 coffee ice creams. We focused on "premium" and "superpremium" products—unofficial categories used to describe products that, according to the International Ice Cream Association, generally contain from 40 to 80 percent more milk fat than the minimum government standard for ice cream. We included several of the new "homemade style" products, which promise a creamy taste similar to that of hand-cranked ice cream. And because limiting fat in the diet *is* still important, we added a "light" ice cream in each flavor to see how it would compare.

3   All the ice creams we tested were at least good. But only *Häagen-Dazs* was consistently excellent. Also notable: *Breyers Vanilla* and a new arrival that was too late for our main test, *Godiva Belgian Dark Chocolate.*

Premium Taste?

4   The quality of an ice cream depends on what it's made of (see "Inside the Scoop") and how it's made. To make ice cream, a manufacturer pasteurizes and homogenizes milk, cream, sweeteners, and other ingredients such as gums and emulsifiers; cools the mixture; adds flavors and colors; and whips air into it as it freezes.

Too much air and too many gums can result in a light, airy ice cream; too little air makes for an extremely dense and heavy product. An ice cream's texture can also be affected by how it's handled between the plant and the store. Sharp variations in temperature, for example, can turn a smooth ice cream into an icy one. 5

As for flavor, here's what our panelists looked for in each category, and what they found: 6

Vanilla. A high-quality vanilla ice cream should be mild but not bland, sweet but not overpoweringly so. The dairy should be balanced with a vanilla-bean, quality vanilla-extract, or other real vanilla flavor. There might be a slight alcohol note from the extract. There may also be a slight egg flavor. The ice cream should be creamy smooth with little or no iciness, and it should melt in your mouth to almost the thickness of heavy cream, but with no obvious gums or thickeners. 7

Breyers Vanilla and *Häagen-Dazs Vanilla* were both excellent—and quite different from each other. *Häagen-Dazs* was more creamy smooth with a very full dairy flavor and very distinct vanilla-extract flavor; *Breyers* had a fresh, clean dairy flavor with a somewhat milder, high-quality, real vanilla flavor, which more than offset its slightly icy texture. 8

Breyers Light actually tasted better than most full-fat vanillas (though it had just 20 calories per serving less than 9

regular *Breyers*). *ShopRite Premium Vanilla Bean,* the best of the store brands, was a good value.

As for the "home-made" vanillas, they were nothing special. In fact, *Breyers Homemade*—which, unlike its regular brandmate, contains gums—had a generic vanilla flavor and was rather light and airy.... 10

The Price You Pay

Ice cream contains protein, calcium, vitamin A, and other vitamins and minerals. But there's no getting around it: With every spoonful of the full-fat products you also get a hefty dose of fat and calories. A standard half-cup serving (but who are they kidding?) of most of the tested ice creams ranged from 140 to 170 calories, with 8 to 10 grams of fat. The same serving of a superpremium such as *Häagen-Dazs* or *Ben & Jerry's* has about 100 more calories and twice the amount of fat. 11

Part of the reason is that superpremiums are denser—less air and more ice cream. You get more ice cream per half-cup serving than you get with premiums or regular ice creams. Finish 12

A powerful chocolate hit
Godiva Belgian Dark Chocolate ice cream has the intense flavor of a Godiva Dark Chocolate bar and a texture that's a cross between a frozen ganache and a very high quality chocolate pudding. Had it been part of our main study, it would have rated excellent. But at $1.06 per serving, it would have also been the most expensive.

IN SHORT

Some "homemade style" ice creams taste more processed than their regular brandmates.

Breyers Light Vanilla has a better overall flavor than many full-fat premium ice creams.

All three flavors of *Häagen-Dazs* are excellent.

INSIDE THE SCOOP   *A guide to ingredients*

Breyers Vanilla **contains just milk, cream, sugar, and natural vanilla flavor. You can't get more basic than that. Other ice creams may also be made with gums, emulsifiers, and other unpronounceable ingredients that enhance or detract from the ice cream's quality, depending on how the ingredients are used. Here are some items you're likely to find on a label:**

Ingredients: Milk, cream, sugar, high fructose corn syrup, corn syrup, eggs, natural and artificial vanilla flavor, cellulose gum, vegetable gums (guar, carrageenan, carob bean), salt.

INGREDIENTS: MILK, CREAM, SUGAR, NATURAL VANILLA FLAVOR.
BREYERS ICE CREAM

Sweeteners. Most manufacturers use corn-based sweeteners in place of or in addition to more-expensive sucrose (a.k.a. sugar). Corn-syrup solids improve shelf life and enhance firmness. Sweeteners such as dextrose and high-fructose corn syrup also help lower a product's freezing point, which can result in smaller ice crystals and a smoother texture.

Milk products. Whole milk and cream contribute to a rich, full, creamy flavor and creamy texture. But other milk products may play an equally important role in determining an ice cream's quality. Buttermilk can enhance the whippability during processing and contribute to a rich flavor. Nonfat milk solids con-

tain protein that contributes to a smooth texture. These milk solids may come from liquid nonfat milk, nonfat dry milk, or dry whey. While all are inexpensive sources of milk solids, nonfat dry milk may produce off-flavors.

Emulsifiers and stabilizers. Emulsifiers enhance smoothness, help keep ingredients well-blended during and after processing, and increase the ice cream's resistance to melting. Common emulsifiers include egg yolks, mono- and diglycerides, polysorbate 80, and lecithin. Stabilizers prevent ice crystals from forming as temperatures fluctuate during storage. They also contribute to a product's uniformity and smoothness and increase its resistance to melting during serving. Common stabilizers are carrageenan, guar gum, and locust bean gum. Used excessively, as in some lower-rated ice creams, they make a product unnaturally slow-melting as well as thick and gummy.

Flavorings. "Natural" vanilla flavor may come from vanilla beans, pure vanilla extract (derived from vanilla beans using alcohol), or other non-alcohol-based vanilla flavors. "Imitation" vanilla contains vanillin, a flavor component of real vanilla. For commercial purposes, it may be derived from wood pulp. Sometimes the simple term "vanilla" is used when the flavor is a combination of natural and artificial. Chocolate ice cream may contain chocolate liquor (from pressed cacao beans), cocoa (chocolate liquor minus the cocoa butter), or both. Based on our test results, the source of the chocolate doesn't seem to make a difference in quality. In the products we tested, the source of the coffee flavor came primarily from coffee extract or brewed coffee.

off a pint of *Häagen-Dazs Chocolate* in one sitting, which some people have been known to do, and you will have consumed 72 grams of fat—more than the government's daily recommended limit of 65 grams of fat for people who eat about 2,000 calories in a day—and 1,080 calories.

One bit of good news: Ice cream may cost a bit less this season. Last summer, a domestic butterfat shortage hiked consumer prices on high-fat dairy products, ice cream included. This year, however, there's a glut, and butterfat prices have plunged. Ice cream prices should follow suit.

13

Tasters' choice Häagen-Dazs, at 73 cents a serving, was consistently excellent. Breyers Natural Vanilla was excellent, too. And at only 23 cents a serving, it's a CR Best Buy.

RATINGS & RECOMMENDATIONS *Ice Cream*

Overall Ratings *Within types, listed in order of flavor and texture score*

Key No.	Product	Flavor and Texture Score	Container Size	Cost	Calories	Fat	Comments
		0 P F G VG E 100					
	VANILLA ICE CREAM						
1	**Breyers**: A CR Best Buy		½ gal.	23¢	150	9g.	Big fresh dairy, notable cream, and distinct real vanilla flavors. Slightly icy, a slightly thinner melt than most, no gumminess.
2	**Häagen-Dazs**		pt.	73	270	18	Big full dairy with a notable cream flavor, very distinct vanilla flavor with a strong alcohol note, hint of egg. Very dense, creamy smooth, with no gumminess.
3	**Ben & Jerry's**		pt.	73	250	16	Full dairy with a notable cream flavor, very distinct real vanilla flavor with a distinct alcohol note, hint of egg. Very dense, little gumminess.
4	**ShopRite** Premium: A CR Best Buy		½ gal.	18	160	8	Big fresh dairy and distinct real vanilla flavors. Noticeably icy with a thinner melt than most and no gumminess.
5	**Breyers** Light		½ gal.	24	130	4	Distinct vanilla flavor, very sweet. Slightly thinner melt than most and little gumminess.
6	**Sensational** Premium		½ gal.	21	150	8	Distinct real vanilla flavor. Little gumminess. (Sold at Stop & Shop, Giant, Bi-Lo, Edwards, and Tops.)
7	**Blue Bell** Homemade		½ gal.	23	180	9	Distinct vanilla and slight custardlike flavors, very sweet. Slightly thin melt and little gumminess.
8	**Newman's Own**		qt.	48	170	10	Overpowering vanilla flavor with a harsh alcohol note.
9	**Dreyer's/Edy's** Homemade		½ gal.	23	140	7	Slight cooked-milk flavor with a caramellike note, imitation vanilla flavor, very sweet.
10	**America's Choice** Premium (A&P-owned stores)		½ gal.	19	150	9	Slightly low vanilla flavor. Somewhat light and airy.

The Tests behind the Ratings

Flavor and texture score is based on blind taste tests by trained panelists. One product goes by two brand names—*Dreyer's* in the West and *Edy's* in the rest of the country. In a **half-cup serving** (4 fluid oz.), **cost** is calculated from the national or regional average price of the most common **container size**. **Calories** and **fat** come from manufacturers' label information. About two-thirds of the fat is satu-

rated. **Caffeine** per half-cup serving, listed only for the coffee ice creams, is based on analyses in our laboratories. For the *Starbuck's Coffee Italian Roast*, which differed greatly from sample to sample in its caffeine content, we list a range. **Comments** are based on the judgments of our trained panel.

Flavor and texture notes: Most of the ice creams were quite sweet, moderately dense, and had no noticeable iciness. Melted, they had

a texture like heavy cream and a very slight to slight gumminess. Most vanilla ice creams had distinct dairy and vanilla flavors with a slight cream flavor. The chocolates generally had a distinct chocolate flavor with a maltlike note, and a moderate dairy with a slight cream flavor. Most coffees had a distinct coffee flavor and a moderate dairy with a slight cream flavor.

RATINGS & RECOMMENDATIONS *Ice Cream*

Overall Ratings *Within types, listed in order of flavor and texture score*

Key No.	Product	Flavor and Texture Score	Container Size	Half-cup Serving Cost	Calories	Fat	Comments
		0 100 P F G VG E					
	VANILLA ICE CREAM						
11	**Breyers** Homemade	▬▬	½ gal.	23	150	8	Slight cooked-milk flavor, very sweet. Somewhat light and airy.
12	**Dreyer's/Edy's** Grand	▬▬	½ gal.	21	140	8	Very sweet. Somewhat light and airy.
13	**Prestige** Premium (Winn Dixie)	▬▬	½ gal.	23	160	9	Very sweet.
14	**Turkey Hill** Premium	▬▬	½ gal.	17	140	8	Low dairy flavor. Light and airy, noticeably thick, gummy melt.
15	**Publix** Premium	▬▬	½ gal.	20	160	9	Low dairy, poor-quality vanilla flavor, very sweet. Light and airy, noticeably thick, gummy melt.
16	**Albertsons**	▬▬	½ gal.	23	150	8	Low dairy and vanilla flavors, slight chemical note. Somewhat light and airy, noticeably thick, gummy melt.
17	**Safeway Select** Premium	▬▬	½ gal.	28	160	10	Low dairy and vanilla flavors. Somewhat light and airy, noticeably thick, gummy melt.
18	**Texas Gold** Premium (Kroger)	▬▬	½ gal.	28	170	10	Low dairy and imitation vanilla flavors, very sweet. Somewhat light and airy, thick, gummy melt.

Commercial "homemade" ice cream Of the homemade-style vanilla and chocolate products we tested, only Blue Bell Homemade Vanilla was very good. Breyers Homemade Vanilla, which contains gums (unlike regular old Breyers), was inferior to its brandmate.

Recommendations

Häagen-Dazs was the only brand to have a consistently high-quality flavor and smooth and creamy texture in all three flavors tested. *Breyers,* at a fraction of the cost, fat, and calories of the superpremiums, weighed in with an excellent vanilla ice cream which we've rated [a] CR Best Buy. *Breyers'* coffee ice cream, another CR Best Buy, is also a very good tasting, less fattening 14

Keeping it light *Breyers Light Vanilla* has just 20 fewer calories than *Breyers Vanilla*, but it has half the fat and about one-third of the saturated fat. And it tastes very good.

alternative to *Häagen-Dazs*.

Breyers Light Vanilla is a very good choice for people who watch their fat intake. It was tastier than most other regular vanilla ice creams but had only about half the fat and somewhat fewer calories per serving. 15

You can save money by purchasing a store-brand ice cream. The best were *ShopRite Premium Vanilla* (another CR Best Buy), *Sensational Premium Vanilla* and *Chocolate* (Stop & Shop and other stores), *Prestige Premium Chocolate* (Winn Dixie), *America's Choice Premium Chocolate* (A&P-owned stores), and *Publix Premium Chocolate*. 16

Reflecting on What You Have Read

1 What criteria does *Consumer Reports (CR)* establish for judging vanilla ice cream? Do you think the criteria are clear and appropriate? Would they also be appropriate for readers who prefer different brands of ice cream? Why or why not?

2 Taste is a highly personal, subjective matter. How does *CR* attempt to show that its rankings are not based solely on personal preference? Is this attempt successful?

3 Look closely at the "Ratings" table. In what ways does it help you compare and contrast the Breyers, Newman's Own, and Texas Gold ice creams?

4 In light of the criteria and other information included in this piece, do you feel that *CR* is justified in placing Breyers Vanilla at the top of the list? Why or why not?

5 Notice the inset boxes and sidebars in this evaluation. What different kinds of information do these visual elements contain? Look closely at the information in any two inset boxes. What reasons do you see for separating this information from the main text of the article?

6 Examine the photograph that appears near the opening page of this evaluation. What reasons do you see for (or against) including this picture at the beginning of the evaluation?

Thinking Ahead

In "Cream of the Crop," the authors identify a question that's likely to be on readers' minds: Which full-fat ice creams are "worth the calories"? The *CR* writers answer that question by testing several different brands of the product. For a different product (personal computers or digital cameras, for example), identify one or more questions important to consumers considering buying that product. Would it be possible for you to answer the questions by devising a test?

One of the most important functions of evaluations is helping readers observe closely and pay careful attention to details they might otherwise overlook. This is especially true in reviews of movies or other performances where sounds, images, and actions compete for people's attention. In the following review from the *Chicago Sun-Times,* film critic Roger Ebert revisits a classic film, *Dr. Strangelove.* As you read the review, pay particular attention to Ebert's discussion of actor George C. Scott's performance in the film.

July 11, 1999

Dr. Strangelove

ROGER EBERT

Every time you see a great film, you find new things in it. Viewing Stanley Kubrick's *Dr. Strangelove* for perhaps the 10th time, I discovered what George C. Scott does with his face. His performance is the funniest thing in the movie—better even than the inspired triple performance by Peter Sellers or the nutjob general played by Sterling Hayden—but this time I found myself paying special attention to the tics and twitches, the grimaces and eyebrow archings, the sardonic smiles and gum-chewing, and I enjoyed the way Scott approached the role as a duet for voice and facial expression.

That can be dangerous for an actor. Directors often ask actors to underplay closer shots, because too much facial movement translates into mugging or overacting. Billy Wilder once asked Jack Lemmon for "a little less" so

1 many takes in a row that Lemmon finally exploded: "Whaddya want! Nothing?" Lemmon recalls that Wilder raised his eyes to heaven: "Please God!" Kubrick, whose attention to the smallest detail in every frame was obsessive, would have been aware of George C. Scott's facial gymnastics, and yet he endorsed them, and when you watch *Strangelove* you can see why.

Scott's work is hidden in plain view. His face here is so plastic and mobile it reminds you of Jerry Lewis or Jim Carrey (in completely different kinds of movies). Yet you don't consciously notice his expressions because Scott 2 sells them with the energy and conviction of his performance. He means what he says so urgently that the expressions accompany his dialogue instead of distracting from it. Consider the scene where his character,

Gen. Buck Turgidson, is informing the president that it is quite likely a B-52 bomber will be able to fly under Russian radar and deliver its payload even though the entire Soviet air force knows where the plane is headed. "He can barrel in that baby so low!" Scott says, with his arms spread wide like wings, and his head shaking in admiration at how good his pilots are—so good one of them is about to bring an end to civilization.

Another actor, waving his 4 arms around, might look absurd. Scott embodies the body language so completely that it simply plays as drama (and comedy). In another scene, scurrying around the War Room, he slips, falls to a knee, rights himself, and car- 3 ries on. Kubrick the perfectionist left the unplanned slip in the film, because Scott made it seem convincing, and not an accident.

Dr. Strangelove (1964) is 5 filled with great comic performances, and just as well, because there's so little else in the movie apart from faces, bodies and words. Kubrick shot it on four principal locations (an office, the perimeter of an Air Force base, the "War Room," and the interior of a B-52 bomber).

His special effects are competent but not dazzling (we are obviously looking at model planes over Russia). The War Room, one of the most memorable of movie interiors, was created by Ken Adam out of a circular desk, a ring of lights, some back-projected maps, and darkness. The headquarters of Gen. Jack D. Ripper, the haywire Air Force general, is just a room with some office furniture in it.

Yet out of these rudimentary physical props and a brilliant screenplay (which Kubrick and Terry Southern based on a novel by Peter George), Kubrick made what is arguably the best political satire of the century, a film that pulled the rug out from under the Cold War by arguing that if a "nuclear deterrent" destroys all life on Earth, it is hard to say exactly what it has deterred.

Dr. Strangelove's humor is generated by a basic comic principle: People trying to be funny are never as funny as people trying to be serious and failing. The laughs have to seem forced on unwilling characters by the logic of events. A man wearing a funny hat is not funny. But a man who doesn't know he's wearing a funny hat . . . ah, now you've got something.

The characters in *Dr. Strangelove* do not know their hats are funny. The film begins with Gen. Ripper (Sterling Hayden) fondling a phallic cigar while launching an unauthorized nuclear strike against Russia. He has become convinced that the commies are poisoning "the purity and essence of our natural fluids" by adding fluoride to the water supply. (Younger viewers may not know that in the 1950s this was a widespread belief.) Ripper's nuclear strike, his cigar technique and his concern for his "precious bodily fluids" are so entwined that they inspire unmistakable masturbatory associations.

The only man standing between Ripper and nuclear holocaust is a British liaison, Group Captain Mandrake (Sellers), who listens with disbelief to Ripper's rantings.

Meanwhile, Ripper's coded message goes out to airborne B-52s to launch an attack against Russia. A horrified President Muffley (Sellers again) convenes his advisers in the War Room and is informed by Turgidson, bit by reluctant bit, of the enormity of the situation: The bombers are on the way, they cannot be recalled, Gen. Ripper cannot be reached, and so on. Eventually, Muffley calls the Russian premier to confess everything ("Dimitri, we have a little problem . . . ").

Other major players include the sinister strategist Dr. Strangelove (Sellers a third time), a character whose German accent now evokes Henry Kissinger, although in 1964 nuclear think-tanker Herman Kahn was the likely target. Strangelove's black-gloved right hand is an unruly weapon with a will of its own, springing into Nazi salutes and trying to throttle Strangelove to death. Action in the War Room and on the Air Force base is intercut with the B-52 cockpit, ruled by Major T. J. "King" Kong (Slim Pickens); when he's told by his radio man that the order to attack has come through, he tells them, "No horsin' around on the airplane!"

Major Kong was intended to be Sellers' fourth role, but he was uncertain about the cowboy accent. Pickens, a character actor from westerns, was brought in by Kubrick, who reportedly didn't tell him the film was a comedy. Pickens' patriotic speeches to his crew (and his promises of promotion and medals) are counterpoint to the desperate American efforts to recall the flight.

I've always thought the movie ends on an unsure note. After the first nuclear blast, Kubrick cuts back to the War Room, where Strangelove muses that deep mines could be used to shelter survivors, whose descendants could return to the surface in 90 years (Turgidson is intrigued by the 10-to-1 ratio of women to men). Then the film abruptly ends in its famous montage of many mushroom clouds, while Vera Lynn sings "We'll Meet Again." 12

It seems to me there should be no more dialogue after the first blast; Strangelove's survival strategy could be 13 moved up to just before Slim Pickens' famous bareback ride to oblivion. I realize there would be a time lapse while Russian missiles responded to the attack, but I think the film would be more effective if the original blast brought an end to all further story developments. (Kubrick originally planned to end the film with a pie fight, and a table laden with pies can be seen in the background of the War Room, but he wisely realized that his purpose was satire, not slapstick.)

Dr. Strangelove and *2001: A Space Odyssey* (1968) are Kubrick's masterpieces. The two films share a common theme: Man designs machinery that functions with per- 14 fect logic to bring about a disastrous outcome. The U.S. nuclear deterrent and the Russian "doomsday machine" function exactly as they are intended, and destroy life on earth. The computer HAL 9000 serves the space mission by attacking the astronauts.

Stanley Kubrick himself was a perfectionist who went to obsessive lengths in order to get everything in his films to work just right. He owned his own cameras and sound and editing equipment. He often made dozens of takes of the same shot. He was known to telephone projectionists to complain about out-of-focus screenings. Are his two best films a nudge in his own ribs? 15

Reflecting on What You Have Read

1 Ebert's criteria here may seem implicit and vaguely defined. As best as you can infer them, what are his criteria? Do they seem appropriate?

2 Why does Ebert have such great admiration for George C. Scott? How does he try to justify his admiration? Does he succeed in doing so?

3 Why do you think Ebert includes the story about actor Jack Lemmon?

4 Ebert identifies a "principle" or criterion that explains why he thinks certain performances in *Dr. Strangelove* are funny. Do you agree with that principle? Does his description of events in the movie justify the conclusions he draws about the actors' performances?

Thinking Ahead

When something is well known and highly regarded, it's easy to take it for granted. Consider books and movies that have been widely praised or disparaged. List some that you think deserve a second look that would give a clearer picture of their strengths and weaknesses.

The preceding readings in this chapter evaluate a product and a performance. Writing for the "My Turn" column in *Newsweek* in 1999, Seth Shostak evaluates a social trend: the dramatic increase in people's use of e-mail. Shostak is an astronomer at the SETI (Search for Extraterrestrial Intelligence) Institute in California, a scientific research organization, and he writes frequently on astronomy, film, and technology. As you read, think about Shostak's credibility. Does he seem to be knowledgeable and trustworthy?

You Call This Progress?

SETH SHOSTAK

E-mail has become a steady drip of dubious prose, bad jokes and impatient requests

1 It's as ubiquitous as winter damp. A pernicious miasma that brings rot and ruin to society's delicate underpinnings. I speak of e-mail, the greatest threat to civilization since lead dinnerware addled the brains of the Roman aristocracy.

2 A technical byproduct of the Internet, e-mail lets 10 million Americans pound out correspondence faster than you can say QWERTY. One twitch of the finger is all it takes to dispatch missives to the next continent or the next cubicle at light speed. The result is a flood of what is loosely called communication, a tsunami of bytes that is threatening to drown white-collar workers everywhere. Masquerading as a better way to put everyone in touch, e-mail has become an incessant distraction, a nonstop obligation and a sure source of stress and anxiety. I expect that a public statement by the surgeon general is in the offing.

3 Mind you, e-mail started out cute and cuddly, an inoffensive spinoff from a government defense project. The technically inclined used it to send personal messages to colleagues without the need for a stamp or a wait. Only a small group of folks—mostly at universities—were plugged in to this select network. The amount of traffic was manageable. E-mail was something to be checked every week or so. But technology marches on. Today access to the Internet is widespread, as common and accessible as a cheap motel. Everyone's wired, and everyone has something to say.

4 Unfortunately, this is not polite correspondence, the gentle art of letter writing in electronic form. E-mail is aggressive. It has a built-in, insistent arrogance. Because it arrives more or less instantaneously, the assumption is that you will deal with it quickly. "Quickly" might mean minutes, or possibly hours. Certainly not days. Failure to respond directly usually produces a second missive sporting the mildly critical plaint, "Didn't you get my last e-mail?" This imperative for the

immediate makes me yearn for old-style written communication, in which a week might lapse between inquiry and response. Questions and discussion could be considered in depth. A reply could be considered (or mentally shelved, depending on circumstance). Today, however, all is knee-jerk reaction.

In addition, there is the dismaying 5 fact that electronically generated mail, despite being easy to edit, is usually prose at its worst. Of every 10 e-mails I read, nine suffer from major spelling faults, convoluted grammar and a stunning lack of logical organization. For years I assumed this was an inevitable byproduct of the low student test scores so regularly lamented in newspaper editorials. Johnny can't read, so it's not surprising that he can't write either. But now I believe that the reason for all this unimpressive prose is something else: e-mail has made correspondents of folks who would otherwise never compose a text. It encourages messaging because it is relatively anonymous. The shy, the introverted and the socially inept can all hunker down before a glowing computer and whisper to the world. This is not the telephone, with its brutally personal, audible contact. It's not the post, for which an actual sheet of paper, touched by the writer and displaying his imperfect calligraphic skills, will end up under the nose of the recipient. E-mails are surreptitiously thrown over an electronic transom in the dead of night, packaged in plain manila envelopes.

Still, it is not these esthetic debilities 6 that make e-mail such a threat. Rather, it's the unstoppable proliferation. Like the brooms unleashed by the sorcerer's apprentice, e-mails are beginning to overwhelm those who use them. Electronic correspondence is not one to one. It is one to many, and that's bad news on the receiving end. The ease with which copies of any correspondence can be dispensed to the world ensures that I am "kept informed" of my co-workers' every move. Such bureaucratic banter was once held in check by the technical limitations of carbon paper. Now my colleagues just punch a plastic mouse to ensure my exposure to their thoughts, their plans and the endless missives that supposedly prove that they're doing their jobs.

Because of e-mail's many-tentacled 7 reach, its practitioners hardly care whether I'm around or not. I'm just another address in a list. So the deluge of digital correspondence continues irrespective of whether I'm sitting in my cubicle doing the boss's business or lying on the Côte d'Azur squeezing sand through my toes. Either way the e-mail, like a horde of motivated Mongolians, just keeps a-comin'. Vacations have lost their allure, and I hesitate to leave town. Consider: if I disappear for two weeks of rest and recreation, I can be sure of confronting screenfuls of e-mail upon my return. It's enough to make a grown man groan. The alternative is to take a laptop computer along, in the desperate hope of keeping up with e-mail's steady drip, drip, drip. Needless to say, there's something unholy about answering e-mails from your holiday suite. A friend recently told me that he can't afford to die: the e-mail would pile up and nobody could handle it.

Today I will receive 50 electronic 8 messages. Of that number, at least half require a reply. (Many of the others consist of jokes, irrelevant bulletins and important announcements about secret cookie recipes. I actually like getting such junk e-mails, as they allow the pleasure of a quick delete without guilt.) If I spend five minutes considering and composing a response to each correspondence, then two hours of my day are busied with e-mail, even if I don't initiate a single one. Since the number of Internet users is doubling about once a year, I expect that by the start of the new millennium, I—and millions like me—will be doing nothing but writing e-mails. The collapse of commerce and polite society will quickly follow.

I'm as much in favor of technology as the next guy. Personally, I think the Luddites should have welcomed the steam looms. But if you insist on telling me that e-mail is an advance, do me a favor and use the phone.

9

Reflecting on What You Have Read

1 What are Shostak's main criticisms of e-mail?

2 Given his criteria and evidence, do you agree with Shostak's criticisms?

3 Assess Shostak's evaluation of e-mail. Do his criteria seem appropriate? What other criteria might he have considered? What experience have you had with e-mail, and does your experience support or challenge Shostak's claims?

4 Compare the overall visual appearance of Shostak's essay with that of "Cream of the Crop." Think of the different circumstances in which each piece was intended to be read. How might those circumstances justify the different visual formats of the two pieces?

Thinking Ahead

Consider trends you're aware of, especially trends that affect you directly. How would you evaluate the changes those trends represent? Do they constitute "progress"? What criteria would you use to evaluate those trends?

This restaurant review originally appeared in the Rensselaer Polytechnic Institute's college newspaper. Patrick Vitarius wrote this evaluation as part of a series on things to do near campus for five dollars or less. As you read this review and the one that follows from *Vermont Magazine*, try to imagine the kinds of readers the authors had in mind for their evaluations.

Breakfast at Manory's

PATRICK VITARIUS

1 If there's one thing I've missed since I left home, it's breakfast.

2 See, I have the less-than-admirable habit of getting up at the last possible moment—typically, fifteen minutes after my first class of the morning starts. (I should take this opportunity to thank Professor Kapila for starting each class with a twenty minute review of the previous class; otherwise, I surely would not have passed Advanced Calculus.)

The unfortunate side effect to this sleeping (or rather, waking) schedule is that there is never time for breakfast. How I missed the salty sensation of sizzling bacon! How I longed for the tangy taste of tantalizing sausage! What I wouldn't have said or done for a single sniff of sumptuous egg! I had thought that that chapter of my life was over and done with upon the first droning sentences of my college courseload.

4 Then I discovered Manory's Restaurant, home of the all-day breakfast.

3 Have you ever had pancakes after dark? Have you ever dined over eggs and bacon as the sun set over the Hudson River? Have you ever danced with the devil in the pale moonlight? If your answer to either of the first two questions was "no," you must go to Manory's right away. If your answer to the third question was "yes," you should look in the Yellow Pages under "Help—Psychiatric" and call the first local number you come to.

6 Now, some of you may have observed by now my tendency to single out a single reason to visit a downtown business—Music Shack only for their used CD bin, China Pagoda only for their lunch buffet, Aquilonia Comics and Cards only for their "three for a buck" boxes. I am about to do the same thing here. Because even though Manory's has a perfectly wonderful breakfast, lunch, dinner, and dessert menu, I am not even going to tell you about them. Oh, you act indignant. If you're so interested, you'll go

there for yourself. I'm just going to talk about their all-day breakfast specials. Live with it.

The $2.09 breakfast special is, if nothing else, aptly named—it is a breakfast, it is "special," and it costs two dollars and nine cents (plus tax and tip). This breakfast is comprised of two eggs (cooked any style), toast, coffee, and juice. Just the right size for the student watching his calories and his budget. As if such a student exists. The only students I know don't even know what a calorie is (chem majors excluded) and have no budget to speak

of, unless change found in friends' cars can be called a budget.

The meal for us is the Big Breakfast. This is a meal near and dear to my own heart. At $3.95, it comes in right under the mark—tax and a 15 percent tip put it exactly at five dollars. And what a well-spent five dollars it is. Again, two eggs cooked any style. With two sausage links. And a couple strips of bacon. And three (count 'em, three) huge pancakes, with butter and syrup. And coffee. And juice. No "one from Column A" breakfast, this. You get it all. The eggs are fresh off the grill. The bacon is thick, just the right crispness, and salty enough to disinfect gunshot wounds. The sausages are spicy and cooked to perfection. The pancakes are fluffy and sweet, and served with enough whipped butter and maple syrup (on the side, by default) to make a meal in themselves. The

Things to Do on Your Way to Manory's (from the RPI campus)

1. Play a fun variation on the road game "Padiddle": every time you see a green-roofed, ivy-covered building on campus, you get to hit your friend.
2. On your way past West Hall, pop in and look for the Rocks and Fossils Room. Neat horse skull.
3. Cross 8th Street, and race down the Fulton Footpath. Last one to the bottom buys everyone breakfast.
4. On your way down Fulton Street, stop in front of the Gurley Building. In your best Schwarzenegger accent, say "Hey, look at the Gurley Building."
5. At the intersection of Fulton and Fourth, make fun of all the high school punk gangstas hanging out in front of "Nite Owl News." Then, quickly, make a left onto Fourth. Run.
6. Stop at the corner of Fourth and Congress. You're there. Hurrah.

coffee is bad for you, so I never order it. I get water instead. (The water, incidentally, ain't bad.) And the juice? Well, I wouldn't know. I've never gotten enough to actually taste it.

See, Manory's has got these teeny little juice glasses. You know the ones I'm talking about. These things make shot glasses look like two-handed beer mugs. These glasses are not big enough to trap fireflies in, not even one at a time. If they made "Fight cancer, Fight harder" commercials with these glasses, the caption would say "Tick cancer off just a wee bit."

9 Man, I've seen OJ defense theories that hold more water than these glasses would. I've seen people walk into emergency rooms with their thumbs stuck in these glasses.

Okay, I'm done ranting 10 about the size of the juice glasses. The rest of the meal more than makes up for this slight, if common flaw. Take my advice. Go to Manory's. Go there. Go now, no matter what time of day it is. After all, if I wanted more juice for my money, I'd buy a half gallon at the convenience store.

And if I did that, it wouldn't 11 come with all the rest.

Reflecting on What You Have Read

● **1** Did you find this restaurant review engaging? Why or why not? Cite examples from the text to support your answer.

● **2** Vitarius includes some background information in his review, including his tendency to sleep late and his fondness for breakfast (paragraphs 2 and 3). What reasons do you see for including this background information?

● **3** What was your reaction to the photographs that accompany this review? What details in these photos made you react in that way?

This restaurant review was published in *Vermont Magazine,* a special-interest monthly for readers who want information on leisure activities and interesting people in this small, picturesque northeastern state. Julie Kirgo's piece aims to appeal both to residents of Vermont and to the tourists who come from nearby cities such as New York and Boston to shop, ski, enjoy the scenery, and eat well. Before you start reading, glance briefly at this evaluation—reproduced as it originally appeared—and consider these questions: What initial impressions does the general layout of the page create? Does it create particular expectations for this evaluation? As you read, think about whether the review meets or defies those expectations.

IN GOOD TASTE

A Storm Brings Culinary Clear Sailing

ould there be a prettier setting in Vermont than the Storm Café's? Nestled into the bottom floor of an elegantly restored stone mill building at the edge of Otter Creek, its flower-bedecked terrace affords views of the sparkling waters of the creek as they move from the tumult of the falls to gentle flow. Inside, the dining room is echt bistro: small, cozy, with a tiny bar, a black-and-white checked floor, a changing panoply of art on the walls, and a lustrous café mirror reflecting the clientele—locals, students and faculty from neighboring Middlebury College, an ongoing rondelay of tourists—like a painting by Tissot.

Question is, can the food live up to the setting? Can it possibly have the same sort of sparkle, the variety, the piquance? As the Storm's loyal and growing customer base can fortunately attest: yes, indeed. Under the imaginative and caring hand of former owner/chef Kay Rentschler, the Storm built a following dedicated to its fresh and eclectic lunch menu; in the last year, its fortunes have taken a turn for the even better, thanks to the talents of new owner/chefs Karen Carney and John Goettelmann. The Goettelmanns (an energetic young couple who met while attending the renowned Culinary Institute of America) have enlarged the menu and added regular dinner service, while wisely retaining the best of the old Storm.

Between them, Karen and John have worked everywhere from the Jersey Shore (John did eight seasons at The Shrimp

BY JULIE KIRGO

The Storm Café serves up great bistro food in Middlebury

Box, which may help to account for his sure hand with seafood) to the coast of California, in restaurants specializing in a dazzling array of cooking styles and ethnicities. "We have lots of influences," says John, while describing their food as "innovative American cuisine."

Take lunch, for example, the meal that made the Storm. Soups, salads, and sandwiches are here in abundance, but they are far from standard fare. The house hum-

The deck of the Storm Café overlooks the swiftly flowing Otter Creek.

mus ($6.50) is rich and creamy, served with roasted eggplant, red peppers, feta, cucumbers, red onions, greens, and a delightfully chewy French bread. The fatoush—I just love saying that—is a tangy mix of wild greens and romaine tossed with tomato, cucumber, thinly sliced radishes, chunks of feta and pita chips, all perfectly dressed in a lemon-mint vinaigrette ($5.50). The soup du jour ($2.95 cup, $3.95 bowl) might be a corn chowder

thick with tender vegetables, slightly smoky with bacon, or a smooth, unctuous purée of squash, cream, and spices.

Sandwiches are justifiably famous. There's the vegetarian hero ($6.75), a luscious combo of provolone, roasted peppers, onion jam, lettuce and pickles on Storm-made focaccia with honey-mustard dressing. The Tri-State ($7.95) is a Philadelphia-style cheesesteak—but what a cheesesteak! A baguette stuffed with thin-sliced New York strip steak sautéed with onions, wild mushrooms, and hot cherry peppers is topped with nothing less than Vermont cheddar. Straying beyond the soup/salad/sandwich triumvirate, the Storm offers lunch specials ranging from a spectacularly tender fruit-wood-smoked salmon ($7.95) to the popular El Bandito ($7), temptingly seasoned corn and other vegetables rolled with house-refried beans, shredded lettuce, and melting cheddar in a nicely warmed flour tortilla.

Good as lunch at the Storm Café happens to be, it's at dinner time that the Goettelmanns really get to stretch out, be expansive, and show off their culinary gifts with a tantalizing range of dishes. You might start with the charcuterie plate ($6.95), a selection of creamy house-made pâtés and spicy sausages, or calamari puttanesca ($6.50), a savory combination of sautéed calamari, tomatoes, kalamata olives, garlic, roasted red peppers, red onions, capers, anchovies, and herbs. I love the rich smashed potatoes ($5.95), pan-fried red bliss spuds mixed with caramelized onions, roasted garlic, and bacon, served with a chevre-and-sour-cream spread. But what I love best are the

DENNIS PARKER

spicy steamed mussels ($6.50), an ambrosial concoction of PEI mussels cooked in a white wine, lime, garlic, and cilantro broth with julienned vegetables and chili paste. These are so tender, so flavorful, I've been known to forego the rest of dinner in their favor.

But I'm an addict. More stalwart souls have lots of other gems to choose from: entrées might include prosciutto-wrapped shrimp ($17.95), grilled and served on a vegetable ratatouille with a roasted plum tomato sauce; a sublime penne carbonara ($11.95), pasta tossed with pancetta, tomatoes, garlic, and black pepper, napped with cream and parmesan; an extraordinary New York strip steak ($15.95) marinated in molasses and black pepper, grilled and served with a compote of wild mushrooms, onions, glazed sweet potatoes, smoked bacon, and pecans; a simply braised lamb shank ($14.95), slow-cooked in a red wine sauce, offered with Brunoise vegetables and mashed potatoes; or pan-seared filet of salmon ($16.95) encrusted with fennel, cumin, and coriander, served over wilted spinach tossed with roasted tomatoes, onions, and garlic.

Venison can be had au poivre ($16.95), quickly sautéed and served in a brandy cream sauce with sundried cranberries and apricots. A special risotto ($12.95) combines arborio rice with portobello and oyster mushrooms. And tuna steak ($16.95), glazed with balsamic chili paste, is served over zucchini "noodles."

Then there are the desserts ($4): chocolate banana cream pie, strawberry rhubarb crisp, a lemon tart artfully piled with fresh strawberries, a perfect crème brûlée, its creamy custard nestled beneath its warm caramel crust. Go ahead; make room.

And be glad that the Goettelmanns allowed themselves a second thought. "When we first saw the ad for the restaurant," John recalls, "it just looked too good. I said, 'Don't even call.'" But Karen nudged him; "Finally," she says, "we called." The result: a perfect marriage of lovely setting and spectacular food. For which we can all be grateful. **▼**

The Storm Café, 3 Mill Street, Middlebury, 802-388-1063. Open Tuesday-Saturday 11-3; Tuesday-Thursday 5-9; Friday-Saturday 5-10.

Reflecting on What You Have Read

● 1 What kind of audience do you think Kirgo has in mind for her review? In what ways do your knowledge, needs, and values make you feel like (or unlike) a member of that audience?

● 2 In "A Storm Brings Culinary Clear Sailing," Kirgo mentions how the owner/chefs of Storm Café met and where they have worked. Why do you think she includes this background information? What does it say to you about the context of the review?

● 3 Try to visualize a scene in which someone is reading this review. Imagine the visual appearance of both the place in which the review might be read and the person doing the reading. Look again at the language and content of the review. In what ways is it consistent (or inconsistent) with the scene you imagined?

● 4 What was your reaction to the photograph on the first page of this reading? What details in the photo made you react in that way? Describe what the picture and its caption tell you about Kirgo's intended audience.

Thinking Ahead

● This restaurant review contains a wealth of details that convey a distinct impression of a specific place. Imagine a place you'd consider evaluating, and assume that *place* can refer to a variety of things—a ballpark, concert venue, chat room, or dormitory, for example. Think about that place from different perspectives, such as a first-time visitor, for example, or someone who uses a wheelchair. What details about the place impress you? How might those details add up to your overall evaluation of the place?

Despite ongoing criticisms and debates over their safety and fuel economy, SUVs continue to be very popular. This review by Ron Sessions, from *Motor Trend* magazine, evaluates one of the most popular—and largest—of these vehicles, the Ford Expedition. As you read, try to determine what the author assumes about his audience's knowledge, values, and needs.

Ford Expedition

RON SESSIONS

Outfitted for more comfort

When the Ford Expedition was introduced in '97, it quickly topped the full-size SUV sales charts. As an SUV derivative of the F-Series pickup, the best-selling vehicle in the land, the Expedition had a lot going in its favor. Mo-bigger-better.

But as scores of fresh competitors piled into the market, buyers had many new ways to spend their SUV dollar: truck-based SUVs, car-based SUVs, wagons, and even all-wheel-drive minivans. And last year, Ford's own Explorer, featuring third-row seating and a smoother-riding independent suspension, began nipping at the Expedition's heels.

Hence, an all-new second-generation Expedition for '03. It may not look that different from

an '02, but the skin's fresh, and there are myriad changes inside. The Expedition still represents the large, full-frame, truck-based side of the SUV spectrum, but for '03, the frame is hydro-formed to provide a stiff base for the suspension and body.

Given that SUVs spend most of their time on the road, one of Ford's major goals with the '03 Expedition was to improve its everyday ride and handling. The Expedition (and its Lincoln Navigator sibling) is the first full-size SUV to get independent rear suspension [IRS], and the improvement in ride quality, particularly over rough and uneven pavement, is quite noticeable. Freeway expansion strips and washboard surfaces can still excite the structure and give a good case of the truck jigglies, but the big guy feels more settled, more predictable when that surprise curve pops up all of a sudden or the radius tightens unexpectedly on an exit ramp. Nicely weighted, precise-acting, speed-sensitive rack-and-pinion steering helps the driver place it on the road.

Keeping it on the road for '03 are bigger brake rotors and an emergency-brake-assist system that can reduce real-world stopping distances by 20 percent. A new AdvanceTrac stability-control setup can enhance control on tricky curves or low-friction surfaces by cutting engine power and selectively applying the brakes on a slipping wheel or wheels. Brakes have stiffer calipers and what Ford claims are the largest rotors among full-size SUVs, 13-in. front and 13.5-in. rear. These haul the rig down from speed with confidence.

Using IRS also allowed Ford to lower the floor height. Not only does this aid ingress and egress, but it frees up some adult-size room in the 60/40 split third-row-seat area. Third-row headroom increases by 3 in. and legroom shoots up by nearly 7.

Using the third-row seats is a breeze with the power-fold option. Each seat section can be raised or lowered at the push of a button. Both the second- and third-row seats fold completely flat, creating a 7-ft-long cargo floor behind the front seats.

This being the most trucklike of our assembly of multipurpose vehicles, we expected the Expedition to press on, regardless of conditions. And it did. The big Ford was the only one of our group to cleanly pick its way to the top of a rocky 200-ft precipice. And the Expedition managed to extricate itself from the deep sand we purposely plowed it into. We'd expect the same outcome in deep snow. Aside from

PERSONALITY PROFILE

'03 Ford Expedition

Cargo capacity 9
More capacious than an Explorer, less than a Suburban

Passenger capacity 9
Almost as accommodating as a minivan

Ride/comfort 6
IRS helps articulation, but still truck-jiggly

Driving ease 7
Won't park in "compact only" spaces; new steering is precise

Performance 7
5.4L V-8 does the job, but won't press you back in the seat

Image Projected 8
Truck-tough yet civilized enough to drive to the opera

Beyond pavement 8
Despite its size and weight, surprisingly capable off-road

Competitors
Chevy Tahoe, GMC Yukon, Toyota Sequoia

brute power and decent ground clearance, the new Expedition 4WD model's optional AdvanceTrac stability control combined with its standard ControlTrac four-wheel-drive setup takes the credit here. With ControlTrac managing traction front to rear and AdvanceTrac using the brakes to do the same side to side, our Expedition was able to keep moving even if two wheels were grabbing nothing but air.

The 5.4L/260-hp Triton V-8 develops 9 90 percent of its 350 lb-ft of maximum torque down low, from 1870 to 4280 rpm, where you use it every day. But when overtaking traffic at 60 mph and above, you're reminded that the engine has 5686 lb of truck to deal with, so plan your moves ahead.

On balance, Ford's added some civi- 10 lizing touches to the Expedition without taking away from its tough-truck appeal. Engineers improved the Expedition's rough-road ride and fine-tuned its high-speed dynamics while actually increasing its towing and payload capabilities. We could argue the wisdom of driving around suburbia in a large, hard-to-park vehicle that gets real-world fuel economy in the low teens, but the ability to use one vehicle to take eight friends, their gear, and the trailer to a log cabin 15 miles down a muddy, bumpy dirt trail is an impressive one. And those very same buyers might feel safe and secure being in something large should the laws of physics make a rude and unexpected visit.

Reflecting on What You Have Read

1 What questions does Sessions answer in his review of the Ford Expedition? What criteria are implicit in those questions? What do the questions tell you about Sessions's assumptions about his audience?

2 Look closely at the largest picture in the group of photos of the Expedition. What details do you notice? What observations can you make about the photo's composition? What attitudes are implied in its details and composition?

3 Now look closely at the smaller pictures of the Expedition. What questions do they answer?

4 Notice the contexts in which the Expedition is pictured. What reasons do you see for showing the SUV in these contexts?

5 *Motor Trend* articles are often written in a personal, almost conversational voice. Is that how you would describe the voice or tone of Sessions's piece? What is there in the text that creates the voice you hear?

Thinking Ahead

Sessions's evaluation focuses on a product that he believes does a good job of meeting users' expectations. What other products—such as computers or exercise machines—are surprisingly good (or bad) at meeting the needs of users? Instead of consumer products, you might consider activities, services, or programs sponsored by schools, governments, or other organizations.

The preceding evaluations focused on a product, performance, or recent trend—the kinds of topics about which many evaluations are written. But in the following evaluation, undergraduate student Ryan Flori focuses on an organization—the Reserve Officer Training Corps (ROTC). His basic concern is whether ROTC represents a good choice for college students, especially those who never considered joining until they encountered ROTC students in uniform on campus. As you read this evaluation, notice how Ryan considers the pros and cons of his topic.

Ryan Flori

Where Is Your Future Going?
Is ROTC for You?

For me it started in the first semester of my freshman year at   1
college. On a Tuesday early in the fall, I asked a new acquaintance
why he was wearing a uniform rather than shorts and a tee shirt like
just about everyone else on campus. He told me that he was enrolled
in the U.S. Navy ROTC program on campus and that he was required
to wear a uniform every Tuesday. My first thought was "ROTC?
What's that?"

Fig. 1. ROTC students on campus.

Since that time, I've   2
learned a good deal about
ROTC, having spent the
last four years as a mem-
ber of the Navy Reserve
Officers Training Corps on
my campus. The training
includes both elective
academic courses on mili-
tary history and strategy
and physical training in
military maneuvers. ROTC
members commit them-
selves to serving as

officers in their chosen branch of the military after graduation. In my years in the ROTC, a lot of students have asked me about the program. (See Fig. 1.) Since I'm now about to graduate and take a commission in the Navy, I can honestly tell them that ROTC is not for everyone. The program involves a number of challenges, but it also offers undergraduates unique opportunities to take on responsibilities that develop important leadership skills. In addition, ROTC offers financial advantages that can make the program very attractive.

Leadership Opportunities

ROTC offers extensive opportunities that help students develop   3
as leaders. In most ROTC programs, every graduate is required to hold at least one leadership position. Most students have held two or three such positions by the time they graduate. Some introductory leadership positions are available even to sophomores. At first, as a new member of an ROTC unit, you train under the supervision of upperclassmen. As you learn more and get older, you gain more responsibility within the program.

Eventually, as you enter the upperclassmen ranks, you will be   4
leading the underclassmen, making sure they are staying in good physical shape, maintaining good academic standing, keeping up with their military training, and overcoming any major personal issues. This means that you are the first contact if a fellow ROTC midshipman or cadet has a problem. As an underclassman's superior you can either deal with the problem or, if it is a personal problem beyond your control, refer him or her to proper counseling. As a superior and officer in training, it is your job to take care of your cadets. For example, when I was a squad leader I had a squad member who failed the physical readiness test because he could not run fast enough. It was my job to train him—and train with him—until he could pass the test. Two months later he retook the physical test and passed. But if he had failed the second test, I would not have done my job and would have looked very bad.

Above the squad leaders are the company commanders, leaders of three or four squads, each including twenty to thirty people.   5

At a still higher rank are the student commanding officer and the student executive officer, who oversee all training and work directly with the active duty military officers in charge of the ROTC unit. My recent position within the ROTC unit has been that of Joint Service commanding officer. This position puts me in control of any event that involves all the Army, Navy, and Air Force ROTC services at my school. This is a pure management job. I have had to coordinate among the services to set up sports competitions and have also put together a $15,000 budget for the annual military ball. Dealings with military protocol, hotels, caterers, deadlines, and hundreds of people are bound to go not exactly as planned, and I've learned valuable firsthand lessons in dealing with the managerial tasks that are an important part of being a leader.

ROTC military experience is one of the single best things you can put on a résumé. As Stephen H. Solomson of the law firm O'Connell, Flaherty, & Attamore in Hartford notes: 6

> Much of the training in the ROTC program is directed into just that area which serves a later employee very well. We have found that graduates of ROTC are much more mature for their age and demonstrate a consistent loyalty to our organization. Presently there are three members of our firm who are ROTC graduates and we have been very pleased with their performance within our law firm. We would not hesitate to hire other graduates of the ROTC program, as we consider them very desirable employees. (Solomson)

Financial Advantages

One aspect of ROTC that is almost entirely an advantage is the money involved. For example, the cost of a four-year education at Duke University is currently $160,000 ("Tuition") and the same education at Carnegie Mellon University is almost $164,000 ("HUB Enrollment"), according to their Web sites. The ROTC programs will pay full tuition to any affiliated college or university. If you were to 7 join during your freshman year, your scholarship would begin at the start of your sophomore year, as mine did. The pay doesn't end with tuition, however.

In addition to tuition, full college fees (such as health center,   8
health insurance, and activity fees) are covered and a book stipend is provided each semester. There is also a cash stipend paid every month ranging from $200 to $400, depending on your year in school (U.S. Department of the Navy). At a few select schools, when an ROTC program pays the tuition, the college or university will pay room and board each semester, resulting in an all-expenses-paid education. Actual payment amounts depend on one's specific branch of service.

Many people point out that military pay after graduation is   9
much lower than someone can make in the civilian sector. Historically, this has been the case and remains true for base pay. However, with the extensive benefits packages provided, including allowances for housing and living expenses, an officer in the armed forces ends up making approximately the same salary as a civilian with an undergraduate degree (U.S. Dept of Defense, 1–2). Another benefit is that the job does not depend on how well the economy is doing. Table 1 shows some of the financial advantages that ROTC graduates enjoy. Notice not only the total pay amounts but also the last two columns, which show that graduating from most ROTC programs leaves the student with no college bills and a job independent of the economy, whereas a non-ROTC graduate faces college loan payments and an economy-dependent job market.

In addition, raises and promotions in the armed forces are vir-   10
tually guaranteed by the fourth year in service, including a substantial increase in salary and benefits. For example, a first-year military officer with a college degree would earn $36,720. By the fourth year, that same officer would earn $55,920. The projected salary increase in the first four years for that officer would be 52% (U.S. Dept of Defense, 1–2).

Table 1   Financial Statistics for College Graduates, ROTC and Non-ROTC

Status	Base Salary	Additional Allowances	College Bills?	Job Dependent on Economy?
First-year military officer (with college degree, regardless of type)	$25,000	• Housing $9480[a] • Living expenses $2040	No	No
	Total $36,720			
First-year civil engineer	$40,000 to $45,000	None	Yes	Yes
First-year liberal arts graduate	$27,000 to $30,000	None	Yes	Yes

Sources: Information in this table compiled by author from U.S. Department of Defense, Defense Finance and Accounting Basic Pay, *2003, and Milwaukee School of Engineering, "Average Starting Salaries of MSOE Graduates,"* MSOE, *2003.*

[a]For upstate New York. Housing allowances for officers located in other parts of the United States will vary with cost of living.

Challenges

Despite these advantages, there are several challenges and   11
problems associated with ROTC. For one thing, it is not easy to get
into an ROTC program. You will need a strong academic record and
the ability to pass a series of interviews, during which interviewers
will attempt to determine why you want to be in the program and
how motivated you are. Also, you will have to be prepared to under-
go difficult physical training.

Once you are admitted to ROTC, you will find that time issues   12
almost always present a disadvantage. While you are in college, the
time required for ROTC events—in addition to extra college courses,
physical training, and drilling sessions—will cause you to miss other
events with friends or will make the usual time crunches even harder.
Once you are commissioned into the active duty military, unit
deployments overseas will pull you away from your family for
months or years at a time.

Finally, you have to realize that military service often entails   13
extreme risk to yourself as well as to others. During training, as well as
during battle, you always face the chance of injury and even death. Further, military service will put you in charge of war machines—ships,
planes, tanks, missiles, and guns—that are meant to deliver destruction
to other people and places. They are for protection and peace, and in an
ideal world they would never be used. However, when called upon, will
you have the ability to fire that weapon, even if there is a chance of
harming civilians as well as enemy soldiers? That is a necessary thing in
the military, and a taxing thought. For this question, individuals have
their own ideas and their own decisions to make.

Deciding if ROTC Is for You

ROTC programs can bring you many advantages and awesome   14
opportunities while you are in school as well as after graduation. But all
of these advantages also come with disadvantages, many of which can
be weighted very heavily. It takes the right person with the right
mindset to excel in the military. From my perspective, ROTC is an
experience that cannot be had anywhere else. The most difficult decision is whether the military and the ROTC program are right for you.
From there it gets easier, as you can decide among the branches of service and the type of work you want to do. Perhaps, like me, you'll decide
that ROTC is the way for you to take your future anywhere you want to
go. If you want to find out more, branches of the military services have
the most complete ROTC information as well as contact information for
further inquiries.

Works Cited

"Average Starting Salaries of MSOE Graduates." *MSOE.* 2003. Milwaukee
    School of Engineering. 4 Jan. 2003 <http://www.msoe.edu/
    placement/salary.shtml>.
"HUB Enrollment Services." *Carnegie Mellon.* 2002. Carnegie Mellon
    University. 18 Nov. 2002 <http://www.cmu.edu/hub/tuition.html>.
ROTC Students. Personal photograph by author. 17 Nov. 2002.
Solomson, S. H. E-mail interview. 15 Jan. 2003.

"Tuition and Financial Assistance." *Duke University*. 2002. Duke
    University. 18 Nov. 2002 <http://www.duke.edu/web/
    ug-admissions/finaid.htm>.
U.S. Department of Defense. Defense Finance and Accounting Service.
    Defense Finance and Accounting Basic Pay. 2002. 22 Nov. 2002
    <http://www.dfas.mil/money/milpay/pay/2003-REV2.pdf>.
U.S. Department of the Navy. Office of Naval Reserve Officers Training
    Corps. *Naval Reserve Officers Training Corps*. 2002. 18 Nov. 2002
    <http://www.navy.com/nrotc>.

Reflecting on What You Have Read

1 Why does Ryan begin his evaluation by talking about his personal experience as someone who knew little about ROTC?

2 In an early draft of his evaluation, Ryan had included large photographs of an aircraft carrier, a tank, and a jet fighter—images associated with the various branches of the military—but ultimately decided to replace those photographs with one showing ROTC students on campus. Do you think his decision was a good one? Why or why not?

3 In justifying his evaluation of ROTC, Ryan shows how the organization meets two criteria: (a) opportunities for responsibility and leadership and (b) financial advantages. If you would use different criteria, what are they and why would you use them?

4 Ryan compares financial statistics for graduates of an ROTC program with those of graduates of an engineering program and a liberal arts program. He could have omitted this table and just summarized this information. If you had been reviewing an early draft of his essay, explain why you would have recommended one strategy over the other.

5 On pp. 298–299, Ryan discusses some of the reasons one might not want to enroll in an ROTC program. Would you recommend that he omit this discussion? Why or why not?

Thinking Ahead

Most college students are involved in or know about any number of organizations—both on and off campus. What are the criteria by which you might evaluate one of these organizations? Who might need to read your evaluation of this organization?

ssignment

Evaluation

Write an evaluation of a product, service, performance, trend, or organization that a specific person or group needs or wants to have evaluated. The topic you choose should be one that affects your readers and that you are competent to evaluate. In carrying out this evaluation, formulate or identify criteria that seem appropriate, given your readers and their values, and then look closely at the subject, identifying specific details that clearly relate to the criteria you are using. Your evaluation should assert a clear judgment without oversimplifying.

Your instructor may have specific requirements about how long the evaluation should be, what sort of subject you should write about, whether you should prepare the evaluation as a print or online document (or as an oral presentation), and whether you should include or exclude any particular visual elements or use a particular documentation style to cite sources. Be sure you understand those requirements before you start working on the assignment.

Guide to Writing an Evaluation

In the early stages of working on your evaluation, you may find yourself rethinking the criteria on which you base your evaluation. That happens sometimes, because criteria for evaluation can be very slippery. You may think you know what your criteria are, but when you actually try to articulate them, you may have trouble finding the right words. Moreover, you may realize that the criteria you intended to use aren't really appropriate for your subject or that they won't mean much to the audience you are trying to address. If you find yourself rethinking your criteria (or even abandoning some and finding new ones), don't be alarmed. This simply means that you are thinking carefully about what you are doing and that, therefore, you probably have a good chance of composing an evaluation that others will find balanced, honest, and useful. The remainder of this chapter will help you identify and effectively use appropriate criteria.

As you work through the assignment for this chapter, you can read a little bit about how student Ryan Flori wrote "Where Is Your Future Going? Is ROTC for You?" In the Student Dialogue box on p. 304, you will find the first of several brief conversations that Ryan had with one of the authors of this text.

Guide to Writing an Evaluation

Getting Started

Sometimes one of the most difficult parts of writing an evaluation is identifying a topic about which someone will actually need or want to read an evaluation. The next several pages will help you select a topic for your evaluation and then analyze the context in which your evaluation will be read.

Selecting a Topic

When you look at the readings in this chapter, you'll find a workable but conventional set of topics for evaluation: consumer products, technological advances, restaurants, and movies. To help you expand your possibilities a bit further, you might consider the following list of topics that writers chose to evaluate when a magazine asked them to identify the best things of the past millennium: trials, toys, magic tricks, leaders, feats of engineering, mistakes, fashions, speeches, land deals, escapes, medical advances, revolutions, and judicial decisions.

Selecting a Topic

To choose a focus for your own evaluation, you don't need to worry about the best of the past millennium, although you might think back over the past several years and see what really stands out in your experience as "best" or "worst." To identify a workable, interesting topic, you might also get some ideas by trying these activities.

> **Look back at the Thinking Ahead prompts after each reading.** Even if you haven't read the evaluation that accompanies the Thinking Ahead prompts, see if one of the prompts gives you ideas about possible topics.

> **Brainstorm.** Try focused brainstorming, responding to the suggestions in one of the Thinking Ahead sections. Or take a more general approach, thinking of things that you have had a strong reaction to or an especially clear sense of. Consider things that happen at school, at work, in social organizations, in politics, in life in your neighborhood or town. Consider objects, performances, decisions, or actions. With these options in mind, begin writing about some possible topics without taking a lot of time to contemplate any of them. Complete sentences such as the following: "One thing I really like/dislike is _____." "The best/worst thing I can think of is _____." "Another thing I like/dislike is _____." "Another good/bad thing I can think of is _____." Whether you take a focused or a more general approach, don't worry about essay form or even about spelling or punctuation. Just write as fast as you can, getting down as many ideas as possible.

> **Review what you have written.** Identify several topics that matter to you and will matter to someone else.

> **Discuss these topics with a small group** or the entire class. Who might be interested in reading an evaluation of these topics? What criteria might you use in evaluating each of these topics?

> **Focus on one topic and brainstorm a list of statements about it.** Try answering the following questions: "What experiences have I had with this subject? What did I observe? What aspects of the subject struck me as significantly good or bad—and why? What criteria am I (consciously or not) using to make my evaluation? How has this subject affected other people? How have they reacted to it? Where or how might I get additional information about it?"

> **Explain what you have come up with.** Talk with a small group of classmates, and then describe the group's reaction to the thing you are thinking about evaluating. Would your classmates have any need to read this evaluation? Can they think of anyone else who might have such a need?

Sometimes students wonder, "Do I really need to do all this? Isn't it just a lot of wasted effort?" It may be a lot of effort, but it won't be wasted if it keeps you from getting stuck with a topic that bores you and that doesn't matter to anyone else. You'll do best to select a topic you think will be interesting to you and important to a particular audience. After you do so, you'll need to begin thinking about the context in which your evaluation will be read.

STUDENT DIALOGUE: SELECTING A TOPIC

Writing in a Visual Age: What other topics did you consider writing about? Why did you decide on ROTC?

Ryan Flori: I also considered writing evaluations of the Rensselaer program that requires students to buy or rent laptop computers, as well as of popular brands of hiking shoes because my family and I do a lot of hiking. Eventually, though, I decided on ROTC because I had more personal experience and knowledge to offer about it and because it seemed a more relevant topic given current world issues.

Analyzing Context

Up to this point, you've probably been thinking about your topic from your own perspective, using criteria that seem important to you. You likely recorded your own impressions of the subject (movie, product, plan, or idea) you want to evaluate. Now, if you haven't already begun doing so, you need to start thinking about the larger context for your evaluation— the readers you hope to reach, the circumstances in which they will encounter your evaluation, and the purposes you hope to accomplish in writing for them. To develop a good sense of your context in writing an evaluation, you should write out answers to the questions that follow.

Questions for Analyzing Context

> bedfordstmartins.com/
visualage

To download these questions as a worksheet, click on
**CHAPTER 5 >
WORKSHEETS**

● **Audience knowledge, values, and needs**

> What sorts of experiences (personal or secondhand) have my readers had with my topic?

> How does my topic relate to things my readers know, value, or care about?

> Do my readers have any biases or preconceptions concerning my topic? If so, what are they?

● **Audience expectations for content**

> What kinds of questions are my readers most likely to want to have answered?

> What kinds of criteria are they likely to find important?

> What kinds of information will they see as credible?

● **Audience expectations for layout or format**

> Which reading in this chapter comes closest to looking the way my readers will expect my evaluation to look?

> Are there any visual features (for example, photographs, charts, or bulleted lists) that my readers are likely to expect or appreciate?

> Are there ways in which my evaluation will need to look different from the readings in this chapter?

- **Circumstances**
  > Are there any recent events that might motivate my audience to read my evaluation? If so, what are they?
  > If not, what sort of background information should I provide at the beginning of my evaluation?
- **Purposes**
  > What purposes am I trying to accomplish in writing my evaluation? (See discussion of purposes on p. 266.)
  > What sort of voice do I want readers to hear when they read my evaluation? (For a discussion of voice, see p. 320 of this chapter.)

Working on the Assignment

Analyzing Context

As you work on your evaluation, your understanding of audience, circumstances, and purposes may change. But now is the time to begin developing that understanding. We recommend that you begin your context analysis by identifying one or two specific individuals who are typical of the people you hope will read your evaluation. Then do the following.

Talk with someone who is a member of your intended audience (or who in some important ways resembles a member of that audience). Has this person had any experience with the thing (product, performance, organization) you are evaluating? What sort of experience? firsthand or indirect? positive or negative? extensive or limited? What values or criteria does this person seem to have? (If, for example, you are reviewing a movie this person hasn't seen, ask the person to describe the qualities he or she expects in a good movie.) Is this person going to live vicariously by means of your evaluation, wondering what it might be like to own a new BMW? Or is the person about to make a decision and, therefore, interested in finding the most reliable information possible? What personal consequences might your evaluation have for your reader?

Put yourself in your reader's place. Ask yourself such questions as these: *If I were a member of the intended audience, why would I want to read an evaluative piece on this topic? What criteria would matter to me? How would I feel if the evaluation were strongly negative or strongly positive?*

Draw on your knowledge of yourself. What are the criteria that underlie your own attitudes toward the thing you are evaluating? Are there any points at which you and your audience might share some of the same criteria? What are the points at which you and your audience differ most with respect to the criteria that matter to you?

Determine the layout or format your audience will expect. Will readers expect an evaluation that looks like a conventional essay, or are they likely to prefer a Web site or a brochure? Will readers appreciate visual elements? pictures? graphs? subheadings? bulleted lists?

Imagine the circumstances in which your readers will encounter your evaluation. Will your evaluation appear as printed text or on a computer screen? What recent events might prompt readers to look at your evaluation? Have readers heard people discussing the topic and felt the need to read an evaluation? What kinds of decisions or actions are open to your audience after reading your evaluation?

As you work on the evaluation, your sense of your audience may change. You may, for example, develop a clearer idea about your readers' values. As a result, you may want to revise your responses to the Questions for Analyzing Context. For now, be as specific as possible.

STUDENT CONTEXT ANALYSIS

Here's how Ryan Flori answered these questions for his evaluation, "Where Is Your Future Going? Is ROTC for You?" (p. 294).

Audience Knowledge, Values, and Needs

What sorts of experiences (personal or secondhand) have my readers had with my topic?

My readers have had very little experience with this topic. They are curious. They have seen ROTC members on campus in uniform and in the gym, but they probably do not know why the ROTC students are here or how they are involved with the military. My readers perhaps have heard a little about the program through friends or roommates.

How does my topic relate to things my readers know, value, or care about?

My readers care about the welfare and protection of their country. They are curious about the military and interested in what they would have to give the military as well as how they would benefit by being in the military. They also want careers that are financially and personally rewarding.

Do my readers have any biases or preconceptions concerning my topic? If so, what are they?

My readers may have preconceived biases about the military, the most important one being that recruiters won't give them the whole truth about military service.

Audience Expectations for Content

What kinds of questions are my readers most likely to want to have answered?

The major questions my readers have pertain to what they will owe the military and what they will get in return for their service. Furthermore, they will want to know what the military is like, beyond the pure-pro view they can get from a recruiter. They want a nonbiased view from someone with military experience.

STUDENT CONTEXT ANALYSIS

What kinds of criteria are they likely to find important?	*The criteria come down to a comparison of "what I get" versus "what I have to do to get it." Other criteria are experiences they will have and what will happen to them during the program—again, a trade-off between what I have to do and what I can get.*
What kinds of information will they see as credible?	*Since I will be completing the four-year program this semester, I believe my readers will see me as a credible source. If any readers do not believe that I am a nonbiased source of information, they will see that I have not limited my evaluation to just pros; I also include cons, which recruiters would not usually talk about, as well as verifiable facts about finances.*

Audience Expectations for Layout or Format

Which reading in this chapter comes closest to looking the way my readers will expect my evaluation to look?	*My evaluation will look somewhat like the piece from* Consumer Reports *in that it will include a table that lets readers make comparisons.*
Are there any visual features (for example, photographs, charts, or bulleted lists) that my readers are likely to expect or appreciate?	*They may not expect a table, but they will probably appreciate one that lets them understand the financial pros and cons of military service.*
Are there ways in which my evaluation will need to look different from the readings in this chapter?	*Although the opening of my evaluation includes a picture, it will not be as flashy as the one on the first page of the* Consumer Reports *article. My photo will simply show ROTC students on campus.*

Circumstances

Are there any recent events that might motivate my audience to read my evaluation? If so, what are they? If not, what sort of background information should I provide at the beginning of my evaluation?	*Presently, a war is taking place. In the not-so-distant past were the terrorist attacks against the World Trade Center towers in New York City. Both of these events can spark patriotism in my readers.*

continued

STUDENT CONTEXT ANALYSIS	
continued	

Purposes

What purposes am I trying to accomplish in writing my evaluation?

The purpose I am trying to accomplish with this paper is to present clear, concise ideas of the advantages and disadvantages of the ROTC program. In doing so, I want to give my readers the tools with which to make an educated decision about whether or not the program is right for them.

What sort of voice do I want readers to hear when they read my evaluation?

I want my readers to hear a very matter-of-fact voice. I don't want to sound like I'm trying to sell anyone on the program. Although I think ROTC is a good program, I want to present the information clearly and then evaluate the most important aspects of the program. From there it is up to readers to make their own decisions.

Drafting

The next few sections of this chapter will help you write your draft evaluation by showing you some of the strategies other writers have used. Don't be concerned if you try a particular strategy and it doesn't pay off for you; the examples in this section will suggest a lot of possibilities. You can further expand your choice of strategies by analyzing other evaluative pieces that you think are effective.

Developing Your Topic

There are several useful approaches to developing your topic: using secondary sources, identifying and defining criteria, and observing and testing.

Using Secondary Sources

Much of what you have to say in your evaluation will come from your own observations and, perhaps, from some of the testing described on pp. 312–314 of this chapter. But don't neglect the background information that can come from secondary sources, especially if your firsthand experience with the topic is somewhat limited.

How to Use Secondary Sources

Strategies	Examples
Read background material that accompanies your topic. This material could include advertising and promotional items as well as any print or Web-based technical specifications provided by the product manufacturer or service provider. Look especially for photographs that suggest your attitude toward your subject and statistical data that can be represented in a chart or table.	*In "Cream of the Crop" (p. 273) the* Consumer Reports *authors indicate that they obtained some information (ingredients lists, calories per serving) from the labels on the ice cream containers.*
Interview people associated with your topic. Talk with people whom your readers will recognize as having some expertise on the subject of your evaluation.	*"A Storm Brings Culinary Clear Sailing" (p. 289) quotes the owners of the restaurant in explaining the influences on the restaurant's cuisine. It also provides some information about the owners' background, information that seems likely to have come from the author's conversations with the restaurant owners.*

STUDENT DIALOGUE: USING SECONDARY SOURCES

Writing in a Visual Age: What sort of background reading did you do? Where did you find your sources?

Ryan Flori: I did a Google search to learn about the costs of education at other schools like Rensselaer. Also, I went to several Navy and government Web sites. As a member of ROTC, I get a paycheck each month from the Navy. I noticed that there was a URL on my paycheck stub, so I checked it out, and that's where I got a lot of my information about finances.

Using Secondary Sources

Keep careful notes on what you learn from reading or from talking with people who know something about your topic. For the reading you do, keep a working bibliography. As you talk with people, be sure to write down memorable comments they make, especially if these comments reflect attitudes you hear from several people. Also listen for anecdotes about their experiences with your topic.

⟩ For more on keeping a working
bibliography, see **Chapter 9.**

Identifying and Defining Criteria

One key to the success of your evaluation will be your ability to identify criteria that your readers will find clear and appropriate. In other words, you'll need to provide readers with the reasons underlying your judgment that something is good or bad, desirable or undesirable, and so forth. Here are some strategies you can use in identifying and defining those reasons or criteria.

How to Identify and Define Criteria

Strategies	Examples
Begin by thinking about your own values. If you are reviewing a movie, for example, ask yourself what matters most to you in a movie and what distinguishes a really good movie from a mediocre one. Is it realistic special effects? a plot that takes surprising twists? witty dialogue?	*"Breakfast at Manory's" (p. 286) gives readers a very clear sense of what the author admires in Manory's "Big Breakfast": quantity, reasonable price, and intensity of flavors (as in the bacon that is "salty enough to disinfect gunshot wounds"). The author seems to assume—probably with justification— that his readers will also admire these qualities.*

How to Identify and Define Criteria

Strategies	Examples
Consider your readers' perspective. What qualities are likely to matter to your readers? How are those qualities similar to or different from the qualities that are important to you?	*Sessions seems to assume in "Ford Expedition" (p. 291) that his readers value ease of handling, safety, and comfort in an SUV in addition to performance in off-road conditions. His evaluation focuses on how the SUV handles in city driving as well as how it performs in deep sand and in steep, rocky terrain.*
Define ambiguous terms by identifying the specific qualities that distinguish between good and bad examples of what you are evaluating. Ambiguous terms have different meanings for different readers. One way to define such terms is to point out contrasts that indicate exactly what distinguishes an excellent product, social trend, or idea from one that is not quite so good. (For more on pointing out contrasts, see Chapter 3, p. 159.)	*In "Cream of the Crop" (p. 273), the Consumer Reports writers set out to explain which vanilla ice creams taste good. Because "tastes good" is open to many interpretations, the writers are careful to define it precisely, pointing out specific ways the various vanilla ice creams differ with respect to balance of flavor, texture, and the consistency of the ice cream when it melts.*

Working on the Assignment

Identifying and Defining Criteria

> List the criteria you plan to use in evaluating your subject.

> Explain those criteria to some classmates; then ask them to identify any terms that could have different meanings for different people.

> Ask them whether your criteria seem appropriate given your subject and audience.

If you have questions about whether you need to define a particular word or phrase, ask members of your audience how they would define it. If different people in your intended audience give you the same definition, you probably do not need to include a definition in your evaluation.

Observing and Testing

Most of the evaluations you write will rely heavily on your experiences with the subject you are evaluating. Sometimes these experiences may consist of personal observations. At other times, these experiences may reflect careful, systematic testing carried out not only by you but by several others as well. When you set out to observe (view, read, listen to, or use) the thing you are evaluating, you should make a point of doing so on several different occasions. On each occasion, try to add to your list of details.

If you want to convey a favorable impression of your subject, you can show how it is similar to things your audience knows and values. Conversely, if your evaluation is unfavorable, you can contrast your subject with things that your audience will recognize as being superior, or you can show how it is similar to something about which your audience has negative feelings. Whether you are evaluating a product, a service, or a policy, you might also make use of some or all of the following strategies.

How to Observe

Strategies	Examples
Observe or work with the subject you are evaluating on several different occasions, each time noticing what happens and whether the subject lives up to the criteria you have established.	*In "You Call This Progress?" (p. 283), the criticism of e-mail is based not on a single, isolated experience but on numerous experiences, all of which reinforce the writer's view that e-mail does not constitute progress.*
Make comparisons. When you make comparisons, you answer such questions as these: Is the subject as good as something else? better than something else? worse? in some ways better and some ways worse?	*"Cream of the Crop" (p. 273) makes detailed comparisons among items belonging to the same general category—in this case, vanilla ice cream.*
Consider both positive and negative aspects of the topic being evaluated. It's rare that something is completely good or completely bad. You'll gain credibility with most readers when you acknowledge both pros and cons.	*Although his evaluation of ROTC is basically positive, Ryan Flori ("Where Is Your Future Going? Is ROTC for You?" p. 294) is careful to point out (in paragraphs 10–12) the "challenges and problems associated with ROTC."*

STUDENT DIALOGUE: OBSERVING

Writing in a Visual Age: You mention disadvantages associated with ROTC. Why did you mention these?

Ryan Flori: The purpose of my evaluation of the ROTC program is to provide both the pros and cons and let my readers decide for themselves whether the program is for them. If I were to include only the good things I have observed about the program, I would simply be a military recruiter.

If you are evaluating a product or service, you may want to supplement your personal observations with additional testing. In this case, you systematically gather information from a group of judges who have expertise with the subject you are evaluating and whom you train to use the criteria you have established. Strategies that will work for many forms of testing are listed below. All of the examples are drawn from "Cream of the Crop."

How to Test

Strategies

Define your criteria, using the strategies mentioned on pp. 310–311.

Examples

According to "Cream of the Crop" (p. 273), a good-tasting vanilla ice cream includes balanced flavors of milk and "real vanilla," with perhaps a hint of egg flavor; it has a smooth texture and, when it melts, is about the thickness of heavy cream. Not all readers will accept CR's definition—for instance, readers who are deathly allergic to eggs will likely read "a slight egg flavor" as a strong warning to stay away. However, this doesn't invalidate CR's judgment. The careful definition gives readers a good sense of how the judgment was arrived at and where they can and cannot accept CR's conclusions.

continued

How to Test

continued

Strategies	Examples
Choose and train your judges carefully. Look for people who will set aside their personal preferences and work within the guidelines you establish.	*Results reported in this article are derived by "blind taste tests by trained panelists"—that is, the judges did not know the brand names of the ice creams they tested.*
Have the judges practice using the criteria until they can apply them consistently.	*The judges on the CR panel have been "trained" to look for particular flavors and textures.*
Have your judges rate the product or service you're writing about.	*The* Consumer Reports *judges gave highest ratings to brands with "consistently high-quality flavor and smooth and creamy texture." They also considered cost, fat content, and calories.*

Working on the Assignment

Testing

When you conduct tests of your subject, keep careful notes in response to the following questions.

> Whom did you choose as judges?
> Why did you choose these people? What makes you think they will give you honest, unbiased information?

> What instructions will you have them follow in making their judgments?
> How often do they agree with each other?

> For more information on creating charts, tables, and graphs, see **Chapter 8.**

Testing often results in some sort of numerical data (the number of people, for example, who found a product easy or difficult to use). Record your data carefully, and determine the kind of chart, graph, or table that will represent them most clearly and accurately in your written evaluation. To be fair, your test must use the product or service under the conditions for which it is intended. If a software program is designed to be used with a computer with a lot of memory, for example, do not test the program on an old computer with insufficient memory. If you cannot replicate the conditions for which the product or service was designed, you probably should find another topic or try to develop your evaluation in another way.

Creating an Exploratory Draft

After you have identified and defined criteria for your evaluation—and determined if your subject meets these criteria through observation and testing—you should be ready to write an *exploratory draft* that will help you determine what you currently know and what you still need to find out in order to write an effective evaluation.

Working on the Assignment

Creating an Exploratory Draft

Use or observe your subject on at least two different occasions, keeping detailed notes about how well (or whether) your subject meets the criteria you have established. You will use these notes in writing an exploratory draft of your evaluation.

Before you begin writing an exploratory draft, take a close look at the context analysis you completed, answering the questions on p. 306. Are there some questions that aren't completed very well? For example, are you lacking information about your readers' knowledge, needs, and values? Do you have a good sense of what your readers will expect in terms of content, both visual and verbal? At this point, complete your responses to the best of your ability.

After revising your context analysis, set aside twenty to thirty minutes to write as rapidly as you can, without interruption, in response to the following sentences.

> "Basically, I think the thing I am evaluating is good/bad (admirable/not admirable, desirable/undesirable, attractive/unattractive). Or it is good in that it _____, but bad in that it _____."

> "One of my criteria is _____."

> "My subject meets/fails to meet this criterion in that _____."

> "Another criterion is _____."

> "My subject meets/fails to meet this criterion in that _____."

> "Another criterion is _____."

After you have completed this exploratory work, read or show what you have written to other students (perhaps in a small group or perhaps to the entire class). Describe your audience to your classmates, and then ask them to answer the following questions.

> Can you think of an audience that would want or need to read an evaluation of this subject?

> Are my criteria clear? Do they reflect my audience's values?

> Do I have sufficient evidence to show how my subject meets (or fails to meet) those criteria?

> What other types of information might I look for in order to explain how my subject meets/fails to meet the criteria I mention in my exploratory writing?

continued

continued

> Where might a picture, chart, table, or graph make my points clearer or easier to understand?

> Does my draft contain any information that might be set off in inset boxes or pull quotes?

> Where might I use one or more of the strategies explained earlier in the chapter to make my evaluation more credible or useful for readers? What strategies should I use?

Use your classmates' responses to guide you in deciding whether or how to add to, delete, or modify information you have included in your exploratory draft.

Engaging Your Audience: Writing an Introduction

People will be more likely to read your evaluation when your topic matters to them. They will probably, for example, read an evaluation of a particular automobile if they are considering buying that automobile. But choosing your topic is only the first step in engaging your readers' interest. You also have to make sure your introduction accomplishes two important tasks.

> It should let readers see how your topic relates to what they know, need, or care about.

> It should establish a conflict (problem, question, uncertainty, dissonance), especially one that can be resolved by reading your evaluation.

Consider, for example, the beginning of "Cream of the Crop." The subtitle and first paragraph refer to a trend readers are likely to be aware of: many people are once again choosing "full-fat" ice creams in preference to "reduced fat products." The subtitle also poses a question that is likely to matter to people who eat full-fat ice creams: "Which ones are worth the calories?" That is, if someone is going to indulge in ice cream containing a lot of fat and calories, which brands taste good enough to justify the indulgence?

Relating to Readers

The evaluations in the Reading to Write section of this chapter display a variety of strategies for relating to readers. Here are five strategies that will help your own writing relate to—or develop common ground with—your readers.

How to Relate to Readers

Strategies	Examples
Create an image readers can recognize or appreciate. You can do this with pictures or photographs that will encourage a strong emotional reaction, or you can create a verbal picture with specific details that readily conjure up images in readers' minds.	*Anyone with a weakness for ice cream will notice the ice cream sundae photo at the beginning of "Cream of the Crop" (p. 273). "A Storm Brings Culinary Clear Sailing" (p. 289) creates a verbal picture in the first paragraph: the "flower-bedecked terrace [that] affords views of the sparkling waters of the creek."*
Refer to an experience your readers probably share. Mention shared experiences that might prompt readers to read or see or buy or visit the thing you are evaluating.	*"Breakfast at Manory's" (p. 286) begins by mentioning a tendency (sleeping late) that many of the author's readers, fellow college students, probably share. This experience creates a problem, the lack of a full, satisfying breakfast, which might make readers receptive to what the writer has to say about the restaurant.*
Make an assertion your readers will probably agree with.	*"Dr. Strangelove" (p. 280) begins with an assertion: "Every time you see a great film, you find new things in it." Film buffs are likely to have seen Dr. Strangelove (and many other classic movies) a number of times, delighting in new things they discover with each viewing.*
Mention a question or problem that is probably on your readers' minds. Specifically, mention a question or problem that might be answered or solved by the subject you are evaluating.	*"Cream of the Crop" asks a question in the subtitle that readers are presumably eager to have answered: "Full-fat ice cream is back in style. Which ones are worth the calories?"*

continued

How to Relate to Readers

continued

Strategies

Use a format that your readers will expect and appreciate.

Examples

Readers of Consumer Reports *expect to find detailed information laid out in tables and graphs that allow detailed comparisons among products being reviewed. They also anticipate that key points will be highlighted (often in pull quotes) and that specialized and background information will be set off in boxes, where readers can readily find that information but where it will not get in the way of the main points of the evaluation. (See "Cream of the Crop.") In contrast, readers of movie reviews usually expect relatively long passages of written text, followed by some sort of rating system (five stars for "excellent," four for "very good," and so on).*

STUDENT DIALOGUE: RELATING TO READERS

Writing in a Visual Age: You talk a good bit about your personal experiences in ROTC. Given your audience, why did you do this?

Ryan Flori: The audience I have chosen is the exact audience that I was a part of four years ago. At the time, I was really interested in what ROTC was like on a personal level. So I figured that my audience might have the same interest.

Establishing Conflict

In addition to letting readers see how your topic relates to what they know, care about, or need, you should create a conflict that will motivate them to read your evaluation. Following are four strategies for doing this.

How to Establish Conflict

Strategies	Examples
Suggest a disparity between what appears to be true and what might actually be true. One way to do this is to mention a strongly positive (or negative) impression and then consider whether that impression is valid.	The introductory paragraphs of "A Storm Brings Culinary Clear Sailing" (p. 289) describe a picture-perfect setting for the restaurant and then, playing on readers' awareness that things can sound too good to be true, pose a question: "Can the food live up to the setting?"
Mention a difference between an initial impression and the insight that comes from repeated experiences with a subject. Initial impressions are not always reliable. Make note of what your first reaction is, and then take a second (or third) look. Does your initial reaction hold after careful observation and/or testing? Do you notice anything after repeated experiences that you did not notice at first?	"Dr. Strangelove" (p. 280) begins with the statement, "Viewing . . . Dr. Strangelove for perhaps the 10th time, I discovered what George C. Scott does with his face."
Present information that conflicts with what readers know, value, or care about. Use this conflict to pose a question or problem that you will answer or solve in your evaluation.	"Where Is Your Future Going? Is ROTC for You?" (p. 294) begins with the writer's memories of a day, early in his first year of college, when he saw a friend dressed in a uniform rather than the shorts and tee shirts most other students were wearing. Puzzled, the author asked the same questions other students subsequently asked him: Why the uniform? What is ROTC? What are the advantages and disadvantages of joining ROTC?
Present two or more contradictory or incompatible facts, situations, or points of view.	The second paragraph of "Dr. Strangelove" recounts a conflict between Jack Lemmon, an actor, and Billy Wilder, a film director, who have different notions as to how a scene should be played.

Engaging Your Audience

> Look on the Web, in magazines, and in books to find an evaluation in which the first few paragraphs do a good job of engaging a reader's interest. Be prepared to show this evaluation to your classmates and explain your answers to the following questions: What assumptions does the writer appear to be making about the reader's knowledge, needs, and values? What aspects of the beginning of the evaluation would appeal to a person with the knowledge, needs, and values you have identified?

> Review—and, if necessary, revise—your context analysis, being careful to describe your readers' knowledge, needs, and values.

> Using one or more of the strategies for relating to readers and creating conflict, write one or more introductory paragraphs that seem likely to engage the attention of the audience you have described.

> Bring this introductory material to class, along with your context analysis. Ask your classmates to tell you whether the introduction you have written seems likely to engage the intended audience. Also ask your classmates whether they can think of other strategies to engage your audience.

Creating an Appropriate Voice

Authors can sometimes give you a sense of how a passage sounds; as you read their written work, you can almost hear them talking to you. As you read a passage, you may think "this sounds angry" or "this sounds very sincere," even though no one is literally speaking. This implied sound is one important aspect of voice. But in the evaluative articles included earlier in this chapter, the term *voice* can also refer to a writer's personality, attitude, point of view, or implied relationship to the reader and the subject. Seth Shostak, for example, seems irritated with e-mail, but he also sounds like someone with a sense of humor (p. 283). By contrast, the voice in "Cream of the Crop" (p. 273) sounds relatively impersonal; there is no indication of who wrote this article, and the authors appear to be expressing the opinions of "highly trained judges" rather than giving their own opinions. And in "A Storm Brings Culinary Clear Sailing" (p. 289), Julie Kirgo conveys a personal voice and sounds almost breathless with excitement.

Which of these authors should you emulate? What kind of voice should you try to create in your evaluation? That depends not only on your topic and audience but also on your awareness of yourself and of the attitudes and personality you want to convey. You'll have to get reactions and further guidance from your instructor and classmates as you develop a voice that makes sense for your topic, audience, and purpose.

One way writers create voice is by carefully selecting the pronouns they use. The first-person pronouns *I* and *we* and the second-person pronoun *you* can suggest a relatively informal relationship between reader and writer. Third-person pronouns (*he, she, it, they*) often suggest a more formal, more impersonal relationship. In addition to their selection of pronouns, the authors of the evaluative pieces in this chapter also create their distinctive voices by using one or more of the strategies listed here.

How to Create an Appropriate Voice

Strategies	Examples
Choose words with connotations that imply or reinforce your attitudes and that are appropriate for your audience.	*In "A Storm Brings Culinary Clear Sailing" (p. 289), Kirgo's enthusiasm comes through in her use of such terms as "rich and creamy," "delightfully chewy," and "unctuous purée." Sometimes her vocabulary ("echt bistro") seems intended to exclude certain readers, narrowing her readership to a relatively small subset of restaurant goers and identifying herself as a member of that group.*
Make comparisons that imply or reinforce the attitudes you want to convey. If your attitude is positive, compare your subject to things your readers know and respect. If your attitude is negative, make the reverse sort of comparison.	*Shostak indicates his low opinion of e-mail in "You Call This Progress?" (p. 283) in this remark: "Today access to the Internet is widespread, as common and accessible as a cheap motel."*
Make conscious choices about what sort of information to include or exclude. Another way to say this is to make conscious choices about the kinds of questions you answer in your evaluation. These choices will not only help reveal the relationship you want to have with your audience, but they will also help reveal your attitude toward your subject. Do you want to be seen as an authority? Then you have to answer the kinds of questions your readers will expect an expert to answer.	*Kirgo frequently includes information about food ingredients and about her own personal reactions, thereby taking on the role of a sophisticated restaurant reviewer, one who is knowledgeable about food and who expects people to listen to her authoritative opinion. "Breakfast at Manory's" (p. 286) makes a number of references to students' experiences (oversleeping and missing part of a class, for example) to help the writer identify with his student readers and gain credibility with them.*

continued

How to Create an Appropriate Voice

continued

Strategies	Examples
Use visuals that convey your feelings toward and your evaluation of your subject. Make sure the visuals suggest attitudes that are consistent with those you want to convey in the written text.	*"A Storm Brings Culinary Clear Sailing" includes a photo of Storm Café's deck on a sunny day that suggests the restaurant would be a pleasant place to have a leisurely lunch. This suggestion is in keeping with the author's overwhelmingly favorable comments about the quality of Storm's food.*

STUDENT DIALOGUE: CREATING AN APPROPRIATE VOICE

Writing in a Visual Age: You say you wanted to create a matter-of-fact voice. Why?

Ryan Flori: I wanted to create a voice my readers could trust. That might not happen if I came across as though I was trying to recruit or "sell" ROTC. Also, with recent events in the Middle East, deciding on a military career is something people need to do thoughtfully, not emotionally.

Working on the Assignment

Creating an Appropriate Voice

If you have not already done so, you should now begin thinking carefully about the voice you want to convey in your evaluation. Here are some suggestions that can help you do this. Keep in mind that as you think about voice, you may discover a need to change the substance of your evaluation. For example, if you have come to be enthusiastic about your topic, you may need to gather additional information that will justify that enthusiasm.

› Review your context analysis—and revise it if you need to.

› List some of the words and phrases you hope readers would use to describe the voice in your evaluation. Do you want your voice to sound personal or impersonal? formal or informal? serious? sarcastic? friendly? knowledgeable? enthusiastic? reserved? excited? calm and reflective?

❯ Check with a classmate or your instructor to see whether the voice you hope to create makes sense given what your context analysis says about your audience and purposes.

❯ Using what you learn from your classmate or instructor, revise the list of words that describe the voice you want to create.

❯ Ask someone (a classmate, your instructor, or a friend) to read a section of your draft aloud, and listen to the sound of his or her voice. Can you hear the attitude you want to create in the sound of this reader's voice? If you can, good. If you

can't, look closely at your draft to see what words and phrases you need to change in order to create the voice you want.

❯ Ask someone to read your introductory paragraph(s) (aloud or silently), and then list the words he or she would use to describe the voice you have created. Does this reader's list match yours? On the basis of what this reader tells you, decide whether you need to revise either your conception of the voice you want to create or your introduction. Or do you need to revise both?

Providing Structure

Like readers of reports, readers of evaluations rarely read every word. Instead, they look for specific pieces of information or try to answer questions that are on their minds. Writers of evaluations therefore need to provide the cues that help readers find the information they are looking for. That is, writers need to make their work accessible. And to accommodate those readers who are reading straight through a text rather than searching for specific pieces of information, writers need to create expectations as to what they will say next and provide links that indicate how any given paragraph relates to those that precede and follow it. The sample evaluations in Reading to Write illustrate a number of strategies that professional writers have used to make their work accessible, create expectations, and link paragraphs. In your own writing, try a strategy (or combination of strategies) to see how it works out. If it isn't helpful, try another strategy—one identified in this chapter or one you notice in something else you have read.

Making Information Accessible

When people read evaluations, they may be looking for information that answers specific questions. Consequently, you should make this information as accessible as possible. The following are strategies you can use to help readers find the information they are looking for.

How to Make Information Accessible

Strategies	Examples
Use explicit thesis statements and topic sentences. Place them "up front," where readers can easily find them.	*The end of the introduction to "Where Is Your Future Going? Is ROTC for You?" (p. 294) asserts the thesis—and forecasts the content of the evaluation—by saying that ROTC "involves a number of challenges, but it also offers . . . unique opportunities to take on responsibilities that develop important leadership skills. In addition, ROTC offers financial advantages that can make the program very attractive."*
Use one or more visual cues. *Subheadings* clearly indicate what comes next in subsequent sections of text. *Pull quotes* are highlighted sentences taken from the text. *Boxed insets* may contain background or other information. *Charts, graphs,* or *tables* enable readers to see how your subject meets (or fails to meet) your criteria or allow readers to compare and contrast your subject with other subjects.	*All of these types of visual cues appear in "Cream of the Crop" (p. 273). For example, the "Ratings" table clearly and concisely presents numerical data about calories, cost, and fat content alongside descriptive information in the "Comments" column and a bar graph representing a "flavor and texture score." To find out more about visual cues, see Chapter 8.*

Creating Expectations

For those who are reading your evaluation straight through, here are several strategies that will help them see what to expect in a given section of your evaluation.

How to Create Expectations

Strategies	Examples
Use a subtitle that indicates your basic point of view.	*The subtitle of "You Call This Progress?" (p. 283) clearly indicates that the evaluation will be critical of e-mail, and even if you overlook that cue, the main point is repeated in the first paragraph.*
Use forecasting words or phrases. These terms tell readers what topic they can expect you to talk about in a passage they are about to read.	*Paragraph 4 of "Ford Expedition" (p. 291) mentions that one of the manufacturer's goals was to improve the new SUV's handling. The remainder of that paragraph focuses on how well the Expedition handles.*
Use visuals that imply a point of view or attitude readers may expect to find in the written text.	*The large group of photos in "Ford Expedition" implies that the SUV will handle well in off-road conditions, and this implication is made explicit in the written text. The photograph of the terrace in "A Storm Brings Culinary Clear Sailing" (p. 289) suggests a relaxed elegance that is reflected in the author's review of the restaurant.*
Create a distinctive voice or tone that implies your values or attitudes.	*It's hard to say the title of the evaluative piece on e-mail—"You Call This Progress?"—without sounding annoyed. Even when read silently, the implied sound of this title leads readers to expect an evaluation that expresses irritation.*

Creating Links

To help make your writing more coherent, here are several strategies you can use to link a given paragraph with the paragraphs that precede or follow it.

How to Create Links

Strategies	Examples
Use transition words or phrases.	Paragraphs in "You Call This Progress?" (p. 283) routinely begin with transition words to indicate a relationship between paragraphs: "unfortunately" (moving from good news to bad); "in addition" (adding one more item to a list); "still" (indicating a conflict between what might seem to be true and what actually is true); and "because" (indicating a cause-effect relationship).
Refer to a topic mentioned in a previous passage, and then go on to add some new information to that topic.	The first paragraph under "Premium Taste?" in "Cream of the Crop" (p. 273) ends with this sentence: "To make ice cream, a manufacturer pasteurizes and homogenizes milk, cream, sweeteners, and other ingredients such as gums and emulsifiers; cools the mixture; adds flavors and colors; and whips air into it as it freezes." The next paragraph begins by mentioning two terms from the previous paragraph: "Too much air and too many gums can result in . . ."

Working on the Assignment

Providing Structure

Bring to class a copy of an evaluation that does a good job of making its structure very clear. Be prepared to show your instructor and classmates how the author(s) enabled you to see the structure of the evaluation.

After identifying strategies other writers have used, review your exploratory draft, looking for ways you might use some of these strategies to make the structure of your own evaluation clear.

Concluding Your Evaluation

People may read evaluations for any number of reasons. Perhaps they just want to daydream about buying a new car or visiting an exotic vacation spot, even though both the car and the vacation spot are completely outside their budget. They may even read a movie review after seeing the movie just to discover what someone else thought about it. However, most often people read evaluations because they want guidance in making a decision. Consequently, one good way to conclude your evaluation is to make a recommendation. In "Breakfast at Manory's," for example, Vitarius does this emphatically: "Go to Manory's. . . . Go now, no matter what time of day it is." The authors of "Cream of the Crop," though less emphatic, conclude with a "Recommendations" section in which they briefly restate their findings as to which of the ice creams they reviewed are the best choices. The other selections in the Reading to Write section of this chapter illustrate still other strategies for concluding evaluations. Which of these evaluations has the best conclusion? Probably they all do. That is, each evaluation ends in a way that makes good sense given its subject and the context for which it was written.

How to Conclude

Strategies	Examples
Frame your evaluation. That is, return to a topic mentioned near the beginning of the evaluation.	*"A Storm Brings Culinary Clear Sailing" (p. 289) ends by returning to a topic—the owners of the restaurant—mentioned near the beginning and then adding an anecdote that gives a new insight into these owners' personalities.*
Ask a provocative question.	*The end of "Dr. Strangelove" (p. 280) poses a question that suggests a possible attitude toward the film: "Are [Stanley Kubrick's] two best films a nudge in his own ribs?"*
Mention a potential benefit of the subject you are evaluating.	*After acknowledging that some readers might question the "wisdom of driving . . . a large, hard-to-park" SUV, "Ford Expedition" (p. 291) concludes by noting that those same readers might also appreciate the safety and security the vehicle offers in the event of an accident.*

Exercise

Bring to class an evaluation you find interesting and informative. Does its conclusion reflect any of the strategies identified above? If not, how does it conclude? What strategy or strategies are apparent in the conclusion? Be prepared to explain your answer.

Working on the Assignment

Concluding Your Evaluation

Using a strategy or strategies identified earlier (or a different strategy from an evaluation you have analyzed), write a conclusion for your evaluation. Share your draft with your instructor or some classmates. Ask them to identify the strategy or strategies you have used in your conclusion and to tell you whether the conclusion reinforces or extends the basic value judgment you have been trying to convey in your evaluation.

> For tips for thinking about effective uses of visual elements, see p. 268.

Designing Your Evaluation and Integrating Visual Information

At several points in this chapter you might have begun thinking visually, looking for pictures, designing tables or charts, or using headings and other devices to make your work accessible to readers. If you have not already begun to do so, now is the time to think in more detail about the appearance of your evaluation. Will you have more than one column of text on each page? Will you include pictures? Will you use headings or other visual cues—inset boxes, pull quotes, bulleted lists, and so on—to call readers' attention to some specific point or fact?

As you consider these questions, notice the design of some of the evaluations reprinted in this chapter. Look not only at the visual elements themselves, but also at the way each visual element functions. Review the questions related to reading visual information in evaluations (p. 268). Keep these questions in mind as you consider using the following strategies to present visual information.

How to Design Your Evaluation and Integrate Visual Information

Strategies	Examples
Look for images that will serve a specific function, such as appealing to readers' emotions or providing objective information. Well-chosen images can add to the authority of your text.	*The photo of ice cream accompanying "Cream of the Crop" (p. 273) will entice most readers. On the other hand, the images of ice cream cartons and ingredient labels illustrate information literally and unemotionally.*
Use subtitles, headings, and pull quotes to make your work accessible. Words that draw the readers' eye should give them a clear sense of the point being made or the kind of information they will find in a section of the evaluation.	*The lead-in question "Full-fat ice cream is back in style. Which ones are worth the calories?" in "Cream of the Crop" provides specifics that are lacking in the article's title. Later, the heading "Premium Taste?" indicates that the section will give information about criteria for selecting the best ice cream.*
Include a sidebar (inset box) to give related information too specialized or detailed to interest all readers.	*The box "Inside the Scoop" in "Cream of the Crop" tells everything readers might want to know about ice cream ingredients.*
Include visual information such as a table or bar graph to help readers make comparisons and contrasts for themselves.	*Consumer Reports' ratings table orders the ice creams from the highest rated to the lowest and provides comments about the general taste of each brand. It also includes a bar graph showing the flavor and texture score.*

Working on the Assignment

Designing Your Evaluation and Integrating Visual Information

> Find an example of an evaluation (from an article in a magazine or scholarly journal, a Web site, a brochure, a book, or a pamphlet) that you think does a good job of using visual information. Work with a partner to figure out what visual elements (pictures, graphs, headings, and so on) are used in the evaluation and why each one is appropriate for the intended audience.

> Check with your classmates and your instructor to see what sort of page or screen layout might make sense given your topic and the information in your context analysis. Remember: *don't use visuals just for the sake of making your work look unique.* Make sure that all visual elements in your evaluation are helpful to and appropriate for your intended readers.

STUDENT DIALOGUE: INTEGRATING VISUAL INFORMATION

Writing in a Visual Age: In the first section of your evaluation, you include a photograph of uniformed ROTC students talking with other students. Why did you choose to use that photograph at that point?

Ryan Flori: This photo helps establish a relationship with other students [at my university] by showing something they have seen on campus. Also, it fits in with my own experiences that I describe in the first paragraph of my evaluation.

Finishing Up

As a result of the work you've done thus far, you should now have a clear understanding of the good and bad points of the subject you are evaluating. You should also be ready to write a review draft of your evaluation. After completing this draft, you will need to assess it carefully not only by critiquing it yourself but also by getting others' perspectives. This means that you will subject the review draft to a final review (from one or more of your classmates or from your instructor). Then you will use this assessment to make revisions in content, organization, style, and format.

Creating a Review Draft

In preparation for writing the review draft, look back at the context analysis you did for your evaluation. Has your understanding of any part of that context changed? If so, revise the context analysis and keep your revisions in mind as you decide what to say and how to say it in the review draft. Also, look back at your exploratory draft. Do you need to modify any of the value judgments expressed there? Are there any places where you need to add information that would make your judgments clearer or answer questions the audience is likely to ask?

As you work on your review draft, examine the introductory and concluding paragraphs. Does the introductory material establish the voice you want to create? Does it seem likely to engage the intended audience? Does the conclusion reinforce the basic value judgment you want to convey? Do your introduction and conclusion still seem appropriate for your audience and topic? If not, modify them by using one or more of the strategies identified in this chapter.

In addition, take some pains to make the structure clear. It might help to write an informal outline indicating the main points about how your subject does or does not meet your criteria. You should also use the strategies described on pp. 324–326 to make your work accessible, create clear expectations for your readers, and link paragraphs or larger sections of text.

Getting a Final Review

Once you have revised your review draft to make it as complete and polished as possible, have it reviewed by one or more people who understand the principles (analyzing context, engaging readers, and so on) that you have been working with in this chapter.

> ❯ Give the reviewer a copy of your draft, one he or she can make notes on.
>
> ❯ Give the reviewer a copy of your context analysis. If necessary, revise that analysis before giving it to the reviewer.
>
> ❯ Ask the reviewer to begin his or her response by answering the following question: Given what I say in my context analysis, how likely does it seem that my evaluation will be informative and helpful to the audience I am trying to reach?
>
> ❯ Ask the reviewer to adopt the perspective of the audience described in your context analysis and to use the following checklist in commenting on your work.

Checklist for Final Review

❯ bedfordstmartins.com/ visualage

To download this checklist as a worksheet, click on CHAPTER 5 ❯ WORKSHEETS

1 In my context analysis, please highlight any statements that give you a good sense of the knowledge, values, and needs of my intended audience. (For an example, see p. 306.) Please indicate any statements that need to be clarified.

2 In my context analysis, please highlight any statements that give you a good sense of the circumstances, purposes, and expected format for my evaluation. (For an example of a good context analysis, see p. 306.) Please indicate any statements that need to be clarified.

3 In what specific passages have I developed my topic thoroughly, especially by making sure my criteria are clear and appropriate for my audience? What are some passages in which I give specific details that relate to my criteria and answer readers' questions? What are some passages where I mention different perspectives (positive and negative) on the thing I am evaluating? In which passages could I make my evaluation clearer or more useful to readers? What are some strategies I might use to do this? (See pp. 309–314.)

4 What portions of my introduction seem likely to engage the interest of my intended audience? What are some strategies (explained on pp. 317 and 319) that might make the introduction more engaging?

5 How would you describe the voice I have created? At what points does that voice seem appropriate, given my intended audience and topic? What strategies (explained on p. 321) might help me make the voice clearer or more appropriate?

6 What are some words and phrases that provide a clear structure for my evaluation, making my information accessible, creating clear expectations for readers, and indicating links between paragraphs or larger sections of text? What strategies (explained on pp. 324–326) might I use to make the structure of my evaluation clear?

7 How does the conclusion reinforce or extend the value judgment I am trying to convey in my evaluation? What strategies (explained on p. 327) might I use to make my conclusion more effective?

8 If the evaluation includes photographs or other visual elements, what does this material contribute to the clarity and usefulness of my evaluation? Do I need to add or revise captions for pictures or legends for charts, graphs, or maps? Are there any places in the draft where I need to add visual information? If so, what kind(s) of visuals should I add?

If possible, ask your reviewers to talk with you about your review draft as well as make notes on it. Listen to what your reviewers say but also to the way they say it. Do they sound annoyed? convinced? skeptical? Try to find out as much as you can about why they react as they do. Also watch your reviewers' facial expressions and body language. If they show a reaction, try to find out what they are reacting to and why (for example: "I noticed that you were frowning when you read that second paragraph. Can you tell me about that reaction?").

Since reasonable people often differ in their evaluations of the same subject, it's possible that your reviewers will disagree with one or more points you make. When this happens, your strong impulse will be to argue with the reviewers, showing them where they are wrong or have missed the point. Resist this impulse, at least at first. Instead, try to find out why they disagree with you. Once you have a good idea of their concerns or objections, you might respond to what they have said, asking how clear and reasonable they find your responses.

Revising Your Evaluation

Up to this point, you have been advised to listen to reviewers' comments without explaining, arguing, or making judgments about the validity of those comments. But once you have a good idea of how your reviewers respond, it is time to go back through your notes on those comments. Bearing in mind your intended audience and purpose, decide which comments are most valid. Then use the strategies referred to in the Checklist for Final Review.

After resolving all the issues that need attention, proofread carefully and correct any typographical or formatting errors. Then submit this final draft to your instructor.

> bedfordstmartins.com/
> visualage
>
> *To download these questions as a worksheet, click on*
> **CHAPTER 5 >**
> **WORKSHEETS**

Taking Stock of Where You Are

Once your instructor has returned the final draft of your work, think back over all the comments you received—from classmates as well as your instructor—and write out answers to the following questions. (You might want to keep these in a journal or in a special section of a notebook.)

Questions for Assessing Your Growth as a Writer

- What appears to be my greatest area of strength?
- Where am I having the greatest difficulty?
- What am I learning about the process of writing?
- What am I learning about giving and receiving feedback on writing?
- What have I learned from writing an evaluation that I can use in my next assignment for this course, for another course, or for work?

SAMPLE STUDENT ASSESSMENT

Here's how Ryan Flori answered these questions for his evaluation, "Where Is Your Future Going? Is ROTC for You?" (p. 294).

What appears to be my greatest area of strength?

My greatest area of strength for this evaluation was my personal experience. Having been through the exact program I was writing about ensured that the information I provided was clear in my mind and truthful.

Where am I having the greatest difficulty?

My greatest difficulty was to present my points in a concise manner so as to include examples and explanations without rambling on with information not needed to get my point across.

What am I learning about the process of writing?

I am learning that a paper is never actually done. It is like a living thing, forever being molded; it can always be made better the more it is worked on. Also, I'm learning that the more feedback I can get from reviewers, the better the paper will ultimately get.

What am I learning about giving and receiving feedback on writing?

Again, I've learned that the more people I get to read and give feedback, the better the paper will become in the long run. Everyone has different ideas; it is up to the writer to choose which ideas he likes, which ideas work well together, which ones to incorporate into the paper—and then work from there.

What have I learned from writing an evaluation that I can use in my next assignment for this course, for another course, or for work?

I have learned that a paper can never be proofread enough times and that it is imperative to always keep the main idea in mind when writing about details. It is far too easy to get sidetracked on an issue that may seem important when in reality it may not even contribute to the main objectives of the paper. No matter how great a tangent may seem, if it doesn't coincide with the goals of the paper, it isn't needed and is only clutter.

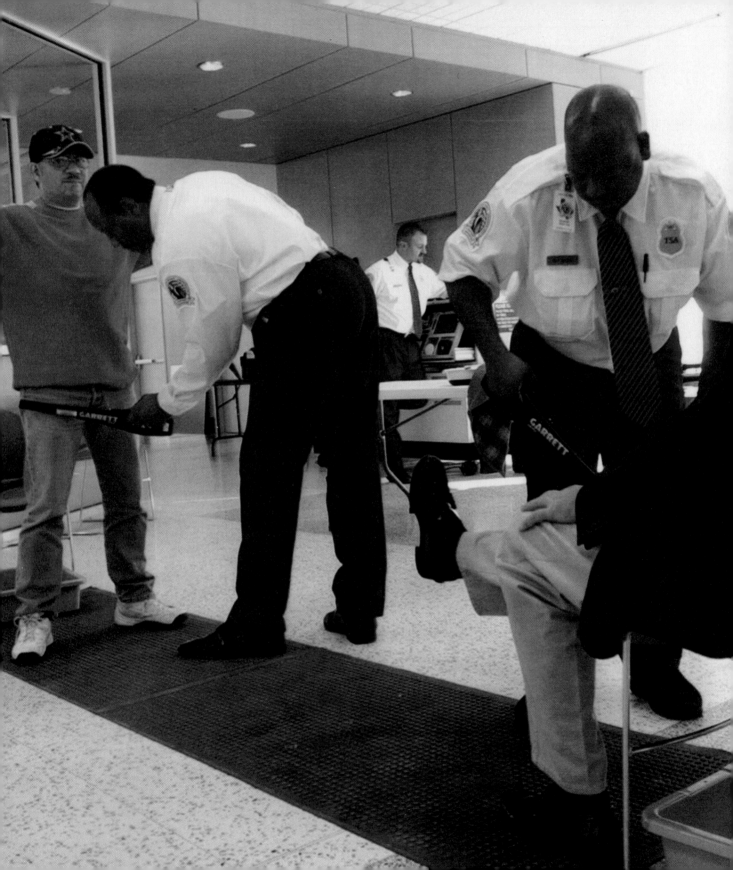

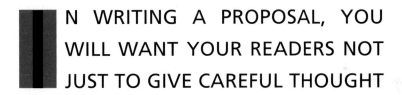

6

Proposals

IN WRITING A PROPOSAL, YOU WILL WANT YOUR READERS NOT JUST TO GIVE CAREFUL THOUGHT

to what you have to say, but also to make some change, to implement your ideas. More than with any of the other types of writing covered in this book, you will be writing in order to make an observable difference in the world around you. One of the best ways to do this is to identify a problem that an organization or group is having and come up with a practical, attractive solution.

When people think about solving problems—at school, at work, or in society—it is easy to go to extremes, ranging from a wild optimism, in which it seems possible to change anything, to an extreme pessimism, in which any efforts to make change seem hopeless and futile. Both extremes are right, and both extremes are wrong. Occasionally, there really are simple solutions to problems, and all you have to do to bring about change is to point out an answer that seems obvious to you. There are also problems so complicated that they are insoluble—especially during the relatively short time you will have to work on your assignment for this chapter. Yet things do get done, changes are made, and students manage to have some influence on what goes on around them.

Before you decide whether or not a particular problem might be solved, remember that even long-standing situations can be changed if your proposal convinces enough people to act. Some changes can be quite dramatic. For example, you may know that many colleges and universities in the United States held investments in South Africa during the era of apartheid, a time when South African policy gave white citizens rights and privileges that black South Africans did not have. Students at major American universities proposed that their schools put some economic muscle behind official U.S. opposition to apartheid. The students argued that by investing in South Africa, the schools were unintentionally helping to pay for the continuation of discrimination; their view was that economic pressure from the United States might help solve the problem. Eventually, colleges and universities withdrew millions of dollars from South Africa. The economic effects of this withdrawal are often credited with helping to end apartheid, which was abolished in 1993.

On the other hand, not every proposal has to save lives or influence global human rights. Effective proposals may result in minor improvements that still satisfy the people affected by them. Assume, for example, that a student group at a local community college proposes to collect donations of blankets and canned food to help impoverished victims of a hurricane in the Caribbean or residents of a local shelter. These efforts don't influence national policy, but they can make substantial changes in some people's lives.

Proposals aren't just for situations that might make the nightly news, of course. In fact, much of the world's work happens because people make and carry out proposals for change. In some companies, for example, a substantial part of employees' work might be to come up with new projects they (and perhaps the company) ought to undertake. No one expects that every proposal will be accepted. In fact, at least one major corporation expects that some percentage of any employee's proposals will not succeed. Managers at this corporation assume that if all of an employee's proposals succeed, the employee is not being ambitious or daring enough. Success with seven of ten ideas is considered a very good track record. This view removes a little pressure, but not too much. Compare this expected level of performance with baseball, where players are considered excellent hitters if they get a hit in only three of ten turns at bat. In the work you do for this chapter, you will not be expected to bat a thousand. But you should come up with a proposal that your intended audience will seriously consider adopting or implementing.

Bringing About Change

This chapter builds on many of the concepts and skills introduced in earlier chapters on reporting, taking a position, and evaluating. For example, your proposal has to show a thorough understanding of pertinent facts and provide good reasons for the claims you make. But when you propose a solution to a problem, you also may be asking the members of your audience to change something (the way they do their job, for example), and change is not always easy or pleasant. Consequently, you should be prepared to address a variety of questions from your audience—questions ranging from the hostile or defensive to the purely practical. These questions, whether stated implicitly or explicitly, will likely include some or all of the following.

> What makes you think a problem exists? Things seem all right the way they are.

> Don't we already have a good solution to this problem?

> How do you propose to solve it? (What exactly needs to be done, and how do we go about doing it?)

> Is your proposal feasible? Do we have or can we acquire the resources to implement your ideas?

> Is there any precedent for what you are proposing? Has your solution been successfully implemented in other situations?

> What are the alternatives? What makes your proposal better than the other options?

> In what ways is your proposed solution attractive or desirable? For example, if we do adopt your solution, how will it benefit us? Will it be consistent with what we need or care about?

Of course, you probably won't have to deal with all the questions above in solving a single problem. But no matter what situation you find yourself in, you should think through all the questions and determine whether your audience is likely to ask them so that you can be prepared to answer them if you need to. Furthermore, you should be prepared to deal with the particular obstacles in the way of solving the specific problem your proposal will address. In some cases, for example, people who are affected by the problem may be ignoring it either because they cannot solve it or because doing nothing benefits them in some way. Or perhaps they may genuinely never have considered the possibility that things could be any different. In such cases, you will need to demonstrate first and foremost that the problem exists and that ignoring it is a bad idea. You will improve the chances of bringing about change if you also show that you have a practical solution ready to implement.

In other cases, the audience may have tried to solve the problem and given up after one or more failed attempts. If this has happened, your primary job may be to discover why previous solutions failed and to explain how your proposal will succeed. Perhaps the audience was trying to implement a solution that did not address the real causes of the situation. If this is the case, you should demonstrate that you have a good understanding of what's causing the problem. Or perhaps the solution had different consequences than the audience expected—or no real consequences at all. In such cases, you should be prepared to show that you have thought through the effects of your proposal and that it will do what you say it will. Finally, perhaps the obstacle for your proposal is that it must compete with one or more other solutions to the problem. In this case, your goal is clear: you must explain the limitations of current efforts at solving the problem, identify your solution, and prove to your audience that your proposal is the best way to meet their needs.

Proposals in Context

An understanding of context—of audience, circumstances, and purposes—is important in all writing. But with proposals, your understanding of context is crucial. You may come up with a proposal that is imaginative and potentially workable. But for that proposal to be accepted and implemented, your readers will have to see that it makes sense, given the circumstances in which they find themselves. Therefore, you will have to work especially hard to put yourself in your readers' place, trying to understand their values and needs and their perceptions of their circumstances.

Audience

Understanding your audience is almost always challenging, especially when that audience differs greatly from you in what they know, value, and need. But the audience for your proposal may be especially difficult to assess. Members of that audience are likely to have a great deal of power: they can allow (or even help) you to do what you want, or they can stop you in your tracks, either by rejecting your proposal outright or by subtly undermining its implementation. In addition, they may be threatened by the changes you propose, since change often forces people to act in new ways they may find uncomfortable or undesirable. Finally, your audience may be more complex than you initially anticipated, since it may include *stakeholders* who may or may not be part of your primary audience but who will be affected by your proposal and thus have a stake in its outcome. For your proposal to have a chance of being accepted and actually being implemented, you must have a thorough understanding of the audience(s) you hope to reach: who they are; what they know, need, and care about; and the circumstances in which they will encounter your proposal.

Circumstances

Since your proposal will attempt to solve a problem, you need to find out whether members of your audience are aware of the problem and whether they have seen other efforts to solve it. Are they feeling any special pressures (from a particular interest group, for example) to solve (or ignore) the problem? Will your proposal be one of several competing proposals from which your audience will select a winner? Also consider whether you will make your proposal orally or in writing. Will your audience expect you to include images or other visual elements? When will your audience encounter your proposal? in the course of a heated debate about possible solutions? after reading a series of relevant news stories or editorials?

Purposes

Your main purpose is to get your audience to adopt your proposal, to implement the changes you want. But to accomplish this, you will also have to accomplish several related goals. First, you will have to demonstrate to your audience that you are aware of the circumstances in which they encounter your proposal. If, for example, the readers are aware of several failed attempts to solve the problem, you need to show them you are also aware of these efforts and that your proposal has qualities other proposals did not have. If they are feeling pressure to avoid making changes, you need to do what you can in your proposal to alleviate the pressure or to provide your readers with the means to resist it. Further, you will probably have to gain the goodwill of your audience. You will likely need to get the members of your audience to like you or at least trust that you have their best interests in mind. You will have to demonstrate to your audience that you are well informed, thoughtful, and competent. If you don't accomplish these related goals, you will have virtually no chance of accomplishing your main goal, solving a problem that you feel needs to be solved.

> ❯ For more advice on demonstrating thoughtfulness, see the discussion of ethical appeals, p. 398.

For Collaboration

Choose one of the proposals in Reading to Write, beginning on p. 344 of this chapter. Working with one or more classmates, list the questions this proposal answers, as well as the questions it does not answer. Does the proposal answer any questions not found in the list on p. 337? In light of these questions and answers, decide what assumptions the proposal makes about what the intended readers know, need, or care about.

Visual Information in Context

In most contexts, proposals use relatively few visual elements. Nevertheless, it is possible for proposals to incorporate most of the visual elements you've seen elsewhere in this book: headings, white space, graphs, sidebars (inset boxes), and variations in type size and style, for example. In some specialized contexts, such as funding or patent proposals made to government agencies, it is not uncommon to make use of photographs and line drawings.

Both when you are reading proposals and when you are writing them, you should ask yourself several questions about the use—or absence—of visual elements and effective design.

❯ For more information on the effective uses of these visual elements, see **Chapter 8.**

Questions to Ask When Reading Visual Information in Proposals

● **Does the layout (arrangement) of the page or screen make it easy for the intended readers to find the information they want or need?**

> ❯ Do visual elements (columns, headings, white space, bulleted lists, and so forth) make the information in the proposal accessible to readers?

> ❯ Are there headings? If so, do they give a clear idea of the information that will appear in the text that follows?

> ❯ Are there sidebars (inset boxes of text) or pull quotes (highlighted quotations from the text)? If so, what purposes do they serve (such as making appeals to readers' emotions)?

> ❯ Are there variations in the size and style of type? What functions do these variations serve?

> ❯ How many columns are there? Does the width of each column make the text easy to read? What sorts of texts or publications regularly use this column style?

> ❯ Do these elements of the layout give the pages or screens an overall look that is consistent with the voice created in the written text and with the expectations of the intended audience?

● **If there are images (photographs, diagrams, or other drawings), what kinds of appeals do they make? To what extent do those appeals make sense, given the context in which the proposal will be read?**

❯ For further discussion of logical, emotional, and ethical appeals, see pp. 395–398.

> ❯ Do the images appeal to readers' emotions? What feelings do the images evoke?

> Do the images appeal to readers' desire for or interest in factual information? Are they arranged and given space in a logical way?

> Do the images try to demonstrate that the author is a person of good character and, therefore, credible? What authorities or symbols do the images use to demonstrate credibility?

> What kinds of details are included in the images? Are there any significant details missing?

> What viewing angle is represented? What is in the center, at the top, and at the bottom of the image? What is in the foreground? in the background? What effects do these placements have on the image?

> What colors are used? Is there anything surprising or distinctive about them?

> Are the images clearly explained in captions or the accompanying text? Is the relationship between images and text clear? Do the words and images work together to make a claim?

● **If there are charts, graphs, maps, or tables, how informative and relevant are they?**

> Can the reader easily see the point of a given chart, graph, map, or table? Is it clearly related to the text? Does it help the reader compare and contrast different data?

> Can the reader easily find the most important information?

> Does any chart, graph, map, or table contain distracting colors or special effects?

> Is each chart, graph, map, and table clearly labeled and explained with a title, legend, or key?

> Are the units of measurement clear and consistent? If symbols are used, is their meaning clear?

 Exercise

Bring to class a proposal that presents information in a visual and interesting way. Try browsing newspaper op-ed pages or magazines and Web sites concerned with politics, causes, or issues for an effective proposal. The proposal might contain images, graphs, or tables. Or it might make special use of text, by setting it off in columns, with color, as pull quotes, or boxed in sidebars, for example. Consider the effects these visual elements create by answering the questions listed above. Then try to determine how these effects are created. Be prepared to explain how the visual elements create a particular effect and how they add to the impressions conveyed through the proposal's written text.

● **Layout** Single column and heading give appearance of community newsletter.

FIGURE 6.1
Visual Elements in "From America's Front Line against Crime," a Proposal from the Web

● **Image** Viewing angle puts reader on equal footing with police officer.

● **Image** Soft blue color suggests tranquility; pose and lack of detail make officer appear friendly and nonthreatening.

● **Layout** Bold type highlights important facts.

● **Layout** Large, bold type emphasizes subheading and numbered recommendations.

● **Graph** Title indicates purpose of graph.

● **Graph** Clearly labeled spike in graph gives important information quickly.

● **Graph** Footnote provides specific information about crimes; caption gives source of data.

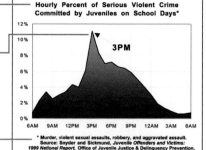

FIGHT CRIME: INVEST IN KIDS

President
Sanford A. Newman

Vice Presidents
Amy R. Dawson
David Kass
Jeff Kirsch

From America's Front Line Against Crime: A School and Youth Violence Prevention Plan

AS AN ORGANIZATION OF MORE THAN 2,000 POLICE CHIEFS, SHERIFFS, PROSECUTORS, CRIME SURVIVORS AND LEADERS OF POLICE OFFICER ORGANIZATONS, we are determined to see that dangerous criminals are put behind bars. But anyone who thinks that jailing a criminal undoes the agony crime leaves in its wake hasn't seen crime up close.

America's anti-crime arsenal contains no weapons more powerful than the proven programs that help kids get the right start in life—programs like early care and education for preschool-age children, youth development programs for the after-school and summer hours, child abuse prevention, and intervention programs proven to help get troubled kids back on track.

Yet today, inadequate funding for Head Start, and other early care and education programs, after-school youth development programs and counseling for troubled kids leaves millions of children at needless risk of becoming violent or delinquent teens and adult criminals—and leaves every American at needless risk of becoming a crime victim.

We call on all public officials to adopt a four-part plan to dramatically reduce crime and violence, and help young people learn the skills and values they need to become good neighbors and responsible adults. While no plan can prevent every violent act, this common-sense plan—based on our experience and the latest research about what really works to fight crime—can make all of us safer.

Four Steps to Dramatically Reduce School and Youth Violence

1. Assure all school-age children and teens access to after-school, weekend and summer youth development programs to shut down the "Prime Time for Juvenile Crime."

In the hour after the school bell rings turning millions of children and teens out on the street with neither constructive activities nor adult supervision, violent juvenile crime soars and prime time for juvenile crime begins. On school days, **the peak hours for such crime are from 3:00 PM to 6:00 PM.** These are also the hours when kids are most likely to become victims of crime. Being unsupervised after school doubles the risk that 8th-graders will smoke, drink alcohol or use drugs.

Quality youth development programs can cut crime immediately and transform this Prime Time for Juvenile Crime into hours of academic enrichment, wholesome fun and community service. They protect both kids and adults from becoming victims of crime, and cut teen pregnancy, smoking, and drug use, while they help youngsters develop the values and skills they need to become contributing citizens. For example:

Hourly Percent of Serious Violent Crime Committed by Juveniles on School Days*

3PM

6AM 9AM 12PM 3PM 6PM 9PM 12AM 3AM 6AM

* Murder, violent sexual assaults, robbery, and aggravated assault. Source: Snyder and Sickmund, *Juvenile Offenders and Victims: 1999 National Report*, Office of Juvenile Justice & Delinquency Prevention.

Fion 1/11/2003

2000 P Street, NW • Suite 240 • Washington, DC 20036 • (202) 776-0027 • Fax (202) 776-0110 • www.fightcrime.org

• Five housing projects without Boys & Girls Clubs

● **Layout** Bullet and extra white space set off supporting study.

Sample Analysis | From America's Front Line against Crime

Later in this chapter, the proposal "From America's Front Line against Crime: A School and Youth Violence Prevention Program" presents some actions the United States might take to reduce crime and violence among young people. This proposal appeared as a downloadable document, published on the Web site of the advocacy organization Fight Crime: Invest in Kids. As is apparent in Figure 6.1 and in the rest of the article, which appears on p. 353, this proposal uses a wide range of visual elements.

The layout of this page makes it easy for readers to see key pieces of information and, at the same time, helps create an ethical appeal. Headings and subheadings appear in large bold type set off from the rest of the text with white space so that readers will quickly understand the point of the article as a whole and of each section within it. Recommendations ("1. Assure all school-age children and teens access . . . ") are numbered and set in large bold type so readers can immediately see the "Four Steps" recommended. Similarly, important facts ("the peak hours for such crime are from 3:00 PM to 6:00 PM") are highlighted with bold type. Studies that support the proposal's recommendations are briefly summarized and set off by bullets and extra lines of white space just before and after each summary. Readers can see at a glance the main points made in the proposal, and they can readily find examples that support those points.

(Look at the second page of this newsletter, found on p. 354, to see how layout can be used to make an emotional appeal, in the form of pull quotes from two law enforcement officials. These quotes are set off from the rest of the text by their appearance—both are in large bold italic type—and by lines that physically separate them from the text of the body of the newsletter.)

An ethical appeal comes from two visual elements on this page, both of which seem intended to suggest that the organization and its recommendations are trustworthy. The use of a single, page-wide column helps give this proposal the familiar look of

a newsletter one might receive from any community organization, especially an organization trying to promote some admirable cause on a relatively limited budget. This is not the work of some slick, high-powered public relations firm. It's put out by an organization working under some of the financial constraints most of its readers will recognize and appreciate. The very look of this page, then, helps build some common ground with readers, saying, in effect, "We're a lot like you, so trust us."

A further ethical appeal—and an emotional appeal as well—comes from the image in the upper left-hand corner of the page. The viewing angle in this picture (that is, the position from which the viewer is looking at the image) puts the reader on an equal footing with the officer and children shown in the picture. The angle here adds to the friendly feel of this image. Both literally and figuratively, the reader is not looking down at the figures in this picture. Nor is the reader looking up at the officer, a viewing angle that might make him seem powerful or threatening.

A potential sense of threat is further minimized by the details that are missing from this picture. The large figure can be identified as a police officer solely by what appears to be a police cap and a blue dot that might be a badge. Invisible in this image are details—a gun belt, a baton, handcuffs—that might be construed as menacing. Instead, the police officer is made to appear kind and helpful, holding hands with a small child, his face turned slightly as though talking with the child. In the background are trees and the roofline of the sort of house one might find in any middle-class neighborhood. All this is set in a soft blue color that suggests feelings of tranquility rather than emotions (anger, fear, uncertainty) people are likely to associate with the proposal's topic—juvenile crime and violence. For some audiences, this image might seem unrealistic, serving therefore to undermine claims made in the written text. But if the authors—who represent "more than 2,000 police chiefs, sheriffs, prosecutors and victims of violence"—want police officers to be seen as public servants and if the audience values the apparent safety of conventional middle-class neighborhoods, this image seems likely to contribute to the intended effect of the proposal.

By contrast with other visual elements on this page of the proposal, the graph in the lower left-hand corner makes a clear, effective logical appeal. At what time on school days are young people most likely to commit crimes? The clearly labeled spike in the graph makes the answer obvious. The title of the graph leaves no doubt as to what it indicates, the footnote marked with an asterisk identifies the specific crimes referred to in the title, and the caption indicates the source of the data represented in the graph. Everything about this graph provides factual detail to show that the problem addressed in the proposal is very serious indeed.

Exercise

> **bedfordstmartins.com/visualage**
> *Click on CHAPTER 6 › VISUALS*

For practice analyzing the visual information in another sample proposal, see the visual exercises on the companion Web site for this book.

Reading to Write

In your principal assignment for this chapter, you will identify a problem that affects a specific audience and then write a proposal that offers a detailed, practical solution. Your instructor may advise you to present your proposal in writing, orally, or both.

> **bedfordstmartins.com/ visualage**

For additional examples of proposals, click on
CHAPTER 6 › PROPOSALS

The following proposals will help you see not only some of the strategies you might use, but also the different kinds of topics about which you might write. Each reading is followed by questions (Reflecting on What You Have Read) that will help you start thinking about what is involved in making a credible, effective proposal; also, a Thinking Ahead prompt will suggest ways to decide on a topic for your own proposal. The subsequent sections of the chapter will focus on starting your assignment, composing a draft, and assessing and revising that draft.

For a lot of students, the process of applying to college is no simple matter, especially if they apply to several schools. In the following proposal, high school senior Nathan Burstein examines this problem and offers a way to solve it. As you read his proposal, bear in mind that it appeared on the op-ed page of the *New York Times*, a page usually reserved for the opinions of nationally known journalists and leaders in politics, government, academia, and business.

Applying to College, Made Easy

NATHAN BURSTEIN

Each day, with the arrival of yet more mail from colleges around the country, I get a clearer picture of what the next few months hold for me: late nights spent battling both my parents' moody old typewriter and a pile of applications that now threatens to topple over on innocent civilians standing below.

It wasn't always like this. Applying to college used to be fairly simple, with most university-bound students aiming for just a few in-state schools. However, as a greater percentage of 18-year-olds head off to college each year, the admissions process has grown increasingly competitive. No longer is it wise to apply to just one or two schools. Many students now apply to a minimum of four or five colleges to insure acceptance at one.

1   My complaint isn't with the increased competitiveness. What bothers me are the number of forms we must fill out. Why hasn't the college application been standardized?

2   Some will point out that the National Association of Secondary School Principals has created a "common application" form, and nearly 200 colleges accept it and evaluate it as equal to their own. The problem is that this application isn't common enough. Fewer than 20 national universities ranked in the top 50 in this year's *U.S. News & World Report* survey accept it, and almost no public universities accept it.

5   Colleges, instead of spending time and money to create their own forms and mail them out to students, could pool their funds to create one universal application that students could pick up at 3 their schools. Teachers and guidance counselors, who often must write individual recommendations for each school to which a student applies, could conserve their energy and write one excel-4 lent recommendation for each student.

6   Saving time, effort and money—if these aren't reasons enough to ease the load on us high school seniors, then colleges should do it for the sake of our collective sanity!

Reflecting on What You Have Read

1 In paragraph 1, Burstein argues that the process of applying to college is a problem for high school students. To what extent does this paragraph persuade you that this is a significant problem that needs to be solved?

2 What stakeholders does Burstein identify in his proposal? How successful is he in showing that his proposal will benefit them?

3 Suppose that this proposal had been published in the letters-to-the-editor column rather than on the op-ed page. In what ways might that influence your response to it?

4 How well informed does Burstein sound? What does he say that makes him seem well—or poorly—informed?

5 How do you think this proposal would be received by administrators at your school?

Thinking Ahead

This proposal identifies a problem faced by many young people applying to college. Think of other problems you and your friends face, especially problems associated with misguided policies or procedures. What could be done to change this policy or procedure? What audience might be in a position to implement the changes?

Several days after Nathan Burstein's proposal "Applying to College Made Easy" appeared on the op-ed page of the *New York Times*, it received a response in the letters-to-the-editor section of the editorial page. Like most letters to the editor, this one has probably been edited to make it as brief as possible. Although the letter is not nearly as long as Burstein's op-ed piece, the writer's credentials are impressive. The author, Paul Oyer, was a faculty fellow at the Institute for Policy Research at Northwestern University at the time his letter was published and subsequently became a professor at Stanford University.

Barriers to College

PAUL OYER

To the Editor:

Many of us can sympathize with Nathan Burstein's frustration at filling out individual forms for different colleges (Op-Ed, Sept. 21). However, the current system may be quite efficient, since the key to college applications is not just minimizing people's effort but finding the right match.

If the process were made too easy with a standardized college application form, admissions offices would be flooded with applicants who know little about each school.

Requiring some amount of school-specific effort makes it likely that prospective students have invested the time to determine a reasonable interest in a given school. Also, since this cost is in time, it does not put students from less wealthy backgrounds at as much of a relative disadvantage.

Evanston, Ill., Sept. 21, 1999

Reflecting on What You Have Read

1   As a rule, editors do not publish every letter to the editor they receive. They often choose two or three that represent the basic sentiments of all the letters they receive on a given topic. In light of this policy, would you argue that Burstein's proposal is a success? Just how would you define *success* in this case?

2   How does Oyer's letter affect your reaction to Burstein's proposal in "Applying to College, Made Easy"?

Thinking Ahead

Read the letters-to-the-editor page of a local newspaper—or perhaps a nationally distributed paper such as the *New York Times*. What issues are raised by these letters? Do any of these letters suggest a topic you might write about?

The events of September 11, 2001, made it clear that security measures then in place at U.S. airports were not adequate to protect airline travelers. In an effort to help remedy this situation, Robert W. Poole Jr. and Viggo Butler published the following proposal about two weeks later, on September 21. Poole is the director of transportation studies at the Reason Public Policy Institute, a libertarian think tank whose members tend to believe that private enterprise is better suited to solve social problems than is the federal government. Butler is the retired CEO of Lockheed Air Terminal and the former chair of a security subcommittee at the Federal Aviation Administration (FAA). As you read, notice what the authors say was the primary cause of poor airport security. Also consider whether their credentials influence your willingness to accept their argument.

Address [▼] Go

FIXING AIRPORT SECURITY

21st-Century Strategies for 21st-Century Threats

Robert W. Poole Jr. and Viggo Butler

The recent terrorist attacks on the Pentagon and the World Trade Center have 1
forced us to rethink the issue of airport security. It's become quite clear that the present system is not adequate to the task. In the past few years, both the General Accounting Office (GAO) and the Department of Transportation (DOT) Inspector General have issued scathing reports on airport security. One FAA official told *USA Today* that Boston and Newark "leak like a sieve." In 1999, federal agents were able to sneak through security doors 46 times at four major airports and walk around on the tarmac or board planes unchallenged.

Thus, while all parts of the system need improving, the biggest hole in the system concerns access to 2 "secure" areas behind the scenes, not the flow of passengers through metal detectors at screening points. The new passenger-focused regulations like those announced within days of the bombings (banning remote bag check-in, keeping cars away from terminals, restricting the use of e-tickets) will do little more than add to already long delays at airports; they would have done nothing to stop the terrorists.

Instead of imposing such new burdens on passengers, a better approach is to make use of improved 3 technology, such as the following:

• More sophisticated luggage-screening devices, used on every single bag;
• New people-scanners that can detect even ceramic knives under people's clothes;
• Biometric systems for access control to secure areas at airports, to ensure that only those individuals authorized to go there can actually do so.

Internet

Address ▼ ➔ Go

These kinds of devices would be far more useful than today's inane security questions and more requirements for passengers that will mean waiting in even longer lines.

But the most fundamental problem with airport security is its fragmentation. Security today is the joint responsibility of the FAA, airport operators, and airlines. The airlines handle the security-screening checkpoints for passengers, hiring contractors that often pay minimum wage for what are inherently boring and repetitive jobs. Turnover in those positions is typically well above 100% per year. Additionally, control of access to secure areas is shot through with loopholes. Everybody is responsible for airport security—which means nobody is really in charge. 4

In response to these problems, some have called for creating a federal security service to take over several or all of these functions. But merely changing the uniforms will not change either the nature of the work or the incentives to cut corners in the name of everyday convenience. (In fact, most federal security is also provided by relatively low-wage contract personnel.) What's needed is a single point of responsibility at each airport, held accountable for every aspect of security. That responsible and accountable party should be the airport owner/operator. 5

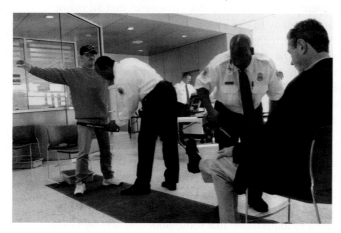

We already can see how much better this model works, because it's already done this way in Europe. London's airports, especially Heathrow, have long been extremely sensitive to the terrorist threat. Yet security there is first-rate. Airport owner/operator BAA employs all the passenger screening people itself, and pays them decent wages. Turnover, not surprisingly, is but a fraction of what is typical of U.S. airports. Some of these employees eventually move up to other positions within the company. At the London airports, every single bag is X-rayed (which has never been done for domestic flights in this country), and there is positive matching of bags with passengers (again, unheard of in this country). 6

London typifies a large-scale trend in Europe toward a more professional model of airport management. In Europe today, an airport is seen as a business: an enterprise run by qualified (and highly paid) professionals, serving a number of different customers, and expected to make a profit (and pay taxes!) by doing so. A growing number of these airports have been shifted into private ownership over the past decade. Since Margaret Thatcher converted the former British Airports Authority into the publicly traded BAA in 1987, a total of 17 U.K. airports have shifted into the private sector. 7

On the continent, privatized airports include Athens, Copenhagen, Dusseldorf, Frankfurt, Hamburg, Naples, Rome, Turin, Vienna, and Zurich, with Amsterdam and Berlin soon to follow. In each case, the corporate model has led to more professional management and increased resources for meeting numerous customer needs—including security.

By contrast, the United States is still stuck with the old model: the airport as a no-frills place to get   8
people on and off planes, at the lowest possible cost. Run by civil servants, it is not expected to take (entrepreneurial) risks, or to take major responsibilities, or seek profits—but simply to do what is expected of it by the airlines and the FAA. Although there are dedicated professionals running some U.S. airports, all too often we have positions filled by political appointees like the former governor of Massachusetts' driver (who is the current chief of airport security at Boston's Logan Airport, where two of the doomed flights originated).

Thus, one way to improve U.S. airport security is to shift from the nonprofit, bureaucratic, civil-   9
servant model of airport management to the emerging global corporate model. An airport becomes a major business enterprise, run by world-class professionals who take on the full responsibilities of ownership, including a serious pro-active commitment to security. This does not mean that all major airports would be sold or leased to private companies. Many of the European airports now being privatized (e.g., Amsterdam and Frankfurt) have been run for years as government corporations, with one or more units of government as their shareholders. The important thing is that they were run as real businesses: controlling their assets, taking entrepreneurial risks, making profits, and paying taxes. It would not be that difficult to "corporatize" U.S. airports, and then allow their state or municipal shareholders, over time, to decide whether or not to sell shares to the public or to sell a significant stake to one of the global airport companies.

Until that kind of institutional change comes about, we can still take immediate measures to provide   10
much stronger incentives for security accountability. Instead of trying to micromanage security procedures from Washington, the FAA should set forth stringent *outcome-based* requirements, and make each airport operator solely responsible for compliance. (That would relieve the airlines from the unwanted duty of running passenger screening and farming it out to the lowest bidder.) The FAA should carry out far more frequent security tests, on a random basis, like those done recently by GAO and the Inspector General's Office. Airports that flunk should face hugely increased financial penalties, and even the threat of shut-down. If the FAA can yank the operating certificate of an airline that doesn't measure up on safety compliance, why not hold airports accountable in the same way?

Airports now run by political appointees who are not really qualified to cope with such levels of   11
responsibility would have newly powerful incentives to make changes. They could either hire managers and staff with much greater qualifications or they could hire one of the global airport firms to manage the airport for them. Either way, responsibility and accountability for airport security would be where it belongs: with those who own and operate the airport.

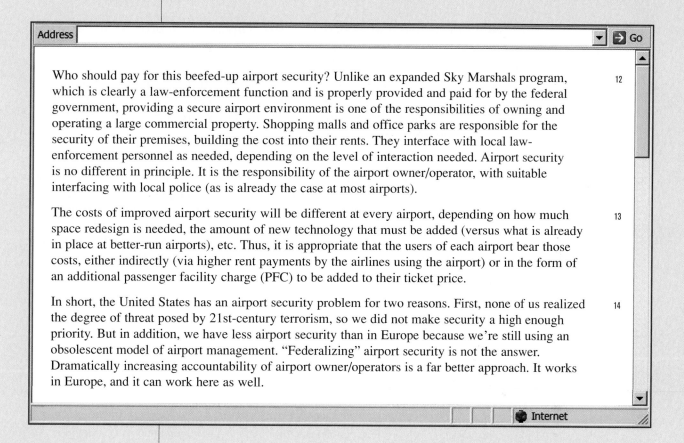

Address [ ] ▼ → Go

Who should pay for this beefed-up airport security? Unlike an expanded Sky Marshals program, which is clearly a law-enforcement function and is properly provided and paid for by the federal government, providing a secure airport environment is one of the responsibilities of owning and operating a large commercial property. Shopping malls and office parks are responsible for the security of their premises, building the cost into their rents. They interface with local law-enforcement personnel as needed, depending on the level of interaction needed. Airport security is no different in principle. It is the responsibility of the airport owner/operator, with suitable interfacing with local police (as is already the case at most airports). 12

The costs of improved airport security will be different at every airport, depending on how much space redesign is needed, the amount of new technology that must be added (versus what is already in place at better-run airports), etc. Thus, it is appropriate that the users of each airport bear those costs, either indirectly (via higher rent payments by the airlines using the airport) or in the form of an additional passenger facility charge (PFC) to be added to their ticket price. 13

In short, the United States has an airport security problem for two reasons. First, none of us realized the degree of threat posed by 21st-century terrorism, so we did not make security a high enough priority. But in addition, we have less airport security than in Europe because we're still using an obsolescent model of airport management. "Federalizing" airport security is not the answer. Dramatically increasing accountability of airport owner/operators is a far better approach. It works in Europe, and it can work here as well. 14

🌐 Internet

Reflecting on What You Have Read

● 1 What do Poole and Butler claim is the fundamental cause of inadequate airport security in the United States? Do you agree with their claim? Why or why not?

● 2 Poole and Butler propose that the "owner/operator" of each airport should be "held accountable for every aspect of [airport] security," noting that this system is used successfully at London's Heathrow Airport. Do you find this supporting example persuasive? Why or why not?

3 The writers also propose that every airport should become "a major business enterprise, run by world-class professionals" (paragraph 9). What do you see as the strengths and limitations of this proposal?

4 What reasons do Poole and Butler give for their objection to "'federalizing' airport security"? How valid do their reasons seem? To what extent do the authors' credentials add to or detract from the credibility of their proposal?

Thinking Ahead

Security is an issue in many aspects of contemporary life—in many neighborhoods, for example, and in school buildings or college dormitories. Identify a place where inadequate security affects you or people you care about. Consider what is currently being done there to address the security problem and why that effort is inadequate. Then propose a plan that will eliminate the cause(s) of inadequate security and thereby increase safety.

What can be done to reduce crime in the United States? Should we hire more police officers? build more prisons? increase the length of prison sentences? Arguably, any or all of these actions may be necessary. But the following proposal takes a different approach, arguing that "America's anti-crime arsenal contains no weapons more powerful than the proven programs that help kids get the right start in life." It appears as a downloadable document on the Web site of Fight Crime: Invest in Kids (www.fightcrime.org), a nonprofit organization whose membership includes both law enforcement officials and victims of violence and whose mission is to prevent children from becoming criminals. Acknowledging that "no plan can reduce every violent act," this proposal claims that adequate funding of key programs can reduce violence among young people and thereby "make all of us safer." As you read, notice the kinds of evidence the proposal cites in support of its claims.

FIGHT CRIME: INVEST IN KIDS

President
Sanford A. Newman

Vice Presidents
Amy R. Dawson
David Kass
Jeff Kirsch

From America's Front Line Against Crime:
A School and Youth Violence Prevention Plan

AS AN ORGANIZATION OF MORE THAN 2,000 POLICE CHIEFS, SHERIFFS, PROSECUTORS, CRIME SURVIVORS AND LEADERS OF POLICE OFFICER ORGANIZATONS, we are determined to see that dangerous criminals are put behind bars. But anyone who thinks that jailing a criminal undoes the agony crime leaves in its wake hasn't seen crime up close.

America's anti-crime arsenal contains no weapons more powerful than the proven programs that help kids get the right start in life—programs like early care and education for preschool-age children, youth development programs for the after-school and summer hours, child abuse prevention, and intervention programs proven to help get troubled kids back on track.

Yet today, inadequate funding for Head Start, and other early care and education programs, after-school youth development programs and counseling for troubled kids leaves millions of children at needless risk of becoming violent or delinquent teens and adult criminals—and leaves every American at needless risk of becoming a crime victim.

We call on all public officials to adopt a four-part plan to dramatically reduce crime and violence, and help young people learn the skills and values they need to become good neighbors and responsible adults. While no plan can prevent every violent act, this common-sense plan—based on our experience and the latest research about what really works to fight crime—can make all of us safer.

Four Steps to Dramatically Reduce School and Youth Violence

1. Assure all school-age children and teens access to after-school, weekend and summer youth development programs to shut down the "Prime Time for Juvenile Crime."

In the hour after the school bell rings turning millions of children and teens out on the street with neither constructive activities nor adult supervision, violent juvenile crime soars and prime time for juvenile crime begins. On school days, **the peak hours for such crime are from 3:00 PM to 6:00 PM.** These are also the hours when kids are most likely to become victims of crime. Being unsupervised after school doubles the risk that 8th-graders will smoke, drink alcohol or use drugs.

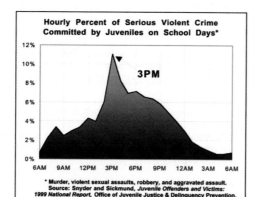

Hourly Percent of Serious Violent Crime Committed by Juveniles on School Days*

3PM

* Murder, violent sexual assaults, robbery, and aggravated assault.
Source: Snyder and Sickmund, *Juvenile Offenders and Victims:*
1999 National Report, Office of Juvenile Justice & Delinquency Prevention.

Quality youth development programs can cut crime immediately and transform this Prime Time for Juvenile Crime into hours of academic enrichment, wholesome fun and community service. They protect both kids and adults from becoming victims of crime, and cut teen pregnancy, smoking, and drug use, while they help youngsters develop the values and skills they need to become contributing citizens. For example:

• Five housing projects without Boys & Girls Clubs

Plan 1/31/2003

2000 P Street, NW • Suite 240 • Washington, DC 20036 • (202) 776-0027 • Fax (202) 776-0110 • www.fightcrime.org

> *"When the peak hours of violent juvenile crime are between the end of school and 6:00 P.M., it's just common sense to provide the after-school programs that give kids the values and skills they need to say 'no' to crime and violence."*
>
> — Sheriff Patrick Sullivan (R-Arapahoe County, CO)

were compared to five getting new clubs. At the beginning, drug use and vandalism were the same. But by the time the study ended, the projects without the programs had 50% more vandalism and scored 37% worse on drug activity.

- High school freshmen were randomly selected from welfare families to participate in the Quantum Opportunities four-year, after-school and graduation incentive program. Six years later, compared to those who received the program, boys left out averaged six times more criminal convictions, and girls and boys left out were nearly four times more likely to be without a high school degree.

- Young people given a Big Brothers/Big Sisters mentor were almost half as likely to begin illegal drug use and nearly one-third less likely to hit someone, compared to applicants randomly assigned to a waiting list.

> *"America's fight against violence must begin in the high chair, not the electric chair. Anything less leaves America's police fighting with one hand tied behind our backs."*
>
> — George Sweat, Director, North Carolina Office of Juvenile Justice; former Police Chief, Winston-Salem (NC)

In short, failing to provide programs like these multiplies the likelihood that at-risk kids will become delinquent.

2. Guarantee all families access to early care and education programs proven to dramatically reduce crime.

Rigorous studies, hard experience, and brain scans tell the same story: In the first few years of life, children's intellects and emotions, and even their ability to feel concern for others—a prerequisite to "conscience"—are being permanently shaped. When parents are at work trying to make ends meet, programs providing nurturing, early care and education for babies and toddlers can not only prepare children to succeed in school but also reduce crime. For example:

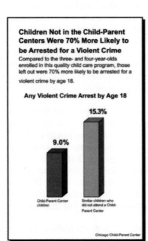

Children Not in the Child-Parent Centers Were 70% More Likely to be Arrested for a Violent Crime
Compared to the three- and four-year-olds enrolled in this quality child care program, those left out were 70% more likely to be arrested for a violent crime by age 18.

Any Violent Crime Arrest by Age 18

9.0% Child-Parent Center children

15.3% Similar children who did not attend a Child-Parent Center

Chicago Child-Parent Center

- In Ypsilanti, Michigan, three- and four-year-olds from low income families randomly assigned to attend the High/Scope Educational Research Foundation's Perry Preschool program were **only one-fifth as likely** to be chronic lawbreakers by age 27, compared to similar children not offered this educational child care.

- In Syracuse, at-risk infants and toddlers enrolled in a quality child development program, with parenting support for their mothers, **were only one-tenth as likely** as similar children to be delinquent ten years later.

- Chicago's government-funded Child-Parent Centers have served almost 100,000 three- and four-year-olds since 1967. Researchers tracked 989 of those children and 550 similar children not in the program for 14 years. The children who did not participate were 70% more likely to be arrested for a violent crime by age 18. This program also cut child abuse and neglect (see next page).

When millions of struggling parents are forced to leave their children in inadequate child care, we all pay a terrible price.

3. Help schools identify troubled and disruptive children at an early age, and provide children and their parents with the counseling and training that can help kids get back on track.

When children are disruptive and troubled, it is a warning signal that it is time to start looking for causes, and to provide the proven social skills training, counseling or other help for the children and their families that can lead the children back to a healthier path. For example:

- A Montreal study showed that providing disruptive first- and second-grade boys with services like these nearly cut in half the odds that they would later be rated highly disruptive by a teacher or by peers and be either in special classes or held back in school— all signs that the risk of future violence has been sharply reduced.

- Five years after randomly-assigned, disruptive, low-achieving seventh-graders completed a three-year program involving behavioral therapy and rewards, they were only one-third as likely to have a juvenile record as those who did not receive these services.

4. Improve deficient parenting and prevent child abuse and neglect by: a) Offering high-risk parents in-home parenting-coaching; and b) making sure child protective, foster care and adoption services have policies and enough well-trained staff to protect and heal abused and neglected children.

Being abused or neglected multiplies the risk that a child will grow up to be violent. Almost three million children are reported abused or neglected each year. Child protective and foster care services in most states lack adequate staff, and often the training or policy support, to protect children and to see that those who have been maltreated get the nurturing care and treatment needed to help them heal. We must also act *before* abuse takes place to expand parenting-coaching and family support programs that prevent children from being abused and neglected, prevent subsequent delinquency, and improve other outcomes for children. For example:

- The Nurse-Family Partnership randomly assigned half of a group of at-risk families to receive visits by specially trained nurses who provided coaching in parenting skills and other advice and support. Rigorous studies showed the children who were not in the program were almost five times more likely to be abused in the first two years. Fifteen years after the services ended, the mothers who were not in the program were five times more likely to have been arrested while their children were twice as likely to have been arrested.

- Chicago's Child-Parent Centers preschool program for three- and four-year olds from poor neighborhoods includes a strong parental involvement requirement. For 14 years, a large scale study tracked children who participated in the preschool program and similar children who did not participate. It found that children who were enrolled were half as likely to be abused or neglected as children who did not attend.

The Bottom Line: Investing in Kids Saves Lives and Money

When America fails to invest in its children and youth, we pay far more later—not just in lives and fear, but also in tax dollars. The federal treasury will actually have *more* money to dedicate to other uses a few years from now—whether for social security or prescription drug benefits—if we invest *today* in programs to help kids get the right start in life. For example:

"We could be saving thousands of lives–and sparing thousands of families unimaginable heartbreak–by investing up front in the proven early childhood care and youth development programs that can turn kids away from crime."

— Jean Lewis, Past President, National Organization of Parents of Murdered Children

"No one can approach crime reduction and public safety procedures today without considering early intervention. The public understands that we need more after-school programs to fight crime. We in the DA's office understand, and the police understand. What we need now is for elected officials to understand."
— District Attorney Charles Hynes, Kings County (Brooklyn), New York

- Economist Steven Barnett found that the High/Scope Foundation's Perry Preschool program saved $150,000 per participant in crime costs alone. The project produced a *net savings of $7.16*—including more than six dollars in crime savings—for every dollar invested.

- Barnett estimates that the cost, including increased crime and welfare costs, of *failing* to provide at least two years of quality educational child care to low-income children is approximately $100,000 per child. That's a total of about $400 billion for all poor children now under age five.

- A study by Professor Mark A. Cohen of Vanderbilt University estimates that for each high-risk youth prevented from adopting a life of crime, the country would *save $1.7 million*.

Law Enforcement United in Calling for Crime-Prevention Investments in Kids

Who says these four steps are among our most powerful weapons to fight crime?

- The more than 2,000 law enforcement leaders and crime victims who make up FIGHT CRIME: INVEST IN KIDS.

- The **International Association of Chiefs of Police, the Fraternal Order of Police,** the **Major Cities [Police] Chiefs' Organization,** the **Police Executive Research Forum,** the **National District Attorneys' Association** and the **National Organization for Victim Assistance** have adopted forceful calls for boosting critical crime prevention investments like these.

"We'll win the war against crime when we're ready to invest in America's most vulnerable children without waiting for them to become America's Most Wanted criminals."

—Seattle Police Chief R. Gil Kerlikowske
Board Chairman, Fight Crime: Invest in Kids

- In a George Mason University poll, 86 percent of police chiefs nationwide said, "expanding after-school and child care programs like Head Start will greatly reduce youth crime and violence." Nine out of ten chiefs agreed with the statement, "If America does not make greater investments in after-school and educational child care programs to help children and youth now, we will pay far more later in crime, welfare and other costs."

For citations of studies referred to above or for a free subscription to research and policy updates, visit www.fightcrime.org

 FIGHT CRIME: INVEST IN KIDS

Launched in 1996, FIGHT CRIME: INVEST IN KIDS is led by more than 2,000 police chiefs, prosecutors, sheriffs, crime victims, and leaders of police officer organizations. Major funding for its operations is provided by:

David and Lucile Packard Foundation, William T. Grant Foundation, Pew Charitable Trusts, W.K. Kellogg Foundation, Charles Stewart Mott Foundation, Robert Wood Johnson Foundation, Afterschool Alliance, Naomi and Nehemiah Cohen Foundation, Garfield Foundation, Freddie Mac Foundation, Ewing Marion Kauffman Foundation, J.P. Morgan Chase Foundation, Rockefeller Brothers Fund, and Rockefeller Family Fund.

Reflecting on What You Have Read

1 This proposal begins by identifying the organization from which it comes: Fight Crime: Invest in Kids is "an organization of more than 2,000 police chiefs, sheriffs, prosecutors, and victims of violence." What do the authors accomplish by beginning the proposal in this way?

2 The proposal mentions several programs—such as "pre-kindergarten and educational child care programs"—but provides few details on how to implement them. Instead, each program is accompanied by details that demonstrate its effectiveness. Why do you think the authors have omitted details about implementation but provided details about effectiveness?

3 Choose one of the four steps outlined in this proposal. What claims does that step of the proposal make? What reasons and evidence does the proposal give in support of these claims? Do you find this evidence and reasoning persuasive? Why or why not?

4 The proposal highlights quotations from several sources—Leroy Baca, George Sweat, Jean Lewis, Charles Hynes, and Gil Kerlikowske—and gives each of them a title. Jean Lewis, for example, is identified as the "Past President, National Organization of Parents of Murdered Children." Does this information add to the credibility of the quoted sources or to the arguments in the proposal? Why or why not?

Thinking Ahead

School violence is a surprisingly vast and serious issue. One recent Internet search turned up almost two million sites devoted to the topic; a search with just the keyword *bullying* turned up almost four hundred thousand sites. Think about your own experience in elementary and secondary school. What forms did school violence take? What measures did administrators take to prevent school violence? Based on your reading and your experience in school, can you propose a plan to reduce violence at a school you have attended?

In confrontations between police and citizens, the citizens often claim police brutality, whereas the police officers often deny the claims or argue that force was necessary to subdue a suspect or protect the officers involved. In this proposal, Richard D. Emery, a civil rights lawyer in New York City, observes that reports of these confrontations are usually confusing, even contradictory. In some situations, it may be impossible to obtain clear, reliable records of an incident. But Emery argues that, at least in some instances, videotaping could eliminate much of the confusion and uncertainty. This article appeared in *Criminal Justice Ethics,* a journal published for both the general public and a specialized audience of criminal justice professionals and scholars.

Cameras in the Station House

RICHARD D. EMERY

Video cameras operating 24 hours a day in police precincts are the most important component of police oversight that is now missing in efforts to stem police brutality and abuse of authority. No other device or procedure can substitute for an instant replay of events that are alleged to constitute police misconduct. Only in this way can both the public and the accused police officers be more assured of a fair assessment of police actions.

Inevitably, every accusation of police misconduct includes ambiguous and confusing events. Police most often either deny that they abused a victim or claim that their physical actions were necessary as proper restraint of their accuser. Accusers invariably deny any improper conduct that warrants a physical restraint, let alone abuse. And invariably the interactions between police officers and people in custody are ambiguous, subject to interpretation and, at a minimum, confusing in the sequence of events that led to physical injuries.

The result is that subsequent testimony of witnesses is often nearly useless. Witnesses contradict each other and allow emotions to color the interpretation of events. These events in normal time happen very quickly, and the mind is a fundamentally flawed recorder. Most often the victim does not even know exactly what happened, let alone nearby witnesses who are not part of the action. Of course the police officers involved are so biased by the fear of accusation and punishment that their story quickly becomes totally unreliable.

Put simply, the best way to sort these complicated confrontations is the same way we look at instant replays in slow motion for basketball and football. Often, with multiple parties coming in close physical contact to one another, the only way that a true version of events can be gleaned is [by] painstakingly analyzing video tape. Certainly with a video tape more can be determined about who did what to whom than in any other after-the-fact method. Thus the value of video tape in sorting out police/citizen confrontations can not be overestimated. As we have learned repeatedly from events that were caught on video tape, far more can be determined in subsequent court proceedings than through witnesses whose memories are highly suspect even on day one, let alone months or even years after the event. And even recorded corroborative activity that will show who was in the area, the witnesses' vantage points, and who was with whom will be valuable in the event that the actual physical confrontation is not caught on tape.

The question then is, "[W]hat is the cost of videotaping police activities?" The answer is: very little. Video cameras placed at locations in precinct houses that are not invasive of personal privacy—[not, for example] in locker rooms where personnel change or in the actual stalls of restrooms—do not trample expectations of privacy. In a public precinct, police officers who are public officials should not and can not have any expectation of privacy. After all, their superior officers at a minimum, and more likely even the press and public, have general access to these areas in precinct houses. Certainly any police officer knows that any other fellow officer would have an obligation to report misconduct that he or she saw in a precinct, to which all fellow officers presumably have full access in any event. Therefore, no police officer can argue that expectations of privacy within a precinct predominate over the value of video recordings of alleged police misconduct.

Similarly, police officers should have video cameras placed in police cars to record scenes of confrontation on the street or in the car itself. Certainly there can be no expectation of privacy that outweighs the value of a record of such confrontations that occur in the street or even in a police car where the interior can always be viewed from the outside anyway. Consequently, claims of expectations of privacy in these contexts are even slimmer.

Whether the same can be said for audio tape is a somewhat closer question. It may well be that police officers have a right to audio privacy even in a police precinct or in a police cruiser. But the simple fact is that audio recordings are far less important than video recordings. I for one would certainly advocate that audio recordings should be made along with video recordings both in police precincts and in police cars, notwithstanding that the intrusion into police privacy is somewhat greater in the context of audio recordings.

It is for this reason that police departments in Florida and California employ video cameras. We see them on television shows frequently and they are now commonplace as evidence in proceedings involving police chases, arrests, and precinct activities.

Of course the main value to video cameras is to assure the public that what their police do is legitimate. In all likelihood, in most instances, false accusations of police misconduct can be quickly disposed of by virtue of a video tape vindicating the version of events of a police officer wrongly accused. In those cases where police officers abuse their authority, of course the video tape is crucial to hold officers accountable, especially when they are presumptively thought to be innocent.

Finally, there may in fact be some modest deterrent effect on police officers if they do not become accustomed to constant video tape and ignore cameras as part of their everyday life. However, all too often, police officers are not deterred whatsoever by video cameras when they abuse their authority and physically mistreat citizens. Nonetheless, many officers who would cross the line if no cameras were watching may be restrained in the face of knowing that they will be caught red-handed.

In conclusion, it is hard to imagine a convincing argument that civil liberties expectations of privacy outweigh the value of video tape in what is essentially the recording of the public functions of police officers. Moreover, given the value and the accuracy of such video tapes in these highly publicized and hotly contested controversies, the case for installation of video cameras to record almost every aspect of police life is compelling.

Given the urgency of controlling police violence and assuring the public that their police operate humanely and fairly, video tape is our best weapon as a salutary response to the current police brutality crisis.

12

Reflecting on What You Have Read

❯ bedfordstmartins.com/
visualage

*For an example of
supporting evidence for
Emery's proposal,
click on*
CHAPTER 6 › EXAMPLES

1 In the second paragraph of this proposal, Emery makes some sweeping generalizations ("Inevitably . . . " "Police most often . . . " "Accusers invariably deny . . . ") without providing factual support. Given his audience, readers of the journal *Criminal Justice Ethics,* should Emery have elaborated on his generalizations? Do you find these generalizations credible? Why or why not?

2 What objections does Emery anticipate? How well does he respond to these objections?

3 Do you believe that his proposal will bring the benefits Emery claims? Why or why not?

Thinking Ahead

As Emery's proposal suggests, some problems exist because participants in any given situation can have widely divergent impressions of what took place. Think of another problem that arises because of people's different impressions. Can you propose something that would reduce these differences? Also think of anecdotes (that is, complaints) you've heard from friends or family members about difficulties they've had because other people perceived the same events in different ways. What were the difficulties? What were the differences in perception? Does one of these anecdotes or complaints focus on a problem for which you might be able to propose a viable solution?

Within a month or so after the day the World Trade Center was destroyed, people began thinking about what to do with Ground Zero, the site on which the twin towers stood. The following essay, from the September 23, 2002, issue of the *Nation*, was written by Amanda Griscom, an energy analyst for the firm GreenOrder and a columnist for *Grist,* an online environmental magazine, and Will Dana, a deputy managing editor at *Rolling Stone.* Acknowledging some of the diverse interests that any new development must accommodate, Griscom and Dana propose a form of development that they believe would "reclaim Ground Zero in the spirit of the twenty-first century." As you read, notice how the authors work to make their proposal attractive and feasible to readers of the *Nation,* a progressive weekly magazine generally supportive of energy conservation and environmental protection.

A Green Ground Zero

AMANDA GRISCOM AND WILL DANA

The debate over how to redevelop the World Trade Center site has revolved around several key concerns: the commercial interests of the real estate industry, the public's desire to embolden Manhattan's skyline with exciting architecture and the historic obligation to memorialize thousands of lost lives. As we continue to address and balance these concerns, let's also seize the chance to reclaim Ground Zero in the spirit of the twenty-first century, showcasing one of today's most inspiring and politically meaningful industrial movements: the revolution in clean energy.

Imagine for a moment that the structures surrounding the memorial will be sheathed in an invisible skin of electricity-producing solar cells. During the day, while electricity demand is peaking, the buildings will silently, automatically produce energy. No power plants or transmission lines necessary. No greenhouse emissions. No need for oil, coal, natural gas or nuclear energy. No risk of blackouts. No spiking electricity prices. Computer and phone networks, elevators, clocks, air conditioners and ATMs will all run simply, cleanly, like a crop of corn or a grove of trees, on sunlight. (The complex will be connected to the grid, drawing electricity when necessary—at night or on cloudy days—and pumping power back in when it creates a surplus.)

These high-tech buildings will supply all the services and comforts of a traditional commercial or residential complex but require less than half the electricity because of their green design features: superinsulated walls and windows; highly efficient appliances and lighting, heating and cooling systems; and a motion-sensing laser system that will automatically switch off lights and equipment when not in use. Whereas the original World Trade Center complex guzzled nearly 100 megawatts of electricity a day on peak days, with associated emissions, the new complex will be a net-zero-emission development. Moreover, this mini–El Dorado of energy independence and its surrounding neighborhood will be designed to have minimal need for cars and trucks. Once there, visitors will be in the greatest walking neighborhood in the world. The three airports, Kennedy, La Guardia and Newark, will be connected by train to the downtown terminal, making it an easy commute. An expanded network of ferries connecting lower Manhattan with Brooklyn, Queens, New Jersey and uptown will provide a fast and pleasurable way to get around. The heart of lower Manhattan will be knitted together by a clean, quiet street grid restored for use by pedestrians alone.

"From both a technological and cost standpoint, this scenario is entirely possible," says Ashok Gupta, an energy economist at the Natural Resources Defense Council. Solar systems, fuel cells and energy-efficiency measures have already been implemented in the design of several skyscrapers in Manhattan, including the Condé Nast building at Times Square and the residential tower at Battery Park currently under construction. As clean-energy technologies become rapidly more sophisticated and affordable, a large-scale application at Ground Zero would galvanize their acceptance in the marketplace. As for transportation, fuel-cell-powered buses and taxis may be too expensive today, but already they're technologically feasible. The Lower Manhattan Development Corporation (LMDC) and the Port Authority have approved additional rail connections for commuters beneath the new complex; they are also considering plans to depress the West Side Highway for a more pedestrian-friendly environment, and to add new ferry lines at Battery Park and on the East River. 4

The opportunities are real, but they can't be realized without leaders. Yet neither Governor George Pataki, site developer Larry Silverstein nor Mayor Michael Bloomberg has expressed much interest so far. "Mr. Silverstein isn't really thinking about this," says his spokesperson. "It's just too early to get bogged down in these kinds of details." Pataki's office expressed a similar lack of initiative, saying the issues are important but not yet a priority. Alex Garvin, vice president of planning for the LMDC, was more assertive in his commitment: "We plan to establish standards for sustainability and green technology that architects will be not only encouraged but required to meet. But we can't get started on this now; it's too early to determine the details." 5

Prominent green architects disagree. Robert Fox, senior principal of Fox and Fowle, the architecture firm that designed the Condé Nast building, says planners should adopt the Leadership in Energy and Environmental Design rating system, the gold standard for sustainable building practices. "Now is the time to address this, at the beginning of the planning process," stresses Fox. "Sustainability measures must be incorporated into every aspect of the design, from the infrastructure of the water, sewage and electricity systems to the external PV-integrated paneling." 6

It's a safe bet that the public will support much if not all of the larger zero-energy vision. In addition to the LMDC, two coalitions—Civic Alliance, representing more than 100 institutions, and New York New Visions, representing dozens of local architecture firms—have endorsed principles for downtown redevelopment that promote sustainable design and clean energy. Furthermore, there's impressive evidence that supports the use of clean-energy systems: Richard Perez, a scientist at SUNY Albany who's been tracking sunlight in New York City for more than ten years, has found that the average amount of sun that hits the city annually is only 12 percent less than that in cloudless Tucson. 7

Right now the Pataki administration is considering a proposal to limit power-plant emissions of carbon dioxide 30–40 percent below 1990 levels by 2010. Building a zero-energy complex and a state-of-the-art transportation system would advance these goals and address the mounting crisis of global warming, while making a clear statement about America's commitment to energy independence. Since September 11 many energy experts have called for a massive, government-funded research project, a "Manhattan Project of 8 alternative energy" to alleviate our dependence on foreign oil. The opportunity for such an initiative now lies at the foot of Manhattan. Nothing would be more appropriate for a memorial to a traumatic past than one that points us in the direction of a sustainable future.

Reflecting on What You Have Read

1 Review the job titles of the authors (listed in the green marginal note at the beginning of the essay) and the people they cite in support of their proposal. Also note the job titles of the people who disagree with the authors. Do these job titles influence your attitude toward Griscom and Dana's proposal? If so, in what ways do they influence you? If not, why not?

2 Consider the title of this proposal. What assumptions does the title seem to make about the audience? about readers' knowledge and values?

3 How do Griscom and Dana try to make their proposal sound desirable? Do you think their efforts are successful, given their intended audience? Are they successful with you? Why or why not?

4 How do the authors try to make their proposal sound feasible? Are you convinced of its feasibility? Why or why not?

5 What evidence do Griscom and Dana provide to support this claim: "It's a safe bet that the public will support much if not all of the larger zero-energy vision" (paragraph 7)? Explain why you do or do not find their evidence persuasive.

6 Look back at the proposal "From America's Front Line against Crime." Would you recommend that Griscom and Dana incorporate some of the same kinds of visual elements found in that proposal? Why or why not?

Thinking Ahead

Few of us will ever be in a position to make a proposal on a project as enormous as the redevelopment of Ground Zero. But we might very well have a chance to influence smaller developments—the remodeling of dormitories or fraternity or sorority houses, for example. Think about the places where you live, work, or play. How might one of those places be improved upon? What changes are needed—and why? How would you gain the attention of the people or groups in a position to implement those changes?

The other proposals in this chapter deal with large-scale issues—college admissions proce-dures, airport security, and school violence, to name a few. While there is a lot to be learned from these proposals and the strategies their writers employ, your proposal will likely have a more limited scope, as in the following proposal written by a Rensselaer Polytechnic Institute student, Max Zujewski. Max wrote this proposal for a college writing course. In it he proposes a solution to a problem that he and other students frequently encounter on campus—their difficulty finding enough coins to operate washing machines in their dormitory. One obvious solution to this problem would be to install more change machines in campus laundry rooms. But as you will see, Zujewski takes a comprehensive approach to the problem.

Max Zujewski

Making the Most of the Rensselaer Advantage Card: Plan for Finishing the Original RAC Project

Seven years ago, a very beneficial project for the faculty, staff, and students of Rensselaer Polytechnic Institute was started. The Rensselaer Advantage Card, or student ID project, was a success for both the staff of RPI and for the students. Not only did the student ID card generate more profits for Rensselaer and make student dorms more accessible and safe, but it also propelled RPI to the forefront of student ID card technology. 1

Yet the Rensselaer Advantage Card project has been left only half complete. Today it sits as a listing on only a single section of a single Web page entitled "Details of Historical Projects." Point eight of this listing states that the Rensselaer Advantage Card's future uses will be for banking applications, credit and debit functions, vending machines, and laundry services. It has been seven years since the inception of the Rensselaer Advantage Card project, but none of these features is yet available on campus. 2

Other colleges and universities across the nation are literally 3
cashing in on self-supporting smart card systems, which not only
create profit, but also expand student convenience drastically when
compared to the magnetic stripe card systems such as the one currently in use at RPI. The University of Arizona's CatCard incorporates
chip technology that allows students to make small payments at the
campus bookstore, parking garage, and unattended locations such as
vending and laundry machine areas. The card's chip is also accepted
by ten different on-campus vendors. Currently the CatCard system
has processed over $1 million in transactions. Another amazing
example is Texas A&M's smart card system. Students can use the
Aggie Bucks on their ID cards to buy items from "the bookstore,
vending machines and snack bars on campus, as well as an ever-
increasing number of off-campus retail locations" ("Case Study"). The
school has reported annual sales of over $12 million dollars.

The added conveniences, profit potentials, and technological 4
innovations of the smart card have made the fact that Rensselaer's
ID card system is needlessly out of date impossible to ignore.

Problem

Several years ago, the high costs of purchasing new ID card 5
technologies forced RPI to place the Rensselaer Advantage Project
on the back burner. But today those same technologies are less
expensive, more versatile, and more functional, and RPI is at the back
of the pack in ID card technology rather than at the forefront. Students don't even have the convenience of using their ID cards at
vending or copy machines—options that students at other schools
have had for years. For these reasons, the Rensselaer Advantage Card
just isn't giving Rensselaer students very much of an advantage.

The list of colleges and universities with new ID card services 6
has been growing by leaps and bounds. Campus polls show that
these new services are indeed beneficial to the students as well. At
Northeastern University in Boston, student ID cards can be pro-
grammed as debit cards that allow students to withdraw cash from
bank accounts; the cards can also be used to obtain "discounts on

rail tickets, shoes, sandwiches, and other goods and services" on and near the campus (Ackerman F1).

The Yale identification card, a smart card introduced in 1999, was recognized by the executive director of Yale's Student Financial and Administrative Systems as "one of the most technically sophisticated among universities and corporations" (Bialik). The DukeCard was implemented as early as 1985, and by 1988 the magnetic stripe card system could be used for vending and laundry services. Today, the DukeCard system has been updated to a smart card system, and, as student Emmanuel Chang notes in response to an on-campus poll, the card "basically ends up being your life" (Bialik). According to the poll:

> Today, the DukeCard is used for nearly every on-campus trans-
> action. . . . [S]tudents can put as much money into their food
> accounts as they wish, and then spend that money on any food
> item, including candy bars from vending machines and pizzas
> delivered from the local Domino's. [For] copying, laundry, or
> buying computer supplies from the university store, the money
> is deducted from their non-food account. (Bialik)

With factors such as profitability, convenience, and the con-
quest of staying on the ID card technology forefront, there shouldn't
be any reason why the Rensselaer Advantage Card project should go
unfinished. With a few clear-cut steps, the project can be placed back
on the table and RPI restored to the forefront of ID card technologies.

Solution

The solution to turning the outdated Rensselaer Advantage
Card system into an up-to-date, profitable, and more convenient ID
card system lies in purchasing a new smart card system. The cost of
new ID card technologies has been declining steadily for the past five
years. The lower cost means that real profits and added student conveniences can now be obtained from a system upgrade. In addition, a
little background on the history of smart card technology clearly
shows why the time is right to purchase a smart card system.

ID card technologies of the past were not cost-effective, as can   10
be seen by looking at the cost of a single card reader unit and the
cost of an individual plastic smart card. In 1998, a single smart card
reader cost between $1,000 and $4,000 (Christie). According to Dave
Wamback, manager of Harvard's Identification and Data Services in
1998, "an ID card with an embedded computer chip would cost
approximately $15, and right now, that's not cost-effective." Wamback
also recognizes the potential of the smart cards, adding: "When
banking goes to smart cards, and costs go down, I can see a lot of
people going to smart cards" (qtd. in Bialik).

Today the same smart card that was not cost-effective to imple-   11
ment has dropped in price dramatically. A recent article in the online
business magazine *Enterprise Kentucky* states, "At one time, a smart
card cost ten dollars [or more] to produce. The per unit cost is now
approaching $3.50 or less" ("Magnetic Stripe Card"). Administrators
at the University of Colorado at Boulder acknowledge the cost-
effectiveness of today's ID technologies. As the housing ID card
manager noted, a new card system is "a daunting expense, so it will
have to come in phases." Nevertheless, Susan Dorsey of the ID
Projects Team stated that "in the long run, this card is going to
generate revenue through long-distance calling and increased use in
the vending machines" (qtd. in Christie).

With that said, it is proposed that Rensselaer purchase the   12
Diebold CS Gold system for its campus. The Diebold card system is a
two-part system. The first part is the hardware part, which provides
plastic smart cards and card readers for various applications across
campus. The second part is the software part, which provides a central database and software for specific-use card readers. According
to the Diebold Web site, the Diebold CS Gold system provides the following advantages:

- Access control
- Alarm monitoring
- Copy machine charges

- Credit/debit functions
- Guest meals and shopping
- Laundry services
- Library checkout
- Off-campus merchant access
- Vending

Along with the hardware and software, Diebold offers an annual   13
support contract with help available twenty-four hours a day
(*Diebold*). Under this support contract, Diebold will provide all service and installation and a full warranty on all Diebold products for
the life of the contract. In addition, the manufacturer will replace
broken and malfunctioning parts of the CS Gold system within
twenty-four hours of receiving a service request. Clearly, Diebold's
system covers what Rensselaer needs to update its system and to
keep it up-to-date in the future.

Some may argue that there must be a cheaper alternative for   14
creating profit and adding student convenience to on-campus facilities. The fact is that there isn't a cheaper alternative that would create as much profit or as much convenience. Furthermore, any alternative besides upgrading the ID card system would still leave the
Rensselaer Advantage Card project unfinished and leave RPI at the
bottom of the ID card technology world.

To make the point about alternatives stick, it's best to examine   15
a couple and discover their particular flaws. The first alternative
would be to add more change machines on campus. Change
machines would allow students to get quarters for laundry and vending services quickly and would be available twenty-four hours a day.
The problem with this is that these change machines must be
restocked often, which in turn means someone has to be paid to do
the job. Another problem is that most on-campus students don't
carry money with them, and if they do, would prefer not to carry
around change. As an obvious example, it would be much more convenient to carry around a card with $22.58 on it than to carry around
"a ten-dollar bill, two five-dollar bills, two one-dollar bills, a quarter,

two dimes, two nickels, and three pennies" ("Magnetic"). This first alternative also doesn't address the issue of technology: No technological advancements would be gained.

A second alternative would be to stick with the current magnetic stripe card system at RPI and just upgrade the cards to handle the new types of transactions occurring on campus. To do this, a new system would have to be implemented. One of these systems is the AT&T Optim9000 magnetic stripe system, which is compared to the Diebold CS Gold system here:

16

- **Diebold CS Gold**
  - Multiple card types supported
    - Smart cards
    - Magnetic stripe cards
    - Barcode cards
  - Ability to integrate with proven software packages
    - Oracle
    - Windows NT
    - Crystal Reports

- **AT&T Optim9000**
  - Only one card type supported
    - Magnetic stripe
  - Ability to integrate only with Oracle software package

The problem with the AT&T system is that it doesn't have the capability of upgrading to smart cards in the future, and it doesn't easily integrate with multiple proven computer technology platforms (*AT&T*). Why are smart cards preferable to magnetic stripe cards? Smart cards hold more information on the card itself. A typical magnetic stripe card can hold only about 1KB of information, but a smart card can hold megabytes of information. Even if the central database goes down, transactions can still occur and be updated on the central database later. Smart cards are also faster than magnetic stripe cards, since each card reader and each card itself contains a microprocessor, which lowers transaction completion times. Finally, smart cards are safer.

It may be thought that this new smart card service just can't be 17
safe; that a card is much easier to lose than money and that because
it uses a microprocessor to store information, a card has a real
value—in other words, if the card is lost then so is the money. In
today's world this is undeniably false. Smart card systems can use a
central computer system for total redundancy and reliability. Once a
smart card is swiped, the amount is deducted from the student's
account information, which is stored locally on the card and on a
remote computer. Therefore, if a card is reported lost or stolen, it
can be immediately deactivated and a new card can easily be issued.
The contents of the card are placed on a new card from the old
card's redundant information on the central computer system. The
latest technologies also include the option for having a PIN (personal
identification number) associated with each smart card. Just as with
a debit or ATM card, the person who owns the card must enter his or
her PIN number before any transaction can take place ("Magnetic").
This gives an added level of security for the user.

The implementation of this proposed solution is straightfor- 18
ward. The ID card services director at Rensselaer needs to fill out a
Request for Proposal (RFP) for a Diebold CS Gold system and send it
to Diebold sometime in the spring. Diebold will examine the RFP and
send back an actual proposal to implement a new smart card system,
along with pertinent pricing information. If the proposal from
Diebold is accepted by RPI, then implementation would begin in the
summer to minimize the impact on students.

This may seem a huge and expensive task to undertake, but it 19
isn't as big or as expensive as one might think. Diebold fills out the
RFP almost completely beforehand. The only things the ID card services director needs to do are review the RFP, add or subtract items
from the proposal to suit Rensselaer's needs, and attach pertinent
information about the current ID and meal plan structure at RPI.
Once the RFP is completed and Diebold's proposal is accepted,
Diebold takes over most of the work. Diebold will install the system
and set up training sessions to train on-campus employees to run the

system. Finally, each smart card will cost no more than $3.50, which can be attached to a student's activity fee at the beginning of his or her freshman year. As for the expense to RPI, it will be a daunting one at first, as directors of ID card services commonly know. Yet numerous schools across the nation—such as Yale, Harvard, Duke, Penn State, and the University of Colorado—have overcome this obstacle by phasing in the project over a couple of years. One summer, the central database could be put in place and dorm access readers changed. Then, during the school year, card readers could be placed on vending machines and laundry machines, which, by the way, will not need to be replaced since card readers can simply be attached to the current machines. By slowly implementing the new smart card system, Rensselaer can budget money efficiently and minimize inconvenience while the new system is being installed.

After looking at the alternatives and their benefits, it is easy to   20
see why the Diebold CS Gold system is the right choice for Rensselaer. The benefits of upgrading the outdated ID card system at RPI far outweigh any initial overhead costs. Selecting this smart card system establishes a single point of contact with an ID card system vendor, making installation, equipment sales, and repairs easier to facilitate. In addition, new ID card system services can be phased in and the extra profits created by the increased system usage will offset the initial cost of implementing these new ID card services. The increased system usage will not only boost profits for Rensselaer, but will boost profits for all vendors on campus. Finally, in addition to increased sales, students will be able to use their ID cards to buy food, make copies, do their laundry, and check out books—all without having to carry around a fistful of change or multiple forms of credit. After all, the goal of the Rensselaer Advantage Card project was, and still is, to create a source of revenue for Rensselaer while making campus facilities more convenient for the students and staying at the forefront of ID card technologies ("Details"). It's time to finish the project, achieve those goals, and restore RPI to the forefront of yet another technological field.

Works Cited

Ackerman, Jerry. "BMOC: Big Marketers on Campus." *Boston Globe* 23
Aug. 1998: F1.

AT&T. 2001. 10 Apr. 2001 <http://att.com>.

Bialik, Carl. "The Future of the ID Card." *Yale Herald* 23 Oct. 1998. 1 Apr.
2001 <http://www.yaleherald.com/archive/xxvi/10.23.98/exclusive>.

"Case Study: More Than a Student ID." *Diebold.com.* 2001. Diebold, Inc.
28 Apr. 2001 <http://www.diebold.com/opccsol/Documents/
Case_Studies/cardsystems_casestudy_texas.htm>.

Christie, Lisa. "Easy-Access ID Cards Coming to Campus." [University of
Colorado-Boulder] *Campus Press* 18 Apr. 1996. 10 Apr. 2001.
<http://bcn.boulder.co.us/campuspress/1996/april181996/
cards41896.html>.

"Details of Historical Projects." Rensselaer Polytechnic Institute. 2001.
28 Mar. 2001 <http://www.rpi.edu/dept/rem/historic.html>.

Diebold. 2001. 28 Apr. 2001 <http://diebold.com>.

"Magnetic Stripe Card, Smart Card, and Point of Sale." *Enterprise
Kentucky.* State of Kentucky. 1 Apr. 2001 <http://www.state.ky.us/
agencies/emgtech/magcard0.htm>.

Reflecting on What You Have Read

1 In his introduction to his proposal, Max makes no reference to the problem (the lack of enough change machines on campus) that originally concerned him. Why do you think he begins his proposal the way he does, rather than by addressing the problem he and other students encounter on campus?

2 The conclusion makes several claims about the ways this proposal will benefit its audience. How plausible do these claims seem?

3 In what ways does Max seem (or fail to seem) well informed about the topic?

4 In what ways does his proposal seem feasible (or not feasible)?

Thinking Ahead

The best proposals are likely to arise from a problem, a sense that something is wrong or that something is not working as well as it could. Think about your daily experience in school, at work, or in social situations. What problems do you experience in these settings? Do they affect other people? If you think you can propose a practical, workable solution to one of these problems, can you identify an audience that would be in a position to implement your solution?

Proposal

Identify a problem (either a problem of your choice or one selected by your instructor) that affects a specific audience. Then formulate a detailed, practical solution that your audience members will be able and willing to implement or at least consider seriously. Probably the most interesting kind of proposal to write is one that will solve a problem that matters greatly to you—especially when you can show that solving the problem matters to your audience as well.

Your instructor may have specific requirements about how long your proposal should be, what sort of topic you should write about, whether you should prepare your proposal as a print or online document (or as an oral presentation), and whether you should include visual elements or use a particular documentation style to cite sources. Be sure you understand these requirements before you start working on the assignment.

Guide to Writing a Proposal

❯ If your instructor asks you to prepare the proposal as an oral presentation with overhead slides, see **Chapter 16**.

Even when you have strong ideas about a topic for your proposal, it's not always easy to come up with a clear statement of the problem. You may at first have a strong sense that something is wrong, but you may not know exactly what the problem is, or your ideas may change as you work on the assignment. You have to be willing to reformulate your statement of the problem as you go along.

Also, don't become fixated on one solution. You may start out with what you think is a practical or workable solution to the problem—and it may well be. But more typically, as you discuss your solution with your classmates and instructor, you will become more aware of its weaknesses, others' objections, even information that might make your solution impossible to implement. If you were to avoid discussing your solution with anyone, you would prevent the discouragement that comes when people shoot holes in ideas you are proud of; you would also virtually guarantee that your proposal will fail. On the other hand, if you listen carefully to what others have to say about your proposed solution, you may be able to strengthen your argument by anticipating and responding to criticisms your intended readers are likely to raise.

The remainder of this chapter will help you through the process of creating a proposal that aims to solve a problem and bring about change—that is, a proposal that others will actually want to implement. The first step is covered in Getting Started—selecting a topic (in this case, a problem with a viable solution) and analyzing the context in which your proposal will be read. Then you will experiment with many of the verbal and visual strategies illustrated in the proposals you were introduced to in Reading to Write, and you will use them in the Drafting section. These strategies can help you work toward the writer's objectives of developing your topic (that is, finding something to say), writing an introduction that will engage readers' interest, creating an appropriate voice, providing clear structure, concluding your proposal effectively, and designing your proposal and integrating visual elements. Finally, in Finishing Up, you will receive guidance in creating a review draft, assessing your work carefully, and using that assessment to revise your proposal.

Guide to Writing a Proposal

Getting Started

Almost all proposals entail helping people solve a problem that matters to them. There are plenty of problems that need solving and, therefore, plenty of potential topics for your proposal. But, as you might expect, some problems may not be solvable, at least not within the time and length limits of this assignment. Moreover, the context within which a given problem must be solved can be a bit tricky; you must, for example, figure out whether your readers know there is a problem and whether they are willing to try to solve it.

Selecting a Topic

Almost all of the readings for this chapter deal with enormously complex problems that affect hundreds of thousands or millions of people. But do not let the scope of these problems mislead you. Even if you are prepared to devote the rest of your life to, say, understanding and remediating school and youth violence, you should choose a much more limited topic for this assignment. How limited? Your topic should be one that allows you to do the following.

> Talk frequently with people involved in the problem and its solution.
> Draw upon your own experiences.
> Develop some expertise that will put your experiences and ideas in a broader context (for example, by doing background reading, interviewing or surveying groups of people, and finding out how others have tried to solve the same problem).
> Devise a practical solution that others will actually be willing to adopt.

Even though you cannot solve the large-scale problems addressed in most of the proposals found in the Reading to Write selections, you can follow their example in several ways.

Choose a problem that matters. Select a problem whose solution would make life better, not just for yourself but for others as well. We know one student who proposed that a video camera be installed near a dormitory fire alarm that people were using to send in false alarms, usually in the middle of the night. After the housing bureau on campus read this proposal, the camera was installed, the culprits were caught, the false alarms ended, and it became a lot easier to get a night's sleep in the dorm.

Think twice about trying to solve long-term problems. For example, there are probably complex reasons why no one has solved parking problems on your campus. To make any headway on solving this problem, you would have to learn a lot about campus politics, academic finance, and, possibly, civil engineering. You would also need a huge amount of good luck. Where luck is concerned, you should accept it when it comes. But don't count on it.

Working on the Assignment

Selecting a Topic

To identify a workable, interesting topic for your proposal, try some of the following activities.

> **Read back over the Thinking Ahead passages** that follow each of the proposals in Reading to Write, looking for a problem you might try to solve in your proposal. You might also try to think of things that bother people in all aspects of your life—in class, in the dormitory, in a campus or summer job, in clubs, or in other organizations.

> **Brainstorm.** Write quickly a list of complaints, irritations, or gripes you or others have expressed. Even if they seem silly—such as "my friend is annoyed because campus dining halls won't eliminate all meat dishes and replace them with tofu"—just jot them down in brief phrases.

> **Work with a small group to create a list of promising topics.**

> **Choose a topic from this list and make some notes.** Write your responses to the following questions: What seems to be bothering people—and why? For which people or group of people is this a problem? Who might be in a position to implement a solution to this problem?

> **Get a sense of what is possible.** Share your responses with the entire class or the members of a small group. See if anything they say gives you fresh ideas. (If one of your classmates is intrigued by the problem you have come up with and would also like to work on it, check with your instructor. It may be that the problem is complicated enough that each of you can work on solving different aspects of it. Or it may be that the problem is significant and complex enough to require the efforts of a small group.)

Once you have identified a topic that seems promising, do some preliminary data gathering to make sure the topic is workable.

> **Examine your own experience.** Have you had any personal experience with the problem? How did it affect you? How did it affect others? So far as you know, have others tried to solve this problem? If so, what happened? Why didn't the attempted solution actually work?

> **Talk with others who may know something about the problem.** Are they aware of the problem? Can they tell you any good stories about how the problem affects them or how others attempted to solve it?

> **Do some reading.** Look for published materials by doing a preliminary search in your library's databases (such as LexisNexis, Readers' Guide Abstracts, or Wilson Select) and on the Internet. Also look for such unpublished materials as memos, handbooks, bylaws, or statements of policy related to your topic.

> **Look for visual information**—images, charts, graphs, and so forth—that might help persuade readers that the problem you are trying to solve is, in fact, a serious problem.

> For advice on conducting library and Internet searches, see **Chapter 9.**

STUDENT DIALOGUE: SELECTING A TOPIC

Writing in a Visual Age: Why did you choose to write a proposal recommending the use of smart cards for campus vending machines?

Max Zujewski: It was an important issue on campus and seemed like one that could actually be changed, something that could actually be implemented, rather than some general topic that students could only rant and rave about.

Analyzing Context

If you are trying to solve a problem that really matters, it's almost certain that you will have to appeal to two different (but sometimes overlapping) groups.

> Your *primary audience*, the person or group in a position to implement or approve your proposal

> Various other *stakeholders*, meaning the people who will actually have to do the work of carrying out your proposal or who otherwise have a stake in the outcome you are proposing (see p. 339).

Consequently, your proposal is likely to have at least two different purposes: to persuade decision makers and, at a minimum, to avoid annoying or alienating other stakeholders. For example, you want to make sure your proposal does not needlessly complicate the work of people who will have to implement your suggestions.

Most of the proposals in Reading to Write are addressed to multiple stakeholders. These people are not always specifically identified, but you can get a sense of who they are when you notice the kinds of questions or objections the proposal writers anticipate. For example, you might assume that Nathan Burstein's proposal for standardizing college application forms is addressed solely to college administrators. But Burstein is also addressing the likely concerns of several other stakeholders. Think about it this way: If Burstein's proposal were adopted, what groups of people would likely be affected?

> College administrators (especially deans of admissions), the primary audience, because they have the authority to accept or reject Burstein's proposal

> Parents of college-age students who might pressure colleges to support or reject Burstein's proposal

> A national association of secondary school principals, who may feel the problem is already solved

> Secondary school teachers and guidance counselors

> High-school students, particularly juniors and seniors, preparing to apply to colleges

What indicates that Burstein is considering all these different groups of people? Consider the kinds of information he includes and the types of objections he anticipates. Imagine Burstein's proposal as a dialogue between himself and various stakeholders.

College administrators and parents: Wait a minute. Aren't you just whining about the competitive nature of college admissions?

Burstein: No. It's not the competition I object to. It's wasting time by filling in a lot of forms that strike me as redundant [paragraph 3].

Secondary school principals: Do your homework, kid. We've already solved this problem.

Burstein: I appreciate what you have already accomplished with the "common application form." It's a great idea, but it just doesn't cover enough schools [paragraph 4].

College administrators: What's in this for us? Why is it to our advantage to do this?

Burstein: Not having to create and mail your school's form will save you time and money [paragraph 5].

Teachers and guidance counselors: How will this change affect us? We already have a procedure that seems to work pretty well.

Burstein: You would have less paperwork to do and more time to write the kind of thoughtful recommendations students need [paragraph 5].

High school students: How will this benefit us? We have more than enough to think about already.

Burstein: My proposal would make picking up and completing applications easier and faster, so it would reduce the load on students who are already under pressure [paragraph 6].

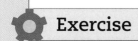 Exercise

Read some op-ed pages of a newspaper, looking for pieces that recommend a course of action or propose a solution to an important public issue. Bring a copy of one of these pieces to class, and be prepared to explain the various stakeholders the author addresses.

STUDENT DIALOGUE: ANALYZING CONTEXT

Writing in a Visual Age (WVA): How did you determine who you should address your proposal to?

Max Zujewski (MZ): I first talked to a lady at the ID card services desk in the Union. I thought she would be in charge of ID card services. She referred me to K. E., her boss. When I talked with K. E., I told her what I was looking for and she said, "Look no further." She has the final word on any ID card services and plans.

WVA: Who are your stakeholders?

MZ: K. E. chairs a committee that's looking into this problem. There are two people from Residence Life, one from the maintenance department, and one from the academic dean's office, as well as two professors and a couple of Student Senate representatives.

WVA: What do you know about this committee?

MZ: K. E. seemed to think the committee members are also concerned with student convenience, with making sure students can actually use the cards for campus transactions—vending machines, laundry machines, bookstore purchases, and so on. I guess the biggest thing the students and professors asked for was a card that would allow access to buildings on weekends and at night.

Questions for Analyzing Context

❯ **bedfordstmartins.com/ visualage**

To download these questions as a work- sheet, click on **CHAPTER 6** ❯ **WORKSHEETS**

● **Audience knowledge, values, and needs**

❯ What sorts of experiences (personal or secondhand) have my readers had with my topic?

❯ How does the topic of my proposal relate to things my readers know, value, or care about?

❯ Do my readers have any biases or preconceptions concerning my topic? If so, what are they, and do I have any information that will correct (or reinforce) those attitudes?

● **Audience expectations for content**

❯ What kinds of arguments are my readers likely to value?

❯ What counterarguments are my readers likely to raise?

❯ What questions or objections are my readers likely to want to have answered?

❯ What kinds of information will they see as credible?

● **Audience expectations for layout or format**

❯ Which reading in this chapter comes closest to looking the way my readers will expect my proposal to look?

❯ Are there any visual features (for example, bulleted lists, charts, or photo- graphs) that my readers are likely to expect or appreciate?

〉 Are there ways in which my proposal will need to look different from the readings in this chapter?

● **Circumstances**

〉 Are there any recent events that might motivate my audience to read my proposal? If so, what are they?

〉 If not, what sort of background information should I provide at the beginning of my proposal?

● **Purposes**

〉 What purposes am I trying to accomplish in writing my proposal? (See the discussion of purposes on p. 339.)

〉 What sort of voice do I want readers to hear when they read my proposal? (For a discussion of voice, see p. 395 of this chapter.)

The activities in the Working on the Assignment box below will help you think through and prepare to answer the Questions for Analyzing Context on p. 380.

Working on the Assignment

Analyzing Context

As with any assignment, you should think about the audience for your proposal as concretely as possible. Try to identify one or more individuals who are reasonably typical of the larger group of readers you hope to reach with your proposal. Then take the following steps.

Talk with members of your primary audience and with any key stakeholders you can identify. Try to become friendly with them, and work to create a favorable impression. Find out what they know, think, or feel about the situation with which you are concerned. Also find out how your proposal might relate to other things they value. You might begin by saying something like "Lately I've been noticing that [briefly describe the situation]." Then follow up with questions such as these: Have you heard or read anything about this? If so, what was your reaction to what you heard or read? Do you know of anyone who is trying to remedy this situation? If so, how successful have these previous remedies been? If they have failed, why or how have they failed?

Listen to *what* people say and *how* they say it. When you talk with members of your primary audience and others who may be affected by your proposal, do they seem hostile? doubtful that the problem can be solved? indifferent? Or do they come across as supportive? enthusiastic? eager to help? Your answers to these questions will help you decide how much work you will have to do in order to engage and maintain your audience's interest.

Put yourself in your readers' place. Use what you are learning about your reader to answer such questions as these: *If I were in my readers' place, how would I react to the recommendations in the proposal? What questions would I want answered? What objections would I raise—and why?*

Identify the circumstances in which your readers will encounter your proposal. Are they aware of any recent events that might influence their understanding of the problem? Are they likely to read several proposals on this problem, or is your proposal the first one they will encounter on this topic?

Answers to the Questions for Analyzing Context may help refine your sense of purpose in writing the proposal. If your readers are hostile or anxious, part of your purpose may be to reassure them that you want to help and that you are not going to threaten their interests. If your audience is eager to help, then part of your purpose may simply be to show that you have a good way to accomplish what you both desire. If your audience seems indifferent, part of your goal may be to dramatize the problem, thereby forcing readers to see why a solution is so important.

As you work on your proposal, your understanding of your audience may change. You may, for example, get a clearer idea of what your audience knows or expects, or you may revise your ideas about the sort of format that is appropriate. Consequently, you may want to revise your context analysis as you work on your proposal. But for now, be as specific as you can.

STUDENT CONTEXT ANALYSIS

Here's how Max Zujewski completed his context analysis for the proposal he wrote, "Making the Most of the Rensselaer Advantage Card" (p. 364).

Audience Knowledge, Values, and Needs

What sorts of experiences (personal or secondhand) have my readers had with my topic?

My readers know about past ID card projects, specifically our school's system. They also know that a few years ago, a system upgrade was very high priced and would not produce revenue.

How does the topic of my proposal relate to things my readers know, value, or care about?

My readers value student convenience, but they are only willing to upgrade the system if the price is right. They value making a profit for the school and generating more revenue through new technologies.

Do my readers have any biases or preconceptions concerning my topic? If so, what are they?

They are interested in having just one point of contact for ID equipment and installation because that would make the job easier.

STUDENT CONTEXT ANALYSIS

Audience Expectations for Content

What kinds of arguments are my readers likely to value?

They want evidence that the plan is practical, that it could actually be implemented on campus.

What counterarguments are my readers likely to raise?

They want to see precedents, especially evidence that other schools have successfully used this technology.

What questions or objections are my readers likely to want to have answered?

How do you know this system will work and be reasonably economical?

What kinds of information will they see as credible?

Data showing that other schools have successfully implemented the smart card system.

Audience Expectations for Layout or Format

Which reading in this chapter comes closest to looking the way my readers will expect my proposal to look?

It will look sort of like the "From America's Front Line against Crime" proposal, incorporating headings and bulleted lists.

Are there any visual features (for example, bulleted lists, charts, or photographs) that my readers are likely to expect or appreciate?

My audience, K. E., is involved with a lot of day-to-day stuff, and she's got many projects going, so she'll appreciate attention-grabbers like bulleted lists and headings that will let her go right to the sections she's most interested in.

Are there ways in which my proposal will need to look different from the readings in this chapter?

Unlike "From America's Front Line against Crime," my proposal won't make use of illustrations or logos.

continued

STUDENT CONTEXT ANALYSIS

continued

Circumstances

Are there any recent events that might motivate my audience to read my proposal? If so, what are they? If not, what sort of background information should I provide at the beginning of my proposal?

K. E. is currently working on a generic Request for Proposal for a new card system on campus. This RFP is approximately 85 percent complete.

Purposes

What purposes am I trying to accomplish in writing my proposal?

I want to overcome K. E.'s belief that smart card technologies are not reliable or cheap enough to warrant purchasing such a system for our campus.

What sort of voice do I want readers to hear when they read my proposal?

I want to sound serious and well informed, not like someone who is just complaining without any facts to back up the complaint.

Drafting

As you have seen in earlier chapters, you can learn a lot about writers' strategies by examining the written texts they create. You can't always determine how much time the writers spent talking to other people, yet many of your best ideas will come from conversations with others. So again we emphasize: talk with your primary audience and other stakeholders to determine their ideas, perceptions, and feelings. Don't worry about whether you agree with them or whether they agree with each other. For now, just ask questions, listen, and learn.

Developing Your Topic

Proposals often begin by describing a personal experience that the writer witnessed or was involved in, an experience that demonstrates why the problem needs to be remedied. Consequently, you may want to rely in part on your own experience as you develop your proposal. But you should also consider using secondary sources. As you develop your proposal, you want to show that the problem exists, define the problem, and demonstrate that your solution is feasible and desirable.

Showing That a Problem Exists

In some situations, readers may already know that the problem exists and may have sent out a Request for Proposal (RFP) to solve the problem. Frequently, however, readers may be unaware that there is a problem and may even be reluctant to admit that a problem exists. In such cases, you will have to make use of evidence and argumentative strategies to persuade readers that a problem exists and needs to be solved. The proposals in Reading to Write suggest several effective strategies for doing this.

How to Show That a Problem Exists

Strategies	Examples
Identify a difficulty felt by someone the readers know and care about. Not all difficulties and problems are equal; the problems that matter most to readers are those that affect the people, institutions, animals, or objects that readers know and care about.	*In "Applying to College, Made Easy," Burstein (p. 345) exaggerates the size of the stack of college applications on his desk. But readers—especially parents—who are familiar with the pressures faced by college applicants should have at least some sympathy for the difficulty Burstein describes.*
Describe a need that is not currently being met. The more readers care about the need that is not currently being met, the more likely they are to think that the problem you're addressing is significant.	*"Cameras in the Station House" (p. 358) begins by citing the need for a "fair assessment" of the actions of police officers.*
Point out a conflict between what readers originally intended to do and what they actually did.	*In proposing that the university adopt smart cards for campus transactions, "Making the Most of the Rensselaer Advantage Card" (p. 364) points out that this sort of service was envisioned in the early development of the school's student ID card but has not yet been realized.*
Acknowledge existing efforts to solve the problem, and show why they are inadequate. If the problem is significant, others have probably tried to solve it, and their solutions, although flawed, also have their strengths. If you can acknowledge those strengths, you may avoid putting readers on the defensive. You might also learn something that you can build on in proposing your own solution.	*"Applying to College, Made Easy" acknowledges the existence of a "common application form" for college admission but points out that relatively few schools accept that form.*

Showing That a Problem Exists

Now is a good time to explore what you already know, believe, or feel about the topic you have chosen for this chapter's assignment.

List everything you can think of that indicates that a bad situation needs to be corrected or that a good situation could be made even better.

Show your list to a classmate or a friend. Ask this person to help you identify statements that seem factual or documentable, eliminate statements that sound like rumor or whining, and identify new sources of information.

Write a brief paragraph explaining what the problem is and identifying a specific individual who has the authority to implement your solution.

Discuss this paragraph with your classmates and instructor. Get their responses to the following questions: *Have I identified a problem that's serious to people other than myself? Is it a problem for which I can probably come up with a plausible solution in the time I have to work on this assignment? If I can come up with a good solution, can I also identify someone who would be willing and able to implement it?*

If you answered "no" to any of these questions, you probably should consider a different topic for your proposal. But if the answer to each of these questions is "yes," you can begin gathering information to show that the problem is serious, that it has severe consequences, or that a solution to the problem would provide significant benefits. To do this, talk with the people who are affected by the problem, especially people with whom readers are likely to sympathize. Also talk with a range of people to make sure the problem is not limited to just one or two people. Look for articles demonstrating that the problem occurs elsewhere.

As you read and talk with people, make notes in response to the following questions.

> What difficulties are these people encountering?

> What needs are not being met?

> What evidence demonstrates that these difficulties or needs are significant?

> Is the problem caused by a conflict between two groups of people? between what someone claims is the case and what actually is the case? between what someone intended to do and what he or she actually did do?

> Have there been previous efforts to solve the problem? Why didn't those solutions work?

Defining the Problem

People may be aware of a problematic situation, but they may be unsure—or mistaken—about what is wrong. Consequently, it is usually necessary to articulate the problem carefully. A good problem statement will identify the cause of the problem and imply what needs to be done to solve it.

How to Define the Problem

Strategies	Examples
Identify the cause of the difficulty people are having. For example: Does the difficulty exist because someone lacks needed information? because a policy is inherently flawed? because someone is trying to make life difficult for someone else? Does it exist because people are not aware of possible solutions or of the consequences of their actions? Each of these questions (and this list is by no means exhaustive) implies a different cause, and each cause implies a different solution.	*"Fixing Airport Security" (p. 348) argues that "[e]verybody is responsible for airport security—which means nobody is really in charge." If you accept the claim that the inadequacy of airport security is caused by fragmented responsibility, the basic solution becomes apparent: get rid of the fragmentation by giving one group or person sole responsibility for ensuring airport security.*
State the problem as something that can be acted upon. Indicate, explicitly or implicitly, what people need to do, stop doing, or do differently.	*"Making the Most of the Rensselaer Advantage Card" (p. 364) points out that the university has not followed through on its plan to provide students with ID cards that can be used with campus vending machines, at the campus bookstore, for banking services, and so on. It then proposes adopting a type of smart card that can be used in these various ways.*

Working on the Assignment

Defining the Problem

Once you have collected information about your audience and problem, you should work to define the problem.

> **Write out a problem statement** that identifies the cause(s) of the problematic situation and implies a course of action.

> **Show this statement to others,** including your instructor, your classmates, and various stakeholders. Ask them to tell you whether you have identified a fundamental cause of the situation, a cause that could actually be remedied.

> **Be willing to revise your problem statement** as you gain additional information and insight from others.

Thinking of Solutions

Throughout the process of gathering information and defining the problem, you have probably been thinking about possible solutions. Now is the time to focus on solutions in earnest.

Thinking of Solutions

To come up with workable solutions, consider the following possibilities.

> **Brainstorm for ten minutes and list every solution you can think of.** Don't worry about how good the solutions seem right now. You will think more about that as you go along.

> **Get a classmate or friend to help you think of other possible solutions.** Consider as many different solutions as you can, even far-fetched solutions that might contain an idea that could develop into something useful.

> **Keep a list of all the solutions that occur to you.** Add to this list as you think of new possibilities.

> **Do some quick reading.** Survey your library's databases and search the Internet to see if others have attempted to solve this problem. Skim the materials you find. Can you see ways to benefit from others' successes or failures? (Remember: you don't want to reinvent the wheel.)

> **Review the options and choose the solution that seems best.** After looking over all of the solutions you have considered, choose the single option that seems most feasible.

> **Do a reality check.** Write a two- to three-paragraph explanation of how you intend to solve the problem.

> **Get feedback.** Ask a classmate to read these paragraphs and tell you where you need to add explanations or anticipate questions and objections.

Demonstrating Feasibility

One of the easiest ways for a hostile audience to criticize a proposal is to point out that its writer has not thought things out carefully and, therefore, has not demonstrated the feasibility of the proposal. Often, this criticism is justified: the writer fails to anticipate exactly what would be involved in implementing the solution—the financial costs, for example, or the amount of time and energy required. In such cases, the audience's response is likely to be something like, "Don't give me any grand-sounding, half-baked ideas. Show me that what you're proposing can actually be implemented." To avoid this sort of response, consider using the following strategies for demonstrating feasibility.

How to Demonstrate Feasibility

Strategies	Examples
Explain the logistics involved in implementing your solution. Consider costs; explain who will need to do what, when, and how. Do this work very carefully. One reason proposals get rejected is that they just don't seem feasible.	*"Making the Most of the Rensselaer Advantage Card" (p. 364) explains the precise steps the audience will need to take in order to obtain the new smart card system.*
Identify precedents that suggest your proposal will work. Solving a problem involves change, which for many people implies risk. To reduce this sense of risk, mention ways people in other situations succeeded in solving similar problems. You might recommend modifying what others have done, so that their solution fits the specific situation with which you are concerned.	*"A Green Ground Zero" (p. 361) cites examples of recent building projects—including New York's Condé Nast building in Times Square and a residential building in lower Manhattan—that have successfully incorporated many of the technologies recommended in the proposal.*
Anticipate and respond to questions and objections your audience is likely to raise. Audience members may be hostile or they may simply want to make sure your solution is well thought out. When presenting your proposal—orally or in writing—anticipate and respond to their questions and objections before they have a chance to raise them.	*"Cameras in the Station House" (p. 358) anticipates that readers may object to installing video cameras in police stations. Emery responds by arguing that cameras placed in public areas of police stations do not conflict with public officials' "expectations of privacy" (paragraph 5).*

Demonstrating Desirability

Most audiences need to be persuaded that a proposal is attractive as well as feasible. To enhance the appeal of your proposal, try the following strategies.

How to Demonstrate Desirability

Strategies	Examples
Identify plausible alternatives and explain why they are less attractive than your solution. If you want your audience to accept your solution, you'll have to show how it is preferable to alternative solutions.	*"Making the Most of the Rensselaer Advantage Card" (p. 364) identifies two alternatives to the smart card and then points out how neither alternative would be as useful to students as the smart card system.*

continued

How to Demonstrate Desirability

continued

Strategies

Point out ways your proposed solution will benefit your audience. It may seem selfish, but there's a good chance your audience will ask, in effect, "What's in this for me?" or "How will this benefit someone or something I care about?" When you can answer these questions persuasively, you dramatically increase the chance that your audience will accept and want to implement your solution.

Examples

"A Green Ground Zero" (p. 361) lists the benefits of the proposal in paragraphs 2 and 3. Typically, however, a proposal mentions such benefits near the end, as in "From America's Front Line against Crime" (p. 353), in the section headed "The Bottom Line."

Creating an Exploratory Draft

At this point, you have spent a good bit of time developing your topic—using the preceding strategies to gather information and define what the problem is, show that the problem exists, and think of a solution to the problem. Your reading, note-taking, and reflecting have prepared you to write an *exploratory draft* of your proposal.

Working on the Assignment

Creating an Exploratory Draft

Before you begin writing your exploratory draft, review the information you have gathered. Identify any places where your notes are unclear or sketchy and where you need to go back and find more information. Also confirm the accuracy of quotations you might use.

In preparation for writing the exploratory draft, take a close look at the context analysis you completed, answering the questions on p. 382. Are there some questions that aren't completed very well? For example, are you lacking information about your readers' knowledge, needs, and values? Do you have a good sense of what your readers will expect in terms of content, both verbal and visual? At this point, complete your responses to the best of your ability.

After completing your research and context analysis, review the information you have developed. Then set aside twenty to thirty minutes and write as rapidly as you can (without interruption), completing the following sentences.

> "The main problem is _____."
> "The causes of this problem are _____."
> "One reason this problem needs to be solved is _____."
> "Another reason is _____."

> "To solve this problem, the first thing that will have to happen is _____." (Be as specific as possible: say who will need to do what, when, where, and how.)

> "The next thing that will have to happen is _____."

> "The next thing is _____."

> "The main questions or objections my audience might raise are _____."

> "My responses to these questions or objections are _____."

After you have done this exploratory work, read or show what you have written to other students (in a small group or to the entire class). Describe your intended audience to your classmates, and ask them to answer the following questions.

> Do I have an audience that would want or need to read a proposal on this topic?

> Is my statement of the problem clear? Does it identify the causes of the problem?

> Do I show that the problem really is a problem?

> In what passages do I do a good job of explaining what needs to be done to solve the problem?

> Where do I need to be more explicit about how to solve the problem?

> How can I anticipate and respond to the objections and questions that my audience is likely to raise?

> Where might I use one or more of the strategies explained earlier to develop my topic more thoroughly?

Use your classmates' responses to guide you in deciding whether or how to add to, delete, or modify information you have included in your exploratory draft.

As you work on your proposal, reread what you've written from time to time, just to make sure that the information you use supports your claims. Perhaps you'll want to modify something you've said, provide some new evidence or arguments, or even come up with a completely new statement of the problem or explanation of the solution. If so, that's fine. Initial drafts are rarely more than a good starting point. As new ideas occur to you, write them down and try to incorporate them into your exploratory draft.

Engaging Your Audience: Writing an Introduction

If you hope for readers to accept—or even pay attention to—your proposal, you have to persuade them to recognize the existence and seriousness of the problem. More specifically, they will have to recognize some sort of conflict—between two groups, between what currently is happening and what should or could happen, or between what they currently know and what they need to know or understand. You also need to relate to your readers. It's crucial to make readers aware of a conflict in your proposal, but it's not enough. As with position papers (Chapter 4), you have to make your readers see how the conflict relates to them—to their personal, social, or professional lives, to their values, or to people or situations they care about.

For some topics, proposal writers don't have to work hard to get their audience's attention. For example, when "Fixing Airport Security" (p. 348) first appeared, ten days after the September 11, 2001, terrorist attacks, people had different ideas about how to improve airport security, but no one argued that it was as effective as it needed to be. Therefore, in their title and first two sentences, Poole and Butler simply remind the audience of a conflict it already knew about: the disparity between the current level of airport security and the needed level of airport security.

> **Fixing Airport Security**
> The recent terrorist attacks on the Pentagon and the World Trade Center have forced us to rethink the issue of airport security. It's become quite clear that the present system is not adequate to the task.

More typically, however, proposal writers need to provide background information, either to prove that a serious problem exists or to demonstrate that they (the proposal writers) are well in touch with a difficult situation. The amount of background information required depends on what the primary audience and other stakeholders already know and how they feel about the topic. Generally, the more readers know about the topic and the more strongly they feel about it, the less background information you'll need to provide in order to engage their attention.

Relating to Readers

The proposals in the Reading to Write section of this chapter display a variety of strategies for making sure readers see how a topic relates to them. Here are two strategies that will help your own writing relate to—or develop common ground with—your readers.

How to Relate to Readers

Strategies	Examples
Create a scene that readers can recognize and that helps them visualize the problem. Try to be specific enough so that readers can imagine themselves—or someone they care about—actually involved in the scene.	*"Applying to College, Made Easy" (p. 345) sets the scene somewhat whimsically, conjuring up an image of the writer late at night facing "a pile of applications that now threatens to topple over on innocent civilians standing below."*
Refer to an accomplishment the audience is likely to value. It's easier to get people to implement change when you can acknowledge a step they have already taken in that direction. If you can recognize some positive move readers have already made, you may find it easier to sympathize with them, and they may be more willing to listen to you.	*In proposing the adoption of a smart card system for student transactions on campus, "Making the Most of the Rensselaer Advantage Card" (p. 364) begins by referring to the initial success of the current system used on campus.*

Establishing Conflict

To establish conflict, try using one or more of the strategies for showing that a problem exists (p. 385). You might also consider using the following strategies.

How to Establish Conflict

Strategies	Examples
Refer to an ongoing debate that the audience is familiar with.	*"A Green Ground Zero" (p. 361) mentions several "concerns" that have fueled the debate over how to redevelop the site where the World Trade Center stood.*
Show that current efforts are inadequate. This can be especially effective when you can show that the current situation is not inevitable, that alternatives to current efforts are well proven and readily available.	*"From America's Front Line against Crime" (p. 353) notes that some of the most effective programs for combating juvenile crime are in danger of vanishing.*
Recount factual events or actions that conflict with what the audience expects, values, or is willing to accept. Most readers can tolerate a certain amount of annoyance before they become willing to take action. So don't write about things the audience can dismiss as minor irritations. Instead, mention events or actions that go beyond what readers will see as fair or reasonable.	*"From America's Front Line against Crime" points out that effective crime-prevention programs are jeopardized by "inadequate funding," a situation that "leaves every American at risk of becoming a victim." Most readers will consider the elimination of effective programs unreasonable and unacceptable.*
Refer to events or actions the audience is likely to see as typical or part of a widespread pattern. Because it's easy to dismiss something that happens infrequently and that bothers only a few people, look for examples that show not just that something undesirable has happened but that it happens repeatedly and affects a lot of people, including people the audience cares about.	*"Applying to College Made Easy" (p. 345) points out that college applicants today must apply not to "just a few in-state schools," as in years past, but to "a minimum of four or five colleges to insure acceptance at one." Most readers will see the increased competitiveness of college admissions, and the increased burdens on applicants, as part of a pattern that affects many people.*

STUDENT DIALOGUE: ENGAGING AN AUDIENCE

Writing in a Visual Age (WVA): Sometimes writers begin proposals by discussing the disadvantages of the current system. Why don't you do that in your proposal?

Max Zujewski (MZ): Because the disadvantages are obvious. My primary audience is the person in charge of a committee that's trying to think of an alternative to our present system. She already knows the limitations of our ID cards.

WVA: Why do you start out by commenting on the original Rensselaer Advantage Card project? Doesn't your audience already know about that?

MZ: When Rensselaer originally started this project, the University was gung ho about the project being able to do this, this, and this. And here it is seven years later. I just want my readers to know I'm aware so they take me seriously.

Engaging Your Audience

> Review—and, if necessary, revise—your context analysis, being especially careful to describe your readers' knowledge, needs, and values.

> Using the strategies for relating to readers and establishing conflict, write one or more introductory paragraphs that will engage your intended audience. You might want to try more than one approach.

> Bring your draft introduction to class, along with your context analysis. Ask several classmates to comment on whether it includes enough details—and the right kind of details—to make your audience appreciate the severity of the problem and see how the problem relates to them or people they care about.

> Also ask your classmates whether they can think of other strategies that you might use to engage your audience.

Creating an Appropriate Voice

Another important way to engage and keep readers' attention is to create an appropriate voice—that is, to make sure that the attitudes, personality, and even the literal sound of the voice the audience hears fits with the message you convey. Sometimes a detached or impersonal voice is best; at other times, a very personal voice—one that seems to be talking directly to a reader, one person to another—may be most convincing. In all cases, however, your voice must make readers believe that your proposal is well informed and thoughtful.

To create an appropriate, effective voice, you have to be aware of alternatives and choose wisely among them. Some choices involve wording; as a rule, if you can think of several synonyms for a given word, you should choose the one that connotes the right personality or attitudes. For example, you will convey one personality or attitude by evaluating a *weekend getaway* and another by rating a *road trip*.

The work you have done so far will already have helped you create the voice for your proposal. You should be able to present yourself as someone who is well informed, credible, and aware of your audience's knowledge, needs, and values. These qualities are essential to the success of any proposal you will ever write. They are not optional. They are obligatory.

Beyond meeting these obligations, however, you do have a range of options—not only as to the tone, attitudes, and personality you display in your proposal, but also as to the strategies you use to create an appropriate voice. To make these decisions, you should first answer this question: What kinds of appeals are likely to be most appropriate for your audience? Do you want to engage their reason (a logical appeal)? Do you want to induce an emotional response (an emotional appeal)? Or do you want to make readers like and trust you (an ethical appeal)?

Making Logical Appeals

In appealing to readers' reason and intellect, you can use any of the strategies described earlier in Defining the Problem and Demonstrating Feasibility (pp. 387–389). In addition, the following strategies are especially helpful.

How to Make Logical Appeals

Strategies	Examples
Cite an appropriate level of detail to show that your proposal is feasible. Readers will require varying amounts of detail. Those who are unfamiliar with a solution will need a lot of detail about implementation, whereas readers with a good idea of how to implement the solution will need to know exactly what you are proposing.	*"Making the Most of the Rensselaer Advantage Card" (p. 364) recommends adopting a technology the audience is not familiar with and explains exactly what needs to be done to adopt the smart card system at the University. In "From America's Front Line against Crime" (p. 353), the assumption is that readers understand the various programs advocated in the proposal but need evidence that these programs are proven to reduce juvenile crime.*
Cite credible precedents. Most proposals entail a degree of risk if only because they represent a departure from the way things have traditionally been done. Readers are more likely to accept your proposal if they know that other, similar proposals have been successfully implemented in the past.	*"A Green Ground Zero" (p. 361) shows how the writers' ideas for integrating "green technology" into new buildings at Ground Zero have been successfully implemented in other large buildings in New York City.*
Acknowledge and refute different points of view. On almost any important subject, it is possible for reasonable people to hold different points of view. One way to show that your proposal is reasonable is to show that you understand different viewpoints and can explain why they are not valid in the situation you're concerned with.	*"A Green Ground Zero" points out that at the time the proposal was written, some of the people charged with redeveloping Ground Zero felt it was "too early" to begin thinking about how "green technologies" could be integrated into buildings there. The proposal then cites architectural authorities who stress that such technologies have to be considered "at the beginning of the planning process."*

Making Emotional Appeals

People can be resistant to change, so sometimes it helps to engage readers' emotions as well as their logic. Of all the proposals in Reading to Write, "From America's Front Line against Crime" shows the widest array of strategies for making emotional appeals.

How to Make Emotional Appeals

Strategies	Examples
Choose words and details that relate directly to readers' values. Values and emotions are closely linked; when you refer to things readers value, you stand a good chance of engaging their sympathies as well as their intellects.	The introductory section of "From America's Front Line against Crime" (p. 353) includes such phrases as "help kids get the right start" and "help young people learn the skills and values they need to become good neighbors and responsible adults." Right start, good neighbors, responsible adults— these are all things that are likely to be highly valued by adult readers concerned about ending juvenile crime.
Use visual devices to highlight facts that will have a strong emotional impact on readers. In other words, make it easy for readers to see—literally *see*—facts that either dramatize the severity of a problem or emphasize the desirability of a proposed solution.	In "From America's Front Line against Crime," the graph titled "Hourly Percent of Serious Violent Crime Committed by Juveniles on School Days" (p. 353) dramatically illustrates the increase in juvenile crime between the hours of 3 P.M. and 6 P.M. Bullets and white space set off and emphasize the results of studies that support the recommendations made in the proposal.
Use moving quotations from respected sources to appeal to readers' emotions. Readers are most likely to be convinced and moved by comments from people who have firsthand knowledge of the topic and who share their values.	"From America's Front Line against Crime" uses emotional pull quotes to support its logical claims. For example, a former police chief's remark that the solution "must begin in the high chair, not the electric chair" offers a stark contrast in figurative language. A past president of Parents of Murdered Children states that early prevention programs could "spar[e] thousands of families unimaginable heartbreak."
Cite benefits that appeal to the readers' values. Readers are more likely to be emotionally committed to your proposal if they can see how it achieves results they value.	Near the end of "From America's Front Line against Crime," the proposal goes into some detail to show that "Investing in Kids Saves Lives and Money," thereby appealing not only to readers' humanitarian values but to their pragmatic values as well.

Making Ethical Appeals

An ethical appeal is an effort to get your audience to like and trust you. In part, this means using the strategies described under logical appeals; when readers see that you have thought out your proposal carefully, you are likely to increase your credibility with them. But there are several other things you can do—or perhaps as important, avoid doing—in order to gain your audience's goodwill and respect.

▵ How to Make Ethical Appeals

Strategies	Examples
Avoid being too emotional about your own experiences. Don't whine or gripe about an experience that has annoyed or inconvenienced you. While it is appropriate to talk about your experience, describe it matter-of-factly or with a degree of humor.	*"Applying to College, Made Easy" (p. 345) is concerned with the difficulty of completing separate college application forms, but the situation is conveyed humorously when the writer says he confronts "a pile of applications that now threatens to topple over on innocent civilians standing below."*
Be fair to stakeholders. There is a good chance that you are making your proposal because others' efforts have not succeeded. But the people who have made those efforts may be among your primary audience or among your other stakeholders. So be careful to acknowledge the value of their past work.	*Paragraph 4 in "Applying to College, Made Easy" acknowledges that the National Association of Secondary School Principals has developed a "common application form" that is accepted at about two hundred colleges. Only after acknowledging the value of this effort does the proposal point out that "[f]ewer than 20 national universities ranked in the top 50 in this year's U.S. News & World Report survey accept it, and almost no public universities accept it."*

❯ For more information about strategies that can help you make logical, emotional, or ethical appeals, see pp. 244–246 of **Chapter 4.**

Other useful strategies for creating an appropriate voice include the following.

> ❯ Choose words and details that reinforce or imply the attitudes you want to convey (see Chapter 3, p. 167).
> ❯ Select appropriate personal pronouns (see Chapter 3, p. 167).

> Decide what sort of information to include and exclude (see Chapter 3, p. 167).

> Make comparisons that imply or reinforce the attitude you want to convey (see Chapter 5, p. 321).

> Use visual elements (images, charts, graphs, and so on) and a page layout that are consistent with the attitude you want to convey in the written text (see Chapter 5, p. 322).

Working on the Assignment

Creating an Appropriate Voice

Consider the impressions writers leave on you as a reader. Working with one or two classmates, choose one of the proposals in Reading to Write that you feel has a clear voice. What words would you use to describe the writer's voice in this proposal? What attitude or personality does the proposal convey? Does it sound personal or friendly? formal or businesslike? concerned? enthusiastic? practical or impractical? something else?

> List words that describe the attitude or personality created in this proposal.

> Underline the specific passages that convey this attitude or personality.

> Try to state how or why these passages help create the voice.

Think about the impression you want your proposal to leave on your readers. To clarify and perhaps revise the voice of your proposal, try the following activities.

> Review your context analysis (revise it if you need to).

> List some of the words and phrases you hope readers would use to describe the voice in your proposal.

> Show both your context analysis and the list of words and phrases to someone else (a classmate or your instructor); ask this person to tell you whether the voice you hope to create makes sense, given what your context analysis says about your intended audience and purpose.

> Using what you learn from your classmate or instructor, revise the list of words that describe the voice you want to create.

> Ask someone (a classmate, your instructor, or a friend) to read a section of your draft aloud, and listen to the sound of his or her voice. Can you hear the attitude you want to create in the sound of this reader's voice? If you can, good. If you can't, look closely at your draft to see what words and phrases you need to change in order to create the voice you want.

STUDENT DIALOGUE: CREATING AN APPROPRIATE VOICE

Writing in a Visual Age: From talking with you about your proposal, it's clear that you're irritated about Rensselaer's lack of progress in fully implementing the original plan for the smart card. But you don't convey that irritation in your proposal. Why not?

Max Zujewski: It is irritating that we don't yet have the smart card system, especially since we said we were going to have one seven years ago. But there's no point in getting irritated. I wanted to come across as sounding professional, as trying to give a lot of facts, and as being very straightforward. I think if I chose a voice that sounded irritated, my audience would dismiss it; she wouldn't want to read it. My audience is concerned about all these different things—money, convenience, and all that—and here I would be complaining and sounding like I don't know what I'm talking about. I didn't want my essay to sound like a hastily written, angry editorial in the college paper. I wanted to sound like I really did my research. That way she'll take me more seriously.

Providing Structure

No matter how original or useful your proposed solution may be, readers may fail to appreciate it if they encounter difficulty in finding the information they need, anticipating what you're going to say, or seeing how comments in any one passage relate to comments in subsequent passages. Consequently, you will need to make the structure of your proposal clear, just as you have done for the writing assignments in other chapters of this book. You'll need to make your work accessible, create clear expectations, and provide links between paragraphs or larger sections of text. The proposals in Reading to Write illustrate a variety of strategies for structuring your work.

Making Information Accessible

As is the case with other types of writing, your readers may not read every word of your proposal. Instead, they may look for information about specific points they are interested in. Consequently, part of your responsibility as a writer is to make it easy for readers to find what they are looking for. Here are several ways you can do this.

How to Make Information Accessible

Strategies	Examples
Use thesis statements and topic sentences to get to the point quickly. The thesis statement of a proposal usually explains the solution in clear terms. In some cases, the thesis may also be expressed or implied in a title. Although topic sentences are not required in every paragraph, it is a good idea to let readers know what to expect near the beginning of each paragraph.	*"Cameras in the Station House" (p. 358) begins with a straightforward thesis: "Video cameras operating 24 hours a day in police precincts are the most important component of police oversight that is now missing in efforts to stem police brutality and abuse of authority." Every paragraph but one begins with a topic sentence. The exception starts with a question—"[W]hat is the cost of videotaping police activities?"—and immediately offers the reply "very little."*
Highlight key pieces of information. Use bold print, bulleted lists, boxed insets, and charts or graphs.	*All of these strategies appear in "From America's Front Line against Crime" (p. 353). You can also find many other examples throughout this textbook. (For a more detailed discussion of these and other visual cues, see Chapter 8.)*
"Chunk" information, grouping related facts together and separating them from other groups of facts.	*"Cameras in the Station House" opens with a recommendation for handling conflicting accounts of police brutality. Then it presents several chunks of information: descriptions of conflicts that cause the problem (paragraphs 2–3), justification for the solution proposed (4), responses to possible questions or objections (5–8), benefits of the proposal (9–10), a summary of the basic argument (11), and a reiteration of the solution (12).*

Creating Expectations

Readers often try to anticipate what a writer is going to say next. To help your readers form clear, accurate expectations, you can draw on the strategies for making information accessible (using thesis statements and topic sentences and visually highlighting key points). You can also use the following strategies.

How to Create Expectations

Strategies	Examples
Use headings that forecast what you are going to say.	*In the middle of the first page of "From America's Front Line against Crime" (p. 353) is the heading "Four Steps to Dramatically Reduce School and Youth Violence." The remainder of the proposal lists those steps and elaborates on each one.*
Establish a pattern in the way you present your ideas.	*The first step listed in "From America's Front Line against Crime" is printed in large, bold type and is followed by an explanation of why the recommendation is important and examples showing that the recommendation is beneficial. The other steps follow this basic pattern.*

Creating Links

Even though readers may not read every word of your proposal, they still will want to have a sense of flow, of how a given paragraph or set of paragraphs relates to the passages that precede and follow it. Here are two strategies you can use to give readers this sense of flow.

How to Create Links

Strategies	Examples
Begin paragraphs with transition words.	*The proposals in Reading to Write use a wide variety of transition words and phrases, such as* first, second, but, finally, in conclusion, *and* similarly.
At the beginning of one paragraph, refer to something mentioned in the preceding paragraph. This will increase readers' sense of the flow or cohesiveness in your writing.	*The third paragraph of "Cameras in the Station House" (p. 358) notes that in confrontations between the public and police, perceptions are often contradictory and unreliable. The next paragraph refers to "these complicated confrontations."*

Providing Structure

Bring to class a copy of a proposal that makes its structure very clear. Be prepared to show your instructor and classmates how the author(s) enabled you to see the structure of the proposal. After identifying strategies other writers have used, review your exploratory draft, looking for ways you might use some of these strategies to make the structure of your own proposal clear.

Concluding Your Proposal

Readers looking primarily for information in a report or an evaluation may not always read the conclusion. For instance, in reading a report, members of the audience may just look for key pieces of information they need; in reading an evaluation, they may just read until they can tell whether they are likely to be interested in the specific topic or item being evaluated. But with proposals, readers are likely to look closely at the concluding paragraphs, if only to get a sense of the "bottom line" or "what's in it for me." In your proposal, the conclusion is your last shot at persuading the audience to do what you want. So make it a good shot.

The kind of conclusion you write will depend on the needs and values of your audience. The proposals in Reading to Write employ a variety of strategies that you may consider as you conclude your own proposal.

How to Conclude Your Proposal

Strategies

Reiterate your basic argument, and restate your recommendation. Especially if your proposal is lengthy or complicated, it can help if you summarize your proposal, making sure the basic outline of your ideas is fresh in your readers' (or listeners') minds.

Examples

The next-to-last paragraph of "Cameras in the Station House" (p. 358) repeats the two basic assumptions underlying the proposal: (1) that placing video cameras in police stations and other public places is not an invasion of police officers' or others' privacy, and (2) that video cameras provide a more reliable, accurate record than do eyewitness accounts. The final paragraph restates the recommendation that video cameras be installed in police stations because "video tape is our best weapon as a salutary response to the current police brutality crisis."

continued

How to Conclude Your Proposal

continued

Strategies	Examples
Point out ways your proposal will benefit the audience, thereby ending on a strong, positive note. Only one bit of caution here: be realistic. Don't promise benefits unless you have strong reasons for believing that those benefits will actually materialize. If you promise more than your proposal can deliver, the audience will be skeptical of your entire proposal—and of any subsequent proposal you may make.	*"Making the Most of the Rensselaer Advantage Card" (p. 364) concludes by pointing out the benefits of the proposal: students will enjoy the convenience of the smart card, campus vendors will see increased sales, and the University will gain revenue and regain its position at "the forefront of yet another technological field."*
Show how your proposal will help others achieve their goals.	*"A Green Ground Zero" (p. 361) concludes by noting that the proposed "zero-energy complex" will address the governor's goal of reducing carbon dioxide emissions and will also answer the call from "many energy experts" to reduce U.S. dependence on foreign oil.*

Working on the Assignment

Concluding Your Proposal

Review your exploratory draft proposal, noting all the ways you have revised it. Using a strategy identified above (or a different strategy from a proposal you have analyzed), write a conclusion for your proposal. Share your draft with your instructor or some classmates who have previously read your exploratory draft. Ask your classmate(s) to identify the strategy or strategies you have used and tell you whether the conclusion seems persuasive and appropriate, given what you have said about your audience.

Designing Your Proposal and Integrating Visual Information

As you've seen in "From America's Front Line against Crime" (p. 353), proposals may include any of the visual elements used in other types of writing—headings, graphs, bulleted lists, sidebars (inset boxes), pull quotes, and so on. In planning your proposal, consider whether visual elements might be useful in presenting your ideas effectively to the audience you are addressing. These elements aren't always necessary, nor are they always appropriate. But for some audiences and situations, they can be highly effective. Other potentially useful visual elements include charts, drawings, and photographs.

Review the questions related to reading visual information in proposals (p. 340). Keep these questions in mind as you consider which strategies to use if you decide to include visuals in the proposal you are writing.

Working on the Assignment

Designing Your Proposal and Integrating Visual Information

Look back over the selections in Reading to Write, and identify types of visual features that you might put to effective use in your proposal. As you think about the design of your proposal, check with your instructor about the kinds of visual elements that may be appropriate for your assignment. Keeping your instructor's comments in mind, identify the visual features you want your proposal to have and revise your draft to make sure it incorporates those features.

Finishing Up

It's now time to bring together all the work you've done thus far on your proposal. You should be ready to write a review draft that meets the goals set out in the assignment for this chapter. This draft should clearly identify the problem, present a practical solution, point out the benefits of the solution, and persuade readers to make the changes you propose. After completing the review draft, you'll need a few more days to finish working on your proposal. During this time you'll assess your writing carefully, not only by critiquing your draft yourself but also by getting others' perspectives on your work. Then you'll use what you learn from these assessments to make any needed revisions in the content, organization, style, and format of your proposal.

Creating a Review Draft

In preparation for writing your review draft, look back at the context analysis you completed earlier. Have you learned anything that would lead you to revise your context analysis in any way? For example, have you learned something new about your audience's values, information that might influence the voice you want to create or the type of appeal you want to make? If so, revise your context analysis and keep it in mind as you work on your review draft. Also look back at your exploratory draft. Ask yourself whether you need to change your statement of the problem, be more explicit about how to carry out the solution you propose, or explain why you reject alternative solutions. Notice points at which you will want to improve on this exploratory draft, perhaps adding or deleting details or even rethinking either the problem or the solution.

As you work on your review draft, examine the introduction and conclusion. Do these sections establish the voice you want to create? Does the introduction seem likely to engage the intended audience? Is the conclusion convincing? Will it persuade readers that your proposal should be implemented—or at least considered seriously? Revise these sections as needed, using the strategies discussed in this chapter.

In addition, take some pains to make the structure clear. To do this, it might help to write an informal outline indicating the main reasons you think there is a problem and what needs to be done to solve it. You should also use the strategies described on pp. 401–402 in order to make your work accessible, create clear expectations for your readers, and link paragraphs or larger sections of text.

Getting a Final Review

Once you have revised the review draft to make it as complete and polished as you can, you need to have it reviewed by one or more people who understand the principles (analyzing context, engaging readers, and so on) that you have been working with in this chapter.

> ❯ Give your reviewer a copy of your draft, one he or she can make notes on.
> ❯ Give your reviewer a copy of your context analysis. If necessary, revise that analysis before giving it to your reviewer.

> Ask your reviewer to begin his or her response by answering the following question: Given what I say in my context analysis, how likely does it seem that my proposal will be attractive and practical to my intended audience?

> Ask your reviewer to adopt the perspective of the audience described in your context analysis and then use the following checklist in commenting on your work.

Checklist for Final Review

> **bedfordstmartins.com/ visualage**

To download this checklist as a worksheet, click on **CHAPTER 6** > **WORKSHEETS**

1   In my context analysis, please highlight any statements that give you a good sense of the knowledge, values, and needs of my intended audience. (For an example, see p. 382.) Please indicate any statements that need to be clarified.

2   In my context analysis, please highlight any statements that give you a good sense of the circumstances, purposes, and expected format for my proposal. (For an example of a good context analysis, see p. 382.) Please indicate any statements that need to be clarified.

3   In what specific passages have I developed my topic thoroughly and credibly, especially by showing that a problem exists, defining the problem, thinking of solutions, and demonstrating the feasibility and desirability of my solution? What are some strategies (explained on pp. 385–390) I might use to make my proposal clearer and more compelling?

4   What portions of my introduction seem likely to engage the interest of my intended audience? Which strategies (explained on pp. 392–393) might help make the introduction more engaging?

5   How would you describe the voice I have created? At what points does that voice seem appropriate, given my intended audience and the subject matter of my proposal? What strategies (explained on pp. 396–398) might help me make the voice clearer or more appropriate?

6   What are some words or phrases that provide a clear structure for my proposal, making information accessible, creating clear expectations for readers, and indicating links between paragraphs or larger sections of text? What strategies (explained on pp. 401–402) might I use to make the structure of my proposal clearer?

7   How does the conclusion help make my proposal more attractive to my intended audience? What strategies (explained on p. 404) might I use to make my conclusion more effective?

8   If the proposal includes photographs or other visual elements, how do they help establish the importance of the problem or the nature of the solution? Do I need to add or revise any captions?

If possible, ask the reviewer to talk with you about your review draft as well as make notes on it. In particular, ask the reviewer to pose questions and raise objections to what you have written. Be careful not to argue with reviewers, especially when they pose questions or disagree with points you have made. When this happens, try to find out why they have questions or objections and make notes about what they say.

Revising Your Proposal

Up to this point, you have listened to your reviewer's comments without explaining, arguing, or making judgments about the validity of those comments. Once you have a good idea of how your reviewer responds to your proposal, however, you should go back through your notes on his or her comments. Bearing in mind your intended audience and purpose, decide which comments are most valid. Then use the strategies referred to in the Checklist for Final Review to revise your proposal.

After resolving all the issues that need attention, proofread carefully and correct any typographical or formatting errors. Then submit this final draft to your instructor.

Taking Stock of Where You Are

Although you will find differences among the writing assignments in this book, there are also some important similarities. For example, you always have to analyze the intended audience, write an introduction that will engage that particular audience, and so forth. Consequently, there should be a cumulative quality to the writing assignments you do from this book. Each assignment should teach you strategies that can help you grow as a writer and improve your work on subsequent assignments. But this will only happen if you make a conscious effort to assess your development as a writer as you go along.

After your instructor has returned the final draft of your work, think back over all the comments you received—from classmates as well as your instructor—and write out answers to the following questions. (You might want to keep these in a journal or a special section of a notebook.)

> **bedfordstmartins.com/
> visualage**
>
> *To download these
> questions as a work-
> sheet, click on*
> ***CHAPTER 6*** ›
> ***WORKSHEETS***

**Questions for
Assessing Your
Growth as a
Writer**

- What appears to be my greatest area of strength?
- Where am I having the greatest difficulty?
- What am I learning about the process of writing?
- What am I learning about giving and receiving feedback on writing?
- What have I learned from writing a proposal that I can use in my next assignment for this course, for another course, or for work?

SAMPLE STUDENT ASSESSMENT

Here's how Max Zujewski answered these questions for the proposal he wrote on student smart cards (p. 364).

What appears to be my greatest area of strength?

Researching—getting information that expands my argument and backs it up. Other things—transitions and things like that—were pretty well in place. Also, I'm good at identifying my audience. Once I've done an audience analysis, I just know how to flow through the paper.

Where am I having the greatest difficulty?

I still don't feel confident about conclusions. Sometimes they get too long, and sometimes I don't know exactly what to say. Also, I sometimes have trouble tying things together at the end.

What am I learning about the process of writing?

The main thing I'm learning is the importance of analyzing my audience. I don't think I did that before taking this course. I'd just think about a very broad audience, not a specific person. Also, I'm getting better at gathering facts and weeding out things that are weak or irrelevant.

What am I learning about giving and receiving feedback on writing?

Feedback allows me to clarify points that seem clear to me but are actually vague to other readers. In my first draft, for example, I knew what intrinsic *and* extrinsic *meant, but some readers did not, so I needed to replace those terms with more familiar ones. Feedback also helped me see what I was doing well throughout the proposal, so I know what to do next time.*

What have I learned from writing a proposal that I can use in my next assignment for this course, for another course, or for work?

I'm learning to see how particular facts fit into the flow of my ideas. Also, I've learned how important it is to use key words that mean a lot to the audience and that tell people what I'm talking about.

MaryBeth Rajczewski

The Basics of PowerPoint

Microsoft PowerPoint is the premiere presentation software. It enables you to create professional presentations in a short amount of time. Presentations using PowerPoint are generally more respected than those using standard overhead transparencies. These instructions will teach you how to create a simple PowerPoint presentation.

Who Should Use These Instructions?

You should use these instruction if you:

- need or want to learn to use PowerPoint to create a presentation
- have not used PowerPoint before
- have used PowerPoint before, but have only limited experience
- have lots of PowerPoint experience, but would like a refresher

You should not use these instructions if you:

- are an expert at PowerPoint
- have absolutely no computer experience

What Are the Prerequisites?

- These instructions assume you know som[e] computers; for example, you know how t[o] through a menu of options, you know how mouse, and you know terms such as click
- If you want to add charts or graphs to yo[ur] must know how to create charts and grap[hs in]

Excel or a similar spreadsheet application. If you want to learn how to create charts and graphs, there are many Microsoft Excel reference books available.

What Equipment Is Necessary?

- A PC that has Microsoft PowerPoint loaded on it.
- A working mouse.

Once you complete the steps in these instructions, you will be able to create basic PowerPoint presentations. You will also know how to use some of the key features that enable you to make more professional presentations. Since PowerPoint is such a powerful tool, there are many features that cannot be discussed in these basic instructions. Once you become familiar with the basics, you are encouraged to learn about some of the more sophisticated features. You'll be amazed at all you can do with PowerPoint.

Creating a New Presentation

Opening Power Point

1. **Click on the Start icon** in the bottom left corner of the screen.
2. Use your mouse to **move the cursor up to Programs**.
3. From Programs, **move your cursor over to Microsoft PowerPoint**.
4. **Click on Microsoft PowerPoint** when this box is highlighted.

7

Instructions

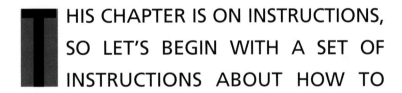

THIS CHAPTER IS ON INSTRUCTIONS, SO LET'S BEGIN WITH A SET OF INSTRUCTIONS ABOUT HOW TO write instructions. To write a good set of instructions that others can actually use, you have to follow two basic steps.

> ❯ Understand what readers are trying to accomplish.
> ❯ Give readers what they need to accomplish their goal.

Perhaps these steps seem too simple. But each one involves a good bit of work on your part. Because this work can seem complex, and because good instructions can take a wide range of forms, it's a good idea to keep these two basic points clearly in mind. If you don't understand what your readers are trying to accomplish, you won't be able to give them what they need. Instead, you'll give them too little information, too much information, or simply irrelevant information. If you ignore these two basic steps in writing instructions, readers will respond by ignoring your instructions, with results that range from inconvenience to disaster.

411

Showing How to Do Something

With most other types of writing, readers will come to your text looking for information, insights, arguments, or possible courses of action they may not have considered. With instructions, however, your readers' goals change. While they may come to new understandings, their primary goal is to do something, to accomplish some task or goal they cannot do on their own. As always, readers will want to have their questions answered. But all of these questions will stem from one basic question: How do I . . . ? How do I create an effective résumé? get in shape? carry out a laboratory procedure? Your readers may need to use instructions to accomplish any one of these tasks or goals. Consequently, readers of instructions are often referred to as users.

Because your users' questions will focus primarily on doing something, you have to approach your writing with questions that differ from the questions that guide your writing of a report (where you focus on the topic's significance or recent developments concerning the topic). Instead, you need to answer questions such as those listed below. If you think about your own experience with trying to follow instructions someone else has written, you'll see why these questions are important.

What is the first step? What comes next? Think back to the last time you got lost while trying to follow someone's directions to a place you had never been before. Almost invariably, it turns out that the person has left out one or two small steps: "Oh, yeah. I forgot. You have to turn left just past the gas station." Don't do this to your users. Don't skip from point A to point C without taking users through point B, and don't take them from point A to point C and then to point B.

How will users know if they are doing the work correctly? Have you ever assembled a piece of prefabricated furniture—a cabinet for your CDs, for example? If the instructions were well done, they probably included pictures of the finished product and of what the cabinet should look like at various stages of construction. Similarly, instruction manuals for computer software often include "screen capture" images of what you should see on the computer screen. Not everyone needs these pictures. A carpenter might not even glance at them—in fact, an expert carpenter probably wouldn't be using a prefabricated kit in the first place. But people who are not experts often need pictures of where they are headed and how they are doing. Experts often carry these pictures in their heads. Others may need them on the page in the instructions they are using.

What if a user makes a mistake? People make mistakes. Good instructions anticipate those mistakes and show users how to recover from them. Think about your experience with working on a computer. You accidentally press the wrong key—or the right keys in the wrong order—and the screen goes blank. Then what do you do? Granted, you probably should have been more careful in the first place. But if you think you may have just lost all the work you have done on an assignment, you don't want to hear that you should have been more careful. You want to know how to make all your work reappear on the screen.

What, if anything, could go seriously wrong? Will the computer crash? Will the mixture of chemicals blow up or create noxious fumes? Will the CD cabinet collapse if your user puts a television on top of it? Readers of instructions don't always think to ask such questions. They just do something that, at the moment, may seem reasonable and then find out they have a serious problem on their hands. You have to do your best to keep this from happening. You do this by anticipating dangers and problems and warning readers at the appropriate point in your instructions.

What if a user still has questions? No matter how good a set of instructions may be, there is still the chance that users will have questions. It's your job to figure out what those questions are likely to be and to answer them—either in the text of your instructions or in a set of frequently asked questions (FAQs) at the end of your document. A later section on anticipating readers' needs (pp. 458–460) will help you figure out what these questions are for your particular readers. Remember that you don't necessarily have to answer all possible questions in every set of instructions you write. Your job is to figure out which questions users can answer for themselves and which you will probably have to answer for them—and to do that, you need a thorough understanding of the context in which your instructions will be used.

Instructions in Context

Virtually no one reads instructions just for pleasure. It's hard for us say this, because we admire instructions that are engaging and pleasant to read, and your teacher certainly hopes you'll write instructions that your audience will find not only useful but enjoyable—or at least not needlessly difficult and annoying. But it's true that people usually read instructions because they need to, not because they want to, and they do so under circumstances that are not necessarily conducive to leisurely, thoughtful reading. You cannot anticipate every context in which your instructions may be used. But you can make informed guesses about the people who are most likely to use your instructions as well as about the time, place, and situations in which readers will use them. The more thoughtful your guesses are, the more likely your audience is to use your instructions successfully and perhaps even appreciate your efforts on their behalf.

Audience

Your audience consists of people who know less than you do about how to carry out a task or accomplish a goal. Any people who know as much as or more than you do won't be among your audience for long; if they pick up your instructions at all, they'll soon put them down, and you'll be left with people who need your help. But how much help do they need? and what sort of help? Some readers may need a detailed explanation to get through a new, complex procedure, whereas others may need only brief reminders about certain parts of a procedure they already know fairly well. Still other readers, worried about making mistakes, will need encouragement and reassurance. Other readers, by contrast, may be confident and willing to experiment; they will need from you only the steps they should follow and the shortcuts they might take.

Circumstances

People will rarely read your instructions under ideal circumstances. They may be working under physical constraints, perhaps trying to read your instructions while holding a key part in one hand and a wrench in the other, or in a difficult psychological context—attempting to recover files after their computer has crashed while they are working on a project that is due in a few hours. Or maybe they just dislike reading instructions and are doing so only because they couldn't find anyone to help them carry out the procedure you are explaining. Whatever the case, you have to be aware of the various circumstances in which your audience will work with your instructions so you can make them as useful as possible.

Purposes

The primary purpose in writing instructions is to enable your readers to complete a task or accomplish a goal as easily and effectively as possible. But the needs of your audience will probably lead you to formulate additional purposes. For example, if your audience members are apprehensive, you may want to reassure them. Your sense of your audience and purpose will also influence the voice you choose to create in your instructions.

❯ For more on creating an appropriate voice, see pp. 463–464.

Visual Information in Context

As you'll see in the Reading to Write section, visual elements must be more than mere decorations—and especially with instructions, where the emphasis is on "reading to do" rather than on "reading to understand." Writers of instructions may use a range of visual elements in order to accomplish a wide range of purposes. As always, you should choose visual elements that are appropriate for your audience, the subject you're explaining, and the purposes you're trying to accomplish.

The visuals you select should help readers accomplish the task at hand and reassure them that they are performing each step correctly. To anticipate readers' needs in terms of visual information, consider two basic questions.

> ❭ Do all the visual elements help the intended readers carry out this procedure?
> ❭ Does the visual information provide reassurance readers may need?

To answer these basic questions, you will need to consider several more specific questions.

❭ For more information on the effective uses of these visual elements, see **Chapter 8.**

Questions to Ask When Reading Visual Information in Instructions

● **Does the layout (arrangement) of the page or screen make it easy for users to see exactly what they need to do?**

❭ Are there useful headings and subheadings? Do they pose questions readers are likely to ask? indicate the major steps readers must take? refer to goals readers are trying to accomplish or actions they must perform?

❭ Are there variations in the size and style of type? What functions do they serve? Do they highlight actions users should take or passages that contain warnings?

❭ Does the layout create a clear visual hierarchy? Can users easily recognize which passages are more important than others? Is it easy to tell which passages provide background information and which ones indicate the steps in the procedure?

● **If there are images (photographs, diagrams, drawings) or other illustrations such as charts, graphs, maps, or tables, how informative and relevant are they?**

❭ Do the images show users what will (or should) happen when they perform a given step?

❭ Is each image clearly connected to the written instruction that accompanies it?

❭ Are charts, graphs, maps, and tables clearly labeled and, if necessary, explained with a title, legend, or key?

❭ Are symbols used consistently?

● **If colors are used, do they make the instructions easier to understand?**

❭ Are colors used appropriately?

❭ Are colors used consistently?

 For Collaboration

Bring to class a set of instructions that presents information in a visual and interesting way. It might contain graphs, tables, and images such as photographs or drawings. Or it might make special use of text, setting it off in columns or sidebars, for example. Working with a small group of students, consider the effects these visual elements create. Then try to determine how these effects are created by referring to the questions listed above. Discuss how the visual elements create a particular effect and how they add to the impressions conveyed through the instructions' written text.

FIGURE 7.1
**Visual Elements in
"The Basics of
PowerPoint,"
Instructions Written
by a Student**

● **Image** Illustration is clearly related to accompanying text.

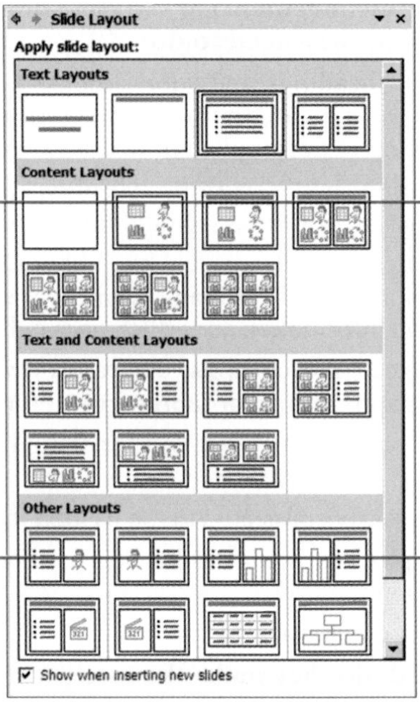

● **Layout** Bulleted list refers to subheadings that follow, beginning on the next page.

● **Layout** Boldface type and white space set off action to be performed.

● **Layout** Headings and sub-headings create a clear visual hierarchy.

New Presentation

Open a presentation
Presentations...

New
Blank Presentation
From Design Template
From AutoContent Wizard

New from existing presentation
Choose presentation...

New from template
Blends.pot
Watermark.pot

Slide Layout

Apply slide layout:

Text Layouts

Content Layouts

Text and Content Layouts

Other Layouts

☑ Show when inserting new slides

Getting Started

1. The task pane to the left will appear. Under the heading **New, click on Blank Presentation**.
2. If the task pane shown here does not appear when you open the program, move on to "Creating Slides," the next step in these instructions.

Creating Slides

Choosing a Type of Slide

PowerPoint lets you create many different types of slides, including:

- text-only slides
- slides with charts
- slides with tables
- slides with clip art or pictures

Each time you create a slide, you first need to choose the type of slide you want to create. You will see a box that shows pictures of different kinds of slides. The pictures are organized into categories in the task pane at left. PowerPoint calls these different types of slides AutoLayouts.

1. In the Slide Layout box, choose the type of slide (AutoLayout) you want to create.
2. **Click on the picture showing the type of slide you've chosen**.

NOTE: There are some very sophisticated types of slides available in the dialog box. They are more difficult to create and are beyond the scope of these instructions.

● **Layout** Distinct typefaces are used for explanations, actions, and technical notes.

● **Layout** Numbered list points out steps to take.

Sample Analysis | # The Basics of PowerPoint

Later in this chapter, in "The Basics of PowerPoint," student MaryBeth Rajczewski explains how to use the presentation software PowerPoint to create slides for an oral presentation. The following analysis of one page of MaryBeth's work will help you see how the preceding questions can be applied to a set of instructions.

The layout of this page (Figure 7.1) is very user-friendly. It creates a clear visual hierarchy: the main heading, Creating Slides, is larger than the subheading Choosing a Type of Slide. In addition, different types of information are made visually distinct through the use of italics for introductory material and numbers to indicate specific steps users are to take. The action to be performed is set off through the use of boldface type and white space (one or two blank lines) before and after each step. Finally, the different types of slides are highlighted in a bulleted list in the middle of the page.

The connections between visual and verbal information are easy to see. A task pane illustrates the material under the subheading Getting Started, where users are told what they will see and what they should do to begin creating a presentation. Later, the instruction for Choosing a Type of Slide is accompanied by a screenshot that shows users the choices they will see when they create slides.

Colors are used to differentiate the levels of headings on the page. The colors used clearly highlight the beginnings of new sections and instructions.

Exercise › bedfordstmartins.com/visualage
Click on **CHAPTER 7** › **VISUALS**

For practice in analyzing the visual information in another set of instructions, see the visual exercises on the companion Web site for this book.

Reading to Write

In your principal assignment for this chapter, you will write a set of instructions that shows someone how to carry out a specific task or procedure or accomplish some goal. The task or goal should be complex and important enough that your intended readers will need substantial help in accomplishing it.

The following readings will help you see not only some of the different strategies you might use in creating your own instructions but also the different kinds of topics about which you might write. Some of the instructions are highly visual; others are primarily verbal. Some are meant to help people create a tangible item, whereas others are intended to help people carry out a procedure or use a technological tool. All of the selections aim to enable people to do something they need or want to do. Each reading is followed by questions (Reflecting on What You Have Read) that will start you thinking about what is involved in creating a useful set of instructions; also, a Thinking Ahead prompt will suggest ways to decide on a topic for your own paper. The subsequent sections of the chapter will help you start your assignment, compose a draft, and assess and revise that draft.

› bedfordstmartins.com/
visualage

*For additional examples
of instructions, click on*
CHAPTER 7 › **EXAMPLES**

In the following instructions, technical writer Crystal Gilson is addressing an audience of medical students—bright, hardworking people who have to perform under stress, often with very little sleep. The instructions explain how to begin a neurological examination, one of a number of exams that medical students must learn to perform. Gilson knows her instructions must be both technically accurate and as simple as possible, given the demands on her student readers' time and energy.

Crystal Gilson

Assessing the Cranial Nerves

What You Will Learn

This set of instructions explains how to perform the first part of the five-part neurological exam. These instructions tell you how to test the 12 cranial nerves and show you expected results as well as abnormal findings. 1

Start the exam with an assessment of the cranial nerves. It is the least intrusive from the patient's point of view. In other words, you are not poking patients with your fingers or prodding them with unfamiliar instruments. By starting with the cranial nerve assessment, you are allowing yourself and the patient time to get used to each other. 2

What You Need to Know

These instructions assume you are familiar with cranial nerve anatomy. If you need to refresh your memory, refer to your neuro-anatomy textbook. Remember that all cranial nerves have *at least* a left and a right branch. In these instructions, "left" and "right" refer to the *patient's* left and right, not yours. 3

Note that you do not test the 12 cranial nerves in the order in which they are labeled. In other words, you do not test cranial nerve I, then II, then III, etc. Some cranial nerves lend themselves to testing in clusters. For example, vision can be crudely assessed while testing ocular movements. That is, patients must be able to *see* in order to follow the movement of your fingers with their eyes. 4

What Materials You Will Need

The following equipment is optional: 5

- some object with a distinctly identifiable aroma, such as an orange (Step 1)
- a tongue depressor (Step 6)
- a pen light (Step 6)

Examination	**Evaluation**

Examination

1. Optional.* Test cranial nerve I (olfactory):

   ❏ ask the patient to close his or her eyes

   ❏ wave an orange below the patient's nose and ask the patient *(with eyes still closed)* to identify the aroma

   *Because most physicians do not have an orange or other distinctly aromatic item handy, they simply ask patients if they are having difficulty smelling.

2. Test cranial nerve II (optic), cranial nerve III (oculomotor), cranial nerve IV (trochlear), and cranial nerve VI (abducens):

   ❏ ask the patient to follow your index finger with his or her eyes without moving the head

   ❏ while you observe the patient's eyes, use your index finger to trace a large letter "N" approximately five inches away from the patient's face *(use the figure below as a guide)*

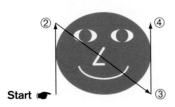

Evaluation

Expected Result:

   • ideally, the patient correctly identifies the aroma, or the patient smells *something**

Abnormal Result:

   • the patient smells *nothing**

*You are testing the patient's ability to smell, not his or her ability to identify the aroma.

Expected Results:

   • the patient sees your finger
   • the patient's eyes follow your finger correctly

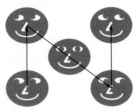

Abnormal Results:

   • the patient cannot see your fingers *(indicates a problem with cranial nerve II)*
   • the patient cannot look up and outward with the right eye and/or up and outward with

Examination	**Evaluation**
	the left eye *(indicates a problem with cranial nerve IV)* • the patient cannot look outward with the right eye and/or outward with the left eye *(indicates a problem with cranial nerve VI)* AND/OR • the patient cannot look in any other direction *(indicates a problem with cranial nerve III)*
3. Test cranial nerve V (trigeminal): ❑ with your index finger, gently stroke the right side, then left side, of the patient's forehead ❑ ask the patient if the strokes feel similar ❑ stroke the patient's right cheek, then the left cheek ❑ ask the patient if the strokes feel similar ❑ stroke the right side, then the left side, if the patient's chin ❑ ask the patient if the strokes feel similar	**Expected Result:** • the patient feels similar* sensations in all six areas you tested **Abnormal Result:** • the patient has no sensation in any or all of the six areas tested *Minor gradations in sensation are probably not important. Lack of sensation is significant and should be noted.*

continued

Examination	Evaluation
4. Test cranial nerve VII (facial):	**Expected Results:**
❑ ask the patient to smile	• the patient has a symmetrical smile
❑ ask the patient to raise his or her eyebrows	

Examination

4. Test cranial nerve VII (facial):

❑ ask the patient to smile
❑ ask the patient to raise his or her eyebrows

Evaluation

Expected Results:

• the patient has a symmetrical smile

• the patient can raise his or her eyebrows symmetrically

Abnormal Results:

• the patient cannot smile or has an asymmetrical smile

• the patient cannot raise the eyebrows or raises them asymmetrically

Examination	**Evaluation**
5. Test cranial nerve VIII (vestibulocochlear): ❏ gently rub your fingers together next to the patient's right ear ❏ gently rub your fingers together next to the patient's left ear ❏ ask the patient if they sound similar	**Expected Result:** • the brushing noises of your fingers being rubbed together sound similar* to the patient **Abnormal Result:** • the patient cannot hear in one or both ears *Minor gradations in sound are probably not important. Lack of hearing is significant and should be noted.*
6. Test cranial nerve IX (glossopharyngeal), cranial nerve X (vagus), and cranial nerve XII (hypoglossal): ❏ ask the patient to open his or her mouth and stick out the tongue ❏ ask the patient to say "ah" while you observe the uvula and the posterior aspect of the roof of the mouth **Hint:** A tongue depressor and pen light may help you see the back of the patient's throat.	**Expected Results:** • the patient can stick out the tongue without deviation to either side of the mouth • there is symmetrical elevation of the patient's uvula and roof of mouth 

continued

Examination	Evaluation
	Abnormal Results: • the patient cannot stick out the tongue *(indicates a problem with cranial nerve XII)* • the tongue deviates to either the left or right side *(indicates a problem with cranial nerve XII)*  • there is either no elevation or asymmetrical elevation of the uvula and roof of mouth **No Elevation of the Uvula** 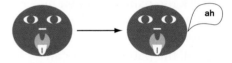 **Asymmetrical Elevation of the Uvula** 
7. Test cranial nerve XI (spinal accessory nerve): ❏ ask the patient to shrug his or her shoulders	**Expected Result:** • the patient can symmetrically raise both shoulders **Abnormal Result:** • the patient cannot raise one or both shoulders

Reflecting on What You Have Read

1 The facial drawings are strikingly simple, appearing as if they were created by a child, not by a professional. Should these drawings be more realistic? Why or why not?

2 If you were a medical student about to conduct a neurological examination, how confident would you be in your ability to diagnose a problem with a patient's optic nerve (cranial nerve II)? How would Gilson's instructions inspire or undermine your confidence?

3 Do you know what the "trigeminal" nerve is? Would you recommend that this term be explained in the instructions? Why or why not?

4 In the Evaluation column, Gilson consistently explains the expected results and the abnormal results. What rationale do you see for this sequencing of information?

Thinking Ahead

The instructions for assessing cranial nerves identify an important job-related procedure that medical students must learn to carry out accurately and efficiently. It's often the case that such procedures are not written down; people have to learn them by talking with other employees and going through a certain amount of trial and error. Can you identify such a procedure at a place where you have worked? Talk with the employees and their supervisors. Would they find it helpful to have a carefully written set of instructions for carrying out this procedure?

One of the main themes of this book—the importance of integrating visual information into your writing—is especially relevant to writing instructions. When you are trying to *show* people how to do something, they often need a clear visual image of how to do it—of the thing they want to create or the procedure they need to carry out. In most cases, visual images are accompanied by written text. But here is an exception: a set of visual instructions that explains through pictures how to assemble a model airplane from a box of about forty pieces. An image of the completed item is followed by several other images that detail steps in the procedure.

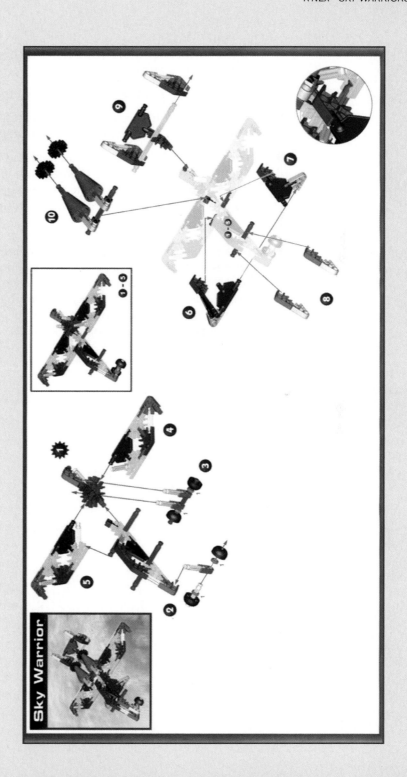

Sky Warrior

**Reflecting on
What You
Have Read**

1 One audience for these instructions is children. How do the instructions appeal to this audience?

2 Why might the instructions also appeal to parents of young children?

3 Why do the instructions break the process of assembling the Sky Warrior into two segments: steps 1–5 and steps 6–10?

4 Look closely at the wing section depicted in step 5 of the instructions. Spend ten minutes writing a paragraph in which you explain, without using visuals, how to assemble this section of the wing. What difficulties do you encounter as you try to write this paragraph?

**Thinking
Ahead**

For many children, building things—airplanes, robots, castles—out of plastic pieces is a hobby; in some cases, it is almost an obsession. Think of other hobbies or pastimes that involve assembling or creating something. Consider creating a set of instructions, perhaps combining words and pictures, that introduces beginners to a hobby or shows experienced users an advanced technique for refining their skills.

While instructions typically aim to help users build something or carry out a technical process, sometimes they focus on solving complex problems of everyday life, problems that do not always lend themselves to neat, tidy solutions. Consequently, when people try to show how to solve these real-life problems, they often oversimplify or make suggestions that are impractical. As you read Caroline Rego's instructions on "The Fine Art of Complaining," which first appeared in a series of articles Rego wrote on consumer empowerment, think about whether you could follow her advice for making "effective" complaints.

The Fine Art of Complaining

CAROLINE REGO

You waited forty-five minutes for your dinner, and when it came it was cold—and not what you ordered in the first place. You washed your supposedly machine-washable, preshrunk T-shirt (the one the catalogue claimed was "indestructible"), and now it's the size of a napkin. Your new car broke down a month after you bought it, and the dealer says the warranty doesn't apply. 1

Life's annoyances descend on all of us—some pattering down like gentle raindrops, others striking with the bruising force of hailstones. We dodge the ones we can, but inevitably, plenty of them make contact. And when they do, we react fairly predictably. Many of us—most of us, probably—grumble to ourselves and take it. We scowl at our unappetizing food but choke it down. We stash the shrunken T-shirt in a drawer, vowing never again to order from a catalogue. We glare fiercely at our checkbooks as we pay for repairs that should have been free. 2

A few of us go to the other extreme. Taking our cue from the crazed newscaster in the 1976 movie *Network,* we go through life mad as hell and unwilling to take it anymore. In offices, we shout at hapless receptionists 3 when we're kept waiting for appointments. In restaurants, we make scenes that have fellow patrons craning their necks to get a look at us. In stores, we argue with salespeople for not waiting on us. We may notice after a while that our friends seem reluctant to venture into public with us, but hey—we're just standing up for our rights. Being a patsy doesn't get you anywhere in life.

It's true—milquetoasts live unsatisfying lives. However, people who go through the day in an eye-popping, vein-throbbing state of apoplectic rage don't win any prizes either. What persons at both ends of the scale need—what could empower the silent sufferer and civilize the Neanderthal—is a course in the gentle art of *effective* complaining. 4

Effective complaining is not apologetic and half-hearted. It's not making one awkward attempt at protest—"Uh, excuse me, I don't think I ordered the squid and onions"—and then slinking away in defeat. But neither is it roaring away indiscriminately, attempting to get satisfaction through the sheer volume of our complaint. 5

Effective complainers are people who act businesslike and 6

important. Acting important doesn't mean puffing up your chest and saying, "Do you know who I am?"—an approach that would tempt anyone to take you down a peg or two. It doesn't mean shouting and threatening—techniques that will only antagonize the person whose help you need. It *does* mean making it clear that you know your request is reasonable and that you are confident it will be taken care of. People are generally treated the way they expect to be treated. If you act like someone making a fair request, chances are that request will be granted. Don't beg, don't explain. Just state your name, the problem, and what you expect to have done. Remain polite. But be firm. "My car has been in your garage for three days, and a mechanic hasn't even looked at it yet," you might say. "I want to know when it is going to be worked on." Period. Now it is up to them to give you a satisfactory response. Don't say, "Sorry to bother you about this, but . . . " or "I, uh, was sort of expecting. . . . " You're only asking people to remedy a problem, after all; that is not grounds for apology.

If your problem requires an immediate response, try to make your complaint in person; a real, live, in-the-flesh individual has to be dealt with in some way. Complaining over the telephone, by contrast, is much less effective. When you speak to a disembodied voice, when the person at the other end of the line doesn't have to face you, you're more likely to get a runaround.

Most importantly, complain to the right person. One of the greatest frustrations in complaining is talking to a clerk or receptionist who cannot solve your problem and whose only purpose seems to be to drive you crazy. Getting mad doesn't help; the person you're mad at probably had nothing to do with your actual problem. And you'll have to repeat everything you've said to the

clerk once you're passed along to the appropriate person. So make sure from the start that you're talking to someone who can help—a manager or supervisor.

If your problem doesn't require an immediate response, complaining by letter is probably the most effective way to get what you want. A letter of complaint should be brief, businesslike, and to the point. If you have a new vacuum cleaner that doesn't work, don't spend a paragraph describing how your Uncle Joe tried to fix the problem and couldn't. As when complaining in person, be sure you address someone in a position of real authority. Here's an example of an effective letter of complaint.

Ms. Anne Lublin
Manager
Mitchell Appliances
80 Front Street
Newton, MA 02159

Dear Ms. Lublin:

First section: Explain the problem. Include facts to back up your story.

On August 6, I purchased a new Perma-Kool freezer from your store (a copy of my sales receipt is enclosed). In the two weeks I have owned the freezer, I have had to call your repair department three times in an attempt to get it running properly. The freezer ran normally when it was installed, but since then it has repeatedly turned off, causing the food inside to spoil. My calls to your repair department have not been responded to promptly. After I called the first time, on August 10, I waited two days for the repair person to show up. It took three days to get a repair person here after my second call, on August 15. The freezer stopped yet again on August 20. I called to discuss this recent problem, but no one has responded to my call.

Second section: Tell how you trust the company and are confident that your reader will fix the problem. This is to "soften up" the reader a bit.

I am surprised to receive such unprofessional service and poor quality from Mitchell Appliances since I have been one of your satisfied customers for fifteen years. In the past, I have purchased a television, air conditioner, and washing machine from your company. I know that you value good relations with your customers, and I'm sure you want to see me pleased with my most recent purchase.

Third section: Explain exactly what you want to be done—repair, replacement, refund, etc.

Although your repair department initially thought that the freezer needed only some minor adjustments, the fact that no one has been able to permanently fix the problem convinces me that the freezer has some serious defect. I am understandably unwilling to spend any more time having repairs made. Therefore, I expect you to exchange the freezer for an identical model by the end of this week (August 30). Please call me to arrange for the removal of the defective freezer and the delivery of the new one.

Sincerely,

Janice Becker

P.S. (Readers always notice a P.S.) State again when you expect the problem to be taken care of, and what you will do if it isn't.

P.S. I am confident that we can resolve this problem by August 30. If the defective freezer is not replaced by then, however, I will report this incident to the Better Business Bureau.

Notice that the P.S. says what you'll do if 10 your problem isn't solved. In other words, you make a threat—a polite threat. Your threat must be reasonable and believable. A threat to burn down the store if your purchase price isn't refunded is neither reasonable nor believable—or if it *were* believed, you could end up in jail. A threat to report the store to a consumer-protection agency, such as the Better Business Bureau, however, is credible.

Don't be too quick to make one of the 11 most common—and commonly empty—threats: "I'll sue!" A full-blown lawsuit is more trouble, and more expensive, than most problems are worth. On the other hand, most areas have a small-claims court where suits involving modest amounts of money are heard. These courts don't use complex legal language or procedures, and you don't need a lawyer to use them. A store or company will often settle with you—if your claim is fair—rather than go to small-claims court.

Whether you complain over the 12 phone, in person, or by letter, be persistent. One complaint may not get results. In that case, keep on complaining, and make sure you keep complaining to the same person. Chances are he or she will get worn out and take care of the situation, if only to be rid of you.

Someday, perhaps, the world will be 13 free of the petty annoyances that plague us all from time to time. Until then, however, toasters will break down, stores will refuse to honor rainchecks, and bills will include items that were never purchased. You can depend upon it—there will be grounds for complaint. You might as well learn to be good at it.

Reflecting on What You Have Read

1 What is your assessment of Rego's instructions? Do you feel you could or would use them in making a complaint? Why or why not?

2 Why does Rego begin by listing several of "life's annoyances [that] descend on all of us"?

3 Gilson begins "Assessing the Cranial Nerves" by stating exactly "what [users] will learn." Would you recommend that Rego begin her instructions in a similar fashion? Why or why not?

4 Rego uses italics in several passages. What reasons do you see for her use of italics? Do these reasons vary from one passage to another? If so, how?

5 In what ways do the pages of Rego's instructions look different from Gilson's instructions? What reasons do you see for these differences?

Thinking Ahead

Many real-life problems are dealt with in advice columns that offer commonsense recommendations. Other problems, however, require a plan of action—a series of steps one needs to take to train for a competitive sport or manage a club or organization, for example. Think about the organizations (clubs, sports, businesses) to which you belong. What are some problems these organizations face? Are there any that could be solved by following a plan of action comparable to the one Rego recommends?

You may never perform a neurological examination or build a Sky Warrior model. But as a student, you will probably make oral presentations that involve the use of PowerPoint or similar presentation software. The following set of instructions—written by MaryBeth Rajczewski, a math major taking her first technical writing course—introduces PowerPoint users to some of the basics of using the program, including how to create visuals or "slides" for an oral presentation.

MaryBeth Rajczewski

The Basics of PowerPoint

Microsoft PowerPoint is the premiere presentation software. It enables you to create professional presentations in a short amount of time. Presentations using PowerPoint are generally more respected than those using standard overhead transparencies. These instructions will teach you how to create a simple PowerPoint presentation.

Who Should Use These Instructions?

You should use these instruction if you:

- need or want to learn to use PowerPoint to create a presentation
- have not used PowerPoint before
- have used PowerPoint before, but have only limited experience
- have lots of PowerPoint experience, but would like a refresher

You should not use these instructions if you:

- are an expert at PowerPoint
- have absolutely no computer experience

What Are the Prerequisites?

- These instructions assume you know some basics about computers; for example, you know how to navigate through a menu of options, you know how to use a mouse, and you know terms such as click and drag.
- If you want to add charts or graphs to your slides, you must know how to create charts and graphs in Microsoft

Excel or a similar spreadsheet application. If you want to learn how to create charts and graphs, there are many Microsoft Excel reference books available.

What Equipment Is Necessary?

- A PC that has Microsoft PowerPoint loaded on it.
- A working mouse.

Once you complete the steps in these instructions, you will be able to create basic PowerPoint presentations. You will also know how to use some of the key features that enable you to make more professional presentations. Since PowerPoint is such a powerful tool, there are many features that cannot be discussed in these basic instructions. Once you become familiar with the basics, you are encouraged to learn about some of the more sophisticated features. You'll be amazed at all you can do with PowerPoint.

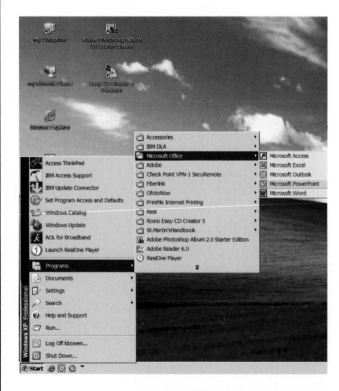

Creating a New Presentation

Opening PowerPoint

1. **Click on the Start icon** in the bottom left corner of the screen.

2. Use your mouse to **move the cursor up to Programs**.

3. From Programs, **move your cursor over to Microsoft PowerPoint**.

4. **Click on Microsoft PowerPoint** when this box is highlighted.

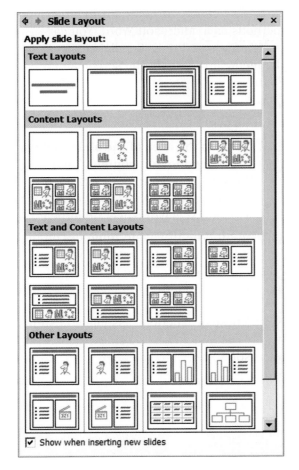

Getting Started

1. The task pane to the left will appear. Under the heading New, **click Blank Presentation**.

2. If the task pane shown here does not appear when you open the program, move on to "Creating Slides," the next step in these instructions.

Creating Slides

Choosing a Type of Slide

PowerPoint lets you create many different types of slides, including:

- text-only slides
- slides with charts
- slides with tables
- slides with clip art or pictures

Each time you create a slide, you first need to choose the type of slide you want to create. You will see a box that shows pictures of different kinds of slides. The pictures are organized into categories in the task pane at left. PowerPoint calls these different types of slides AutoLayouts.

1. In the Slide Layout box, choose the type of slide (AutoLayout) you want to create.

2. **Click on the picture showing the type of slide you've chosen**.

NOTE: There are some very sophisticated types of slides available in the dialog box. They are more difficult to create and are beyond the scope of these instructions.

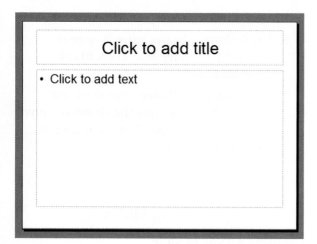

Adding Information to Your Slide

There are different instructions for each type of slide you can create. Follow the instructions for the type of slide you chose in the previous step.

Text-Only Slides

1. Add text to different areas of the slide by **clicking in areas that say "Click to add..."** and then **typing your text**.

NOTE: Text can be formatted using the same methods as in Microsoft Word. You can modify fonts and sizes by clicking Format on the menu at the top of the screen and then Fonts.

Slides with Charts

1. **Click on the area of the slide that says "Click icon to add content,"** and select the small icon that looks like a bar graph. A sample chart will be displayed with an Excel worksheet underneath.
2. **Modify the titles and numbers** on the Excel worksheet. The chart will automatically change to include the new information.

NOTE: These instructions assume you know how to create and modify charts using Microsoft Excel.

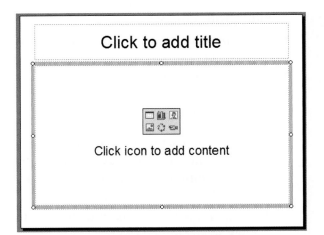

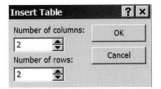

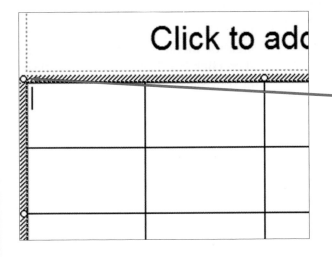

Slides with Tables

To Create a Slide

1. **Click on the area of the slide that says "Click icon to add content,"** and select the small icon that looks like a table. The Insert Table dialog box will appear.

2. **Enter the number of columns.**

3. **Press Tab** on your keyboard.

4. **Enter the number of rows.**

5. **Click OK.** The table will appear on your slide.

To Modify a Slide

1. To add information, **click the cell you want** or **press Tab** to move from one cell to the next.

2. To resize a table:

   a. **Click and hold** a box in any corner.

   b. **Drag your mouse** until you have made the table smaller or larger.

Slides with Clip Art

Microsoft makes available many types of clip-art images that you can import into your Power-Point presentation. You can also insert any other pictures into a slide that you have stored on your computer.

1. To view clip art options, **Click on the area of the slide that says "Click icon to add content."** A dialog box labeled Select Picture will appear.

2. An alternate way to insert pictures is to **click Insert** on the toolbar at the top of the screen. Then **click Picture** and then **Clip Art**. An Insert Clip Art task pane will appear.

3. Use the search box to use keywords to search. All the pictures available in that category will appear.

4. **Use the scroll bar on the right** to search through the pictures.

5. If you find a picture you want to insert, **click the picture.** A menu will appear. Then **click OK**. The picture will appear on your slide.

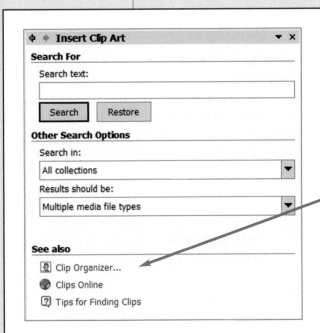

6. If you don't find a picture that you like:

   a. **Click the Clip Organizer**. A dialog box will open with a collection list. You can browse categories of clips under Office Collections.

   b. **Click Clips Online** to connect to Microsoft's library of additional clip art, searchable and organized by category.

Inserting the Next Slide

1. To create the next slide in your presentation, **click Insert** on the toolbar at the top of the screen.

2. **Click New Slide.**

3. Go back to the instructions for "Creating Slides" and complete the steps for "Choosing a Type of Slide" and "Adding Information to Your Slide."

4. Repeat this process for each new slide you want to create for your presentation.

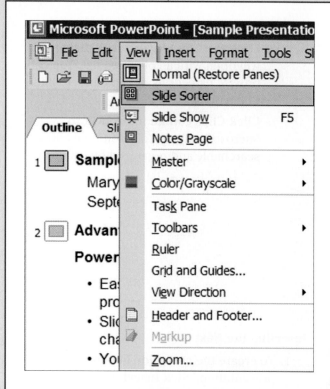

Looking at Your Presentation

Viewing All Your Slides

Once you have created all the slides you need, you can view all of them on the screen at the same time. This enables you to determine if any changes need to be made and helps you prepare for the order and timing of the presentation.

1. **Click View** on the toolbar at the top of the screen.
2. **Click Slide Sorter.** You will see small versions of all your slides.

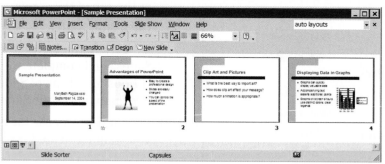

NOTE: In Slide Sorter View, you can delete slides, hide slides, change the order of slides, modify slides, and perform other tasks. These advanced features are beyond the scope of these instructions; assistance can be found in PowerPoint's Help feature.

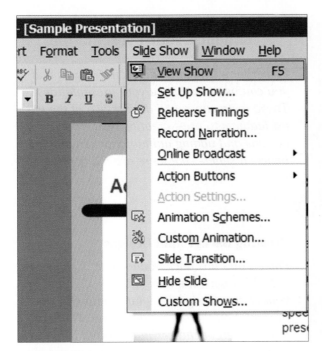

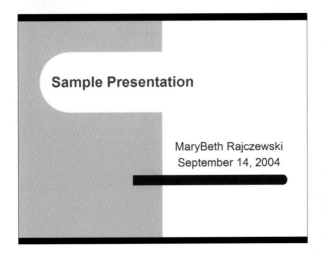

Viewing Your PowerPoint Presentation

You will show your completed presentation as a slide show. Your slides will appear one at a time on a full computer screen or an overhead projection screen, depending on how you give the presentation. You should practice viewing your show as a slide show at least once before you give your presentation to prepare your timing and coordinate the slides with any comments you want to make.

1. **Click Slide Show** on the toolbar at the top of the screen
2. **Click View Show.** The first slide in your presentation will appear on the screen.
3. **Use the spacebar or click the mouse to move from one slide to the next.** (To back up a slide, use the left arrow key.)

NOTE: The rectangle that sits in the bottom left-hand corner of the screen during your presentation allows you to view your slides in a different order or to end the show immediately. Click on the rectangle during the presentation to see these options.

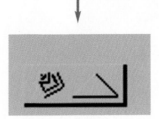

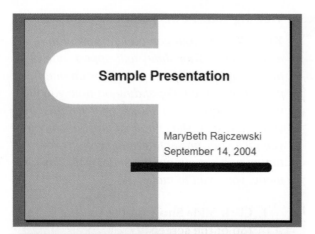

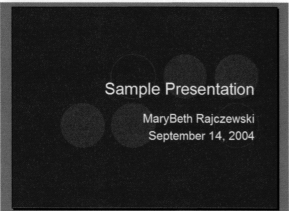

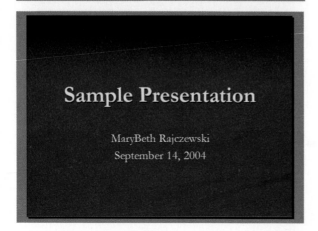

Using PowerPoint Features to Enhance Your Presentation

PowerPoint has many different features that you can use to enhance your presentations. These instructions will discuss two of the easiest features to use—creating background designs and adding animation when moving between slides—but there are many others.

Creating Background Designs

PowerPoint has background slide designs called Design Templates that you can add to your slides. Design Templates help give your presentation the appropriate tone. There are many different choices in PowerPoint—I have demonstrated three in the accompanying pictures. Each Design Template can also be customized using color schemes.

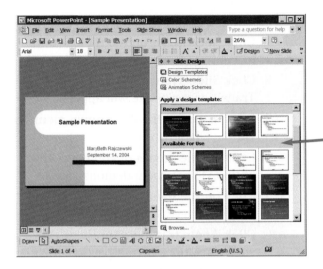

Choosing a Design Template

1. **Click Format** on the toolbar at the top of the screen.

2. **Click Slide Design.** A task pane showing design templates will appear.

3. **Click on the picture of a template.** The design will be applied to all the slides in your presentation.

4. To apply a different color scheme, **click Color Schemes**. To apply a color scheme only to specific slides, click on the box at the right of the design's picture and **click on Apply to Selected Slides**.

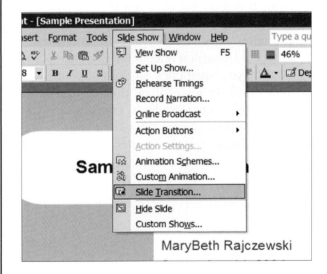

Adding Animation When Moving between Slides

When you move from one slide to the next, the next slide will simply appear on the screen. PowerPoint allows you to make your presentations more interesting by adding animation when moving between slides. The animations are called Slide Transitions; they allow you to choose how the slide will appear on the screen. For example, if you choose the transition Wipe Right each slide will appear as though it is starting on the left side of the screen and slowly moving right until it is centered on the screen.

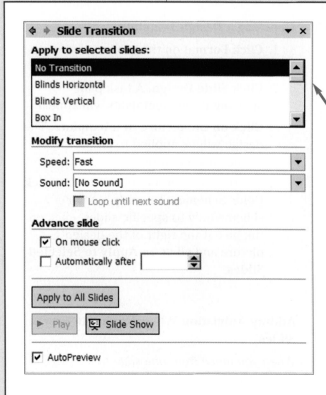

Choosing a Slide Transition

1. **Click Slide Show** on the toolbar at the top of the screen.

2. **Click Slide Transition.** The Slide Transition task pane will appear.

3. **Scroll through the drop-down menu** to view available options.

4. **Click on the names of some transition options** to see them demonstrated.

5. **Click on the name of the transition** you want to use.

6. **Click Apply to All** if desired, or vary your transitions to suit particular slides or sections of your presentation.

NOTE: If you do not click Apply to All, only the current slide selected will have this transition effect. Some users prefer to create different transition effects for each slide. To do this, you must click on each of your slides in Slide Sorter View, then complete the steps for "Choosing a Slide Transition." Continue this process until all of your slides have different transition effects.

Reflecting on What You Have Read

1 Assume that you have never used PowerPoint and you want to learn how to create slides incorporating clip art. Which sections in MaryBeth's instructions would you need to read? Is it easy to find the information you need? Why or why not?

2 Skim through "Assessing the Cranial Nerves" and "The Basics of Power-Point." Both make extensive use of visuals. What important differences do you see in the way each set of instructions uses visuals? What do these differences reveal about each author's understanding of her audience?

3 "The Basics of PowerPoint" begins with background information about the presentation software and information about who should and should not use this set of instructions, whereas "Assessing the Cranial Nerves" does not. Why do you think MaryBeth chose to begin with these sorts of information? What assumptions about her audience and purpose can you use to justify your answer?

Thinking Ahead

Technology-based products, especially computer-related items, too often come with instructions that are incomplete or confusing, leaving consumers struggling to figure out how to use the products. Think of a technology-based product—such as a computer application, digital camera, or MP3 player—that came with such poorly written instructions that you had to rely on trial and error or help from friends or a technical support person to figure out how to use it. Consider writing a clear set of instructions for that item for future users.

Instructions

Create a set of instructions that will enable someone to carry out a complex procedure or accomplish a challenging goal. Provide a detailed, helpful answer to the question, "How do I do this?" As you saw in the Reading to Write selections, the question may be about a specific procedure ("The Basics of PowerPoint") or a more abstract topic ("The Fine Art of Complaining"). Similarly, the answer to this question may take different forms, ranging from an instruction manual to a magazine article. In all cases, your work is not finished until the intended readers can actually carry out the procedure or accomplish the goal they have in mind.

Your instructor may have specific requirements about how long the instructions should be, what sort of topic to write about, whether to prepare a print or online document, and whether to include or exclude any particular visual elements. Be sure you understand these requirements before you start working on the assignment.

Guide to Writing Instructions

You may find that your plan for writing clear, complete instructions will work out perfectly, but you shouldn't be discouraged if it doesn't happen on the first try. Your understanding of your audience, circumstances, and purposes may shift as you work on your instructions, or you may discover that your original topic does not work well for some reason. That's fine. Projects do not always end up exactly the way you expect them to. Your ideas should develop over the course of working on the project.

The remainder of this chapter will help you through the process of creating a clear set of instructions that others can use to carry out a procedure or accomplish a goal. The first step is covered in Getting Started— selecting a topic and analyzing the context in which your instructions will be used. Then you'll learn some strategies that can help you in Drafting. Specifically, you'll learn things you can do in order to develop your topic (that is, find something to say), write an introduction that engages your readers, create an appropriate voice, provide a clear structure, conclude your instructions effectively, and design your instructions, using visual elements appropriate to your subject and audience. Finally, in Finishing Up, you will receive guidance in creating a review draft, assessing your work carefully, and using that assessment to revise your instructions.

Guide to Writing Instructions

Getting Started

Choosing a workable topic for your instructions can be problematic. Some topics are too straightforward, involving so few steps or so little complexity that users need little in the way of instruction. Other topics may be too complex, requiring a complete manual rather than several pages. Like Goldilocks, you may have trouble selecting a topic that is "just right" in terms of its length and complexity. And even when you identify a procedure that might be a workable topic, you still have the problem of understanding the context in which your instructions will be used. The following sections will help you solve both of these problems.

Selecting a Topic

One conventional bit of advice might be to write instructions for a procedure you understand thoroughly. Such a topic might work well for you. But consider an alternative: a topic about which you know something but still need to learn a good bit more. This sort of topic may actually help you do a better job on this assignment. If you thoroughly understand a procedure and can do it without much conscious effort, you may find it hard to understand the difficulties a less experienced person may have in carrying out the procedure. You may also find it easier to help someone else get past the tricky spots if some of them are still fresh in your own mind.

As you think of possible topics, keep the following guidelines in mind.

> Choose a procedure or goal that a specific person or group actually needs or wants to learn to do. Don't write about how to tune an automobile engine unless you know someone who intends to use your instructions to save on auto repair bills.

> Choose a procedure or goal that your audience will find challenging because it involves a number of steps that must be carried out in a specified sequence or in a particular manner.

> Make sure your audience can carry out the procedure or accomplish the goal successfully and within a relatively short period of time, perhaps within an hour or so.

STUDENT DIALOGUE: SELECTING A TOPIC

Writing in a Visual Age (WVA): What topics did you consider writing about?

MaryBeth Rajczewski (MBR): At first I was going to explain how to book a trip online. But that didn't seem complicated enough, and the instructions already available were pretty sufficient, so I didn't think anyone needed new ones.

WVA: Why did you choose PowerPoint?

MBR: I remembered a job where I did a couple of PowerPoint presentations and the other people thought it was a good idea. But a lot of them didn't know how to use PowerPoint. Then I realized that PowerPoint is software that a lot of people have on their computers but might not necessarily know how to use. Also, I wanted a topic that would let me give a good amount of information but that would also let people accomplish something useful by reading just a few pages.

Selecting a Topic

As you think of possible topics for this assignment, look back at the Thinking Ahead prompts that follow the readings in this chapter. Also think of times when you learned how to do something new or taught someone else how to do something.

Brainstorm, drawing on your own experience and observations.

> Do you have a hobby—photography, for example—that requires you to carry out complex procedures? Do you know anyone who is new to the hobby and needs to learn how to carry out some of the procedures?

> Have you ever been responsible for organizing an event, one that required a lot of careful preparation? Is there anyone who would benefit from knowing exactly what has to be done, when it has to be done, and how to avoid likely pitfalls?

> Have you taught a younger sibling or a classmate how to do something that other people may need to learn how to do?

> Have you ever taught new employees how to carry out a complicated procedure, such as operating a computer system or supervising a restaurant for a day?

> Have you (or has someone you know) had to use a set of instructions that were needlessly difficult, confusing, or incomplete?

> What tasks are you currently having difficulty with? Is there a laboratory procedure you and your classmates don't quite understand? a piece of computer software you need to learn how to use?

Work with a group of classmates and compare your lists. Once you have a list of a half-dozen or more topics, work with a few other students to identify the most promising ones. Look for topics that meet the guidelines suggested earlier (p. 448).

Choose one topic based on the conversation with your small group.

Brainstorm, writing quickly and informally a list of statements about the topic. Who needs help in carrying out this task? Why? When and for what purposes would someone need to perform this task?

Explain your choice to your classmates and instructor, stating why you have chosen to write about this particular task or goal. Make sure you can explain how the topic meets the three guidelines listed in Selecting a Topic.

Once you have identified a topic that you might like to write instructions for, you need to do some preliminary data gathering, making notes about what you learn.

Examine your own experience. Where and how will you get the information you need to show someone else how to do this task or accomplish this goal? Will you be able to draw on your own experience? Do you have any anecdotes or information that seem relevant?

Talk with others. Are there people you can consult about how to do the task correctly? What are their experiences?

Do some reading. Are there some existing instructions that explain the task poorly? Don't try to read everything carefully at this point. Read enough to confirm that your topic is worthwhile and that there is plenty of instructional material for you to consult.

Look for visual information that provides insight into the procedure or task.

Analyzing Context

On the face of it, writing instructions might seem like a fairly simple assignment. All you have to do is figure out the specific steps people need to take in order to carry out a procedure or accomplish a goal. But how much detail do you have to give readers about each step? How can you get them to persevere, performing each step exactly as it needs to be done? To answer these questions, you need to understand the physical and psychological contexts in which your instructions will be used.

Assessing Physical Context

Assume that you are writing a set of instructions for assembling the pre-fabricated parts of a relatively large piece of furniture, such as a desk or a computer stand. You can make several assumptions about the physical context in which your instructions will be used. First, your readers are probably not highly accomplished woodworkers; such people could build their own desks from scratch. So your users will probably be assembling pieces at home rather than in a workshop, and they may have access to only the most basic tools. Second, the instructions will likely be set out on a worktable or the floor and glanced at occasionally as the user attempts to line up pieces of wood or attach brackets to a desk drawer. Finally, you know that the printed text and accompanying visuals will have to be relatively large and simple—and this, in turn, means that each page can contain only a small number of steps, each illustrated so clearly and specifically that a person who is not an expert can follow the steps with a minimum of frustration.

STUDENT DIALOGUE: ASSESSING PHYSICAL CONTEXT

Writing in a Visual Age: In what physical context will your readers use your instructions? How did you decide what format to use?

MaryBeth Rajczewski: One thing I always notice, when you're using instructions with the computer, is you have to do a lot of looking back and forth between the printed instructions and the computer screen. So I knew it would be important for my instructions to be easily visible. That way when my readers glance at the computer and then glance back at the instructions, they can pick up on the page where they just left off.

Assessing Psychological Context

In addition to considering the physical circumstances, you need to consider the psychological context in which your instructions will be used. That is, you need to take into account the knowledge, preconceptions, misconceptions, and attitudes with which your user is approaching the task. Sometimes readers may be intimidated by the procedure you're explaining, in which case they may be feeling stressed and dubious about their ability to carry it out. Even competent and confident people may feel this way. For example, the instructions for carrying out a neurological exam (p. 419) are intended for a sophisticated group of users—medical students—who are under a great deal of pressure to learn how to perform specialized tests quickly and accurately. Consequently, they need to have an unfamiliar procedure laid out so clearly and simply that they cannot make a mistake. In other situations, your users may be feeling relatively little stress. For example, the instructions for building the Sky Warrior (p. 427) assume that users are eager to begin the task of assembling the model plane and need only to be shown what parts fit where.

> ### STUDENT DIALOGUE: ASSESSING PSYCHOLOGICAL CONTEXT
>
> **Writing in a Visual Age:** How would you describe the psychological context of the audience you're writing for?
>
> **MaryBeth Rajczewski:** Let's say your boss says, "You have to do a presentation on Tuesday, and it would be good if you used PowerPoint." You're motivated, but there may be some anxiety if you haven't worked with PowerPoint before. So you want instructions to ease your mind—to make you feel that you can get through this. So the instructions have to ease any anxieties or pressures you're feeling.

Your sense of the psychological context will shape the purposes you want to achieve in your instructions. Your basic purpose, of course, will always remain the same: helping users do something they need or want to do. But in order to accomplish that basic purpose, you may have to achieve related purposes—trying to reassure users, for example, or motivating them to complete a task they may be reluctant to undertake.

In order to analyze the physical and psychological contexts in which your instructions will be used, think in terms of one or two individual readers who will work through your instructions. Once you've identified a typical individual, you need to answer questions about his or her knowledge, values, and needs; expectations for content and layout or format; and the circumstances in which he or she will encounter your instructions. You should also answer questions about your own purpose for doing this type of writing. By asking and answering these questions, you analyze the context for your instructions and establish a basis for making wise decisions about what to say and how to say it.

Questions for Analyzing Context

Audience knowledge, values, and needs

> What sorts of experiences (personal or secondhand) have my readers had with the procedure I am explaining?

> How will this procedure help my readers accomplish some goal associated with doing a job or pursuing a hobby?

> Do my readers have any biases or preconceptions concerning the procedure I am explaining? If so, what are they, and do I have any information that will correct (or reinforce) those attitudes?

Audience expectations for content

> What aspects of the procedure are likely to be confusing or difficult for my readers?

> What questions are my readers likely to want to have answered?

> What kinds of information are my readers likely to value?

Audience expectations for layout or format

> Which reading in this chapter comes closest to looking the way my readers will expect my instructions to look?

> Are there any visual features (for example, photographs, charts, or numbered lists) that my readers are likely to expect or appreciate?

> Are there ways in which my instructions will need to look different from the readings in this chapter?

Circumstances

> Where, when, and why will my readers be using my instructions?

> What physical or psychological circumstances might make it difficult for my readers to follow my instructions?

Purposes

> Beyond helping someone carry out a task or accomplish a goal, what purposes am I trying to accomplish in writing my instructions? (See discussion of purposes, p. 414.) Do I, for example, need to reassure or motivate my readers?

> bedfordstmartins.com/
visualage

To download these questions as a work-sheet, click on
CHAPTER 7 >
WORKSHEETS

❯ What sort of voice do I want readers to hear when they read my instructions? (For a discussion of voice, see pp. 463–464 of this chapter.)

The activities in the Working on the Assignment: Analyzing Context box below will help you think through and prepare to answer the Questions for Analyzing Context.

Working on the Assignment

Analyzing Context

The following activities will help you develop a thorough understanding of the context in which your instructions will be used.

Draw on your own experiences and observations. Jot down some notes in response to the following questions. Where are readers likely to be when they carry out the procedure you are explaining—at an office, a construction site, home workshop, or computer lab? Is there anything about that physical setting that makes it easy or difficult to perform the task? Under what circumstances will they be working? Is there a time deadline? Will readers have to complete the procedure you are explaining before they can complete some larger task? What does this procedure accomplish? Why is it important that readers do it correctly? Think back to the first time you tried to carry out the procedure you are explaining. How confident were you in your ability to carry out the procedure? Did any prior experiences influence your feelings?

Talk with other people who have to perform the procedure. Talk not only with people who understand the procedure thoroughly but also with those who are just beginning to work with it. In what ways are their experiences similar to or different from your own? What questions did they have when they first began? What problems did they need help solving?

After you have thought through the preceding questions, complete your own context analysis. As you work on the instructions, your understanding of your audience may change. You may, for example, get a clearer idea of what the audience knows or expects, or you may revise your ideas about the sort of format that is appropriate. Consequently, you may want to revise your responses to the Questions for Analyzing Context as you work on your instructions. But for now, be as specific as possible.

STUDENT CONTEXT ANALYSIS

Here's how MaryBeth Rajczewski answered
these questions for the instructions she wrote,
"The Basics of PowerPoint" (p. 433).

Audience Knowledge, Values, and Needs

What sorts of experiences (personal or secondhand) have my readers had with the procedure I am explaining?

Members of my audience have seen PowerPoint presentations but have never tried to use PowerPoint to make slides.

How will this procedure help my readers accomplish some goal associated with doing a job or pursuing a hobby?

My readers will likely want to create an effective oral presentation, either for a class or for their job.

Do my readers have any biases or preconceptions concerning the procedure I am explaining? If so, what are they, and do I have any information that will correct (or reinforce) those attitudes?

Some people in my audience may feel that the program is too "high tech" for them to use easily.

Audience Expectations for Content

What aspects of the procedure are likely to be confusing or difficult for my readers?

The part about adding information to slides may be confusing, since there are slightly different procedures for adding information to each type of slide.

What questions are my readers likely to want to have answered?

How do I get started? Will this be difficult?

Am I experienced enough with computers to use this program?

Once I've created the slides, how do I actually give the presentation?

What kinds of information are my readers likely to value?

They are likely to value shortcuts or anything that will make their task as uncomplicated as possible.

STUDENT CONTEXT ANALYSIS

Audience Expectations for Layout or Format

Which reading in this chapter comes closest to looking the way my readers will expect my instructions to look? Are there any visual features (for example, photographs, charts, or numbered lists) that my readers are likely to expect or appreciate? Are there ways in which my instructions will need to look different from the readings in this chapter?

They will expect my instructions to look sort of like "Assessing the Cranial Nerves" (p. 419)—a step-by-step guide, including both text and images.

Circumstances

Where, when, and why will my readers be using my instructions?

My instructions will be used at a desk with a computer, either at home or at work. Readers will have to look back and forth from the instructions to the computer screen.

What physical or psychological circumstances might make it difficult for my readers to follow my instructions?

They may feel nervous and stressed about getting the task done on time. However, they will be highly motivated to complete the task.

Purposes

Beyond helping others carry out a task or accomplish a goal, what purposes am I trying to accomplish in writing my instructions? Do I, for example, need to reassure or motivate my readers?

I designed these instructions for people who use the computer primarily for word processing and are nervous about using PowerPoint. As they work through the instructions, they should feel that they know exactly what they are supposed to be doing. And that is what I was going for, the feeling that "I can do this. I'm not worried about this."

What sort of voice do I want readers to hear when they read my instructions?

I don't want to talk down to my users, but I want to be as clear and helpful as possible. I want them to feel that they have a friend who is taking them through the process.

Drafting

The instructions you write for this chapter will likely look very different from other assignments you have done. For example, you may include more illustrations or make more extensive use of graphic elements such as inset boxed text or bulleted and numbered lists. In addition, as noted earlier, your readers will be reading more to do or accomplish something than to understand. This means that they may be less interested in understanding why or how something functions and more concerned with finding out exactly what they have to do in order to complete the task or accomplish the goal.

In spite of these differences, your responsibilities as a writer remain the same: to develop your topic, engage your audience, create an appropriate voice, and so on. You may or may not have to provide a conclusion, but you will need to design your instructions effectively, giving users visual cues that will help them carry out the task you are explaining. As in other chapters in this book, you will be working with strategies that will assist you in meeting these responsibilities.

Developing Your Topic

In order to create a good set of instructions, you will, of course, have to know exactly what readers will need to do in order to carry out their task or accomplish their goal. But you will also have to understand your topic well enough to clarify points at which readers are likely to become confused and to help them recover from mistakes and avoid dangers they might not be aware of. To develop this understanding, you will need to draw on your personal experience with your topic and on secondary sources as well.

Drawing on Personal Experience

The single most important way to develop your topic for this assignment is to carry out the procedure yourself. Ironically, the more difficulty you initially have in carrying out the procedure, the better chance you'll have of writing useful instructions. When you are thoroughly experienced in a

STUDENT DIALOGUE: DRAWING ON PERSONAL EXPERIENCE

Writing in a Visual Age: How did you go about developing your topic?

MaryBeth Rajczewski: Just to make sure I knew exactly what steps I wanted to include, I went through and made a sample PowerPoint presentation. I asked myself, "What would I do first? What would I do second?" And I jotted down notes to make sure I was actually doing it the way I thought I would.

procedure, you may forget to mention actions that have become almost second nature to you, and you may even find it hard to remember ever having trouble with the task. But when you struggle to learn how to do something unfamiliar, you have a much clearer sense of both the difficulties others may have and the kinds of information they need to know.

Using Secondary Sources

Although your instructions will be largely based on what you learn by carrying out the procedure yourself, you should also consult secondary sources—that is, any existing instructions for your procedure. Pay careful attention to especially helpful passages as well as incomplete or confusing ones. If you find that the existing instructions are basically clear and complete, you should probably consider a different topic. Also consider whether any existing instructions written for experienced users might be substantially revised for novice users. However, in this case check with your instructor to be sure the revisions will satisfy the requirements of the assignment.

In addition, consult with people who understand the procedure better than you do. Ask them to talk you through it. Make notes about problems you encounter while trying to follow their instructions and about the helpful tips they offer.

STUDENT DIALOGUE: USING SECONDARY SOURCES

Writing in a Visual Age: Did you use any secondary sources in preparing your PowerPoint instructions?

MaryBeth Rajczewski: I was pretty sure there were easy ways to create a PowerPoint presentation, but I asked my father for advice because he uses PowerPoint a lot. I wanted to make sure I really was telling my readers the easiest way to do this.

Creating an Exploratory Draft

As you work through the procedure for which you will write your instructions, keep careful notes about every step you have to take, everything that goes wrong, and every helpful hint you receive from a secondary source. Once you have reached a point where you can carry out the procedure correctly, you will be ready to write an exploratory draft that will help you determine what you currently know and what you may still need to find out in order to write effective instructions.

Creating an Exploratory Draft

Before starting the exploratory draft, take a close look at the context analysis you completed earlier (p. 454). Do you have questions that aren't completed very well? For example, are you lacking information about your readers' knowledge, needs, and values? Do you have a good sense of what readers will expect in terms of content, both verbal and visual? At this point, complete your answers to the best of your ability.

Now read over the materials you gathered. Then take twenty to thirty minutes to write as quickly as you can, answering the following questions one at a time in as much detail as possible.

> Will readers need any special equipment in order to carry out this procedure? If so, what is it?
> What is the first step readers will need to take?
> Exactly how will they go about doing it?
> What is the next step?
> Exactly how will readers go about doing it? (Keep answering these questions for every step in the procedure.)

> What is one problem readers are likely to encounter in carrying out this procedure?
> What do readers need to do in order to solve or avoid this problem?
> What is another problem readers are likely to encounter?

After completing this exploratory work, read or show what you have written to other students (in a small group or to the entire class) and ask them to answer the following questions.

> Which readers will be most likely to need help carrying out this procedure?
> In which passages are my instructions especially clear and helpful?
> Which passages did you find confusing or difficult to understand?

Using your classmates' responses as a guide, decide whether or how to add to, delete, or modify information in your exploratory draft.

Anticipating Readers' Needs

At this point you should have a good understanding of how to carry out the procedure you are attempting to explain. But how do you make that understanding accessible and useful to readers? The Reading to Write selections suggest several strategies you can use to anticipate and meet readers' needs.

How to Anticipate and Meet Readers' Needs

Strategies	Examples
Inform readers of any required background knowledge and equipment *before* they begin the procedure. By anticipating readers' needs, you ensure that your instructions will be helpful to readers, rather than a source of frustration.	*"Assessing the Cranial Nerves" (p. 419) opens with two brief sections on "What You Need to Know" and "What Materials You Will Need."*
Keep the primary focus on readers' actions. Especially in instructions for using high-tech products, writers often tend to start by explaining how the technology works. This is almost never the main thing the audience really wants to know. Remember: people are reading primarily to do rather than to understand. So make sure your instructions focus primarily on actions a user needs to take in order to perform the task or procedure correctly.	*Although "The Basics of PowerPoint" (p. 433) is about a complex software application, it rarely comments on how the software works; instead, the focus is on the actions or steps readers need to take to use the program.*
Try to anticipate *all* the actions readers will need to perform. Although many steps may seem obvious and intuitive to you, they probably will be unfamiliar to your readers.	*"The Fine Art of Complaining" (p. 429) not only recommends that readers make their complaints in person, but also advises readers on how to direct their complaints to the right people.*
Give examples to clarify exactly what should be done. Novice users will require examples, whereas more experienced users will not. To accommodate all readers, you want to make it easy for users to find or ignore information as needed (see How to Make Information Accessible, p. 465). As a general rule, if you are in doubt about whether to put in an example, include it in early drafts; later, you can remove any that your reviewers deem unnecessary.	*Even though "Sky Warriors" (p. 427) contains few words, the instructions contain a series of examples that show where each colored piece should go.* *"The Fine Art of Complaining" outlines the main points readers should make in a letter of complaint and then illustrates each point with excerpts from a sample letter.*

continued

How to Anticipate and Meet Readers' Needs

continued

Strategies	Examples
Create scenarios or brief narratives that state exactly what the reader needs to do and, if necessary, what will happen when the reader performs each action.	*"Assessing the Cranial Nerves" relies almost entirely on scenarios that tell readers first what to do (in the "Examination" column) and then what results to expect (in the "Evaluation" column).*
Anticipate problems, mistakes, and sources of confusion. Identify the problems and mistakes that arose when you carried out the procedure. Keep in mind that other problems may arise later on when you have your review draft tested (see Getting a "Use-Aloud," p. 470).	*"Assessing the Cranial Nerves" anticipates a mistaken assumption that medical students may bring to one part of their examination: they are not to assume that failure to correctly identify a smell as that of an orange means that the patient has failed that part of the examination. The instructions point out that medical students are "testing the ability to smell, NOT [patients'] ability to identify the aroma."*

STUDENT DIALOGUE: ANTICIPATING READERS' NEEDS

Writing in a Visual Age: Did you see any limitations to your instructions in terms of who could and who could not use them?

MaryBeth Rajczewski: The instructions wouldn't necessarily have been correct for everybody. So I thought it would be only fair to let people know in the beginning whether they should or shouldn't be using them. You don't have to be an advanced computer user, but you have to know what a mouse is and how to click on something and where a menu is. It wouldn't be fair to somebody who didn't know this. On the other end of the spectrum, with advanced computer users I just wanted to make sure people knew this wasn't advanced PowerPoint.

Anticipating Readers' Needs

Show your exploratory draft to one or more classmates, and ask them to look for ways you can use the preceding strategies to improve your instructions. Your classmates should keep the following questions in mind while evaluating your draft.

> To follow these instructions, what additional background knowledge or special equipment would you need?

> Are there places where the instructions give too much information or information not relevant to the task at hand?

> Are there places where the instructions do not give enough information or seem to skip one or more steps?

> Are there places in the instructions where an example or a scenario would help you understand what is required?

> Can you identify any points of confusion or anticipate any mistakes you might make while following these instructions?

Engaging Your Audience: Writing an Introduction

When you write instructions, it may seem that you don't need to work on engaging readers' interest or motivating them to pay attention to what you have to say. After all, you're showing them how to do something they already need or want to do. This assumption may be justified, especially if readers' need is strong and their confidence level is high. Much more frequently, however, readers approach instructions reluctantly: they doubt their ability to master something new, or they are skeptical because of their prior experiences with incomplete or poorly written instructions. Therefore, you may need to motivate your readers to pay attention to what you have to say.

Reducing Conflict

As you've seen in earlier chapters, one way to motivate readers is to create a conflict (mention a problem or question, for example) that will prompt them to read what you have written. In the case of instructions, however, it's likely that your readers are already aware of the conflict. They recognize the gap between what they want or need to do and what they are able to do, or they know they need to use instructions but past experience tells them they don't want to. Your job is to reduce conflict.

How to Reduce Conflict

Strategies	Examples
Make the instructions look approachable. Use white space and other visual cues to reduce users' possible misgivings; avoid using a gray-looking page that seems to hide the specific steps readers must perform.	*"Assessing the Cranial Nerves" (p. 419) and "The Basics of PowerPoint" (p. 433) are useful examples of this practice.*
Create an appropriate voice.	*For examples and a discussion of voice, see pp. 463–464 in this chapter.*

Relating to Readers

Other chapters in this book suggest a variety of ways to relate to readers. (See, for example, Chapter 3, pp. 163–165.) But in writing instructions it's especially important to let readers know that you understand the goals they are trying to accomplish and that you are aware of problems they may have experienced.

How to Relate to Readers

Strategies	Examples
Immediately indicate how your instructions will help readers accomplish what they want to do. Refer to the goal they hope to achieve, the problem they hope to solve, or the procedure they want to complete.	*The "Sky Warriors" (p. 427) instructions are elegant in their simplicity: they show the assembled plane in full color.* *More typically, instructions identify a task users have to accomplish, as in "Assessing the Cranial Nerves" (p. 419): "This set of instructions explains how to perform the first part of the five-part neurological exam."*
Refer to problems readers are likely to have experienced.	*"The Fine Art of Complaining" (p. 429) opens with a series of problems (slow restaurant service, cars that have unexpected mechanical problems while they are still new) that readers have probably experienced. These references to "life's annoyances" should motivate readers to continue reading.*

Engaging Your Audience

> Bring to class a set of instructions in which the first few paragraphs do a good job of engaging readers' interest. Be prepared to show these instructions to your classmates and to explain your answers to the following questions: What assumptions does the writer appear to make about readers' knowledge, needs, and values? What aspects of the beginning appeal to a person with the knowledge, needs, and values you have identified?

> Review—and, if necessary, revise—your context analysis, being careful to describe your readers' knowledge, needs, and values.

> Using one or more of the strategies for reducing conflict or relating to readers, write one or more introductory paragraphs that seem likely to engage the attention of the audience you have described. You may want to try more than one approach.

> Bring your draft introduction to class, along with your context analysis.

> Show your classmates the introduction and the context analysis. Ask them to tell you whether your introduction seems likely to engage the intended audience.

> Also ask your classmates whether they can think of other strategies to engage your audience.

Creating an Appropriate Voice

The most appropriate voice for instructions is one that is clear and helpful. One way to create such a voice is to use some of the strategies for anticipating and meeting readers' needs—especially giving examples; creating scenarios; and anticipating problems, mistakes, and sources of confusion (see pp. 458–461). You should use the sort of language with which your audience is familiar.

In addition, you may have to reassure readers if they are apprehensive about their ability to carry out the procedure. The less knowledgeable your readers are, the more reassuring your voice may need to be. In order to determine how much and what sort of reassurance your readers require, consider using the audience testing procedure described on pp. 470–471 of this chapter. Also consult the earlier sections on "Anticipating Readers' Needs" (p. 458) and "Reducing Conflict" (p. 461) for useful strategies for creating a reassuring voice.

How to Create an Appropriate Voice

Strategies

Use language with which your readers are familiar. Any specialized terms should probably be defined with language and examples to which your reader can readily relate. But use good judgment about which terms need defining and which terms readers are already familiar with.

Choose an appropriate tone. Decide what effect you want to have on your readers. Addressing readers with the second-person pronoun *you* can make your instructions sound friendly and familiar; using imperative verbs lends an air of authority to what you say.

Show readers how to achieve their goals. Instructions may include a very specific scenario, but they typically illustrate a process that can be applied in a variety of situations.

Examples

"Assessing the Cranial Nerves" (p. 419) refers to the names of the cranial nerves ("optic," "oculomotor," and so on) without defining them, thereby acknowledging the medical expertise of readers.

"The Basics of PowerPoint" (p. 433) directly addresses readers in the questions at the beginning: "You should use these instructions if you . . ." Later, the instructions use imperative verbs such as choose and click.

"The Fine Art of Complaining" (p. 429) includes a hypothetical letter of complaint about a "Perma-Kool freezer." The first paragraph provides a nonemotional account of the actions that document the "unprofessional service" mentioned in the second paragraph of the letter.

Creating an Appropriate Voice

Review your context analysis, and decide on the kind of voice you want to create in your instructions. Will it be helpful to your users if you use (or avoid) specialized language that assumes your users have expertise in a particular field (medicine, for example)? To what extent do you need to reassure them?

In three or four sentences, describe the voice you want to create in your instructions. If it helps, compare that voice to the voice you hear in one of the readings in this chapter. Then revise your introduction to give it the voice you intend.

Finally, give the revision to a classmate or your instructor and ask that person to do the following.

⟩ Describe the voice he or she hears in your instructions.
⟩ Mark passages where that voice is especially clear.
⟩ Mark passages where that voice seems to change in ways that users might find confusing.

Providing Structure

Although instructions may not look like other types of writing you do, readers still need a clear sense of the structure of your instructions. You need to give them cues to this structure so they can do what readers always need to do: find what they are looking for, anticipate the kind of information they will find in a segment of text, and see how different sections relate to each other. To give these cues, as in any other type of writing you can use forecasting terms, transitions, and so forth.

> For more examples of ways to provide structure, see **Chapter 3**, pp. 168–171.

Making Information Accessible

Instructions are likely to contain several different types of information—background information and warnings, for example, as well as the actions users must perform in completing their task or achieving their goal. Because readers should be able to locate the information they need, you should make your instructions as accessible as possible.

How to Make Information Accessible

Strategies	Examples

Highlight the actions or steps readers should take. Make it easy for readers to see—literally see—exactly what they need to do at each step of the procedure. As a rule, precede each action with a number or a bullet, and highlight the action in boldface or other eye-catching type, surrounded by extra white space.	*"Assessing the Cranial Nerves" (p. 419) numbers each main action and presents related steps in indented bulleted lists, as in the following example.*
	
	4. Test cranial nerve VII (facial):
	   • ask the patient to smile
	   • ask the patient to raise his or her eyebrows

Use headings that refer to goals readers want to accomplish or actions they need to perform.	*"The Basics of PowerPoint" (p. 433) includes a main heading that refers to the user's goal of "Creating a New Presentation," followed by subordinate headings that refer to related actions ("Opening PowerPoint" and "Getting Started").* *Following a brief introduction, every two-column page of "Assessing the Cranial Nerves" contains two headings—"Examination" and "Evaluation"—each of which indicates actions readers should take.*

continued

How to Make Information Accessible

continued

Strategies

Break up long lists of steps into more manageable groups. If you have more than five or six steps in a series, try to organize them into related groups. Although it is not always possible to divide steps into groups, most lists that contain more than five or six items can usually be made clearer when they are broken up into shorter lists.

Examples

"The Basics of PowerPoint" breaks the series of steps for "Creating Slides" into three groups of steps: "Choosing a Type of Slide," "Adding Information to Your Slide," and "Inserting the Next Slide." The author subdivides "Adding Information to Your Slide" even further, giving one set of actions for "Text-Only Slides," another set for "Slides with Charts," another for "Slides with Tables," and a fourth for "Slides with Clip Art."

STUDENT DIALOGUE: PROVIDING STRUCTURE

Writing in a Visual Age: How did you organize the various steps in your instructions?

MaryBeth Rajczewski: The headings outline the big picture of what you're going to be doing, and the subheadings break things down even further so that you don't have such a long list of steps to carry out. If you have too long a list of steps, you get lost. The longer the list of steps, the more lost you can become.

Working on the Assignment

Providing Structure

Bring to class a set of instructions that makes its structure very clear. Be prepared to show your instructor and classmates how the author(s) enabled you to see the structure clearly. After identifying strategies other writers have used, review your exploratory draft, looking for ways you might use some of these strategies to clarify the structure of your own instructions.

Concluding Your Instructions

Occasionally, instructions include a brief conclusion, something on the order of, "at this point you have successfully assembled (installed, repaired) your stereo cabinet (computer software, carburetor). Congratulations." However, when the audience is reading to understand as well as to do, instruction writers will use one of the concluding strategies described in Chapter 3, Reports (see pp. 171–172). "The Fine Art of Complaining" (p. 429), for example, uses a "framing" strategy. In the first two paragraphs, Rego mentions several of "life's annoyances" that her readers are likely to have felt. Then, in the final paragraph, Rego returns to the annoyances theme, mentioning additional annoyances that reinforce her claim that people need to be able to complain effectively.

Most often, however, instructions just end with the last step required to complete the procedure. The conclusion takes the form of the completed task.

Exercise

Bring to class a set of instructions you find clear and helpful. Does it have a conclusion? If so, what strategies has the author used? For a list of useful strategies, see Chapter 3, pp. 171–172.

Working on the Assignment

Concluding Your Instructions

Using a strategy or strategies from Chapter 3, pp. 171–172 (or a different strategy from a set of instructions you have analyzed), write a conclusion for your instructions. Share your draft with some classmates or your instructor, and ask them to tell you: (1) what strategy you used in your conclusion and (2) whether that conclusion adequately sums up and completes your instructions.

Designing Your Instructions and Integrating Visual Information

Part of what you need to understand about designing your instructions is explained in Providing Structure (pp. 465–466). As you use headings, provide numbered or bulleted lists, and break up long lists of items, you can make your instructions more inviting and user-friendly. But to create a really effective design there are several additional steps you need to take.

How to Design Your Instructions and Integrate Visual Information

Strategies	Examples
Choose a layout that is appropriate for your audience, purpose, and topic. Consider the formats of other sets of instructions your readers admire and are accustomed to working with as well as those modeled in Reading to Write.	*The audience for "The Fine Art of Complaining" (p. 429) is reading to understand as well as to do. Consequently, the first few paragraphs look like a conventional essay. The extended example of how to write an effective letter of complaint follows the layout of a typical business letter, interrupting that layout only to include italicized, boldface type to highlight the general principle illustrated in each paragraph.*
Create a clear visual hierarchy. Use visual cues—white space, headings, different sizes of type, clearly labeled pictures, indents—to give different types of information a distinctive appearance and to make it easy for readers to find or ignore information as needed. (For more on creating a visual hierarchy, see Chapter 8.)	*"The Basics of PowerPoint" (p. 433) presents information in various visual styles: italics for introductory background information; numbered, indented sentences to refer to steps the user must take; and slightly smaller type printed "flush left" (that is, with each line beginning at the left-hand margin) for each "Note." To help inexperienced computer users see the actions they are to perform in creating PowerPoint slides, the author not only prints each action in bold type but also precedes and follows each action with an extra line of white space.*
Maintain a consistent layout.	*"Assessing the Cranial Nerves" (p. 419) uses the left-hand column to list the actions the examiners should take; in the right-hand column the author lists the results the examiner is likely to see. In listing these results, she consistently moves from normal or "expected" results to "abnormal" and consistently follows each abnormal result with an explanation of the problems it indicates. Consequently, the readers always know exactly where to look for specific types of information.*

How to Design Your Instructions and Integrate Visual Information

Place images near the written text that refers to them.

"The Basics of PowerPoint" places every screenshot to the left of the text that discusses the material depicted in the screenshot. When the written text mentions part of an image, an arrow points to the relevant part.

Working on the Assignment

Designing Your Instructions and Integrating Visual Information

Design and bring to class at least one page of your instructions. If you plan to incorporate images, you do not need to include them at this time, but at the point in your page where a picture will appear, draw a rectangle that is the size and shape of the picture you intend to use in your final draft. Ask your instructor and classmates to tell you whether you have used enough visual cues to create a clear visual hierarchy.

STUDENT DIALOGUE: DESIGNING YOUR INSTRUCTIONS AND INTEGRATING VISUAL INFORMATION

Writing in a Visual Age: How important do you think the visual elements are in your instructions?

MaryBeth Rajczewski: I found that there were some places where it was much easier for people to glance at a screenshot in the instructions and say, "Oh, yeah. This is what my screen is supposed to look like." And if the screen doesn't look right they know they're not doing it right. I don't have a screenshot for every single step, but every critical step is illustrated so that readers know they're going in the right direction.

Finishing Up

By now you should have developed a thorough understanding of the topic about which you are writing your instructions. If you have not already begun to move beyond your exploratory draft, now is the time to do so. To make sure that your instructions are useful to others, you'll need to create a review draft. After completing this draft, you will assess it carefully not only by critiquing it yourself but also by getting others' perspectives. This means that you will subject the review draft to an audience test, or "use-aloud," and a final review (from one or more of your classmates or from your instructor). Then you will use these assessments to make revisions in content, organization, style, and format.

Creating a Review Draft

In preparation for writing the review draft, look back at your context analysis, your exploratory draft, and any additional notes you made. Has your understanding of any part of that context changed? If so, revise your context analysis and keep your revisions in mind as you decide what to say and how to say it in your draft.

Before you begin work on your review draft, make an informal outline listing the main steps you want readers to take or the main tasks they will need to perform. Then, for each main step or task, indicate exactly what readers will need to do to accomplish that step or task. As you write the review draft, be as thorough as possible, not only indicating the steps readers will need to take but anticipating questions or problems that may arise and giving readers some idea of what they will see upon completing important steps. Be especially careful to make your information as accessible as possible.

Getting a "Use-Aloud"

In other chapters of this book, audience testing focuses on how well your audience understands what you have said and whether your ideas seem credible, persuasive, and insightful. But with instructions, the emphasis shifts from understanding to doing. That is, the primary question is not so much whether people understand or agree with what you have written, but whether readers can use your instructions to carry out the task. To answer this question, you need to have someone do a "use-aloud" procedure. That is, you will observe someone think out loud while trying to carry out your instructions.

The process of thinking aloud can be tricky, inviting several potential problems. One problem is that a few people find it almost impossible to do this sort of work, usually because they find it distracting to think out loud while they follow instructions. Other people sometimes become so involved in the task that they simply forget to think aloud. These problems are relatively easy to solve: you find someone else to do the testing, or you prompt your tester with such comments as "I notice that you hesitated when you read that passage. Can you tell me what you were thinking?" and "Would you tell me in your own words what you think that passage is telling you to do?"

A much more serious problem is likely to arise when the tester makes a mistake or asks a question and your impulse is to jump in, explain what the tester should do, answer a question, or correct a mistake. Do not do any of these things. Listen, watch, and take notes. Pay careful attention to places where the person stumbles in thinking aloud. But do not talk, except to prompt the tester to explain what he or she is thinking. You will probably find this self-restraint difficult. You know how the procedure should be done, and it's almost painful to watch someone struggle with what is perfectly clear to you. But if you pay careful attention to where and why your tester struggles, you'll get a good sense of how to revise your instructions.

Working on the Assignment

Getting a "Use-Aloud"

› Find someone who is typical of the users for whom you are writing your instructions, preferably someone who does not already know how to do what your instructions explain how to do.

› Ask this tester to read the instructions aloud and perform the task as he or she reads. Ask the tester to think aloud while reading and performing the task. (You want the person to verbalize questions and reactions that occur while he or she is performing the task.)

› Explain that, even though you want to hear the tester's questions, you will not be able to provide answers until after he or she completes the task successfully or comes to a point where it is impossible to proceed farther.

› Take careful notes on where and why the tester encounters difficulties with your instructions.

STUDENT DIALOGUE: CREATING A REVIEW DRAFT

Writing in a Visual Age (WVA): I noticed that your final draft includes the heading "Choosing a Type of Slide," which did not appear in your review draft.

MaryBeth Rajczewski (MBR): The "use-aloud" was the first time I realized my headings were all off. I had the stuff about different types of slides, but I didn't have a heading about selecting a slide. My tester was confused. He didn't see why he needed to know about the types of slides, and he didn't realize he had to choose a type of slide before creating a slide. So I added the section "Choosing a Type of Slide" to make these points clear.

WVA: In your final draft, the different slides are color-coded to go with the text. Why?

MBR: My user didn't understand which type of slide was which. I had to do something to show the connections.

WVA: There are more subheadings in your final draft than in your review draft. Why is that?

MBR: In my use-aloud, my tester kept getting lost and making mistakes. Putting in subheadings helped prevent that.

WVA: In the review draft, you discussed special features and then explained how to view the entire presentation. Why did you change the sequence of two sections in the final draft?

MBR: In the use-aloud, my tester was much more interested in learning how to view the presentation than in learning about the program's special features. So I put special features last so that people could quit after they had viewed their presentation. This let people finish without having to skip over material they didn't need.

Getting a Final Review

Once you have tested and revised your review draft to make it complete and polished, have it reviewed by one or more people who understand the principles (analyzing context, engaging readers, and so on) that you have been working with in this chapter.

> Give the reviewer a copy of your draft, one he or she can make notes on.
> Give the reviewer a copy of your context analysis. If necessary, revise that analysis before giving it to the reviewer.

> Ask the reviewer to begin his or her response by answering the following question: Given what I say in my context analysis, how likely does it seem that my instructions will be clear and useful to my intended audience?

> Ask the reviewer to adopt the perspective of the audience described in your context analysis and to use the following checklist in commenting on your work.

Checklist for Final Review

> **bedfordstmartins.com/ visualage**

To download this checklist as a worksheet, click on **CHAPTER 7** > **WORKSHEETS**

1 In my context analysis, please highlight any statements that give you a good sense of the knowledge, needs, and values of my intended audience. (For an example, see p. 454.) Please indicate any statements that need to be clarified.

2 In my context analysis, please highlight any statements that give you a good sense of the circumstances, purposes, and expected format for my instructions. (For an example of a good context analysis, see p. 454.) Please indicate any statements that need to be clarified.

3 In what specific passages have I developed my topic thoroughly, especially by advising readers of any required equipment and background knowledge, explaining exactly what should be done at each step of the procedure, giving helpful examples, and anticipating readers' problems or questions? What are some strategies (explained on p. 459) that might make my instructions clearer, more complete, and more helpful?

4 What portions of my introduction seem likely to engage the interest of my intended audience? What are some strategies (explained on p. 462) that might make the introduction more engaging?

5 How would you describe the voice I have created? At what points does that voice seem appropriate, given my intended audience and subject matter? What strategies (explained on p. 464) might help me make the voice clearer or more appropriate?

6 What are some words or phrases that provide a clear structure for my instructions, making information accessible, creating clear expectations for readers, and indicating links between paragraphs or larger sections of text? What strategies (explained on pp. 465–466) might I use to make the structure of my instructions clear?

7 Do my instructions need a conclusion? If so, what strategies might I use to make my conclusion more effective?

8 How do the visual elements (white space, numbered or bulleted lists, images, headings, and so on) contribute to the clarity and usefulness of my instructions? Are there any points at which I need to add more visual elements to improve the clarity and usefulness of my instructions? If so, what strategies might I use for designing my instructions and integrating visual information (explained on pp. 468–469)?

If possible, ask your reviewer to talk with you about your review draft as well as make notes on it. Be careful not to argue with your reviewers, especially when they raise questions or disagree with something you have written. When this happens, try to find out why they have questions or objections and make notes about what they say.

Revising Your Instructions

Up to this point, you have listened to your reviewer's comments without explaining, arguing, or making judgments about the validity of those comments. Once you have a good idea of how the reviewer responds to your instructions, however, you should go back through your notes on those comments. Bearing in mind your intended audience and purpose, decide which comments are most valid. Then use strategies referred to in the checklist in revising your instructions.

After resolving all the issues that need attention, proofread carefully and correct any typographical or formatting errors. Then submit this final draft to your instructor.

Taking Stock of Where You Are

Each of the assignments in this book should teach you strategies that can help you grow as a writer and improve your work on subsequent assignments. But this will only happen if you make a conscious effort to assess your development as a writer as you go along.

Once your instructor has returned the final draft of your work, think back over all the comments you received—from classmates as well as your instructor—and what you learned from your audience testing. Then write out answers to the following questions. (You might want to keep these in a journal or in a special section of a notebook.)

**› bedfordstmartins.com/
visualage**

*To download these
questions as a work-
sheet, click on*
**CHAPTER 7 ›
WORKSHEETS**

**Questions for
Assessing Your
Growth as a
Writer**

- What appears to be my greatest area of strength?
- Where am I having the greatest difficulty?
- What am I learning about the process of writing?
- What am I learning about giving and receiving feedback on writing?
- What have I learned from writing instructions that I can use in my next writing assignment for this course, for another course, or for work?

SAMPLE STUDENT ASSESSMENT

Here's how MaryBeth Rajczewski answered these questions for the instructions she wrote on using PowerPoint (p. 433).

What appears to be my greatest area of strength?

After completing the PowerPoint instructions, I have a good understanding of the need to use white space, headings and subheadings, and short lists of steps. All of these things result in instructions that are more accessible or "user-friendly." I also learned a lot about creating an appropriate voice for my instructions—in this case, a friendly, helpful tone.

Where am I having the greatest difficulty?

The organization of the instructions has been my greatest difficulty in this assignment. It was difficult to determine the exact, correct order of steps so that it would make for the easiest set of instructions possible. I had to be sure that each step followed naturally from the previous one so that nothing important got left out.

What am I learning about the process of writing?

I learned that my first draft is extremely important because it gives me a starting point. The organization of any document, especially instructions, is also important, but sometimes I can't organize until I get my ideas down on paper. Probably the most important thing I learned from this assignment is that I need to really think about my audience. Their needs should shape my writing.

What am I learning about giving and receiving feedback on writing?

The "use-aloud" test really helped me see how my instructions would be used. My classmates pointed out a lot of spots in the instructions where the working headings and the organization were confusing or ineffective. Their feedback allowed me to create a better finished product. Also, the experience of testing other people's instructions was helpful. I was able to think about comments others had given me and look for those same kinds of issues in other people's work.

What have I learned from writing instructions that I can use in my next writing assignment for this course, for another course, or for work?

Most of the lessons I learned from writing these instructions also apply to other forms of writing. I know that from this point on, I'll carefully consider my audience and really think about their attitudes and what they need. I will also try to use headings and white space to create a visually pleasing document. Headings also help to cue readers in to what's coming next, which helps to keep their interest and attention. Finally, good organization is one of the most important elements of a good set of instructions and any other form of writing as well.

2 Strategies for Design and Research

8

Designing Pages and Screens

S THE READINGS AND INSTRUCTION THROUGHOUT THIS BOOK SHOW, WRITING INVOLVES A LOT MORE

than putting words on a piece of paper or a computer screen. Today there is an expectation that writers will produce documents that incorporate a wide range of visual features or that writers will "write visually." The software tools for creating such documents are changing more rapidly than anyone ever thought possible. Thus this chapter outlines general principles for effective design as well as techniques for using software and other tools. This chapter provides a quick guide to basic design concepts that will help you create both print and online documents that work for your purposes.

The most important thing to think about when planning the appearance of a print or online document is what purpose you want the design to achieve. You can use design to accomplish many of the writer's objectives described throughout this book. For example, do you want to use a visual element to engage the members of your audience? (Choose something that will capture their attention, that is appropriate to the topic, that makes them curious about what you might have to say, that surprises them, that is consistent with what they expect.) Are you trying to make information more accessible to your readers? (You may want to create a table or chart, use bulleted or numbered lists, add headings in a distinctive font.) Can design help you create an appropriate voice? (Choose photographs that convey the emotion you want readers to feel, use a font that reflects the voice you want to convey, create a layout that emphasizes that voice.) The design and visual elements of a text always affect the way the message is interpreted by the reader. If the design is applied appropriately and the visuals are well chosen, they will be helpful in fulfilling your objectives as a writer. However, if the design is inappropriate or the visuals are chosen haphazardly, they may interfere with your ability to reach those objectives.

For Collaboration

Bring any magazine to class. With a small group of classmates, look through the magazines and choose one article or advertisement from each that has a lot of visuals. See if you can figure out what the creator of that article or ad wanted the visuals to convey about the subject. What do the visuals say about the author's view of the readers of that particular magazine? See if you can identify differences in the readership of the various magazines on the basis of the visuals. Hint: You might start with ads for automobiles—these are often quite different depending on readership.

❯ bedfordstmartins.com/
visualage

*For links to further
resources on designing
pages and screens,
click on*
CHAPTER 8 ❯ *LINKS*

This chapter is not divided into separate sections about designing print and online documents. Although there has been much research on what makes a printed page effective, similar research on Web pages has not yet yielded definitive guidelines. There are still plenty of conflicting ideas about what works best when designing for the Internet. However, the *concepts* that will help you to arrange words and images effectively on a sheet of paper also apply to arranging words and images for Web text. When there are certain strategies or options that work better for Web design, this chapter's text will point them out. Meanwhile, the chapter is divided into sections that focus on those concepts that you need to think about when designing either print or online documents.

Throughout the chapter are figures that demonstrate some of the concepts, principles, and visual attributes described in each of the following sections. In particular you will learn how to read visuals from the perspective of a writer, which will be useful when you are integrating visuals into your own documents.

> ❯ **Design principles:** basic concepts that provide guidance in planning the appearance of a text
> ❯ **Layout:** the arrangement of words and images on a piece of paper or a computer screen
> ❯ **Images:** pictorial representations
> ❯ **Representations of information:** graphical forms for presenting data
> ❯ **Color:** a visual aspect that draws attention but that should be used with caution and care
> ❯ **Typefaces and fonts:** the different shapes and sizes of letters and other characters

Design Principles

This section covers five essential principles of design that are important for creating effective documents: alignment, chunking, contrast, consistency, and tension. For each of these principles, you will find a detailed definition and examples to illustrate how the principle affects documents.

Alignment

Professional document designers typically use grid lines to help them align, or line up, the elements on a page effectively. If you've ever used document design software (for example, PageMaker or Quark), you are familiar with the grid that automatically appears on the screen when you open a new document. But with any document you can imagine or impose a grid to reveal the alignment of all the text and visual elements. There are several important points to remember about alignment.

Align similar elements. Generally, all the like elements on a page should be aligned with one another because they go together. For example, in a document with several lists, even though the lists might contain different types of information, they should be aligned because they're all lists. The same idea holds true for headings (see Figure 8.1). All headings of a particular level should be aligned (for a definition of levels of headings, see p. 501).

FIGURE 8.1
Use of Aligned
Headings in This Book

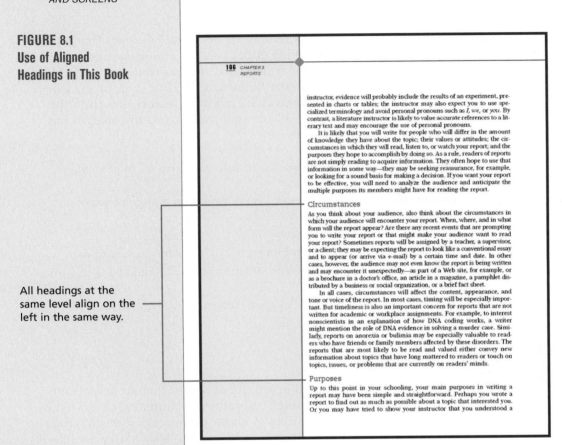

All headings at the
same level align on the
left in the same way.

Avoid having too many vertical "lines" in your document. In any document, your mind's eye can draw vertical lines at each indentation. Look at the résumé in Figure 8.2 for an example of a document with too many implied vertical lines. The reader's eye gets confused by the complexity of the layout. This is particularly inappropriate in a résumé, which is a document that readers often need to scan quickly. When you create such a document, you want the reader's eye to be able to easily find the most important information; therefore the layout must be fairly simple with a minimal number of implied vertical lines.

The best Web sites are created with a fairly simple grid. For example, consider the simplicity of the homepage in Figure 8.3. This community site has a horizontal banner across the top and three vertical columns. The most important information is in the wide center column, the index is in a narrow column to the left (a conventional position for indexes on

FIGURE 8.2
Ineffective Use of
Vertical Alignment

Joshua Patrick Brien
jpbrien@unity.ncsu.edu

Permanent address: School Address:
6209 Carlyle Drive   2213 Hoot Owl Ct.
Raleigh, NC 27614   Raleigh, NC 27603
(919) 518-1463   (919) 931-0394

OBJECTIVE: An internship in the computer industry in an IT department where I can utilize
                skills gained from work experience and gain practical IT knowledge.

EDUCATION: North Carolina State University
                Bachelor of Science in Business Management, concentration in Information
                Technology
                Expected May 2005

WORK
EXPERIENCE: Cisco Systems, RTP, NC   Summers 2003, 2002, 2001, 2000
                Dev-Test engineer intern
                   • Performed series of tests in the MWG
                   • Assisted various groups in lab maintenance

                Cisco Systems, RTP, NC   June 1999 – August 1999
                Engineering Lab Assistant
                   • Participated in the planning and implementation of transferring an engineering
                      lab from San Jose, CA to the RTP location
                   • Inventoried all non-Cisco lab equipment for Y2K purposes
                   • Monitored the engineering labs and restocked basic cable supplies

                Cisco Systems, RTP, NC   June 1998 – August 1998
                Engineering Lab Assistant
                   • Member of IBD Engineering Lab Move team
                   • Contributed to the planning and implementation of a move of several engineering
                      labs and many engineers to a new building
                   • Maintained and updated engineering documentation databases

SKILLS: • HTML Experience and Web Site design
                   • **Software:** Microsoft Word, EXCEL, PowerPoint, Outlook, Outlook Express,
                      Internet Explorer, Netscape, Eudora
                   • **Platforms:** Windows 95\98\00\XP, Unix

ACTIVITIES: • Alpha Phi Omega, National Service Fraternity
                        *Brother of Iota Lambda chapter (Fall 2001 – Present)
                        *Chapter officer for four semesters (Treasurer, Service VP, President)
                        *Chapter Outstanding Brother (Spring 2003)
                   • Member of the Catholic Campus Ministry leadership team at NC State (2002)
                   • Representative to the Inter-Residence Council (Fall 2000)

AWARDS &
HONORS: BSA Eagle Scout

Web pages), and special announcements are in a narrow column to the right. Readers of this Web page can easily find the information they need because the layout is simple and familiar, with items aligned in rows and columns.

One common design for Web sites uses multiple frames—distinct boxes that divide the screen into discrete scrollable areas. The frames may overlap several columns and rows of a Web site's grid. For example, you might be able to scroll through an index in a frame on the left without moving the rest of the page or scroll through the main column without moving the index. Frames are not easily displayed on all browsers and systems, so they should be avoided unless you are creating a document for a specific audience that you know will have the capability of viewing and using the frames. Also, frames make it more difficult for readers to bookmark and print the pages of a site.

FIGURE 8.3
Web Site Aligned on a
Simple Grid

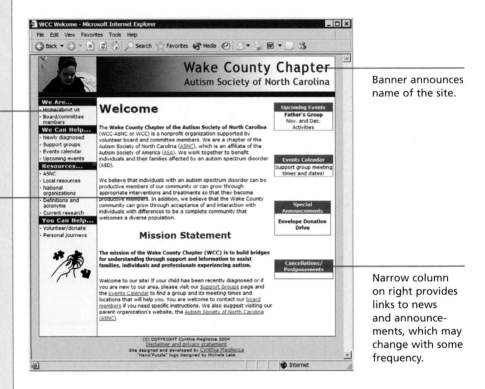

Banner announces
name of the site.

Narrow column on left provides index with links to other
pages within the site. This
information is fairly stable
over time.

Wide center column provides
main message and featured
sponsors.

Narrow column
on right provides
links to news
and announce-
ments, which may
change with some
frequency.

Do not ignore the alignment of any graphic elements. Photos, tables, charts, and so forth need to be aligned, not just randomly placed. After you have determined why the graphic is necessary and how it supports or clarifies the reader's understanding, then you should visually link the graphic to the words it supports by aligning it (vertically or horizontally) with those words. For example, consider the excerpt from a *Consumer Reports* evaluation of ice cream shown in Figure 8.4. There are two images stacked on top of one another and also aligned with a narrow column of text. The images show the packaging from two brands of ice cream, and the text describes how these brands "stack up" in comparison to one another. The vertical alignment of the images reinforces the message of the text, and the horizontal alignment of images and text connect them to one another.

Chunking

Chunking, or clustering, means arranging parts of the text that go together—the words, sentences, lists, paragraphs, graphic elements, and so forth that are related to one another and in some way are distinct from other parts of the text—and *visually separating* them from other parts of

FIGURE 8.4
Use of Aligned
Graphics and Text

Commercial "homemade" ice cream Of the home-made-style vanilla and chocolate products we tested, only Blue Bell Homemade Vanilla was very good. Breyers Homemade Vanilla, which contains gums (unlike regular old Breyers), was inferior to its brandmate.

the text. Aside from aligning these elements, you need to make sure that they are set apart in some meaningful way. There are several options for creating the chunks that will enable readers to distinguish one part of your text from another. Here are three examples.

> Insert a heading (see Figure 8.5).
> Use indentation to group related items, such as items in a list.
> Use white space to separate chunks of information (see Figure 8.5). For example, add space around visuals to set them apart. Or when writing for the Web, set your line length to allow for ample margins and add space between chunks of text.

Chunking makes it easier for readers to see the logical structure of your text and find the information they need.

When designing a Web text, be sure that your chunks of information are fairly short. Although research suggests that readers are becoming more tolerant of pages that go beyond one screen, they still prefer to read short paragraphs and lists.

Contrast

The variations in appearance that are used to create contrast can increase readability and accessibility while adding visual interest to a text. The most obvious type of contrast is color contrast, a clear distinction between colors based on differences such as dark and light, bright and dull, and distance from one another on the color spectrum (see Figure 8.6). Although black type on white paper creates a strong contrast, the combination is so common that it is barely noticeable (until someone takes it away—such as when a dark gray background reduces the contrast and makes reading more difficult).

FIGURE 8.5
Web Site Using
Headings and White
Space to Create
Chunks of Information

Red subheadings
create chunks of
information.

Wide white space
between exhibits
listed creates
obvious chunks
of information.

Smaller amount of
white space indicates
break within elements
in an exhibit.

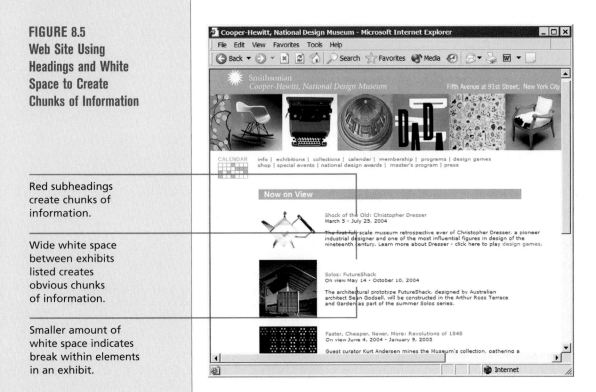

FIGURE 8.6
Color Contrast

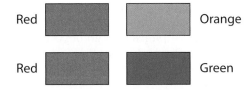

Red and orange do not provide a strong contrast, but red and green do.

Gray and yellow are both light colors, but there is still some contrast
because they are so different from one another.

There are many ways to create contrast in a document. The following suggestions describe some of the most common (and easiest) ones. (Since academic writing projects often require very specific layouts and designs, before using these suggestions you should check with your instructor.)

Use color to add emphasis in either the background or the type (or both). A colored background (or *screen*) emphasizes the text it anchors. (See, for example, the green How-To boxes throughout Part 1 of this book.) Using color behind text makes that important information more obvious. Notice, however, that it is easiest to read black type on a background that is a light color. Both in print and on screen, readers have less eye strain reading dark type on a light background. For documents outside of school, you don't have to stick with black for your type; you can try any dark color on a white or any light background. One of the advantages of online documents is that you can easily try an almost endless variety of color combinations.

Choose dramatically different typefaces and fonts (style, size, color). Everyone is familiar with the use of large type in titles and headings as a way to cue the reader about the divisions within a book or article, but type can also be used to create all kinds of contrast. For example, look at the various styles and sizes of type in the article "Weapons of Mass Disruption" in Figure 8.7. The article opens with several paragraphs describing a scenario, and this section is set in italics to separate it from the rest of the article. Within that section, you see a few sentences that are not italic and that are much larger than the rest—and they are set in red. The readers' eyes will be pulled to those sentences first, and the content will engage their attention. The title uses two different type styles— a large, bold style in red for the word *Weapons* and a smaller, less dense style in black for the rest of the title. Again, this draws the readers' eyes to the crucial word in the title. If you look closely at other pages of the article (see pp. 127–134), you can see how type size and style (including uppercase letters, bold, italics, and serif and sans serif fonts) and color are used to create contrast among sections of the article.

❯ For more on typefaces and fonts, see p. 524.

Systematically vary the amount of space between, around, or within chunks. If you look at the Old El Paso package in Figure 8.8, you'll notice that the first two columns are compressed—there's not a lot of extra space around words or between lines. But the larger right column, the one that is most important to the user of this product because it provides instructions for its use, looks quite different. There is a contrast between the columns in part because of the amount of space that is left open around the right column and between numbered steps in that column.

Combine large and small graphics on the same page or in the same document. Look at the *Time* cover in Figure 8.9 on p. 490—there is a marked

FIGURE 8.7
Use of Fonts to
Create Contrast

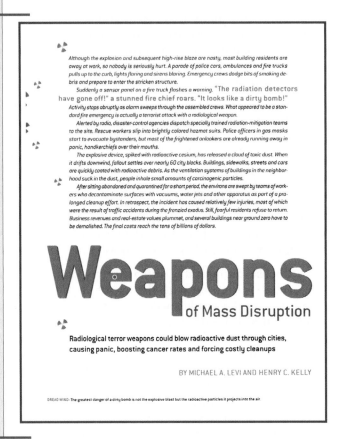

contrast between the size of the shoe and the size of the people running through the field. This dramatic contrast reinforces the sense of foreboding or threat that the designer of the cover wanted to create. The designer also sets the viewing angle—from beneath the shoe—to emphasize the danger to the smaller people.

Consistency

Consistency does not mean that every print page or Web page should be identical, but that once you have figured out the basic grid for the document, all the pages should fit on that grid in such a way that they all look

FIGURE 8.8
Use of Space to Create Contrast

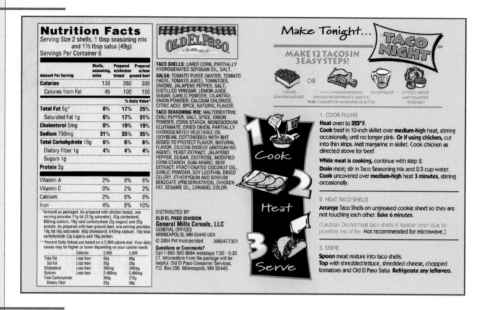

like parts of the same document. Examine the screens in Figure 8.10, a collaborative student Web project, to see how this works. As shown in the first screen, the homepage is based on a grid that consists of a two-tier navigational banner, a title (Gallagher Health Center), and a text area anchored by a black and red border. The homepage for the Health Center also offers an animated announcement about flu shots, along with photos, a map, and contact information.

When you examine the second screen from the site, the site's consistency becomes apparent. The same implied grid is in use, with many of the key navigational features in place such as the location and shape of navigational banners, the link to the homepage, the fonts, and the border around the body of the text. The Services page includes descriptions and links to specific areas at the Health Center. The other pages within the site—including appointment sign-up forms, a staff directory, and so on—vary because different types of information are presented and in each instance the available space must be used efficiently and effectively. However, the same basic grid forms the basis for each page, reinforcing a sense of unity and consistency within the site.

Flip through several books. In any given book, can you see any similarities among the table of contents page, a page with graphic elements,

FIGURE 8.9
**Use of Size to Create
Contrast**

a page with all text, and the index? Whether you notice it or not, all the pages are likely based on the same grid. Similarly, when planning your own document, you will make decisions about format that will be used consistently throughout the document with minor modifications to meet the needs of specific pages.

One thing that is particularly noticeable in Web sites is that home-pages often are much simpler than subsequent pages "deeper" in the site. A homepage is essentially analogous to either a magazine cover or a table of contents. In the first case, the homepage tries to attract the readers' attention and invite them into the site (think of cover art on many magazines with the blurbs and headlines describing the issue). In the second case, the homepage tries to direct the readers to the information they want or need.

FIGURE 8.10
Use of a Grid to
Achieve Consistency
of Layout

The same navigational banner is used for both pages, with an identical logo and placement.

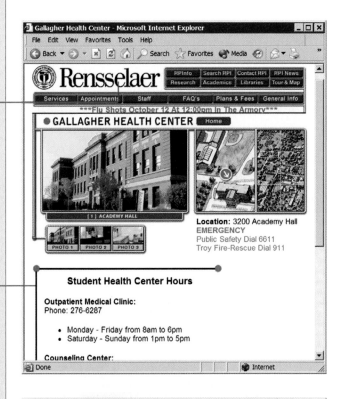

Although the content is different, the border on the left of the main column of text is the same shape and in the same position relative to the margin on both pages.

The title is in the same position, uses the same design, and has the same links to Home.

The wide main column has the most important information, just as on the homepage.

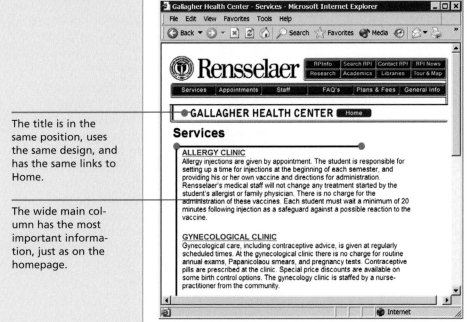

If you are creating a Web site, think about why people might visit it. Is it an entertainment site? Do you need to entice members of the audience to enter and read? Or is it an information site? Are your readers already anxious to read and just needing to know where to go? In either case, the homepage should be clear and fairly simple so that readers know where they are and where they are going.

Tension

Tension is a feeling invoked in readers when they see a well-designed print or online document. It relates to how well the various elements on the page get along: Do they work well together, or do they compete for attention? Do they create a particular mood? Figure 8.11 shows a flyer produced by the White House Project, a political advocacy group, that creates interest by generating tension.

The "weight" of this page is on the right side. Because our alphabet and system of reading moves from left to right, the weight (headings, paragraphs, graphics) is usually more pronounced on the left and the white space (empty space, or lack of weight) is on the right. But on this page most of the white space is on the left, all the photographs are on the right, and even the margin on the right is slightly narrower than the margin on the left. Only the two paragraphs toward the bottom have lines that are balanced, and even they have a narrower margin on the right than on the left.

White space on left of page creates contrast.

FIGURE 8.11
Use of Tension to
Create Interest

Text and headings align on the right. Conventionally, headings and text are either centered or aligned left.

Photos appear in a vertical column. Because we naturally look at visuals first, this flyer encourages us to read from top to bottom.

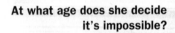

At what age does a girl dream of becoming President?

At what age does she decide it's impossible?

Women have made great strides toward equality in American society. Yet women represent only 20% of elected officials nationwide, even though they are 52% of the U.S. population. No woman has served as president, vice president, or White House chief of staff.

The men and women of The White House Project are dedicated to changing the climate of American politics, so that in the future women will launch successful campaigns for the U.S. presidency. We are working toward the day when our country celebrates its first woman president and women participate fully in leading our nation.

It is time for a change.
Use your voice to make it happen.
Vote inside.

THE WHITE HOUSE PROJECT

This page might first be perceived as off balance—or at least unusual. It certainly attracts the readers' attention, even if they don't know why, and it might make them feel just a bit uncomfortable. This reaction may be what the authors wanted, encouraging readers to question the current role of women in national politics.

The tension on a page is created by the way the elements are positioned in relation to one another and to the page itself. Once again, there is no set way to arrange elements to create tension, but here are some ideas to help you think about how it is created.

Remember that anything unexpected creates tension. The White House Project flyer shows several ways to create tension, the most pronounced of which is the placement of the weight on the (unexpected) right-hand side of the page. In addition, tension can be generated through the use of strong contrasts, unusual colors, or unexpected shapes (think of that giant shoe on the *Time* cover in Figure 8.9).

Use graphic elements that incorporate diagonal lines. Examine the photographs or drawings you plan to use and trace or imagine the lines the elements in these images create. Diagonal lines remind us of motion. However, use caution when adding visuals that include diagonal lines to your texts—make sure they are not "falling" on something important (unless, of course, that's your whole point). Once again, look at the *Time* cover in Figure 8.9. Not only is the giant shoe about to squash some tiny people, but it is coming down at an angle—and squashing the titles as well as the people. The odd thing about diagonal lines in images is that they can create this frightening kind of tension when they are positioned to fall on something, but if they are positioned to lean away from something or someone, they give an entirely different feel to the page. Diagonal lines that lean away give a sense of opening up (think of flowers blooming) or of progress (think of a line graph that goes up and to the right or an airplane taking off).

Incorporate photographs or drawings that face into the page. The amount and kind of tension this creates will depend on the graphic element and its position on the page and the kind of text you are designing. In general terms, photos of people that face off the page will be seen as distant, unfriendly, unhappy, or separate. Photos that face into the text or toward a facing page (as in a magazine spread) will seem friendly, optimistic, inclusive, and natural. When producing a book (or any other document that will be printed on both sides of the page), be sure to think in terms of facing outward and inward as opposed to left and right, respectively.

Exercise

Pick up a popular magazine that has a lot of photographs, such as *People* or *Ebony*. Take a look at where the photographs are positioned on each page, and note especially which way the people face. Can you see any pattern? How do you react to the photos? What causes that reaction?

Layout

Many people use the words *layout* and *format* to mean the same thing. The word *layout* here describes the options you have in designing a print or online document. When writers produced their texts with typewriters, they had very few options for layout. In fact, texts that needed complex visual presentation were turned over to graphic artists. However, with today's word processing and desktop publishing software capabilities, writers now have options for creating complex layouts themselves. Not only can they use Cut and Paste features provided by their software, but they can use other options to create various textual and visual elements and then move those elements to the most appropriate position. You should explore the capabilities of your own software program(s) before starting to design your text. Look through the features under the Insert menu (for features such as page numbers, pictures, textboxes, footnotes, and so forth), the Format menu (for features such as lists, numbering, columns, tabs, justification, margins), and the Table menu (for features pertaining to the creation and design of tables). Your software may also provide drawing tools that enable you to add lines, arrows, boxes or other shapes, background color, and so forth.

With so many options, how do you know what is most appropriate? There is no one correct answer because what is appropriate will depend on the audience, circumstance, and purpose of the text you are creating. However, whether you are designing a report, a brochure, or a Web site, you want to generate a consistent layout that will guide your work for the entire document. This does not mean that every page will look the same. It does, however, mean that every page will have some consistent features that enable readers to understand what is important, know what to expect, and gain access to the parts of the document that they most want or need. When you plan a layout, take into consideration the design principles discussed in this chapter. Of course, when determining the layout for an academic assignment, check with your instructor for design requirements.

In general, most of the elements of layout can be created or modified by using the menus and tools in your software program(s). This section presents a number of suggestions for making decisions about these elements, but keep in mind that you will probably have to revise your options once you see how they all work together.

Lists

Of the several types of lists that you will often see in documents, *numbered* lists and *bulleted* lists are two of the most common. Lists are very useful for bringing the reader's attention to a series of steps or items. Lists are also used a great deal in Web pages because they are easier to scan than paragraphs. Indeed, research has shown that many people read online documents differently than they read paper documents; that is, they are more likely to scan online documents. Yet another common use for lists is in presentation software, such as PowerPoint. Brief lists make excellent visual accompaniments for oral presentations.

❯ For more about creating visuals for oral presentations, see **Chapter 16**.

Numbered lists should be reserved for situations where the sequence is important; that is, if the order in which the items in the list are to be read is critical or significant, use numbers. For example, you would want to use numbered lists when writing for the following situations.

> ❯ the steps in a set of instructions
> ❯ a key that matches labels to images (such as a parts diagram or a campus map)
> ❯ a list of maps or figures for a book or some other lengthy document

Bulleted lists provide a clear, concise way to present information that is not necessarily sequential but is related. Lists are often preferable to paragraphs in some texts because the items in a list are relatively brief. Paragraphs use transitions such as *the first feature, another feature, more opportunities,* and *further ideas* to connect ideas.

Many software packages can create lists automatically. There is usually an icon on the main toolbar or a menu choice that will enable you to transform your typed text into either a numbered or a bulleted list or to automatically format as you type. The software will generally provide an appropriate format, but there may be times when you will want to undo the automatic formatting.

The bullets in a bulleted list are usually a kind of dot (like a bullet hole), but you can look at the different character sets included with your word processing software for other symbols. For most academic and professional writing, you should not get too fancy, but sometimes it's fun and appropriate to use something other than a round bullet as a cue for your readers. For example, you might use the following symbols.

> a checkmark (✓) for items in a checklist
> an empty box (☐) that readers could check off themselves
> a pointing hand (☛) to make a set of instructions more obvious

Lists are conventionally aligned with the left margin or are indented the same amount as the paragraph indent. If your software program does not automatically establish the space to the right of the bullet, you should indent each item (about ¼″ for the most commonly used line lengths and sizes of type). If each or some of the items in your list will include a second line, you can wrap each line under the bullet or under the words.

> When the text hangs under the bullet, the words in subsequent lines of the item line up with the bullet.
> When the text hangs under the previous line of text, the first words of each line in the item line up under one another.

When you align the text under the bullet, each item is distinct, but not dramatically so. Aligning each line of text under the previous line of text makes the symbol you are using as the bullet more obvious and separates each item from the others more distinctly.

For a list that is made up of other lists, such as a directory (perhaps a list of departments with lists of names for each individual within the

For Collaboration

Find a document that has some type of bulleted list, and bring it to class. Try to find a list that uses a symbol other than the standard bullet. With two or three of your classmates, compare the symbols that are used to identify the items in the lists and answer the following questions.

1. How many different symbols did you find?
2. Do you think the symbols are appropriate for the audience, circumstance, and purpose of the document? What makes each symbol appropriate or inappropriate?
3. Would a numbered list have been more appropriate? Why or why not?
4. Does everyone in the group know how to create a bulleted list using each of those symbols? If not, ask the ones who do to share their knowledge with the rest of the group.
5. If the text for any of the items runs to a second line, how is that text aligned? What effect does this alignment achieve?

department), you should use indentation, style of type, and/or color to distinguish the items rather than bullets, which would look too busy. For a list that provides navigation on a Web site, see the navigation index in Figure 8.3 for an example that avoids looking busy. This index is broken down into a series of lists showing the options within each category. The main headings are in a large, bold font on a blue background. The subheadings are bulleted and aligned under the heading, in a slightly smaller font without any bold. In a list like this, bullets are optional and numbers would be inappropriate (there is no ranking of items).

▷ For information about creating and formatting lists of works cited or references, see **Chapter 12.**

Columns

With your word processor you can create many of the types of columns you see in newspapers, magazines, newsletters, brochures, Web sites, and tables. Your software program likely offers you the opportunity to create text in one of two types of columns, most commonly called *newspaper* and *parallel* columns.

Newspaper columns (see Figure 8.12) begin at the top of the first column and continue to the end of the page, then move to the top of the second column on that same page. Depending on the size of the page, there may be as many as five or six columns. Also used in magazines, newspaper columns are most often used in print; they are rarely used in Web texts.

Newspaper columns are typically all the same width, usually dividing the available space on the page into equal columns. When using newspaper columns, be careful not to crowd too many onto the page—the more columns you have, the shorter each line of text will be, possibly making the text harder to read (see the following discussion of line length).

Parallel columns are used to present information that is read across the page. Parallel columns are similar to tables or charts, where the information on the left has a relationship to the information on the right. Think of a table of contents with titles in the left column and page numbers on the right, or the nutritional information on food packaging where each nutrient is listed in the first column and the amount of that nutrient in the food is listed in a column on the right (for example, see the nutritional information on the box in Figure 8.8). You are also likely to see parallel columns in Web texts, especially in directories or other information lists.

Parallel columns can be the same width, but they don't have to be. In fact, the information that will appear in each column can be used to determine the width. For example, in a table of contents the left-hand column holding the chapter titles or section names would need to be much wider than the right-hand column holding the page numbers.

FIGURE 8.12
Newspaper Columns

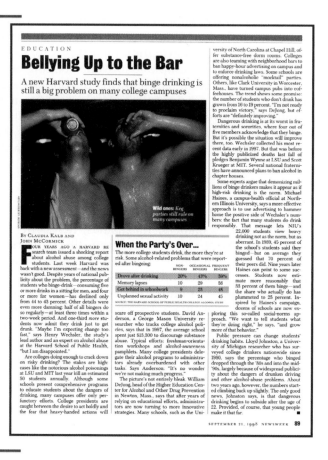

In some software programs, you create parallel columns using the Tables feature. You simply create a table with the number of columns you want. To make it look like columns, you then delete the lines (or borders) that separate the cells of the table. Making borderless tables is also a way to create columns in Web texts.

Line Length

When lines of type are too long or too short, readers have trouble reading—after all, we don't read one word at a time: we cluster the words into meaningful groups (such as phrases and clauses). If a line is too long or too short, readers have trouble creating those clusters. Line length refers not only to the actual measured length of a line of type but also to the number of characters (letters, numbers, punctuation marks, symbols)

FIGURE 8.13
Line Length

This column is quite narrow but it works adequately for this small font (11 point). The second line of text here has only 65 characters, but when you add the 14 blank spaces, you get 79 character spaces. (The Word Count feature on your software program may count words, characters (no spaces), and characters (with spaces) in addition to paragraphs, pages, and lines.)

If we switch to a larger font (this is 16 point), the second line of text has only 46 characters, or 55 including spaces. Although you can read this short passage easily, it would not work well for a lengthy document.

❯ For more about typefaces and fonts, see p. 524.

that appear on that line. Thinking of line length in terms of numbers of characters is useful because different-size fonts will allow for different numbers of characters in the same amount of physical space. For example, a line length that works well for a 12-point font does not work as well for a font that is larger or smaller.

As a rule of thumb, you should create lines that are between 40 and 70 characters long (count the spaces between the words, too) for hard copy and between 40 and 55 characters long for online documents. If you're not sure whether your line length is appropriate, you can manually count the letters and spaces in several lines and average them. Many software programs have a Word Count feature that will also give character counts, making it easy to check average line length (see Figure 8.13).

Headings

Headings are guideposts that help readers find the information they want or need in documents as short as a brochure and as long as an encyclopedia. Headings are particularly important in Web sites, where readers tend to look at headings as they surf. With a Web page, a heading may be the only chance you have to engage the attention of your audience. There are four things to consider when creating headings.

Decide what the heading should say. Headings should be concise. Try to capture the core of what is covered in a section in as few words as possible, but make those words meaningful to the reader as a way of increasing accessibility. If the document you are creating is a reference tool or set of instructions, questions are often appropriate headings. Avoid headings that *name* the section (such as "Introduction" and "Conclusion"), and try to think of headings that *describe* the section (for examples, look at the headings in this chapter).

Headings should be grammatically parallel whenever possible. For example, if you use nouns or noun phrases (like some of the headings in this chapter), use *all* nouns or noun phrases consistently throughout the document. If you use questions or statements, make sure that all your headings are either questions or complete sentences.

Choose an appropriate typeface. Sans serif typefaces (see p. 524) are often used for headings because they attract attention. They tend to look heavier than serif typefaces and stand out against the text.

Determine where to position the heading. There are a lot of options for positioning headings, but the most common position for your first heading (the title) is centered. Secondary headings can appear in four positions: (1) flush left, (2) indented the same amount as your paragraph indentation, (3) outdented (hanging out into the margin), or (4) run-in (continuous with the text). Regardless of its position, the heading should be closer to the text that follows it than to the text that precedes it. A simple way to make sure the heading is positioned appropriately is to double-space before a heading and single-space after it. The lesser amount of space visually ties the heading to the text it describes. Make sure to use consistent spacing before and after headings at each level.

 ## Exercise

Outdented headings hang over into the left margin. You will often see outdented headings in magazine articles and textbooks. *Run-in headings* are on the same line as the text that they introduce. Look through Parts 2 and 3 of this book and see if you can find examples of outdented headings and run-in headings.

Decide how many levels to use. For the most part, the kinds of documents you write in school will not need more than two levels of headings beyond the title—one level for major headings and one level for subheadings.

When choosing the levels of headings, follow the recommendations of the documentation style you are using. MLA style documentation, commonly required in English and many other humanities courses, does not advocate headings within a paper. On the other hand, APA style, used in many social science classes, allows five levels of headings. When in doubt, consult your instructor.

One easy way to think of the levels is to compare them to the parts of an outline. Here is an excerpt from a formal outline.

How I Spent My Summer Vacation
I. July
    A. Summer school
        1. Algebra
           a. Homework
           b. Tests
        2. Geography
           a. Maps
           b. Movies
II. August
    A. Family trip (with appropriate subheadings)
    B. Swimming (with appropriate subheadings)

In this example, the items with upper-case Roman numerals would be level 1 headings, and the upper-case letters would be level 2 headings. If you were to write a lengthy, detailed report, you might add a third level of headings for the items with lower-case numerals (i and ii in this example). It's unlikely that you would go into enough detail for a fourth level of headings; if you did, the items identified with lower-case letters would form those headings.

Notice that in this outline, each level includes two items. When you decide to add a level of headings, make sure to have at least two items at that level. If you can only think of one heading for a particular level, there is not enough complexity in your topic to divide it into subtopics.

Each level should look distinctive enough that readers get a sense of where they are in the hierarchy of your document. The most common ways to create these distinctions are through type size and placement, but you can also use bold, underlining, or italics to make headings distinct from one another. Box 8.1 gives suggestions. For school assignments, check with your instructor for specific recommendations.

BOX 8.1 Creating Different Levels of Headings

1. Figure out what type size you will use for the body of your document.
2. Make your lowest level heading the same type size as the body of the text, but use a bold sans serif typeface.
3. Make your next highest level the same typeface, but two or three points larger.
4. Repeat step 3.

If there will be more than three levels, you may want to use italics, underlining, or caps to give yourself extra options (for more on these forms of emphasis, see p. 524). Most projects—other than books—can be completed with three levels of headings. If you think you need four levels, ask yourself if the text could be organized more simply.

Here is an example of how you might design the title and three levels of headings for a document.

Title
20-pt Helvetica, bold, centered

LEVEL ONE
17-pt Helvetica, caps, bold, centered

Level Two: 14-pt Helvetica, bold, flush left

Level 3: 11-pt Helvetica, bold italic, flush left

Body type: 11-pt Times New Roman

Pull Quotes and Sidebars

Although pull quotes and sidebars are rarely used in academic papers, for this course you may want to break up dense passages of text by positioning some information outside the standard paragraph structure. Pull quotes and sidebars—common features in magazines, Web sites, and other sources—not only make the document more attractive but also draw readers into the text. And they are easy to produce with most word processing software. Check with your instructor before adding these elements.

Pull quotes are short segments from the main text—usually no more than a sentence or two—that are particularly important or intriguing. These segments are highlighted as a way of engaging the readers' attention. You have seen pull quotes (sometimes referred to as callouts) in many of the readings in this book.

FIGURE 8.14
Pull Quote in a Magazine

Pull quote uses a larger, bold typeface, set off with extra space.

THE ROAD TO KABUL
(Continued from page 42)
first trip. After so much war, a grimmer culture could be expected. Instead, the Afghans had retained their openness and their wonderful sense of the absurd. They still loved to laugh. Humor and warmth were the weapons everyday people used to endure what had been for them a very long war.

That isn't to say that the Afghans aren't ferocious warriors. They are. And they are equally ferocious survivors, ingenious when it comes to getting by in difficult times. The colorful satellite dishes pieced together from hair-spray and air-freshener cans, now springing up for sale everywhere, are a testament to this improvisational spirit and to how much the people crave contact with the rest of the world.

Many of Afghanistan's men are gone. In war, a country's best men go first. They die or return home without limbs or eyesight. So it has been in Afghanistan for more than 20 years. So it is today. You see them along the roads, on the streets and in the alleys of villages and cities: the broken men, many begging, some too proud to stick out their hands but begging just the same. You can see it in the eyes.

The many war widows are mostly at home, or at a mosque, weeping, wailing and praying. Sometimes you see orphans running in packs, the smaller ones begging or scavenging for food, the older ones fighting and stealing. Etched in my mind forever are the faces of the children we met as they played among the tombstones at the cemetery outside of Kabul. They all knew which of the graves held warriors and which held victims. They knew how the people had died and when and where. One little girl about 2½ years old sat on a tomb, swinging her legs idly. Two graves over, her brother leaned against a tombstone, gazing at the sky.

Time Warner Cable Manhattan Edition

And then there was 19-year-old Raffi Khetab and his dog-eared English dictionary, tossing out ancient slang like "shake a leg," "don't let the cat out of the bag" and, his favorite, "all that jazz." He wanted to fit in when he made it to the USA. Slim as his chances are, he is absolutely convinced that some way, somehow, he will beat the odds. I hope he does. And I hope that, if he does, he finds America to be all that he wants it to be.

Looking for reporting help, we went to the local television station. There was little help to be had. The station, built by the Russians in the 1970s and 1980s, was a bombed-out, shot-up hulk.

In war, a country's best men often go first. They die or return home without limbs or eyesight. So it has been in Afghanistan.

The station's oversize, typically Russian satellite dish had been disabled by Taliban explosives. What was left of it stood against the sky like a monument from another age. The onetime local TV news anchor—a compact, handsome young man who spoke good English—agreed to help us while he waited to get back on the air with his own work. There was sadness in his tight smiles. I think he thought his anchoring days were finished, but he could not or would not give up hope.

To be in Afghanistan again was to feel anew just how awful, how truly awful, is war. From the Tank Man to the orphans of war to the Northern Alliance foreign minister we interviewed when we first arrived in Kabul, the eyes were vacant but for the hurt and fear of the hunted. Everywhere we went in Afghanistan, day and night, we could feel those haunted eyes upon us. ■

Dan Rather anchors the CBS Evening News.

TV GUIDE/**51**

► For advice on wrapping text around inserted elements, see p. 509.

If you think a pull quote will be effective in the document you are creating, ask someone (your instructor, your supervisor, or a friend) for feedback about both content and placement. Once you know what to include and where to put the pull quote, you can highlight it in one of several ways.

› You can use a larger type size (the same typeface as the body text or a different typeface) and then separate it from the rest of the text with a solid line above and below it.

› You can use your word processing program to create a text box and then type the quote inside the box, again using a larger type size than the body text (see Figure 8.14). (See p. 49 of Chapter 2 for a full-size copy of this page.) The text may have a border around it or not.

FIGURE 8.15
Sidebar in a Magazine

Heading and sub-heading indicate sidebar subject.

Box used to separate from main text.

Sidebar used for extended definitions and diagrams.

DIRTY VERSUS NUCLEAR BOMBS

People sometimes confuse radiological with nuclear weapons

A DIRTY BOMB is likely to be a primitive device in which TNT or fuel oil and fertilizer explosives are combined with highly radioactive materials. The detonated bomb vaporizes or aerosolizes the toxic isotopes, propelling them into the air.

High explosives

Radioactive materials

A FISSION BOMB is a more sophisticated mechanism that relies on creating a runaway nuclear chain reaction in uranium 235 or plutonium 239. One type features tall, inward-pointing pyramids of plutonium surrounded by a shell of high explosives.

High explosives

Beryllium/polonium core

Plutonium pieces

Heavy casing

When the bomb goes off, the explosives produce an imploding shock wave that drives the plutonium pieces together into a sphere containing a pellet of beryllium/polonium at the center, creating a critical mass. The resulting fission reaction causes the bomb to explode with tremendous force, sending high-energy electromagnetic waves and fallout into the air.

This kind of scenario could become a reality in the not too distant future. Defending ourselves from the threat of radiological weapons has become a grim necessity. The components and know-how needed to build a dirty bomb are available, and there are fanatics out there who just might do the deed. The arrest earlier this year of Al Qaeda sympathizer José Padilla (Abdullah al Muhajir) on suspicion of plotting to construct and set off a dirty bomb gives an indication of the interest in building such a device.

A radiological weapon, or dirty bomb, is typically a crude device comprising conventional explosives, such as TNT or a fuel oil/fertilizer mixture, laced with highly radioactive materials. The explosives generate a pulse of heat that vaporizes or aerosolizes radioactive material and propels it across a wide area.

Weapons experts consider radiological bombs a messy but potentially effective technology that could cause tremendous psychological damage, exploiting the public's fears of invisible radiation. Not weapons of mass destruction but weapons of mass disruption, these devices could wreak economic havoc by making target areas off-limits for an extended period. Radiological bombs have never been used, mainly because they have long been considered inappropriate for military purposes: their effect is too delayed and unpredictable to sway a battle.

Although they are relatively simple in principle, constructing and deploying one of these mechanisms is difficult to do. It is more complicated than wrapping stolen materials around a stick of dynamite. Such a clumsy weapon might only scatter large chunks of material, limiting the area affected and making cleanup easy. An effective dirty bomb is, however, much easier to assemble than a nuclear weapon, although it would still require considerable skill. A major problem is that the builder could be fatally exposed to hot isotopes. But a deadly dose of radiation can take weeks to have an effect and so might not deter suicidal terrorists.

Radioactive Rebar
Materials that are highly radioactive are employed in hundreds of medical, industrial and academic applications. There are about two million individual sources

---

Sidebars (see Figure 8.15) contain information that is peripheral to the main text, but not essential. Typically, sidebars are set to the side of the text. Like pull quotes, they can be separated by a line or put inside a box. They can also be set to one side, with the main text wrapping around them.

Paper Size

For most purposes, $8\frac{1}{2}'' \times 11''$ sheets of paper are appropriate, but other choices are useful for different situations. For example, personal stationery is smaller; legal paper, which is used for contracts and other legal documents, is longer ($8\frac{1}{2}'' \times 14''$).

For Collaboration

With several of your classmates, make a list of all the situations you can think of where the paper used—for a school project, flyer, mailing, newspaper, or magazine—was not a standard size. How did the audience, circumstances, or purposes justify an atypical paper size?

In general, you will seldom have to worry or even think about paper size. However, when creating a document such as a brochure, poster, or newsletter, you may want to consider nonstandard papers. Ask yourself the following questions.

> Will my software program be able to create a page that matches the paper size?
> Will my printer be able to accept a nonstandard-size paper?
> Is it likely that anyone will need to photocopy this document? Do photocopiers accept this size paper?
> If the document has to be mailed, will it fit into a standard envelope or will the envelope have to be a special size as well?
> What will the paper (and envelope) cost? If it's a special envelope, will it cost more to mail each piece? Can I (or whoever is paying for the document) afford the extra cost(s)?

Margins

Most instructors require one-inch margins for academic work, and word processing software usually sets default margins of one inch or a bit more. (You should check your settings and the requirements of your course.) But there are times when other margins are used to meet specific purposes. For example, when producing a résumé, you may want to make smaller margins at the top or bottom to give yourself more room (so you can keep the résumé to one page). When producing a document that will be bound or hole-punched, you should make the left margin wider to accommodate the binding. The guidelines below will help you decide if you need to change the margins in your document.

Identify the reason for changing the margins. Are you trying to cram a lot of information onto one or two pages? (This may make the page too busy and unreadable.) Are you trying to accommodate letterhead, graphics, or other formatting needs? Are you trying to meet a page requirement for an assignment by increasing the margins? (Most instructors will not approve.)

> For an example of a student essay following MLA style for margins, see p. 606.

Decide how much white space is appropriate. Including appropriate amounts of white space around the visual and textual elements of the document can make the material stand out and attract attention. Or it can dwarf the text and make it seem insignificant. For example, wide margins do not make a short note more effective or visually appropriate. Likewise, too little white space around the edges can create a page that is dense, overcrowded, and unfriendly. Readers do not like pages that are too full.

Indentation

There are three primary instances where you need to be concerned about indentation: at the beginning of paragraphs, at headings, and in lists. There are no hard-and-fast rules about this, but the following discussion offers guidelines that can help you decide how much to indent.

⟩ For advice on line length, see p. 498. For more on type size, see p. 526.

Traditionally, the first line of every paragraph is indented a fixed amount to give the reader a visual cue that a new topic is being introduced. The length of the indentation, or tab, will depend somewhat on the line length and the type size, but it should rarely be less than three character spaces or greater than five character spaces. If your instructor requires MLA documentation style, the standard indentation is five spaces or one-half inch. APA style also recommends an indentation of five spaces or one-half inch. Sometimes you will see documents that do not use indentations for new paragraphs. These "block style" documents (see Figure 8.16), usually business letters or memos and a great many electronic documents, use an extra line space (extra blank space between the lines) to indicate that a new paragraph is starting. Because of the double space between paragraphs, block style documents are usually single-spaced.

When planning indentations for other elements, such as headings, lists, graphs, charts, tables, and bibliographic entries, think of the entire document and make sure that you do not have too many different indentations. Wherever you plan to have an indentation, mentally draw a vertical line down the whole page. Keep the number of those imaginary vertical lines to a minimum to avoid confusing the reader. For example, the résumé in Figure 8.1 has too many vertical lines that draw the reader's eyes all over the page, making it difficult to focus on the important information.

When you create a Works Cited list for a research project, the entries are typically arranged with *hanging indents:* the first line is typed at the left margin and any additional lines are indented. You should use the same size indentation that you used throughout the paper for paragraphs. A Works Cited entry in MLA style, indented five spaces or one-half inch, would look like the example below.

McNergney, Robert F., and Joanne M. Herbert. <u>Foundations of Education</u>. Boston: Allyn & Bacon, 2001.

FIGURE 8.16
Block-style Memo

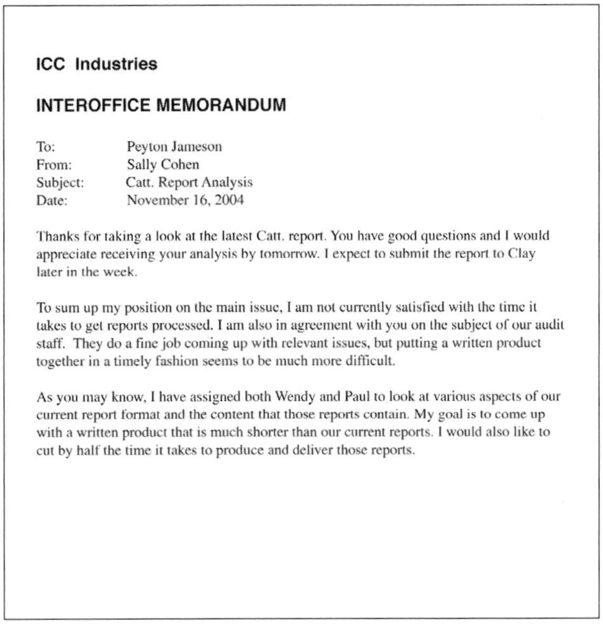

ICC Industries

INTEROFFICE MEMORANDUM

To: Peyton Jameson
From: Sally Cohen
Subject: Catt. Report Analysis
Date: November 16, 2004

Thanks for taking a look at the latest Catt. report. You have good questions and I would appreciate receiving your analysis by tomorrow. I expect to submit the report to Clay later in the week.

To sum up my position on the main issue, I am not currently satisfied with the time it takes to get reports processed. I am also in agreement with you on the subject of our audit staff. They do a fine job coming up with relevant issues, but putting a written product together in a timely fashion seems to be much more difficult.

As you may know, I have assigned both Wendy and Paul to look at various aspects of our current report format and the content that those reports contain. My goal is to come up with a written product that is much shorter than our current reports. I would also like to cut by half the time it takes to produce and deliver those reports.

▷ For more about works cited lists and reference lists, see **Chapter 12.**

Although the information would be arranged slightly differently for APA style, the format (hanging indent) would be the same. When using a different citation style, you will need to check a reference guide to find the correct format.

Spacing

Spacing involves the amount of space between lines of typed words. The most common spacing options are single, 1½, and double. Single spacing has a line of words on every "line" available, 1½ spacing adds an extra half line of space between lines of words, and double spacing adds another full blank line between each line of words.

The choice you make for spacing will probably be determined by some outside source—the instructions from a teacher or supervisor, the conventions of a document type (for instance, MLA-style and APA-style research papers should be double-spaced), or the constraints of the amount of total space available. However, if you are free to make choices, here are some general guidelines.

> ▷ Use single spacing for letters, memos, and other short (one- or two-page) business documents and for most online texts. Add an extra blank space between paragraphs in block-style print and electronic documents (see p. 497).

> Use 1½ spacing for longer documents, especially those with minimal interruption (headings, charts, photographs, and so forth) of word-heavy passages.

> Reserve double spacing for drafts where you or a reviewer may need room to write comments or revision ideas or when your instructor or style guide requires it.

> Add more space between lines when working with especially large type sizes. Many software applications allow you to set a specific amount of space (called leading) between lines of text. The word *leading* should take you to the correct information in a Help system.

Justification

Justification is a term that describes how a document is aligned on its left and right edges. Your software program gives several options: you can create text that is left-, right-, fully-, or center-justified.

In *left-justified* text all the words line up on the left side of the page, but the right side is "ragged." This paragraph is left justified. Left-justified text is one of the most user-friendly formats for readers of English and other languages in which the eyes scan from left to right. Thus left-justified text is the default setting on most word processing software. Left-justified text (or "ragged right," because the right edge of the lines is uneven) will be appropriate in almost every writing situation you encounter. *Never hesitate to left-justify your text.*

Right-justified text is the opposite of left-justified text: all the words line up on the right side, but the left side is ragged. This paragraph is right justified. Right-justified text is not used often because it is hard to read. *Reserve right-justified text for special documents.* You will most often see it in advertising, magazine titles, and Web pages in which the document designers have carefully manipulated the line lengths to get particular words on particular lines.

Fully justified text has the words lined up evenly on both margins, as in this paragraph. Most books are fully justified (as is most of the text in this book), as are many documents written in columns, such as newspapers, magazines, and newsletters (see the columns in Figure 8.12, for example). Some organizations that have internal style guides also require fully justified papers and reports. However, the danger in fully justified text is that distracting rivers of white often appear between the words or sometimes there are big gaps in lines of text—especially if the document contains a significant number of lengthy words or line length is short. You can solve some of these problems by turning on the hyphenation feature, which allows the software program to make decisions about splitting words to even out the lines. Unless specifically requested, *avoid fully justified text.*

Center-justified text aligns each line on the center of the page. For some reason, students and professionals alike tend to overuse centered text. As with right-justified text, *reserve centering for special uses* such as titles, headings, and cover pages, as well as for documents such as formal invitations, advertisements, and posters.

Text Wrapping

One way to incorporate visuals and other elements in your document is to format the text so that it wraps around or close to the visual element—a photograph, a drawing, a pull quote, or even another article. Many software programs allow you to wrap text easily. Just make sure that wrapping the text does not result in a column that is too narrow (a line length that is too short) or make it too hard for the reader to follow your train of thought.

⟩ For more about wrapping text, see the discussion of clip art on p. 514.

 Exercise

Collect some examples of left-, right-, fully, and center-justified texts. See if you can figure out why each text was printed with that type of justification. Do you agree with the author's or designer's decision? Why or why not?

Headers and Footers

Headers (sometimes called running heads) and footers are small sections at the top and bottom of a page in a printed document that may contain the page number (see p. 510), the title or author of the document, and/or the date the document was produced.

The primary function of headers and footers is to remind readers where they are in a document or to give them reference points for returning to information. In academic work, many documentation styles call for headers on each page that include the author's (your) name and page number (MLA style) or a shortened title and page number (APA style). Outside of academic work, since readers should not need reminders on the first page of a document, and since the first page is easy to find, it is

⟩ For an example of a student essay following MLA style for headers, see **Chapter 12.**

conventional to omit the header or footer on the first page. Most software programs make it easy to set "first page different" or "omit header/footer this/first page."

The guidelines for creating headers and footers online, however, are slightly different. Online headers typically appear in the form of a navigation bar. Because the header appears the same on all screens in an online document, it can serve to unify all the Web pages in your site visually. When used as a navigation bar, the header also enables readers to find different parts of the site easily. Unlike print documents, where readers typically look at the first page before moving into subsequent pages, online documents can be entered at any point. A unifying header can enable readers to find the homepage and other important segments of the document. Online footers also may be used to provide navigation (for example, providing links to Home) and to provide information about the editor or sponsor of the page, date of publication, and so on.

❯ To see an example of a header providing navigation information, see Figure 8.10; for an example of a footer giving publication information, see Figure 8.3.

Just as with body text, information in headers can be justified (left, right, or center). Also, you can use any style and size of type available—for example, text appearing in headers and footers can be the same as the body text, an italic version of the body text, a point or two smaller than the body text, or a completely different size and style.

In some software programs, the space for the header and footer is reserved regardless of whether or not you choose to enter anything into that space. In other programs, adding a header or footer decreases the amount of space available on the page. Therefore, it's a good idea to insert headers or footers early in the production of your document so that the total number of pages and the placement of images and text on each page will not be changed by any late additions.

Page Numbers

Page numbers can typically be added to a document in one of three ways: through the creation of a header or footer, by using the software Insert menu, or by clicking on a page number icon.

Page numbers can be centered at the top or bottom, placed in the upper or lower right-hand corner, or (if the pages of the document will be printed front and back) in the upper or lower outside corner. Again, your software program will allow you to place the page number in any of these positions (it will say something like "different odd and even pages" or "alternating pages" for double-sided pages). The upper and lower left-hand corners are seldom used for page numbers except in block-style business letters and reports. Whatever you decide about position, be consistent throughout your document. If you are unsure where to put the page number, check with the person who will review your document (your instructor or supervisor). If you are writing an essay following MLA or APA style, you will need to put the page number in the upper right-hand corner of every page, one inch from the right edge and one-half inch from the top edge, as part of the header (see p. 606). This is the default position for the page number in many word processing programs.

You should develop the habit now of always including page numbers on printed documents. (Page numbers are rarely used in online documents.) The page number can be as simple as the numeral itself (most common), can have the abbreviation "p." in front of the numeral, or can be surrounded by dashes (- 3 -). The version with dashes is most commonly used in centered page numbers.

Links

Links are highlighted words and phrases, buttons, tabs, or other visual cues that connect elements in an online document and improve its accessibility. Links enable readers to make choices about what they read and the order in which they read them. Be sure to plan links carefully to provide obvious cues to readers.

Links can be internal, connecting to other parts of the site, or external, connecting to pages in other sites. Although you do not need to distinguish between internal and external links in your site, you should make sure that readers can get back to their prior position easily. With external links, readers will have to rely on the Back button in their browser. With internal links, they may use the Back button, but thoughtful Web-page designers also provide return links—buttons that say "Return to home" or "Return to top."

A text link should be concise but meaningful. It can be a single word or a simple phrase, but it should not be a lengthy sentence. Pick out a key word or phrase in the sentence to use as the link to decrease the interference with reading for those readers who choose not to follow each link.

You can also create links by using icons, buttons, or other images. For example, look at some of the links in the Gallagher Health Center site (Figure 8.10). The two large set of buttons at the top of the screen very clearly identify links with specific labels that let readers know what they can accomplish by clicking on the link. If you use images, consider adding captions so that readers know what the image will link them to. For example, you might use a photograph of some athletes as a link and create a caption that says, "Click on the photo to learn more about last week's hockey game."

Images

❭ For a discussion of how a photograph or series of photographs contributes to a reader's understanding of a subject, see the analysis of "The Road to Kabul" on p. 35.

There are times when words alone cannot describe an object with sufficient clarity or present an object in its most appealing or useful light. Images—or pictorial representations—are the photographs, drawings, cartoons, and schematic drawings that show what something is actually like.

Not so long ago, it was fairly difficult to include photographs or drawings in papers and reports. Writers could cut them out and paste them onto their pages and then photocopy the result, or they could hire a graphic artist or a printer to incorporate visuals in their work. Today scanners, computer drawing programs, and vast libraries of clip art (drawings and other images that can be "clipped"—cut and pasted—for free or for a fee) enable anyone to include a tremendous variety of images. However, just because you *can* do it doesn't mean you should; and just because you can do it doesn't mean you can do it *right*.

Before including an image (photo, drawing, map, or clip art) in your print or online document, ask yourself the following questions.

❭ **Why do I need to add this image to my document?** Will it engage the reader? Will it make the information more accessible? Will it contribute to the voice you are trying to create?

❭ **Where should I place the image on the page or screen?** Typically, the image should be near the text that refers to it. In academic documents, images should be numbered and labeled and a reference to each should appear in your text: *see Figure 5*. Also think about alignment and tension (see pp. 481 and 492). How does the image line up with other elements on the page? What kind of tension does the image create on the page?

❭ **How big should it be?** The visual should be big enough for the reader to see and understand it clearly. But do you want the visual to overwhelm the reader or just remind him or her of something? Notice the way that visuals throughout this book are presented in a variety of sizes. Some of the model texts are produced as full-page or nearly full-page reproductions. In other cases thumbnails, miniature versions of the larger print or online document, are appropriate.

❭ **Can I use the whole image, or should some of it be trimmed off (cropped)?** What happens to the meaning of the visual if you delete some of the information? How does that affect the message that the visual conveys?

❭ **Does it need a caption?** If the visual is self-explanatory, it may not need a caption. Or if you refer to the visual explicitly in the text and explain it thoroughly there, it may not need a caption. But if your readers are likely to skim through the document without reading the text, and the meaning of the visual isn't obvious, you should add captions so that they know what

⟩ For an example of a student essay that includes captions in MLA style, see **Chapter 12.**

⟩ For advice on citing photographs and other images, see **Chapter 12.**

they're looking at. Note that when you are writing for your courses and using MLA style, you must include a caption and position the visual as close as you can to the reference in your text. Under the visual, include the label *Fig.* (for *Figure*) and a number for the visual, followed by complete source information in a caption. The label and caption should appear directly below the visual. APA style also requires identifying numbers and captions for any visuals; place the number, title, and caption below the image, flush left.

⟩ **Should it be presented in color or black and white?** Which version provides more clarity? How does the meaning change when you go from color to black and white? Are any of your readers going to want to print or photocopy this document? A color visual may not print or photocopy well in black and white.

⟩ **Have I given credit to the originator of the graphic in my text?** Just as you cite the source for quotes, paraphrases, and summarized ideas, you need to cite the source for any visual images used in your text.

⟩ **Do I have permission to use this graphic?** If the graphic was created by someone else, make sure that it is legal to copy it before you use it. Many Web sites provide free artwork, but others will tell you that the material is not to be copied. If you are using someone else's graphic in a text that will be published—in print or online—you must get written permission from the owner of that graphic. Many people do not realize that material published on the Internet is protected by the same copyright laws that protect material published on paper. If you are using the graphic for an assignment that will not be posted on the Web, you may be permitted to use it under the "fair use" exception, which allows use of material for some educational purposes.

⟩ **If I modify a photograph or drawing, will I be distorting an important fact or truth?** For example, imagine you are creating a brochure for a summer recreation program, and you have a series of photographs of participants from prior years. However, the photographs all show white teenagers, and you need to show that teenagers of all races are welcome in this program. Adding color to the skin tones or pasting in photos of teenagers of color who had not participated would be distorting the truth and would therefore be unethical. One solution to this problem would be to take some new photos that show the actual diversity of the program participants. Or, if you are making the brochure after the program has ended, you might choose to use the photos you have, cropping them in interesting ways to emphasize the activities over the participants.

An important consideration when choosing graphics of any kind for online use is the length of time it will take for a reader to load the graphic. Large and complex graphics may be visually appealing, but they may also discourage readers from looking at your site. Avoid large graphics, especially at the top of a Web page, when designing online documents.

❯ For more information about
choosing appropriate visuals,
see **Chapter 2.**

To be on the safe side, limit yourself to image files no greater than 20 kilobytes.

Many writers use images and clip art to add visual interest to their documents. The term *clip art* refers to copyright-free or royalty-free drawings and photographs that are widely available online or integrated in many software programs. It is easy to search for clip art and other images on the Internet through design sites and at photo archives. For example, the Google homepage allows you to search the Web for appropriate visuals (click on the Images tab). Note, however, that if you choose images that are copyrighted, you will need to contact the author or publisher of the site to request permission to reuse the images in any text that will be posted online.

Word processing programs offer various tools for importing or pasting images into your texts. This is fairly easy to do and can be effective. If you work on a PC, you can copy and paste the image directly into your text by highlighting the image you find online, right clicking on it, selecting Copy, positioning your cursor in your document, and right clicking again to select Paste. You can also save a picture as an image file by right clicking on the image and selecting Save Picture As. To place the image in your text in Microsoft Word, for example, position your cursor in the correct place in the document and use the Insert menu, choosing Picture and selecting From File. If you work on a Mac, you can insert a saved image by using the Insert menu, or you can drag the online image from your Web browser to the location in your text where you want to add it. To create higher-quality copies of images or to edit them, there are software tools (such as the freeware program PrintKey) that allow you to easily create screenshots and manipulate images you have on your computer screen. For images from print sources, many campus computer labs offer access to scanners. Image editing programs such as Microsoft Paint or Adobe Photoshop allow users to crop, flip, resize, and edit details in images.

You can position the image so that the text wraps around it in a variety of ways (which vary with different software applications), and you  can change the size of any image—either when you scan it or after you have placed it within the document. However, make sure that when you resize it, you don't inadvertently distort the shape of the drawing. Notice that the clip art image of a windmill is distorted—it's stretched after sloppy resizing. When you resize an image, make sure to maintain the original proportions or the image will be distorted.

Before inserting a visual, however, think about how your audience will respond to a particular image and how it adds to your purpose.

Don't just throw in an image because it's cute (like the lab equipment to the left of this paragraph) or because you're afraid your document is boring. Instead of using images like this appealing but generic lab clip art, Stephanie Guzik chose to use effective photographs of her subject in her profile "Behind a Plain White Lab Coat" in Chapter 2. Use images that have relevance to your subject, and position them so that they go along with the words you have written. Remember to use images responsibly, seeking permission to use copyrighted images if necessary, giving credit for images you use, and taking care not to edit images deceptively. Inserting images can be an effective way to connect with an audience (if it's the only visual on the page, it will be the first thing the audience notices), but you have to make sure that the visual reflects your audience, your topic, and your purpose. The bottom line is that images can be effective when used appropriately and carefully, when they help you connect with your audience.

Representations of Information

There are many instances when the information that you need to convey to readers is too complex to be written in paragraph form or even in lists. In these situations, graphic shortcuts can represent the more detailed information. You need to determine which graphic form will answer the kinds of questions readers will have about your topic. Will they have a great many questions and want detailed answers? (Choose a table or bar graph.) Will they just want to get a general sense of the relationship among a few elements? (Choose a pie chart.) Will they want to see how certain things have changed over time? (Choose a line or bar graph.) Computers have made the creation of tables, charts, and graphs so easy that you will most likely be expected to use them in many situations throughout your academic and professional careers. As with other visual elements, check with your instructor about the appropriate uses of tables, charts, and graphs in your assignments.

Tables

There are two common types of tables. The first type is a *text table*, such as the student context analysis tables in Part 1 of this book (see, for example, p. 74). Because Western readers read from left to right, tables pull the reader across the column to see the related information.

The second type is a *data table*. Data tables present information, usually in columns, that is complex and detailed. Most data tables are not meant to provide information at a glance. The point of such tables is to enable readers to choose the kind of information that is most important, interesting, or relevant to them so they can make their own comparisons. Data tables can present numerical information (see Figure 8.17), textual information, or a combination of data represented in words and numbers. Textual data tables do not try to provide a detailed description; rather, they give succinct facts. An example would be a table that lists the principal products of a variety of countries or the types of jobs in greatest demand in different regions of the United States.

Charts and Graphs

There are many kinds of charts and graphs, and your computer probably has software to help you create a lot of them. Like tables, charts and graphs are visual tools that enable you to present a great deal of information in a succinct way. There are many specialized charts and graphs—such as flow charts and organizational charts—that you might need to read but that you are probably not going to be called on to create in your academic work. The trick to using charts and graphs is to choose the right one for each task.

FIGURE 8.17
Data Table
Active Duty Military
Personnel by Geographic
Area, 1989–1995

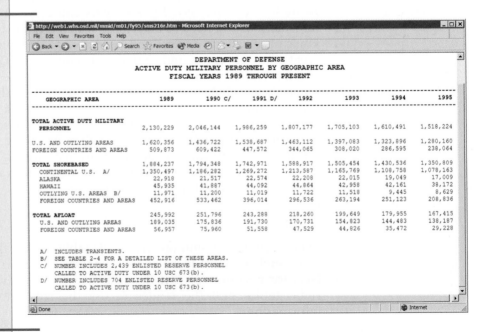

Pie Charts

Pie charts give a quick picture of how some "pie," or whole, is divided. This type of chart is usually used when there are a relatively small number of "pieces" and the important thing is the relationship among those pieces rather than their actual size. For example, if you wanted to give readers an idea of the relative number of shore-based service people working here and abroad in 1990, you could create a pie chart such as the one shown in Figure 8.18 (based on the information in the table in Figure 8.17). This pie chart does not tell how many people were in each location, but it does show that a majority were stationed in the continental United States and that there were very few personnel based in Alaska.

Your software program should have several design options for creating labels, using color, and so on for each type of chart. For example, the pie chart in Figure 8.18 uses color, which is often in the default settings. However, the key to this pie chart will not be useful if the chart is photocopied in black and white—readers would have difficulty distinguishing the different colors for the smaller segments. To produce a pie chart that could be usefully photocopied in black and white, you could choose a black and white option to create distinct visual markings for each segment, as well as labels for each segment rather than a key.

FIGURE 8.18
Pie Chart
Geographic Distribution of Shore-based Military Personnel

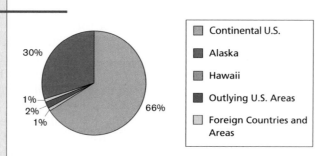

Bar Graphs

Bar graphs are also useful for showing the relationship among quantities, but usually they present slightly more precise information than pie charts (and less precise information than tables). Using the information from the table in Figure 8.17, the bar graph in Figure 8.19 shows the number of military personnel stationed in the United States and abroad from 1989 to 1995. This graph does not show exactly how many troops were in both categories, but a reader can estimate roughly how many and can see how the numbers changed for both categories over time.

Note that the labels on the graph axes indicate the primary information; the labels in the key indicate the secondary information. Looking at

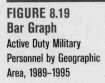

FIGURE 8.19
Bar Graph
Active Duty Military
Personnel by Geographic
Area, 1989–1995

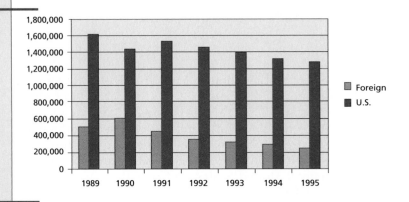

a key requires more work from the reader, so it should contain the less important information.

Line Graphs

Line graphs show change over time. They are commonly used in business, primarily to demonstrate increases (or decreases) in sales, customers, clients, or prices. We can plot some of the same data from Figure 8.17 about active duty military personnel on a line graph to get a representation of the decrease in personnel over time (see Figure 8.20). A line graph with multiple lines could be used to plot more specific information, allowing the reader to compare two sets of data over time. For example,

FIGURE 8.20
Line Graph
Total Active Duty Military
Personnel, 1989–1995

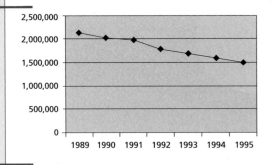

a graph with two lines could show the distinct data for the personnel in the United States and for those abroad.

A simple rule of thumb for creating charts and graphs is: *keep it simple*. Charts and graphs that are cluttered with too many lines or too many labels are hard to read and may confuse the audience. When creating multiple charts and graphs on the same topic, be sure to use colors and symbols consistently. Be careful to choose colors that offer clear contrast, too. The simpler the visual, the more likely it is to convey your message. For additional information on how published authors have used tables, charts, and graphs, see the analysis of "Cream of the Crop" on p. 271 of Chapter 5.

For Collaboration

Assume that you work for a local nonprofit organization with the following income and expenses for 2004:

INCOME
Government grants: $375,000
Fees: $273,467
Contributions: $114,763
Special events: $58,450
Product sales: $12,468
Total income: $834,148

EXPENSES
Program services: $741,935
Administrative costs: $88,500
Miscellaneous: $5,230

Total expenses: $835,665

As directors of the organization, you are responsible for bringing in more money and must present the past year's financial information to two groups of people, as described in the following scenarios.

> Within the community is a core group of consistent contributors who give the same amount each year, even though the cost of running the organization continues to go up. You must convince these contributors to give additional funds during your presentation at the annual fund-raising banquet. You need to create graphic representations of financial data that will convince the contributors of the need for additional funds and that will reassure them that the money they gave in the past has been spent wisely.

> Your organization is eligible to apply for a new grant from a federal agency. You have to write a proposal explaining why your organization needs the money and demonstrating that it is fiscally responsible. There is a strict page limitation, so you must present financial information concisely but in enough detail to make a strong case.

Working with one or two classmates, sketch out the visuals (by hand or using a computer) that you would create for the presentation and the proposal. Be prepared to justify your choice of visuals based on the audience, circumstances, and purposes for each situation.

Color

This section offers advice about using color for print and online documents. It will help you figure out the answers to three important questions.

> When (in what documents) should I use color?
> Where should I position color?
> What color(s) should I choose?

Using Color Effectively

With increasingly easy access to inexpensive color printers, many writers have begun to incorporate color into documents that were formerly produced only in black and white. However, the availability of color technology has not been matched by an increase in writers' understanding of how to use color, so many color documents are difficult to read and visually unappealing. Any random surf around the Internet will bring up Web sites that do not use color appropriately—they have either too much color, or ugly or illegible colors.

Color makes pages (print or electronic) more interesting. It's a fact of human nature that people would rather look at a page that has color on it. But you shouldn't add color just to get people to look at a page. When readers look at that page and see that color, they should see something that they need or want to know.

Check with your instructor for guidance on using color in specific print documents for your courses. Here is a short list of some text elements and kinds of documents that make the best use of color.

> **Titles, headings, and subheadings.** Color can be used effectively to distinguish headings from the main text. You can see this effect in Figure 8.21 and in various places throughout this textbook.

> **Section dividers.** Blocks of color printed along a top or side margin can help readers find chapters or sections more easily. For example, in this textbook the sections that describe MLA and APA documentation styles have color printed along the side of the page so that readers can find them quickly (see Chapter 12).

> **Photographs, drawings, charts, and graphs.** Graphics can be more meaningful, easier to read, and more conspicuous if they are in color.

> **Warnings.** If you are creating a set of procedures or instructions and you need to warn readers about something they ought to know or ought not to do, color will help ensure that readers do not overlook vital information (see Figure 8.22).

> **Attention-grabbers.** You can use unexpected colors to draw extra attention to any element on the page.

Although color is distinctive, no color will contrast as well as black when printed against a white background (see Figure 8.23). Therefore, keep a few things in mind when using color for type.

When using color to emphasize a few words within the text, consider making those words bold. This will make the letters thicker, adding contrast and making them more noticeable.

FIGURE 8.21
Colored Headings

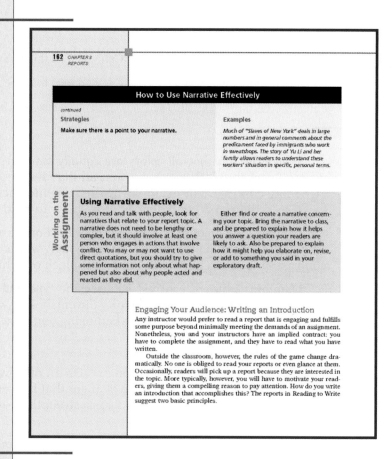

FIGURE 8.22
Colored Warnings in a Child's Car Seat Instruction Manual

FIGURE 8.23
Color Contrast for
Legibility

Can you read this line easily?   Can you read this line easily?

Can you read this line easily?   **Can you read this line easily?**

Can you read this line easily?   Can you read this line easily?

Can you read this line easily?

Remember that not all colors are equally legible (see Figure 8.23). In general, darker colors are easier to read than lighter colors because they give more contrast. For example, against a white background, red is easier to read than pink, and dark blue is easier to read than yellow.

Minimize the amount of text that is printed or presented in a light color on a dark background (reversed). Even though white on black is a strong contrast, it is much harder to read than black on white.

Maintain sufficient contrast between the type and the background. As people grow older, their visual acuity diminishes. As with type size, think about the age of your audience when using contrast.

Positioning Color

Color makes a strong visual statement. On an otherwise black and white page, the reader's eye will go to an element that is in color no matter what color you choose. Because of color's strength, you need to position it wisely.

Use color sparingly, and keep the number of colors to a minimum. Use color for headings, bullets, boxes, images, and graphics. If you use too much color, readers will not know where to look first. Did you ever visit a Web site and leave quickly because you couldn't find what you wanted on the first screen? It may have been because there was so much color that you couldn't really see what was on the screen.

Reserve color for the most important elements on the page. Imagine a grammar handbook where a block of color at the top of the page provides the background for headings such as "Commas" and "Parallelism," or a dictionary where the index tabs are colored. If you use color for trivial details, readers may not find the important information—whether that information consists of actual words typed or printed in color, images, or the background that draws attention to words typed or printed in black or white.

Use color consistently. For example, use the same color for all subheadings to connect them visually. If you use color inconsistently, you will confuse the readers.

Choosing Color

Although there are no hard-and-fast rules about what colors to choose for every purpose, there are some general guidelines for choosing colors that work well together, that don't work well in certain situations, and that carry conventional or cultural meanings.

When using only one or two colors, make sure that they will work in all situations where you want them. For example, imagine you're printing a brochure about a nature preserve and you want to use black for the text and color for certain graphic elements and for the headings. You might choose a shade of green because of the theme of the brochure; just make sure that the shade you choose is dark enough for the headings to be legible.

When using more than one color, choose a combination of strong, dark colors and light colors. You may want to use multiple colors within the same color family—for example, lighter and darker shades of green for the nature preserve brochure. Combining strong, dark colors with lighter, more subtle ones gives contrast that will add interest and provides a palette of colors for various uses (pale tints for background images, darker shades for headings and graphics that need emphasis, contrasting colors for pie charts, and so on).

Get feedback from others. Let others look at the colors you have chosen and the way you are planning to use them. Make sure these readers find the colors comfortable and appropriate. Since different people "see" colors differently, make sure that the people you ask to check your color choices belong to or represent your intended audience.

Check the final product before turning it in or distributing it. Color combinations that look good in a Web text may not look the same when printed. Colors used in electronic texts may not look the same on other browsers or operating systems, so try to check several before posting your pages to the Web.

Remember that if you use color for a document that has to be duplicated, the cost will increase dramatically. Before adding color to such a document, find out how much it will cost to print or photocopy, and make sure that you (or whoever is paying) can afford it.

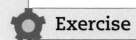 Exercise

Take another look at Figures 8.5, 8.8, 8.15, and 8.21 to see what you think of the colors. Do they make sense? How do they make you feel? Can you think of any reason why the authors or designers might have chosen those colors?

Typefaces and Fonts

Typefaces are families of characters—letters, numbers, and symbols. A typeface, such as Times Roman, might be available with different options for emphasis—italic or bold. A *font* is a set of type in a particular size and style, such as 11-point Times Roman. You might consider three important aspects of typefaces and fonts—style, size, and emphasis—to help you make decisions when designing your print or online documents.

Although most software applications provide users with a variety of font choices, most people don't think much about what style of type to use. People tend to choose on the basis of personal taste, use what they're told to use, or rely on the software's default setting. However, you are likely to have opportunities to choose a font, so this section is designed to help you make that choice on the basis of reasoning rather than just personal preference. Following are some general rules. Keep in mind, however, that you should always follow any specific guidelines that your instructor (or, at work, your supervisor) provides.

In printed documents, reserve sans serif typefaces for headings and short lines of text. Long lines in sans serif typefaces are harder to read on paper. For Web sites, choose a sans serif typeface for all text because the serifs tend to blur, depending on the screen resolution.

Do not mix too many typefaces in one document. One serif and one sans serif should be sufficient.

Use font size and other forms of emphasis to create differentiation. Italics and bold are the most common forms of emphasis.

Use script, handwriting, and decorative typefaces sparingly. These typefaces are often difficult to read, so limit their use to special purposes.

For Web documents, choose a common sans serif typeface, such as Helvetica or Arial, or use default styles to ensure that your text will be legible on a variety of browsers. Some typefaces, such as Verdana, have been created specifically for use on the Web. However, not all monitors and systems are able to deliver new typefaces.

Type Style

Although there are several ways to categorize styles of type, one of the most useful is to identify whether the typeface is *serif* or *sans serif*. The serif is the little "tail" that is readily visible in the letter T—notice the tails that come down from the crossbar at the top and that extend on each side of the bottom. It's easiest to see if you compare it to an uppercase T from a typeface that is sans (or "without") serif, T. A sans serif T is made with just two straight lines. One of the most typical serif typefaces (the default setting in many word processors) is Times. Courier (which looks like typewriter type)

FIGURE 8.24
Serif and Sans Serif
Typefaces

Serif	Sans Serif
Courier	Arial
Palatino	**Chicago**
Cooper Black	Geneva
Times Roman	Helvetica

is also a serif typeface. Popular sans serif typefaces include Arial and Helvetica. Your software may have many different styles of type, but you will always be able to find a selection of styles with and without serifs. (See Figure 8.24 for some examples of serif and sans serif typefaces.)

Serif typefaces are best used for body text in printed documents; sans serif typefaces are used for headings, tables, captions, and legends (in graphs). Sans serif typefaces are also best used for all online documents.

Three additional categories that you should know about are script, handwriting, and decorative. Both script and handwriting typefaces mimic handwritten text. Script typefaces connect the letters the way you see them in cursive writing. (Italic typefaces are *not* script—they are slanted versions of straight, or Roman, ones.) Handwriting typefaces look more like hand-printed text. Here are some examples.

Do you think this looks like it was written by hand? (This typeface is called Sand.)

Do you think this looks like it was written by hand? (This typeface is called Textile.)

Do you think this looks like it was written by hand? (This typeface is called Kidprint.)

Script and handwriting typefaces are most often used in personal or display documents—invitations, announcements, flyers, posters, brochures, advertisements, and so forth.

Decorative typefaces are not intended for books or essays or articles. They're fun and interesting and distinctive—and often hard to read in large blocks. Like script typefaces, decorative ones are most often used for display—for headings or signposts or attention-getters—or for informal, personal documents. Here is an example.

Would you really like to read a whole page in this typeface? (This typeface is called Edwardian Script.)

Size

The bigger the font, the more emphasis the words will get; conversely, the smaller the font, the less attention the words will get. Font size is traditionally measured in fractions of an inch called *points*. Most people are comfortable reading text printed in 10-, 11-, or 12-point type. However, all fonts of the same point size are not the same actual size. Below is a sentence typed in the same font size (11 point), but in two different typefaces.

11-point Courier:

The sentence "The quick brown fox jumped over the lazy dog" includes every letter of our alphabet.

11-point French Script:

The sentence "The quick brown fox jumped over the lazy dog" includes every letter of our alphabet.

Notice that the first version (Courier) takes almost twice as much space as the second version (French Script). You can also look back at the samples of script and decorative typefaces, all of which were typed in 14 point, to see how font choice affects the amount of space used.

As you make decisions about font size, make sure your text is easy to read and appropriate for your audience. For academic texts, 11- or 12-point type is often required. There are situations where you will need to adjust font size—for example, texts written for young children and older adults are typically written in larger fonts.

People often use a larger font size for major text headings. When using font size to differentiate among headings, you need to increase or decrease by at least two points for the difference to be noticeable. That is, if your lowest level heading is in a 12-point font, your next higher level heading should be at least 14 points.

❯ For more information about headings, see p. 499.

Emphasis

There are many ways to add emphasis, but be careful not to use too many ways in any one document or on any one page (of either print or electronic text). The purpose is to engage the readers' attention, to draw them to particular words, phrases, or sections that are important. If you put in too many different kinds of emphasis—bold and italics and color and underlining and capitalization and "special effects"— your readers will become confused and won't know what to look at. They may also have trouble deciding which parts of the text are most important.

The most common methods for creating emphasis are *italics* and **bold.** Used sparingly, these attributes can help your readers see what you think is important. Italics give words emphasis by setting them off from other words in a sentence. Italics are also used to set off titles, to set off terms being highlighted as terms, and to designate words from a foreign language. Bold is best used to draw the readers' eyes to the specific word, to make that word jump out on the page. Bold can be very helpful when it is important for readers to be able to scan a page of text and find key words, such as items that are defined in a glossary. Both italics and bold can be used effectively for run-in headings.

Printing words in a different color can be one of the strongest ways to add emphasis. You probably noticed the word *color* written in red as soon as you turned to this page. However, it is important to use color carefully and consistently (see. p. 519).

Underlining is used as a substitute for italic type—for example, when a text is handwritten. However, it tends to make the text difficult to read, so use italics if available. Underlining is also most effective for short words or phrases that are separate from other lines of text because the underlining can interfere with reading the words *below* the underline if it's used excessively in body text. In the past, underlining was used to indicate titles in documenting sources, and some disciplines and instructors still prefer it. With the current widespread use of personal computers, underlining is gradually disappearing as a means of identifying titles, but check with your instructor to make sure you understand the requirements for your particular course. Today underlining is most often used in low-level headings and, online, to indicate a link.

UPPERCASE, or caps (short for "capital letters"), is also difficult to read because words that are written in all uppercase have fairly similar shapes. In contrast, the distinctive shapes of lowercase words actually help the reader read. Save the use of all uppercase for one- or two-word headings.

Another way to add emphasis is to use SMALL CAPS. These are uppercase letter forms, but they are smaller than the regular caps in any particular font size. You can type using a combination of caps and small caps, a style most often used in headings.

Your software program will undoubtedly have other options, but most of them have specific uses in editing (~~strikethrough~~), math and science (superscript), and advertising (**shadow** or outline). You will certainly want to investigate all the possibilities, but use them only if they add something distinctive, necessary, and appropriate to your document.

In general, keep your use of any sort of emphasis to a minimum or it will lose its effectiveness. Also, be sure to use emphasis consistently. If, for example, you decide to use italics to emphasize key words, do it throughout the entire document.

9

Starting Research and Finding Sources

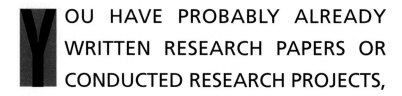OU HAVE PROBABLY ALREADY WRITTEN RESEARCH PAPERS OR CONDUCTED RESEARCH PROJECTS,

and you may know a great deal about using the library and the Internet to find information. Whether you're an experienced researcher or a novice, this chapter will give an overview of the resources that are likely to be available at your school, as well as some suggestions about using them effectively. The chapters that follow will explore specific research skills and strategies, some of which are introduced in this chapter. Even if you think your previous experience has prepared you adequately for doing research, it's a good idea to review the basics presented here. After all, a solid foundation in the basics of doing research will serve you well in all aspects of the process, regardless of whether you conduct research for a college course, an internship or a job, or an independent inquiry. This chapter will focus on a research project assigned as part of a college course.

Starting Your Research

Before you begin to gather information for a research project, be sure to read the assignment carefully (or talk to the instructor) so that you know what's expected. As with any assignment, be sure you have essential information about the required length of the final project, what form it should take (print or electronic), and when it is due. Beyond these basic issues, consider what the assignment specifies or suggests your audience, circumstances, and purposes to be. In other words, is the research project to address your instructor? your classmates? some other group? Will you have to analyze? persuade? compare? Do you need to use a specific number of sources or certain types of sources? Are you expected to do field research? What kinds of visual elements should you include? Knowing the answers to these key questions as you approach the assignment will save time—and trouble—later on in the research and writing process.

> For advice on reading assignments, see **Chapter 13.**

Working with Different Kinds of Sources

To understand what kinds of sources to gather for your research project, you should first consider the different kinds of sources that are available. Some types of sources will be more appropriate for your project than others, and some will lend themselves more readily to one search method than another. In most cases, your instructor will be able to help you decide which types of sources will be most useful—and appropriate—for your research topic and assignment.

Print and Online Sources

These days, Web sites and discussion forums contain a vast amount of material. In fact, by working online you can often get quick access to some sources that also appear in print. Because of the way online sources are published, they can be easily and frequently updated, so some very current information is available online. But because material on the Internet is so easily edited or deleted, information online can change overnight. Therefore, it's important to make print copies of electronic materials you find and to keep accurate bibliographic information for online sources as you locate them.

> For advice on evaluating online sources, see **Chapter 11.**

Print sources, on the other hand, are relatively stable, if not always as readily accessible as electronic ones. Although certain print sources may be available online—for example, in the form of databases, online books, or Web versions of periodicals—many print sources are not found on the Internet. If your search focuses only on online sources, you may overlook a huge number of helpful, appropriate print sources.

BOX 9.1 Style Guides

Most *style guides*—books that provide comprehensive guidelines for writing and documenting research projects—are available only in print form. They offer advice on how to formulate research questions, conduct research, take notes, write grammatically, incorporate references to other sources, and format the list of works cited. Many disciplines follow a unique style, so you may need to use different style guides in different courses. Some style guides, such as the one for the American Psychological Association (APA), exist partially online—the APA has an online guide to citing electronic sources—but the information for citing more traditional materials can be found only in the printed book.

❯ For advice on documenting sources using MLA and APA style, see **Chapter 12.**

Primary and Secondary Sources

The material that you gather during research can come from either primary or secondary sources. A *primary source* is a firsthand account or direct observation by an eyewitness or participant. A *secondary source* is a summary, analysis, interpretation, or evaluation of information gathered from one or more primary sources.

Context may determine what is primary and what is secondary. In historical research, a primary source is material from that historical period—for instance, the text of a speech, a diary or letter, the record of a legal transaction, a newspaper article reporting on an event, even a video recording of a meeting. A secondary source would be a historian's analysis of that period (based on research into original material such as speeches, diaries, letters, legal documents, and news accounts). In literature, a primary source is an original text—such as a novel, essay, poem, short story, or hypertext fiction—whereas a secondary source would be a literary critique or interpretation of a primary text or texts.

If you were doing research on binge drinking among college students, secondary sources would be reports based on research studies, such as the magazine article reprinted on p. 113 of this book (Figure 9.1). For primary information, you might read the original studies cited in this report or conduct a survey of students on your own campus. If you

FIGURE 9.1
Secondary Source:
A Magazine Report

EDUCATION

Bellying Up to the Bar

A new Harvard study finds that binge drinking is still a big problem on many college campuses

Wild ones: *Keg parties still rule on many campuses*

BY CLAUDIA KALB AND JOHN MCCORMICK

FOUR YEARS AGO A HARVARD RE search team issued a shocking report about alcohol abuse among college students. Last week Harvard was back with a new assessment—and the news wasn't good. Despite years of national publicity about the problem, the percentage of students who binge-drink—consuming five or more drinks in a sitting for men, and four or more for women—has declined only from 44 to 43 percent. Other details were even more damning: half of all bingers do so regularly—at least three times within a two-week period. And one-third *more* students now admit they drink just to get drunk. "Maybe I'm expecting change too fast," says Henry Wechsler, the study's lead author and an expert on alcohol abuse at the Harvard School of Public Health, "but I am disappointed."

Are colleges doing enough to crack down on risky drinking? The stakes are high: cases like the notorious alcohol poisonings at LSU and MIT last year kill an estimated 50 students annually. Although some schools present comprehensive programs to educate students about the dangers of drinking, many campuses offer only perfunctory efforts. College presidents are caught between the desire to act boldly and the fear that heavy-handed actions will

scare off prospective students. David Anderson, a George Mason University researcher who tracks college alcohol policies, says that in 1997, the average school spent just $13,300 to discourage substance abuse. Typical efforts: freshman-orientation workshops and alcohol-awareness pamphlets. Many college presidents delegate their alcohol programs to administrators already overburdened with other tasks. Says Anderson: "It's no wonder we're not making much progress."

The picture's not entirely bleak. William DeJong, head of the Higher Education Center for Alcohol and Other Drug Prevention in Newton, Mass., says that after years of relying on educational efforts, administrators are now turning to more innovative strategies. Many schools, such as the Uni-

versity of North Carolina at Chapel Hill, offer substance-free dorm rooms. Colleges are also teaming with neighborhood bars to ban happy-hour advertising on campus and to enforce drinking laws. Some schools are offering nonalcoholic "mocktail" parties. Others, like Clark University in Worcester, Mass., have turned campus pubs into coffeehouses. The trend shows some promise: the number of students who don't drink has grown from 16 to 19 percent. "I'm not ready to proclaim victory," says DeJong, but efforts are "definitely improving."

Dangerous drinking is at its worst in fraternities and sororities, where four out of five members acknowledge that they binge. But it's possible the situation will improve there, too. Wechsler collected his most recent data early in 1997. But that was before the highly publicized deaths last fall of pledges Benjamin Wynne at LSU and Scott Krueger at MIT. Several national fraternities have announced plans to ban alcohol in chapter houses.

Some experts argue that demonizing millions of binge drinkers makes it appear as if high-risk drinking is the norm. Michael Haines, a campus-health official at Northern Illinois University, says a more effective approach is to use advertising to hammer home the positive side of Wechsler's numbers: the fact that many students do drink responsibly. That message lets NIU's 22,000 students view heavy drinking not as the norm, but as aberrant. In 1989, 45 percent of the school's students said they binged—but on average they guessed that 70 percent of their peers did. Nine years later Haines can point to some successes. Students now estimate more reasonably that 33 percent of them binge—and the share who actually do has plummeted to 25 percent. Inspired by Haines's campaign, dozens of schools are now exploring this so-called social-norms approach. "We want to tell students what they're doing right," he says, "and grow more of that behavior."

Public pressure can change students' drinking habits. Lloyd Johnston, a University of Michigan researcher who has surveyed college drinkers nationwide since 1980, says the percentage who binged dropped through the '80s and into the mid-'90s, largely because of widespread publicity about the dangers of drunken driving and other alcohol-abuse problems. About two years ago, however, the numbers started climbing back up slightly. The only good news, Johnston says, is that dangerous drinking begins to subside after the age of 22. Provided, of course, that young people make it that far. ∎

When the Party's Over...

The more college students drink, the more they're at risk. Some alcohol-related problems that were reported after bingeing:

	NON-BINGERS	OCCASIONAL BINGERS	FREQUENT BINGERS
Drove after drinking	20%	43%	59%
Memory lapses	10	29	56
Got behind in schoolwork	9	25	48
Unplanned sexual activity	10	24	45

SOURCE: THE HARVARD SCHOOL OF PUBLIC HEALTH COLLEGE ALCOHOL STUDY

SEPTEMBER 21, 1998 NEWSWEEK **89**

were doing research on the strength of titanium, your secondary sources would be reports from various laboratories or manufacturers. Primary research would involve creating and conducting experiments to determine the strength of the metal.

Often, gathering information from previously published materials will be just the beginning of your research. Many projects will involve going beyond primary and/or secondary sources that you find in the

❯ For advice on conducting field research, consult **Chapter 10.**

library or on the Internet and doing *field research* to investigate how people think or feel about a particular topic. When you are out in the field, the people you interview, survey, or observe become your primary sources.

Popular, Trade, and Scholarly Sources

Popular sources include magazines, newspapers, and books written by journalists and freelancers with a variety of backgrounds. Examples of popular sources are magazines such as *U.S. News & World Report* and *Rolling Stone,* and newspapers such as the *Washington Post* and the *Wall Street Journal.* Although all these sources may be credible, their value to your project will vary according to your audience and topic (as well as the credentials of the individual writer).

Trade journals and magazines are professional publications for practitioners in specific fields. Publications such as the *Government Accountants Journal, AdWeek,* or *Managed Care* feature articles covering news, research, and events about the field, written by experts within that field or by journalists trained to cover it. The articles are often short (though some may be longer, in-depth features) and usually assume that the reader has a great deal of knowledge about the subject.

Scholarly works are also written by experts within their field, usually scholars or researchers. These works usually go through *peer review* by editors and other scholars who decide if the works are acceptable for publication. The authors of articles in scholarly (or academic) journals are not paid by the publication. Examples of scholarly publications include the *New England Journal of Medicine, Middle East Policy,* and *Modern Fiction Studies.*

Popular and trade publications usually accept advertisements, often print unsigned articles, do not usually include lists of sources cited in their articles, and are published daily, weekly, or monthly. Scholarly publications usually do not accept advertisements, rarely if ever print unsigned articles, almost always list cited sources, and are typically published monthly, quarterly, or semi-annually.

Analyzing Your Research Assignment and Choosing a Topic

You usually will have a good deal of notice about when a research project is due—sometimes several months—so your instructor will expect you to "do your homework." That obviously means doing whatever research is required; but even more, it means that your final project should be written clearly, with appropriate transitions, a logical organization, an appropriate voice, and few (if any) grammatical or typographical errors. In most cases the instructor will want a research essay that is

❯ For more information on determining the credibility of different types of publications, see **Chapter 11.**

❯ To see how one student met her instructor's requirements, see the sample essay in **Chapter 12.**

computer-generated or typed, and in many cases you will be expected to include appropriate visual elements, such as charts, graphs, photographs, maps, or other images. You may also be expected to know how to format your essay according to the instructor's specifications, including the use of a particular documentation style, certain fonts (typefaces) and sizes, headings, margins, systems of page numbering, and so on.

You can get a good idea of how much time to spend on the research assignment by checking the course syllabus and by asking yourself the following questions.

> **How detailed are the instructions?** Although this is not a hard-and-fast rule, detailed instructions often indicate higher expectations for the final product, which should indicate a greater amount of time and effort on your part.

> **How much is the assignment worth in terms of the final grade?** A project that will count as 25 percent should demand more of your time than one that will count as 10 percent.

> **How long is the project supposed to be?** Instructors often give page or word-length guidelines. The longer the project, the more time you should spend on it.

> **How much other work is this instructor assigning at the same time?** For all your college courses, you should expect to spend approximately three hours working outside of class for every hour that you spend in class. If the instructor has given you lots of other out-of-class assignments that are due at the same time, that should help you budget your time on the research project.

> **How much advance notice did the instructor give?** If you had a good deal of advance notice (more than two weeks), you are probably expected to spend quite a bit of time on the research project, regardless of how much other work you are assigned.

> For advice on brainstorming topic ideas, see **Chapter 3,** p. 147.

Unless your instructor has assigned a topic, your first challenge will be to come up with a broad topic—a general subject area that you'd like to investigate. If nothing comes to mind, try brainstorming a list of ideas or issues that you want to learn more about. Here are some examples.

> for a course on writing in the sciences: herbal supplements, global warming
> for an American history course: populist movements, indentured servitude
> for a sociology course: the influence of advertising, peer pressure
> for a biology course: invasive species
> for a literature course: modernist writers in the early twentieth century
> for a psychology course: body image in teenagers
> for a physics course: cold fusion

Developing a Research Question and Planning Your Research

Many topics that would make a good starting point for a college research project will require fine-tuning to bring them down to a manageable size that is appropriate for the assignment's audience and time and length constraints.

Narrowing a Topic by Asking Questions

Think of your research as an attempt to answer some questions about that topic. Although you may be thinking of the topic as "herbal supplements," you'll need to formulate questions about it, such as these.

> Do herbal supplements work to relieve symptoms of some ailments?
> Which herbal supplements have been scientifically tested?
> How do scientists distinguish between a genuine result and a placebo effect?
> How safe are herbal supplements?
> What does *natural* mean in relation to an herbal supplement?
> Who regulates the contents of herbal supplements?
> How do supplements interact with pharmaceutical drugs?
> Which herbal supplements, if any, do medical experts recommend, and for which conditions?

Your research project won't necessarily answer each question you initially formulate about the topic. From an initial set of questions, you can focus on just one or two related questions. If you're not sure how many questions to tackle, ask your instructor for guidance.

Developing a Research Question and a Working Thesis

After selecting a topic and thinking of several relevant questions, your next step will be to formulate a focused research question. As you begin to gather and explore sources of information on your topic, you may discover that there is a wealth of information on one aspect of your topic (one or more related questions), but not much on other aspects. If so, you will probably want to focus your research on an area where you can find a lot of sources, and this will help you narrow your topic. In other cases, you may discover that you are more intrigued by one or more of your questions than by others. Whenever possible, choose a question that you care about—a personal interest will make the assignment more meaningful and help you do a better job.

As you refine and focus the research question, you will develop an answer to the question that becomes your working thesis. The purpose of your research paper is to gather sufficient credible evidence to support the thesis. Because the working thesis will evolve as you find sources that support or challenge it, you should be open to refocusing your work as you proceed.

Using a Research Question to Plan Research

While looking for ways to answer the question(s) you have formulated, you will probably need to do more than one type of research to locate different types of sources. Some research questions lend themselves to scholarly sources such as books, academic journal articles, and disciplinary subject guides; other questions may be better answered by popular sources such as recent magazine or newspaper articles, Internet sources, or even original field research. You'll also need to consider whether to include visuals in your project. Does your instructor require visuals or value them highly? Does your topic lend itself to charts, graphs, or tables? Would you be able to answer the research question(s) more clearly or persuasively by adding photos, drawings, diagrams, or maps? If you think ahead about the types of visual information you might want to incorporate, you can look for effective examples (or gather data to create your own) as you search for written information.

Regardless of the way you search for information, be sure to take notes to help keep track of what you've found and where you've found it.

> For advice on creating visuals, see **Chapter 8.**

> For more information on finding and working with visual sources, see p. 559.

> For advice on taking notes, see **Chapter 11.**

Searching for Information Using Your Library's Resources

The information presented in this chapter cannot substitute for a tour of your school's library, but it will give you general information about using library resources. Consider whether you are in a position to take advantage of all the available resources by answering the following questions.

> Do you know how to use the library's online catalog or card catalog?

> Are you familiar with the electronic indexes and databases at the library?

> Do you know how to access the library's online catalog and electronic databases from your own computer or from computers on campus?

> Do you know how to find books and periodicals at the library?

> Are you familiar with the kinds of reference books that might help with your research, including indexes, bibliographies, and annotated bibliographies?

> Do you know what kinds of help the library's reference librarians can provide?

> Do you know the library's interlibrary loan policies?

Once you know all the types of resources you can access, the sheer number of options might appear overwhelming. Many libraries now allow students to create a personal page within the library's Web site, enabling them to keep track of the resources they find most useful. You can create a customized page that displays links to specific databases, electronic journals, and other Web sites, including electronic reference books. Take advantage of such tools or the Bookmark or Favorites features of your Web browser to eliminate some of the confusion that can arise from trying to remember which database you used previously or where you found a particular type of information.

In addition to using the catalog, there are many other ways to search for information in the library. The next few sections explain more about consulting reference librarians, using reference books, and searching for information in a variety of electronic indexes and databases.

Libraries have always been important repositories of information, but today's "wired" libraries are truly amazing. They not only house significantly greater stores of information than libraries could in the pre-digital age but in many cases allow you to access an array of textual and visual resources without even leaving your room. As long as you can use the Internet to connect to your library's homepage, you can find your way to catalogs, databases, image galleries, interlibrary loan forms, and much more. Most libraries have classes, tours, electronic tutorials, and printed handouts that describe the resources and services available at the library itself and through the Internet. If you haven't already done so, take time now to learn about what your library has to offer.

Using the Library Catalog

One of the most familiar and useful tools available at the library is the catalog. A library catalog is a database containing descriptions of material housed in that particular library (or network of libraries), along with information on how to access that material. Most libraries now have their catalogs available online, though some libraries still maintain card catalogs. Both online and card catalogs allow you to search for specific titles, authors, and subjects, but only online catalogs allow you to search by using *keywords*.

Search by keyword. With an online catalog, you can do a keyword search by typing in words that appear anywhere in the record for a

❯ For more advice on keyword searches, see Searching Indexes and Databases, p. 545, and Narrowing Your Search, p. 556.

source—the title, subject words, author's name, or, for some works, a summary or abstract. A keyword search is useful and less restrictive than a subject search because a single source can be located through many different keywords but would only be assigned one subject heading. Also, several keywords can be combined in one search to locate the most specific information. If you don't know what subject heading to look under for your topic or if you don't know the exact title or author of a book you want, a keyword search is likely to locate some relevant sources. Keyword searches can also help you locate a book by a particular author on a certain subject without knowing the title or scrolling through all the listings for that author. Instead, you can simply enter the author's last name as one keyword and enter a single word that might be in the title because it describes the subject as another keyword. Some online catalogs allow you to search for author keywords, subject keywords, or title keywords.

Search by subject. You can also look for resources in an online catalog by typing in a short description of your topic. Libraries catalog their materials according to a list of standard subject headings; most catalogs use the subject headings established by the Library of Congress. Thus you may need to try several different subject searches before you get a useful response. Most electronic cataloging systems will tell you the official subject heading that is most closely related to the subject you have entered. For example, in researching movies, you might do a subject search on *movies* or *film*. *Movies* and *film* are not official Library of Congress subject headings (LCSH), but many online catalogs will tell you that *motion pictures* is the subject heading you need. If your school's online catalog does not give you this information, try typing in synonyms for your subject or asking a reference librarian for a list of all the official Library of Congress subject headings. Then you can browse for headings that seem relevant to your topic.

Once you have found the appropriate Library of Congress heading for the subject you want to research, subject searches can be more precise than keyword searches because they do not require you to think of every possible synonym for the subject. A subject search may also turn up fewer irrelevant hits; for example, it will not bring up cases in which a search term appears as part of a fiction title.

Online catalogs often allow you to set limits on your search. That is, you can specify several other search variables, including the type of material you want (for example, books, dissertations, CD-ROMs, maps, or audiovisual materials), the language and publication date of the material, and the specific library where the material is housed (if the college has more than one library or if your library gives you the option to search the catalogs of public or other college libraries). Since many colleges and universities have more than one library, pay attention to how you set your limits. You can also find location information in the catalog record for each source.

For example, a subject search in the North Carolina State University (NCSU) online catalog on the phrase *violence in motion pictures* returns a list of subject headings that start with the phrase *violence*. The catalog also suggests several other related subject headings that could be searched. Your school's library screen will look different, but Figures 9.2 and 9.3 show typical examples of the kind of search tools and results you will find.

Analyze your search results. After entering your search term(s) and finding a list of entries, you can look at each item individually to see if it's likely to be useful. If the search brings up too many entries, try narrowing the search in some way—for example, by adding another search term, specifying only the most recent material, or focusing on a particular format.

❯ For tips on adding search terms, see Searching Indexes and Databases, p. 545. For suggestions on identifying the most useful sources, see Sorting through Your Sources, p. 558.

FIGURE 9.2
Library Catalog
Subject Search
Request

Limiting the search to the NCSU catalog restricts the search to holdings in the NCSU libraries.

The search type "L.C. Subject" uses Library of Congress subject headings to find sources on *violence in motion pictures.*

Search was limited to materials in English. Additional limits could have been placed on location (library), type of material (such as journal or book), and date.

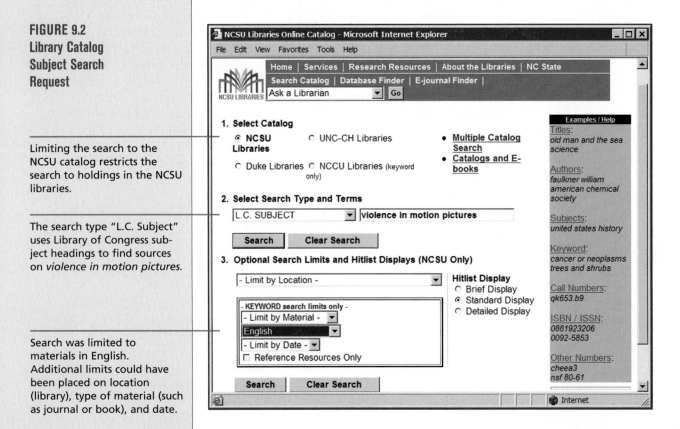

FIGURE 9.3
Library Catalog
Subject Search
Results List

List can be printed or downloaded for future use.

Search found 19 titles under this subject.

Clicking on the title of each entry calls up the complete record for that source.

List of results includes both print and electronic sources.

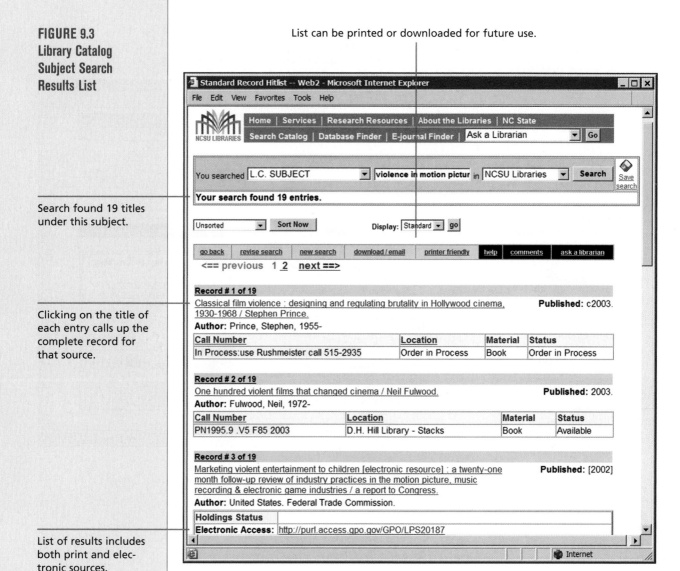

Although the library catalog doesn't tell much about the contents of a book or periodical, it does give a lot of information that might help you decide whether a source is worth pursuing (see Figure 9.4). The individual record for a source lists information that will help you determine whether a work might be appropriate for your topic—or at least worth looking at in the stacks.

FIGURE 9.4
Library Catalog
Record for a Book

Subject headings for this book; clicking on these links leads to a list of the catalog's titles categorized under that subject heading.

Entry 6 in a subject search that returned 19 entries.

Shows the book's title and subtitle, as well as the names of both of its editors.

Shows the publisher's city, publisher, and copyright date.

Clicking on the book's authors/editors will lead to a list of their other works in the catalog.

This line gives the number of pages, including frontmatter in Roman numerals; shows that the book is illustrated; and gives the book's height.

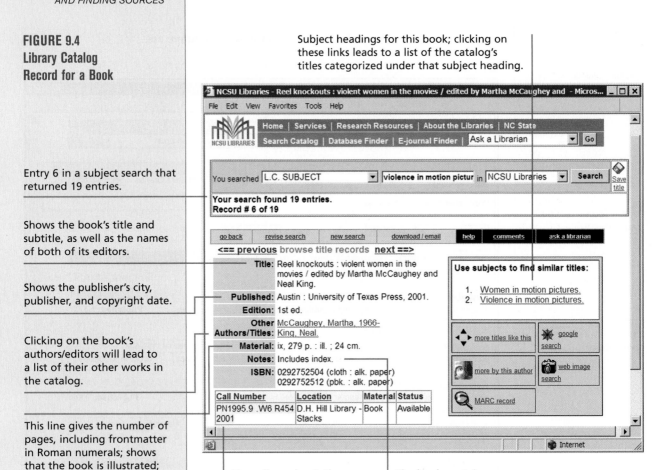

The call number is the locator for this book in the library's stacks.

The book contains an index, suggesting that it is a scholarly work.

Locating Materials in the Library

After analyzing your search results and deciding which books and other sources look the most promising, the next step is to skim a download or physical copy of the source. The online catalog entry will provide a link to materials that are available electronically or the basic information you need to locate books and other print material—namely, the location where the source is shelved (the specific library or collection within a library) and the call number. Books are grouped together by topic, so you should browse the shelves near books you've located to find other books that may also turn out to be relevant to your topic.

Most college libraries permit students to find books and many periodicals for themselves in the stacks, rather than requesting a particular work and waiting for a librarian to retrieve it. Within any library, you should look for a map, chart, or online guide detailing the general location of different call numbers (by floor or section) so that you don't have to wander aimlessly in the stacks looking for what you need.

You should also be careful not to wander aimlessly in a more figurative way: in these days of easy access to the Internet and other electronic resources, it's worth noting that books are often still the best source of information for college research projects. You might be tempted to think that you can find everything you need without getting up from the computer and venturing into the stacks. For some types of research, that may be true, but probably not for the kind of research project you would be doing in a writing class or any other college course. You may not have to read books in their entirety, but you can certainly look through the tables of contents, indexes, and introductions of several relevant books to see if they contain pertinent information on your topic—and if they do, read those specific chapters or sections. You may even have time to read (or skim) a few complete books that are particularly informative. Also keep in mind that many books on scholarly topics are collections of essays or articles by different authors, so you might be able to find a lot of good sources all in one place. If the book has notes or a bibliography or works cited list, you'll probably be able to use that list to find some promising leads for other sources to consult.

❯ For ideas about using citations to find new sources, see Box 9.2 on p. 548.

Consulting Reference Librarians

Reference librarians are trained professionals whose primary job is to help people find the materials they need. These librarians can be an amazingly helpful resource at any stage of the research process. For example, you can ask questions such as these.

> Where can I find information on [specific topic]?
> What databases might have articles about [specific topic]?
> Where could I find statistics (or quotations or facts) about [specific topic]?
> How do I do a search in [specific database]?
> Where could I find a drawing (or diagram, photograph, map, and so forth) of [specific item]?
> I've already tried [specific resources] to search for my topic. Can you think of any other sources I should try?
> I'm having trouble connecting to [the library catalog, a different library's catalog, a database]. Can you help me?

> What journal does the abbreviation in this database listing represent?

> How do I get a book/article through interlibrary loan?

A reference librarian can also help you locate other library resources that you may not have considered.

> **Government documents.** Many reports produced by federal, state, and local government agencies, especially older reports, are available in print or on microfiche in libraries. Many more are now readily available on the Internet, and you can link to them through a variety of databases.

> **Audiovisual materials.** These collections often include audio recordings, films, videotapes, DVDs, slides, and so forth. Such collections could be particularly helpful if you need visuals for a Web project or for an oral presentation.

> **Special collections.** Many libraries have collections of rare books and other documents or artifacts of particular local interest. These collections are not generally open to the public, but a reference librarian can get you access to them.

> **Vertical files.** These are collections of pamphlets, brochures, and annual reports from a variety of organizations, companies, and agencies.

Most libraries allow you to telephone the reference librarians, and many now provide online access to them—either through the library's Web site or by e-mail. These helpful services eliminate the need to visit the library in person each time you have a question. (But, of course, you can't expect a reference librarian to do all your research for you!) As you become more familiar with the library's resources, you may be able to reduce the number of trips you have to make—especially if your research is in a subject area rich with databases providing full-text articles online.

Using Reference Books

Although many people have come to rely on electronic resources, you may be able to obtain some information more easily by looking through reference books, such as encyclopedias, disciplinary guides, or bibliographies. Check with a reference librarian to determine the availability of these resources.

> **Encyclopedias.** Specialized encyclopedias devoted to a particular subject area (for example, the *Encyclopedia of Philosophy*) give a more thorough introduction to and summary of a topic than general encyclopedias (such as the *Encyclopedia Britannica*). Look for specialized encyclopedias rather than general ones.

> **Disciplinary guides.** These guides provide lists of reference tools—books, journals, bibliographies, electronic databases, and so forth—for specific subject areas or disciplines. To find a relevant disciplinary guide, consult a general guide such as Robert Balay's *Guide to Reference Books.*

> **Specialized reference works.** Your library will have many biographical dictionaries and indexes, almanacs, yearbooks, atlases, and other reference works that offer information in depth on particular topics. These resources can be useful to find background information, to narrow your topic, or to find keywords for a search. Check with a reference librarian to determine which specialized reference works are available in the field that relates to your topic.

> **Bibliographies.** Bibliographies are useful lists of published research—journal articles, books, research reports, Web sites, and so forth—on particular topics. An *annotated bibliography* is a reference tool that lists sources of information relating to a specific topic and provides a summary of each source's contents and relevance. To find a specific bibliography, add the term *bibliography* or *annotated bibliography* to your keyword search or ask a reference librarian for help.

Using reference tools such as these may give you a faster start on your research than an electronic search because the book's editors and compilers will already have made informed decisions about what to include and exclude. Also, since not all reference books have been published online, some material may be available only in print. Other reference sources may be available electronically, either on the Internet or on CD-ROM, but your library may not have access. A reference librarian can tell you about resources appropriate to your topic that are not available electronically, are not available at your library, or are simply easier to search in print than in electronic form.

Using Indexes and Databases

The term *index* usually refers to a guide to articles in periodicals or in book collections or to material related to a specialized subject. The term *database* is used more generally to describe a searchable collection of reference material, either in print or electronic form. (In some cases, *index* and *database* are used interchangeably to refer to such a collection.) The indexes and databases in a research library may connect the reader to full-text, downloadable, and printable articles; to abstracts or summaries of material; or to a listing of author, title, and publication information.

When you start to search for material, keep in mind the type of information you're seeking so that you can choose the appropriate index or database. For example, do you need to cite scholarly research that

❯ For more on the differences among popular, trade, and scholarly publications, see p. 532.

reflects expert opinion, or could you use less academic material from the popular press? Alternatively, do you need articles from specialized trade journals and newsletters directed to insiders in a particular field? Many indexes or databases link to only one of these types of sources, so you need to be aware of the differences and then decide which indexes or databases will be the most useful for your particular research.

Choosing Indexes and Databases

Indexes and databases all have limitations—you are unlikely to find all the information you need in one place. Most indexes and databases that you can access through the library will be organized by subject area (discipline), so first you should figure out what subject area is most likely to yield information on your topic. You may need to do some brainstorming or talk with a reference librarian to get ideas. For many topics, you may want to look in the indexes and databases for more than one subject area. For example, in writing a paper about child abuse, you might check specialized indexes and databases on psychology, sociology, social work, and maybe even criminal justice. (Some database services cover several different subject areas.)

Keep in mind that there are hundreds of indexes and databases, but it's unlikely that more than a few will be helpful on any given topic. Unless you stay focused, you might waste a lot of time searching in the wrong subject area. Your library will probably offer the option of choosing databases and indexes from an alphabetical list or by subject area. Unless you know exactly what database or index you need, try starting with a broad subject area and gradually narrowing to the appropriate databases or indexes. For example, the North Carolina State University library lists the following main categories for its electronic databases.

Agriculture and Life Sciences	Medicine and Health
Design	Multidisciplinary
Education and Psychology	Natural Resources
Engineering and Technology	Physical and Mathematical Sciences
Humanities and Social Sciences	Textiles
Management, Business, and Economics	Veterinary Medicine

Choosing any category will bring up a list of electronic resources available under that category (some libraries break down each broad category into subcategories), with links to each source so that you can investigate it further. At some libraries, you can link directly from the category list to the different resources under that subject area—journals, reference books, electronic texts, and so on—without first linking to a specific index or database.

If you have trouble determining which subject areas are relevant to your topic, ask your instructor or a reference librarian for ideas—or for the title of a particular journal that might be useful. Most indexes and databases provide a list of the journals they include; once you have a title, you can choose a database or index that includes the publication and assume that you will find other relevant journals there as well. When linking directly to a list of journals from the library's subject category list (rather than first linking to a specific database or index), you can take the same approach—namely, checking the list to see what other journals are included under that subject area.

Finally, be aware that electronic databases are relatively new; most of them only go back about thirty years. Thus information published before the 1970s is not likely to be referenced electronically. The lack of old material may not be relevant if you're writing a paper on the latest AIDS research, but many other topics will warrant a search into earlier sources—for example, looking at the original coverage of Ronald Reagan's acting career or discovering the origin of a newspaper comic strip. You may be able to use print versions of indexes, many of which have been published for decades, to look for older sources.

Searching Indexes and Databases

> For information on keyword searches, see Narrowing Your Search, p. 556.

Once you've chosen one or more indexes or databases—or linked to a particular journal—you're ready to conduct a search. Most indexes and databases allow you to search by author, title, keyword, or subject heading. Keep in mind that not all electronic databases use the same Library of Congress subject headings employed by library catalogs (see p. 536), so you may need to search for synonyms when conducting a subject search. With some electronic databases you can use phrases or Boolean operators to connect search terms.

If you're accustomed to searching for information via a variety of online search tools, including many online library catalogs and some databases (such as InfoTrac), you may be familiar with search options called *Boolean operators*. Boolean operators (the words AND, NOT, OR, and NEAR), as well as related search limiters like parentheses and quotation marks, define the relationships among keywords by specifying what results to find.

AND limits your search. If you connect two words or phrases with the Boolean operator AND, the search will find only items that include both search terms. For example, if you enter the terms *television* AND *violence*, you might get results about violence on television, or about how television promotes violence. You might also get results that mention both violence and television but that do not discuss the relationship between violence and television.

NOT limits your search. If you put NOT in front of a term, you exclude any results that contain that term. For example, if you want to find information on different kinds of spears without getting many irrelevant hits concerning popular music, you might type *spears* NOT *britney*. Your results would include all references to spears that do not mention the singer Britney Spears.

OR *expands your search.* Adding OR to a search will give you all items that include either one of your terms. This is useful when you want the maximum number of results and you know that two terms related to your topic are often used interchangeably. For example, typing *Holland* OR *Netherlands* will turn up more results than either term would produce alone, since the country can be called by either name in English.

Quotation marks limit your search. Putting quotation marks around two or more words will return only results that include those exact words in that exact order. For example, if you search for *"New York Yankees,"* you will get only items that contain this phrase. Sometimes words such as *in* and *to* will be exempted so that they don't affect the search.

Here are some additional tips for conducting searches.

❯ Before beginning a search, you should find out whether the database you're using requires Boolean operators. If you are unsure, check the site's Help or Search Tips section.

❯ Some databases (such as Lexis-Nexis and FirstSearch) provide Boolean operators as drop-down menu choices. Others let you substitute a plus sign (+) for AND and a minus sign (−) for NOT. Note that you have to type the (+) in front of both terms (+*violence*+*media*).

❯ Boolean operators are used for *keyword* searches—namely, searches for terms that actually appear in the text, title, or abstract of a document. But you can also use them to combine search categories, such as author and title. For example, you might search for the author's last name as one keyword and for a single word in the title of a book or article as another keyword, connected by a Boolean operator.

❯ If you're searching for information on a certain topic and getting too many results, you can narrow the search by adding AND followed by another search term. If you're not getting enough results, you can expand the search by adding OR followed by another search term. If you're getting too many results on an unrelated topic, you can eliminate the irrelevant results by adding NOT followed by another search term.

> Try putting a long phrase, or even a proper name, in quotation marks. For example, *"Treaty of Paris"* will give you more relevant results than *Treaty of Paris* because you'll be searching for the exact phrase rather than the individual words. Without the quotation marks, the Boolean operator AND is usually assumed, so you would get results that are about treaties and that also happen to include the word *Paris*—for example, any treaty that was signed in Paris (such as the Treaty of Versailles).

> You can also use a Boolean operator and quotation marks to connect two phrases or a phrase and a word: *"violent media"* AND *aggression.*

If all goes well, your search will result in a list of sources relevant to your topic. If the database provides a full-text version of articles, you can skim through each one online to see if it is definitely useful. To avoid wasting paper and ink, time, and money (if your school or library charges printing fees), try to read as much as possible online and print only the material you really need.

If the database provides only an abstract or a citation for a source, you may not be able to tell if it will be helpful. Check the library's catalog to see if you have easy access to the print version. If the library doesn't own the book, subscribe to that periodical, or have the issue in which the article appears, you might want to request it through interlibrary loan.

Once you have at least one really good, in-depth source on your topic, you have one more way to search for additional information that could be the most useful of all. Box 9.2 explains how to use citations—both *within* and *to* a source—to locate other relevant sources on your topic.

 For Collaboration

With a small group of classmates, talk about what it means if the original article you found has been cited frequently in a citation index. How would this affect your opinion of the article?

Searching for Information on the Internet

The Internet provides access to a vast array of information on virtually any topic you can imagine. Unfortunately, Internet sources are not necessarily reliable—in fact, you need to be extra cautious when evaluating the credibility and determining the viewpoint (and possible bias) of material located on the Internet. Chapter 11 offers detailed suggestions for assessing the accuracy and perspective of content you find in books

---

BOX 9.2   Using Citations and Citation Indexes

When reading an article, you should make a note of any statements or quotations that seem particularly relevant to your topic. If you find quotations or evidence from a source other than the author of the article, check to see if the author has *cited*—included a reference to—the source. The sources listed at the end of every scholarly article (and some trade and popular press articles as well)—variously titled Works Cited, References, or Bibliography—can be a valuable resource because the entries in this list point you to the original material cited in the article, providing everything you need to find that source material. Often, you can find several good new sources for your topic just by reading one relevant article carefully.

You can also track all the references in other works to your chosen article by using a *citation index*. These specialized indexes are lists of published articles that have been cited in other articles. For example, you may have found a useful article that was originally published in 1999. You can check a citation index to find articles that were published later that include references to the 1999 article. Because the more recent articles referenced the article you consider relevant to your topic, many of them will likely be on the same topic—and some may prove useful to you as well. Before beginning a search, check with a reference librarian or view the list of journals included in a particular citation index to make sure you're using one that includes the original article you found.

---

and periodicals and on Web sites. However, before we consider these important issues, it will be useful to look at some good ways to go about searching for information on the Internet.

Using Search Tools

Everyone has a favorite search tool. Search engines are not all the same—and they're constantly reinventing themselves as companies buy one another, develop partnerships to use someone else's search technology, or tinker with the design and philosophy of their own sites.

In fact, some popular search tools, such as Yahoo!, MSN, and Lycos, are actually *portals* (online destination sites) that provide access to a search engine plus other kinds of content (such as news, stock quotes, shopping channels, message groups, and free e-mail). Some search tools, such as Yahoo!, were originally built around subject directories, using human editors to compile search information and organize it into categories. Many search sites, such as HotBot, offer users a choice of engines. Dogpile and Search are *metasearch engines* that simultaneously search a variety of search engines and compile the results.

A *search engine* relies on automated searching software that "crawls" through the Internet and adds Web pages to its database. It then ranks and organizes these pages within its search results on the basis of a particular set of criteria or mathematical instructions. The search methodologies and ranking systems vary and are constantly changing. That's why different search engines yield such different results. Therefore, you shouldn't rely on just one search tool: try a few and see which one works best for your particular research needs.

The mark of a good search tool is getting relevant results within the first page or two, so that you don't have to scroll through hundreds (or even thousands) of hits to find the information you need. Choose a search tool that provides *enough* good results; theoretically, the more Web pages and other kinds of files a search engine indexes, the better your chances of finding appropriate hits. Another consideration is the quality of the searching experience—how the site looks, how easy it is to use, and what kinds of *filters* or *preferences* it offers, such as being able to limit your search by geographical region, language, or date. The table on the next page lists some popular search tools.

❯ For more advice on setting preferences, see Narrowing Your Search, p. 556.

BOX 9.3 Google: Star Search Engine

What's the best search engine? That's hard to say. But in 2003, Google was by far the Web's most popular search engine, handling 75 percent of all searches—through both its own site and the partner sites that license its search technology.

Google is also the largest search engine in terms of the number of Web pages it indexes (about 3 billion), as well as a variety of other kinds of files (such as images and Usenet newsgroups). In fact, Google is now so popular—and the only search engine that many people ever use—that the word *Google* as a verb has become a synonym for *search the Web*.

Google may be the Web's dominant search engine, but you shouldn't think it's the only option. In fact, Google's unparalleled popularity has forced its competitors to redesign their sites and refocus their search technology, so it's worth experimenting to see what else is out there.

Popular Search Engines and Search Sites

Search Engines	
AlltheWeb	**www.alltheweb.com** Multimedia search engine with image, audio, FTP (file transfer protocol), and advanced searches.
AltaVista	**www.altavista.com** Very complete search engine with a news page, "people finder," and various multimedia searches, including images, audio, and video.
Google	**www.google.com** World's largest search engine—more than 200 million searches a day. Search by subject, keyword, or image. Offers a news page with links to different news sources—CNN, UPI, BBC News, the *Washington Post,* and others.
Teoma	**www.teoma.com** Search by keywords or phrases. Advanced search function features a breakdown by language, region, date modified, and so on.
WiseNut	**www.wisenut.com** Search by keywords or phrases. Features "WiseSearch" (search by exact phrase) and audio searches.
Search Sites	
AOL	**www.aol.com** Search function of this site is powered by Google search engine. "Matching site" feature links user with sites of related interest.
Ask Jeeves	**www.ask.com** Site features keyword, image, news, and product searches, along with a children's search function. Powered by Teoma search engine, which it owns.
Lycos	**www.lycos.com** Features topic searches as well as keyword or phrase searches. Leading Spanish and Portuguese language site.
MSN	**www.msn.com** Search function of this site is powered by Yahoo!
Netscape	**www.netscape.com** Powered by Google search engine.
Yahoo!	**www.yahoo.com** Comprehensive, multimedia search site. Search by subject, field of interest, or keyword.

Metasearch Sites	
Dogpile	www.dogpile.com Metasearch site powered by Google, Yahoo!, AltaVista, Teoma, and other search engines. Very quick multimedia searches with "refine your results" sidebar function.
HotBot	www.hotbot.com Site with multiple search engines. Features custom "WebFilter" to help narrow search.
Ixquick	www.ixquick.com Multimedia, metasearch site. Features searches in many different languages.
Search.com	www.search.com Site similar to Ixquick, with many of the same search engines.
WebCrawler	www.webcrawler.com Metasearch site uses Google, Yahoo!, AltaVista, Ask Jeeves, and others. Specific search options include exact phrase, Boolean terms, domain filter, last page update, and language filter. Owned by Excite.

Trying Different Search Sites: A Case Study

Because different search sites have different capabilities and return different results, you should probably try more than one—particularly if you are dissatisfied with the kind of sources found on your first search. Try your favorite search tool first, and then move on to others to compare results and make sure that you have gained access to the best available material.

First-year student Chris Dwyer was concerned about an outbreak of mononucleosis on her college campus. She (and her friends and parents) wanted to find answers to some questions about this disease, including the ones listed below.

How is it transmitted?

What are the symptoms?

Can it be prevented?

What is the incubation period?

How long does it last?

What kind of medical care is necessary?

Can it be cured?

Are there any long-term effects?

Chris knew that one way to get answers would be to do a Web search on the keyword *mononucleosis*. (In Web pages, keywords are words that actually appear in the text, title, or abstract of a document or page.)

FIGURE 9.5
Google Keyword
Search on
Mononucleosis

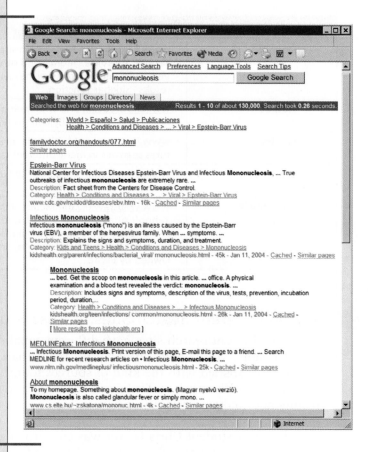

❯ For more tips on refining a
search, see Narrowing Your
Search, p. 556.

For her search, Chris first used Google. Her search yielded about 130,000 hits, the first five of which are shown in Figure 9.5.

Chris could have scrolled through these thousands of results or checked out the first few—namely, those sites that Google considered the most relevant. She also could have refined her search by clicking either on Advanced Search or on Preferences at the top of the page or by clicking on the Search Within Results option at the bottom of any Google page. Instead, she decided to postpone that step and try a different search site.

Chris tried her next search on Yahoo! because she knew it has subject directories. Scrolling to the bottom of Yahoo!'s homepage, she found a section called Web Site Directory. Under that heading were fourteen broad subject categories (with a few subcategories under each one). She decided to try the main subject Health. Clicking on this link brought her to the screen shown in Figure 9.6.

FIGURE 9.6
Yahoo! Directory Page on Health

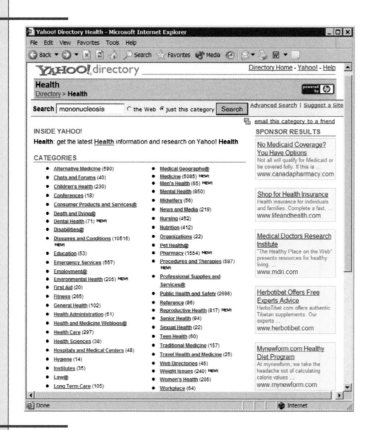

Once she got to this page, Chris first had to distinguish between the directory information and the "screen junk." The Yahoo! screen shows sponsored search results alongside its directory categories. (As you search the Web, it's important to recognize the difference between the information you are searching for and the commercials trying to get your attention, many of which feature flashing or animated images. On some Web sites, pop-up ads even open as separate windows.)

After tuning out the sponsored results, Chris noticed that the page was divided into two sections: Inside Yahoo! and Categories. Inside Yahoo! pointed to a link to a Yahoo! page devoted to Health, whereas Categories was followed by a bulleted list of fifty alphabetical subtopics relating to health. Not sure which category or subtopic to select, Chris decided to search all of Yahoo! Health (the general directory category) rather than clicking on one of the narrower subtopics (such as Medicine or Teen Health). She typed the keyword *mononucleosis* in the search field at the top left. Because she wanted to search the Yahoo! Health directory

FIGURE 9.7
Keyword Search of
the Yahoo! Health
Directory

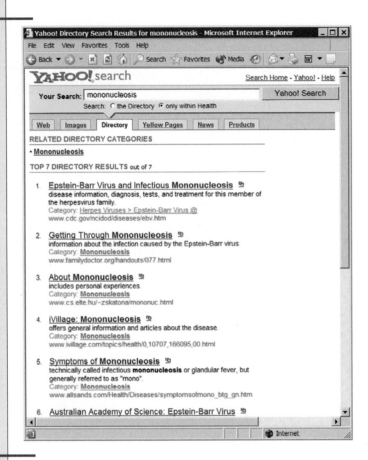

rather than the whole Web, she selected the "just this category" option in the search field. That choice brought her to the screen shown in Figure 9.7.

This screen also offered two options: a Related Directory Category, and seven Directory Results. As all this was potentially useful information, and as there were only eight matches, Chris wanted to investigate them all. Clicking on the Related Directory Category Mononucleosis led to an Inside Yahoo! page that she guessed was content provided by Yahoo! itself (or one of its partners)—and she wanted to find a different source. Scrolling through the other choices, Chris noticed that the first two listings under Top 7 Directory Results were in fact the same Web pages as the first two listings from her Google search: www.cdc.gov/ncidod/diseases/ebv.htm and www.familydoctor.org/handouts/077.html. She decided to start with these results because she was impressed by the fact that the Web sites Google had ranked first in its search results were also the first two sites that the Yahoo! directory editors had chosen. Chris chose to start with "Getting Through Mononucleosis" from familydoctor.org because she had a feeling that this site would be more easily understood than the government site.

Exercise

Simply finding a source through a reputable search engine does not guarantee that it is a credible source for academic research. For instance, the sixth match on the Google search results page (Figure 9.5), *About mononucleosis,* is from the personal Web site of a Hungarian college student who had mononucleosis. Why do you think this source is not likely to be very useful for academic research?

> For more information on judging the credibility and usefulness of sources, see **Chapter 11.**

But what if Chris were not simply an interested college student, but a college student writing a research project about mononucleosis? Would this search method and the familydoctor.org site be sufficient? Probably not. First, although she could be fairly confident that the American Academy of Family Physicians would not publish false information, she would want to find out something about this organization before making that assumption. Second, and more important, the content provided here would probably not be sufficiently credible or in-depth to satisfy the professor who assigned the project. It probably does not answer the precise kinds of questions a student would need to address in a research project—questions such as these.

> What is the history of mononucleosis? When was the disease first identified? What precipitated the earliest investigations into the causes and cures for this disease?

> What is the role of mononucleosis in popular culture?

> How do doctors detect and diagnose mononucleosis? How accurate is the diagnosis? Is mono ever confused with other diseases?

> How accurate is the public perception of this disease? What are the myths that surround what is commonly known as "the kissing disease"? How do the myths match the reality?

If Chris wanted to expand her search to find more information for a research project, she could (1) use databases that would find other types of information (scholarly/medical journal articles, newspaper and magazine articles, books), (2) check the government site and some of the other matches on the first page of her Google search and the other Yahoo! directory listings, or (3) use other search engines.

FIGURE 9.8
Google Image Search

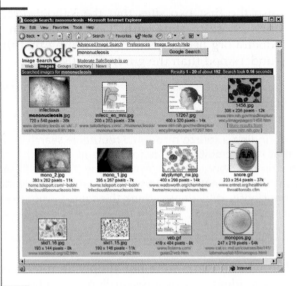

Chris's decision about what to try first would depend on the nature of her research. For example, if she were writing a paper on how doctors detect and diagnose mononucleosis, she might incorporate visuals showing what the virus looks like or some of the obvious physical symptoms. To find this type of visual information, she could use one of the tools that offers the option to search for visuals. For example, clicking on Google's Images option under *mononucleosis* would result in 192 images, many of which show how mono affects infected individuals and what an infected blood sample looks like. (See Figure 9.8 for the first 12 images returned by this search.)

Narrowing Your Search

If your Web search results in hundreds or thousands of hits, you may need to modify the search terms to refine the results. You can narrow the search by specifying multiple keywords that must be included on a Web page to show up in your results. For example, if you were particularly interested in the antiviral drugs used to treat mononucleosis and you turned up too many sites by looking for *mononucleosis* and *treatment*, you could narrow the search by adding *antiviral* as one of the required search terms. Specifying a complete phrase (such as *antiviral drugs to treat mononucleosis*) may narrow the results even more. You can also exclude irrelevant sites by specifying words that may not appear. For example, if you were researching the causes of mononucleosis but turning up too many sites that contained information on a variety of diseases,

FIGURE 9.9
Google Advanced
Search

you might instruct the search tool to exclude any site that included the phrases *West Nile virus* or *Epstein-Barr syndrome*.

❯ For a discussion of Boolean operators, see p. 545.

One way to narrow your search in these ways is to use Boolean operators, such as AND, OR, and NOT. However, most current Web search tools allow you to narrow your search by using an Advanced Search option with step-by-step guidance (Figure 9.9).

Most search engines also have Preferences settings that let you customize how you search by choosing *filters*—controls that limit the search by language, geographical region, or date (among other options). For example, you might limit your *mononucleosis* search to Web sites written in English, from the United States, and modified within the last year (so that the information is current). You can also tell the search engine to filter out Web sites with offensive content or to return only those results that contain image or audio files. If you usually search for exact phrases rather than keywords, you can often specify that as your default search setting. Different search tools support different filters. (You can find guidance under Search Tips or Help.)

Some search sites suggest either Related Searches or Categories that draw on subject directories to narrow a search automatically. For example, Teoma's Refine section presents Suggestions to Narrow Your Search that help whittle down extremely long lists of sources. When these results need further refining in order to be useful, you need to think of a way to make the topic even narrower. By adding words and phrases to the original string of search terms, you can then search only within the results already obtained. Once your list is narrowed down, you can scan the first few hits to find additional phrases to add to your search terms. A short list of thirty to fifty sources is a size that a researcher could look at without wasting too much time. And narrowing down search results in this way will help you to focus on a topic that is much more specific.

Sorting through Your Sources

Once you have used the library and Internet to find potential sources, you need to make decisions about which ones to pursue. This section provides advice on making those decisions while keeping audience, circumstances, and purposes in mind. It also offers suggestions for thinking about visuals. Remember, while choosing sources you need to keep track of bibliographic information so that you can find the sources again and also create a list of works cited. Many instructors call this list of potential sources a *working bibliography;* it is always subject to revision because you are constantly working on it.

❯ For more information on in-text citations and lists of works cited, see **Chapter 12.**

Making Decisions about Sources

As you begin to look through your sources, think carefully about how many you will need. When working on an assignment for school, your instructor will probably give an idea of how many sources to incorporate into the final project, as well as what types of visuals to include. When doing research for some other purpose—for a job, a community organization, an extracurricular activity, or a personal project—you won't have the same kind of guidance. In those situations, you will need to decide how much information will make your work credible.

If you have access to the Internet and a variety of databases, you will likely have more problems narrowing your search and sorting through the results than finding sources. Here are some suggestions for determining which sources are most relevant for your purposes.

Read enough of the source to determine if it adds something of value to your research project. Is the source focused narrowly on your topic? Does it help answer your research question? Does it support your main point? Does it provide an important argument against your main point that you will need to refute? Does it help establish your credibility with readers?

Determine if the material is from popular, trade, or scholarly sources. Are sources from this category appropriate for your audience, circumstances, and purposes?

Consider the date of publication. Does your topic require a focus on the most recent material available? If not, would older, historical material be preferable? Should your sources relate to one another chronologically?

> For a more detailed discussion of these issues, see **Chapter 11.**

Evaluate the credibility of the author and publisher. Are you as certain as possible that your sources are accurate, honest, and fair? If you decide to use information from a source you're not sure about, have you acknowledged that doubt in your research paper?

Analyze the type of evidence the author uses to back up his or her claims. Does the source include statistical data or some other type of research data? Does the data come from an impartial, reputable source such as a university (as opposed to a corporation or a special interest group, which might present biased or incomplete information)? Does the author quote recognized experts or provide reasonable examples?

> For more on recognizing perspective, see **Chapter 11.**

Identify the perspective of the source. Have you figured out what perspective each source represents to ensure that your research project examines multiple points of view?

Choose sources from more than one medium. Have you incorporated a mix of reference materials: books; magazine, newspaper, and journal articles; Web sites; and so forth?

Thinking about Visual Sources

> For more advice on crediting visual sources, see **Chapter 12.**

As you sort through sources, think about what visuals will help achieve your purpose. You may want to print or photocopy pages with the visuals you want to incorporate; just be sure to keep a record of where the images come from so that you can properly credit them.

As you research your topic, the types of visuals you need should become clearer. If you are citing statistics, you may want to create or adapt a table. If you are analyzing how something has changed over time, you may want to create a bar or line graph. If you need to show what something or someone looks like, a drawing or photograph will probably be most effective. One of the best ways to determine what visuals you need is to look closely at the elements incorporated into the sources you are selecting. How do those authors and publishers use visuals to convey information? Do you have data or ideas that could be presented in a similar way? Remember also to analyze key sources for their use of visual elements such as headings, color, and so forth. You may want to use those sources as models for your own project.

> For more information on layout and design elements, see **Chapter 8.**

Preparing to Take Notes

Research involves synthesizing a lot of facts, ideas, and opinions before coming to conclusions of your own about a topic. To *synthesize* means to bring different parts together into a whole. Your research will lack credibility if you don't find out what other people have said, written, or done that is relevant to your topic—but your project will lack coherence if you don't figure out how to unify these concepts and voices.

❯ For suggestions on what type of notes to take, when to take them, and how to organize them, see **Chapter 11.**

❯ For advice on MLA and APA documentation styles, see **Chapter 12.**

❯ **bedfordstmartins.com/ visualage**

To download these forms as worksheets, click on **CHAPTER 9** ❯ **WORKSHEETS**

No matter what you are writing about, you cannot expect to remember everything you read or see during your research—you have to take notes about important facts, ideas, and visual elements. Specifically, you will look for memorable statements that you can quote, key concepts that you can paraphrase, complex information that you can summarize, and data that you can present graphically. The success of your project—whether it's a research project, oral presentation, annotated bibliography, or one of the writing genres covered in Part 1 of this book—will depend on your ability to find good sources and take accurate notes. Sources must be documented properly—both in the text and in a bibliography (often called either References or Works Cited). The information you need to gather will depend on the documentation style your instructor requires, so make sure to find out whether you're expected to use MLA, APA, CSE, Chicago, or another style for your research.

You will be most successful at taking notes if you create an organized system for gathering information—either on paper or in your computer. The system can be as simple as a file of index cards or as complex as a computer database. (A notebook without removable pages is not a good choice because at some point you will want to sort through your notes and rearrange them.) Whatever format you choose, it will be helpful to use a template (form) with spaces for all the types of information required. The sample forms in Figures 9.10 to 9.12 provide spaces for recording bibliographic information from different types of sources. You can adapt the forms to suit your particular project.

FIGURE 9.10
Working Bibliography Form for Books and Parts of Books

Author_____

Editor (if any)_____

Title (and subtitle)_____

Chapter title _____

Place of publication _____

Publisher_____

Page numbers (for the part you've read)_____

Date of publication _____

Call number_____

Other information (for example, translator, edition, volume) _____

Why the source is important _____

FIGURE 9.11
Working Bibliography
Form for Periodicals

Author_____

Title (and subtitle) _____

Periodical title _____

Volume number _____

Page numbers _____

Date of publication _____

Other information (for example, translator, issue)_____

Why the source is important _____

FIGURE 9.12
Working Bibliography
Form for Online
Sources

Author (if available)_____

Title (and subtitle) _____

Site name_____

Page numbers (if available) _____

Paragraph numbers (if available)_____

Date of publication or posting_____

Name of sponsoring institution or organization _____

Date of your access_____

Electronic address (URL) _____

Why the source is important _____

Once you have established a system for your working bibliography (see p. 560), you are ready to start looking through your sources and taking notes. Here are a few tips that will make your efforts more efficient and productive.

Skim through the article, book, or Web site once before you start to take notes. Doing research is time consuming, and you don't want to waste time making notes about an article that turns out to be irrelevant or inappropriate.

Write down all the bibliographic information as soon as you decide that a source will be useful. Then read the selection (article, Web page, section of a book, etc.) carefully, looking for information that relates to your project.

Print or copy pages with pertinent visual elements if you cannot describe the visuals succinctly or summarize the data they present. For a chart or table, it may be sufficient to write, for example, "table of population statistics for 1995–2003." However, for diagrams and photographs, it's unlikely that verbal descriptions will be clear enough for you to choose later on which visual is best suited to your purpose. By printing or copying pages and marking each with the source, you can easily sort through the images when you're ready to make a final selection.

Continuing Your Research

The whole idea behind research is to gather information, synthesize it into a coherent whole, and in the process learn something that you didn't understand before. But doing research is a repetitive process: you go through cycles, many of which have the same steps. First you think of a topic, then you formulate a research question based on that topic, and then you look for information to help answer the question. But as you conduct this research—in the library, on the Internet, or in the field—you may find that the topic has to change or that you have to modify the original question. For example, you may discover that the kind of information you need is unavailable or that your research question has already been discussed so thoroughly that there's no room for new ideas. You may realize that it would take too long to meet the time frame of a school assignment or that your topic is too broad for a single research project. You may come across some new information that sends you back to the library, onto the Web, or into the field in pursuit of verification, contradiction, or another point of view. You may decide that only field research will produce the kind of information you need, in which case you will find help in Chapter 10. Regardless of the kind of research you conduct and of the number of times you feel compelled to search for more information, however, at some point you will need to *just start writing*.

How will you know when to start writing? Only you can make that decision. You probably have some idea of how long it takes you to write a paper of a certain length and complexity. Remember to leave time to go back and do additional research if it becomes necessary or if you decide that you do not have sufficient credible evidence to support your point. You will also need time to compose your bibliography—regardless of the documentation style you use, producing a correct list of references is a time-consuming chore. The ideal time to start writing, then, is when you have enough material to begin your project and enough time left to finish it.

❯ For tips on evaluating sources, see **Chapter 11.**

❯ For advice on using and documenting sources, see **Chapter 12.**

10

Conducting
Field Research

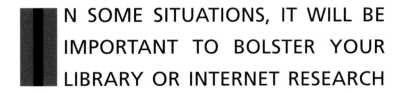N SOME SITUATIONS, IT WILL BE
IMPORTANT TO BOLSTER YOUR
LIBRARY OR INTERNET RESEARCH

with field research. Internet and library research generally involve looking at information from secondary sources—material created by people who were not witnesses to the events they describe. Field research, on the other hand, requires the researcher to turn to primary sources, usually the people directly involved, for information. You may need to do field research if you want data that does not yet exist in another form—information about a hot issue on your campus or the habits of its current students, for example, or about local people or practices in a community today.

This chapter presents guidelines to help you conduct the type of primary field research you may be asked to do for an English class. You will find information here about *interviews* in which you talk one-on-one with a subject, *surveys* in which you ask many people for information about themselves, and *observations* of a place or situation.

563

Interviews

Interviews can be extremely useful sources of information and opinions, especially in the early stages of an investigation. You can use interviews to accomplish the following tasks.

> ❯ gather new information on a topic, based on a person's firsthand experience or expertise
> ❯ identify varying opinions or perspectives on a topic
> ❯ gather interesting and relevant quotes to add to your project
> ❯ gather anecdotal evidence to support your position on a topic
> ❯ get suggestions and advice on additional sources of information to pursue

Figure 10.1 is a good example of an article that incorporates information from interviews. All the highlighted sentences are based on interviews—and so are many of the other sentences presenting facts the writers learned about from the experts they interviewed. Only one paragraph in the entire article does not present information obtained from an interview. Notice that in each case the authors give the name of the interviewee and explain why that person is a credible source for that particular topic. Indeed, the credentials of the researchers and other experts add a great deal of support to the article. Also notice that the authors use two techniques to present the information they obtained from their interviews: they *paraphrase* the interviewees and *quote* them directly. By using these two approaches, Kalb and McCormick keep the article from becoming a monotonous series of quotations.

 For Collaboration

With one or two of your classmates, make a list of all the people Claudia Kalb and John McCormick interviewed and included in the article from Chapter 3, p. 113, shown in Figure 10.1. What makes each person a credible source for this topic?

Without the interviews *Newsweek* probably would not have found this article worthy of publication, even though the topic of binge drinking is important and likely to be of great interest to readers. The interviews strengthen the story by providing factual information as well as a variety of perspectives from numerous areas of expertise.

FIGURE 10.1
Article That Relies on
Information from
Interviews

EDUCATION

Bellying Up to the Bar

A new Harvard study finds that binge drinking is still a big problem on many college campuses

Wild ones: *Keg parties still rule on many campuses*

BY CLAUDIA KALB AND
JOHN MCCORMICK

FOUR YEARS AGO A HARVARD RE-search team issued a shocking report about alcohol abuse among college students. Last week Harvard was back with a new assessment—and the news wasn't good. Despite years of national publicity about the problem, the percentage of students who binge-drink—consuming five or more drinks in a sitting for men, and four or more for women—has declined only from 44 to 43 percent. Other details were even more damning: half of all bingers do so regularly—at least three times within a two-week period. And one-third *more* students now admit they drink just to get drunk. "Maybe I'm expecting change too fast," says Henry Wechsler, the study's lead author and an expert on alcohol abuse at the Harvard School of Public Health, "but I am disappointed."

Are colleges doing enough to crack down on risky drinking? The stakes are high: cases like the notorious alcohol poisonings at LSU and MIT last year kill an estimated 50 students annually. Although some schools present comprehensive programs to educate students about the dangers of drinking, many campuses offer only perfunctory efforts. College presidents are caught between the desire to act boldly and the fear that heavy-handed actions will

When the Party's Over...

The more college students drink, the more they're at risk. Some alcohol-related problems that were reported after bingeing:

	NON-BINGERS	OCCASIONAL BINGERS	FREQUENT BINGERS
Drove after drinking	20%	43%	59%
Memory lapses	10	29	56
Got behind in schoolwork	9	25	48
Unplanned sexual activity	10	24	45

SOURCE: THE HARVARD SCHOOL OF PUBLIC HEALTH COLLEGE ALCOHOL STUDY

scare off prospective students. David Anderson, a George Mason University researcher who tracks college alcohol policies, says that in 1997, the average school spent just $13,300 to discourage substance abuse. Typical efforts: freshman-orientation workshops and alcohol-awareness pamphlets. Many college presidents delegate their alcohol programs to administrators already overburdened with other tasks. Says Anderson: "It's no wonder we're not making much progress."

The picture's not entirely bleak. William DeJong, head of the Higher Education Center for Alcohol and Other Drug Prevention in Newton, Mass., says that after years of relying on educational efforts, administrators are now turning to more innovative strategies. Many schools, such as the University of North Carolina at Chapel Hill, offer substance-free dorm rooms. Colleges are also teaming with neighborhood bars to ban happy-hour advertising on campus and to enforce drinking laws. Some schools are offering nonalcoholic "mocktail" parties. Others, like Clark University in Worcester, Mass., have turned campus pubs into coffeehouses. The trend shows some promise: the number of students who don't drink has grown from 16 to 19 percent. "I'm not ready to proclaim victory," says DeJong, but efforts are "definitely improving."

Dangerous drinking is at its worst in fraternities and sororities, where four out of five members acknowledge that they binge. But it's possible the situation will improve there, too. Wechsler collected his most recent data early in 1997. But that was before the highly publicized deaths last fall of pledges Benjamin Wynne at LSU and Scott Krueger at MIT. Several national fraternities have announced plans to ban alcohol in chapter houses.

Some experts argue that demonizing millions of binge drinkers makes it appear as if high-risk drinking is the norm. Michael Haines, a campus-health official at Northern Illinois University, says a more effective approach is to use advertising to hammer home the positive side of Wechsler's numbers: the fact that many students do drink responsibly. That message lets NIU's 22,000 students view heavy drinking not as the norm, but as aberrant. In 1989, 45 percent of the school's students said they binged—but on average they guessed that 70 percent of their peers did. Nine years later Haines can point to some successes. Students now estimate more reasonably that 33 percent of them binge—and the share who actually do has plummeted to 25 percent. Inspired by Haines's campaign, dozens of schools are now exploring this so-called social-norms approach. "We want to tell students what they're doing right," he says, "and grow more of that behavior."

Public pressure can change students' drinking habits. Lloyd Johnston, a University of Michigan researcher who has surveyed college drinkers nationwide since 1980, says the percentage who binged dropped through the '80s and into the mid-'90s, largely because of widespread publicity about the dangers of drunken driving and other alcohol-abuse problems. About two years ago, however, the numbers started climbing back up slightly. The only good news, Johnston says, is that dangerous drinking begins to subside after the age of 22. Provided, of course, that young people make it that far. ∎

Quotations taken from interviews are highlighted.

The following guidelines will help you prepare and conduct your own interviews.

Setting Up the Interview

The first step is to decide who would be the most appropriate person or people to interview. This choice will depend on your audience and purpose. For a research report on a disease, such as mononucleosis, you might want to interview a doctor who is an expert in diagnosing and treating the disease as well as a patient who has had it. For a project on an environmental issue, such as the effects of recycling programs on a particular community, you might want to interview a town official, an environmental activist, and a local resident. You should also think about how many people to interview. Is the topic extremely controversial? If the answer is yes, you cannot simply present one point of view—you'll need to interview at least two people. Even for a profile, you'll probably want to interview not only the person being profiled but also some friends, colleagues, and/or family members who can offer additional insight into your subject's life or work.

Next figure out how you are going to approach each person you want to interview. Do you already know this person? If not, do you know someone who does and who would be willing to make the initial contact for you? Do you think this person would be willing to talk to you? Keep in mind that most people—even busy professionals—are happy to talk about themselves and their work and are often enthusiastic about helping students (as long as those students sound motivated and polite). Before you contact each person to schedule the interview, be sure to think about exactly what you want to say and how you want to say it. You might even consider preparing a script requesting an interview, but be sure to rehearse it so that you don't actually have to read it awkwardly over the phone. (See Box 10.1 for an overview and example of this approach.)

Decide if you will be able to conduct the interview in a face-to-face setting. You'll get the most information from this type of interview because people communicate a great deal through facial expressions, gestures, and body language; thus you can more fully "read" a person's responses when you are talking face to face. You can also learn a lot by observing a person's home or office (if the interview takes place there), and then you can add descriptive, personality-revealing details of setting. If such a meeting is impossible or impractical, consider conducting the interview over the telephone. You can still establish rapport with your interviewee and can learn a lot from his or her tone of voice, general attitude toward you and the topic, and the pauses in the conversation. If all else fails, you can conduct the interview by e-mail, sending questions that the interviewee will respond to in a Reply message. Recognize, however, that you will lose a great deal of the richness of human communication with an electronic interview.

BOX 10.1 Requesting an Interview

It's often helpful to prepare exactly what you're going to say before you contact a potential interview subject. If you use a script for requesting an interview, try to include the following types of information.

> ⟩ your name and why you are calling ("Hi, my name is Dan George, and I'm writing a research report on campus safety for my English class at North Carolina State University.")

> ⟩ any connection you have to this person and what you want from him or her ("My instructor, Professor Fetzer, suggested that you might be willing to talk to me about the new call-box system that has been installed on campus this year.")

> ⟩ a specific suggestion about how long the interview will take ("I would like to talk with you for about thirty minutes.")

> ⟩ a few alternative dates and times, as well as a suggestion for where the interview might take place ("I could meet with you at your office any time next Tuesday or Thursday morning or after 3:00 p.m. next Wednesday.")

> ⟩ a specific request for an appointment ("Would you be able to meet with me at one of those times next week?")

> ⟩ a sincere thank-you at the end, and a repetition of the date, time, and meeting place that you've both agreed on ("Thank you for your help with my project. I look forward to talking with you at 4 o'clock next Wednesday afternoon at your office.")

Preparing for the Interview

Create a schedule that allows time for you to set up, prepare for, conduct, and analyze your interview. Contact your interviewee well in advance of the actual date when you want to conduct the interview—this allows for the possibility of a last-minute cancellation or postponement. You should also allow enough time for a follow-up phone call or e-mail because as you review your interview notes or tape recording, you may find that you need to clarify a point or ask another question.

Prepare a list of questions that are relevant to your topic, that are appropriate for the person you are interviewing, and that elicit meaningful answers. This list will vary greatly depending on the topic, so it is difficult to generate precise guidelines. You can start by reviewing the lists of questions at the beginning of Chapter 3 (p. 104) and Chapter 5 (pp. 262–263). Those lists may help you brainstorm questions for the interview. As you prepare your list, make sure to avoid writing questions in such a way that you tell the person what you want (or expect) to hear. Also avoid questions that can be answered by a simple "yes" or "no" or with a brief factual

Exercise

Read the following questions, and think about what makes them inappropriate for an interview. Then see if you can figure out a way to request the same type of information without letting the interviewee know your perspective.

> Whose bright idea was it to have the clock tower chime all night long?
> Don't you agree that the dorms need to be renovated?
> Why doesn't someone solve the parking problem on campus?
> Doesn't it bother you that your medical research involves killing innocent animals?

Now read the next group of interview questions. All of them could be answered with a simple one-word answer, which would not give you much to put into a report. Try rewriting these questions so they are phrased to solicit more detailed, informative answers.

> Do you like your job?
> Was it hard to be a working mother during the 1960s?
> When did you start designing robots?
> How many physicians are on staff at the university's health center?

response. Ask open-ended questions that inspire longer answers full of details, opinions, anecdotes, and analysis. Try asking the interviewee to describe, explain, or simply tell you about something. Also keep in mind that your list of prepared questions is just a starting point; once the interview gets going, you should reassess your questions on the basis of the interviewee's responses and the flow of the conversation. Keep sight of your goals for the interview—the questions you want answered—but don't proceed slavishly to the next question in your script if the interview is moving in a more intriguing but unexpected direction.

Practice your interview questions with a friend or family member so that you feel comfortable. You can also practice by tape-recording yourself asking the questions and then playing back the tape to hear how you sound. (You can get even more feedback by videotaping yourself.)

Decide if you're going to tape-record the interview or just take notes. Keep in mind that even if you record the interview, you should also take notes as a backup; recording devices can malfunction, and some people are hard to understand on tape. (Also be aware that transcribing a tape can be extremely time-consuming.) If you decide to use a recording device, be sure to get the permission of the person you're interviewing, even if you're taping a phone interview. (Be aware that some people dislike being recorded, so you may need to rely entirely on notes.) This is also a good time to think about using photographs. Depending on the type of research project and the expectations of the assignment, you may want to add the visual impact of a well-chosen photo—either of the interviewee or of a setting or object that is important to that person. Again, be sure to ask permission before taking any photographs of your interviewee or their environments.

Contact your interviewee again the day before the interview to confirm the appointment. (A brief phone call or e-mail is best.) If you've decided to take photographs or tape-record the interview, now is the time to ask permission. If the person says no, be gracious and agreeable. If the person says yes, be sure your tape recorder is working properly: practice turning it on and recording with it, and make sure you have extra batteries and blank tapes. Also make sure to have good note-taking equipment—a pad, notebook, or laptop computer, as well as several sharpened pencils or working pens.

For Collaboration

With one or two classmates, make a list of all the different types of interviews (or articles based on interviews) that you've read, seen, or heard. Are some of them more informative or revealing than others? Why? Which interviews seem like credible reporting, and which ones seem like publicity puff pieces?

Conducting the Interview

On the day of the interview, arrive on time, dressed appropriately, with all the equipment and writing tools you need. If you have to wait, be patient. If the person originally gave you permission to record the interview or take photographs, ask again before turning on the tape recorder or taking out your camera.

During the interview, speak slowly and clearly and try to establish friendly eye contact (rather than looking down at your notes the whole time). Remember to write down not only what the interviewee says but also *descriptive details* about his or her appearance, voice, body language, gestures, or setting that might enliven your report. Also remember that your list of prepared questions is just a starting point—so be flexible, and allow the interview to move in a new direction if necessary (without going completely off course). Do, however, keep within the time limits you agreed upon in your initial request for an interview (unless the person invites you to stay longer), and be sure to say a sincere thank-you before you leave. You might also ask for permission to call or e-mail in a few days if you have any additional questions.

Writing Up the Interview

After the interview, write up your notes as soon as possible. If you do this within an hour or two, you'll remember a lot of details that would otherwise become fuzzy. In addition to fleshing out your notes about what the interviewee actually said, be sure to write down your own analysis of the interview. Did the person seem knowledgeable and insightful? Did he or she demonstrate any strong opinions or reactions to your questions or to the general topic? Did the person say or do anything to indicate a particular bias? If so, does that bias seem strong enough to affect his or her credibility as a source for your research project, or is the bias something you could simply point out in your project? Also reflect upon what you learned during the interview, and write down your own response to what the interviewee said. Looking back at the interview, do you think you asked the right questions? Did you stick too rigidly to your script? Is there a point you should have pursued more aggressively or a fact you still don't understand? If so, consider calling or e-mailing with a follow-up question.

It's also a good idea to send a thank-you note after the interview, particularly if it took place at the person's home or lasted a long time. In your note, offer to send copies of any photographs you took (or perhaps even your finished research project).

Surveys

Surveys (sometimes called questionnaires) typically consist of a series of questions that can be asked and answered in writing, in person, or over the phone. Surveys are used all the time by marketing consultants who want information about the public's response to new products and services. Those surveys are scientifically designed and conducted, and they lead to quantitative results—the kind that are often trumpeted in ads with claims such as "Four out of five dentists surveyed recommend product X." (See Box 10.2 for a discussion of the difference between *quantitative* and *qualitative* data.) A survey that you conduct for this course will probably not allow you to make generalizations about large groups of people because you will not have the time or the resources to develop a scientifically valid survey instrument and collect a large number of responses. However, the answers to the questions in a simple survey can help you generate information for localized populations about topics such as the following.

> the prevalence of a particular practice ("How many people in this class have e-mailed the instructor about an assignment?")
> varying points of view ("What do people in this dorm think of the food in the dining hall?")

BOX 10.2   Quantitative and Qualitative Data

Quantitative data is any data that can be reported in numbers. Quantitative data tells how many ("Nine out of ten participants in the study showed improvement on this medication") or how much ("Thirty percent of the precipitation fell as sleet before turning to rain") or how likely ("Forty percent of all marriages in the United States are likely to end in divorce"). Quantitative data deals in generalizations; it clusters facts together and counts them. Most people have a lot of confidence in quantitative data, which typically comes from surveys or experiments.

  Qualitative data is descriptive and specific. It can give a more vivid picture of how people think, feel, or behave than quantitative data. (See the vivid detail, obtained from interviews and observation, that adds emotional impact to "Slaves of New York" on p. 120.) It is not generalizable, but it can add the type of detail that makes writing more interesting or more believable. Qualitative data typically comes from interviews, open-ended survey questions, and observations.

> preferences for particular products ("What brand of running shoes do men between the ages of eighteen and twenty-five prefer?")

> the beliefs of a particular group with regard to a particular topic ("Do students on this college campus believe that President George W. Bush won the election fairly in 2000?")

> the feelings of a particular group ("How do first-year students feel about being away from home?")

Consider the article "Invisible to VCs" (reprinted from the Web site ABCNEWS.com), which begins with a photograph and a narrative about a specific person but quickly moves into a report of the results of a survey (Figure 10.2). The second section of the article (beginning with the subhead "2% Into 38% = Woe") contains a lot of information derived from a survey. We learn, for example, that 38 percent of U.S. businesses are owned by women but that only 2 percent of all venture capital investments go to women-owned firms. These survey-based facts enabled reporter Michael Liedtke to write an informative article that starts with

 Exercise

Look back at the article on binge drinking (Figure 10.1) taken from Chapter 3, p. 113. Reread it to find one or two examples of information derived from a survey or a study.

FIGURE 10.2
Article Based on
Information from
a Survey

a specific individual (as a way to engage the audience) and moves on to describe a problem. Without the survey data, this piece of writing might have been a human-interest story. With this information, however, the author broadens the article to discuss trends and repercussions. Notice how he uses interviews in combination with the survey information to add interest and credibility to the article.

Planning the Survey

The first step is to figure out the characteristics of the people you want to survey. These characteristics will vary according to your audience and purpose. For a report requested by the Dean of Advising on the reasons students drop out of your college, you'll need to find people who have dropped out. For a workshop for instructors on the advantages and disadvantages of lecture-based courses versus discussion-based courses, you'll need to survey students who have taken both types of courses. There may be other considerations, too: Are you writing about a topic that has a particular geographical limitation? Are you writing about a topic that has a gender, race, or age limitation?

Your next step is to decide how many people need to complete the survey. For statistically significant studies, there are scientific ways to determine the number of participants (respondents) needed. However, for your purposes, you will probably be able to survey a relatively small population as a representative sample. For the purposes of a writing course, you can probably get credible information if you survey at least twenty-five participants.

Decide whether the participants can remain anonymous. If you're asking questions about a sensitive topic (such as sexuality, weight, drug or alcohol use, depression, or domestic violence), you will get a more honest response if you can guarantee that you will not reveal the identity of any participants. To do so, you must come up with a way to gather, store, and code the survey data so that no one can possibly know any of the respondents' names. Keep in mind that even if the respondents remain anonymous, you may still want them to identify their age, gender, race, ethnicity, or other characteristics. Also keep in mind that, theoretically, surveys conducted in person or over the phone can be anonymous in the sense that names and other identifying information will not be connected to the data. As a practical matter, however, participants usually will not feel that their survey responses are truly anonymous if, for example, they are your own classmates or relatives.

Consequently, a key step in the planning process is to decide if you want to conduct the survey in writing, in person, or over the phone. Each method has advantages and disadvantages. One advantage of a written survey is that participants usually answer more honestly when they are not speaking directly with the researcher. However, you may have a better chance of getting people to answer the survey (and not forget to send it back to you) if you sit down with them in person or ask your questions over the phone. Another important point to consider is how much time you can expect the participants to spend responding to the survey. Many people are willing to take a few minutes to complete a survey, but very few will respond if they think it will take more than fifteen or twenty minutes.

After deciding on the format of your survey, you need to determine how to find and contact potential participants. Do any of your friends or relatives have the appropriate characteristics? Do you belong to a group that would allow you to survey its members? Would classmates or students who live in your dorm be suitable respondents? Think about how you will convince people to participate. You'll need to tell prospective participants why you need this information and what you plan to do with it. (You might also want to assure them that the survey is brief and won't take too much of their time.) For a written survey that you will mail or e-mail, you should write a cover letter or e-mail message supplying this information, asking people to complete the survey and giving them a deadline or due date. Include postage-paid, self-addressed envelopes for the return of mailed surveys. If you can guarantee their anonymity, include that information in the cover letter or message.

Writing the Survey Questions

Writing a first draft of a survey is very hard to do well. One important concept is to avoid asking two questions at the same time ("Do you think you eat a healthy diet and get enough exercise?"). The problem with such *double-barreled questions* is that respondents might have different answers to the two parts. Just as with interviews, you also have to avoid asking *leading questions*—questions that give participants cues about the answers you want. After all, people tend to give responses they think the researcher wants to hear, and they also tend to give answers that cast their behavior in a favorable light. For example, they might exaggerate how often they exercise or read books and underreport how often they eat junk food or play video games. One way to combat these tendencies is to ask questions in a neutral and nonjudgmental way, with no emotionally loaded terms. Another approach is to ask a key question in two different ways—in different parts of the survey—and then check to see if the participant answered both versions consistently.

Suppose you wanted to find out about students' eating habits. You might ask a series of questions about the types of food they eat regularly. In one section of the survey, you might have multiple-choice and checklist questions (see Box 10.3 for a discussion of different types of survey questions) like the one that follows.

At a fast-food restaurant, I am likely to order (check all that apply):

☐ hamburger	☐ chicken nuggets	☐ regular soda
☐ cheeseburger	☐ taco	☐ diet soda
☐ salad	☐ French fries	☐ other
☐ chicken sandwich	☐ milkshake	

BOX 10.3 Survey Questions

There are two basic categories of survey questions: closed questions and open-ended questions. *Closed questions* ask participants to choose an answer from a set of fixed choices. *Open-ended questions* ask participants to explain or describe something in their own words or to provide a specific factual response (such as a number or an age). Typically, open-ended questions require a short answer, usually no more than a few sentences.

You are probably familiar with several types of closed questions from tests and quizzes.

> *Multiple-choice questions* ask participants to choose one from among several options.

> *Checklist questions* ask participants to place a checkmark next to all the choices that apply. (The fast-food restaurant question on p. 574 is an example.)

> *Ranking questions* ask participants to rate a statement or question on a scale, which usually has five points. For example, to assess behavior you might include a scale like this: 1 = never, 2 = rarely, 3 = sometimes, 4 = often, and 5 = very often. To assess opinion you might use a scale like this: 1 = agree strongly, 2 = agree somewhat, 3 = neutral, 4 = disagree somewhat, and 5 = disagree strongly. With ranking questions it is usually better to move sequentially from a lower to a higher level of response or from agreement to disagreement.

> *True/false* and *yes/no* questions ask participants for a specific response (and sometimes for an *agree/disagree* response, if the choice is clear and does not involve the levels offered in a ranking question).

When designing a survey, consider including more than one type of question—this is a good way to increase the reliability of your data. However, you should probably use mainly closed questions because they are easiest for participants to answer and the results are easiest for you to analyze. On the downside, you may not get the most accurate or nuanced answers—for example, if a respondent is frustrated by the choices, misinterprets the question, or rushes through the survey. Although open-ended questions are hard to analyze, they often elicit the most thorough and thoughtful responses and can provide information that you never considered when you designed the survey.

Then, in a later section of the survey, you might ask an open-ended question such as the following and then compare the two answers to see if the respondent answered consistently.

Describe the menu items in a typical meal that you would eat at a fast-food restaurant.

Keep in mind that when you write two versions of the same question, you need to make sure that you really are teasing out inconsistencies. For example, if you instead worded the open-ended question to ask people to describe a typical meal that they eat off campus, you'd be introducing a new, confounding element—because students might eat off-campus meals at a variety of places other than fast-food restaurants.

Make sure your questions don't become too complex or require too much expertise for participants to answer (unless you are specifically trying to measure their level of knowledge). For example, asking them to estimate how many calories they consume in a typical fast-food meal would be problematic because most people know too little about the caloric content of foods to give a correct answer. Also be careful to avoid questions that are vague, ambiguous, or open to different interpretations. For example, if you want respondents to indicate how often they engage in a certain activity, such as eating at a fast-food restaurant, it would be better to provide a range of specific numbers of visits per week or month rather than subjective choices such as *often, sometimes,* and *rarely.* (For more on ranking questions, see Box 10.3 on p. 575.) Finally, phrase questions carefully to avoid sexist language or unwarranted assumptions about respondents' gender, race, ethnicity, marital status, sexual orientation, and so on.

If you will be conducting a written survey, you should also think about its visual design. Make sure to use a typeface and layout that are attractive and legible; the design should make it easy for respondents to complete their answers fully and accurately. For example, provide enough space for them to write out the responses to open-ended questions. (For more on open-ended questions, see Box 10.3 on p. 575.)

Testing the Survey

Whether you plan to conduct your survey in writing or on the phone, once you've drafted all your questions you should test the survey with friends or family members who won't be participating. Ask them to tell you if there are questions that they cannot understand or that are too hard to answer (perhaps because there is no suitable answer choice, the choices overlap, or the question requires too much specialized knowledge). If the survey is written, find out how much time they needed to complete the survey. If it's a phone survey, keep track of the time so you know how long it takes to ask all the questions. If the survey requires more than fifteen to twenty minutes to complete, you may need to eliminate some of the questions. Read through the results of your test survey, looking for answers that indicate a problem with a particular question—for example, whether it was leading or biased, or whether it was misinterpreted. Revise any questions that have caused or revealed problems.

Conducting the Survey

After revising problematic questions, you're ready to conduct the survey. If you're using a written format, determine whether you will be able to distribute the survey in person (for example, by handing it out in the dining hall) or will instead have to mail it to participants. If you can think of a population that is appropriate for your topic and can be reached by e-mail, you might save time and money by distributing the survey electronically (or by using a Web site so that participants can respond online). For any written survey, make sure to ask participants to return it to you (or complete it online) by a specific date. You'll get the best response rate if you include a stamped, self-addressed return envelope.

Analyzing and Presenting the Results

For multiple-choice, checklist, and ranking questions, you can simply tally the results—in other words, count how many participants gave each possible answer. For example, for the checklist question about fast food on p. 574, you would count the number of people who reported that they order hamburgers, cheeseburgers, salads, and so on. For yes/no and true/false questions, just count the number of each answer. If you asked for a specific fact ("Which fast-food restaurant do you go to most often?"), you could list all the responses and then record the number of times each response occurs. If you survey a lot of people, a computer spreadsheet application such as Excel can help you add up the data, calculate percentages, and so on.

For open-ended questions, you will need to read all the responses to see how many types of answers were given. You may decide to cluster the answers into categories. For example, if you asked twenty-five students "Why do you eat off campus?" you might get answers such as the ones that follow.

1. better food
2. shorter lines
3. takes less time
4. can get breakfast at 10 a.m.
5. costs less
6. better variety
7. can eat with my off-campus friends
8. open late at night
9. fresher salads
10. quieter
11. dining hall closes before my evening classes, and I don't have time to eat earlier because of sports practice

12. save money by skipping some meals and preparing others (eat breakfast in my dorm)—so I don't have to buy a meal plan
13. dining hall closes for breakfast too early (I get up late!)
14. dining hall is too crowded
15. can't stand running into my old boyfriend

You could cluster these responses into categories such as *Quality of food* (#1, 6, 9), *Convenience* (#2, 3, 4, 8, 11, 13), *Cost* (#5, 12), *Social reasons* (#7, 15), and *Environment* (#10, 14).

When you report your results, you can refer to the quantitative data—the things you have counted—in percentages ("Fifty percent of all participants order hamburgers or cheeseburgers in fast-food restaurants, whereas only 8 percent order salads") or in actual numbers ("Only 2 out of 25 participants reported ordering salads in fast-food restaurants"). If you asked participants to identify their gender, age, or other characteristics, you might also choose to break down the data more specifically if you have noted significant differences ("Only women order salads").

If you cluster the data from open-ended questions, you can quantify it and present it the same way you present the other quantitative data. For example, using the data from the question above, you can calculate the percentage of respondents who eat off campus for convenience. You can also use actual quotes from the open-ended questions to add credibility and detail to your report. (See Box 10.4 for tips on what to do with surveys that are filled out improperly or incompletely.)

After analyzing and summarizing the survey results, you need to consider how to incorporate them into your research project. You should also determine whether you will present the data visually—for example, by using pie charts or bar graphs. (If you used a spreadsheet program to

> For advice on presenting data visually, see **Chapter 8.**

BOX 10.4 Incomplete and Invalid Surveys

It is possible—in fact, likely—that you will not be able to use every survey that gets returned. Some participants might not take the survey seriously—for example, they may check off every answer to a multiple-choice question or write an implausible or flippant response to an open-ended question. Other participants might not complete the entire survey. Use your judgment to decide whether to include the results of such surveys. If a participant made inappropriate responses, you'll probably decide to discard that survey. However, if the participant simply failed to respond to certain questions, you can still use the data that he or she did provide. When you write about your research, it's a good idea to include information about the total number of surveys you received and how many were not fully completed.

analyze the data, you can also have it generate graphic elements based on that data.) Most important, you must come up with a way to summarize your results, making generalizations and drawing conclusions about what you think the survey revealed. In other words, you must present not only the data but also your interpretation of that data in relationship to your topic and research question(s). You also have to explain how your survey results compare or contrast with the information you found in other sources.

Observations

Before reading this chapter, you probably already knew that interviews and surveys are frequently used as research strategies, but you may not have realized that it is also possible to conduct research by simply *observing* the behaviors of others. In fact, observations can be a useful way to accomplish the following research tasks.

> see how people behave in their natural environment
> collect data without influencing the participants
> gather *anecdotal evidence* (see Box 10.5) that will make your research report more realistic
> generate questions and ideas that can be investigated further through interviews and surveys
> verify the information gained through interviews or surveys
> collect data without relying on the interpretation, memory, accuracy, or honesty of interviewees or survey participants
> gain a great deal of information about specific groups or situations, often in a short amount of time

---

BOX 10.5   Anecdotal Evidence

An *anecdote* is a little story; thus, anecdotal evidence uses a story or stories to prove a point. Often anecdotal evidence comes from your own experience, but it can also come from observations. An anecdote makes a great opening paragraph because a story is a good hook to get the reader interested in your topic. You can also intersperse anecdotes throughout the report to support specific points. A memorable anecdote may even work well as a conclusion.

In Bill Buford's *New Yorker* article "Sweat Is Good," excerpted in Figure 10.3 on p. 581, you can see how one writer uses his own observations as evidence to increase the credibility of his report. In this section of the article, Buford suggests that sweatshops are not as bad as some people claim. The highlighted sentences describe how he gained admission to several sweatshops and what he saw there. Notice that several elements strengthen Buford's credibility. First, he tells us how many sweatshops he visited (a dozen), so that we won't think he based his opinion on just one or two observations. He also tells us that he took someone else with him, so we understand that his companion can verify what he reports. Finally, he contrasts what he actually saw with what he had expected to see, so we know that he did not allow his preconceived ideas about sweatshops to influence his reporting.

Although Buford seems to have made his observations fairly quickly, some researchers, such as anthropologists, conduct very detailed, long-term observations of groups of people. For example, many researchers visit remote parts of the world to live with and observe aboriginal peoples and then report on their observations. Many issues of *National Geographic* contain reports based largely on observation. This type of study is done with the permission of the people being observed and may involve years of field research. It also requires years of training.

However, it is possible to conduct some types of observation in a short amount of time, without any formal training, and without asking for permission. For example, if you are researching the number of people who drive the wrong way down a poorly marked one-way street, you can stand on the corner of the street and keep track of how many people make the attempt during a certain period. You won't be doing anything wrong, and you won't be bothering anyone. (You'll also get more accurate information than if you surveyed people about how often they engage in this behavior.) But if you want to observe the number of people who order salads in a particular fast-food restaurant at lunchtime, you'll need to ask the manager for permission to sit at a table and take notes.

In another type of observational research, you might want to watch a specific person or group of people over an extended period. For example, you might be interested in writing a report on students' attentiveness in large lecture courses at your college. To do this, you would need permission to attend several different lecture courses. Then you would sit quietly and observe the students, lecturer, and classroom (or lecture hall) setting, taking notes about your observations of details such as those in the following list.

> how many people are in attendance

> how big the room is

> how the room is arranged, as well as the types of furniture, lighting, ventilation, and acoustics

> what kinds of media are used to support the lecture (for example, chalkboard or white board, videotapes or DVDs, slides, overhead transparencies, or software presentations such as PowerPoint slides)

❯ **bedfordstmartins.com/ visualage**

To read the complete text of Buford's essay, click on
CHAPTER 3 ❯ EXAMPLES

FIGURE 10.3
Excerpt from "Sweat Is Good," an Article Based on Information from Observations

I wanted to see the sweatshops in Sunset Park but didn't know how I'd able to get inside. An idea presented itself. I would just walk in. 1

The idea was proposed by a P.R. person from UNITE. The union has an outpost in the heart of the district, at Seventh and Sixtieth, a "workers' justice center," and the P.R. person had also been curious to see first-hand what the conditions were like. I suggested we might go together. It's one thing, I felt, to walk in off the street on your own: "Hi, I know you run a horrible sweatshop and I'd just like to have a look around." It's a bit easier when you can do it with company. 2

We visited a dozen plants, maybe more, enough to get a picture. Laws were being broken. Time cards were not being kept. People were working overtime and not gettinig paid for it. And we suspected that the wages were close to the legal minimum, if not below it—and they were getting paid in cash. These were not foursquare on-the-up-and-up, apple-pie, American-flag businesses (even though we found several American-flag labels there—J.C. Penney, Bradlee, Diane von Furstenberg). But they weren't all that bad, either. The bathrooms, which I had been warned would be disgusting, were clean. The fire exits were marked, and the aisles were clear. There were windows and light. And there was plenty of space, not a feature of Manhattan garment factories. And while we did spot one child—I had been told to expect underage laborers—it was a small boy, hiding shyly beneath the table of his mother while she sewed (an illegal practice but scarcely a heinous one). 3

Silant Chung runs the Sunset Park justice center—she had given us our list of sweatshops—and when we returned I reported that the places had looked, well, 4

not so bad. This was not the impression she had assumed the visit would make. Earlier she had arranged an interview with a garment worker, and that, too, hadn't quite left the impression she was hoping for. He had invited me to call him Xie Zhin, fearing that if he used his real name it might get him in trouble with the local factory owners. Zhin was forty-three, a sewer on a Merrow machine, the most elementary kind of machine, a labor not normally undertaken by men. His wife was a sewer as well, and they lived in a two-bedroom Brooklyn apartment with two children, paying five hundred and fifty a month—not cheap, in the circumstances. They were from the countryside ("peasants"), about twenty-five miles from Fuzhou, and had come here, illegally, five years ago, and then contrived to secure political asylum. I asked Zhin about the conditions of the factories (reasonable), his workday (often twelve hours long, during busy periods), and his pay, which averaged out to something a little less than minimum wage but on which he paid no tax: his take-home, then, wasn't all that different from what some union workers get. This fly-by-night, stuff-it-in-the-mattress existence sounded about right; this was life in Sunset Park.

I asked him what he would like to see changed. In fact, what I said was: "Of all the possible conditions, what would you like to see improved?" I was expecting a union answer: health care, a minimum wage, overtime pay. Or an attack on profiteering owners. 5

"We want more work!" he said, with Silant Chung translating. "We want more business. The factories don't have the business they once did. Because of that, we are all under pressure. I am here because I want people to know about our plight. We'll do anything. But the work is not coming our way." 6

. . .

> whether students take notes, ask questions, or seem to listen carefully

> what kinds of opportunities are presented for interaction

> how many students engage in an unrelated activity during the lecture (for example, talking, sleeping, e-mailing, using instant messaging, surfing the Web, or playing hand-held video games)

> what students say to one another about the class on their way out

In your report, you might present a chart or table summarizing some of this information. You might also want to make sketches to show how certain physical and environmental features affect students' attentiveness.

Planning the Observation

The first step is to figure out what you want to accomplish by conducting an observation. What research question(s) do you hope to answer? What will you need to observe to get your answer(s)? How much time will be required?

> For more advice on formulating a research question, see **Chapter 9,** p. 534.

Next you'll need to select an appropriate site at which to observe the relevant phenomena. If you choose a public site (such as a city park), you will not have to ask permission. If the site you choose is private, you must contact someone who is authorized to give you permission to conduct the observation. (Keep in mind that shopping malls and stores are private, not public.) When asking for permission, be sure to say who you are, what you plan to observe and why, when you want to conduct the observation, and how long you will be there.

After selecting a site, make a plan for recording your observations. Visit the site to get a sense of the available space. Will you be able to sit down and use a table to take notes? How obvious will you be to those you are observing? Is there adequate lighting for note-taking, or should you bring a pen light (for example, at a theater)? If you plan to plug in a piece of equipment, are there electrical outlets? The answers to these kinds of questions will help you with the next step of planning: Should you take notes on a laptop computer; dictate your observations into a tape recorder; or use a pad, notebook, or clipboard and pre-formatted data charts to log in your observations? Should you try to tape-record, videotape, or photograph any parts of the observation? Remember that in order to photograph people or electronically record their words and actions, you must get their permission (in addition to getting permission from an authorized person at the site, if it's private property).

Before you start the observation, decide exactly what you want to focus on. For example, an observation for a report on food preferences might involve sitting in a fast-food restaurant for several hours and keeping track of the kinds of food people order. Do you want to answer questions about the number of people who order salads? French fries? Diet versus regular soft drinks? If so, you would need some kind of chart to keep track of all the orders; and because most fast-food restaurants offer a lot of variety, you would probably need to group your observations into broad categories. These categories would vary according to the research questions. For example, if you were only interested in salads versus burgers, you could have three categories: *Salads, Burgers, Other*. If you were interested in the soft-drink question, you could again have three categories: *Regular soft drinks, Diet soft drinks, Other beverages*. You would also have to record the total number of people who order anything so that you could say, "*X* percent of all customers ordered . . ." or "*X* out of *Y* customers ordered. . . ."

Conducting the Observation

On the day of the observation, arrive in plenty of time with all your tools and equipment (working pens, sharpened pencils, notebook or pad, camera, tape recorder, and so on). If the site is private, immediately announce yourself to the person who gave you permission, and restate your project and purpose. Next find a position where you can observe without interfering with other people. Try to be unobtrusive—it may help to think of yourself as a spy or plainclothes detective trying to blend into the scene. Take notes on everything you see or hear. If you write down someone's actual words, put quotation marks around them so you can remember later which words are your own and which ones are someone else's. Be sure to take notes about the people, place, and actions you observe, making sketches or taking photographs if those types of visuals will make your work more effective. You can also make some notes about your own thoughts and feelings as you observe the situation and setting.

Thinking about the Observation

Soon after conducting the observation, read through your notes and add any other ideas that occur to you. Now is the time to flesh out your observations by writing down your thoughts about what the observation revealed, as well as additional details about the people, setting, and actions—things you may have been too busy to record as they were happening. If you used a lot of abbreviations to speed up your note-taking, now is also the time to clarify what you jotted down. Do this as soon as possible after conducting the observation—preferably within an hour or two—while your memory is still fresh.

After looking over your notes, decide if you need to conduct additional observations. Perhaps during your observation you didn't see much that was relevant to your research question(s). If so, think carefully about what was missing. What did you expect to observe that you didn't see? Would it be helpful to go back to the same place at a different time of day or a different day of the week? Or would it be better to try a different site? Do you just need to collect more of the same type of information, or should you focus on a slightly different research question? Is there any type of preparation that might make a follow-up observation more successful?

Analyzing and Presenting the Data

You will probably have gathered a great deal of information. Don't feel overwhelmed; for this type of observation, let your research question(s) guide your analysis. What did you see that might help answer one or more of these questions? Read through your notes carefully to find any patterns (for example, more men than women ordered cheeseburgers, or more people ordered salads at lunch than at dinner). It may be helpful to use a highlighter or colored pen to mark patterns or particular observations that provide evidence to support the claims you plan to make in your report. In looking for patterns, pay attention to the exceptions—the information you gathered that does not fit the pattern—to see if it sheds an interesting light on the topic. For example, if in fact you observed that more men than women ordered cheeseburgers, you might want to take a look at the women who *did* order cheeseburgers: Did they have any characteristics in common?

If you conducted more than one observation, were the data from the different sites consistent? If not, can you draw any conclusions about the differences? For example, if you conducted observations at several fast-food restaurants, you might have observed significant variations in the physical settings, types of food ordered, hours of operation, or employee-customer interactions. In analyzing the data, you might suggest possible causes or effects of these differences. Here are some other questions to consider as you analyze your data.

> What did I observe that I expected to see?
> What did I observe that surprised me?
> Did I observe anything that upset or angered me?
> How did my observation support or amplify what I learned through my other research (including interviews and surveys)?
> Did my observation contradict any of my other sources?
> As a result of my observation, do I need to conduct additional research?

Finally, think about how to incorporate your observational research into your project. Will you present the data as anecdotal evidence or in a more formal way? How will you use this data in conjunction with the information you gathered from other sources? Will the results of your observation provide backup for your other research or represent a major element of your project?

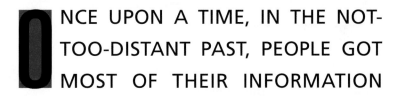

11

Evaluating Sources and Taking Notes

ONCE UPON A TIME, IN THE NOT-TOO-DISTANT PAST, PEOPLE GOT MOST OF THEIR INFORMATION

from newspapers, radio, and three major television networks. Network television provided entertainment and news for eighteen or twenty hours per day, computers were used for word processing and spreadsheets, and everyday objects such as cereal boxes told you what was inside them. Times have changed, and so have our sources of information. These days, television provides news, entertainment, and information around the clock; the Internet offers access to millions of information sites around the world (see Figure 11.1); and cereal boxes sometimes present footnoted articles about nutrition and high blood pressure.

FIGURE 11.1
Web Sites Offer Vast
Amounts of
Information

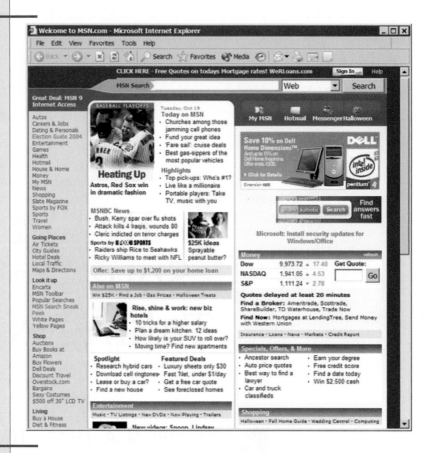

❯ For advice on finding sources,
see **Chapter 9.**

Everywhere you look, you are bombarded by information. What does this bombardment mean?

On the one hand, you have access to a great many more sources of information than people of any generation ever had before. On the other hand, you cannot get away from a constant stream of information, often on topics that are of no interest to you. You may feel overwhelmed at times—there is so much coming at you from so many different sources that you may have trouble figuring out what information is worth paying attention to. The availability of so much material also means that even though you can easily find information on any topic, you may have a hard time sorting through and evaluating everything you find.

Once you have used the library and Internet to find potential sources for your project, and perhaps done field research as well, you will need to start making decisions about which possibilities to pursue more seriously. This chapter will provide advice on evaluating sources. It will also provide suggestions for taking notes and for thinking about the visuals you may need for your project.

EVALUATING SOURCES

With today's easy access to the Internet and a variety of databases, you may wind up with more sources than you need. What do you do with so many sources that seem to support your work? You evaluate them in two important ways: (1) to determine if they fit your research project and (2) to determine if the sources themselves are trustworthy. Here are some suggestions that will help you choose the best sources.

Evaluating the Appropriateness of Sources

Regardless of how interesting or timely a source may be, it must be appropriate for your research. Think about your purpose, audience, and research question to make sure each source fits your research topic.

Considering General Purpose and Audience

As you look at your sources, think about your overall reason for writing. For example, if you're writing to *persuade* people to act on a proposal, you'll need sources that will convince readers of the thoroughness of your understanding of the problem and the feasibility of your proposed solution. You would therefore want sources (1) that the audience recognizes and believes and (2) that reflect different perspectives on the proposal to show that you have taken various approaches into consideration. On the other hand, if you're writing to *describe* or *explain* this proposal, you would undoubtedly use some different kinds of sources. Your focus might be more factual or statistical. You might include excerpts from the proposal itself or compare the proposal to similar ones in an effort to help readers understand your explanation.

Also keep in mind who your audience is and what sources your readers will consider most credible and persuasive. If you're writing for an academic audience (such as biology or psychology instructors), you would probably include scholarly works and journal articles. If you're writing for specialists in a particular field (such as auto mechanics or graphic designers), you may need to seek out journals aimed at that field. If you're writing for enthusiasts of a particular sport or hobby (such as golfers or bird watchers), you should look for magazines or Web sites that focus on that activity. Imagine, for instance, a research paper you might have written in the fall of 2003 in which you were urging readers to support Howard Dean in his bid for the Democratic presidential nomination in 2004. Your sources might vary considerably, depending on whether your audience consisted of fellow students, political science professors, supporters of Dick Gephardt, or registered voters over sixty-five years of age.

Focusing on the Research Question

To guide your research, focus on the question that the main point of your paper will answer. The question should help you zero in on specifics instead of broad, general ideas and should help you take a more objective approach to finding possible sources.

Keep in mind the specific question your research is about. As you skim potential sources, ask yourself if the source helps you answer the research question. Does it support your main point? Does it provide an important argument against your main point that you will need to refute? Does it help establish your credibility with readers? Suppose, for example, that you are researching the following question: "Why did the flu vaccine supply run so low in the 2003–2004 flu season?" While doing your research, you find a number of good analyses of the vaccine shortage (see Figure 11.2), and you consult drug company news releases as well. You also run across pieces describing side effects of flu shots. However, although these articles may be interesting and well thought out, you realize they have nothing to do with your research question, and you decide not to use them.

Determine whether you have found the right kinds of sources. Given your research question, do you have enough primary or secondary sources? Do you need both? As you recall, a *primary source* is a firsthand account by an eyewitness or participant, whereas a *secondary source* is an analysis based on primary sources. In the research project about flu vaccine, for example, you would mostly use secondary sources. However, you might rely on primary sources as well—accounts of physicians who administered vaccination programs and comments of government and public health officials who analyzed the flu season. Most research projects require a mix of primary and secondary sources. It is also a good idea to use sources from several media, choosing from Web sites, reference works, magazines, newspapers, books, scholarly journals, and so forth. If all your sources are from only one kind of media—popular magazines, for instance—chances are you have overlooked important sources elsewhere.

❯ For more on primary and secondary sources, see **Chapter 9**, pp. 530–531.

Decide how important the publication date of your sources is. Does the topic require you to focus on the most recent material available? For example, in writing a research project on the influence of France on the

**FIGURE 11.2
Google Search
Results List on Flu
Vaccine Supply**

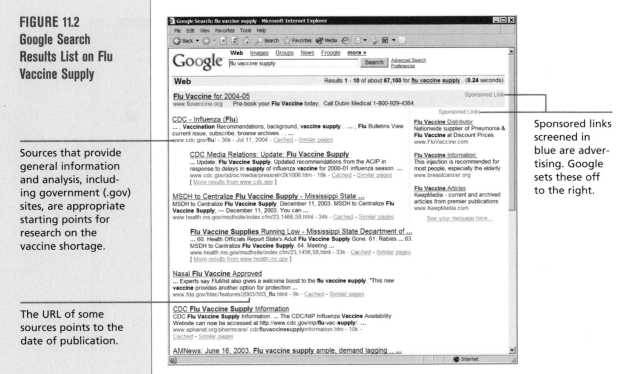

Sources that provide
general information
and analysis, includ-
ing government (.gov)
sites, are appropriate
starting points for
research on the
vaccine shortage.

Sponsored links
screened in
blue are adver-
tising. Google
sets these off
to the right.

The URL of some
sources points to the
date of publication.

American Revolution, you would probably use a lot of older, historical sources as well as more recent analyses by historians. In this instance, the publication date of each individual source would not be critical. However, in writing an evaluation of today's Web publishing software, your sources would need to be current. Keep in mind that Web pages are not always up to date. Information on the Internet may appear to be current but actually be too old for your purposes (see Figure 11.3). Take time to determine the publication date of each Web source and the date when it was revised. Internet sources that regularly list the dates when content is updated are generally the most reliable.

Be sure you have found sources that agree as well as disagree with you. Think again about the paper in which you urged readers to support Howard Dean in his bid for the Democratic presidential nomination in 2004. Ideally, such a paper would include sources that bolster your position, sources that disagree with you, and your own rebuttal to those who disagree. As you evaluate sources, make sure to cover more than one side of an issue.

Look for sources with visuals. As you evaluate sources, think about the visuals in them and whether they will help achieve your purpose. How do

FIGURE 11.3
Yahoo Search Results
List with Some
Inappropriate Sources

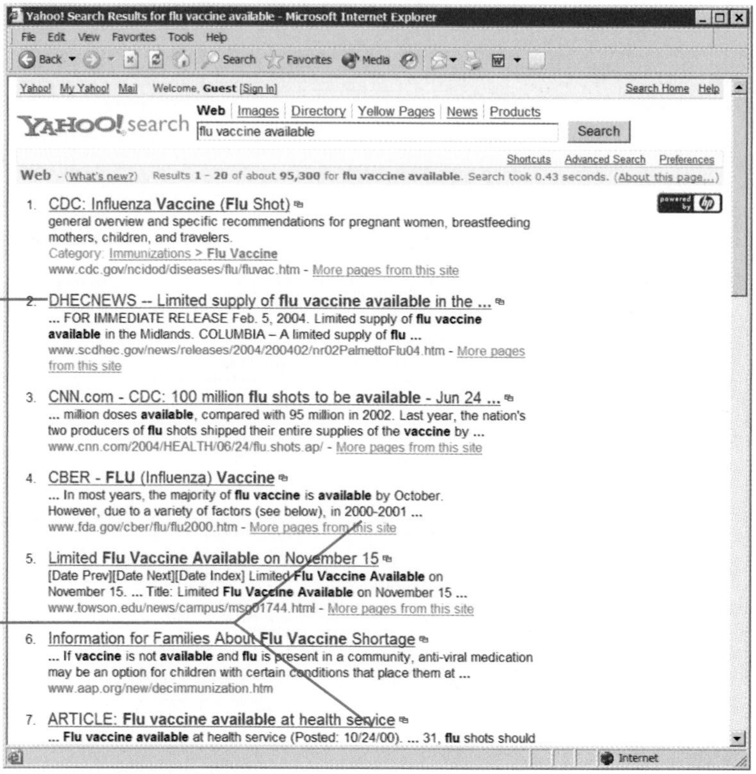

Sources specific to one region
may be too narrow in focus.

Sources updated in 2000
or 2001 are likely too old
to be useful.

your sources use visuals to convey information? Do the visuals enhance what the authors are saying? Do you have data or ideas that you could present in a similar way? If you're citing lots of statistics, you may want to create or adapt a table. If you're analyzing how something has changed over time, you may want to create a bar or line graph. If you need to show what something or someone looks like, a drawing or photograph will probably be most effective. If you haven't already done so, it's a good idea to print or photocopy pages with the visuals you might want to incorporate; just be sure to keep a record of exactly where the images come from so that you can properly credit them in your project.

❯ For more advice on creating visual representations of information, see **Chapter 8**.

❯ For more advice on crediting visual sources, see **Chapter 12**.

Evaluating the Trustworthiness of Sources

The sources you choose must not only be appropriate for your research; they must also be trustworthy—accurate, honest, and fair. You can determine the trustworthiness of a source by taking a close look at both the author and the publisher.

Considering the Author

Consider what you know about the authors of potential sources. A careful assessment of an author's credibility will point you to sources with expertise and authority.

Examine the author's credentials and/or experience. Finding out such information can help you determine whether the author is qualified to write on your topic. For example, in 2003, Madeleine Albright's book *Madam Secretary: A Memoir* was published. Because Albright had been secretary of state during the Clinton administration, had served as the U.S. representative to the United Nations, and was a former professor of international affairs at Georgetown University, she clearly had the credentials and experience to write about foreign policy. Whether or not you agreed with Albright's positions, she would still be considered a trustworthy source. And if you were not familiar with her background, you could easily find information about her by searching the Web for interviews or visiting governmental sites such as secretary.state.gov or sites with reviews of her book such as BarnesandNoble.com.

However, some authors are not well known. In fact, many magazines and newspapers recognize that their readers cannot possibly know every author's background, so they provide information. If you look at articles in magazines like *Newsweek* and *Time,* you often see a blurb at the end of each article that tells a little bit about the author. Other magazines, like the *New Yorker* and *Vanity Fair,* provide information about authors in a separate section at the beginning of the magazine. In many books, too, a section at the back (or at the beginning or end of each chapter) may tell about the author(s). On Web sites, look for links titled About the Author. If author information is not available, use an author's name for a Web search.

Review the types of evidence the author uses. As you evaluate each source, consider the factual information the author includes. Where did he or she get that information—and can you verify the facts? Does the author name his or her sources? If statistics are included, are they accurate and used fairly? Or does the author use statistics selectively to prove a point, overlooking data that might weaken the argument?

Also, look at the author's opinions. Is the author's main thesis backed up by solid evidence and presented in a logical, persuasive argument? Does he or she cite recognized experts? If the author makes assertions but doesn't back them up with evidence and examples, the argument may be weak. In written sources and in personal interviews, be on the lookout for phrases such as *It is obvious, We all realize,* or *It is a fact.* If an author or interviewee makes such assertions without supporting evidence, you should look for a more trustworthy source.

Evaluate whether the author seems to understand the topic thoroughly, including any opposing viewpoints. In the most effective arguments, authors present more than one perspective. In order to persuade readers to agree with their point of view, they try to predict what readers' objections might be and then try to counter those objections. Be cautious of sources that do not take possible objections into account. Be wary of those who contradict themselves or who simply dismiss those who disagree with them.

Determine the author's perspective or bias. Learning about an author's credentials or experience may also reveal his or her point of view or bias. Imagine, for example, three articles about gun control. One is written by the president of the National Rifle Association, one is written by a senator who led the fight in Congress for tougher handgun laws, and one is written by the parent of a child who was killed in a drive-by shooting. Clearly, the role and experience of each author would affect his or her article.

Another clue to an author's perspective is the kind of language—or tone—he or she uses. If a piece of writing contains strong, emotional language, the author may have a deep personal investment in the topic. For example, if your neighbor is angry about a new landfill being proposed in your county and she writes a letter to the editor of the local newspaper, you would expect some emotional language. In this instance, the strong language might be appropriate. The question to ask yourself is this: Does the letter provide a solid argument against the landfill, or is the letter just a series of emotional outbursts?

Just because an author has a particular perspective or bias doesn't mean that you should automatically disregard the source. All of us bring some point of view to our writing, especially in persuasive pieces. It is important to determine an author's bias and to judge the author's argument on its own merits, based on evidence, logical presentation, and so forth. If you disagree with the perspective of a source, you may still want to use the source as an opposing viewpoint to your own opinion.

Considering the Publisher

Consider carefully what you know about the publisher or sponsor of a source. Doing so will help you determine which sources are most appropriate to your research project.

Identify the publisher. The text you are evaluating may have been published in a magazine, newspaper, or book, or it may have been published on a Web site. Regardless of medium, some organization or person decided that this text should be either printed or distributed electronically. If the publisher is an organization, it might be a commercial or scholarly book publishing company (Random House, Oxford University Press), a newspaper (*Chicago Tribune*), a magazine (*Sports Illustrated*), a nonprofit organization (American Heart Association), a political or special interest group (Republican Party), or a government agency (Food and Drug Administration). A commercial publisher might also be part of a larger company, and a periodical might be part of a chain of newspapers or magazines—which, in turn, might be owned by an even larger corporation.

There are no firm rules about evaluating the credentials of a publisher. Some newsmagazines, newspapers, and Web sites are commercial enterprises, ideally making a profit for the publisher. Most academic journals are backed by the authority of their discipline or by an academic publisher. Books may be published by large commercial companies or by academic or small presses. Knowing the motivation of a publisher, whether it is profit or dissemination of information, gives you hints about the appropriateness of a publication for your research purposes.

With printed materials, it's usually easy to figure out who the publisher is. In books, look for this information (name, address, telephone number, Web site, and e-mail address) on the title page and copyright page. In magazines, newspapers, and journals, look for a masthead listing the editors and other important staff members, as well as subscription, reprint, and contact information. If you want to learn more about a particular publisher, ask your reference librarian to show you sources such as *Literary Market Place, Working Press of the Nation, Ulrich's International Periodicals Directory,* or *The Serials Directory.*

On Web sites, examining the domain in the URL carefully will tell you about the kind of group sponsoring the site: governmental (.gov), educational (.edu), commercial (.com), or nonprofit organization (.org). Also, look for a link offering more information about the people or organization sponsoring the site. To find this link, you might first need to go to the homepage of the Web site (look for a Home link at the bottom, top, or left side of the page), and then find the About Us or About This Site link.

Disclosure of this type of publication information shows that the publisher is open to scrutiny and can be contacted. If you cannot find such information, particularly on a Web site, you should be suspicious of the source. But clearly, just knowing who the publisher is and how to contact an organization or person isn't necessarily sufficient to establish that publisher's trustworthiness.

Identify the standards or guidelines the publisher follows. Keep in mind that different publishers may have very different guidelines about what they publish. For example, academic journals have review boards composed of experts who judge whether each article is worthy of publication. Thus articles that appear in professional or scholarly periodicals such as the *Journal of the American Medical Association* are scrutinized by medical experts before being accepted for publication. Newsmagazines like *Time* or *Newsweek* and most newspapers also adhere to certain standards, such as checking the facts in their articles, avoiding sensational language, and printing corrections when they make a mistake. On the other hand, some publishers have little regard for the standards of the mainstream. Some newspaper Web sites, for instance, publish rumors, wild speculation, and whatever else they choose, whether or not any evidence supports their claims. Check to see what is said about a publisher, particularly when it is cited by other sources. Consider whether the publisher seems to respect integrity and good reporting or if its apparent standards might make it inappropriate as a source.

Determine how long the publisher has been in business. Another indicator—but not a guarantee—of trustworthiness (or lack thereof) is the number of years a publisher has been in business. Common sense tells us that periodicals focusing on the Internet, computers, or other aspects of electronic communication are not going to have a long history of publication, but many of the most credible publications (such as the *New Yorker, The Atlantic,* and the *Washington Post*) have been around for a long time, as have book publishers such as Macmillan and Random House. The longevity of a periodical or book publisher can give you a sense of confidence, but this confidence may be misplaced if the publisher fails to meet other criteria for trustworthiness.

Consider the perspective or bias of the publisher. Many publishers try to be fairly neutral. Publications of U.S. government agencies, for example, usually provide straightforward information or statistics regardless of which political party is in power. Many commercial publishers also publish books or articles from a variety of perspectives rather than advocating a particular position. Other publishers, however, have a definite slant. Web sites may also range from neutral to biased. Suppose, for example, that your research question is "What is the best way to treat the common cold?" A commercial (.com) Web site sponsored by a vitamin company will probably advocate natural treatments (such as its own vitamins) for a cold. But a commercial (.com) site sponsored by a manufacturer of cold pills will probably advocate its own product and might not even mention vitamins. A government (.gov) site, however, sponsored by an agency such as the U.S. Department of Health and Human Services, might discuss a whole range of cold remedies—taking vitamins and

**FIGURE 11.4
Online Source
Showing an Obvious
Bias**

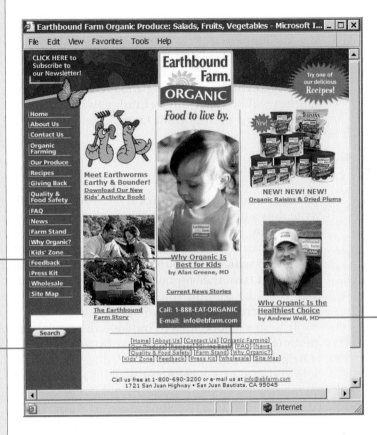

Articles on benefits of
organic food present
claims this company
promotes to sell
its products.

News stories and
resources are pre-
sented in the context
of a commercial
(.com) site.

Credibility of
information may
be enhanced
because articles'
authors are
doctors.

medicine as well as getting plenty of rest, drinking liquids, eating properly, and so forth. It may be perfectly fine to use sources that have a
definite bias as long as you are aware of what the bias is. For example,
Figure 11.4, a commercial Web site for a company selling organic produce, promotes the health benefits of food grown without pesticides or
other chemicals—and the information about food safety found on the
site is likely to reflect this point of view.

Bringing It All Together

Research involves synthesizing a lot of facts, ideas, and opinions before
coming to some conclusions of your own about a topic. To *synthesize*
means to bring different parts together into a whole. Your research will
lack credibility if you don't find out what other people have said, written,
or done that is relevant to your topic—but your project will lack coherence if you don't figure out how to work these different concepts and

❯ For more on creating a working bibliography, see **Chapter 9,** pp. 560–562.

voices into a unified piece of writing. Your next step will involve going beyond familiarizing yourself with all the information in your sources to actually synthesizing it into a coherent research project.

As you find and evaluate sources, you have probably been keeping track of them in a *working bibliography*. When you decide that some sources will be especially helpful, you also need to take notes so that you have a record of important facts, ideas, and visual elements.

TAKING NOTES

❯ For more on creating in-text citations, see **Chapter 12.**

❯ For advice on organizing research notes, see pp. 602–603.

❯ For more advice on avoiding plagiarism, see pp. 600–602.

When recording information from your research, always remember to write down the source—something that will help you link each item to its appropriate bibliographic data. For example, you could write down the author's name or the title (or a shortened form of the title) and the page(s) on which you found the material. Recording this information as you find it (whether on notecards or with a computer program) ensures that you'll be able to find it again and that you'll have all the details needed to create *in-text citations*.

It is also a good idea to indicate the kind of note you're taking. Is it a quotation, paraphrase, summary, or some other kind of information? It is helpful to include a subject heading for each note as well, which will help you organize your notes by subtopics later. Also, take care to avoid inadvertent plagiarism by accurately noting quotation marks. Be sure to summarize and paraphrase only in your own words. You may not remember all the major points of a source later on, so be sure your notes are complete. Double-check notes for accuracy, especially for statistics and factual information.

❯ For MLA and APA guidelines on information to include for sources you cite, see **Chapter 12.**

Quoting, Paraphrasing, and Summarizing

As you take notes, be on the lookout for memorable statements that you can quote, key concepts that you can paraphrase, complex information that you will have to summarize, and data that you can best present graphically. The success of your project—whether a research project, an oral presentation, an annotated bibliography, or one of the writing genres covered in Part 1 of this book—depends on your ability to find good sources and take accurate notes about what you find in them.

Quoting

Quoting another person's exact words can strengthen a research paper, but it's a strategy that writers tend to use too frequently. A good guideline is to save quotations for situations where an author has said something so clearly or so memorably that you cannot imagine any other way to say it. Another effective use of quotations is to introduce or conclude your writing. If you find a memorable quote that asks a question you're going to answer in your project, it may be a good way to engage the reader right away. If you find a solid quote that supports your conclusions, it may be a dramatic way to end your project.

When you find a direct quotation that you might want to use, copy it down word for word and include the exact punctuation (see Figure 11.5). Make sure to enclose it in quotation marks and indicate the source and page number(s) for print sources or date retrieved for electronic sources. Double-check your notes against the original source to make sure you wrote the quotation exactly as it appears. If the author misspelled a word or made a grammatical error, add the Latin word *sic* (meaning "thus") in brackets directly after the error to show that it was the writer's mistake and not yours. If you are sure (at the note-taking stage) that you want to use only part of a quote, use ellipsis points (. . .) to indicate where you omitted words or whole sentences within the original passage. Use brackets to introduce changes or new words to the quotation. After shortening the quotation, carefully reread the original text to make sure you haven't taken the quote out of context or changed the author's meaning by omitting parts of the passage.

Often, rather than writing down the words of the original writer, you will want to take a different kind of note. For example, instead of writing down quotations from highly technical material to use in a report for teenagers on the dangers of cigarette smoking, it would probably make more sense to *paraphrase* or *summarize* the information.

> For guidelines on integrating quotations into your writing, see **Chapter 12.**

FIGURE 11.5
Quotation Note

ACL injuries—women

Lang, "Clue to Female Athletes' Greater Knee Injury Risk," retrieved May 3, 2004

"Studies have shown that the injury rate to the knee's anterior cruciate ligament, or ACL, is up to eight times higher for women than it is for men, particularly in sports requiring stopping and jumping tasks."

Quotation

Paraphrasing

When you paraphrase, you state someone else's ideas in your own words without changing the meaning or adding your own opinion. Paraphrasing is useful when you want to make sure that readers understand what someone else has to say, but the author's original wording is not particularly important. For example, if the author of your source material is writing for an academic journal and you are writing for a school newspaper, you would probably want to use different language and a different style. By paraphrasing the original, you could relate all the author's key points and details in a way that your readers would understand.

One way to paraphrase is to make an *outline* of the section of the original text you want to use—that is, make a list of the writer's key points in order and any details that support each of those points. Then rewrite one point at a time in your own words. It may help to explain the key points to someone else or aloud to yourself. By doing so, you may come up with new ways to write the key points and supporting details.

When you paraphrase, you are still presenting someone else's ideas even though you are rephrasing them. So, just as with a direct quotation, keep track of the source and page number(s) or date retrieved for Internet sources (see Figure 11.6). You must also make sure that you are not simply "translating" the author's words and phrases into your own synonyms while maintaining the basic sentence structure of the original. If you need to include some of the author's words within the paraphrase, be sure to enclose them in quotation marks. If you present another writer's ideas as your own without acknowledgment, even if they are paraphrased, or if you offer a paraphrase that is too close to the original, even if you credit the source, you are guilty of *plagiarism*—stealing someone else's words or ideas. If you are unsure of what constitutes a paraphrase

FIGURE 11.6
Paraphrase Note

ACL injury prevention

Reuters Health, "Muscles to Blame," retrieved May 5, 2004

A recent study points to particular weakness in the knee muscles of women who participate in basketball and similar jumping sports, with less strength than men and other kinds of female athletes. This study may indicate a need for much better training and strengthening of knee muscles in these women athletes.

Paraphrase

that is too close to the original, check with your instructor. The following examples show some inappropriate and some effective paraphrases.

Original
Fall is when many women take to the field for soccer, volleyball, or field hockey, and that makes it prime time for women's athletic injuries. In fact, as increasing numbers of females have become active in fall sports at all levels of competition, their rates of injury have reached or exceeded those of males in the same or similar sports.
–*HealthDayNews*, "Injuries Abound for Women Athletes"

Unacceptable Paraphrase
Autumn is the time when a lot of women take up field hockey, soccer, or volleyball, so fall is the peak season for injuries to female athletes. As more and more women play fall sports at all competitive levels, their injury rates have matched or surpassed the rate for men in identical or comparable sports.

Acceptable Paraphrase
More women participate in fall sports than ever before, but there are also more injuries to women athletes than ever before. Women now have injury rates that match those of men in comparable sports.

Here is another passage from an original source. Figure 11.6 shows one student's note paraphrasing it, and Figure 11.7 on p. 600 shows another note summarizing it.

Women who participate in jumping and pivoting sports, such as basketball, volleyball and soccer, are eight times more likely to rupture a knee-stabilizing ligament than are men.

The reason women are more likely to injure the anterior cruciate ligament (ACL) may be weakness in the muscles surrounding the knee, according to a new study. Women who participated in jumping and pivoting sports had knee muscles that were weaker not only than those of men who played the same sports but also than knee muscles of women who participated in other sports, such as bicycling, crew and running, according to a study published in the *Journal of Bone and Joint Surgery*.

The results show that training for women who participate in sports that carry a higher risk of this type of knee injury may not be adequate, study co-author Dr. Edward M. Wojtys said in an interview with Reuters Health.
–Reuters Health, "Muscles to Blame for Women's Knee Injury"

Summarizing

Unlike a paraphrase, which relates all of an author's main points, a summary presents an abbreviated version of an original passage or whole work (see Figure 11.7). When you summarize, you want the readers to understand basic ideas, but you don't think they need a lot of detail.

To summarize a passage, read it carefully once or twice. Jot down the key points and any supporting details you might want to include in your

FIGURE 11.7
Summary Note

ACL injury prevention

Reuters Health, "Muscles to Blame," retrieved May 5, 2004

The <u>Journal of Bone and Joint Surgery</u> study suggests that muscle weakness around the knee may be to blame for ACL injuries, pointing to a need for better training for many women athletes.

Summary

paper. As you write, make certain that the words in the summary are all your own, but don't change any specific ideas or the overall meaning. As with paraphrasing, you may find it helpful to talk about the passage before starting to summarize it.

Because a summary is a presentation of someone else's ideas, you must cite that original source in your work. However, you may not need to give precise page numbers when summarizing a lengthy passage. If you are uncertain about whether to include page numbers for a particular summary you have written, check the style guide you're using or ask your instructor.

You can create another type of summary by taking statistics or other data that are presented as text and summarizing them in a table, chart, graph, bulleted list, or other visual element. Depending on your topic and the specific type of data you want to convey, a visual summary can be an effective and concise way to present a lot of information. When you create a visual summary, be sure to acknowledge the source of the data.

> For samples and advice on creating graphs and tables, see **Chapter 8**.

Avoiding Plagiarism

In some cultures, it is not considered unethical to borrow the words or ideas of others. However, in the United States and many other countries, presenting another person's words or ideas as your own is considered plagiarism. Plagiarism is improper—and often illegal, whether it is intentional or not. Plagiarism occurs when a writer, speaker, or artist "borrows" (steals) someone else's words, ideas, or images without giving credit to the original creator. In most schools, plagiarism is a serious academic offense; students who plagiarize are subject to disciplinary action—they may fail a course, be suspended, or even be expelled.

Perhaps because of the ease with which computers and the Internet enable writers to cut and paste, plagiarism seems to be on the rise. Schools all across the United States now report that plagiarism has become a serious problem, not only at colleges but at high schools and middle schools as well.

While some plagiarism is intentional, often it is the accidental result of sloppy note-taking and a poor understanding of what it means to copy someone else's work. Fortunately, plagiarism can be avoided. Just remember that you *must* credit the source of any specific words (quotations), general ideas (paraphrases and summaries), or visual elements (charts, graphs, diagrams, drawings, photographs, and so on; see Box 11.1) that you use in your paper.

> For advice on crediting the sources of visual elements, see **Chapter 8.**

If an idea or fact is common knowledge (for example, "the Earth rotates around the sun" or "the Declaration of Independence was written in 1776"), you don't have to provide a reference or citation. However, any ideas that are not your own or any facts that the general public would not be likely to know must be attributed to a source. If you are unsure whether certain information needs to be credited to a source, check with your instructor.

As you take notes, make sure that you clearly differentiate between direct quotations and your own rewording of original source material. If you don't make this distinction, you could run into problems when it comes time to write. You might mistakenly think that these notes were your own paraphrase or summary, and you might present the passage or even a few key phrases as your own writing. Even if you do credit the source, you would be guilty of plagiarism.

Another way to avoid plagiarism is to make sure each paraphrase does not borrow too heavily from the original writer's words, phrases, and sentence structure. It is not enough to acknowledge the source; you must come up with a paraphrase that is truly different from the original, in both wording and overall structure.

To combat the rise in plagiarism, a number of Internet-based services now make it easier for instructors and other readers to detect plagiarized work. For example, a service might compare the text of a specific student paper to millions of documents held in a database. Instructors can also use search engines such as Google to check suspicious passages or phrases in their students' work, especially if they think a student has plagiarized an electronic source. Some instructors have developed their own anti-plagiarism software. At the University of Virginia, for example, forty-eight students were expelled in November 2002 after their physics professor created a computer program to detect plagiarism in the term paper for his class.

Copying an essay or even a phrase or idea from another writer is never a good idea, even if that writer has willingly provided such a service for a fee and even if you're in a hurry. The time you spend trying to avoid doing work—and avoid getting caught—would be much better spent developing your own ideas and doing your own research and writing. If you feel overwhelmed by an assignment or a deadline, talk to the instructor rather than resort to cheating.

BOX 11.1   Using and Adapting Visuals

If you find a good visual that you want to use "as is" or adapt in some way, check carefully for any information about copyright. Copyright law protects visual elements just as it protects verbal passages. If the document you're producing is an assignment for a course that doesn't post assignments to the Web, you can use the visual as long as you give credit to the source, just as if you were quoting someone's words. However, if the assignment will appear on a Web site or if you plan to publish your work (in print or electronic form), you may need to get permission from the source. In some instances, especially on Web sites, you may find that it is easy to ask for permission. Often there is a Contact Us link or a statement about whether visuals on the site are available for use by others. When the visual you want to use is published in print, you will need to write to or e-mail the publisher.

It is important to remember that if you modify someone else's visual, you still need to give credit to the originator. You would cite the original source, introducing it with the words *based on* or *adapted from* and then explaining how you modified it.

❯ For more information about
using and modifying visuals,
see **Chapter 8.**

Organizing Notes

The organizing scheme for your research notes should be based on your research question and on the subtopics that follow from that main question. Think about the possible categories of information that you might try to gather. As you take notes, try to sort your research into these categories. For example, Steve Jacobs wrote the following research question for a course project on organizational culture:

> How do newcomers learn about an organization's culture?

Steve used this question to create a list of subtopics (his organizing scheme) that he thought would be relevant to his research question.

> ❯ what newcomers learn from consumer, customer, or member literature, such as posters, brochures, Web sites, and so on
>
> ❯ what they learn from orientation and training sessions
>
> ❯ what they learn from employee, member, or team handbooks

> For more on creating a working
bibliography, see **Chapter 9,**
pp. 560–562.

> To see how one student's
research results came together
in an essay, see **Chapter 12.**

On his computer, Steve set up a separate file for each subtopic. He had already set up a file for his working bibliography. When he found an idea or a quote that fit one of these subtopics, he recorded the bibliographic data in a computer file he named "bib file," and then he made notes in the relevant subtopic file (making sure to add information such as author or title, page number(s), or URL, so he would be able to identify the source later). Keeping all information about sources in one working bibliography file saved Steve a lot of work: if a particular source had information on more than one subtopic, he needed to type the bibliographic data only once.

As he proceeded with his research, Steve discovered that he needed to add another subtopic.

> what newcomers learn by communicating with other employees, members, or teammates

Because of his organizing scheme, he could easily open a new file and start gathering data on the new subtopic.

You can also organize your notes when working with index cards. Use different-colored cards or pens, or simply give each subtopic a number and put the relevant number on each card. If you plan an organizing scheme ahead of time, your note-taking will be more logical and you will be able to sort through the information more easily when it's time to start writing. Moreover, you may discover that the subtopics you created make good subheadings within your project. Be sure, however, not to limit yourself to the subtopics you start out with. As Steve discovered in his research, you will probably find additional ideas that should be included.

Alternatively, you may want to use a software program specifically designed to keep track of research notes and bibliographic data.

At some point, you will decide that you have found enough sources and taken enough notes. You will have organized a lot of facts, ideas, and opinions in some sensible way based on your research question. Now it's time to bring the various parts of your research together—to *synthesize* them—into a whole. In other words, you are ready to combine the voices of others with your own voice, and to do so in a way that results in a unified piece of writing.

12

Using and Documenting Sources

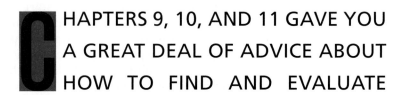C HAPTERS 9, 10, AND 11 GAVE YOU A GREAT DEAL OF ADVICE ABOUT HOW TO FIND AND EVALUATE

sources. Now that you have a list of credible sources and some notes from those sources, you need to figure out how to use the material in your writing and how to document the sources you use. If you are using the sources for an assignment based on one of the chapters in Part 1 of this book, you can use that chapter to guide you through the integration of sources into your paper. But you may be asked to write what is known as a "research paper" or "research project," either for this course or for another one. The first part of this chapter presents (1) a student research project (in the form of an essay) which demonstrates the effective use of sources and (2) some guidelines for the parts of a research project that are a little different from other kinds of writing. The second part of this chapter offers a brief guide to two of the most widely used systems of documentation, MLA (Modern Language Association) style and APA (American Psychological Association) style. This guide will help you create in-text citations and a bibliographic list of the works you have cited so that your readers will be able to identify where the information is from and refer to the original if they choose to do so.

USING RESEARCH IN A PROJECT

When a college instructor assigns you a research project, regardless of the discipline or topic, you can count on certain basic requirements. For example, you will be expected to do the following.

> Write about a topic that bears scrutiny—usually a topic that others have investigated before.

> Conduct research to answer specific question(s) about the topic.

> Synthesize information that you find through library and Internet research (and sometimes through field research).

> Present your findings clearly so that others can see what you have learned.

> Cite your sources so that others can find and consult them and make decisions about the credibility of the information you present.

If you've read any of the chapters in Part 1 of this book, you already have ideas about how to do some of these things. The process and objectives that are described in all the chapters in Part 2 apply to the research project just as readily as they apply to reports, position papers, evaluations, and other kinds of writing. In other words, when you are assigned a research project, you still need to select a topic, analyze context, develop the topic, engage the audience, create an appropriate voice, provide structure, conclude effectively, integrate visual elements, get representative audience members and peers to assess your work, and revise your writing. The following sections of this chapter, which include examples from a sample student research project, show how these by-now-familiar tasks relate specifically to writing a research project.

Sample Essay, MLA Style

The following pages show a sample research paper. Amanda Zimpfer followed MLA guidelines for formatting her paper and for documenting sources. The annotations in the margins point out how various kinds of sources are integrated into the work and documented according to MLA style. Note that the essay is shown in reduced format to allow for these annotations.

½"
Zimpfer 1

1"

Amanda Zimpfer

Professor Katz

English 398

13 October 2003

½" — Would You Like to Teach in a Waldorf School?

Choosing which kind of school to teach in is a decision that can have career-long consequences. As a potential teacher, imagine this scene.

• Long introductory quotation to engage readers

The first thing one notices upon entering a fifth-grade classroom at the Rudolf Steiner School, in New York City, is how remarkably polite the children are. They step up with 1" — firm handshakes, looking me directly in the eye and enunciating, "How do you do, Mrs. Prescott?". . . A young boy inquires as to how I prefer my tea--"With sugar, lemon, or milk?" and bounds off to prepare it. This is a fifth-grade boy? (Prescott 21)

• For set-off quotation, parenthetical citation follows final punctuation.

In today's schools, well-mannered children are not always the norm. It is not surprising, then, that Jennifer Prescott was so impressed by the polite children she first encountered at Rudolf Steiner, a Waldorf school. She concluded that the children's model behavior was a result of the distinctive education offered at Waldorf schools, a type of education she applauds. To some parents and educators, however, a Waldorf education is not without drawbacks. This paper will explain the history, philosophy, and curriculum of

• Preview of the paper's organization

Waldorf schools; describe typical school activities; explain required teacher training; look at some of the pros and cons of the Waldorf program; and provide information for you to use to decide whether a Waldorf teaching career might be right for you.

1"

Zimpfer 2

History and Philosophy of the Waldorf System

The first Waldorf school was established in Stuttgart, Germany, in 1919. Emil Molt, director of the Waldorf-Astoria cigarette factory, asked Austrian scientist and philosopher Rudolf Steiner to start a school for the workers' children. Steiner agreed as long as the teachers could run the school according to "a highly ambitious curriculum" (Oppenheimer 73).

Steiner (1861-1925) developed a system of thought called anthroposophy "in which the heightened capacities of thinking, feeling, and willing are seen as key to unlocking enormous human potential" ("Introduction"). He believed that humans have not only the five familiar senses--sight, hearing, touch, smell, taste--but seven others: "thought, language, warmth, balance, movement, life, and the individuality of the other" (Oppenheimer 73). And he developed a curriculum that tapped these senses at what he felt was the appropriate time in children's lives. Steiner believed in the power of children, their willingness to learn, and their ability to learn through exploration with the guidance of teachers. Steiner said that education revolved around "the need for imagination, a sense of truth, and a feeling of responsibility" (qtd. in Oppenheimer 73).

In 1928 the first Waldorf school opened in the United States, the same school that Jennifer Prescott visited in New York City in 1999. There are now 800 Waldorf schools worldwide, with about 150 in North America (Barnes).

The Waldorf Curriculum

The curriculum of the Waldorf schools is designed to engage the heart as well as the mind, with the goal of "awakening imagination and creative powers [and] bringing vitality and wholeness to learning" ("Waldorf Education," Saratoga Springs). The arts--music, speech,

---

Annotations (left margin):

- Centered headings in bold identify sections of the paper—not standard MLA style, but can be used effectively with instructor approval.

- Quotation from a print source smoothly integrated into the sentence

- Definition of an important term that readers may find unfamiliar

- Direct quotation cited according to MLA style with the author's name and the page number

- Indirect source of a quotation identified with the abbreviation *qtd. in*

- Site name (Saratoga Springs) helps distinguish between two articles with identical titles.

Zimpfer 3

and drawing--are integrated in the Waldorf curriculum at all levels (see fig. 1). Listening rather than rote textbook learning is emphasized, and this demands from the teacher the ability to tell the stories that form the core of the curriculum, especially in the early grades. "Waldorf schools use a developmental curriculum that follows the progress of civilization as the child ages. First-graders learn fairy tales and folk tales; second-graders get legends, fables, and nature stories; third-graders study Old Testament stories; fourth-graders focus on Norse and Native American myths" (Beem).

- Parenthetical reference directs reader to figure.

In prekindergarten and kindergarten, the Waldorf curriculum is based on creative and imaginative play ("Frequently Asked Questions").

- In-text citation consisting of only the author's last name for a source from an unpaginated Web site

Very little of a traditional academic content is apparent because according to the Waldorf philosophy, children are not "developmentally ready for academic work" until first grade (Hetzner).

- Student artwork demonstrating integration of artwork into curriculum

Fig. 1. Painting by Zoë Mena, a sixth grader at the Housatonic Valley Waldorf School. From Housatonic Valley School, 2003, 26 Oct. 2003 <http://www.waldorfct.org/html/open_house.html>.

In grades one to three, storytelling and creative and imaginative play are still the main methods of delivering the educational content. It is not uncommon to have students in third grade who cannot read but who can relate with accuracy everything the teacher has read or recited or who can express what they have learned in detailed drawings or beeswax forms. "Waldorf children learn to listen really well," according to Sarah Van Fleet, a teacher in Merriconeag Waldorf School in Freeport, Maine. "Much of the curriculum is delivered orally by the teacher. It's not lecture. It's done in story" (qtd. in Beem).

Zimpfer 4

In the middle grades and through high school, the Waldorf teachers impart a more traditional curriculum, covering literature, history, mathematics, and the sciences, but the basis for most of the instruction is still storytelling and creative interaction with the content through drama, music, and artwork.

Waldorf classes are usually larger than the public school norm, with classes of 25 to 30 not uncommon. Waldorf teachers usually remain with one class from first grade through eighth grade. According to the Waldorf philosophy, a "deep human relationship . . . is the basis for healthy learning." By keeping one teacher with one class through eight grades, "the teacher and the children come to know and understand each other in a deep way. The children, feeling secure in a long-term relationship, are better able to learn. The interaction of teacher and parents also can become more deep and meaningful over time, and they can cooperate in helping the child" ("Frequently Asked Questions").

A Day in the Life of a Waldorf School

A day spent in the classroom of a Waldorf school is quite different from a day in a typical American public school. Students first enter an attractively colored room, shake the hand of the teacher, and recite the morning verse, a poem written by Steiner that varies by grade level. The main lesson follows for two hours. During this block of time each day, teachers present the basic academic content, focusing on one subject or topic--such as Old Testament stories or math or science--for a week or more at a time (Hetzner). This concentrated time gives the students an in-depth understanding of the subject and "allows the teacher to develop a wide variety of activities around the subject" ("Classroom and Curriculum").

The students in the lower grades do not use textbooks but instead create "main lesson books" that contain notes about

● Ellipsis points indicate that one or more words have been removed from the quotation.

● Source of paraphrased material cited parenthetically

Zimpfer 5

activities and experiments in the classroom, field trips, the teachers' regular oral presentations, and summaries of material that the students gather from primary sources (see fig. 2). "Playfulness is encouraged in these books, because Waldorf teachers believe that imaginative wonderings can be just as educational as objective facts and conclusions, if not more so" (Oppenheimer 72).

● Caption explaining illustration and documenting its source

Fig. 2. Page from a main lesson book by a third grader at Hawthorne Valley School, Ghent, NY. From <u>Tucson Waldorf Education Association</u>, 21 June 2002, 10 Oct. 2003 <http:// iwhome.com/twea/wesd.htm>

Music, art, and handwork are included from the earliest grades, and they are integrated in all aspects of the curriculum. For example, all children learn to play the recorder, and they also learn to knit or crochet cases to store their recorders in. This type of learning through creativity is one of the foundations of the Waldorf system, and it can be found in all grades.

Although all Waldorf schools follow the philosophy of their founder, Rudolf Steiner, each Waldorf school develops a mission statement that reflects the vision of that particular school in its particular community. For example, here is the mission statement of the Housatonic Valley School in Newtown, Connecticut:

● Long quotation (more than four typed lines) indented and cited without quotation marks

> The mission of the Housatonic Valley School is to educate, inspire, and instill in each child courage, integrity, and a passion for learning. Out of reverence for the individual spirit and a commitment to the principles of Waldorf Education,

Zimpfer 6

we lead the children into an experience of true community, meaningful work, and awe for the rhythms of nature. The living Spirit of the School draws warmth from and radiates light into the community, to feed continuously the spark of creation. (Housatonic Valley School)

Training for and Teaching in a Waldorf School

Teachers must go through a special training program to teach in a Waldorf school. There are thirteen Waldorf training institutes in the United States, from New England to California to Hawaii. All offer a Foundation Year, a one-year program that serves as an introduction to the basic works of Rudolf Steiner and to Waldorf education. Enrolling in this introductory program would be one way to determine if you are suited to the Waldorf model. For those who decide to become Waldorf teachers, the Foundation Year is followed by one to two years of additional study, after which teachers receive a diploma in Waldorf education. Some of the institutes also offer a master's degree program ("Teacher Education"; "Waldorf Teacher Training").

Besides the study of Steiner's philosophy and educational system, the teacher training curriculum includes child development, Waldorf methodology, traditional subjects (language arts, literature, mathematics, history, social studies, the sciences), and study of all the other elements of a Waldorf education: the arts (including painting, drawing, clay modeling), eurythmy (the art of movement), singing, woodworking, handwork, sports, and games. Student teachers can focus on early childhood (prekindergarten and kindergarten), elementary school, or high school. A typical Waldorf institute, Kula Makua in Hawaii, says that its program

combines a study of the fundamentals of Waldorf education with training in the academic disciplines and the development

● More than one source cited in the same parenthetical reference and separated with semicolons

● Signal phrase prepares readers for the quotation that follows.

Zimpfer 7

of skills for imaginative classroom management. Equally stressed are the arts and crafts in many of their various forms--as vehicles for intellectual development, creativity, and imagination. ("Kula Makua Programs")

One element of Waldorf education that a prospective teacher must consider is that elementary school teachers remain with the same group of students from first to eighth grade. They thus must learn to plan and prepare a new curriculum each year and guide the students at each new stage of development. This is challenging but potentially rewarding; it "means time to really know the children and help them unfold their gifts, as well as the challenge and freshness which can come with working with a new curriculum each year" ("Waldorf Education," Saratoga Springs). Early childhood teachers focus primarily on creative expression and storytelling; high school teachers focus on specific subject areas, as they do in traditional high schools.

Pros and Cons of the Waldorf System

Waldorf education has garnered testimonials from numerous parents and students. Kenneth Chenault, president and CEO of American Express, is one of Waldorf's most visible graduates. He credits his adult success to his early Waldorf education:

> I am convinced that Waldorf schools deliver an essential alternative to our existing systems. A Waldorf education provides students with an approach to learning which successfully integrates the arts and sciences with the practical tools necessary to succeed in these challenging times. I am personally very grateful for the foundation that was laid during my formative years at Waldorf. (qtd. in "Waldorf Education," Rudolf Steiner College)

Zimpfer 8

Many parents and students who were disenchanted with traditional public education have found a civility in Waldorf education that they find lacking in other schools. A student at the Merriconeag Waldorf School in Maine said, "My old school was scary. Kids swore a lot. There was no such thing as a friend" (qtd. in Beem). Lynne Espy, a parent at Merriconeag, said, "Everything is very deliberate in a Waldorf school. The children imitate [their teachers'] kindness. It's not talk; it's do. They just do it" (qtd. in Beem).

Todd Oppenheimer, a writer for <u>Atlantic Monthly</u>, observes the positive effects that a Waldorf teaching style has had on at-risk students in a public school for juvenile offenders. Oppenheimer cites students who respond to the oral storytelling, the music program, and the emphasis on handwork and artwork. He finds hope in the Waldorf system for other educational environments: "The daily experiences of one creative education system [Waldorf] ought to tell us something about the challenges and possibilities for other schools, both alternative and traditional" (Oppenheimer 72).

Not everyone agrees that the Waldorf system is appropriate in public education. Some Waldorf schools that have been established as charter schools within a public school system have met intense opposition. An organization called People for Legal and Nonsectarian Schools (PLANS), a coalition made up of evangelical Christians and secular humanists, sued two California school districts in 1998 to stop the districts from giving public funding to Waldorf schools. Members of PLANS argued that because Steiner's anthroposophical beliefs amounted to an "occult theory," the schools were private religious institutions and ineligible for taxpayers' money (Archer). Steiner's views, as Oppenheimer notes, amount to "his own brand of

- Signal phrase introduces a paraphrase and a quotation.

- Square brackets indicate a change needed to clarify the quotation.

- Opposing viewpoints indicate that the research has been thorough and objective.

Zimpfer 9

spirituality" (80). Waldorf teachers deny teaching anthroposophy to their students, and the regulations of Waldorf schools prohibit religious teaching (Oppenheimer 80). Nevertheless, Waldorf teacher training requires considerable study of the philosophy of Rudolf Steiner, as PLANS member Dan Dugan has demonstrated. The Skeptic's Dictionary notes that "anthroposophical ideas are not part of the standard Waldorf school curriculum, but apparently are believed by those in charge of the curriculum. Waldorf schools . . . tend to be spiritually oriented and are based on a generally Christian perspective" (Carroll). The PLANS lawsuit was dismissed by a federal court in 2001 (Hetzner), but an appeals court reinstated the case in February 2003 (Lindelof).

Is Waldorf Right for You?

• Conclusion summarizes the Waldorf system and suggests follow-up actions.

If you are searching for an alternative to traditional public education and would like to be part of an organized system that is designed to educate "the whole child, hand and heart as well as mind" ("Waldorf Education," Rudolf Steiner College), then becoming a Waldorf teacher may be for you. You could visit a Waldorf school in your area or talk with people who have been involved in the Waldorf system. Discussing the Waldorf philosophy with both its supporters and its opponents may clarify your views of the spiritual aspects of the program and allow you to determine whether you can accept them. You might even want to enroll in Waldorf's Foundation Year to find out more about the program and to experience firsthand what would be involved for you as a teacher. Ask questions and observe the program, if possible, to determine if it is a good match for your interests and abilities.

● Works Cited list begins on a new page.

● Entry for an article from a Web site includes the article title in quotation marks, the underlined title of the site, the date of access, and the URL of the site.

● Entry for a print article retrieved from a library subscription service includes the print publication information, the name of the subscription service, the name and location of the library, the date of access, and the URL.

● Entries begin at left margin. Entries that run more than one line indent one-half inch.

Zimpfer 10

1"

Works Cited

"Anthroposophy." <u>Great Lakes Teacher Training</u>. 10 Oct. 2003

    <http://67.29.153.233:30451/steiner.htm>.

Archer, Stephan. "Public Schools Teaching Occult Religion?"

    <u>WorldNetDaily.com</u> 1 Oct. 1999. 10 Oct. 2003 <http://

    www.worldnetdaily.com/news/article.asp?ARTICLE_ID=17206>.

Barnes, Henry. "Waldorf Education . . . An Introduction." <u>AWSNA</u>

½"   (Association of Waldorf Schools of North America). 9 Oct. 2003

    <http://www.awsna.org/education-intro.html>.

Beem, Edgar Allen. "The Waldorf Way in a Nation Obsessed with

    Measurement." <u>Boston Globe Magazine</u> 15 Apr. 2001: 13.

    Lexis-Nexis. U of North Carolina, Chapel Hill Lib. 8 Oct. 2003

    <http://lexis-nexis.com>.

Carroll, Robert Todd. "Anthroposophy, Rudolf Steiner (1861-1925),

    and Waldorf Schools." <u>The Skeptic's Dictionary</u>. 2002. 11 Oct.

    2003 <http://www.skepdic.com/steiner.html>.

"Classroom and Curriculum." <u>AWSNA</u> (Association of Waldorf

    Schools of North America). 9 Oct. 2003 <http://www.awsna.org/

    education-class.html>.

Dugan, Dan. "Why Waldorf Programs Are Unsuitable for Public

    Funding." <u>Cultic Studies Review</u> 2.2 (2003). 11 Oct. 2003

    <http://www.waldorfcritics.org/active/articles/

    dugan_dan_csr0202j.htm>.

"Frequently Asked Questions." <u>AWSNA</u> (Association of Waldorf

    Schools of North America). 9 Oct. 2003 <http://www.awsna.org/

    awsna-faq.html>.

Hetzner, Amy. "Serving Up Waldorf Learning: Private School Takes a

    Different Approach to Education." <u>Milwaukee Journal Sentinel</u>

    13 Jan. 2002: 01Z. Lexis-Nexis. U of North Carolina, Chapel

    Hill Lib. 8 Oct. 2003 <http://lexis-nexis.com>.

Zimpfer 11

Housatonic Valley School. 10 Oct. 2003 <http://www.waldorfct.org>.

Housatonic Valley School. Painting by student. 10 Oct. 2003 <http://
www.waldorfct.org/html/open_house_dates_and_times_le.html>.

"Introduction." Rudolf Steiner College. 8 Oct. 2003
<http://www.steinercollege.edu/introduction.html>.

"Kula Makua Programs." Honolulu Waldorf School: Kula Makua.
9 Oct. 2003 <http://www.honoluluwaldorf.org/kulamakua/
English/Programs.htm>.

Lindelof, Bill. "Lawsuit against Waldorf Revived." Sacramento Bee
31 Mar. 2003. 10 Oct. 2003 <http://www.sacbee.com>.

Mena, Zoë. Painting. Housatonic Valley School. 26 Oct. 2003
<http://www.waldorfct.org/html/open_house.html>.

Oppenheimer, Todd. "Schooling the Imagination." Atlantic Monthly
Sept. 1999: 71-83.

Prescott, Jennifer O. "A Day in the Life of the Rudolf Steiner School."
Instructor 109.4 (1999): 21-25.

"Programs." Rudolf Steiner College. 8 Oct. 2003 <http://
www.steinercollege.edu/programs.html>.

"Teacher Education." Sunbridge College. 10 Oct. 2003 <http://
www.sunbridge.edu/programs/teacher.htm>.

Tucson Waldorf Education Association. Page from main lesson book. 21
June 2002. 10 Oct. 2003 <http://iwhome.com/twea/wesd.htm>.

"Waldorf Education." Rudolf Steiner College. 8 Oct. 2003
<http://www.steinercollege.edu/waldorf.html>.

"Waldorf Education." The Waldorf School of Saratoga Springs.
9 Oct. 2003 <http://www.waldorfsaratoga.org/wedu_t.html>.

"Waldorf Teacher Training." Antioch New England Graduate School:
Education Department. 10 Oct. 2003 <http://
eddept.antiochne.edu/EDDegrees/waldorf>.

- Newspaper article accessed online

- Article in a monthly magazine

- Entry for a journal article includes volume and issue numbers separated by a period, and the publication year in parentheses.

- Photograph obtained from a Web site

Finding a Topic

As you know from Chapter 9, the first steps in beginning a research project are to choose and narrow a topic. Before you begin, you should read the assignment carefully (or talk with the instructor) so that you know exactly what is expected. Do you need to cite a specific number of sources? Do you need specific types of sources (a textbook that has been assigned for your course, perhaps, or scholarly journals)? Do you need to do any type of field research? Does the instructor want you to include visual elements? Is there a page-length requirement?

❯ For more on analyzing a research assignment and choosing a topic, see **Chapter 9**, p. 532.

In some cases, your instructor will assign the research topic or give you a choice of topics. However, if you need to come up with a topic on your own, many of the brainstorming strategies found in Chapters 2 through 7 of this book can help. Think of your research as an attempt to answer a specific question about your topic.

In Amanda's class, the assignment was to select a type of school from a short list provided by the instructor, determine—through research on its history, philosophy, and practices—whether teaching at that school was an appealing career choice, and write a paper based on that research. Amanda's instructor handed out instructions that told students to include information on the goals and mission of the school, the population that the school served, and the programs that were offered. The students were also told to include a description of at least one example of this type of school and to illustrate that description by reference to some type of literature from the school, such as a brochure or Web site. The instructions specified that students had to include at least five sources, of which at least three were to be print (not electronic), and that they had to write a paper that was eight to ten double-spaced pages long. Although the instructions did not specify any particular use of visuals, the instructor told the students that their work should be "visually appealing."

Amanda did not know much about any of the schools on the list. The Waldorf schools were intriguing because she'd babysat for a family with children enrolled in one. She chose Waldorf schools because she wanted to find out more about them from the point of view of a prospective teacher.

Once Amanda had decided on a topic, her next step was to analyze the context of her research project. In other words, she had to think carefully about the audience, circumstances, and purposes for this assignment.

In "Would You Like to Teach in a Waldorf School?" Amanda's audience included her instructor and her classmates. Amanda was aware that her instructor already knew a great deal about Waldorf schools and would be reading her assignment critically to see if she had done a thorough research job. She also knew that among her classmates were other students who were thinking about careers as elementary school teachers, but that most of them had probably never heard of Waldorf schools. Because she is a member of this audience, Amanda could predict the kinds of questions her classmates would have about this topic. They would want to know something about the history of the program, how many schools follow this method, what the curriculum is like, what it is like to teach in this type of school, and what kind of special training the teachers need.

The circumstances for this assignment were provided by the instructor. Amanda knew that she was expected to produce a print essay that the instructor would read and grade, but she also had to submit the paper electronically so that it could be mounted on the secure course Web site. (If she had been asked to post her paper to a site that was available to the public, she would have needed to obtain permission to use the art she included in her paper, which she could probably have done by contacting those responsible for the Web sites where she found the art.)

The purpose of the assignment was also given by the instructor: the students were to write about their topic so that everyone in the class could learn about a variety of educational philosophies and systems. The research would also serve a second purpose when groups of students collaborated on the oral presentation.

Developing a Topic

Once you have a topic, you can begin to think about how to develop it. In the case of a research project, this means formulating some research questions and beginning to answer them. Your questions may change as your research progresses, but you should start out with at least a few questions that you want to answer in your final project. The work you have done on analyzing the context is a good start. Based on your assignment, your topic, and your questions, you will conduct some of the library, Internet, and field research activities described in Chapters 9 and 10. By keeping the assignment, topic, and questions clearly in mind, you will be able to do your research more efficiently, making notes about relevant information and organizing it as you go.

After Amanda chose the type of school she was going to write about, one of the first things she did was to search the Internet for images. Like many writers, she often starts by looking for visuals because they give her "something to talk about." Searching for visuals also provided her with a wealth of Internet sites that had information about Waldorf schools. In

❯ For more on developing a research question, see **Chapter 9**, p. 534.

fact, Amanda found that there was too much information, so she took a step back from her research and started thinking about the kinds of questions she had considered when analyzing her audience.

The work that Amanda had done on analyzing context not only gave her a list of questions to answer in her essay, but it also gave her a good way to develop her topic. She organized her questions and then reviewed all the notes she had taken when she was starting her research. Next she drafted a section of her essay about each one of these questions.

> ❯ Where did Waldorf schools begin? (see "History and Philosophy of the Waldorf System")
> ❯ How are students taught there? (see "The Waldorf Curriculum")
> ❯ What is a typical routine at a Waldorf school? (see "A Day in the Life of a Waldorf School")
> ❯ What kind of training would I need to teach in a Waldorf school? (see "Training for and Teaching in a Waldorf School")
> ❯ Are any aspects of the Waldorf system controversial? (see "Pros and Cons of the Waldorf System")

Finally, Amanda framed her essay by focusing on one main question that was directly linked to her readers: "Would You Like to Teach in a Waldorf School?" The questions and answers that form the body of the essay provide the kind of information that can help readers answer the main question—posed in the title—for themselves.

Establishing Credibility

As you learned in the chapters in Part 1, no matter what your topic is, you have to convince readers that they need to pay attention to what you have written. Once you understand the context for your research project, you should work on creating an appropriate voice. Are you trying to be scientific and objective? friendly and personable? or something else entirely? The voice you create will depend on your topic and purposes as well as on your audience and its circumstances. For example, for academic research projects, instructors often prefer a voice that is authoritative, somewhat formal, and objective. You should choose words and visuals carefully to enhance your credibility.

The attention you pay to correctness and clarity can add to your authority. Texts that are grammatically correct and clearly presented demonstrate that the writer is attentive to the reader's need to understand, often without the reader being conscious of the effect. Clear,

❯ For more on creating in-text citations, see p. 628 and p. 644.

correct prose says that the writer has taken some care with the production of the document and that the writer is conscientious. Documents that are not grammatically correct and clear are often seen as unreliable. Readers don't have a lot of confidence in the content if they see a lot of problems with the presentation. If you have trouble spotting grammatical problems or recognizing sections of your paper that aren't clear, be sure to ask your reviewers for help.

As discussed in Chapter 11, referring to experts is one way to establish credibility. When you quote, paraphrase, and summarize—and provide the in-text citations to support those features—you are building credibility. You are demonstrating that the information and views in your paper are supported by evidence from reliable sources.

Because Amanda knew that her classmates would be reading and using the information in her essay, she wanted to create a clear, credible voice that her audience could relate to. Notice how her title, opening, and closing explicitly address the reader. She says, in the opening, "This paper will . . . provide information for you to use to decide whether a Waldorf teaching career might be right for you." Amanda's use of the second person pronoun *you* emphasizes her relationship with her classmates.

Amanda knew that there are some words and phrases, such as "curriculum" and "rote textbook learning," that her readers would understand, so she didn't need to define them. However, she does explain terms that are unique to the Waldorf schools, such as "anthroposophy" and "main lesson books." These explanations provide the clarity and support that her readers need in order to understand what she is describing.

Amanda's use of visuals also enhances her essay's clarity and credibility. The first two figures—a painting by a student and one from a "main lesson book"—illustrate points in the text. All of the images—drawings produced by students at Waldorf schools—aid the reader's understanding of the importance of art to this unique educational system.

Integrating Research

When you use a quotation from a source, you insert the original author's exact words in quotation marks and tell readers where you found the material. Consider adding a quotation to your writing when you find a source that says exactly the right thing in exactly the right way, or when you want to use the exact words of a noted authority. Be aware, however, that integrating quotations into your writing requires you to follow certain conventions to make the quotations fit your own material smoothly and clearly.

> You should usually include a *signal phrase* that gives the author's name or provides other information about the source. (See p. 611.)

> You can insert a quotation anywhere in a sentence—before or after a signal phrase or in the middle of a sentence. You can even interrupt a quotation with a signal phrase.

> When you need to omit words from a quotation to make it more concise or to make it fit the structure of your own sentence, mark the omission with ellipsis points.

> When you need to add a word or part of a word to make the quotation fit the structure of your sentence or to clarify the material, enclose the added letters or words in square brackets.

> When you use a quotation that is longer than four typed lines (or more than three lines of poetry), format it as a *block quotation* if you are using MLA style documentation. Begin a block quotation on a new line and indent each line an additional several spaces. You should not enclose a block quotation in quotation marks, but you should conclude with a parenthetical citation, as MLA style requires. For more information on MLA style documentation, see pp. 626–642.

Be careful not to overuse quotations. A paper containing too many quotations may strike readers as boring, unoriginal, or incoherent.

When you want to use information from your research but do not need to use the exact words of an original source, consider a paraphrase or summary instead. A paraphrase includes all of the details of the original material but is stated in your own words. A summary, too, uses your words to condense the main ideas of an original passage that is too long to include in your paper.

> For more information on paraphrasing and summarizing, see **Chapter 11.**

Finally, remember that you must cite the sources of material you borrow from another source—whether you quote words exactly or paraphrase or summarize the original—unless the material you are using can be considered common knowledge. If a fact can be found in many general sources, or if your research turns up the same information again and again, it may be so commonly known that a citation is not necessary. Check with your instructor if you are not sure whether to cite a source, or be safe and include the citation. For more information on documenting your research, see pp. 626–642 (for MLA style) or pp. 643–654 (for APA style).

Amanda integrated a variety of sources. Although she was only required to have five sources, she used many more. Some provided visual as well as textual data. Amanda carefully cited each source in the text, identifying the pages for actual quotations and the source for information that was paraphrased or summarized. Amanda chose to quote phrases and sentences when she had trouble thinking of a better or different way to say something that she thought was important. You may have noticed that there are many short quotations scattered throughout the essay. For example, Amanda directly quoted some of the statements that describe the philosophy of the Waldorf schools.

Mostly, however, she paraphrased and summarized passages from different sources. For example, the first paragraph in the section describing a day in the life of a Waldorf school is paraphrased from a description in a magazine article. The section "Training for and Teaching in a Waldorf School" summarizes information found on Web sites for several teacher training institutes.

Providing Structure

As you will recall from the chapters in Part 1, there are a variety of ways to provide structure for your readers. In a research project, as with many other types of writing, you may want to use thesis sentences, forecasting terms, headings and subheadings, and transitional words. Furthermore, you may want to use charts, graphs, boldface type, white space, or other visuals to help readers locate those sections of your project that most interest them.

In Amanda's project on Waldorf schools, there are two obvious structural features: the preview in the opening paragraph and the headings that divide the essay into sections. Notice in the final sentence in the first paragraph how the order of the words and the actual words themselves are mirrored in the headings. The headings are informative—they tell the reader what type of information will be presented in each section, and they highlight aspects of the Waldorf schools that would be relevant to someone thinking about becoming a Waldorf teacher.

Amanda's conclusion also plays a structural role. Some readers of research essays read the first and last paragraphs before focusing on the pages in between. Typically, a concise summary of the main research findings works well as a conclusion. You might want to look through Chapters 2 through 7 to find other concluding strategies that would make sense for your research project. In Amanda's essay, the conclusion acts as a frame—it returns to the purpose mentioned in the introduction. Amanda concludes with a section titled "Is Waldorf Right for You?" She reminds her readers that Waldorf teaching is a viable option, and she summarizes some of the most distinctive features of the Waldorf program to give readers a succinct way of deciding if they want to investigate further. Amanda also makes suggestions for what they might want to do next if they are interested in pursuing a career as a Waldorf teacher.

Designing a Research Project and Integrating Visual Elements

Although you should be thinking about designing your research project and integrating visual elements throughout the drafting process, you may want to take a close look at your project as a final step before creating your review draft. Many of the research projects you've read or written probably did not have a wide variety of design features. However, as with all your other writing, you will have to make layout decisions on such elements as margins, font size, and spacing. You also have to think about the practicalities of including charts, graphs, tables, photographs, drawings, and other visual elements that are commonly found in research papers.

Whether your visual elements are taken from one of your sources or created by you, they need to be integrated with your text. There are two parts to the integration of visual elements: (1) verbal connection and (2) position. You make a verbal connection by making an explicit reference to the visual element. This can be as simple as a parenthetical comment (for example, "See fig. 1") or a more detailed explanation of the purpose of the visual (for example, "The table below presents the findings of this study"). The visual should be positioned as close to the verbal reference as possible, preferably on the same page, but ideally no more than one page after the reference. The visual should not appear before the verbal reference.

All visuals copied from another source should be cited, either in the caption or in the text, according to the documentation style you are using. Many styles require a caption for every visual, so be sure to check with your instructor or the style manual before completing your assignment.

Check with your instructor to find out if there are guidelines on some of these choices (such as font size and spacing). If there are no guidelines, refer to the guides to the documentation style of your discipline.

Amanda printed her essay in an 11-point sans serif font with standard margins. Her name, the course information, and the date are flush left, and her title is centered, following MLA style. She has incorporated a number of visual images in her essay, including paintings and drawings produced by students at Waldorf schools. She found all these images on various Web sites and integrated them carefully into her essay. Amanda has used images to emphasize the highly artistic nature of the Waldorf system and to support or introduce specific facts. Notice how she alternates the positioning of the figures to add variety to the pages and how she wraps the text around each image and its caption.

❯ For more information on page layout and text wrapping, see **Chapter 8.**

Reviewing the Project

After refining your draft, it is time to assess and revise it. You will need to find a representative of your audience to read and comment on your draft. Pay careful attention to what this reader has to say about your text. Ask him or her to point out any places where it was difficult to understand what you are saying. A lack of clarity can be disruptive to the reader and can also affect your credibility as a writer. You may want to provide a series of questions about your research to see if this reader understands the main points you hoped to present. On the basis of feedback from this reader, revise your project to make it as clear and as polished as possible.

If you need help with mechanics or grammatical errors, ask a peer reviewer, a friend, or your instructor. If the instructor approves, you may want to visit your school's writing or tutorial center for extra help.

Then, ask a peer to review your draft. Ask a classmate to read it and make sure you have met the expectations for the assignment. It may be a good idea to swap projects with at least one other classmate so that you are getting feedback on your project from more than one person. By performing a peer review for a classmate, you reinforce your own understanding of the requirements for a good research project. Your final revision, based on the peer review, should focus on meeting those requirements.

Amanda asked a classmate who is also thinking of becoming a teacher to conduct a peer review for her. She asked the classmate to talk with her as she read the paper, asking questions or making comments whenever a passage was unclear. The most important thing that Amanda learned from the classmate was that there was not enough information about teacher training. After the peer review, Amanda reviewed her notes, gathered more information, and added a new section, "Training for and Teaching in a Waldorf School." In addition, the classmate noticed that Amanda had not provided in-text citations for all of her sources, which Amanda corrected before submitting the final draft.

DOCUMENTING SOURCES

Throughout Chapter 11, we emphasized the researcher's need to rely on work that has been done by others. As the writer of a research paper, you need to *document your sources* for readers who are truly interested in your topic and who may want to do further reading and investigation on their own. Proper documentation provides the information that will enable your readers to find additional sources of information—the sources that you have used in preparing your research paper. You can provide that information through *in-text citations* and *reference lists*. The nuts and bolts of citing sources in the text and formatting the entries in your list of references will vary depending upon your academic discipline. Check with your instructor or academic department to find out what documentation style your assignment requires. If you need to locate information on documentation styles, the following table will help you get started.

The examples of in-text citations and entries in reference lists in this chapter will show you how to properly document many of the kinds of sources that you are likely to use in your research papers. For the purposes of your first-year writing class, you probably will not be required to master all the conventions for academic work in a particular discipline, but (especially once you have chosen a major field of study) you should know that disciplinary style manuals offer scholars and writers important editorial and formatting information in addition to documentation guidelines. Such information typically includes topics as diverse as the types of research being published in the discipline, preferred formats for tables and graphs, acceptable units of measurement, conventions for pronoun usage, and more.

Formal conventions for citing material from electronic sources evolve rapidly, and the information in the print versions of style guides is frequently updated online. Sometimes you will not be able to find

> bedfordstmartins.com/
visualage

For links to up-to-date documentation guidelines, click on
CHAPTER 12 > LINKS

Commonly Used Documentation Style Manuals

Discipline	Style Manual
English and General Humanities	*MLA Handbook for Writers of Research Papers*, 6th ed. (New York: MLA, 2003)
History and Some Humanities	*The Chicago Manual of Style*, 15th ed. (Chicago: U of Chicago P, 2003)
Psychology, Social Sciences, and Nursing	*Publication Manual of the American Psychological Association*, 5th ed. (Washington: APA, 2001)
Biology and Natural Sciences	*Scientific Style and Format: The CBE Style Manual for Authors, Editors, and Publishers*, 6th ed. (New York: Cambridge UP, 1994)
Chemistry	*The ACS Style Guide: A Manual for Authors and Editors*, 2nd ed., ed. Janet S. Dodd. (Washington: American Chemical Society, 1997)
Law	*The Bluebook: A Uniform System of Citation*. Comp. editors of *Columbia Law Review* et al., 17th ed. (Cambridge: Harvard Law Review, 2000)

> bedfordstmartins.com/
visualage

For a list of links to useful Web sites that offer additional documentation advice for a variety of disciplines, click on
CHAPTER 12 > LINKS

instructions for the exact type of source that you want to use, so you will have to improvise. In those cases, refer to the generic description of the way the information should be organized that is typically introduced in each section of the appropriate style guide, and then pick the closest thing you can find as a model. Always use your sense of what your audience will need to know as a guide in determining what information to include.

Documenting Sources: MLA Style

MLA style is typically used for research papers in English and the general humanities, particularly in the fields of study of various languages and literatures. MLA style is used in books, journal articles, and electronic materials produced by scholars in these fields as well as by students taking courses in these fields. The MLA system for citing sources requires documentation within the text for all materials you quote, paraphrase, or summarize. MLA style then requires that you include all of the works that you have cited in a list of Works Cited at the end of your project.

For more advice on documenting sources according to MLA style, see the *MLA Handbook for Writers of Research Papers,* 6th ed. (New York: MLA, 2003). For more information on MLA style, you can also consult the MLA's Web site at www.mla.org.

⟩ For a more detailed discussion
of quoting, paraphrasing, and
summarizing, see **Chapter 11**,
pp. 596–600.

MLA In-Text Citations

MLA style suggests that you include the author's last name and the page number for the referenced information in the sentence where the work is cited. The basic format is the same whether you are providing a direct quote, paraphrasing, summarizing, or referring to the original source. For example:

> One of the key principles of visual design is alignment (Williams 14).

If you include the author's name in the sentence, you can simply put the page number in the parentheses:

> Williams says that one of the key principles of visual design is alignment (14).

As in these examples, in-text citations usually consist of *signal phrases* and *parenthetical references*. A signal phrase introduces the cited material, indicating that something has been taken from a source and may include the author's name. A parenthetical reference is placed after the material you are citing and includes page numbers and, sometimes, other information to direct the reader to more information in the Works Cited list. If your parenthetical reference includes a title (or a shortened version of a title), you can always safely underline the title, as specified in MLA style. If you want to use italics, ask your instructor first.

Generally, it is best to keep parenthetical references brief and as close to the material cited as possible. For any sources you cite, the choice between author in parentheses and author indicated in a signal phrase is yours. Always think about what you've already told the members of your audience and what they will want to know or may need to be reminded of. Note that you do not put the word "page" or the abbreviation "p." in front of the page number in MLA style.

The following examples of in-text citations will help you see how to refer to different kinds of works and how to avoid confusing your readers when you cite more than one work by an author, works by two different authors with the same last name, and so on.

1. Work with one author

> Beowulf's disposition has been called "strange and not entirely safe" (Ker 166).
> Ker calls Beowulf's disposition "strange and not entirely safe" (166).

2. Work with more than one author

List all last names in a signal phrase or include the names in a parenthetical reference: (Gross and McDowell 162).

> According to Gross and McDowell, Eliot sees poetry as striving to attain the emotional heights of music: "To Eliot 'the music of poetry' means a great deal more than melodious verse, achieved through smooth textures and verbal tone color" (162).

3. Two or more works by the same author

Provide enough information so that the reader knows which work is being cited, including the title of the work in a signal phrase or in the parenthetical reference. To include both the author and the title in parentheses, put a comma after the author's name, then insert the title of the work (if it's short) or a shortened version of the title.

> On the contrary, Gordon tells us that Sartre and Fanon were both "acutely aware of the simultaneous fluidity and rigidity of institutional power" (<u>Fanon and the Crisis</u> 25).

4. Work by a corporate author

Give the group's or corporation's name either in the signal phrase or in the parenthetical reference.

> The National Center for Health Statistics points out that measuring the longevity of a population is easier than assessing overall health status (1).

5. Works by two or more authors with the same last name

Add the initial of the first name to distinguish between authors with the same last name.

> Van Gogh's works "lacked the elegant sinuosity of the line that informs even Gauguin's most 'primitive' figures" (B. Collins 75).

6. Work with an unknown author

Cite the title of the document if the author is unknown.

> One local newspaper argues that "sometimes it takes just one generous-minded individual to get the ball rolling" ("A $20 Million investment" 4).

7. Indirect source (source quoted in another source)

Begin with the abbreviation "qtd. in" (for "quoted in"), followed by the author and page number for the source where you found the quotation.

> Expressing the anger of many teachers, a school principal complained, "We teach to the test. We'd be idiots not to. But school, real education, is not just about taking tests" (qtd. in Ivins and Dubose 91).

8. Electronic or nonprint source

Treat material from the Internet in the same way as printed material. If you do not know the author, include the title of the document. If the document has numbered paragraphs instead of stable page numbers, include those numbers with a comma and the abbreviation *par.* If the source has no numbered pages or paragraphs, omit the number.

> Shakespeare's Globe Theatre "was actually the first to be built specifically for an existing acting company and financed by the company itself" (Gurr).

9. Multivolume work

In the parenthetical reference, put the volume number after the author's name. Separate it from the page number with a colon and one space.

> Cook notes that during World War I, Eleanor Roosevelt "organized the Red Cross Canteen, and with Addie Daniels organized the Navy Red Cross. She knitted and distributed free wool to the Navy League, entertained troops in and out of Washington's Union Station, and made coffee and sandwiches" (1: 215).

10. Two or more works in the same reference

Put the author and page information in the citation in the same order as the works appear on the Works Cited page. Separate the citations with a semicolon.

> Poetry's emotive effects can be traced to the way its syntax creates feelings apart from meaning, much like the arrangement of tones to produce a certain abstract emotion (Gross 82; Snodgrass 1).

11. Entire work or one-page source

Include the author's name in a signal phrase rather than in a parenthetical reference.

> Malcolm Gladwell suggests that we can understand how and why cultural changes occur by thinking about these changes as social epidemics.

12. Work in an anthology

Include the name of the author of the anthologized work and the page number(s). Do not refer to the name of the editor or compiler of the anthology in an in-text citation.

> Oliver uses vivid sensory details, notably color: "I make coffee and walk from window to window, lifting the shades, watching the pink, tangerine, apricot, lavender light dart and sail along the eastern horizon" (219).

13. Work without page numbers

If a work has no page numbers, include only the author's name.

> Pissarro's innovation of dividing colors can be seen in <u>The Garden of Les Mathurins at Pontoise</u>, "where the sunlit path is made up of brushstrokes of pink, blue, white and yellow ochre" (MacDuffee).

14. Literary work

Literary works, especially those that are well known, often come in many different editions. First put the page number(s) from the edition you used, followed by a semicolon, then give other information that would help readers find the passage in any edition. For a novel, indicate the page number, followed by a semicolon, then the section or chapter.

> When the undead finally appear in Stoker's <u>Dracula</u>, they lure human prey with voices that are "diabolically sweet" (37; ch. 16).

For a play, indicate the page number, followed by a semicolon, and the act and scene. For a verse play, you need only cite the act, scene, and line numbers.

> Thomasina tells her tutor that "if there is an equation for a curve like a bell, there must be an equation for one like a bluebell" (Stoppard 327; act 1, sc. 3).

For a poem, cite the section (if there is one) followed by a period and the line(s); page numbers are not required. If you cite only line numbers for a poem, use the word "line(s)" in the first citation; for subsequent citations, just cite the number.

> The use of repetition reinforces the "silent and endless" suffering in Whitman's "Hours Continuing Long" (line 21).

15. Sacred text

To cite a sacred text such as the Bible or the Qur'an, give the title of the edition, the title of the book, and chapter and verse separated by periods. Use abbreviations for books of the Bible included in parenthetical references.

> She was fond of reminding him that "a foolish son is a sorrow to his mother" (<u>New American Standard Bible</u>, Prov. 10.1).

MLA List of Works Cited

> For a complete sample of a student Works Cited page written using MLA style, see p. 615.

At the end of a research paper, the author needs to include a list of all the sources that were cited within that paper. In MLA style, this reference list is called Works Cited. The information in the list contains all of the relevant publication information that will enable readers to locate specific books, journals, Web sites, and other original sources that they are interested in reading.

For most documentation styles, you will need the same general information to complete an entry in any reference list or bibliography. However, the form and order of that information will vary. Figures 12.1

through 12.4 show four different types of entries that are typically found in an MLA-style Works Cited list: books, journal articles, works from Web sites, and articles from online periodicals. The annotations explain the information presented, including sequence of elements, punctuation, and acceptable or required abbreviations. In the section following these annotated examples, you'll see sample entries for a variety of other sources in MLA style.

FIGURE 12.1
Typical MLA Works
Cited Entry for a Book

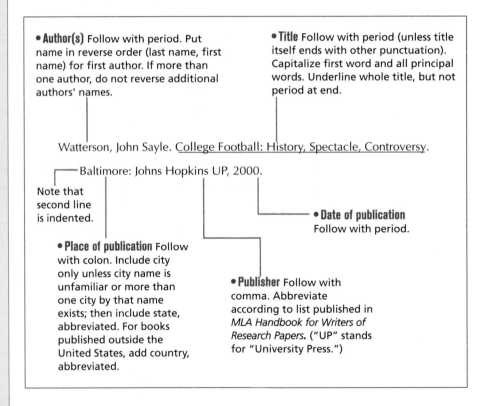

• **Author(s)** Follow with period. Put name in reverse order (last name, first name) for first author. If more than one author, do not reverse additional authors' names.

• **Title** Follow with period (unless title itself ends with other punctuation). Capitalize first word and all principal words. Underline whole title, but not period at end.

Watterson, John Sayle. <u>College Football: History, Spectacle, Controversy</u>.

Baltimore: Johns Hopkins UP, 2000.

Note that second line is indented.

• **Place of publication** Follow with colon. Include city only unless city name is unfamiliar or more than one city by that name exists; then include state, abbreviated. For books published outside the United States, add country, abbreviated.

• **Publisher** Follow with comma. Abbreviate according to list published in *MLA Handbook for Writers of Research Papers.* ("UP" stands for "University Press.")

• **Date of publication** Follow with period.

**FIGURE 12.2
Typical MLA Works
Cited Entry for a
Journal Article**

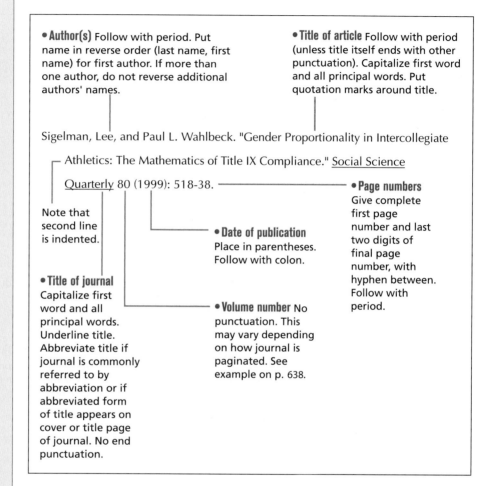

• **Author(s)** Follow with period. Put name in reverse order (last name, first name) for first author. If more than one author, do not reverse additional authors' names.

• **Title of article** Follow with period (unless title itself ends with other punctuation). Capitalize first word and all principal words. Put quotation marks around title.

Sigelman, Lee, and Paul L. Wahlbeck. "Gender Proportionality in Intercollegiate

Athletics: The Mathematics of Title IX Compliance." Social Science

Quarterly 80 (1999): 518-38.

Note that second line is indented.

• **Title of journal** Capitalize first word and all principal words. Underline title. Abbreviate title if journal is commonly referred to by abbreviation or if abbreviated form of title appears on cover or title page of journal. No end punctuation.

• **Date of publication** Place in parentheses. Follow with colon.

• **Volume number** No punctuation. This may vary depending on how journal is paginated. See example on p. 638.

• **Page numbers** Give complete first page number and last two digits of final page number, with hyphen between. Follow with period.

FIGURE 12.3
Typical MLA Works
Cited Entry for a
Work from a Web Site

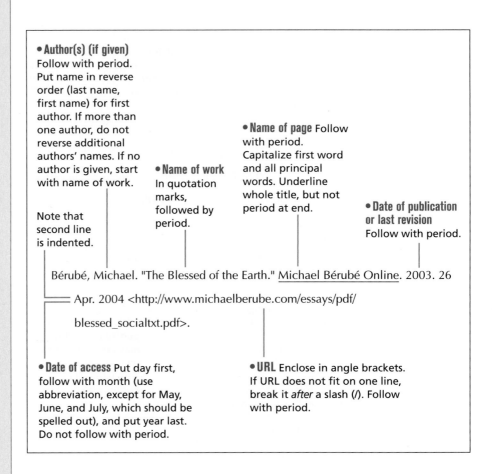

● **Author(s) (if given)**
Follow with period.
Put name in reverse
order (last name,
first name) for first
author. If more than
one author, do not
reverse additional
authors' names. If no
author is given, start
with name of work.

Note that
second line
is indented.

● **Name of work**
In quotation
marks,
followed by
period.

● **Name of page** Follow
with period.
Capitalize first word
and all principal
words. Underline
whole title, but not
period at end.

● **Date of publication**
or last revision
Follow with period.

Bérubé, Michael. "The Blessed of the Earth." Michael Bérubé Online. 2003. 26

Apr. 2004 <http://www.michaelberube.com/essays/pdf/

blessed_socialtxt.pdf>.

● **Date of access** Put day first,
follow with month (use
abbreviation, except for May,
June, and July, which should be
spelled out), and put year last.
Do not follow with period.

● **URL** Enclose in angle brackets.
If URL does not fit on one line,
break it *after* a slash (/). Follow
with period.

**FIGURE 12.4
Typical MLA Works
Cited Entry for an
Article from an Online
Periodical**

• Title of periodical
Capitalize first word and all principal words. Underline title. Abbreviate title if periodical is commonly referred to by abbreviation or if abbreviated form of title appears on cover or title page of periodical. For journals, add volume and issue numbers after title. No end punctuation.

• Author(s) (if given)
Follow with period. Put name in reverse order (last name, first name) for first author. If more than one author, do not reverse additional authors' names. If no author is given, start with article title.

• Title of article
Follow with period. Capitalize first word and all principal words. Put quotation marks around title.

• Date of publication
For journals, give year only; enclose within parentheses, follow with period. For magazines and newspapers, give full date (day month year). Do not enclose in parentheses. Follow with period.

Note that second line is indented.

McEachern, William A. "Stadium Will Revive City." <u>USA Today</u> 14 Dec. 1998.

15 Dec. 1998 <http://www.usatoday.com/news/comment/ncoppf.htm>.

• Date of access Put day first, follow with month (use abbreviation, except for May, June, and July, which should be spelled out), and put year last. Do not follow with period.

• URL Enclose in angle brackets. If URL does not fit on one line, break it *after* a slash (/). Follow with period.

Note: If stable page numbers or paragraph numbers are given, insert after date of publication and prior to date of access. Give total number of pages or paragraphs. Specify *pp.* (for pages) or *pars.* (for paragraphs). Insert colon after page or paragraph number.

❯ For an annotated example of
citing a book, see Figure 12.1.

Books

1. Book by one author

> Wright, Esmond. <u>Fabric of Freedom: 1763-1800</u>. New York: Hill and Wang,
> 1961.

2. Book by two or three authors

> Hales, Steven D., and Rex Welshon. <u>Nietzsche's Perspectivism</u>. Urbana: U of
> Illinois P, 2000.
> Porter, Lewis, Michael Ullman, and Ed Hazell. <u>Jazz: From Its Origins to the
> Present</u>. Englewood Cliffs: Prentice Hall, 1993.

3. Book by four or more authors

When a book has four or more authors, the *MLA Handbook* gives you
a choice. You can list just the first author's name followed by "et al."
(meaning "and others"), or you can list all authors as they are listed on
the title page of the book. Some people feel that it is more appropriate to
list all the authors so that all who contributed to the book are given credit
for their work. You may want to check with your instructor if you have a
book with four or more authors.

> Grand, Gale, Rick Tramonto, Julia Moskin, and Marty Tiersky. <u>American Brasserie</u>.
> New York: Macmillan, 1997.

4. Book by an unknown author

If the author is unknown, alphabetize the work by its title.

> <u>Art Meets Science and Spirituality</u>. London: Academy Editions, 1990.

5. Book by a corporate or group author

> American Heart Association. <u>To Your Health! A Guide to Heart-Smart Living</u>.
> New York: Clarkson Potter, 2001.

6. Translation

List a translated book by its original author. Insert the abbreviation
"Trans." (for "Translated by") after the title, and then insert the first and
last name of the translator.

> Alighieri, Dante. <u>The Inferno of Dante</u>. Trans. Robert Pinsky. New York: Farrar,
> 1994.

7. Book by an author and editor

List an edited book by its original author. Insert the abbreviation "Ed."
(for "Edited by") after the title, and then insert the first and last name of
the editor.

> Warhol, Andy. <u>The Andy Warhol Diaries</u>. Ed. Pat Hackett. New York: Warner,
> 1989.

8. Anthology or collection with an editor

List an edited collection or anthology by the first editor's last name; after all of the editors' names, insert a comma and "ed." or "eds." (for "editor" or "editors").

> Keller, Michael, ed. <u>Reading Popular Culture: An Anthology for Writers</u>. Dubuque: Kendall/Hunt, 2002.

9. Book in a series

Provide the title of the series (with no underlining or quotation marks) after the title of the book, followed by the number of the book within the series.

> Larkin, Bruce D. <u>War Stories</u>. Conflict and Consciousness: Studies in War, Peace, and Social Thought. Ser. 10. New York: Lang, 2001.

10. Multivolume work

If you use one volume of a multivolume work, give the volume number after the title and give the total number of volumes after the date.

> Cook, Blanche Wiesen. <u>Eleanor Roosevelt</u>. Vol. 1. New York: Viking, 1999. 2 vols.

If you use two or more volumes, give the total number of volumes after the title.

> Cook, Blanche Wiesen. <u>Eleanor Roosevelt</u>. 2 vols. New York: Viking, 1999.

11. Work in an anthology or collection

List the author of the work, then the title of the work in quotation marks. After the title of the anthology or collection, identify the editor(s).

> Oliver, Mary. "Dust." <u>The Best American Essays 2001</u>. Ed. Kathleen Norris and Robert Atwan. Boston: Houghton, 2001. 218-20.

12. Entry in a reference book

List the author's name if it is given; otherwise, begin with the entry's title. If the reference book alphabetizes entries, no volume or page numbers are needed.

> "Cinderella." <u>Encyclopedia of Folklore and Literature</u>. Ed. Mary Ellen Brown and Bruce A. Rosenberg. Santa Barbara: ABC-CLIO, 1998.

13. Introduction, preface, foreword, or afterword

> Holman, Bob. Foreword. <u>Burning Down the House: Selected Poems from the Nuyorican Poets Café's National Poetry Slam Champions</u>. By Roger Bonair-Agard et al. New York: Soft Skull, 2000.

> Keynes, Sir Geoffrey. Introduction. <u>Songs of Innocence and Experience</u>. By William Blake. Oxford: Oxford University Press, 1989. 7-15.

14. Multiple works by the same author

List the works in alphabetical order by title. (Titles are alphabetized letter-by-letter.) Put the author's name as the first item in the first work.

After that, use three hyphens followed by a period in place of the author's name.

> Angelou, Maya. <u>And Still I Rise</u>. New York: Random, 1978.
>
> ---. <u>A Song Flung Up to Heaven</u>. New York: Random, 2002.

15. Title within a title

When a book title includes the title of another book, the title within the title is not underlined.

> Kinnamon, Keneth, ed. <u>New Essays on</u> Native Son. Cambridge: Cambridge UP, 1990.

16. Sacred text

> <u>Bhagavad-Gita: The Song of God</u>. Trans. Swami Prabhavananda and Christopher Isherwood. New York: Signet, 2002.

17. Edition other than the first

> Smith, Charles D. <u>Palestine and the Arab-Israeli Conflict</u>. 4th ed. Boston: Bedford/St. Martin's, 2001.

Periodicals

❯ For an annotated example of citing an article from a journal, see Figure 12.2.

18. Article in a journal paginated by volume

> Basney, Lionel. "Teacher: Eleven Notes." <u>American Scholar</u> 71 (2002): 75-88.

19. Article in a journal paginated by issue

Insert a period and the issue number after the volume number.

> Godwin-Jones, Bob. "Blogs and Wikis: Environments for Online Collaboration." <u>Language Learning and Technology</u> 7.2 (2003): 12-16.

20. Article in a magazine

If the magazine is published once a month or less frequently, include the month and year of publication. Abbreviate the name of any month except May, June, or July.

> Wilson, Ann Lloyd. "Architecture for Art's Sake." <u>Atlantic Monthly</u> June 2001: 85-88.

If the magazine is published weekly or biweekly, include the day, month, and year of publication—in that order.

> Cagle, Jess. "The Women Who Run Hollywood." <u>Time</u> 29 July 2002: 52-57.

21. Article in a newspaper

> Angier, Natalie. "Science Is Finding Out What Women Really Want." <u>New York Times</u> 13 Aug. 1995, sec 4: 7.

22. Unsigned or anonymous article

> "Producers Give Thanks for a Windfall of Family Films." <u>New York Times</u> 1 Dec. 2003: E5.

23. Review

List the reviewer's name and the title of the review. Then add the abbreviation "Rev." (for "Review") and the word "of" followed by the title and a comma, then the word "by" and the creator of the work being reviewed. Provide publication information for the review, not for the work reviewed.

> Meadows, Susannah. "Son of a Sort of Goddess." Rev. of <u>The Impressionist</u>, by Hari Kunzru. <u>New York Times Book Review</u> 12 May 2002: 27.

24. Editorial

> "Volunteer Opportunity." Editorial. <u>Boston Globe</u>. 30 Sept. 2002: A18.

25. Letter to the editor

> Jeffords, Jim. Letter. <u>New Yorker</u> 23 Sept. 2002: 9.

Electronic Sources

26. Entire Web site

If you can determine the name of the person or organization that created the site, begin your entry with that name; otherwise begin with the title of the site, underlined. If there is no title, write a description such as "Home page." Do not underline the description. Follow the title with the date of the last update (you may have to search the site to find this), the name of the organization sponsoring the site (if there is one), the date that you accessed the site, and the URL (address of the site) in angle brackets. Put a period at the end of each component of the entry except the date of access.

> Auerbach, Nina. <u>Nina Auerbach's Home Page</u>. 2004. 15 April 2004 <http://www.english.upenn.edu/~nauerbac/>.
>
> <u>A Guide to Electronic Beowulf</u>. Ed. Kevin Kiernan. 2003. U of Kentucky. 15 April 2004 <http://www.uky.edu/ArtsSciences/English/Beowulf/eBeowulf/guide.htm>.
>
> The Nature Conservancy. <u>The Nature Conservancy</u>. 2004. 15 April 2004 <http://nature.org>.

❯ For an annotated example of citing a work from a Web site, see Figure 12.3.

27. Work from a Web site

> Breuer, János. "Bartók and the Third Reich." Hungary.Network. 1995. 30 Aug. 2004 <http://www.hungarianquarterly.com/no140/p134.html>.
>
> Renan, Ernest. "Poetry of the Celtic Races I." <u>Bartleby.com</u>. 2002. 15 June 2004 <http://www.bartleby.com/32/302.html>.

❯ For an annotated example of citing an article from an online periodical, see Figure 12.4.

28. Article in an online periodical

> Jewett, Thomas. "Terrorism in Early America: The U.S. Wages War against the Barbary States to End International Blackmail and Terrorism." <u>Early America Review</u> 4.1 (2002). 30 Jan. 2002 <http://earlyamerica.com/review/2002_winter_spring/terrorism.htm>.

29. Article in an online newspaper

> Aletti, Vince. "On the Road." <u>Village Voice</u> 27 Sept. 2002. 4 May 2004
> <http://www.villagevoice.com/issues/0240/aletti.php>.

30. Online book

> Aaron, Henry J., ed. <u>Behavioral Dimensions of Retirement Economics</u>.
> Washington, D.C.: Brookings Institution P, 1999. 13 May 2004 <http://
> www.brookings.nap.edu/books/0815700636/html/R3.html>.

31. Online government document

List the name of the government and then the name of the agency that issued the document.

> United States. Census Bureau. <u>Bucks County QuickFacts from the U.S. Census</u>
> <u>Bureau</u>. 24 Sept. 2002. 10 Oct. 2004 <http://quickfacts.census.gov/
> qfd/states/42/42017.html>.

32. Material accessed through an online subscription service

> Cutler, Maggie. "Whodunit--the Media?" <u>Nation</u> 26 Mar. 2001: 18-20. EBSCO-
> host. New York Public Research Lib. 25 July 2004 <www.ebsco.com/home>.

> Sipe, Thomas Owen. "Beethoven, Shakespeare, and the 'Appassionata.'"
> <u>Beethoven Forum</u> 4.1 (1995): 73-97. <u>RILM</u>. FirstSearch. Moravian Coll. Lib.,
> Bethlehem, PA. 24 Sept. 2004 <www.firstsearch.org>.

33. Material published on CD-ROM, magnetic tape, or diskette

Include the date of a document's original publication and the date of the publication or last update of the CD-ROM, tape, or diskette.

> <u>The North American Bird Reference Guide</u>. CD-ROM. Seattle: Multimedia
> 2000, 2004.

> Bushman, Brad J., and Joanne Cantor. "Media Ratings for Violence and Sex:
> Implications for Policymakers and Parents." <u>American Psychologist</u> 58.2
> (2003): 130-141. <u>PsycARTICLES</u>. CD-ROM. Ovid. Sept. 2003.

34. E-mail message

> Burns, Monica. "Re: Penn State Main Campus." E-mail to the author. 15 Sept. 2004.

35. Instant message

> Betro, Elizabeth. Conversation about Picasso. 24 Apr. 2002. AOL Instant
> Messenger.

36. Online posting

> Oosthoek, K. "New Jersey's Environments: History and Policy." Online posting.
> 7 Oct. 2002. H-Environment. 10 Oct. 2004 <http://www.h-net.org/~environ/>.

> Langly, Ringo. "Minimum Wage Going Up--What Good Will It Do?" Online post-
> ing. 17 July 2004. 27 July 2004 <Google newsgroup: soc.politics>.

37. Computer software

Practica Musica. Computer Software. Kirkland, WA: Ars Nova, 1999.

Other Sources

38. Television or radio program

Include the title of the episode or segment (if any) in quotation marks, followed by the series title. Give information about the writer ("By"), director ("Dir. "), performers ("Perf. "), or host ("Host"), as appropriate. List the series title (if any), network, local station, and date aired.

"The Jesus Factor." Frontline. By Raney Aronson. PBS. KETC, St. Louis.
    29 Apr. 2004.

39. Film, videotape, or DVD

Include the title, director, lead actors, the company releasing the film, and the release date. For video, include the original release date followed by "Videocassette" or "DVD," the name of the distributor, and the release date of the tape or DVD.

Pollock. Dir. Ed Harris. Perf. Ed Harris, Marcia Gay Harden. Sony Picture
    Classics, 2000.

Bonnie and Clyde. Dir. Arthur Penn. Perf. Warren Beatty, Faye Dunaway. 1967.
    DVD. Warner, 1999.

40. Music or sound recording

Beethoven, Ludwig van. String Quartets: Op. 127, 130, 131, 132, 133, 135. Perf.
    Alban Berg Quartet. EMI, 1997.

41. Cartoon or comic strip

Roberts, Victoria. Cartoon. New Yorker 8 Mar. 2003: 44.

42. Advertisement

Secret. Advertisement. Cosmopolitan Sept. 2002: 248.

43. Interview

Blackburn, Simon. "The Seven Deadly Sins: Envy." Interview. Talk of the Nation.
    NPR. WBEZ, Chicago. 4 Sept. 2003.

Graves, Denise. Personal interview. 27 Apr. 2004.

44. Survey

Moravian College Food Services Questionnaire. Personal survey. 2 Feb. 2004.

45. Lecture

Kress, Gunter. "Gains and Losses: New Forms of Texts, Knowledge, and Learn-
    ing." Conf. on Coll. Composition and Communication. Hyatt, San Antonio.
    26 Mar. 2004.

46. Performance

Chamber Dance Project: Dancers and Musicians. Choreographed by Ann Carlson, Adam Hougland, and Stanton Welch. Dir. Diane Coburn Bruning, Stanley L. Corfam, and Stacy Caddell. Perf. Chris Bandy et al. Kaye Playhouse, New York. 6 June 2002.

47. Work of art or photograph

List the artist or photographer, the title of the work, the name of the museum or other institution, and the city. Include the year the work of art was created after the title, if this information would be of use to your reader. To cite a photograph or a work that you have not seen in person, include the publication information for the source where the photograph or reproduction appears, and conclude with the number of the page, slide, plate, or figure. For an online photograph of the work, include the date of access and URL.

Becker, Otto. Custer's Last Fight. Anheuser-Busch Archives. On the Rez. By Ian Frazier. New York: Picador, 2000. 120.

Millais, John. Ophelia. 1851-52. Tate Gallery, London. 27 July 2004 <http://www.artchive.com/artchive/M/millais/millais_ophelia.jpg.html>.

Van Gogh, Vincent. Self-Portrait. 1886-87. Art Institute of Chicago, Chicago.

48. Unpublished doctoral dissertation

Bauer, George. "Perpetual Displacements as a Creative and Critical Strategy of Inquiry into Sites of Meaning." Diss. Texas Tech U, 2002.

49. Published doctoral dissertation

Jones, Anna Maria. Problem Novels/Perverse Readers: Late-Victorian Fiction and the Perilous Pleasures of Identification. Diss. U of Notre Dame, 2001. Ann Arbor: UMI, 2001. ATT 3028783.

50. Government document

› For advice on citing online government documents, see p. 640.

United States. Federal Bureau of Investigation. United States Government Interagency Domestic Terrorism Concept of Operations Plan. Washington: Federal Emergency Management Agency, 2001.

51. Pamphlet

American Cancer Society. Making Strides against Breast Cancer. New York: American Cancer Society, 2002.

52. Personal letter

Antoinette, Meghan. Letter to the author. 13 Feb. 2004.

Wyatt, Liza (Faber and Faber Ltd.). Letter to Dr. Claire Polin. 30 May 1972. Claire Polin Archives, Harrington Park, NJ.

Documenting Sources: APA Style

APA style is typically used for research papers in the social sciences. It is used in books, journal articles, and electronic materials produced by scholars in a variety of fields, including psychology, sociology, and technical communication, as well as by students taking courses in these fields. The following pages describe the APA system for citing sources within the text of a paper as well as the format for listing the works cited at the end of the paper. In APA style, this list is called References.

For more information on APA style, refer to the *Publication Manual of the American Psychological Association,* 5th ed. (Washington: APA, 2001). For up-to-date advice on documenting electronic sources, consult www.apastyle.org/elecref.html.

Directory to APA Style

continued

APA In-Text Citations

The key elements in APA style for in-text citations are *author* and *date*. Writers using APA style include the author's last name and the publication date for the referenced information in the sentence where the work is cited. The name may be used in a signal phrase followed by the year in parentheses, or both name and year can be placed in parentheses at the end of the sentence if the name does not appear earlier. For example:

> Williams (1994) observed that one of the key principles of visual design is alignment.
>
> One of the key principles of visual design is alignment (Williams, 1994).

❯ For a detailed discussion of quoting, paraphrasing, and summarizing, see **Chapter 11,** pp. 596–600.

If you are paraphrasing, as in the previous examples, you are not required to include the page number in parentheses (although you may do so if you think it will be helpful to the reader). If you are quoting, however, you do need to include it. Note that APA style requires a "p." in front of the page number. Notice, too, that APA style requires you to use a verb in either the past tense (such as *observed* or *explained*) or the present perfect tense (*has observed, have explained*) in the signal phrase.

> Williams (1994) observed that one of the key principles of visual design is alignment, which "creates a clean, sophisticated, fresh look" (p. 14).
>
> One of the key principles of visual design is alignment, which "creates a clean, sophisticated, fresh look" (Williams, 1994, p. 14).

❯ For more on signal phrases, see p. 621.

When using a signal phrase in a sentence with a quotation, put the page number after the quotation.

The following examples of in-text citations illustrate how to cite various types of works in APA style. They will help you avoid confusing the reader when you cite a single source more than once, when you cite more than one work by an author, and so on.

1. Work with one author

Claxton (1994) pointed out that "the 1960s and 1970s sparked attempts to relate birth order to differences in attitudes and opinions, creativity, job selection, personality, sex-role identity, socialization, and psychiatric problems" (p. 477).

2. Work with two authors

Ceci and Williams (1997) found a "high correlation between general intelligence and years of schooling" (p. 1052).

When both authors' names appear in parentheses instead of in a signal phrase, use an ampersand instead of the word "and" to join the two names.

Schooling has been called "primarily a marker for intelligence" (Ceci & Williams, 1997, p. 1052).

3. Work with three to five authors

The first time you cite a work with three to five authors, list all authors by last name only, in the order listed in the publication.

Tucker, McHale, and Crouter (2001) noted that "younger siblings whose parents have lower education levels rely on older siblings for support with schoolwork" (p. 327).

If you refer to the same text a second time, include only the last name of the first author, followed by "et al." (Latin for "and others").

Tucker et al. (2001) observed . . .

4. Work with six or more authors

Cite only the first author's name, followed by "et al." in either a signal phrase or a parenthetical reference.

As Dohrenwend et al. (1992) noted, "We found that rates of major depression in women and antisocial personality and substance use disorders in men are higher in Israelis of North African background" (p. 951).

5. Work with an unknown author

Include the title of the work or the first few words of the title, either in parentheses or in a signal phrase. Titles of books should be italicized; titles of articles and short works are placed inside quotation marks.

People succumb to shock from a variety of causes, including massive infections called sepsis ("Treating Shock," 2004).

6. Work with a group author

If the group name is long, use the full name in a signal phrase or parenthetical reference the first time you cite the source. If the group is known by a familiar abbreviation, include the abbreviation in brackets after the full name. In subsequent references to the source, use the abbreviation alone.

first citation   (Environmental Protection Agency [EPA], 2004)

second citation   (EPA, 2004)

7. Web site or electronic document

If an electronic source's date of publication is unknown, use *n.d.* ("no date"). If there is no author, either include the document title in a signal phrase or use a shortened version of the title in parentheses.

> According to the World Health Organization, there is no significant threat to the public in China from new outbreaks of SARS ("China," 2004).

If page numbers are unavailable, use paragraph numbers to document quotations.

> Through the use of brain imaging, Tapert, G. Brown, Baratta, and S. Brown (2003) have demonstrated that "craving can influence treatment of substance use disorders, but is difficult to measure objectively" (para. 1).

8. Two or more works in the same reference

Present the works in the parenthetical reference in the same order that they appear in the References list, separated by semicolons.

> The confluence hypothesis expanded the idea that firstborns had a higher IQ due to extended contact with their parents, to include the effect that their relative position to their younger siblings and family size had on their intelligence (Ernst & Angst, 1983; Zajonc, 1975).

9. Two or more works by the same author

When your References list includes two or more works by the same author, the date will provide the information needed to identify the source. However, if the References list contains two or more works by the same author *published in the same year*, you need to distinguish among them. List them in alphabetical order (by title) within that year, adding the lower-case letter "a" after the date for the first source entry, "b" for the second entry published in the same year, "c" for the third entry published in the same year, and so on. In the parenthetical reference, be sure to include the lower-case letter that identifies the appropriate source.

> According to Hawking (2002a), the concept of an expanding universe was not seriously theorized before the twentieth century.

10. Works by two or more authors with the same surname

Use the authors' initials along with their last names for each citation.

> S. Johnson (2004) described with fascination the results of his own MRI scan.

11. E-mail or personal communication

Include the initials and last name of the author of the communication, and give as exact a date as possible. Do not include personal communications in the list of references.

> D. W. George (personal communication, December 19, 2002) listed fourteen different billing errors that had occurred since the first of the year.

12. Indirect source

To use information from a source that was cited in another source (a secondary source), cite the original source in a signal phrase. Include the secondary source in the list of references and, in the in-text citation, include it after the words "as cited in."

> In an earlier report, Gellman describes "the first known acquisition of a nonconventional weapon other than cyanide by al Qaeda" (as cited in Shafer, 2004, para. 6).

APA List of References

In APA style, the list of all sources cited in a research paper is called References. The information in the list contains all the relevant publication information that would enable readers to locate specific books, journals, Web sites, and other sources that they are interested in reading.

For most documentation styles, you will need the same general information to complete an entry in any list of references. However, the form and order of that information will vary. Figures 12.5 through 12.8 show annotated APA-style references for four different types of entries: books, journal articles, works from a Web site, and articles from an online periodical. The annotations explain the way the information must be presented, including the sequence of elements, punctuation, and acceptable or required abbreviations. One of the most common errors that students make when using APA style is in the capitalization of titles. In APA style, only the first word, proper nouns, and the first word following a colon are capitalized in the titles of books and articles. All important words are capitalized in the titles of journals. In the section following these annotated examples, you will see sample entries for a variety of other types of sources in APA style.

FIGURE 12.5
Typical APA Reference
List Entry for a Book

FIGURE 12.6
Typical APA Reference
List Entry for a
Journal Article

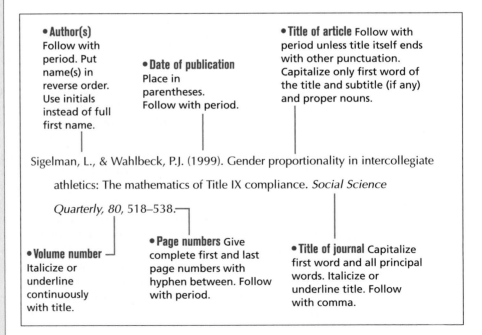

FIGURE 12.7
Typical APA Reference List Entry for a Work from a Web Site

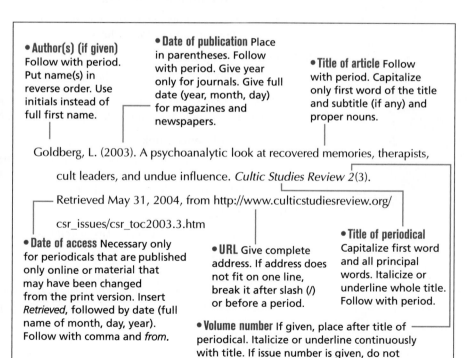

- **Author(s) (if given)** Follow with period. Put name(s) in reverse order. Use initials instead of full first name.

- **Date of publication (if given)** Enclose in parentheses and follow with period. Give complete publication date. If the date is not available, use *n.d.*

- **Name of work** Follow with period unless title itself ends with other punctuation. Capitalize first word of title and subtitle (if any) and proper nouns. Italicize or underline whole title.

Gandhi, A. (2002, November 29). *Nonviolence—A way of life*. Retrieved April
26, 2004, from http://www.gandhiinstitute.org/nonvwylife.html

- **URL** Give complete address. If address does not fit on one line, break it after a slash (/) or before a period.

- **Date of access** Necessary only for periodicals that are published only online or material that may have been changed from the print version. Insert *Retrieved*, followed by date (full name of month, day, year). Follow with comma and *from*.

FIGURE 12.8
Typical APA Reference List Entry for an Article from an Online Periodical

- **Author(s) (if given)** Follow with period. Put name(s) in reverse order. Use initials instead of full first name.

- **Date of publication** Place in parentheses. Follow with period. Give year only for journals. Give full date (year, month, day) for magazines and newspapers.

- **Title of article** Follow with period. Capitalize only first word of the title and subtitle (if any) and proper nouns.

Goldberg, L. (2003). A psychoanalytic look at recovered memories, therapists,
cult leaders, and undue influence. *Cultic Studies Review 2*(3).
Retrieved May 31, 2004, from http://www.culticstudiesreview.org/
csr_issues/csr_toc2003.3.htm

- **Date of access** Necessary only for periodicals that are published only online or material that may have been changed from the print version. Insert *Retrieved*, followed by date (full name of month, day, year). Follow with comma and *from*.

- **URL** Give complete address. If address does not fit on one line, break it after slash (/) or before a period.

- **Title of periodical** Capitalize first word and all principal words. Italicize or underline whole title. Follow with period.

- **Volume number** If given, place after title of periodical. Italicize or underline continuously with title. If issue number is given, do not italicize; place in parentheses.

❯ For an annotated example of
citing a book, see Figure 12.5.

Books

1. Book by a single author

Stewart, L. (1992). *Changemakers: A Jungian perspective on sibling position and the family atmosphere.* New York: Routledge.

2. Book by two or more authors

Pollock, D. C., & Van Reken, R. E. (2001). *Third culture kids: The experience of growing up among worlds.* Yarmouth, ME: Intercultural Press.

For a book with more than six authors, list the first six authors and abbreviate the rest as *et al.* (for "and others").

Huston, A. C., Downerstein, E., Fairchild, H., Feshbach, N. D., Katz, P. A., Murray, J. P., et al. (1992). *Big world, small screen: The role of television in American society.* Lincoln: University of Nebraska Press.

3. Book with an unknown author

The Spanish republic—A survey of two years of progress. (1933). London: Eyre & Spottiswoode.

4. Book with an author and an editor

Woolf, V. (1989). *Congenial spirits: The selected letters of Virginia Woolf.* (J. Trautmann, Ed.) London: Hogarth.

5. Book by a group author

When publisher and author are the same, use "Author" as publisher.

National Research Council. (2002). *Effectiveness and impact of corporate average fuel economy (CAFE) standards.* Washington, DC: National Academy Press.

6. Article in a reference book

Resick, P. A., & Calhoun, K. S. (2001). Posttraumatic stress disorder. In D. H. Barlow (Ed.), *Clinical handbook of psychological disorders* (3rd ed., pp. 60–113). New York: Guilford Press.

7. Edited collection

Gates, H. L. (Ed.) (2002). *Classic slave narratives.* New York: Signet.

8. Article or chapter in an edited book

Adams, M. (2001). Core processes of racial identity development. In C. L. Wijeyesinghe & B. W. Jackson III (Eds). *New perspectives on racial identity development: A theoretical and practical anthology* (pp. 209–242). New York: New York University Press.

9. Multivolume work

Give the number of the volume you cite after the title or the number of volumes total if you are citing all volumes, in parentheses.

Katz, S. H. (2003). *The encyclopedia of food and culture* (Vol. 2). New York: Scribner.

If you cite a volume with a separate title, use the title of the volume, followed by a colon, the abbreviation "Vol.," and the volume number. Then include the title of the multivolume work.

Johnston, L. D., O'Malley, P. M., & Bachman, J. G. (2003). *College students and adults ages 19–40: Vol. 2. Monitoring the Future national survey results on drug use, 1975–2002.* Bethesda, MD: National Institute on Drug Abuse.

10. Edition other than the first

Randall, D., Burggren, W., & French, K. (2002). *Animal physiology: Mechanisms and adaptations* (5th ed.). New York: W. H. Freeman.

11. Translation

Freud, S. (1999). *The interpretation of dreams.* (J. Crick, Trans.). Oxford: Oxford University Press. (Original work published 1900)

12. Multiple works by the same author

When you have used more than one work by the same author, list the sources by year of publication with the earliest first, beginning with the author's name each time. When you have used two or more works by the same author *published in the same year*, alphabetize by title within that year, adding the lower-case letter "a" after the date for the first entry, "b" for the second entry published in the same year, "c" for the third entry published in the same year, and so on.

Gould, S. J. (2002a). *I have landed: The end of a beginning in natural history.* New York: Harmony Books.

Gould, S. J. (2002b). *The structure of evolutionary theory.* Cambridge, MA: Belknap Press of Harvard University Press.

Gould, S. J. (2003). *Triumph and tragedy in Mudville: A lifelong passion for baseball.* New York: Norton.

Periodicals

13. Article in a journal paginated by volume

› For an annotated example of citing an article from a journal, see Figure 12.6.

Dingfelder, S. (2003). Tibeten Buddhism and research psychology: A match made in nirvana? *Monitor on Psychology, 34,* 46.

14. Article in a journal paginated by issue

Underwood, R. L., & Klein, N. M. (2002). Packaging as brand communication: Effects of product pictures on consumer responses to the package and brand. *Journal of Marketing Theory & Practice 10*(4), 58–69.

15. Article with more than six authors

If an article has more than six authors, list the first six names followed by *et al.* ("and others").

> Dorhenwind, B. P., Lerav, I., Shrout, P. E., Schwartz, S., Nevah, G., Link, B. G., et al. (1992). Socioeconomic status and psychiatric disorders: The causation-selection issue. *Science, 255,* 946–952.

16. Article in a magazine

> Lemonick, M. (2003, December 1). Is Alzheimer's in the family? *Time,* 86–87.
>
> Langewiesche, W. (2003, November). Columbia's last flight. *Atlantic Monthly,* 58–87.

17. Article in a newspaper

If the article appears on discontinuous pages, list all the page numbers, separated by commas.

> Jolly, M. E. (2001, October 8). Traditional families still the norm: Census 2000. *The Intelligencer,* pp. B1, B4, B7.

18. Article with an unknown author

Alphabetize by the first important word in the title.

> Setting the stage. (2003, December). *Scientific American,* 32.

19. Editorial

> Deregulation's weakness (2002, September 30). [Editorial]. *The Washington Post,* p. A18.

20. Letter to the editor

> Datnow, A., & Hubbard, L. (2002, March/April). Getting it right. [Letter to the editor]. *Psychology Today,* pp. 6–7.

21. Review

> Shenk, J. W. (2003, May/June). Think different. [Review of the book *Saying yes: In defense of drug use*]. *Mother Jones,* 81–82.

Electronic Sources

❭ For an annotated example of citing a work from a Web site, see Figure 12.7.

22. Document from a Web site

Include the author, publication date, title of the document (in italics), and retrieval information. To cite a whole Web site, give the URL in a parenthetical reference and do not include the site on the References page.

> Devlin, K. (2003, December 1). *John Von Neumann: The father of the modern computer.* Retrieved December 4, 2003, from http://www.maa.org/devlin/devlin_12_03.html

❯ For an annotated example of citing an article from an online periodical, see Figure 12.8.

23. Article from an online periodical

List the retrieval date and the URL after the title if the article appears only online or if it is likely to differ from the print version.

> Behncke, L. (2004, March). Mental skills training for sports: A brief review. *Athletic Insight* 6(1). Retrieved September 16, 2004, from http://www.athleticinsight.com/Vol6Iss1/MentalSkillsReview.htm

If the material is based on a print source and is an exact duplicate of the print version, put the words "Electronic version" in square brackets after the article title. You do not need to include an access date or a URL.

> Rose, F. (2003). The second coming of Philip K. Dick [Electronic version]. *Wired, 11*(12), 198–209.

24. Article from an online newspaper

Give the URL for the newspaper site, not the exact source, if you access the article from a newspaper's searchable Web site.

> Zakaria, T. (2004, April 28). Terrorist threat center tackles technology, privacy. *Washington Post.* Retrieved April 30, 2004, from http://www.washingtonpost.com

25. Article or abstract from a database

> Tucker, C. J., McHale, S. M., & Crouter, A. C. (2001, June). Conditions of sibling support in adolescence. *Journal of Family Psychology,* 254–271. Retrieved February 6, 2002, from PsycARTICLES database.

26. E-mail

As with other forms of personal communication, e-mail messages are cited in the text but are not included in the list of references.

27. Online posting

Cite a posting to a newsgroup or other forum only if you can access it in an online archive. Otherwise, treat it as personal communication and cite it in a parenthetical reference.

> Oosthoek, K. (2002, October 7). New Jersey's environments: History and policy. Message posted to H-Environment electronic mailing list, archived at http://www.h-net.org/~environ/

28. Online government document

> National Center for Infectious Diseases. (n.d.). *Viral hepatitis a.* Retrieved November 22, 2003, from http://www.cdc.gov/ncidod/diseases/hepatitis/a/index.htm

29. Computer software

> Gray, P. (1999). Psychology 3e: Student activity CD-ROM [Computer software]. New York: Worth.

Other Sources

30. Television program

Zuiker, A. E., & Donahue, A. (Writers), & Fink, K. (Director). (2002). Identity crisis [Television series episode]. In J. Berman (Producer), *CSI: Crime Scene Investigation*. New York: CBS Worldwide.

31. Film, videotape, or DVD

Ball, C. J. (Producer), & Nolan, C. (Director). (2000). *Memento* [Motion picture]. United States: Columbia Tristar.

32. Music or sound recording

Eminem. (2002). Cleanin out my closet. On *The Eminem show* [CD]. Santa Monica, CA: Interscope Records.

33. Interview

As with other types of personal communication, interviews are cited parenthetically within the text, but they are not listed in the References.

34. Photograph, table, figure, or graph

Include all of the information about the print or electronic source where you found the photograph, table, figure, or graph as a caption under the image where you insert it. The caption should resemble a References entry for the publication, beginning with a title (if any) and ending with a page number or reference marker for the location of the image. Do not include an entry for the photograph, table, figure, or graph on the References page.

❯ For advice on citing online government documents, see p. 653.

35. Government document

U.S. Senate. (2003). *Homeland security federal workforce act of 2003*. Washington, DC: U.S. Government Printing Office.

36. Technical or research report

Association of Certified Fraud Examiners. (1996). Report to the nation on occupational fraud and abuse. Austin, TX: Author.

37. Personal letter

As with other forms of personal communication, personal letters are cited in the text but are not included in the References.

Strategies for Special Writing Situations

13
Writing for the Classroom

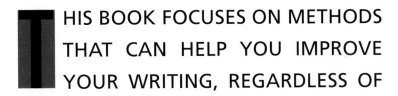**T**HIS BOOK FOCUSES ON METHODS THAT CAN HELP YOU IMPROVE YOUR WRITING, REGARDLESS OF

the type of writing you want or need to do. It highlights the types of writing, such as reports and proposals, that you are likely to write in both academic and professional careers. This chapter, however, discusses the kinds of essay writing that primarily occur in academic contexts—responding to essay questions for assignments or exams. Essay questions assigned by instructors may provoke anxiety among students because such questions often have stricter time constraints than many other types of academic writing. This chapter will suggest tips to help you understand your audience's expectations and use your time wisely to organize and draft your responses.

This chapter also offers advice on the types of online communication that many academic instructors require, including e-mail, listservs, and other online discussions.

657

ESSAY ASSIGNMENTS AND EXAMS

Essay questions are common in courses in nearly every academic discipline. Whether you write a response to an essay question outside of class or in class, as homework or as an examination, the instructor's goal is to give you an opportunity to demonstrate what you have learned. In an academic essay, you not only describe or explain what you know about a topic but also expand on that knowledge. In other words, you have the opportunity to demonstrate that you can make connections, see distinctions, synthesize information, or reach conclusions. When an instructor asks you to respond to an essay question (whether in class or at home), he or she generally gives you instructions describing what is expected. This chapter helps you read those instructions more carefully and use the information they contain to provide the kind of response that the instructor expects.

Although essay questions have many common characteristics regardless of the academic discipline, the criteria (standards) that are used to evaluate essays vary according to the discipline. Thus no single format or outline will work in every situation. In fact, you may find that the essay your instructor asks you to produce has many of the features of a report (Chapter 3), an evaluation (Chapter 5), or one of the other types of documents described in earlier chapters of this book. If you find that an essay you are asked to write for another course is similar to one of the types of writing described in this book, you should review the appropriate chapter for more ideas on how to respond.

This section of the chapter presents examples of essay questions from exams in fields such as economics, computer science, and English, and for assignments in sociology, zoology, and geography. As you will see, the instructions for in-class essay exam questions are virtually identical to those for take-home essay assignments and exams. However, there is one important difference: in class, you will have a set amount of time in which to write. In this situation, it is easy to become rattled and waste precious time. Reading the instructions closely will enable you to determine what you are being asked to do and make the most of your limited time. The first part of this section provides specific advice for in-class exam situations. The second part is relevant primarily to essays written outside of class. The rest of the section is equally useful for responding to any essay question.

Responding to Essay Questions in Class

When you know that you will be taking an essay exam, your preparation is different from the studying you would do for a short-answer test. To prepare for an essay exam, you need to spend time focusing on the type of information that will enable you to respond fully and appropriately to the assigned essay question(s). Although you may not know exactly what will be asked, you can do several things ahead of time to improve your performance on the exam.

Identifying the Format

Before the exam, learn as much as possible about what you will be expected to do. Sample questions from previous exams can be helpful study aids if the instructor is willing to share them. Some instructors even provide sample student answers. If your instructor has created a Web site for the course, look there for sample exam questions and answers.

Practicing with Sample Questions

If you are fortunate enough to see sample questions from old exams, or if the instructor gives information about the questions ahead of time, you may want to practice responding. Depending on your level of confidence in the material and your writing, you could analyze the question, write a thesis sentence, draft an outline, write a rough draft, or actually write a full essay. When you practice, keep an eye on the clock to see how long each step takes. Practicing with sample questions can improve the speed with which you move through the initial stages so that you can spend more time writing and revising your essay.

Managing Your Time

One crucial thing to consider when you write in-class essay exams is the amount of time you are expected to spend on each essay. (Remember, in-class essays are not expected to be as polished as essays assigned ahead of time.) You will have a fixed amount of time to work on each essay, and there will probably be limitations on your ability to do research, format your essay, and add visual elements. If the class meets in a computer classroom you might have access to some formatting options, but you will probably be discouraged from spending much—if any—time on formatting (unless it's a technical writing course and the purpose of the exam is to demonstrate your ability to format).

Given the fixed amount of time for writing essays in class, you must budget your time carefully. Most instructors will indicate how much the question is worth (toward the total score of the exam), which gives an idea of how much time they expect you to spend answering it. For example, if you have three hours for the exam and one question is worth 20 percent of the grade, you should spend 20 percent of the time (approximately thirty-five minutes) writing your response. In thirty-five minutes, you would probably be expected to write a fairly coherent essay of at least five paragraphs.

Exercise

Read the following two essay questions from an in-class economics exam.

> Discuss the relationship between bond prices and the interest rate.

> Suppose that Congress increases government spending by $100 billion this year but the public anticipates a $200 billion increase in government spending. If the new classical view of the economy is correct and government spending does affect aggregate demand, predict what will happen to aggregate output and the price level. How would the answer change if the traditional model is the correct description of the economy? Be sure to include the appropriate diagram.

Do you think the instructor would expect you to put in the same amount of time on each essay? If you think he or she would recommend spending more time on one essay than on the other, explain which one would take longer and why you think so.

Taking Notes

Use the first few minutes of in-class exam time to read the question *slowly* and make notes. It may help to underline important words in the question as you read (see pp. 666–672 to figure out which words are the most important). If you have thirty-five minutes to write an essay, use five to ten of those minutes to read, make notes, and plan your essay.

Responding to Essay Questions at Home

❯ For guidance with assignments that include significant amounts of research, see **Chapter 9**.

If you are asked to respond to an essay question outside of class, you usually will have a good deal of advance notice about when the assignment is due, so your instructor will expect you to "do your homework." That means doing whatever research is required; but more important, it means that your essay should be written clearly with a logical organization, an appropriate voice, appropriate transitions, and few grammatical errors. In most cases the instructor will expect your essay to be typed and formatted according to his or her specifications, including the use of certain font types and sizes, margins, headings, systems of page numbering, and so on. In many cases you will be expected to include appropriate visual elements such as charts, graphs, photographs, or other images.

In terms of how much time to spend on an out-of-class writing assignment, you can get a good idea by checking the course syllabus and asking yourself the following questions.

> **How detailed are the instructions?** Although this is not a hard-and-fast rule of thumb, detailed instructions often indicate higher expectations for the final product, which implies a greater amount of time and effort on your part.

> **How much is the assignment worth in terms of my final grade?** An essay that will count as twenty-five percent should demand more of your time than an essay that will count as ten percent.

> **How long is the essay supposed to be?** Instructors often give page or word-length guidelines. The longer the essay, the more time you should spend on it.

> **How much other work is this instructor asking me to do at the same time?** For all your college courses, you should expect to spend approximately three hours working outside of class for every hour that you spend in class. If the instructor has assigned lots of other homework that is due at the same time, that should help you figure out how much time to spend on the essay.

> **How much advance notice did the instructor give?** If you were given more than two weeks' advance notice, you are probably expected to spend a good deal of time on the essay regardless of how much other work is assigned.

On a take-home exam the amount of time is not as fixed as on an in-class exam. However, you still have a set number of days, and you need to make sure to allocate time within those days. It's easy to put off a task when you don't have to do it immediately, but you only increase the pressure on yourself by putting it off to the last minute. When you get the exam, be sure to read it right away—even if you will not be doing the work immediately. The instructor may have added certain requirements (such as incorporating charts and graphs, reading a particular text, or doing some research) that take additional time before you begin to write the essay. Also, he or she may have indicated how much time you should spend writing the exam.

Identifying Expectations

When it comes to essay exams and other writing for class, it is important to define, analyze, and describe your audience. Throughout your academic career you have undoubtedly had a lot of practice adjusting to new instructors—new audiences—with every new school year or course. By now you probably adapt your writing style to each new instructor without even realizing it. To be successful in writing for the classroom, think about the specific instructor you are writing for. What does he or she focus on? What topics come up in class discussions, assigned readings, and homework or exam questions?

Essentially, you must pay attention to the expectations built into every assignment. You must answer the questions that are asked. Expectations can be explicit (spelled out, obvious, clear) or implicit (implied, unspoken, understood), so be sure to read carefully and think about every word in the question or assignment.

Finding and Understanding Explicit Cues

Some instructors will tell you very clearly what they expect you to write. Read carefully the following essay assignment for a sociology course. As you read, think about the instructor's expectations.

> Suppose you are writing a set of recommendations for the planners and curators of a museum exhibition and an accompanying catalog on Jamaican culture. Based on the materials presented in this course so far, choose *five* things that you would want to incorporate into your recommendations. State your five recommendations clearly, describe their implications, and explain why you think they are important.
>
> Note: (1) While I do not have a "checklist" of my own, I will be looking at *your* list in terms of whether it reflects an understanding of and engagement with *all* the class discussions and readings so far, including the assigned readings by Clifford, Marcus and Fischer, and Argun Appadurai. (2) While no specific detail about Jamaican culture is necessary for your essay, you may want to take into account certain characteristics it shares with many other cultures today, such as its diasporic nature.

Explicit cues in the assignment indicate that this instructor expects students to write an essay that meets the following criteria.

> ❭ The response should make *five* different recommendations based on the students' understanding of Jamaican culture. This is a crucial piece of information; if you come up with four (or six), this instructor may take away credit regardless of the quality of your work.
>
> ❭ The response should make reference to "*all* the class discussions and readings so far." Furthermore, certain readings are mentioned specifically, so the instructor is making sure you understand exactly what he means by *all*. Realistically, you can't make reference to all class discussions and readings, so which readings did he talk about the most? What topics did he emphasize most in class?
>
> ❭ A successful response should compare characteristics of Jamaican culture and other cultures. Item (2) in the final paragraph says, ". . . you may want to take into account." This is an important hint about what the instructor wants to see in the essay. Whenever an instructor advises "you may want to [include something, refer to something, describe something]," you should strongly consider taking that advice.

Exercise

Read carefully this final essay exam for a management course on organizational behavior in a multicultural business context. As you read, make a list of the expectations you find for any one of the three possible exam questions. Be prepared to discuss those expectations in class.

The final exam will be in the form of an in-class essay exam. Please bring a "blue book." You may also bring a dictionary and/or thesaurus, and up to two pages of written notes. I will choose one of the three following questions for you to write on at the time of the exam.

Your writing will be evaluated on the following criteria.

> integration of reading concepts

> creative, analytical individual contributions

> freedom from errors

> illustration and specifics

1. How would one set about to modify his or her interpersonal style if he or she wanted to develop and maintain truly supportive interpersonal relationships? Discuss the attributes of supportive communications that one would strive to develop in his or her communications style. Pay particular attention to the roles of listening skills and conflict management styles in developing and maintaining supportive relationships.

2. Compare and contrast the paths of Native Americans, African Americans, Latinos, Asian Pacific Americans, and white immigrants in their struggles to close the gap between the promise of democratic principles and actual American history and practice. What key views and differing attitudes on race and racial progress are currently held by members of these communities?

3. Analyze a traditional and/or innovative university course learning experience that you have had.

   > Describe the leadership philosophy of the instructor or the course structure using McGreggor's Theory X and Theory Y assumptions. Which assumptions applied in that circumstance? With what effects?

   > Also do an analysis of the learning styles (Kolb) supported most by the course, with specific examples.

   > Use Herzberg's model to provide ideas for generating a more truly motivational climate for the course.

Finding and Understanding Implicit Cues

Many instructors are not nearly as explicit about what they expect as the sociology instructor whose essay assignment appears on p. 662, so you need to read carefully to find the implicit cues. You can often identify the instructor's expectations by looking at the first word or words of the question, especially if that first word is *who, what, when, where, why, which,* or *how.* Each one of these questioning words signals a way to start thinking about the topic and about your essay.

If the question does not begin with a questioning word, check to see if one (or more) is buried further inside the question. If you cannot find one, read the question over carefully and try to complete the following sentence: "The instructor wants to know _____." When you complete the sentence, you will most likely use one of the questioning words. For example, read the following computer science essay exam question and see if you can figure out what this instructor wants to know.

> These days, some information about everyone is stored on a computer somewhere. If you fill out forms online, send in warranty cards, answer questionnaires, give out information on the phone or at the cash register, your personal information is collected somewhere. Do you think there should be a law to stop the accumulation of personal information in databases? Are there benefits to collecting this information?

Here, the instructor asks two questions that technically could be answered with a "yes" or a "no." This type of closed question does not seem to require a lengthy or varied response; however, since the instructor has explicitly labeled it as an essay question, we know he is looking for a detailed response. In other words, he wants to know *what* kinds of problems might result from the collection of personal information in databases and *what* the benefits of such collection might be. The first question implies a problem by asking if there should be "a law to stop the accumulation of personal information in databases." (If someone is suggesting a law might be needed to stop an activity, he or she must think there are negative effects of that activity.) By asking if there are "benefits" to the activity, the second question suggests the possibility of another point of view. The two questions represent two possible positions, and the instructor wants students to think (and write) about both. In answering this question, you would use your knowledge and understanding of class discussions and readings to establish your personal point of view and decide how best to respond.

Once you've located the questioning word(s) in an assignment or exam question, you will have a good idea of how to incorporate the course content in your response. The following table provides suggestions for using questioning words to shape your essay.

Finding and Using Questioning Words

Questioning Word	Suggestions for Shaping Your Essay	Examples
Who	*Who* questions ask you to describe a person or a group of people. Be sure your answer provides the specific information about an individual or group responsible for or connected to the topic in the question.	"Who is best suited to work in virtual space?"
What	*What* questions want you to demonstrate that you can define and/or explain a topic or some aspect of a topic.	"What key views and differing attitudes are currently held by members of various ethnic communities?"
When	*When* questions may want you to show that you know the date/time of an event ("When did something happen?"). However, be careful because these could be questions that are looking for a consequence ("When *X* happens, what is the result?").	"When businesses work virtually, what will happen to the professional and personal lives of the workers?"
Where	*Where* questions are not very common. If you encounter one, you can be fairly certain that the instructor wants to know the location (geographical, temporal, sequential) of some event.	"With complete freedom to live anywhere and work for anyone, where would you live?"
Why	*Why* questions call on you to explain or analyze a topic, often focusing on the causes of events (why something happened) or the thinking that supports your answer (why your response is valid).	"Explain why you think your recommendations are important."
Which	*Which* questions ask you to make a choice between two or more events, aspects, components, and so on. Read the rest of the question carefully; you are probably being asked to make a choice and then argue for your choice.	"Describe the philosophy of an innovative course you have taken, using assumptions from these two theories. Explain which of those theories applied."
How	*How* questions are closely related to *why* questions. Both require you to provide some kind of explanation or analysis. *How* questions may focus on causes, but they may also be testing your understanding of a process or sequence of events.	"How would you set out to modify your interpersonal style in order to develop and maintain truly supportive interpersonal relationships?"

Recognizing Important Words

❯ For more advice on analyzing
the voice of an essay question,
see p. 672.

In addition to identifying the questioning words, you should read instructions and questions very closely to locate two other types of words: the *verbs* that tell how to approach the essay and the *nouns* that suggest what to write about. Finally, be sure to notice the level of formality or informality of the instructor's wording; this cue to *voice* will help you determine whether to use technical or conversational language in your essay.

Analyzing the Verbs

Imperative verbs in instructions or questions tell you what the instructor wants you to do. An imperative verb is a word that commands or requests (*examine, argue, explain, be*). Many essay questions include several such verbs, so be sure to read each question completely and find all the verbs that tell you what to do. For example, in the following directions for an assignment from a zoology course, see how many imperative verbs you can find and what you think they mean.

> Study the two images below. The first is a low magnification of tissue from the nasal septum (the partition between the nostrils). The second is a higher magnification of the same tissue. Write a short essay describing the epithelium of this tissue, using the terminology you have learned from the online lesson and/or the reading assignment. Describe the epithelium as completely as possible, but only regarding aspects that are *visible* in these images.

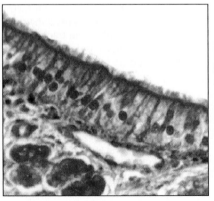 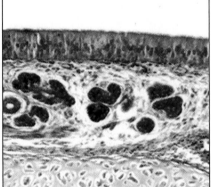

There are three imperative verbs in the zoology assignment.

> ❯ ***Study.*** This assignment asks students to notice and identify ("Study") specific visual information ("two images below") before they write anything.

Exercise

Take a look at the imperative verbs in the following example, an essay assignment for a geography course. List the imperatives in the three questions. Rewrite one of the questions using questioning words, but do not change its meaning. Bring your revised question to class to compare with those of your classmates.

The following list contains a choice of topics for the essay. Only one topic is to be chosen from this list.

1. Critically examine Canadian migration policies and their role in the changing of Canadian society. Support your discussion with examples, statistics, and policy documents.

2. Is it likely that human numbers will stabilize at some point in the future? Discuss the conditions that can contribute to the solution of the population explosion.

3. It is argued that geopolitics gave way to geoeconomics. Explain the context and evolution of ideas about global security.

The instructions also say exactly what the two images are. Why do you think there are two images? Perhaps the first one creates a context for the second one; because the second one is at a higher magnification, students might not recognize it easily without the first one. Or perhaps elements that are visible or clearer in one of the images will help students identify all aspects of the epithelium.

❯ *Write.* Notice that the assignment asks students to "write a short essay describing the epithelium . . . [and] using the terminology . . ." The instructor could have been more direct, saying "Describe the epithelium of this tissue. Use the terminology . . ." In this instance, *describe* and *use* are hidden imperatives. Read your essay assignments carefully to find the hidden imperatives that are crucial to your success.

❯ *Describe.* Here the imperative verb *describe* is explicit, which reinforces its importance. The students' essays must be descriptive if they are to meet the instructor's expectations. In their description, students would name the various aspects of the epithelium, perhaps explaining their role or relationship or describing their unique characteristics.

You will find imperative verbs in most essay exam questions. Following are some of the most common of these verbs, along with suggestions for using the verbs to understand what you have to write.

Analyze. When you are asked to analyze, you are expected to write a fairly substantial answer; after all, analysis is not something you could have memorized (like a definition). When you analyze something, you break it down to talk about components or attributes and then put it back together with some kind of synthesis or conclusion. For this type of question you will probably have to spend time planning your response. Read the question carefully for other cues: an analysis question generally gives information about what to analyze and how to analyze it. Use that information to get started.

Argue (*see also* Critique). An essay question that asks you to argue requires you to make a claim about something and to back it up with evidence. The instructor might tell you what kind of evidence to use, but he or she might simply expect you to figure that out on the basis of what you've been studying in class. When you argue, you take a position. Questions that ask for your opinion expect you to take a stand and argue for that stand. You might also consider presenting opposing points of view and responding to that opposition.

Compare *and* Contrast. When you are asked to compare (or compare and contrast), you are expected to describe similarities and differences. Technically, *compare* means to describe the similarities and *contrast* means to describe the differences, but not every instructor will make that distinction. Read the question carefully to see if the instructor wants you to describe both similarities and differences. If so, you can describe all the ways the things are similar and then describe all the ways they are different. Alternatively, you could describe each thing fully and then summarize the similarities and differences in a conclusion.

Critique *or* Criticize (*see also* Argue). A critique is a type of argument. When you are asked to critique, you must find the flaw (or flaws), state your claim about the flaw, and provide evidence to support your claim.

Define. A question calling for definitions is usually asking for a short essay, although technically a definition could be as short as one sentence for a simple term (especially if the question isn't worth a lot of points). You don't want your answer to be as brief or as fragmented as a dictionary definition, but that type of definition does give you a way to think about your response. A definition provides the meaning for a word or phrase, so you will need to write complete sentences showing the instructor that you know what he or she is asking about. Sometimes definitions describe unique characteristics and also tell what something is *not*; for example, abstract art is art that is not a realistic representation of its subject. In some situations, it may be important to show how the definition changes under different circumstances (time, place, culture, and so on). For example, how old does something have to be in order to be considered an antique? In terms of furniture, the standard is one hundred years; in terms of cars, it may be as little as twenty-five years.

Describe. Descriptions demonstrate that you understand what something "looks like." The something could be a physical object, a relationship, or a process (for example, a particular chemical reaction). When you write a description you will most likely need to label the attributes of your subject, usually using terminology appropriate to the field (see, for example, the zoology assignment on p. 666). Descriptions often answer *how* questions.

Discuss. A discussion can be similar to an argument but would likely present more than one point of view and would try to persuade readers to accept one particular point of view. Read the question carefully. If the instructor doesn't give specific instructions on how to shape the discussion, you are probably free to write it as a comparison, a description, an explanation, or even an analysis. Try rewording the question to focus your response. Also, class discussions and readings can help you decide how to shape your essay.

Evaluate (*see also* Argue). When you are asked to evaluate, you are expected to examine a topic, issue, object, person, place, or process and determine its value. An evaluation should establish the criteria you use to make your judgment (unless the instructions give you the criteria), make claims about the subject's positive and negative attributes, provide evidence to support those claims, and come to a conclusion about the worth of the subject.

Examine (*see also* Analyze). In an essay question, *examine* means to look closely at a topic, as you would in an analysis.

Explain. An explanation requires you to demonstrate your understanding of a concept, process, or event. You need to go beyond definition, but a definition may be a good way to start. Once you have defined the subject, you then must show that you understand a particular aspect of it such as its significance, behavior, effects, or causes. The wording of the question should give cues about what is expected; for example, it might ask you to explain *how* something works (which would be similar to a description) or to explain *why* something happened (which would be similar to an analysis).

Identify. Identifying an item or a list of items involves defining them and explaining their significance. If you are asked to identify terms that are commonly used in or specific to a particular academic discipline, you will need to show that you know what they mean and why they are important to that field.

Illustrate. When you see the verb *illustrate*, you are expected to describe something that exemplifies a general principle or concept. *Illustrate* is often used in conjunction with *define*. You might be asked to define a general concept (such as "class system") and then illustrate it with an example (such as the formal caste system of India or the less formal class system of Great Britain). Note that the word *illustrate* is unlikely to mean "include a visual"—although it could have that meaning if you're taking a course in design, art, architecture, or many of the sciences.

Refer. If the question includes the verb *refer*, the instructor expects you to use a specific text, event, or issue as evidence to support your answer. *Refer* will not be the primary focus of the question; rather, it will likely appear toward the end of the question.

Summarize. When you summarize, you touch briefly on the most important points about a topic. You could plan your answer by making a list of everything you know about the topic, choosing aspects you think are most important, and writing a paragraph on each of them.

Support (*see also* Argue *and* Refer). When you see the verb *support* in an essay question, the instructor wants you to provide evidence to back up any claims you are making. The evidence may be in the form of statistics, examples, personal experience, citations from course readings, or other sources appropriate to the course.

Synthesize. When an instructor asks you to synthesize, you are expected to blend material from different sources or different perspectives. A synthesis demonstrates a thorough understanding of the topic because it shows that you can identify its components and combine them into a meaningful whole. For example, you might be asked to synthesize the ideas presented in a series of readings on a particular topic. Your essay would not summarize each of those readings in turn; rather, it would present the various viewpoints on key elements of the topic covered in each reading. Your essay would be organized by the elements, not by the readings. If you are asked to synthesize, read the question carefully for cues about what the instructor wants you to synthesize and how he or she wants you to organize the information. The nouns used in the question are crucial in figuring out how to write a synthesis.

Examining the Nouns

The nouns in a question can provide important cues to help you think about your essay. In the following example from an entomology exam, the nouns are underlined along with the adjectives that modify them.

Because they have different <u>types</u> of <u>sensory receptors</u>, <u>insects</u> and <u>humans</u> may perceive the same <u>environment</u> very differently. What <u>types</u> of <u>stimuli</u> can <u>humans</u> detect more easily than <u>insects</u>, and what can <u>insects</u> detect that <u>humans</u> cannot?

This question requires students to demonstrate an understanding of the differences between the way two species (insects and humans) perceive their environment. To answer this question, you could first use the nouns to make notes about the following information.

> what types of sensory receptors insects and humans have
> how insects and humans use their sensory receptors to perceive the environment
> what types of stimuli humans detect
> what types of stimuli insects detect

Your notes, a simplified outline describing what you know about the sensory receptors of insects and humans, could form the basis for your response to the question.

As you make notes to guide you in answering an essay question, you should also think about class discussions or readings. What words and phrases in the question are familiar? What was emphasized about those topics? What other topics were related to them? These notes will be especially important in planning a response to more complex questions, such as this one from a nursing education course.

You are spending a <u>clinical day</u> in a <u>homeless shelter</u>. The <u>nurse</u> at the <u>shelter</u> explains that many <u>homeless women</u> come to the <u>shelter</u> from <u>abusive relationships</u>. The <u>women</u> have been abused as <u>children</u> (by <u>parents</u>) and as <u>adults</u> (by <u>spouses</u>, <u>boyfriends</u>). Many times they lack <u>education</u>, <u>employment</u>, and <u>support systems</u>. You learn that many of these <u>women</u> also lack <u>education</u> about <u>HIV transmission</u> and engage in <u>intravenous drug use</u> and <u>unprotected sex</u>. Using the <u>Health Belief Model</u>, describe why these <u>women</u> behave in this <u>manner</u>.

This question is based on a scenario, a common technique in essay questions. Scenarios set a context for the question and the relevant response, but they also give cues about what the response should address. Often, students fail to read such questions carefully and end up writing lengthy responses that are inappropriate. Here, for example, they might write about the relationship between a history of abuse and homelessness, or between lack of education and unemployment. Although the sample question includes a lot of information about homeless women, it is really only asking students to use a particular model to explain the reasons for two types of behavior: intravenous drug use and unprotected sex.

Be careful not to fall into the trap of writing about a scenario. The nouns and noun phrases give cues about topics to include in your discussion. In this example you would undoubtedly mention homeless women, abusive relationships, and education, but those topics would not be the focus of your essay. The final sentence of the instructions—which contains both an imperative verb (*describe*) and a questioning word (*why*)—provides the focus. Always read through the whole question before you begin to make notes or write your essay.

Analyzing the Voice of the Question

The *voice* of the question is another cue to the kind of answer you should provide. Is the instructor's voice formal or informal? Does he or she use technical terminology or everyday language? The zoology question on p. 666 includes technical words (*magnification, nasal septum, epithelium*); given a question like that, you would use appropriate technical words in your response. The computer science question on p. 664, however, is conversational: the instructor asks a series of questions directed to "you." Because his voice is informal, your essay can probably assume a similar voice (you can write, "I would . . ." or "I think . . ."). If the assignment has an informal voice, check with your instructor to make sure that you can respond with a similar informal voice.

Organizing Your Essay

After determining what information to include in your essay, you face the challenge of deciding how to organize that information. Again, the instructions themselves often give suggestions. Sometimes they are very clear and precise, as in the English essay exam that follows. Read through the instructions, and see if you have any questions about how to proceed.

> Use the following quotation as the starting point for your discussion of a major theme in the works we have read.
>
> "Let me hear no smooth talk of death from you, Odysseus, light of councils. Better, I say, to break sod as a farm hand for some poor country man, on iron rations, than lord it over all the exhausted dead."
>
> Suggested itinerary: First discuss in two to five sentences the context of the quote for the work it comes from (who is talking to whom about what; what has just happened; what is about to happen). This is the only place in the answer where you need to give plot synopsis.
>
> Next, discuss in three to ten sentences the general theme that the quote embodies. (Note: A statement of theme is a complete sentence/thought—for example, "death is final.") In this stage, define major terms/concepts.

Next, discuss how the work containing the quote develops this theme throughout; pay particular attention to any change or development that the work makes by its conclusions. (about one to two pages)

Finally, discuss how the other works we've read treat the same theme (about 1/4–1/2 page per work); spend more time on the works we spent more time on in class. (That is, if the quotation comes from the *Odyssey*, then discuss how *Medea* treats the same theme, and vice versa.)

This instructor has provided a detailed outline for students to follow: he tells them what to write in each section, how much to include in each section, and what order to put the information in, and he even provides parenthetic definitions for terms such as *context* and clarification of potentially ambiguous instructions (see the final paragraph).

The students in this class were fortunate to have an instructor who provided so much information, but you shouldn't expect your instructors to give this much help. More likely, the assignments or exam questions you receive will be similar to those provided for the final essay exam in the management course on organizational behavior on p. 663. Consider again question 2 from that exam:

> **Compare** and **contrast** the <u>paths of Native Americans, African Americans, Latinos, Asian Pacific Americans, and white immigrants</u> in their <u>struggles</u> to close the <u>gap</u> between the <u>promise of democratic principles</u> and <u>actual American history and practice</u>. **What** <u>key views</u> and <u>differing attitudes</u> on <u>race and racial progress</u> are currently held by <u>members of these communities</u>?

The words printed here in bold (the imperative verbs *compare* and *contrast* and the questioning word *what*) tell what the assignment expects you to do, but they also give a cue about organization. First you could describe the similarities and differences, then move on to describing current views and attitudes.

The words underlined here (the nouns and noun phrases) tell what kind of information to include, but they also suggest an organizational scheme: describe the paths of each group in the order suggested, compare and contrast them with one another, and then describe the current views and attitudes of each group—again, in the order suggested. Note that this wouldn't be the only way to organize your essay, but it's acceptable because the question suggests it.

Drafting Your Essay

Responding to an essay question has some benefits that more open assignments lack. For example, there is no need to spend time brainstorming to find a topic or thinking about a research question because the topic has been selected for you (or the instructor will provide a limited choice). Moreover, the context for your response has been identified (the audience, circumstance, and purpose are either known or have been given within the instructions).

Analyzing the question will give you ideas about the direction of your response as well as a list of key words or phrases. With this information you can quickly draft a thesis sentence (a sentence that succinctly states your main point) and then create a brief outline that will guide the drafting of your essay. The outline also serves another purpose. If you run out of time completing the essay, your instructor can read the outline to see the other ideas you had planned to cover. An outline that demonstrates an understanding of the topic and a detailed plan for responding to the question may influence the instructor's review of your work.

Careful planning before you start to write should help the paragraphs fall in a logical order the first time through, making your response neat and easy to read. Try to focus on the topic and stick to your outline. However, stop a few times and reread what you have written to make sure you're staying on track. Also, be sure to leave margins on both sides of the page so you can add details as you reread and review the essay. Write as neatly as you can so that the instructor doesn't have to struggle to decipher your handwriting.

If there is time and if it's appropriate, you may want to create a small chart or graph to illustrate an important point. Just don't spend so much time creating visual elements that you don't write enough to completely respond to the question.

Reviewing Your Work

In a timed situation, keep an eye on the clock as you write so that you have time to do a final review of your work. There will be limited opportunity for revision, but you can proofread for misspelled or inappropriate words, add details, make deletions, and correct grammatical or punctuation errors. You should also reread the essay question before reviewing your work so that the question is fresh in your mind. With the question in mind, you may see opportunities to add key words or phrases or respond more fully to the instructions embedded in the question.

If essay exams cause you difficulty or undue stress, you may want to look for on-campus or electronic sources for assistance. Many schools have writing, learning, or counseling centers that offer information to help students feel more comfortable about taking tests. Furthermore, a great many Web sites are devoted to helping students do well on essay exams. For example, the University of Chicago Counseling and Resource Service Web site (http://counseling.uchicago.edu/vpc/) has links to many such sites under the heading *Test Taking*.

Sample Student Essay Exam

You may find it helpful to see how one student responded to an essay question. The question presented here was one of ten essay questions on a final exam in organizational communication. The students had to answer all ten questions, and each one was worth ten points. The final exam counted for twenty-five percent of the final grade. This was a take-home exam that the students were given one week in advance.

The question begins with an unusual imperative (*imagine*) that hints that this question will describe a situation. In this way, it is similar to the question on p. 671. It is also similar to that example because in both cases it would be easy for students to answer the wrong question if they did not read carefully. If students stopped reading at the second sentence of this sample, they might write an essay about how to change the employee culture to empower employees. However, the final sentence asks students to make recommendations to *implement* the desired change.

Colleen Kanet earned all ten points for her response because she gave several recommendations and explained the value of each recommendation. She gave enough detail to demonstrate that she understood the question and knew how to answer it without overwhelming the reader with irrelevant or superfluous information. Even though this essay is only one paragraph, she gives a brief introduction (the first sentence) and a conclusion (the final sentence) that use words from the question to frame her response, and she uses transitions to move from one recommendation to the next (*first, also, further*) within the body of the essay.

Organizational Communication Final Exam Question

Imagine that a company that has been structured according to the principles of scientific management for seventy-five years has decided that they should adopt a more modern approach to organizing. They turn to you as a consultant and ask how they can change the employee culture so that employees will be empowered to solve their own problems rather than always approaching a supervisor for decisions. Based on your understanding of organizational culture and communication, what recommendations would you offer this company to help them implement this change?

Colleen Kanet's Response

Since scientific management has been the structure of this organization for seventy-five years it is important to take great care in assuring that this change will go as smoothly as possible. First of all, it is highly important to inform the organization of this change as early as possible. This will allow employees to get used to the idea. To make workers view the change positively, it is important to point out the advantages of the change. You could discuss how the change will benefit the organization as a whole (increase organization's reputation) and how it will affect employees individually (health benefits, job stability, increased technology to make jobs faster, easier and more organized). It would also be wise to create training sessions to allow employees to have hands-on experience and understand how the new operation will work before it is actually implemented. It is also imperative to make sure that employees have what they need to make a smooth transition, such as software or communication needs. Employees would be kept updated on ongoing changes. Further, it is essential that management makes sure that employees are committed to making this change and that they have all the skills and resources to do so. Using these methods will ensure a much smoother transition to the modern approach of organizing.

ONLINE COMMUNICATION

Instructors and students communicate online with one another about administrative matters (attendance, due dates, assignments) and substantive concerns (academic content of the course). Even in courses that are not entirely online, many instructors use e-mail, bulletin boards, and course chat rooms to reinforce face-to-face classroom meetings. The guidelines in this section will help you produce and distribute texts that are appropriate for the electronic environments commonly found in college courses today. The way you communicate online can have a significant impact on how you are perceived by your classmates and your instructor, which in turn can affect how well you perform in the course.

Although you may have been communicating online for years, take a moment to examine the ways you communicate and make sure they are appropriate for an academic environment. Many people use e-mail for keeping in touch with friends and relatives and visit chat rooms to talk with people with similar interests. Just as a casual face-to-face conversation with a friend is different from a conversation with an instructor or a supervisor, your online communication should reflect its context. This section will present guidelines for using e-mail in academic and workplace environments. Then it will discuss considerations to keep in mind when responding to class chats or bulletin boards.

Using E-mail

Although e-mail has become easy and commonplace today, in an academic context it is important to respect rules of conduct, grammar, and style and to know how to regularly use the organizational features of your e-mail system. As the following pages explain and as Figure 13.1 illustrates, carefully prepared e-mails can enhance your interactions in the academic environment.

Netiquette

There are a lot of issues to consider when you use e-mail to respond to academic or workplace messages, not the least of which are basic rules commonly referred to as netiquette.

FIGURE 13.1
Sample of an
Effective E-mail

> Limit the use of all uppercase letters (caps) to emphasize one or two words; never type an entire message that way. Text that appears in all caps in e-mail is the equivalent of shouting.

> Limit the use of italics for emphasis. They may not be visible on some e-mail programs, and they are difficult to read on the screen.

> Avoid sending angry messages. Conflicts can accelerate quickly in the faceless electronic medium. You're usually better off handling conflicts in person.

> Only send messages that people need. Although people commonly send jokes and games by e-mail, send them only to those you know will appreciate receiving them.

> Send copies of your messages only to people who need the information or have requested copies.

> Limit each message to one topic; you get a better response that way.

> Be aware that most e-mail systems automatically include the original message in any reply that you send. If the recipient will not need a copy of the original message, delete it before sending your reply. However, don't reply with just "okay." The reader may not recall what you're saying okay to.

> Do not send mass mailings or copies of a message to everyone in your address book. This is the electronic equivalent of junk mail. Also, sending mass messages slows down the system for everyone—it could even shut down the system if there are a lot of names in your address book.

> Avoid multiple or lengthy attachments. Not everyone has a high-speed Internet connection, so be considerate of your readers' time and patience.

Privacy

One of the most important issues to consider when using e-mail is privacy. Be careful what you say in an e-mail message because you can never know who will see it. Once you press *Send*, you lose control of your text. The recipient can forward it to others, copy and paste it into another message, or copy it and use it in other documents. Furthermore, many organizations (particularly in the workplace) routinely monitor electronic messages that pass through their servers. In fact, electronic messages can even be retrieved by a computer-savvy person after they have been deleted. Follow this good advice: "Don't ever write anything in an e-mail message that you wouldn't want your mother to read."

Grammatical Correctness

Be sure to use appropriate grammar in your e-mail and postings. A friend may not care about punctuation, grammar, or capitalization, but an instructor, workplace colleague, or supervisor may think you're sloppy or careless if you don't use standard English. Many e-mail systems have a spell checker that will catch some, but not all, errors. If yours does not, you can create your message using word processing software that has spell checkers and grammar checkers and then copy it into e-mail. Pay attention to the grammatical and typographical format of messages that you receive from others in your class or work group. Be prepared to modify your messages if the people you work with have higher standards of correctness than you are accustomed to.

Also be sure to notice how those you correspond with use abbreviations and emoticons. It is common practice in informal online communication, especially in instant messaging, to abbreviate common phrases. For example, *by the way* becomes *btw, before* becomes *b4,* and *for what it's worth* becomes *fwiw*. However, these abbreviations are not acceptable in formal academic communication.

Emoticons are characters made up of standard punctuation marks to express emotion, such as the smiling face :-) (to denote humor, happiness, or sarcasm) and the frowning face :-((to denote sadness or anger). Emoticons, also commonly used in instant messaging, are unlikely to be acceptable in academic texts.

Proofreading

Before pressing the Send button, reread your e-mail message. In particular, make sure you typed in the recipient's correct address. It's all too easy to send a message to the wrong person, especially if you are using addresses stored in an electronic address book or folder. If your instructor and your girlfriend are both named Mary, you could easily make an embarrassing mistake.

Subject Lines

Include a subject line that is both specific and helpful. Most people struggle to sort through spam and legitimate messages in their e-mail and will delete any that lack a subject line, especially if they don't know or aren't expecting mail from the sender. When you are writing to a friend, a subject line that says "Hi" is acceptable. But in the classroom or workplace, the subject line on an e-mail message is the equivalent of the subject line in a memo. It should be descriptive enough to convey the main topic of the message. For example, explicit subject lines such as "Visuals for evaluation assignment?" "Is this plagiarism?" and "Due date for evaluation?" make it very clear what the reader can expect in your message.

Greeting and Closing

Most e-mail systems automatically produce To and From headings. In this respect e-mails mimic memo format, which does not require a greeting ("Dear Alice,") or a closing ("Sincerely,"). However, you should put your name and contact information, including your e-mail address, at the bottom of your message to ensure that the recipient knows who sent it.

System Features

Most e-mail systems offer a variety of features that can save you time and frustration. It's a good idea to learn to use the features your particular system offers.

> An *electronic address book* enables you to enter information about people you correspond with regularly. You can usually create an alias, or nickname, for each entry so that you don't have to type in the full e-mail address. You can also create group entries: for example, an alias for your entire family.

> *Folders* enable you to store old messages. Storing them in your inbox will make it overcrowded and unmanageable, and your server may not allow

you an infinite amount of storage space. Creating a filing system to store important messages will become increasingly important as you use e-mail for school and work.

> *Signature files* enable you to automatically insert contact information about yourself—such as name, address, phone number, and so on—at the end of each message.

Participating in Online Discussions

Over the past few years, many instructors have taken advantage of new media to encourage conversation among their students beyond the typical classroom setting. In some cases, courses are taught entirely online and the only opportunity to discuss course content is through an electronic medium. In other cases, electronic media augment in-class discussion and out-of-class work. The following pages describe the differences among various electronic options and provide guidelines on participating appropriately. Be aware, however, that if an instructor asks you to participate in an electronic forum, he or she may have additional guidelines for you to follow.

Such guidelines may go beyond listing conventions for use; they might require a specific amount of participation. Even if an instructor does not require participation, there are benefits to be gained by joining online discussions. For example, you can use the electronic forum to get answers to questions about the course or specific assignments, to clarify your understanding of readings or in-class discussion, or to get feedback from peers about your writing or ideas.

Listservs and Discussion Boards

A listserv is a collection of e-mail addresses for a group of people who sign up to discuss a particular topic. The listserv has an address that enables individuals to post e-mail messages simultaneously to all list members. As a member of a listserv, you would receive all messages posted to the list by other members, and all members would receive all messages that you post to the list.

Listservs are popular in many arenas outside of school, but they are also one way that instructors keep in touch with students and sometimes foster discussion. Instructors routinely use course listservs to send reminders to students, make minor changes to the schedule, or announce class cancellations.

Discussion boards are similar to listservs, but they exist on a Web site. Whereas listserv messages automatically come to your inbox as long as you belong to the list and you can post messages to the list from your e-mail account, with a discussion board you have to visit the Web site to participate in the discussion. Discussion boards often display multiple

FIGURE 13.2
Effective Posting to
an Online Class
Discussion

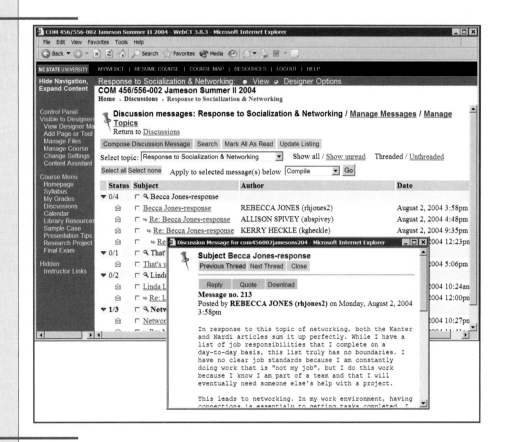

topics (sometimes called threads); you choose the topic you want to discuss. The messages on a discussion board are archived, or kept on file, so that you can read what everyone else has said before posting your own message (see Figure 13.2).

As with listservs, instructors who use discussion boards often require (and sometimes grade) participation. Many instructors use either course discussion boards or listservs to post questions or discussion topics and ask students to respond to the questions outside of class. Participation in these online discussions can be helpful to students as well for generating ideas or getting feedback.

Guidelines for Participating in a Listserv or Discussion Board

Most of the guidelines regarding e-mail (pp. 676–680) apply equally to participation in listservs and discussion boards. In addition, the following suggestions are useful.

> Take the time to compose a fully developed, coherent message that will initiate or contribute to the discussion. When you begin a discussion or respond to your instructor or classmates, you are not communicating in real time, so there's no excuse for sloppy writing or sloppy thinking.

> Feel free to ask follow-up questions or ask for clarification if you don't understand what someone else has written. This is the whole point of discussion—to add to everyone's understanding.

> Stay focused on the topic. Ask questions, add comments, explore tangential ideas, but make sure that everything you write is relevant to the discussion.

> Never present someone else's thoughts or ideas as your own. If you are citing some type of research or external source for support of your ideas, tell readers what that source is. If appropriate, include a link to an Internet source so that readers can verify or examine your support. Be cautious about reposting someone else's copyrighted material; limit the number and extent of such quotes, and make sure to post the content in an environment in which it will be discussed and critiqued.

> Feel free to disagree, but do so politely. Avoid making personal attacks or racist remarks. Do not threaten anyone.

> Do not send spam. Sending spam—unwelcome or excessive messages—clogs up inboxes and discussion board space. Take the time to write a coherent, thoughtful message rather than multiple short messages.

> Do not post jokes, chain letters, personality quizzes, and so forth. If you want to share something with the group that is off topic, create a new thread, or topic space, for that material.

Chats and MOOs

A chat (short for chat room) is a virtual space that provides participants the opportunity to communicate *synchronously:* the communication takes place in real time. (Listservs and discussion boards, in contrast, provide *asynchronous* communication.) Because chats occur in real time, the pace of conversation is much faster than on a listserv or discussion board. It may be difficult or impossible to keep up with all the messages being posted (streaming); but usually they are archived, so you can go back to see what you missed.

Instructors may create one general chat room that can be used throughout the term to discuss any topic pertaining to the course, or they may create topic-specific chats to accompany particular readings or assignments, or they may have both generic and specific chats. Like discussion boards, chats are frequently used in online courses. However, chats enable the class to "meet" in the virtual space at an appointed day and time to discuss a particular topic. Again, in both traditional classroom and online courses, instructors may require or grade participation in the course chat.

A MOO is a MUD (Multi-User Domain), Object Oriented: a text-mediated virtual environment on the Internet in which participants use words to create spaces, often called rooms, where they gather to interact with one another and the virtual objects that they create within those spaces. Using specific codes, sequences of characters, and terminology, participants move from room to room, picking up and examining objects, engaging in conversation, building new spaces, adding objects to spaces, and so forth. MOOs are more commonly used for distance education and for events such as online conferences, but some instructors integrate them into traditional courses as well.

In both chats and MOOs, it is common practice to create an identity for yourself. In other words, you create an online persona with a different name and characteristics from those you have in the real world. Always check with your instructor about the extent to which he or she will allow you to change your identity for a course chat or MOO.

Guidelines for Participating in a Chat or MOO

All the guidelines for using e-mail (pp. 676–680), and all but the first guideline for listservs and discussion boards (pp. 680–682), apply in chat rooms and MOOs. In addition, here are some unique guidelines for chats and MOOs.

> Avoid writing long messages. Because the communication is happening in real time, the longer your message, the more you will miss of what others are saying and the longer you will interrupt the flow of conversation.

> Learn the acronyms that are conventional for the particular group you are chatting with. For example, write *btw* instead of *by the way*, *fyi* instead of *for your information*, *lol* instead of *laugh out loud*. The group may even use shorthand such as *u* for *you* and *b4* for *before*. However, be aware that most instructors do not accept such acronyms and shorthand in assignments and exams.

> Be patient with typographical errors—your own and those of others in the chat room. When people communicate in real time, they type rapidly and are likely to make mistakes. If you cannot understand what has been written, ask a follow-up question or request clarification.

> Remember that if you write something and no one responds, you may repeat it but should not complain about the lack of response. If you still get no response, frame your point or question in a different way, or move on to a different point.

> Be aware that MOO spaces often provide guidelines for acceptable behavior. Check to see if there is a Conventions or Etiquette space that provides information about behaving appropriately in that domain.

14
Writing Portfolios

A *PORTFOLIO* IS A COLLECTION OF WORK ASSEMBLED TO DEMON-STRATE THE RANGE, VARIETY,

and skill of an individual. Portfolios are used by artists, architects, photographers, fashion designers, and other professionals in the visual arts in a variety of situations, such as applying to graduate school, interviewing for a job, or making a presentation to a prospective client. Portfolios are also used by professional writers, such as journalists and technical writers, for the same purposes.

In academic settings, instructors often ask students to create portfolios of their work as a way of demonstrating what they have accomplished during a course, how they have developed as writers, and what they have learned about their own writing processes. If an instructor asks you to develop a writing portfolio, he or she will probably give you instructions on what to do. This chapter offers background information about various types of portfolios, including information about audiences, circumstances, and purposes. It also presents guidelines for constructing a portfolio.

Portfolios may be tangible artifacts (texts printed on sheets of paper and then inserted into a manila folder or fastened into a binder) or electronic documents (individual Web pages forming a personal Web portfolio). Regardless of the medium used to produce the portfolio, the material contained in it is essentially the same. Thus you can use the suggestions in this chapter to create either one.

❯ **bedfordstmartins.com/
visualage**

*For samples of student-
produced portfolios,
click on*
CHAPTER 14 ❯ **EXAMPLES**

Portfolios in Context

As with any document, a writing portfolio exists within a context—for specific audiences, circumstances, and purposes. This chapter focuses on portfolios created in an academic context, but you should be aware that there are other contexts as well. The discussion that follows will mention some of those other contexts as an example of the differences to consider when creating a portfolio for use outside the classroom.

Audience

There are two primary audiences for an academic portfolio: the instructor and the student who creates the portfolio. The instructor will be a critical but supportive reader. Being familiar with the conventions of writing portfolios, he or she will likely provide detailed instructions about what to include, how to organize the material, and how to present it. In some instances instructors give students some freedom in choosing and organizing material, but those choices still must meet certain guidelines for appropriateness.

As a student, you are your own audience in the sense that you can learn a great deal about how to improve your writing through the very act of assembling the portfolio materials. The process of reading, selecting, revising, and writing about one's writing provides an opportunity for reflection that can be a powerful learning experience.

Outside of the composition classroom, portfolios have other audiences. Students who plan for careers as journalists or technical writers, for example, will create portfolios that demonstrate their skill at writing within journalistic or technical genres. They will develop their portfolios for an audience of experienced professionals who have the authority to make decisions about hiring. This type of portfolio demonstrates an individual's suitability for a particular job or career.

Circumstances

It is likely that you will be required to create an academic portfolio as the final project for a writing course. Its purpose will be to illustrate your development as a writer and demonstrate your competency in meeting the course requirements. Your primary reader (the instructor) will have a set of expectations about the portfolio's contents, having read many others in the past. This experience will affect the instructions he or she gives. For example, the instructor may allow a great deal of freedom in choosing pieces to include (sometimes called an *open portfolio*) so that the range of each student's skill is evident. Or the instructor may decide that everyone should follow a similar format and include specific types of documents within the portfolio (sometimes called a *closed portfolio*), making assessment more uniform.

Compiling the portfolio is likely to be a culminating event of the course, occurring at the end of a term, although there may be opportunities for the instructor or your classmates to review the portfolio's contents before you submit it. For example, you may be required to bring the portfolio to a conference with your instructor as a work in progress one or more times prior to the due date.

Occasionally, portfolios are carried over from one course to the next—or even throughout a student's entire college career. In these circumstances, it is important for the portfolio to demonstrate the full scope of a student's writing experiences and development.

❯ **bedfordstmartins.com/
visualage**

For links to more information about this type of portfolio, click on
CHAPTER 14 ❯ **LINKS**

Another use of academic writing portfolios is to gain exemption from a particular course. For example, at North Carolina State University some students are eligible to submit a portfolio of their writing for review prior to taking freshman composition. If the portfolio meets certain criteria, the student gets credit for the course without actually having to take it.

A portfolio for use outside the classroom would demonstrate your skill as a writer to a potential employer. As you gained experience and developed new skills, you would continually revise and update it. In fact, just as you will revise your résumé frequently over the course of your career, in a profession that uses portfolios you will regularly revise that as well. The people who review your portfolio will be assessing what you have accomplished and what you are capable of doing.

Purposes

Your purpose in producing a portfolio is to demonstrate your improvement and strengths as a writer. You want the reader to recognize your achievements and credit your accomplishments. In an academic setting, you're obviously trying to get a good grade; but more than that, you want to impress the reader with your diligence, attention to detail, ability to follow instructions, and overall development as a writer. Because a great deal is riding on your performance in the portfolio, you need to take extra care in gathering, selecting, and organizing the material you include.

If the instructor gives specific guidelines about how to present the material, you should follow them closely. Think carefully about what you are trying to accomplish with your portfolio before you put it together. Spend some time at an office supply store looking at all the options for binders, page protectors, dividers, and so forth. Your portfolio will be a representation of what you are capable of, so be sure to choose the most appropriate way to demonstrate your skills.

If you are creating the portfolio for a class, your instructor will probably tell you whether he or she wants it on paper or electronically. But outside the classroom, you have the opportunity to choose. Before you decide, you should think carefully about the audience, circumstances, and purposes of your portfolio. Who will be reading your portfolio? Why will they read it? How will they gain access to it? Do you want something you can carry with you when you go on job interviews? Do you want something you can link to from a business or personal Web site? By answering these questions, you should be able to determine the type of portfolio that will work best for you.

Creating Your Portfolio

There are three basic steps involved in creating a portfolio. First you have to plan what to include, then you have to choose the materials outlined in your plan, and finally you have to assemble those materials. The rest of this chapter provides detailed guidance for completing these steps.

Planning Your Portfolio

Regardless of the details about content, one thing is certain: you will not be able to create your portfolio overnight. A portfolio, by its very nature, is a collection that develops over time. Therefore, as soon as you know you'll need to create one, you should start thinking about how to keep track of appropriate material.

First, make sure you understand exactly what you are expected to include (see p. 686). Once you know what you need, make a checklist to keep track of what you have already completed and what is still needed. For example, see the following sample portfolio assignment and a checklist as one student might have created it.

Sample Writing Portfolio Assignment
For this course you will complete a report, a position paper, an evaluation, and a proposal. You will receive feedback from me on drafts of all of these assignments and from your peers on three of them. For your portfolio, choose any three of these assignments and revise them to include in your portfolio. For one of the assignments that was peer reviewed, include all your preliminary notes (such as brainstorming activities or other activities from

the "Working on Your Assignment" section of the textbook), your context analysis worksheet, all drafts, the notes from your peer reviewer, and the feedback I provided. For all three assignments, include your response to the "Taking Stock" questions at the end of the relevant chapter in Part 1 of the textbook. You should also include at least five pages of writing from any other course you are taking this semester. This work can be one five-page (or slightly longer, but no more than eight pages) text or a series of shorter assignments.

Create a cover page, a table of contents, and an introduction for your portfolio. In your introduction, explain the audience, circumstance, and purpose for each of the assignments and describe what you learned about writing from completing that assignment. For the material that is not from this course, explain why you chose to include it and add what you think you might do to improve it if you had an opportunity to revise it. Put all materials in a report cover, folder, or thin three-ring binder that will hold the pages in place. Use dividers to separate each assignment, and label the dividers with the type of assignment. Number all pages consecutively throughout the portfolio.

Sample Checklist for a Writing Portfolio

☐ Assignment from this course (Position Paper)

☐ Assignment from this course (Proposal)

☐ Assignment from this course with all peripheral materials (Evaluation)

☐ Assignments from another course totaling at least five pages (Biology 101 lab report, 2 pages; World History 101 essay, 4 pages)

☐ Cover page

☐ Table of contents

☐ Introduction

☐ Binder

☐ Dividers

☐ Numbers on all pages

Second, if the portfolio will be hard copy, develop a system for keeping copies of drafts, revision notes, peer-review responses, instructor responses, and final versions of every text you create that could potentially be included. You may want to invest in a set of folders with pockets so that every document connected to each assignment has its own folder. Be sure to make back-up versions of every document that you create on the computer. This is especially important in developing an electronic portfolio.

Third, throughout the semester keep in mind the criteria your instructor provided for the portfolio. If you have to write descriptions for each entry, write them while the assignment is fresh in your mind. If you have to write reflections on each piece, begin this step as soon as you finish the piece, and add to it as you get feedback from classmates or the instructor. Completing the "Taking Stock" questions at the end of each chapter in Part 1 for which you have completed an assignment will generate a wealth of information for writing a reflective essay.

Finally, if you are allowed to submit material from other courses, regularly analyze all your other writing assignments to see if they meet the criteria for the portfolio. As you find suitable materials, note them on your checklist. Be aware, however, that it's important to be flexible and choose the best materials, so keep an open mind about what to include.

Choosing Materials for Your Portfolio

Your instructor will provide guidelines for what to include in the portfolio—in the course syllabus, a specific assignment sheet, a Web site, or some combination of those. Here are some of the typical materials that you may be asked to include, as well as questions to consider in clarifying your particular situation.

> **Assignments from this course.** Do you need to include every assignment? specific assignments? Do you have a choice about which assignments to include? How many assignments must be included? Is a specific number of pages required?

> **Drafts and revisions.** Should you include all drafts? specific drafts? Can you do additional revision before including them in the portfolio?

> **Peer reviews.** Should you include notes from classmates about your drafts? Do you need to demonstrate how you responded to those reviews?

> **In-class writing or homework.** Are you expected to include any of the less formal writing you did for this course? For example, would you include any of the context analyses that accompany the assignments in Part 1 of this textbook? Do you need to include your brainstorming lists?

> **Reflective writing.** Are you expected to include material written specifically about your writing process in this course? Would you submit that reflective work as an introduction? Should there be a reflection for each piece? Could you use the "Taking Stock" questions from the chapters in Part 1 of this book as the basis for your reflections, or could you just include your answers to those questions?

> **An introduction.** As in most academic portfolios, will yours open with some type of introduction? See the next section of this chapter for suggestions on how to write the introduction.

> **Descriptions of each piece.** Are you required to describe the context for each piece?

> **Materials from other situations.** Can you include documents written for other courses, an internship, or a job? How many such pieces can you include? Should you include drafts?

> **Table of contents.** Do you need to create a table of contents? If so, how should pages be labeled and numbered?

If your instructor has specified what to include, you may not have a lot of choices. However, if he or she has given you some freedom, you may have to think about what you have written that best meets the established criteria. For example, if an instructor for a first-year writing course wants to see your three best papers out of five written for the course using this textbook, you should reread all your papers, compare them to the features of the genre described in the appropriate chapter in Part 1, review the feedback you received from the instructor and your classmates, and determine how well you fulfilled the purpose of the assignment. Alternatively, the instructor might want to see papers that demonstrate how your writing has changed over the term, which suggests a chronological approach. In this case, be sure to include drafts as well as final versions. Or you might do a further revision on an earlier paper to show what you have learned since writing it at the beginning of the course (if the instructor permits further revision).

Writing Specifically for Your Portfolio

Although most of the material that goes into your portfolio will have been written to complete other assignments, you will likely have to create some texts specifically for and about the portfolio. For example, the instructor may require a brief description of the context for each piece. Unless otherwise instructed, one paragraph that explains the audience, circumstances, and purpose for each text should be sufficient. This description should occur immediately before the text. In portfolios created for the workplace, these descriptions are especially useful because they may be the only cue the reader has about whether you achieved your goal in creating a particular text.

Most academic portfolios begin with some type of introductory document written specifically about the portfolio. This document can take many forms, and the instructor will probably give specific directions. Here are some of the types of information you may have to include in your introduction.

> **An overview of the contents.** What will the reader see in this portfolio? What types of documents are included? An overview may be similar to the preface of a book that briefly describes each item, identifying it by title and genre. If the instructor has not requested individual descriptions for each piece, you might mention each one's context instead.

> **A rationale for your selections.** Why did you include each text in this portfolio? What criteria did you use in the selection process? What do you want the reader to see or learn from reading each piece?

> **An evaluation of your work.** What is good about each piece? What might make it better? (If you are required to create an evaluation, be sure to review Chapter 5 so that you include all the necessary information: criteria you base the evaluation on, evidence to support the evaluation, and so

forth. You can also refer to other chapters in this book for determining appropriate criteria for the genres included in your portfolio.)

> **A reflection on your development as a writer.** What have you learned from this course? How do the documents demonstrate changes in your writing? Which one is your best piece? Why is it the best? What weaknesses have you overcome? How did you overcome them? What weaknesses do you still need to work on? What did you learn from suggestions made by the instructor or classmates? (The "Taking Stock" section at the end of each chapter in Part 1 of this textbook can also provide the basis for a reflective essay.)

Figure 14.1 shows how a student created an introduction for a portfolio for a writing class.

Assembling Your Portfolio

Some instructors give specific guidelines for assembling the portfolio, whereas others allow students to use their own judgment. Be sure you check the syllabus or assignment sheet for your instructor's requirements. If there are no instructions about organization, the following suggestions may be useful.

> **Create a cover or homepage.** For a print portfolio, the cover page can be as simple as your name, the instructor's name, the course title and section, and the date. For either a print or an electronic portfolio, it can be a complex, highly visual representation of your work. Unless you have specific instructions, you can design the cover or homepage as a personal expression or representation of your work. However, avoid excessive visuals that are irrelevant and may distract readers from the content. In an electronic portfolio, a homepage should also display an index or menu that links the reader to each item in the portfolio. Subsequent pages should repeat those links or have a special link that returns the reader to the homepage.

> **Create a table of contents for a print portfolio.** Tables of contents enable the reader to see quickly what is included and to easily access the material. The contents should identify each piece and the page number where it starts. You will have to add page numbers, which can be confusing because most of the documents will already have page numbers. Create a system that avoids confusion, such as putting the new numbers in a different position on the pages, using a different font for the new page numbers, or printing the new page numbers in color. Use the new numbering system consistently throughout the portfolio. Wait until the portfolio is complete before numbering the pages and creating the table of contents.

> **Write an introduction.** This should be the first item after the table of contents in a print portfolio. In an electronic portfolio, the introduction may appear on the homepage or on a separate page. If your instructor has not given specific instructions for the introduction, see Writing Specifically for Your Portfolio (p. 690) for ideas.

FIGURE 14.1
Introduction for a
Writing Portfolio

Beth Carson
April 28, 2004
Professor Borgese
Eng. 111

Portfolio

This portfolio represents the best examples of my writing from my first-year composition course. I have included the following papers to demonstrate both my development as a writer and my ability to write for different purposes and audiences: a personal essay, a position paper, an evaluation paper, and a community–based writing project. One of the first writing critiques I received in this class urged me to remember that "thought is motion," and I have been working to develop stronger direction and to be more concise in my own writing ever since.

Writing selections from my first-year composition course:

- *Personal Essay*—titled "Ties that Bind," this piece, based closely on my own experiences, is about the struggles, rewards, and frequent humor of being from a small town. The intended audience for this essay is fellow students who may not be from a small town.

- *Position Paper*—this essay, published in the school newspaper, argues that scholarships at our school should be granted on the basis of academic achievement and financial need only.

- *Evaluation*—a paper that evaluates the effectiveness of using a car safety belt with children 12 and under. Sources include crash statistics, information provided by car manufacturers online, other online information, and articles.

- *Community Writing Project*—from a class assignment on writing for a community organization. Along with some other women in my class, I volunteer at a shelter for mothers and children who are homeless; this piece is a fund-raising pamphlet which I wrote the text for, which is currently being used by the shelter to solicit funding from individuals and corporations.

> **Arrange the material logically.** Your instructor may have prepared guidelines about how to arrange the material, in which case you should make sure you understand those guidelines and follow them closely. If there are no guidelines, think carefully about the purpose of the portfolio that your instructor discussed in class or described in the syllabus or assignment sheet. If the purpose is to show your development as a writer, you could start with your weaker papers and build to your best work. If the purpose is to show your achievement, your best work should come first. If the purpose is to demonstrate relevance to a theme, arrange the papers according to that theme.

> **Label each item.** To avoid confusion, create some type of label for every item in the portfolio, such as Final Draft: Report; Peer Review: Evaluation; or Context Analysis: Proposal. It will be less confusing if you refer to the items by label instead of by title in the introduction, table of contents, and any other descriptive elements. For one thing, the title of a report might have changed from your first draft to your final draft, so just referring to it as a report is easier for the reader. Also, if titles are longer than a single word or short phrase, including several of them in a paragraph or table of contents will be awkward and will take up more space than simpler labels would. In a print portfolio, put the labels on the first page of each item or on dividers that separate the items. In an electronic portfolio, the label will be a link to the item, but it should also appear on the page so that the reader always knows where he or she is in the portfolio.

> **Cluster related materials.** If there are several items for one assignment (for example, a context analysis, an exploratory draft, a peer-review response sheet, and a final draft for the report assignment), assemble those items in chronological order—that is, the order in which you created them. In a print portfolio, you may want to put a divider (with, for example, the label Report written on the tab) before each section. In an electronic portfolio, you may want to create a system of major and minor links, with the name of the assignment being the primary link and labels for any peripheral materials being secondary links.

> **Choose an appropriate container for a print portfolio.** Unless the instructor has specified a type of folder or binder, find something that gives your portfolio a polished appearance and makes it easy for the reader to use. A binder that holds paper with metal fasteners or plastic sleeves is difficult to lay open flat on a desk; this is cumbersome for the reader, who has to hold it open with both hands. A small three-ring binder may be preferable. Be sure that the binder you choose allows the reader to remove pages easily (so that, for example, the reader can compare a draft and a final version by laying them side by side). However, be sure that the pages cannot fall out and get out of order. Another good option is a multi-pocket folder, with a pocket for each item in the portfolio. Sheet protectors, which enable you to use a three-ring binder without punching holes in the actual documents, create a very professional look.

15

Writing for the Community

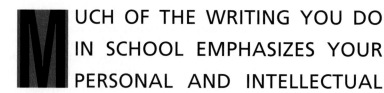UCH OF THE WRITING YOU DO IN SCHOOL EMPHASIZES YOUR PERSONAL AND INTELLECTUAL growth, enabling you to develop new skills, explore new concepts, and reach a better understanding of your own ideas, values, and feelings. In the assignments you have done for this textbook, you have written about subjects that are not directly covered in your courses and you have addressed audiences other than—or in addition to—your instructor and classmates. But the ultimate goal of those assignments was to help you develop as a writer and a thinker, as someone who can understand a complex, important topic and communicate about it clearly, persuasively, and responsibly.

In this chapter, the emphasis changes to focus on writing that serves the needs of some organization in a community beyond the college classroom. You may come to this chapter looking for a resource to help you do some writing for a community group that you are already involved with. Or your instructor may assign this writing as part of your coursework. In either case, there is a significant added dimension to your work: it will not be complete (or successful) until a representative of the organization you've been writing for says, in effect, "This is great. We can use this. We are going to print it, post it on our Web site, mail it out, hand it out, *use* it to get on with the work we do here."

What sort of community organization could you be writing for? And what sort of document could you produce that would be of use? Answers to these questions may vary widely, but almost any significant problem our society faces—homelessness, for example, or poverty, or troubled families, to name just a few—suggests possibilities. If you live in a community of, say, fifty thousand people, there are probably two dozen or more agencies that deal with such problems. All these groups need documents such as brochures describing their mission and services, newsletters to send to contributors, and written procedures for staff to follow. As an administrator with one community service organization commented: "There's so much we need to have done, I just don't have time to get to it all."

Of course, writing for the community is not limited to organizations that work with homelessness or poverty. Unless you live in a very unusual place, there are numerous other organizations that might value your assistance. For instance, is there a YMCA or YWCA near you that could use some help with its newsletter? Is there a community-action group that could use help in researching and reporting on some issue that concerns its members? Is there a local museum or historical organization that needs informative materials to pass out to visitors? Is there a group (perhaps a local visitors' bureau) that can use some sort of marketing materials—brochures, pamphlets, annotated maps, a Web site—to promote tourism in the community?

Other possibilities may exist within your campus community. Although students today are increasingly sophisticated about using computers, many people need help in using new hardware and software. The campus library or computer center probably maintains some sort of help desk, but people who work there may be tired of answering the same questions over and over. Could they use a good set of instructions that would show students how to use the campus computing system more effectively? Could they use a good set of troubleshooting procedures that would let students solve routine problems they encounter in using technology located in the library or computer center?

Diverse as community organizations are, they tend to have several common traits. Most of them are understaffed and underfunded. Most of them need to produce more documents—newsletters, brochures, public service announcements, procedures for staff to follow—than their employees have time to write. Many organizations have documents that badly need to be revised, perhaps because they are out of date or because they were put together hurriedly by someone who was trying to accomplish several other tasks at the same time. These organizations can use your help. And the writing you do for them may help you as well.

In fact, you may find that working with a community organization broadens your perspective considerably. You may learn, as one group of students did, that what they had regarded as a decaying Rust Belt community was once a thriving center of technology with a history that is now beginning to attract international attention and a future that will draw twenty-first-century technology into the area. You may learn that even a relatively affluent community has pockets of homelessness and poverty comparable to those reported in the national media. Or you may learn about the intricate diplomacy and hard work required to bring about what seems like a simple change in the world beyond your classroom.

Such lessons as these are not always easy and fun. Nevertheless, there are many reasons to persevere. Writing for the community can be excellent preparation for the work you will do on co-op jobs and internships and in your career. This last statement may sound strange because the topics you write about may have little or nothing to do with your intended career. And you may assume—as many undergraduates do—that you will have to do little or no writing for your career. But this assumption is wrong. Professionals in virtually every career, even science and engineering, have to do substantial amounts of writing.

One comprehensive report, synthesizing some twenty large-scale surveys, indicates widespread agreement on two points: (1) college graduates spend a good percentage of their time (on average, 20%) in writing, and (2) the ability to write well is extremely important for most college graduates. In a more limited survey, graduates of one technological university reported that the ability to write effectively was either "essential" (50%) or "very important" (40%) to succeeding in their careers. Thus writing for the community can be a way to begin developing the knowledge and abilities needed to function effectively in the world beyond the classroom.

This chapter will present examples of some of the kinds of writing you may be asked to do for an organization in your community, and then it will answer questions students frequently ask when they perform this sort of work for the first time.

Writing Successfully for the Community

If you are asked to choose a community group to write for, make the choice carefully. Nothing is more crucial to your success than the choice of an organization with which to work. Do not automatically decide to

Exercise

Talk with people who are succeeding at the kind of career you hope to have. Talk with students doing co-ops or internships at companies where you would like to work. Ask them what kinds of writing they routinely have to do. Most likely they will report not only that they do a good bit of writing but that the tasks include producing one or more of the following: reports, proposals, evaluations of products or policies, and explanations of procedures they have followed. Do you notice any connections between this list and some of the chapter titles in this book?

work with the first organization that occurs to you or one that happens to be conveniently located. Instead, consider the following questions: Are the organization's goals and activities important to you? Are you willing to spend some time learning about the organization's background and the population it serves? Does your schedule permit you to spend time on-site? Do you have the skills and the temperament to work effectively in this organization? If you are already involved with an organization, chances are that your answer to most of these questions is yes.

The writing you will be asked to do may seem relatively simple; almost certainly it will not be as lengthy as other assignments for your writing course. But as you will quickly learn, these assignments can be surprisingly complex and demanding. They will require an investment of time and energy. Make sure to work with an organization where you feel your investment will pay off for both you and the organization, even if the payoff for you is as intangible as a sense of having contributed to a cause you value.

 I don't think [writing for my organization] has to involve huge amounts of time. But I think it has to be time well spent, [with the writer] taking the task very seriously. . . . The more seriously someone's willing to invest in us, the more we're willing to invest in them."

– *Tracy Neitzel, executive director of Joseph's House, a homeless shelter*

Whether you work for a community organization or a co-op/internship sponsor, your success as a writer—and, indeed, as a participant in that organization—depends largely on your understanding of the following points.

> **The organization has a distinct culture that influences much of what its members do**—not just the way they dress or interact with clients, but the way they write as well. This culture includes people's sense of the organization's mission, their customary ways of carrying out their jobs, and their attitudes toward each other and the people (clients, customers, patients) they serve. This culture also includes a sense of the organization's past and its prospects for the future. You may or may not agree with this culture. But you cannot ignore it. And you cannot write well for the organization unless you understand it.

> **Your writing may not take the form of a conventional academic essay.** At a minimum, you will need to use headings and numbered or bulleted lists. You will probably also have occasion to use pictures, text or image boxes, pull quotes, and charts or graphs. And you may have a chance to work with page layout, setting text in two or more columns and using white space to help readers see—literally—the points you are making.

> For more information on design, see **Chapter 8.**

> **Your writing may remain around the organization long after you have left.** Be aware that your work will probably have a relatively long shelf life. For example, one historical organization still hands out a brochure some undergraduates created in 1999. Another organization still gives new employees a procedures manual a student helped write in 2000.

> **Your writing will be read by a number of different stakeholders,** people who may be affected by what you write. If your writing helps them or doesn't harm them, you may never hear from these people; indeed, you may never know who they are. But if your work harms or confuses or inconveniences them, they will find ways to make their dissatisfaction known to you or, if you are no longer working with the organization, to your supervisor.

> **Your writing will have practical consequences.** People will rely on your writing to make a decision, settle an argument, carry out a procedure. They may react to it—and to you—in ways you may not be able to anticipate.

> **Your writing will become the basis for other people's conclusions about the organization and about you.** It may not be fair to judge a book/organization/person by the cover/brochure/memo. But it happens all the time. When you write for an organization outside the classroom, it will happen to you. Your readers may or may not use your work to draw conclusions about your ability as a writer, but they will certainly use it to determine the value of the organization you represent and your value as a member of that organization.

To show how these points apply to writing for community organizations, the following pages present several pieces of writing for Joseph's House and Shelter, a shelter for homeless people in a small northeastern city. The writing is typical of documents used by almost any community

> I had a woman call me out of the blue. I don't know where she got our name. She said a friend told her about us and she was thinking of giving us some money, but she didn't know anything about us. . . . For some reason I wrote her a letter and sent her a packet of stuff [including copies of a brochure and the newsletter]. About two weeks later we got a thousand-dollar donation. She's been giving us a thousand dollars a year since then. And I still don't know who she is."
>
> *– Tracy Neitzel*

organization. Accompanying each document are comments from Tracy Neitzel, the executive director of Joseph's House. These comments are also typical, not in their content but in their reflection of the attitudes and needs you will likely encounter when producing a document for an organization in the community beyond your classroom.

Sample Writing for the Community

Joseph's House and Shelter is a community-based organization, one that is not part of a state or federal bureaucracy but rather a privately run agency supported by donations and by state and federal grants. Over the course of a year, it offers both short-term and long-term housing to some eight hundred homeless people—individuals and families—some of them addicted to drugs or alcohol, some mentally ill, some victims of calamities that have exhausted the resources offered by friends and family. During the past decade the agency has grown dramatically, expanding not only its physical facilities but also the types of services it provides.

Accompanying this growth, and perhaps contributing to it, is a culture of sensitivity and respect—with regard not only to the people Joseph's House serves but also to the larger community in which it operates. Joseph's House provides homeless people with access to a number of services—programs to treat alcoholism or drug addiction, for example—that have enabled some residents to transform their lives. In fact, former residents now manage two of the major programs offered by the agency. But residents—"guests," as they are referred to by the agency—are not required to enter treatment or to make fundamental changes in their personality or character. Joseph's House is a "low demand" shelter, posing a minimum of restrictions while allowing guests as much autonomy and dignity as possible. In order to spend a night at

Joseph's House, guests must obey certain rules of safety, courtesy, and sanitation. They may not, for example, use drugs or alcohol while at Joseph's House; they may not carry a weapon. If they do, they are "referred out"—in effect, temporarily expelled. But they are not permanently excluded. As soon as they become sober, as soon as they relinquish their weapon, they may re-enter the shelter. The primary goal of the agency is not so much to transform lives as to provide food and safe shelter to people who would otherwise have none.

While maintaining this nonjudgmental, supportive culture within its own walls, Joseph's House must also exist within a larger community that can be very judgmental, even intolerant, of the homeless. As Tracy Neitzel explains, "It's somehow become safe and acceptable to write off [homeless] people, to say that this kind of person has no value so we're not going to help them. Period." Furthermore, some communities are not eager to provide locations for homeless shelters, fearing that problems experienced by the homeless will affect the larger community in which a shelter is located.

As the following pages indicate, many of the documents produced at Joseph's House are available to a wide range of audiences, including guests of Joseph's House. In creating these documents a writer does a juggling act, trying to respect the needs and values of people from very different communities while either gaining support for Joseph's House or enabling the organization to work effectively and humanely. The specifics of this juggling act are probably unique to a writer at Joseph's House. The basic situation, however, applies to writers in any organization. They must work within the culture of the organization to produce a variety of documents that accomplish the organization's purposes with a variety of readers.

The following pages present excerpts from several documents that range from relatively polished, professional work to materials that have been created in an ad-hoc manner to serve a specific need. As is often the case in community organizations, most of the documents are "in progress" or "under construction"—that is, subject to ongoing review and revision.

Brochures

Almost every community organization either wants a new brochure or needs to revise an existing one so that it is more up-to-date, more persuasive, or more professional looking. After all, brochures are one of the principal ways an organization introduces itself to the public and to prospective supporters. A great deal can ride on what the brochure says and how it delivers that message.

As a rule, brochures are organized around a set of topics or implied questions ("Who We Are," "How You Can Help") that are likely to matter to readers with an interest in the organization. Such brochures are relatively brief, often consisting of a single sheet of paper printed on the front and back and folded into three panels, or vertical columns, of text and pictures. Because they are so brief, brochures may seem simple to write. But, in fact, this very brevity makes it difficult to write a good one. There is not enough room for a lot of information, so every detail must strike the reader as significant. Moreover, the brochure's voice must be engaging and consistent with the culture of the organization, as in the two panels from the Joseph's House brochure shown in Figure 15.1.

Even though the Joseph's House brochure is one of the documents Neitzel is eager to have revised, it does do some things well. For instance, the sole statistic it contains is impressive: 7,000 nights of shelter for 800 people. That's shelter for a lot of people. In addition, phrases such as "the most vulnerable members of our community" reflect the nonjudgmental and respectful culture of the agency. Furthermore, the writer of the brochure has made judicious decisions about what information to include and exclude. On the one hand, he or she has been mindful that readers are likely to respond positively to passages such as "a warm and

FIGURE 15.1
Joseph's House and Shelter Brochure

How You Can Help

♥ Become a Sustaining Member of Joseph's House and Shelter. Make a donation on a regular basis and receive a monthly letter describing how your generosity is being used to address the needs of our homeless guests.

♥ Spend time with our guests as a Hospitality Volunteer. Welcome and support guests and share chores that keep the shelter running.

♥ Organize a group of friends or colleagues to prepare and serve a weekend meal.

♥ Seek opportunities to educate yourself and others about homelessness. Being open and honest about homelessness and sensitive to the diversity of experiences and backgrounds will reduce the stigmas and misconceptions attached to shelters and to homeless people.

74 Ferry Street
Troy, New York 12180
Phone: 518-272-2544
Fax: 518-272-9370

Who We Are

Joseph's House and Shelter is located in downtown Troy, New York and has provided shelter for thousands of homeless men, women, and children since 1983.

We offer emergency and transitional shelter and permanent supported housing to the most vulnerable members of our community.

Joseph's House provides homeless single adults and families with a warm and safe place to rest, hot nutritious meals, and access to free medical care, personal items, and laundry facilities. We provide more than 7,000 nights of shelter to approximately 800 homeless men, women, and children annually.

Advocates work with our guests to identify permanent housing opportunities and other resources in accordance with goals our guests set themselves. Our Outreach Team provides support services for adults in the community whose ability to maintain stable housing has been threatened.

Joseph's House depends on loyal volunteers and regional businesses to collaborate with us to provide these services to the homeless of our community.

> There's always the need to vet [review carefully] everything that goes out of here. . . . [D]oes this convey the respect that we want to convey? Does this convey the way we approach the work that we do? Because a lot of people are going to make their decision based on what they read about us."
>
> *– Tracy Neitzel*

safe place to rest, [and] hot nutritious meals." On the other hand, the writer has excluded details that might reinforce some readers' stereotypes of the homeless. What does it mean, for example, to say that someone's "ability to maintain stable housing has been threatened"? The specifics are probably not important or appropriate here. What matters is that readers know the agency is providing help to people who need it.

Descriptions of Policies and Procedures

Every organization—even one that is as nonjudgmental and nonrestrictive as Joseph's House—has rules, procedures, and ways of doing things that enable it to carry out its mission effectively. If the organization is small and serves a limited, homogeneous clientele, the organization may operate on unwritten rules that are part of the culture and that can be conveyed in informal conversations. But the larger the organization and the more diverse its clientele, the greater the likelihood that it will need written documents that not only specify what to do in particular situations but also explain what the organization expects of its employees and clientele and what they, in turn, may expect of the organization.

In many social groups (such as fraternities, sororities, clubs, and religious groups), these documents take the form of bylaws. At Joseph's House, the principal policies and procedures are specified in a set of House Rules and an Employee Handbook. Both documents directly affect the lives and actions of stakeholders, and each can be the basis for action—a decision, for example, about whether someone is allowed to spend the night at Joseph's House or whether an employee has been treated fairly. These internal documents, like other publications, must be consistent with the culture of the organization.

> Everything here says 'working draft'; everything's 'under construction.' Because we constantly change [our documents]. We change them all the time."
>
> *– Tracy Neitzel*

The House Rules document shown in Figure 15.2, which is relatively brief (only two pages long), clarifies what is expected of everyone—employees and volunteers as well as guests. Each rule is stated in a single sentence and elaborated upon in several additional sentences. The elaboration is intended not only to forestall misunderstanding but also to remind everyone—staff and guests alike—of the fundamentally nonjudgmental culture of Joseph's House. Certain kinds of behavior will not be

FIGURE 15.2
Joseph's House and Shelter House Rules Document

WORKING DRAFT
Joseph's House and Shelter, Inc.

House Rules

Welcome to Joseph's House and Shelter, Inc. During your stay with us we hope that you feel both comfortable and safe. To make this possible we have developed the following set of house rules and ask that you make every effort to understand and follow these guidelines. If you have any questions, please feel free to ask any staff member for a more detailed explanation.

Office Hours...9:15 a.m.–5:00 p.m.
Shelter Hours...24 hours per day
Breakfast...7:00 a.m.–8:30 a.m.
Lunch..12:00 noon–1:00 p.m.
Dinner...5:00 p.m.–6:00 p.m.
Check in..10:00 p.m.
Bedtime...11:00 p.m.*
Lights out..11:30 p.m.
Wake up...6:00 a.m.

*Guests are to go to bed but may read for last half hour.

1   **No drugs or alcohol are allowed in Joseph's House. No one who is under the influence of alcohol or non-prescription drugs will be allowed in Joseph's House at any time.** If staff on duty suspects that you have been using alcohol or illegal drugs, you will be referred out for the night. Joseph's House cannot hold a bed for anyone referred out of the shelter; however, you are welcome to return the next day if a bed is still available. We suggest that if you find yourself in this situation, you contact us first thing in the morning to determine if a bed is still available.

tolerated. But staff are expected to judge the behavior, not the person. If someone is denied shelter—for drinking, say, or for using drugs—that person will be admitted on a subsequent occasion if he or she returns to the shelter sober. According to Neitzel, Joseph's House is one of the few homeless shelters in the area that does not maintain a list of people who are permanently barred from receiving food and shelter.

2 **Smoking is not permitted in the building.** We apologize for any inconvenience this may cause. Smoking is permitted in the courtyard; however, we ask that you please utilize the ashtrays located there.

3 **All Staff, Guests, Volunteers, and NEIGHBORS must be treated with courtesy and respect.** Violence and threats of any kind are unacceptable. If you have difficulty with someone, please seek staff intervention. Violence between guests either in or out of the shelter will result in both guests being asked to leave.

4 **Joseph's House will provide shampoo, toothpaste, soap, razors, and combs to all guests.** Towels are available from staff on request. All guests are expected to shower once per day to better accommodate such a large number of people in such a small place. Your cooperation is greatly appreciated.

5 **Sexual activity is not permitted in Joseph's House.** Sexual harassment, innuendo, advances, and jokes are also banned. Even comments that may be meant as harmless can often be frightening or intimidating to others. Please make every effort to be respectful of others in the shelter. Male guests are not allowed in women's bedrooms and female guests are not to enter the men's bedrooms.

6 **Weapons of any kind are prohibited in our shelter.** If you have a weapon, please make staff aware of it and we will hold it for you when you are in the building. Staff retains the right to hold illegal weapons and may ask you to find another place to keep them (outside the shelter).

There's stuff in here that employees need to know. It's all in there for them to look back at. Maybe someone will come to me and say, 'How come we don't have [a holiday for] Rosh Hashanah?' and I'll say, 'Well, look in your Handbook. That's why we have four flexible holidays [i.e., holidays of the employee's own choosing].' It [contains] a lot of information we don't expect people to remember. A lot of this is in writing to protect the agency, especially with regard to unemployment disputes, Department of Labor disputes, lawsuits. Because the first thing that happens when you get into a dispute over unemployment is that the Department of Labor says, 'Did the employee know that?' And we say, 'Well, yeah.' And they say, 'Was it in writing somewhere?' And we have to furnish them a copy."

– *Tracy Neitzel*

An agency's clientele is not the only group that needs rules and regulations to be spelled out. The organization's employees also have a right to know what they can expect of their employer and what it can expect of them. At Joseph's House, these expectations are spelled out in the Employee Handbook, a fourteen-page document that explains pay, sick leave, other benefits, criteria for promotion, and so forth. All employees receive a copy of this handbook; they are asked to read it and sign a statement acknowledging that they have done so. This document is not a legally binding contract. However, it is a formal record that employees and supervisors may consult if a dispute arises. And it may come under legal scrutiny if an employee has a grievance with Joseph's House. An excerpt from the section titled "On the Job" is shown in Figure 15.3.

Organizational Newsletters

As with brochures, almost every organization either has or wants to have a newsletter. Typically, newsletters contain several types of information: announcements of upcoming events, letters to or from readers, and stories about recent activities or people associated with the organization. As a rule, newsletters are periodically sent to people who are involved with or interested in the organization. Consequently, readers are likely to be relatively sympathetic to the organization's goals. However, they probably will not turn to the newsletter for detailed analysis or in-depth reporting. They will most likely be attracted to stories about individuals who either carry out the work of the organization or struggle with (and, preferably, overcome) the kinds of problems the organization addresses. The goal of a newsletter may vary from one organization to another, but often its main objective is to maintain the interest and goodwill of people who have expressed an interest in the organization.

FIGURE 15.3
Excerpt from Joseph's
House and Shelter
Employee Handbook

SECTION FOUR: ON THE JOB

IF YOU ARE INJURED AT WORK

Any injury sustained on Joseph's House property or in the course of Joseph's House business should be reported to the Executive Director immediately, or in her absence, to the designated person.

PERSONAL PROPERTY

Joseph's House is not responsible for theft or damage to personal property brought on to Joseph's House property which is not necessary for performance of your duties.

SMOKING

In compliance with the New York State Public Health Law, Joseph's House has adopted policies regarding the smoking of tobacco products in the workplace. The policies strive to accommodate the needs of smoking and non-smoking employees, volunteers and guests in accordance with state law. Non-smoking employees are entitled to work in an area which is smoke-free, where no smoking occurs and where the drift of smoke from smoking areas is negligible. Smoking is allowed in the private enclosed offices of employees and in shared office space or conference space if everyone using the space agrees. No smoking is allowed in elevators, hallways, restrooms, stairways, and rooms containing photocopying equipment or other office equipment used in common. Signs are posted to identify "smoking" or "no smoking" areas. If you require additional information about the smoking policy, please contact your immediate supervisor.

STANDARDS OF CONDUCT

As an employee of Joseph's House you are expected to treat co-workers, guests and volunteers with courtesy and respect, and to perform duties in a responsible and professional manner as required for the successful operation of the agency. It is expected that your relationship with your supervisor allows for the open discussion of issues and problems. It is also expected that all information regarding guests of Joseph's House be kept strictly confidential.

CORRECTING PERFORMANCE PROBLEMS

It is expected that you work with your supervisor through a process of progressive discipline to document and resolve performance problems. The goals of progressive discipline are to minimize misunderstandings between supervisors and employees, permit employees to develop professionally, and to provide employees with notice of unacceptable conduct in sufficient time to permit self-correction and improvement.

Newsletter stories that are profiles of people who work for the organization or who are served by it are usually brief; the best ones include facts about the individual and perhaps a short quote that reflects not only his or her personality but also his or her understanding of the organization's mission. Sometimes, as in the excerpt from *Our House* (Figure 15.4), the quarterly newsletter from Joseph's House, the written text is

FIGURE 15.4
Newsletter for Joseph's House and Shelter

> Refer to Chapter 2 to review the characteristics of appropriate images.

Our Staff

NEW STAFF ADDS TO JOSEPH'S HOUSE

Adriene Banks, who previously worked at the Families in Crisis program at Unity House in Troy, began working full-time in December as our Family Counselor and Resettlement Services Co-ordinator. It's a long title for a big job that includes working to help families while they're here and staying in contact with them after they leave.

Adriene, on her way with a delivery

Adriene says one of the most satisfying parts of her job is seeing families leave the shelter and establish homes. "I see that hooking them up to community resources makes a real difference in their lives," she says.

amplified by a photograph—in this case, a smiling young woman who appears to be charging off enthusiastically on an errand associated with her job.

Sometimes newsletter pictures are chosen by default, selected from a random collection of pictures the organization happens to have on file. But when possible, it's a good idea to use pictures that capture the spirit of an individual or of the organization. The picture of Adriene Banks in Figure 15.4 is a very good example.

Newsletter stories can also take the form of narratives, usually success stories. In the narrative the person being featured usually faces some sort of problem, with the story telling what the problem was, how the person reacted to it, and how the problem was solved. As a rule, the goal is not simply to report an individual's success but to say something positive about the organization as well. The story in Figure 15.5 gives insight not only into Lenore's character but also into the way Joseph's House works to help people in predicaments like Lenore's.

> **"** [Our newsletter is] certainly not a fundraising tool. . . . It's more to raise friends—strengthen ties, keep connected to people."
>
> – Tracy Neitzel

FIGURE 15.5
Story in Joseph's
House and Shelter
Newsletter

Lenore, a twenty-two-year-old mother, came to Joseph's House with her four-year-old daughter one cold night last winter. Lenore had left an abusive relationship in another part of the state and intended to stay with relatives in Rensselaer County. When she arrived, her aunt was apologetic, but made it clear that since her own daughter, son-in-law, and three grandchildren were staying with her, there was no room for Lenore and her daughter. She suggested Lenore try Joseph's House.

Lenore was upset when she rang our doorbell. She hadn't expected to have to stay in a shelter and she was afraid of what it might be like. Would she be able to stay with her daughter? Would it be dangerous? Dirty? Where would she go next? She knew she did not want to return to her abusive relationship.

Our staff detected Lenore's stress and gently helped her adjust. They showed her around the family shelter - an apartment - like setting off limits to other guests - where Lenore and her daughter could share a room. They recommended a support group for Lenore to attend during this transition in her life, and, perhaps most important, they listened.

Our House

Our House is a publication of Joseph's House & Shelter Inc.

74 Ferry St./ Troy, NY 12180
Editor/Writer: Elizabeth Gallagher
Design: Kristina Almquist Design
Questions and suggestions about *Our House* are encouraged.
Phone: 518-272-2544
FAX: 518-272-9370

Permission to reprint is only provided if credit is given to: Our House, a publication of Joseph's House and Shelter Inc. of Troy, NY.

As Lenore began to trust the staff at Joseph's House, she began to share more of herself, and disclosed a history of abuse that began in her childhood. It was a pattern she desperately wanted to change. Joseph's House staff referred her to a therapist, who helped her begin to deal with her past.

With the help of our family counselor, Lenore and her daughter moved into their own apartment. We knew Lenore had potential to build a stable life for herself and her daughter, but we were aware that her lack of financial and social resources, and her history of abuse, would continue to pose challenges. Our resettlement team stepped in to help ease the transition from homelessness into the community.

Lenore was eager to find a job, but childcare was a concern. The Joseph's House resettlement team helped her identify reliable and safe childcare. Lenore began working at a local fast food restaurant. Soon after, with the support of the Joseph's House resettlement team, Lenore completed her GED and enrolled in a certified nurses assistant program at a local vocational school. Her daughter entered kindergarten.

Today, Lenore works with developmentally delayed adults. She states the staff at Joseph's House inspired her interest in the helping profession. She recently purchased her first new car. "I finally feel as if I am going somewhere," she said.

WISH LIST

Toiletries, especially toothpaste, toothbrushes, and deodorant
Can Opener
Household Cleaning Supplies
Diapers
Bus Tokens
Telephones
Alarm Clocks
Hand Tools

When newsletter stories report on issues, they often do so in dramatic form, focusing on a conflict or problem. The report "Welfare Reform and Homelessness" in Figure 15.6 locates the work of Joseph's House in a larger social context, identifying problems caused by state and federal efforts at welfare reform. The article's basic structure is "good news/bad news." The good news is that welfare rolls are shrinking; the bad news is that the shrinkage comes at a substantial, unforeseen price.

Serious as the problem is, the story does not try to overwhelm the reader with too many details. The chart under the subtitle ("Fewer on Welfare—But at a Cost") is not labeled, nor does it contain specific numbers. As a rule, you should avoid using such a chart; but in this context, it is quite appropriate. The arrow's upward path conveys a sense of dissonance, suggesting a general increase (in costs and demands placed on

FIGURE 15.6
Report in Joseph's House and Shelter Newsletter

Our Guests

WELFARE REFORM AND HOMELESSNESS

Fewer on Welfare—But at a Cost

Welfare reform changes enacted in New York State since 1995 have presented problems for many guests at Joseph's House and other up-state homeless shelters. The intent of these welfare changes was to help recipients move from welfare to work through training and support incentives. However, many recipients are being dropped from welfare and left without any income because of their failure to comply with new stringent eligibility demands. Welfare recipients can lose their benefits for a number of reasons, including failure to submit to mandatory drug evaluations and treatment, leaving a job without sufficient reason and not adhering to workfare training.

"When someone is homeless and is 'esanctioned' from receiving welfare, they are stuck," says Joseph's House program director Kevin O'Connor. "They have no money to secure housing. There is little we can do to help them move out of the shelter and back into the community."

The numbers of sanctioned guests at Joseph's House has been rising steadily. During the first three months of 1999, Joseph's House sheltered 17 'esanctioned' guests. O'Connor notes that 10% of February's shelter guests were sanctioned.

1998 JOSEPH'S HOUSE STATISTICS

Total Guests Sheltered:	695
Number of families sheltered:	76
Individuals receiving homeless outreach services:	128
Patients seen at Joseph's House medical clinic:	268
Tenants at the Inn at Ferry Street:	9

O'Connor says it is particularly difficult watching homeless guests who lack the skills to comprehend or comply with the new welfare standards. He has seen people suffering from mental illness and developmental disabilities dropped from the welfare rolls.

"While the state has mandated screening recipients for drug use, it hasn't taken into account mental health disorders," O'Connor says. "Psychotic symptoms, chronic depression, and mood disorders can be debilitating. Psychiatric illnesses contribute to guests' non-compliance with employment, or workfare and treatment requirements. But because the state hasn't looked for psychiatric illnesses, they've concluded these guests are only 'unmotivated' to work."

Across the state and the country, leaders are pointing to the successes of welfare reform. Nationally, public assistance enrollment is at a thirty-year low. More that 630,000 people have left N.Y. State's welfare rolls since 1995. The state notes that 317,000 former welfare recipients made 'entries to employment' during this period.

However, anti-poverty advocates point out these statistics reveal that nearly half of those who left welfare during this period are unaccounted for. They claim many former welfare recipients are actually poorer and more dependent on private social services since welfare reform. Local emergency soup kitchens and food pantries have noted a 30% surge in demand. Homeless shelters are seeing more guests without entitlements. During the first quarter of 1999, more than half of the adult guests entered Joseph's House without any income.

"People should be wary of accepting the public rhetoric on the successes of welfare reform," O'Connor says. "There are many people who are suffering more because of welfare reform. National and State leaders are trying to place more blame for welfare dependence on the recipients. They've designed the reforms to 'light a fire' under recipients in the hope they'll achieve economic self-sufficiency. This moralizing view avoids the systemic causes of poverty, and diminishes our government's commitment to addressing the needs of the poor."

homeless shelters) in an area where readers might have hoped for a decrease (in the numbers of people needing public assistance). The inset box in the lower left corner provides statistics showing how Joseph's House is responding to the problem created in part by welfare reform. Together, the two visuals imply a claim that newsletter readers are almost certain to find reassuring: in the face of an increasing social need, Joseph's House is rising to meet that need.

> The newsletters we used to put out had a whole lot of text in them, and I don't think people were reading them. Once we pulled some of the text out and started breaking up the pages, we got a lot more response on our newsletters. . . . And I've kind of learned the hard way that it's impossible to force-feed people with all the information they should have to understand homelessness in this community."
>
> – *Tracy Neitzel*

Frequently Asked Questions about Writing for the Community

When students begin writing for the community outside their classrooms, they often have questions. The next few pages present some of the most frequently asked questions, accompanied by answers that reflect practical experience. The questions fall into four categories: finding an appropriate organization, getting started, working on the assignment, and being assessed.

Finding an Appropriate Organization

How do I find an organization that might need to have some writing done?

Use all the resources available to you. One of these is your instructor, who may already have contacts with organizations that need help. But you should also find out if your school has an office that coordinates community-based internships or service projects. Also, draw on your own experience with part-time jobs or organizations, either on or off campus. Do you belong to a group that needs a newsletter or a set of bylaws? Have you worked at a job where employees need a set of procedures for opening the business in the morning or using a new piece of software?

How do I choose the right organization?

Choose an organization that will let you produce a document that your instructor considers appropriate for the course and that you can complete within the time allotted for the assignment. Also, consider logistical issues that will affect you. If the organization is located some distance from campus, do you have a way to get there? Will the hours work with your class schedule?

Consider also what you know about yourself. It can be useful to explore aspects of life outside your everyday experience, but be realistic. If, for example, you have strong negative feelings about homeless people, you may not be able to overcome those feelings in a single project for a homeless shelter. If this is the case, consider working for a different type of community organization.

What if I can't think of an organization?

If you really are stuck, your instructor may be able to make recommendations. Also, listen to your classmates' ideas. They may suggest an option you have overlooked. Or perhaps one of your classmates has identified an organization that can use the efforts of more than one student. In this case, check with your instructor and with the organization to make sure that a collaborative project is appropriate.

Getting Started

How do I make contact with the organization?

Whenever possible, use personal contacts. Your work will be easier if you know someone who knows someone. At the very least, it helps to have the name of a specific person to contact. If possible, find out if someone—your instructor, perhaps, or a friend who works for the organization—can prepare the way so that you can contact a person at the organization and say, "[Mr./Ms./Dr. So-and-so] suggested I contact you about the possibility of doing some writing for your organization."

If you can't find a personal connection, don't give up. You can always go to the main office of an organization, introduce yourself to a receptionist, and say something like, "I'm a student in a writing class at [your school], and I'd like to get some real-world writing experience. Is there anyone at [this organization] who might know whether there are some writing projects I could volunteer to do—an article for a newsletter, maybe, or a brochure?" If you take this approach, you will probably have to talk with two or three people before you find the specific individual who can help you.

Before asking about doing some writing for a particular organization, make sure you know something about it. Check to see if the organization has a Web site, or stop by its main office and ask to see some brochures that describe the organization's mission, the people it serves, and its main programs or activities.

How do I get people in the organization to like and trust me?

The more people like and trust you, the more likely they are to help you find interesting writing projects and the more willing they are to guide you toward resources for carrying out those projects. Remember, you are relying on people's goodwill to carry out your assignment. Chances are that the staff members are not required to help you or even be nice to you.

Your main guide will be your own good judgment and personality, but here are several recommendations.

> **Respect people's time.** When you make an appointment, be on time; in fact, be a few minutes early. As far as possible, try not to reschedule appointments. If you absolutely must change an appointment, notify people as far in advance as possible.

> **Meet deadlines.** If you have agreed to complete a certain piece of work by a certain date, get it done on time.

> **Show some interest in the work of the organization.** In addition to visiting the organization's Web site and reading its promotional material (brochures, flyers), pay attention to current events that may affect

the organization. When the opportunity arises, ask people in the organization what they do. And smile—especially when people are telling you what they do or when they are showing you around the organization.

> **Dress and act appropriately.** It's unlikely that you will be expected to wear a business suit or that you will be asked to leave if you fail to observe some formality. But pay attention to the way people in the organization dress and act. Make a reasonable effort to fit in.

> **Never put things off until the last minute.** As a student, you may be accustomed to living with last-minute crises—for example, spending Sunday night in a panic because you went skiing over the weekend rather than preparing for a test. People in community organizations have their own last-minute crises, some of them personal, some of them work-related. They rarely have time or patience to deal with your crises and their own at the same time.

How do I learn about the culture of the organization? And do I have to do this?

You have to understand the goals of the organization and the attitudes, values, and personality it wants to convey to the people it serves and the larger community. Otherwise you have little chance of creating documents that the organization will be able to use. Because you will probably be working with the organization for a relatively short time, there are limits to what you will understand of the culture. Nevertheless, you need to learn as much as you can.

> **Ask your contact person** to tell you what the organization is working to accomplish and what values underlie its actions.

> **Ask other people in the organization** to explain what they do and how their work fits into the organization's overall goals.

> **Pay attention to what goes on around you;** notice how people in the organization dress, what they talk about, the way they treat each other and their clients.

You [may] know how to write, but do you know how to write in the context of Joseph's House?"

– Tracy Neitzel

What if there's a conflict between the goals or activities of the organization and my own personal values?

This question probably will not come up if you have chosen the organization carefully. But if it does, face it squarely and ethically. First, make sure that you understand your own ethical principles. Second, ask yourself two questions: If I complete this assignment in the way people in the organization want me to, what effects will my work have? Are those effects likely to be consistent with my principles? If you cannot make a reasonable commitment of time, energy, and emotion to the writing you are asked to do for a particular organization, you probably should look for a different organization or at least for a different assignment within that organization.

Working on the Assignment

Where and/or how will I get my assignment?

For all practical purposes, your assignment will come from someone in the organization. This person may have a very clear idea of what is needed ("I want a tri-fold, black and white brochure covering the following topics and based on your reading of the following materials and your interviews with the following people"). In other cases, however, your contact person may have only a general idea of what needs to be done ("We could use a good human interest piece for our newsletter, or maybe some marketing materials for prospective donors"). In the latter case, your assignment may evolve over the course of two or three conversations. You may need to do some background reading and talk with two or three people (if you're writing for a course assignment as well as for an organization, your instructor should be among them) and then come back to your contact person with a more specific idea for the assignment.

Even if your assignment entails some conversation and negotiation, there will come a point at which you feel fairly well set. At this point, make sure that everyone involved (you, your instructor, and the organizational representative with whom you are working) understands and agrees upon the subject, purpose, audience, and format for the writing.

How much freedom will I have to shape my writing assignment?

There is a good chance that your contact person will negotiate your assignment, especially if you have acted in ways that lead people to like and trust you (see pp. 711–712). Most of the time, people in a community organization will understand that you are a student and will try to accommodate your needs and interests. Also, most organizations need so many different written documents that there will likely be a wide variety of projects from which to choose. In general, people will be most willing to let you take the initiative in deciding what to write if you can demonstrate the following characteristics.

> You understand the goals and needs of the organization.

> You have an idea that will help the organization meet those goals and/or satisfy those needs.

> You have a good chance of completing the project you propose.

Can I do something for the Web?

That depends, in part, on whether the organization has Web access. It also depends on the kind of work you want to do. Unless you plan to work with the organization for a semester or more, you may not be able to create a Web site even if you have the technological skills to do so. Good sites take a long time to create; more important, they also require maintenance.

If the organization already has a Web site, you may be able to develop the content for a particular topic they want the site to include. But if this assignment is for your writing class, make sure your instructor agrees that the work will meet the demands of the writing course. Avoid any project that will require you to spend most of your time programming or trying to master some Web-related technology.

How will I figure out what to say?

Chapters 2 to 7 presented a number of strategies to use in developing a topic. Some of those will almost certainly help in this situation. As you use those strategies, also consider drawing on one or more of the following sources of information.

> other materials the organization has produced (pamphlets, brochures, press releases, manuals, statements of policy)

> background readings about subjects related to the organization's work

> interviews with different groups of people: employees, volunteers, people who use the organization's services

Also, look at your topic from several perspectives, including your own: What strikes you as interesting, unusual, or potentially helpful about the information you are finding? Also consider your readers' perspective: What will they need from the document you write? What questions are they likely to have? What aspect(s) of the organization might they see as unique, helpful, or troubling? Finally, consider the organization's perspective: What does it hope to accomplish when it lets people see what you have written?

How will I know whether I'm on the right track—either with what I'm saying or with how I'm saying it?

Throughout your project, talk frequently with your contact person (and with your writing instructor if the project is for a course). In the early stages, summarize what you are learning, ask questions about the material, and seek ideas about other sources to consult or questions to ask. As you create a draft, request feedback from the contact person, from your instructor, and from your classmates. Point to specific passages (or visuals) and ask people to react to the tone, summarize the content, and mention questions they still have after reading your draft. If possible, also have the draft reviewed by a member of the audience for whom it is intended, and ask him or her for similar feedback.

Above all else, don't assume you'll get it right the first time. Sometimes people are not sure what they want until they see something that is not quite to their liking. In the world outside the classroom, important documents may be revised many times before they are ready to be shown to the public. Allow time for revisions. There will surely be some.

Being Assessed

Who will assess my work?

If your writing project is part of a class assignment, it will be assessed by at least two people: the instructor and a representative of the organization with which you have been working. If you are volunteering on your own, one or more people in the organization will assess your work.

How much influence will each of these people have?

If your project is for a writing class, the instructor will decide how much influence each evaluator will have. At a minimum, the instructor will probably want to know how well a representative from the organization thinks you have done on the assignment. Beyond that, your instructor will specify how much and what sort of weight to give the outside assessment.

What criteria will be used?

The organization's representative will likely focus on questions such as these: Can we use this document? Does it accomplish the goal(s) we had in mind for the audience(s) we hoped to reach?

Your instructor will focus on the issues mentioned repeatedly throughout this book: Does the writing show a clear understanding of the context for the work? Given the word choice, content, organization, and visual appearance of the written product, is it likely to accomplish the intended purpose for the intended audience?

What if my instructor and the organization's representative disagree about the quality of my work?

Do everything in your power to keep this from happening. Keep both parties informed about what you are doing, and ask for their advice and guidance as you go along. If you see potential areas of disagreement, identify them immediately and discuss them with both the instructor and the organization's representative. People are not likely to disagree about the quality of your final product if they have approved of the steps you took in creating it.

Yet people sometimes do disagree. What you should do when this happens depends in large measure on what people disagree about. For example, an organization may have a particular stylistic practice—such as avoiding the use of personal pronouns. There are lots of times when personal pronouns are appropriate, and your instructor may think so as well. But assume that writers in the organization you are working with make a habit of avoiding them. Probably your instructor will understand if you explain this practice and show that you know how to use personal pronouns appropriately, even though you avoid them in the writing you do for the organization.

In other instances, people may disagree on what constitutes an acceptable piece of writing. For example, the organization's representative or your instructor may think your text needs one more round of revising and polishing. If that additional work is consistent with the needs and purposes of the organization—and the goals of your writing course—you should be prepared to do it.

16

Making Oral Presentations

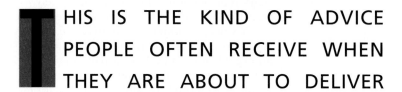

THIS IS THE KIND OF ADVICE PEOPLE OFTEN RECEIVE WHEN THEY ARE ABOUT TO DELIVER

an oral presentation: "Stand up straight." "Make eye contact with your audience." "Don't talk in a monotone." "Don't be so nervous—try to relax." And it's good advice. But it is only part of what you need to know to make a good oral presentation. For a really effective oral presentation, the most important thing is to prepare carefully, using what you have learned from the other chapters in this book: analyze your audience, develop your topic thoroughly, compose an introduction that will engage your audience, and so on. Eye contact and good posture will not do you much good unless you are saying something that the audience realizes is worth listening to. Consequently, this chapter presents some guidelines for adapting what you have learned about writing to make effective oral presentations. It concludes with a discussion of questions students often ask about *delivery*, such as overcoming nervousness, using visual aids, and being aware of body language and eye contact.

Successful Oral Presentations

What you do in making a successful oral presentation depends in part on your personality, the subject you are addressing, and the circumstances in which you are speaking. For example, if you tend to use a lot of gestures when you talk informally with friends, you may find yourself doing the same thing when you make an oral presentation. In most cases, however, there are several basic guidelines that can help you create and deliver a successful oral presentation, especially when you are addressing a relatively large group such as a class. In these situations, it's a good idea to do the following.

> **Create a compelling introduction.** Your introduction should be relatively brief—not more than a minute or two for an eight- to ten-minute presentation. But it has to be effective. Within the minute or two you devote to the introduction, be sure to create common ground with your listeners and give them strong reasons for paying attention to what you have to say.

> **Forecast the main points you are going to make.** As soon as you have engaged the listeners' attention, provide them with a basic outline of your presentation; in effect, give them a road map that indicates the territory you will cover in your presentation.

> **Use visual aids (slides or overheads) to emphasize what you are getting at.** At any point in your presentation, use overheads or slides to help the audience see—literally *see*—what point you are making and how a given detail or example relates to your other points.

> **Elaborate on your visual aids.** Do not just read the words written on your slides or overheads. Supplement the basic structure shown in the visuals with details, examples, stories, or arguments that will be meaningful to the listeners and will clearly demonstrate the idea you are trying to convey.

> **Talk directly to your listeners.** As a rule, the voices people create when they write are different from the ones they create when speaking. Your oral presentation is talk, not written text. Make it sound like talk. When you quote from or paraphrase outside sources, be sure to identify them, but do so as concisely as possible so as not to interrupt the flow of the presentation.

> **Finish strong.** Use the last thirty seconds or so to reiterate your main points in a memorable way, pose a question that will engage your listeners, or emphasize ways that the ideas you presented will affect your audience.

Creating a Compelling Introduction

This sort of opening is almost guaranteed to make you sound like a nervous beginner: "Umm, OK. The topic I'm going to talk about today is . . ."

Maybe you are inexperienced, but you don't want to advertise the fact with such an ineffective introduction. Instead, make use of strategies for engaging the audience's interest.

Think about your topic from the listeners' perspective. Determine how your topic relates to what they know, care about, believe, or expect. Then look for something (a set of facts, an anecdote, a question, a situation) that will conflict with their knowledge, values, beliefs, or preferences. By including this type of element, you will likely capture their attention. A number of the readings in this book do this so well that they might work as well for an oral presentation as they do for a written text. For example, Edward Barnes's report "Slaves of New York" (see Figure 16.1) begins by creating a scene that most readers will find unsettling, even shocking.

FIGURE 16.1
Introduction to
"Slaves of New York"

Many people have become increasingly concerned about sweatshops: factories where employees work long hours for little pay, often in conditions that are unsafe or unsanitary. Americans often assume that sweatshops are located solely in foreign countries, where wages are low and living conditions for most people are miserable. Edward Barnes's report, published in *Time*, challenges this assumption, showing that sweatshops—many employing illegal immigrants—exist here in the United States. As you read this piece, underline passages where the information he provides confirms, adds to, or challenges what you already know about sweatshops. Also, pay careful attention to the photographs and the way people and their surroundings are depicted.

Slaves of New York

EDWARD BARNES

How crime and mismanaged laws have made the city the biggest magnet for Chinese illegals

Autumn in New York may be inviting to most visitors to the city, but the approach of winter is ominous for the transients inhabiting a fourth-floor walk-up on the Bowery. In the heat of summer, a few at least are able to sleep on the fire escapes and the roof of the building—avoiding for a moment the circle of hell they have been assigned. The cramped and airless space within is subdivided into 32 cubicles doled out to at least 100 men. The stink of sweat, unwashed clothing, old shoes and garbage suffuses the narrow makeshift corridors. Cooking noises mingle with the gurgle of kitchen-side urinals. On tiny TV sets, a few men watch home videos of kin and country long left behind, for some as much as a decade ago. Others stare at the

Living in airless, unhygienic cubicles in Manhattan, the Fujianese are isolated by language and fear, their nights lonely and their days occupied by ill-paid labor.

> Autumn in New York may be inviting to most visitors to the city, but the approach of winter is ominous for the transients inhabiting a fourth-floor walk-up on the Bowery. . . . The cramped and airless space within is subdivided into 32 cubicles doled out to at least 100 men. The stink of sweat, unwashed clothing, old shoes and garbage suffuses the narrow make-shift corridors.

Columnist Fred LeBrun's position paper, "Up in Arms over Decision" (p. 211), begins in a way that categorizes potential members of his audience.

> When it comes to the way courts and juries do things in New York, there has always been the upstate way, the downstate way, and Brooklyn.
>
> Brooklyn's otherness was confirmed last week when a jury in federal court there returned a $560,000 liability award against 15 handgun manu-facturers for the harm done to seven victims.

LeBrun's audience of hunters and gun owners, all of whom live in upstate New York, fears any action that would support the anti-gun lobby. LeBrun allies himself with his upstate readers by citing an example of "Brooklyn's otherness," a jury decision that conflicts powerfully with the audience's needs, beliefs, and values.

The evaluation "Breakfast at Manory's," by Patrick Vitarius (p. 286), begins by mentioning a situation most college students can relate to: he tends to sleep in, which conflicts with his fondness for a really good breakfast.

> If there's one thing I've missed since I left home, it's breakfast. See, I have the less-than-admirable habit of getting up at the last possible moment—typically fifteen minutes after my first class of the morning starts.

Forecasting Your Main Points

When people read something you have written, they should be able to quickly get the gist of it by skimming or looking at headings and topic sentences. This effective reading strategy lets readers develop a general framework to which they can relate the details presented in the text. This sort of framework may be even more important for listeners than for readers. Remember, your spoken words essentially disappear once you have uttered them. But if listeners have a sense of the structure of what you're going to say, they will be able to relate specific details to this structure and, therefore, find it easier to remember them.

Chapters 2 through 7 of this book offer tips on how to provide a clear structure for your writing so that readers can find the information they are looking for and/or can anticipate what you will say in any given section. These strategies can also help you produce a well-structured oral presentation. That is, your oral presentations should incorporate all of the following elements: thesis statements and topic sentences, transitional words and phrases that indicate how one point relates to the points that precede and follow it, and forecasting phrases and sentences that announce the topic you are about to discuss.

Useful as these strategies are, you will probably need to supplement them with one further cue to structure: an *outline* or *overview* of the main points you will make. As a rule, you should present this overview early in the presentation, right after engaging the listeners' interest. In the context of an oral presentation, this overview functions like the homepage on a well-designed Web site, one that gives a clear outline of the topics (and sometimes the subtopics) discussed on the site. For example, Chapter 4 contains a Web text, "School Vouchers: The Wrong Choice for Public Education," sponsored by the Anti-Defamation League (p. 206). In addition to asserting the organization's basic position (vouchers are "the wrong choice for public education"), the opening page links to the main points in support of the organization's position: school vouchers are a bad idea because they:

> Are Constitutionally Suspect
> Undermine Public Schools
> Are Not Universally Popular

These brief statements outline the content found in the rest of the Web text. Near the beginning of an oral presentation on any topic, you would need to do something similar. And you should reinforce the outline through the use of visual aids. In your spoken comments, you should use other strategies for providing structure, especially some combination of the following ones.

> Assert or strongly imply your point in the title of your presentation.
> Use thesis statements and topic sentences.
> Use transition words, especially when moving from one section of the presentation to the next.
> Ask and answer questions.

You should also highlight your main points through a series of well-designed visual aids.

Using Visual Aids

In creating visual aids, you might use overhead transparencies or presentation software. This software is especially attractive since it offers many sophisticated design templates and visual effects. For example, you may have seen PowerPoint presentations in which pictures appear, text and graphics move, and one slide flows into another almost magically. Such visual effects can give your oral presentation a polished, professional look. But they are not nearly as important as straightforward visual aids—slides or overhead transparencies—that help listeners see the *structure* of your message. You can make the structure of your presentation clear by following these suggestions.

Guidelines for Making Slides or Overheads

> **Use large type.** Major headings should be in 40-point type or larger. Subpoints should be 24 to 30 points or larger. (The smallest type in the sample PowerPoint slides shown here is 24 points.)

> **Be concise.** Capture the gist of each main point in as few words as possible, without becoming so cryptic that your audience cannot figure out what you are saying.

> **Use brief bulleted or numbered points** rather than long blocks of text. Items in a list should be grammatically parallel.

> **Consider the room where you will be presenting.** Use a light background and dark type if your presentation will take place in a darkened room; use a dark background and light type if the room will be well lit.

> **Avoid choosing overly complex design templates** that come with presentation software such as PowerPoint. Work with designs that complement your subject and do not distract the audience.

> **Choose visuals that are easy to read when projected.** For graphs and other complex visuals, include labels and other text elements that are large enough for the audience to read.

> For more on how to create your own PowerPoint presentation, read "The Basics of PowerPoint," p. 433.

As an illustration of these guidelines, consider how the Web-based position paper on school vouchers (p. 206) might be adapted for presentation software such as PowerPoint. Phrases listed at the left-hand side of the first screen (for example, "Constitutionally Suspect") and at the top of each other screen on the site make it easy to get the gist of this text without reading every word. If this presentation were being presented orally, the speaker might begin by making many of the points that are in the site's introduction and then forecasting the basic structure of the presentation with a slide or overhead such as the one in Figure 16.2.

Subsequent slides or overheads might contain just one of these points, which the speaker would elaborate on in some detail. For example, the next slide (Figure 16.3) might include subpoints.

After elaborating on ways that vouchers might be seen as "constitutionally suspect," the speaker's third slide (Figure 16.4) would move on to the next major point.

The bold, dark type for the second bulleted point focuses listeners' attention on the point the speaker is currently making, while the lighter type for the first bulleted point provides a running summary of the speaker's argument. The next slide might elaborate on how vouchers "undermine public schools."

FIGURE 16.2
Introductory Slide
in a PowerPoint
Presentation

School Vouchers

- Are Constitutionally Suspect
- Undermine Public Schools
- Are Not Universally Popular

Chad Crume
English 102
Professor Susan Katz
November 25, 2003

● Heading is large
and easy to read.

● Bulleted points
are grammatically
parallel, and each
word is capitalized.

● Includes
presenter's name,
course informa-
tion, and date.

FIGURE 16.3
Second Slide in
a PowerPoint
Presentation

School Vouchers

- Are Constitutionally Suspect
  - Compel taxpayers to pay for religious instruction
  - Have only limited support from the Supreme Court

● Bulleted items
show presenter's
main points and
subpoints.

● Dark type on a
light background
is easy to read in
a darkened room.

FIGURE 16.4
Third Slide
in a PowerPoint
Presentation

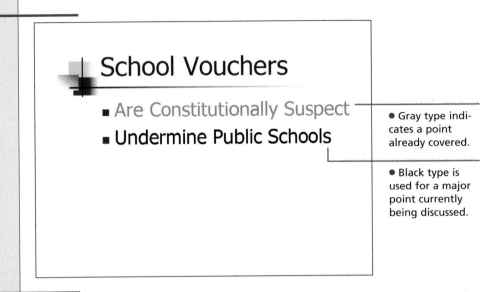

Not all speakers have to provide listeners with this sort of visual structure for their oral presentations. In fact, this sort of structure rarely—if ever—appears in sermons, political speeches, graduation speeches, or comic monologues. But for most of the oral presentations you will make, it's probably a good idea to provide listeners with a visual forecast of your main points. The effort to come up with concise, meaningful headings and subheadings will help you understand exactly what you want to say. And as you improve your own understanding, you will probably improve that of your listeners as well.

Elaborating on Visual Aids

Few things are more boring or ineffective than oral presentations in which speakers simply read the words that appear on their overheads or slides. You should think of overheads or slides simply as a way to present the framework of what you have to say. Your job as a speaker is to flesh out this framework, using strategies presented elsewhere in this book for developing your topic, engaging your listeners' interest, and creating an appropriate voice. In making an oral presentation, it is especially important to elaborate on your points with compelling, credible details—facts, examples, stories, statistics, or quotes. Many of the strategies discussed under Developing Your Topic in Chapters 2 through 7 will be useful as you think of ways to elaborate on the main points of your oral presentation. Here are several that may be especially useful.

› **Look for details that are likely to have validity for your listeners.** Choose details that from the audience's perspective are most likely to make sense. This is especially true in dealing with highly subjective or emotional subjects. For example, the evaluative piece "Cream of the Crop" (p. 273) addresses a highly subjective question: Which vanilla ice creams taste best? The authors identified aspects of vanilla ice cream ("real vanilla flavor," "creamy smoothness," and an absence of "obvious gums or thickeners" when the ice cream melts) that should strike most people as reasonable attributes of a good vanilla ice cream.

> **Choose details that relate clearly to your listeners' view of the world, either confirming or dramatically changing that view.** In criticizing e-mail, the author of "You Call This Progress?" (p. 283) cites details (the proliferation of messages, the fact that people expect an immediate response) that all e-mail users have experienced, even if they do not share the author's view that e-mail demands only "knee-jerk reaction."

> **Create memorable conflicts or contrasts.** Sometimes contrasts are made explicit, but often they need only be strongly implied. In her criticism of SUVs, "SUVs Belong in Car Ads Only" (p. 195), for example, Ellen Goodman outlines a few of the attributes of the Ford Excursion without giving specific data for other automobiles: "It's 7 feet tall, 80 inches wide, weighs four tons, and gets 10 miles to the gallon." Her audience should have little trouble grasping how exceptionally large and inefficient this SUV is.

> **Present the opinion or experience of someone who is likely to have a high degree of credibility for the audience you are addressing.** The authors of "Fight Crime: Invest in Kids" (p. 353) argue that money should be spent on educational programs that will prevent rather than merely punish criminal behavior by young people. They buttress their arguments not only with data from research but also with quotes from law enforcement officials (a sheriff, a former police chief) who speak with authority on what is needed to reduce juvenile crime.

> **Tell a story about someone whose experience typifies the subject you are discussing.** In reporting on the plight of illegal immigrants, Edward Barnes asserts in "Slaves of New York" (p. 120), "Each tale is one of heartbreak." He then tells the story of Yu Li:

Almost immediately after reaching New York, she began working 17-hour days, seven days a week, at a local garment factory. But because she was new and the factory paid piece rate, she made only $1 an hour. . . . She and her husband made so little money they couldn't afford to live together. He continued to sleep on the floor of the restaurant that employed him. She slept in a basement owned by relatives. . . .

[E]ach month Yu has to pay $3,000 on the debt [incurred in bringing their three children from China]. . . . "The hardest thing," she says, "is that I have had to make the children work. They should be in school, but we need the money they bring home."

Yu Li's story gives an immediacy to a situation that is probably quite remote from the experience of most people who read "Slaves of New York."

When you have a wonderful anecdote or a powerful array of statistics, make sure your listeners can see how that information connects to a key point in your presentation. Especially when inexperienced speakers know a lot about their subject, they often get so involved in presenting details that they and their listeners lose sight of the larger points. In some situations, usually when listeners are very familiar with the topic being discussed, they have little difficulty seeing the connection between a detail and the larger point. But you cannot always count on this. In terms of making the connection between details and key points, follow the guideline "When in doubt, spell it out."

Talking to Your Listeners

No matter how anxious you feel about talking in front of a large group, try to give your listeners the feeling that you see them not as a terrifying sea of faces but as individuals who have some of the same feelings, values, interests, and needs that you have. Try to speak in a relatively conversational voice and talk to members of your audience collectively as if you were talking one-on-one with individual listeners. This is not to say you should talk to all audiences as though you were conversing informally with your best friend. Obviously, some situations require you to be more formal, more courteous, more on-your-best-behavior. But in general, talk directly to—better yet, *with*—your listeners.

> **Use personal pronouns, but be careful how you use them.** Pronouns such as *I*, *we*, and *you* are almost always appropriate. They make your presentation a little less abstract, a little more personal. However, be careful not to use *you* in a directive or critical sense. Although there may be some exceptions, by and large audiences do not respond well to being told what to do. Judicious use of personal pronouns, especially *you*, can help you avoid alienating your listeners.

> **Use conversational sentence fragments, but sparingly.** In informal conversations, people don't always speak in complete sentences. They often use fragments, especially for emphasis. Consider, for example, the preceding sentence. It is punctuated as a single complete sentence, using a comma before "especially for emphasis" so that you detect a slight pause before that last phrase. If it were being spoken in an oral presentation, the pause might be a little longer, a little more dramatic, so that the sentence would sound as though it were punctuated like this: "They often use sentence fragments. Especially for emphasis." However, be aware that too many fragments make a presentation sound choppy, so use them sparingly.

> **Ask questions, but don't depend on the audience for answers.** In some situations, especially when the audience is familiar with the topic and comfortable about speaking out, listeners may want to answer a question you have posed. But people are often reluctant to venture a comment

when they are part of a large group. This reluctance (and the silence that usually accompanies it) can cause you trouble if you feel an answer is necessary before continuing. Instead of subjecting yourself and your listeners to long, uncomfortable periods of silence, ask a question listeners themselves might be prompted to ask, either because of something you have just said or because of something that is likely to be on their minds. Then provide a thoughtful answer. If your question is significant and your answer thought-provoking, listeners may want to engage you in further conversation after the presentation.

 ## Exercise

Observe a presentation (or lecture) and take notes. How does the speaker introduce the topic and use forecasting language to signal what is to come? How effective are the visuals used in the presentation? How does the speaker's voice (including tone, word choice, level of formality) affect your response to the presentation? How effective is the conclusion? Write a page or two analyzing the effectiveness of the presentation and bring your analysis to class to report your findings.

Finishing Strong

This sort of conclusion is inappropriate and ineffective: "So . . . umm . . . that's about all I have to say." It certainly does not do justice to all the hard work you put into making your presentation engaging and informative. The chapters in Part 1 of this book include lists of strategies writers have used in concluding their work. Chances are that one or more of these strategies will be appropriate for your oral presentation. In particular, here are several that are widely used in oral presentations.

❯ For an example of summarizing an argument, see the beginning and ending of "SUVs Belong in Car Ads Only," p. 195.

❯ For an example of framing a presentation, see the conclusion of "Yes, Let's Pay for Organs," p. 201.

> ❯ **Summarize your main arguments and conclude by restating your thesis.** Readers can always go back and review a written text. But in an oral presentation it is a good idea to remind listeners of the key points you have made and to end by reiterating your thesis in a powerful or memorable way. Sometimes you can do this by quoting someone else whose statements echo the theme you've been developing.
>
> ❯ **Frame your presentation.** In your conclusion, come back to something (a person, an idea, a set of statistics) with which you began your talk.
>
> ❯ **Mention the implications of what you have just said.** Make sure listeners understand either the positive or the negative consequences of the situation you have described in your presentation.

Frequently Asked Questions about Delivery

If you are saying something thoughtful and interesting, most audiences will forgive you if you sometimes fail to make eye contact or if your posture is less than perfect. But still, if you've invested time and effort in preparing thoroughly, you might as well do justice to that preparation by making a presentation that is as polished and effective as possible. Here are some suggestions for accomplishing that, in the form of answers to questions students commonly ask. These questions and suggestions fall into three major categories: overcoming nervousness, using scripts and visual aids, and being aware of body language and eye contact.

Overcoming Nervousness

Making an oral presentation scares me to death. How do I get over being so nervous?

You never get over being nervous—not if you're like most people. Even when the best public speakers stand in front of a group, they often have nervous reactions: their pulse rate may be high, their hands may be clammy, they may feel queasy or weak in the knees. They probably have as much adrenaline coursing through their systems as you do. If they don't, their presentations likely will be listless, flat, and boring. Rest assured that you're not alone in being nervous.

So other people get nervous too. How does knowing that help me?

Have you ever heard the statement, "We have nothing to fear but fear itself"? That applies for people who have to make oral presentations. You can begin conquering your anxiety by accepting the fact that you may be nervous. Indeed, being nervous does not mean that you're a bad speaker or that you're doomed to failure. If others can feel the same anxiety you do and still make effective oral presentations, so can you.

OK, I'm resigned to being nervous. Isn't there anything else I can do about my nervousness?

> **As you're waiting for your turn to speak, practice breathing.** Take a deep breath and exhale slowly, counting silently as you do so. On your first exhalation, see if you can count to 15 before running out of air. On the next one, see if you can count to 20. Don't just do this once or twice; do it at least five or ten times. This focus on breathing will accomplish several things: it will help your voice sound stronger and more confident (one reason people's voices sound weak or shaky is that they are taking quick, shallow breaths rather than breathing deeply), it will calm your nerves, and it will give you something to think about other than how nervous you are.

> **While you're speaking, concentrate on what you're saying.** Anxiety can easily lead your mind in all sorts of irrelevant and harmful directions: *Why won't my knees stop shaking? That person in the back row seems to be laughing at me—or is she smiling in agreement? This isn't*

going to be nearly as good as the last presentation. Is a carpenter hammering in the next room, or is that my heart pounding? Instead of letting your mind wander like this, focus on what you are saying. Concentrate on the assumption that if you've done the sort of preparation recommended in this book, you will have something interesting and worthwhile to say. Remember your main points (your overhead transparencies or presentation software slides should help). Think—and tell your listeners—about how a set of details helps illustrate a point you want to make. Focus on making sure the listeners see how one main point leads to another. If you make statements that are clear and well thought out, your listeners are likely to appreciate what you're saying—even if they disagree with you. At the very least, they will focus on what you are saying rather than wondering if you are nervous. If the audience is not worrying about how nervous you are, why should you?

❭ **Before—*long before*—the day of your presentation, rehearse.** Don't just imagine what you're going to say; actually give your presentation aloud. Practice speaking by referring to your overheads or slides. Get to the point where you can glance briefly at an overhead or slide, notice a key phrase, and elaborate on that phrase, using quotes, statistics, facts, examples, or stories. Especially rehearse the beginning and concluding sections of your presentation. You want to be able to deliver these sections without looking at notes, overheads, or slides. This way, at the beginning and ending of your presentation you will be able to make good eye contact with the audience and express your points clearly and emphatically.

If possible, also make a videotape of your rehearsal, or practice in front of a friend. Consider such questions as these: *Do the elaborations clearly relate to the phrases I have on my overheads or slides?* (If not, change the elaboration, change the overhead or slide, or change both.) *Are there places where I rush through key points? Do I pause to emphasize certain comments? Do my gestures help emphasize my key points, or am I making random, nervous movements?* Careful rehearsal won't eliminate all feelings of nervousness, but it will let you tell yourself that all you need to do when you stand up to speak is what you were doing all along in rehearsal.

Using Scripts and Visual Aids

In preparing my presentation, should I write out everything I'm going to say and then read what I have written?
This is a point on which experienced speakers have different experiences and perspectives. The following extracts present the approaches followed by the authors of this textbook. See if one makes sense for you.

Susan Katz:
When I was in high school, I did a lot of public speaking—but it was always the type where students competed in presenting a famous speech.

In other words, I was almost always presenting something I had memorized, rarely something I had written myself. Perhaps that experience spoiled me. If I write out my presentation ahead of time, I feel I have to memorize the speech and present it word for word. I actually get more nervous, and the end result is often awkward and stilted.

In the kind of public speaking I have done in my professional life—as an advertising executive and now as a college professor—I prefer to make presentations that sound more spontaneous. I *never* write out my whole presentation. But I very carefully write out my major and minor points. Actually, I write and rewrite those points until each one clearly and succinctly says exactly what I want to say. Then I practice each presentation aloud from beginning to end at least ten times (and sometimes many more than that).

Lee Odell:

At this stage of my career, I do essentially what Susan does. But early on, I would write things out. I'd try to write them exactly the way I would say them if I were talking with an individual instead of addressing a large group. Then I'd practice reading what I had written until I could make my presentation sound as spontaneous as if I were working from notes. This might not have been the best way to do things, but I found that if I relied solely on notes, I would spend a lot of time worrying that I might forget to say something or that what I thought I had to say wasn't as good as I imagined it was. By writing things out, I could be confident that I actually had something worthwhile to say and that I wouldn't be likely to forget to say it while making my presentation.

You've mentioned overhead transparencies and presentation software (such as PowerPoint) slides. Which should I use?
Use the technology with which you are most comfortable. Overhead transparencies are not technologically sophisticated, so they are a better choice if you're uncomfortable with the computer projectors required by software such as PowerPoint. The last thing you need is to worry about some sort of technical glitch involving your disk, a computer, and/or a computer projector.

If you decide to use PowerPoint (or any other presentation software), be careful not to get carried away with the technology. PowerPoint will let you incorporate visual images, create background designs for each visual, and add some animation, especially in the transition from one slide to another. Used judiciously, PowerPoint can help you make a polished, professional-looking presentation. However, a PowerPoint presentation can easily turn into a landslide of visual images in which twenty or thirty slides—each crammed with visuals and text—flash by almost as fast as the presenter can read them. Definitely avoid this.

When you use any presentation software, observe a principle that also applies to overhead transparencies: *Keep things simple*. If you include a picture or chart, make sure it clearly relates to a point you want the listeners to remember. Keep the text on the slide or overhead brief and intuitively meaningful. Use the slide or overhead to provide the kind of structure described on pp. 720–723 of this chapter.

Being Aware of Body Language and Eye Contact

People have told me that when I make an oral presentation I should stand up straight, keep my hands at my sides, and avoid moving around. How important is this?

It's fairly important. You don't want your body language (posture and gestures) to betray any nervousness. When people are nervous, they tend to gesture and move around abruptly. If they are not feeling confident, they may stand with shoulders slumped, chest caved in, and most of their weight on one leg. They may even have their weight back on their heels, almost as though they want to physically pull away from the people they are talking to.

You probably can't—and shouldn't—stand completely still with your hands always at your sides. In fact, as you do more and more presentations, you will find a style that suits your personality and customary ways of speaking. For example, if you normally gesture a lot when talking with an individual or a small group of friends, there's no point in holding your hands rigidly at your sides when you give an oral presentation. The main thing to remember is that you want to project a sense of confidence and enthusiasm. Here are some suggestions that will help you do so.

> **Stand with your feet slightly apart** (maybe six to ten inches, depending on your height and what feels comfortable to you), with most of your weight toward the balls of your feet. Try putting one foot slightly (maybe a couple of inches) in front of the other. This will give you a stable base and suggest, subtly, that you are leaning toward your audience, reaching out in your enthusiasm for what you are saying.

> **Stand straight with your chest up, your shoulders back, and your weight evenly distributed on both legs.** Make your body give the impression that you feel you are saying something important.

> **Try to keep your hands and body relatively still.** The key word here is *relatively*. It's perfectly all right to gesture, to shift your weight, even to move about a little. The important thing is to make sure that when you gesture or move, your actions emphasize the points you are making. Above all, don't move randomly.

> **Be especially careful with your hands.** Don't let them twitch. If you need something to do with them, consider holding some note cards in one hand, keeping them a little above waist height at a level where you can easily glance down at them—but not so high that they cut off your view of your listeners or so low that you can't read them. (If you do use note cards, make sure that the print is large and legible.) If your other hand feels uncomfortable dangling at your side, let the elbow bend a little so that the hand is just below waist level.

What about eye contact? How important is that?

Eye contact is very important, at least in most Western cultures. In some Asian societies, it is considered rude to look people directly in the eye. But in

Western cultures your willingness to make eye contact indicates that you are honest and sincere. If you can't meet people's gaze, it suggests you have something to hide or you are not being entirely honest.

But how do I make eye contact with an entire group of people?

Start by looking in the general direction of the group—not above their heads, not at the floor, not at a visual projected onto a screen in front of the group. Look somewhere toward the middle of the group, preferably with a relaxed expression on your face. As you talk, look toward individuals or small groups of individuals in different parts of the room. You shouldn't focus exclusively on one person or one part of the room, nor should you let your gaze swing mechanically back and forth across the group. Make a statement to one person or small group, and then shift your focus to another small group or individual and, occasionally, back to the middle of the group (the general area you were looking at when you began). Think of eye contact as a form of nonverbal punctuation. When you come to a pause—the oral equivalent of a semicolon or a period—use it as a moment to make eye contact with a different part of the audience. This will let listeners feel you are talking to them individually as well as collectively. It will also give you a way to emphasize key points, especially if you combine a shift in eye contact with a gesture or a shift in posture.

But what if the room is dark because I am using presentation software such as PowerPoint? How can I make eye contact with a group of people if I can't see their faces clearly?

You might not be able to see your listeners, but they can see you. If you don't look in their direction, they will get the impression that you aren't very interested in communicating with them. Follow the procedures suggested above, even if you only focus on different areas of the room rather than on individual listeners.

If I follow all the advice given above, is it guaranteed that I won't be nervous and that I'll give a great presentation?

You can be sure of two things.

> ❭ When you prepare and make your oral presentation, you will have something to think about other than how nervous you are.

> ❭ The more times you follow this advice, the better you will become. It has worked too many times to believe otherwise.

Glossary of Visual and Rhetorical Terms

alignment   in layout and design, the way in which text and *visual elements* are lined up on a page or screen. They might be lined up along the left margin (left-only justified), along the right margin (right-only justified), along both margins (full justified), or in the center (centered or center-justified). See Chapter 8. See also *format*.

analogy   strategy for developing a piece of writing in which the writer explains an unfamiliar thing by comparing it to a more familiar thing; useful for explaining complex ideas or objects clearly. For example, paragraph 4 of Fred LeBrun's essay "Up in Arms over Decision" (Chapter 4) uses the analogy of "ski manufacturers being held responsible for broken legs" to ridicule the idea "that the makers of legally sold guns ought to be held to some degree responsible for illegal acts done with them." See also *figure of speech*.

analyze, analysis   to break a subject down into component parts in order to examine it in depth (*analyze*); a strategy for developing a piece of writing that examines the parts that make up a subject (*analysis*). See also *critical thinking*.

anecdote   a short *narrative* (story or joke), usually based upon personal experience, that provides support for a *claim*.

appeal   a strategy used by writers for persuading readers or listeners to agree with the writers' opinion or *claim*. The three appeals most commonly used are ethical (*You should agree with me because I'm trustworthy*), logical (*You should agree with me because I'm reasonable*), and emotional (*You should agree with me because of how this makes you feel*). See Chapter 4.

argument   the presentation of a *thesis* (point of view) regarding a particular issue, offering *reasons* and *evidence* in order to be persuasive. See Chapter 4.

assumption   a belief or opinion that is assumed or taken for granted. Assumptions, which writers may state or imply and with which they may expect most or all readers to agree, affect both the writers' choices and the readers' reactions to the text. See also *critical thinking, reasons*.

audience   the intended readers (viewers or listeners) of a written, auditory, or visual work. A primary audience includes those who will act or make decisions based upon the information presented. A secondary audience includes those who will be affected by the information but will not directly act or make decisions based upon it. See also *stakeholder*.

authority   an expert providing knowledge that lends *credibility* to a *claim*.

balance   in layout and design, the *principle* by which text and graphic elements are evenly or harmoniously distributed on the page or screen. See Chapter 8. See also *format*.

banner   a *graphics*-based Web advertising display space or unit; often referred to as a banner ad. Standard size is 468 *pixels* wide by 60 pixels tall.

bias   a *perspective* based on a subjective or personal *point of view*, often without regard for opposing points of view. Bias can result in a lack of *credibility* for the writer.

blank space   See *white space*.

bold, boldface   a typographical highlighting technique whereby letters or lines are made heavier and darker than normal type to achieve emphasis through visual prominence. This is **boldface** type.

brainstorming   an idea-generating technique whereby a writer compiles any and all ideas that come to mind concerning a subject without judging the value of the ideas. See also *exploratory writing, freewriting*.

bullet   a marker or symbol used to denote a listed item; this is a standard bullet: •.

caption   a short description or explanation of an *image* or other *visual element*, usually set alongside or underneath, that gives information about the image or element.

cause and effect   a strategy for developing a piece of writing whereby the writer explains why something happened or demonstrates the influence of one event upon another. The effect is the *consequence* of the cause. When using this strategy, the writer must establish a chain of logic and *evidence* to show the relationship between the event and its cause or outcome. For example, "Yes, Let's Pay for Organs" (Chapter 4) describes the potential effects on seriously ill people of not modifying policies on organ donation.

chart   a graphic element that helps readers compare and contrast data by means of a combination of *columns* and rows, *images* and text. See also *graphics, line graph, pictogram, pie chart*.

chunking   a way of clustering sections of text by visually separating those sections that go together (chunks) from other parts of the text; can be achieved by the use of *headings*, indentation, or *white space*. See Chapter 8. See also *balance, sidebar*.

circumstances   the time, place, or form in which the text will appear; part of *context*. See also *audience, purpose*.

claim   a statement or proposition that serves as the foundation for an *argument;* also called an argumentative thesis.

classification   a strategy for organizing information or ideas; can entail grouping related things into a class or category, or dividing ideas, objects, or events into categories. For example, in the review of the Storm Café (Chapter 5), the author evaluates the food in two classes (lunch and dinner) and further divides the dinner class into three categories (starters, entrees, and desserts). See also *division*.

color   design element that draws a reader's eye; useful for adding emphasis and interest to a page or screen.

column   the vertical space in a grid, or items aligned in that vertical space. (The horizontal space in a grid is called a "row.")

common ground   shared experiences, *perspectives*, interests, or goals that serve a writer and an *audience* as a platform for mutual understanding. Identifying common ground enables writers to produce texts that will engage readers. For example, Margaret Tomeo opens her report on ACL injuries (Chapter 3) with an anecdote that would engage her audience of women athletes.

comparison   a strategy whereby the writer examines how two or more related things are similar (and different). Writers can use comparison to organize a text in a variety of ways:

Point by point: The writer moves back and forth between the items being compared. For example, in "Ford Expedition" (Chapter 5), the writer makes a point-by-point comparison between the 2003 model of the SUV and its competitors, discussing details such as the cargo capacity, quality of the ride, off-road capability, and so on.

Block structure: The writer discusses all the points related to one item, and then all the points related to another item. For example, in "Fixing Airport Security" (Chapter 4), the author first describes all the attributes of the European model and then describes the "old model" used in the United States.

Similarities: The writer focuses on features that the items have in common. For example, in "Fight Crime: Invest in Kids" (Chapter 6), the authors frequently compare programs in different parts of the country, focusing on similarities in program results.

Contrast: The writer focuses on dissimilarities between the items. See, for example, Max Zujewski's comparison between two magnetic stripe card systems: the Diebold CS Gold and AT&T Optim9000 (Chapter 6).

composition in *design,* the way in which an *image* is planned and organized to draw attention to certain areas or to evoke specific emotions in the viewer. See, for example, the analysis of the opening page of "The Road to Kabul" (Chapter 2). See also *viewing angle.*

concession an acknowledgment of a valid point in a *counterargument,* often in order to establish the writer's *credibility* and strengthen other *claims.* For example, in "Yes, Let's Pay for Organs" (Chapter 4), the author concedes that Pennsylvania's proposed plan to make payments to the families of organ donors does indeed cross an ethical line, turning body parts into a commodity. However, the author then refutes the second part of the counterargument, which says that crossing the line leads to the establishment of a market for body parts. See also *refutation.*

conflict a sense of dissonance or disagreement, often created purposefully by the writer as a way to engage readers. See, for example, "From Welfare to Washington" (Chapter 2); the title suggests conflict because most readers probably would not think of welfare recipients as becoming powerful politicians.

consequence a result brought about by a cause or by particular conditions. See also *cause and effect.*

consistency in design, a way of making pages appear to belong to the same document by making every page conform to the same basic format or grid.

context the situation within which a text exists. Features of context include the *audience* for whom the text is written and designed, the *circumstances* in which it will be read, and the writer's *purposes* in producing it.

contrast in *design,* the variations in appearance that enhance readability and add visual interest to a text; can be achieved by using different colors, *typefaces,* amounts of *white space, images,* and so forth. See Chapter 8 for more on visual contrast. See *comparison* for a discussion of contrast as a method of organizing a text.

counterargument a persuasive strategy by which a writer anticipates readers' objections and provides *evidence* to overcome those objections. By demonstrating fairness to counterarguments, a writer can establish *credibility.* See also *concession, refutation.*

credibility the degree to which a writer and his or her information can be believed or trusted, based upon specific *evidence.* A credibility analysis involves investigating the veracity of the evidence used in an *argument.* See Chapter 4.

criteria standards used to evaluate an *argument,* product, service, statement, behavior, and so forth. Explicit criteria are stated outright; implicit criteria are suggested or stated indirectly. See Chapter 5.

critical thinking examining a text or an idea carefully to consider its *context,* its *credibility,* the amount and type of *evidence* in support of any *claim* it makes, and the validity of its *assumptions.* Critical thinking allows reasoned judgments about the text or idea. See also *analyze, argument, bias.*

critique an in-depth evaluation of a person's work or idea.

deductive reasoning assuming a general *principle* and then applying it to a particular case.

definition as a strategy for developing an essay, an explanation of a thing, concept, or word by listing one or more features particular to it that distinguish it from another. For example, "Weapons of Mass Disruption" (Chapter 3) distinguishes a radiological weapon from a nuclear bomb. Conversely, a definition may explain what something is not: *An evergreen does not lose its leaves in autumn.*

delivery the manner in which an oral presentation is made to the *audience*; includes type of presentation (memorized, extemporaneous, spontaneous, or scripted) and performance-related factors (pronunciation, enunciation, speed, pitch, and volume). See Chapter 16.

description a method of development whereby the writer explains or illustrates a place, person, event, or thing so that readers can create a mental *image* of it. Descriptions use nouns, adjectives, and adverbs to name parts and provide distinctive details. For example, "Weapons of Mass Disruption" (Chapter 3) includes this vivid description: *Police officers in gas masks start to evacuate bystanders, but most of the frightened onlookers are already running away in panic, handkerchiefs over their mouths.*

design the way in which a text is visually arranged, both logically and aesthetically. Five essential *principles* of design are *alignment, chunking, contrast, consistency,* and *tension.* See Chapter 8.

division a strategy for organizing information or ideas whereby the writer divides an item or group of items into categories. See also *classification.*

evidence support that proves the validity of a *claim*; may include facts, authoritative opinions, data, quotations, paraphrased text, statistics, statements that enhance the writer's *credibility,* testimony, and so forth. See Chapter 4.

example a strategy for developing a piece of writing by giving instances to clarify something. "ACL: The Curse of Women Athletes" (Chapter 3) gives examples of ways a woman's leg structure differs from a man's to illustrate why women are more likely than men to suffer an ACL tear.

exploratory draft an early version of a document that helps the writer to determine (1) whether he or she understands the topic, and (2) what other information should be added or deleted. See also *review draft.*

exploratory writing a *brainstorming* technique whereby the writer refines ideas and plans what to include in a text.

figure of speech descriptive words or phrases used to emphasize the thing described, to create a vivid *image* in a reader's mind, or to make a difficult concept clearer. One common figure of speech is a simile, in which something is compared to something else using the word "like" or "as." An example of a simile appears in "ACL: The Curse of Women Athletes" (Chapter 3), when the action of a woman's femur is compared to a guillotine cutting the ACL (para. 8). Another common figure of speech is a metaphor, in which something is said to *be* something else. An example of a metaphor appears in "School Vouchers: The Wrong Choice for Public Education" (Chapter 4), in which public schools are called "the backbone of American democracy" (para. 7). See also *analogy.*

font a set of type in a particular size and style; see also *typeface.* See Chapter 8.

forecasting term a word or phrase that appears near the beginning of a section of text and indicates the topic to be covered.

format the plan or *design* of a page or screen; includes the arrangement of textual elements and *visual elements* on the page or screen. See Chapter 8. See also *alignment, balance.*

freewriting a *brainstorming* technique whereby the writer concentrates on a single topic or issue, writing down every idea—whether related to the topic or not—that comes to mind.

generalize to draw a conclusion about a group based on a sample of its members. If the sample size is large enough and if the members are truly representative of the group, a generalization can be a useful way to understand *quantitative data;* however, an unrepresentative sample or a sample that is too small can lead to mistaken *assumptions* about the characteristics of individual people, things, or ideas.

graphics *visual elements* used by the writer to present, enhance, or dramatize the message in print and electronic page design. Such elements include line drawings, *bullets,* photographs, *charts,* graphs, tables, *icons,* logos, *banners,* and the like. See Chapter 8.

heading a word or phrase used to guide readers to particular content in a text. See Chapter 8. See also *subheading*.

homepage the introductory or core page of a Web site.

icon a symbol or *image* that visually represents the ideas or activities to which it refers.

image in *design*, a graphic representation of a person, thing, idea, or action; in writing, a *figure of speech*.

inductive reasoning making a generalization based on specific instances.

inset box a section of text or *visual element*, often bordered by lines or a box, inserted into the main text. For example, see "Bellying Up to the Bar" (Chapter 3). See also *chunking, sidebar, text wrap*.

italic a typographical highlighting technique whereby letters are angled to the right to give visual emphasis. This is *italic* type.

layout the arrangement and *design* of text and *visual elements* in a print or electronic document. See Chapter 8.

leading See *line spacing*.

line graph a *chart* used to illustrate disparities in numerical data, with lines visually representing the numbers plotted on the chart. Best used to denote changes over time. See Chapter 8.

line spacing the amount of *white space*, or "leading," between lines of text.

link a highlighted word, phrase, or other visual cue on a Web page that brings the user to another area on the same Web page, another page on the same Web site, or a different Web site. Also called "hyperlink," "hotlink."

medium a written, auditory, or visual means of distributing information, such as a newspaper, magazine, Internet site, television, and so forth; the plural form is "media."

narrative a discourse with plot, setting, characterization, and sequence of events, often involving some type of conflict. Particularly useful in profiles, but often used in other texts to engage or maintain readers' interest. See Chapter 2.

navigation aid the element of a print or electronic document that helps readers to get from one place to another in the text or to find specific information within the text; may include tables of contents, headers, footers, running heads, navigation bars, menus, hyperlinks, indexes, and image maps.

objection a point in opposition to a writer's *claim*. See also *concession, refutation*. See Chapter 4.

objectivity *perspective* and reasoning based on facts rather than on personal beliefs or prejudices. See also *critical thinking, subjectivity*.

paraphrase a restatement of an original text that conveys the original meaning in someone else's words. See Chapter 11.

perspective the way in which an individual relates to an *image*, object, or idea. For example, Ellen Goodman's experience has given her a negative perspective on SUVs (Chapter 4). See also *point of view*. For a definition of visual perspective, see *viewing angle*.

persuasion a strategy for developing a piece of writing that aims to influence another person, using *argument* and *evidence*, toward a particular *point of view*. See Chapter 4.

pictogram a *chart* or graph that uses *icons* as elements.

picture box a four-sided border used to contain an *image*.

pie chart a specialized graph, shaped like a circle or pie, that emphasizes an important relationship among percentages of like elements. See Chapter 8. See also *graphics*.

pixel one of the many tiny dots that make up a computer screen *image;* comes from the phrase "picture element."

plagiarism using someone else's ideas visually and/or words without giving credit to the original source.

point of view the position from which a writer evaluates a subject. See also *perspective.*

presentation software software, such as Microsoft PowerPoint, that is used to prepare and present text- or *graphics*-based information to accompany oral presentations.

principle a fundamental or widely recognized rule: *Appropriate amounts of vitamins are essential for a healthy body. Supply and demand determine pricing.*

pull quote a short selection of relevant text that a writer copies from a source document and places near his or her original text to draw attention to an important point; usually visually distinguished by *font* size or other *typeface* treatment, position, or presentation (such as placing within an *inset box* or separating with *bold* lines).

purpose what the writer hopes to accomplish by producing a particular text for a particular audience in given circumstances. See also *context.*

qualifier wording that restricts the *claims* in an *argument,* decreasing the likelihood that the claims will be too extreme and protecting the writer's *credibility.* Common qualifiers include the words "some," "many," "may," "possibly," "often," and "usually": *Many girls want to play football. Leaves are usually green. Some textbooks have companion Web sites.*

qualitative data descriptive notes and observations about individual actions, events, or responses; typically drawn from interviews, open-ended survey questions, and observations. Cannot be used to prove theory but can add support, explore ideas, or generate questions; also adds the type of detail that makes writing more interesting or more believable. For example, "Slaves of New York" (Chapter 3) relies on personal observation and interviews to describe the situation of many Chinese immigrants in New York City. See Chapter 10.

quantitative data information that can be measured objectively in numbers or specific amounts. Can be persuasive, as most people trust such infor-

mation. For example, see the statistical data in "Cigarette Advertising Expenditures before and after the Master Settlement Agreement: Preliminary Findings" (Chapter 3).

quotation a portion of text copied verbatim (without alteration); must appear within quotation marks, and the source must be acknowledged. See Chapter 11. See also *plagiarism.*

reasons information that supports an *argument* by linking *claims* and *evidence.* For example, Ellen Goodman makes the claim that SUVs belong in car ads only (Chapter 4). Her evidence includes the fact that SUVs cause thousands of deaths every year. The reason that connects the claim and the evidence is that SUVs make driving more dangerous for people in smaller vehicles. See also *warrant.*

rebuttal See *refutation.*

refutation a technique used to discredit an *argument* or *counterargument* by demonstrating a failure in logic, *evidence,* or reasoning. In "Yes, Let's Pay for Organs" (Chapter 4), the author describes several objections to the practice of selling human organs and refutes each one in turn. See especially paragraphs 3 (objection) and 4 (refutation), or paragraph 5 (objection and refutation), for examples. See also *concession.*

review draft an early version of a work that enables the writer to determine how effectively he or she has presented information; alternatively, the version of a text reviewed by someone other than the writer before completion. See also *exploratory draft.*

rhetorical situation See *context.*

scenario a brief description of a hypothetical or real situation.

sidebar a four-sided border that contains text, often surrounded by other text on a page or screen. See also *inset box, text wrap, chunking.*

stakeholder an individual affected by the information contained in a work or text, either directly or indirectly; a person with some investment in the issue, situation, or person being discussed in a work or text. See also *audience.*

subheading a word or phrase, subordinate to a main *heading*, that identifies the content in a section of text.

subjectivity *perspective* and reasoning based on personal beliefs or views rather than objective facts. See also *critical thinking, objectivity*.

summary shortened or condensed material from a longer work; presents the main points of the original text but does not provide all the detail. See Chapter 11.

support See *evidence*.

tension a feeling invoked in readers by a well-designed print or electronic document; determined by the relationship among the text, the *visual elements,* and the *white space* on a given page. See also *design*.

text wrap text that flows (wraps) around an *image* on a page or screen.

thesis the central idea in a work, stating the writer's point of view; supporting a thesis with *evidence* is integral to a writer's purpose. For example, the following is the thesis sentence of "ACL: The Curse of Women Athletes" (Chapter 3): *As the number of women competing in sports continues to increase, understanding the causes of this common injury will enable us to help these athletes to reduce their risk.* See also *claim*.

tone the quality or mood of expression conveyed by the writer. See also *voice*.

topic sentence a statement that briefly describes the point and the content of a paragraph, usually relating the paragraph to the work's *thesis*.

transition a word or phrase used to indicate relationships between ideas or phrases: *Stephanie saw Diana every time she visited the lab; consequently, Stephanie thought Diana spent most of her time in the lab. In fact, Diana also participated actively in her sorority.*

typeface a family of characters—including letters, numbers, and symbols. Typefaces are usually available in different styles (for example, *italic, bold*) and in different sizes (for example, 10-point or 12-point type). See Chapter 8. See also *font*.

viewing angle the vantage point from which an *image* is presented (for example, the angle from which a photograph is taken or the perspective from which a figure is drawn); can give more or less emphasis to the subject. See, for example, the analysis of the photo of workers in "Weapons of Mass Disruption" (Chapter 3). See also *composition*.

visual element a graphic feature that complements or enhances text-based information, such as color, lines, photographs, line drawings, *charts, graphics, icons, inset boxes,* or *pull quotes*.

voice the aspect of a text that reflects a personality, a set of attitudes, or even the literal sound of a person speaking. Related to *tone*. See Chapter 2.

warrant the underlying *assumption* or *principle* that connects *claims* and *reasons*. For example, Ellen Goodman makes the claim that SUVs belong in car ads only (Chapter 4). One of her reasons is that SUVs make driving more dangerous for people in smaller vehicles. The warrant that connects her claim and her reason is that limits should be placed on those things that endanger life. See also *reasons*.

white space the area on a page or screen not occupied by text or *images* (such as margins and other blank space). Used to enhance visual *design* and readability, white space gives emphasis and helps to organize elements in a text. See also *balance, chunking*.

Acknowledgments

Text

Anti-Defamation League. "School Vouchers: The Wrong Choice for Public Education." From http://www.adl.org. Copyright © 2002 by the Anti-Defamation League. Reprinted with permission of the Anti-Defamation League.

Edward Barnes. "Slaves of New York." From *Time*, November 2, 1998. Copyright © 1998 TIME Inc. Reprinted by permission.

Jose A. Bufill. "Human Organ Donation: Gift or Graft?" From *Chicago Tribune*, July 12, 2000. Copyright © 2000 by the Chicago Tribune. Reprinted courtesy of Jose A. Bufill, M.D.

Nathan Burstein. "Applying to College, Made Easy." From *The New York Times*, September 21, 1999. Copyright © 1999 by The New York Times. Reprinted by permission of the New York Times.

Consumer Reports. "Cream of the Crop." From *Consumer Reports*, July 1999. Copyright © 1999 by Consumers Union of the U.S., Inc. Yonkers, NY 10703-1057, a nonprofit organization. Reprinted with permission for educational purposes only. The preceding excerpt contains information only on vanilla ice cream. The complete article rates chocolate and coffee ice cream as well. No commercial use or photocopying permitted. Log onto http://www.ConsumerReports.org.

Roger Ebert. "Dr. Strangelove." From *Chicago Sun-Times*, July 11, 1999. Copyright © Chicago Sun-Times Inc. Reprinted by permission of Universal Press Syndicate.

Richard D. Emery. "Cameras in the Station House." From *Criminal Justice Ethics*, Volume 17, Number 1, Winter/Spring 1998. Reprinted by permission of The Institute for Criminal Justice Ethics, 555 West 57th Street, Suite 601, New York, NY 10019-1029.

Thomas Fields-Meyer, Elizabeth Velez, and Mary Boone. "From Welfare to Washington." From *People*, December 3, 2001. Copyright © 2001 by Thomas Fields-Meyer/People Weekly. All rights reserved by Time Inc.

Fight Crime: Invest in Kids. "From America's Front Line against Crime: A School and Youth Violence Prevention Plan." This material is available to the public for download at http://www.fightcrime.org/reports/schoolviol.pdf. Reprinted by permission of Fight Crime: Invest in Kids.

Crystal Gilson. "Assessing the Cranial Nerves." Reprinted by permission of the author.

Ellen Goodman. "SUVs Belong in Car Ads Only." From *The Boston Globe*, May 9, 1999. Copyright © 1999 The Washington Post Writers Group. Reprinted with permission.

Amanda Griscom and Will Dana. "A Green Ground Zero." From *The Nation*, September 23, 2002. Copyright © 2002. Reprinted with permission from *The Nation*.

Tom Junod. "Can You Say . . . 'Hero'?" From *Esquire*, November 1998. Copyright © 1998 by the Hearst Corporation. Reprinted by permission of the David Black Literary Agency.

Claudia Kalb and John McCormick. "Bellying Up to the Bar." From *Newsweek*, September 21, 1998. Copyright © 1998 by Newsweek, Inc. All rights reserved. Reprinted by permission.

Julie Kirgo. "A Storm Brings Culinary Clear Sailing." From *Vermont Magazine*, July/August 1998. Reprinted courtesy of Vermont Magazine.

Charles Krauthammer. "Yes, Let's Pay for Organs." From *Time*, May 17, 1999. Copyright © 1999 TIME Inc. Reprinted by permission.

Fred LeBrun. "Up in Arms over Decision." From *Times Union*, February 16, 1999. Copyright © 1999. Reprinted by permission of the Times Union, Albany, NY.

Michael A. Levi and Henry C. Kelly. "Weapons of Mass Disruption." From *Scientific American*, November 2002. Copyright © 2002 by Scientific American, Inc. All rights reserved. Reprinted with permission from Scientific American.

Robert Mackey. Excerpts from "E.R. Unscripted." From *The New York Times Magazine*, May 5, 2002. Copyright © 2002 by Robert Mackey. Distributed by The New York Times Special Features. Reprinted by permission of The New York Times Syndicate.

Paul Oyer. "Barriers to College." Letter to the editor of *The New York Times*, September 23, 1999. Reprinted by permission of the author.

Robert W. Poole Jr. and Viggo Butler. "Fixing Airport Security: 21st-Century Strategies for 21st-Century

Threats." From *Reason Public Policy Institute*, Rapid Response No. 106, September 21, 2001, http://www.rppi.org/rr106.html. Copyright © 2001 by The Reason Foundation. Reprinted by permission of the Reason Foundation.

Dan Rather. "The Road to Kabul." From *TV Guide*, February 2, 2002. Copyright © 2002 by Dan Rather. Reprinted by permission of the author.

Caroline Rego. "The Fine Art of Complaining." Reprinted by permission of the author.

Ron Sessions. "Ford Expedition." From *Motor Trend*, June 2002. Copyright 2002 by *Primedia* Specialty Group. All rights reserved. Reprinted by permission of Primedia Specialty Group.

Seth Shostak. "You Call This Progress?" From *Newsweek*, January 18, 1999. All rights reserved. Reprinted by permission of Newsweek.

Sierra Club. "New Roads Are Not the Answer." Downloaded from http://www.sierraclub.org/sprawl/induced.pdf on November 18, 2002. Courtesy of the Sierra Club.

Diane Turner-Bowker, Ph.D and William L. Hamilton, Ph.D. "Cigarette Advertising Expenditures Before and After the Master Settlement Agreement: Preliminary Findings." Preliminary study published May 15, 2000. Reprinted by permission of the authors.

Patrick Vitarius. "Breakfast at Manory's." From *The Polytechnic*, January 15, 1998. Reprinted by permission of The Polytechnic.

Art

Various Microsoft Corporation. Clip art from Microsoft® Clip Art Gallery at http://online.microsoft.com/clipart. Screenshots from Microsoft Internet Explorer® version 6.0, Microsoft PowerPoint® XP Professional, Microsoft Windows® XP Professional, and Microsoft Word® XP Professional. Copyright © Microsoft Corporation. Reprinted by permission of Microsoft Corporation. **2** Jeff Greenberg/Index Stock © 2004. **4 (top left)** © 2003, *Newsweek*, Inc. All rights reserved. Reprinted by permission. Photo: Andrew Hetherington/*Redux* for Newsweek. **4 (top right)** Splash newsletter, Winter 2004. Reproduced with permission of Dynamic Graphics magazine, June/July 2004, V9N3. © 2004 Dynamic Graphics Inc., http://www.dynamicgraphics.com/dgm. **4 (middle)** San Francisco Bay Area Rapid Transit (BART) System Map. Copyright 2004 San Francisco Bay Area Rapid Transit District. All Rights Reserved. Used with Permission. **4 (bottom)** United Way Billboard. Courtesy of United Way of America/United Way of Waco McLennan County and Swift Outdoor Advertising. **5 (top left)** Front page of The Washington Post, May 20, 2004. © 2004 The Washington Post. Reprinted with permission. **5 (top right)** ESPN.com's front page on October 21, 2004. Image courtesy of ESPN. "You + HP" ad courtesy of Hewlett-Packard Company. "Save up to $500" ad courtesy of Samsung Electronics America. Photos from top to bottom: (1) Darren M. Collester/Getty Images, (2) Elsa/Getty Images. **5 (bottom left)** Habitat for Humanity, New York City; Christine Whitney, photographer; Elizabeth Powell, designer. © Christine Whitney. **5 (bottom right)** "At what age does a girl dream of becoming President?" Reprinted by permission of the White House Project. Photos top to bottom: (1) Geri Engberg/The Image Works (TIW), (2–5) Joel Gordon, (6) Joseph Nettis/Photo Researchers, (7) Explorer/Photo Researchers. **6 (top left)** Flagg-Rochelle Community Park District. **6 (top right)** Daniel Boone Regional Library, Columbia, Mo. **6 (bottom left)** Evite invitation used with the permission of Evite.com. **6 (bottom right)** "Panas-Lakeland Teacher vs. Teacher Volleyball Game" flyer created by Michael Helfrich. Reproduced with the permission of Michael Helfrich and the Panthers Parent Teacher Council. **7 (top left)** Columbia Festival of the Arts 2004 promotional flyer. Designed by Fertile Mind Designs, featuring artwork by Columbia Public Schools student Aubriana Nichols. The Columbia Festival of the Arts is a program of the City of Columbia, Missouri, Office of Cultural Affairs. Reprinted with permission from the City of Columbia Office of Cultural Affairs. **7 (top right)** Photographs by Thomas Lewis on http://www.buzznet.com. Reproduced with the permission of Thomas Lewis and Buzznet, Inc. **7 (bottom left)** Courtesy Roberta Bastow, *Perfect Blend* Espresso Bar and Café. **7 (bottom right)** Sahir Azam CD cover. Designed by Sona Ahuja (http://www.audesignz.com). **8 (middle)** Photo: Nick Wass/Associated Press/Wide World Photos (AP/WW). **8 (bottom)** Raghav Sachdev. Portfolio at http://www.rpi.edu/~sachdr2/cep/. Reprinted by permission of the author. **9 (top)** Lake Norman Regional Medical Center website. Used with the permission of Lake Norman Medical Center. College of Medicine at the University of Arizona website. © Arizona Board of Regents. Used with the permission of Arizona Board of Regents. **9 (bottom)** Photos: (1) Dr. Robert Johnson, Johnson Optometric Assn., (2) Alan Lacey, w3 Media Limited, (3) National Eye Institute, (4) American Health Assistance Foundation. **17** Nick Wass/AP/WW. **26** Dan Winters Photography. **34** Alexander Markushev/ AP/WW. **37** Courtesy Sen. Patricia Murray. **38** Melina Mara. **39 (top)** John Froschauer/AP/WW. **39 (bottom)** Melina Mara. **40** Courtesy Sen. Patricia Murray. **42, 43** Naomi Harris. **45** Alexander Markushev/AP/WW. **46 (top)** CBS Photo. **46 (bottom)** Kevin Frayer/AP/WW. **47, 48** Marco Di Lauro/AP/WW. **51–55** Dan Winters Photography. **61, 64** Stephanie

Guzik. **102** Chien-Chi Chang/*Magnum* Photos. **110 (top)** Sara Chen. **110 (bottom)** Yun Jai-hyoung/AP/WW. **113** Andrew Lichtenstein/TIW. **120–123** Chien-Chi Chang/*Magnum* Photos. **126** Art by Catherine McIntyre. **128, 130, 131** Sara Chen. **132** Yun Jai-hyoung/AP/WW. **135 (left)** Art by Catherine McIntyre. **137** Nick Wass/AP/WW. **138** Diagram of the ACL. From "What Is the ACL?" Reprinted from http://www.aclsolutions.com courtesy of Linvatec Corporation. **139** Diagram of the Q-angle. From Stephen Pribut, "Runner's Knee," Dr. Stephen M. Pribut's Sports Pages at http://www.drpribut.com/sports/spknees.html. Copyright © 2004 Stephen M. Pribut. Reprinted by permission of Stephen M. Pribut. **180** Courtesy of the Sierra Club. **195** Washington Post Writers Group. **197** Steve Sack/Star Tribune © 2002. **201** Illustration by Brian Cronin/Renèe Rhyner & Co. **204** Art by Dennis Van-Keersbilck. **211** Courtesy Fred LeBrun. **260, 270 (top)** Barry Runk/*Grant Heilman*. **270 (middle)** McDowell & Piasecki, Inc. **273** Barry Runk/*Grant Heilman*. **274** Godiva Belgian Chocolate Ice Cream courtesy Campbell Soup Co. **276** McDowell & Piasecki, Inc. **278 (top)** Blue Bell Advertising Assoc. **278 (bottom left, bottom right)** McDowell & Piasecki. **281** Everett Collection. **283** Courtesy Seth Shostak. **289** Dennis Parker. **291** Ford Motor Co. **334, 349** David J. Phillip/AP/WW. **426, 427** K'NEX® Corp. **484** WCC Welcome page at http://www. wakecountyautismsociety.org. Copyright © 2004 by Cynthia Magliocca. Reprinted by permission of Cynthia Magliocca. WCC logo and photo reprinted by permission of Michele Lete. **485 (top)** Blue Bell Advertising Assoc. **485 (bottom)** McDowell & Piasecki, Inc. **486** Cooper-Hewitt, National Design Museum homepage at http:// ndm.si.edu. Reprinted by permission of Cooper-Hewitt, National Design Museum, Smithsonian Institution. **489** OLD EL PASO®, a registered trademark of General Mills Cereals Inc. Used with permission. **490** *Time*, Feb. 7, 2000/Getty Images. **492** "At what age does a girl dream of becoming President?" Reprinted by permission of the White House Project. Photos top to bottom: (1) Geri Engberg/TIW, (2–5) Joel Gordon, (6) Joseph Nettis/Photo Researchers, (7) Explorer/Photo Researchers. **498** Andrew Lichtenstein/TIW. **504** Sara Chen. **521** Courtesy Britax Child Safety, Inc. **531** Andrew Lichtenstein/TIW. **538–540** NCSU Library Catalog Subject Search Request, Subject Search Results List, and Record for a Book. Copyright © 2001 North Carolina State University and Sirsi Corporation. Used with permission. **552** Google Keyword Search on Mononucleosis. Google Brand Features are trademarks or distinctive brand features of Google Technology Inc. © 2004 Google. Reprinted with the permission of Google. **553–554** Yahoo! Directory Page on Health and Keyword Search of the Yahoo! Health Directory. Reproduced with permission of Yahoo! Inc. © 2004 by Yahoo! Inc. *Yahoo!* and the *Yahoo!* logo are trademarks of Yahoo! Inc. **556–557** Google Image Search and Google Advanced Search. Google Brand Features are trademarks or distinctive brand features of Google Technology Inc. © 2004 Google. Reprinted with the permission of Google. **565** Andrew Lichtenstein/TIW. **572** Michael Liedtke. "Survey finds women business owners getting little venture capital." From the Associated Press, July 17, 2000. © The Associated Press. All rights reserved. Reprinted with permission. For reorders call Valeo IP, Inc. 651-582-3800. ABCNews.com website elements. Copyright © 2004 ABC News Internet Ventures. Reproduced with permission from ABC News. Photo: Stuart Ransom/AP/WW. **581** Bill Buford. "Sweat is Good." From *The New Yorker*, April 26 & May 3, 1999. Copyright © 1999 by William Buford. Reprinted with the permission of the Wylie Agency, Inc. **586** MSN homepage from October 19, 2004. Copyright © 2004 Microsoft Corporation. All rights reserved. "Save 10% on Dell Home Dimensions™" advertisement. Copyright © 2004 Dell Inc. Reprinted with permission of Dell Inc. FOX Sports logo courtesy of 20th Century Fox Film Corp. Photos from top to bottom: (1) Mike Blake/Reuters America, (2) Lehn/*AGE Fotostock*, (3) Anne Marie Weber/ Getty Images. **589** Google Search Results List on Flu Vaccine Supply. Google Brand Features are trademarks or distinctive brand features of Google Technology Inc. © 2004 Google. Reprinted with the permission of Google. **590** Yahoo Search Results List. Reproduced with permission of Yahoo! Inc. © 2004 by Yahoo! Inc. *Yahoo!* and the *Yahoo!* logo are trademarks of Yahoo! Inc. **595** Earthbound Farm homepage at www.ebfarm. com. Copyright © 2004 Earthbound Farm. All rights reserved. Reprinted by permission of Earthbound Farm. **608** Painting by Zoë Mena, a sixth grader at the Housatonic Valley School, Newtown, CT. Used with the permission of the Housatonic Valley School. **610** Page from a student's third grade main lesson book. Hawthorne Valley School, Ghent, NY. Courtesy of class teacher James Pewtherer and student Katharine Payne, Hawthorne Valley School. **666** Dr. Betty Blake. **701, 703–704, 706–709** "Who We Are," "Draft of House Rules," "Section Four: On the Job," "Adriene Banks," "Coming Home," and "Welfare Reform and Homelessness." Excerpted from Joseph's House and Shelter literature. Reprinted with the permission of Joseph's House and Shelter, Inc. **718** Chien-Chi Chang/*Magnum* Photos.

Index

Note: Numbers in **bold** refer to terms included in the Glossary of Visual and Rhetorical Terms.

Quick Reference Menu

This quick reference guide lists the places in *Writing in a Visual Age* where you can find key information and get answers to frequently asked questions.